Readings in Christian Ethics

Readings in Christian Ethics

Volume 2
Issues and Applications

Edited by David K. Clark
and Robert V. Rakestraw

Baker Academic
a division of Baker Publishing Group
Grand Rapids, Michigan

©1996 by David K. Clark and Robert V. Rakestraw

Published by Baker Academic
a division of Baker Publishing Group
P.O. Box 6287, Grand Rapids, MI 49516-6287
www.bakeracademic.com

Eleventh printing, August 2008

Printed in the United States of America

Library of Congress Cataloging-in-Publication Data
Readings in Christian ethics / edited by David K. Clark & Robert V. Rakestraw.
       p.   cm.
    Includes bibliographical references and index.
    Contents: v. 1. Theory and method. — v. 2. Issues and Applications.
    ISBN 978-0-8010-2581-5 (v. 1: pbk.) — ISBN 978-0-8010-2056-8 (v. 2: pbk.)
    ISBN 10: 0-8010-2581-8 (v. 1: pbk.) — ISBN 10: 0-8010-2056-5 (v. 2: pbk.)
    1. Christian ethics. 2. Christian ethics—Methodology. 3. Evangelicalism. I.
Clark, David K. II. Rakestraw, Robert Vincent.
BJ1251.R385   1994
241—dc20   93-30274

To our children,
Tyler and Ryan,
Joni and Laurie

Contents

Part 2   Human Sexuality

Part 3   Class Relationships

Part 4   Stewardship of Creation

Preface

People in Western societies have lost their moral footing and are adrift in currents they barely understand and cannot control. So say many cultural critics, not only religious, but secular as well. A major book on virtues by a significant American public figure recently topped best-seller charts. Yet this attempt to buck the tide is inundated by many other forces that cater to a violent and narcissistic consumer culture.

Aggravating these problems is the exponentially accelerating complexity of the moral issues we face today. Relieving the suffering of the dying has always placed people in personal turmoil. Now advances in the medical arts have created little-understood twilight zones between life and death. Our society can barely resist calls for physician-assisted suicide and legalized mercy killing. Marital infidelity fractured families in the past. Now the avalanche of divorces, various kinds of abuse, and assorted consensual relationships seems overwhelming. Healthy families where children are deeply loved and taught to serve God and others seem like rare exceptions. War has plagued the human race for centuries. Now threats of nuclear holocaust or atomic blackmail in the wake of the Soviet demise threaten to destroy the human race entirely.

Because of the mind-boggling and gut-wrenching character of these and other questions, traditionally minded Protestant Christians have struggled to resolve these issues effectively. One shortcoming is that evangelicals often reflect on the great moral issues without first giving concerted attention to ethical theory. How can we ground moral norms? How do we approach moral dilemmas in which ethical norms appear to conflict? How can we apply ethical reflection to differing cultural contexts? How should we use the Bible in ethical reflection? How should we work through a process of ethical decision making? How shall we become a people of virtue who truly reflect the image of God?

In *Readings in Christian Ethics, Volume 1: Theory and Method,* a companion to this anthology, we addressed these issues. Several works on ethics by conservative Protestants present only a single introductory chapter on theory before moving directly into specific moral questions. Ethical reasoning can easily succumb to literalism or legalism on the one hand or to situationism, utilitarianism, or egoism on the other. We strongly urge, therefore, that Christians give due consideration to ethical method. We believe that the first volume is critical.

With volume 1 as background, the present collection addresses concrete ethical issues. Since we choose to allow the commitments of the centrist evangelical community to guide our selections, much of this volume tackles questions evangelicals often focus on: abortion, sexuality, divorce and remarriage, war and peace, and capital punishment. Unfortunately, conservative Protestants (with some notable exceptions) too often ignore other pressing issues: environment, materialism, and gender. Evangelical silence on the evil of racism, for instance, and on the need for racial reconciliation in the body of Christ is deafening. We believe that failure to give serious attention to these questions hurts the Christian church. Thus we have included chapters on these more neglected topics.

Our approach is neither strictly philosophical nor exclusively biblical. It is primarily theological. We do interact with philosophical and biblical ethics at many points. Theological ethics, like all systematic theology, interacts with a variety of other disciplines as well. Our selection of topics and readings, however, is controlled theologically, and we engage the other disciplines where they are relevant to that main agenda.

As indicated above, we collected these essays and organized this volume with evangelical interests and perspectives in mind, and so this book will differ from other works in ethics. For example, a mainline Christian anthology in ethics places the chapter on homosexuality in a section on prejudice and oppression, not in the unit on sexuality as we do. Although we explicitly recognize our evangelical orientation, we include essays by Christian authors who are either not evangelical or not Protestant. In this way we illustrate a variety of positions on various topics. At all points, however, we chose issues, views, and persons that are of interest to evangelicals.

Given our historic Protestant stance, a unique feature of these volumes is our interest in the Bible. We want to ground ethics more directly in Scripture than do most contemporary writers—even many Christian ones—on ethics. This does not imply, however, a biblical literalism or biblicism. Indeed, since this is theological ethics, we believe it important to go beyond faithful interpretation of biblical material to theological reflection and synthesis and to relevant cultural application.

We believe this two-volume set is unique. Although many ethicists have collected essays in anthologies, few of these represent an evangelical point of view. Conversely, several evangelical ethicists have written significant works in ethics, but most of this literature represents a single-author viewpoint. We trust, therefore, that a multiple-perspective volume on ethics that grows out of the historic Protestant ethos may make an important contribution.

We introduce each chapter with brief essays. In these we try both to spell out the nature of the various positions or aspects of a problem and, at times, to present arguments and ideas that will push discussion on the issue forward in small ways. In these essays, we put items listed in the glossary in bold print the first time they appear. To each chapter we add case studies and a brief annotated bibliography.

Choosing the readings, given the limitations of space, was a painful process. We resolved to select readings to represent a balanced continuum of views or several facets of a problem. We also kept an eye on "teachability" in order to make the materials suitable for students as well as for others interested in ethics. The essays are those we felt best clarified the options for someone who wishes to understand the issues in a balanced way.

Decisions about gender-inclusive language are difficult. We followed the conventions of inclusive language in our own writing, but we chose to allow the readings to stand as they are. Given that even feminists used traditional conventions in their own work at the time some of our selections were written, we felt we should keep the readings as close to the original as possible.

This volume begins with the issues of abortion, reproductive technologies, and euthanasia gathered in a section on the beginning and ending of life (part 1). Next are chapters on sexuality (including marriage and singleness), homosexuality, and divorce and remarriage in a section on human sexuality (part 2). In a section on class relationships (part 3), we include discussions of human interactions that cross racial and gender lines. Chapters on wealth and economics and on care for the environment comprise the section on the stewardship of creation (part 4). In a section on law and government (part 5), we conclude the volume with discussions of civil disobedience, capital punishment, and peace and war.

Finally, we acknowledge many who helped make this project possible. Bethel Theological Seminary supported the process with a sabbatical leave. The editors at Baker Book House, Jim Weaver and Linda Triemstra, gave freely of their time and expertise. Many students have worked through these issues with both of us in many classes on ethics over the last fifteen years. Teaching assistants Rod Ankrom, Jim Beilby, Paul Eddy, Ken Magnuson,

Justin Sunberg, and Peter Vogt did much legwork for us. We express thanks to all of these friends. We also welcome suggestions from readers about ways to improve this set in any future revisions.

David K. Clark
Robert V. Rakestraw
St. Paul, Minnesota

List of Contributors

W. French Anderson is chief of the Laboratory of Molecular Hematology of the National Heart, Lung and Blood Institute, National Institutes of Health.

Jerram Barrs is professor of Christian studies and contemporary culture, and director of the Francis Schaeffer Institute, at Covenant Theological Seminary.

E. Calvin Beisner is associate professor of interdisciplinary studies at Covenant College.

R. J. Berry is professor of genetics at University College, London.

Donald B. Bloesch is professor of theology emeritus at Dubuque Theological Seminary.

Paul W. Brand served eighteen years at the Christian Medical College in Vellore, India, and was head of rehabilitation at the U.S. Public Health Service leprosy hospital in Carville, Louisiana.

Stephen B. Clark is teaching at Christian Teaching Center, Lansing, Michigan.

Jack W. Cottrell is professor of theology at Cincinnati Bible Seminary.

Richard J. Foster is Jack and Barbara Lee Distinguished Professor of Spiritual Formation at Azusa Pacific University.

Norman Geisler is dean of Southern Evangelical Seminary.

Stanley J. Grenz is Pioneer McDonald Professor of Baptist Heritage, Theology and Ethics at Carey Theological College and professor of theology and ethics at Regent College.

Eric E. Hobbs is an attorney in Milwaukee, Wisconsin.

Walter C. Hobbs is professor emeritus at State University of New York, Buffalo.

David A. Hoekema is academic dean at Calvin College.

Stanton L. Jones is chair of the psychology department of Wheaton College.

Robert E. Joyce is professor emeritus of philosophy at St. John's University.

Craig S. Keener is associate professor of New Testament at Hood Theological Seminary.

Glen Kehrein is executive director of Circle Urban Ministries, Chicago, Illinois.

George W. Knight III was dean and professor of New Testament at Knox Theological Seminary.

Karen Lebacqz is professor of Christian ethics at Pacific School of Religion.

Janet Dickey McDowell is coordinator of education and professional training at Planned Parenthood of the Blue Ridge, Roanoke, Virginia.

Gilbert Meilaender is a professor in the department of religion at Oberlin College.

Virginia Ramey Mollenkott is professor of English at William Paterson College of New Jersey.

J. P. Moreland is professor of philosophy of religion at Talbot School of Theology, Biola University.

Stephen Mott is pastor of Cochesett United Methodist Church of West Bridgewater, Massachusetts.

John Murray was professor of systematic theology at Westminster Theological Seminary.

Ronald H. Nash is professor of philosophy at Reformed Theological Seminary in Orlando, Florida.

James B. Nelson is professor of Christian ethics at United Theological Seminary of the Twin Cities.

Thomas C. Oden is Henry Anson Buttz Professor of Theology and Ethics at The Theological School, Drew University.

Spencer Perkins is one of the pastors of Voice of Calvary Fellowship, Jackson, Mississippi.

John Piper is senior pastor of Bethlehem Baptist Church, Minneapolis, Minnesota.

Robert V. Rakestraw is professor of theology at Bethel Theological Seminary.

Charles C. Ryrie was professor of systematic theology at Dallas Theological Seminary.

Robert L. Saucy is professor of systematic theology at Talbot School of Theology, Biola University.

Ronald J. Sider is professor of theology and culture at Eastern Baptist Theological Seminary and executive director of Evangelicals for Social Action.

Richard K. Taylor is parish services coordinator for St. Vincent de Paul Catholic Church in Philadelphia, Pennsylvania.

Everett Tilson is professor emeritus of Old Testament at Methodist Theological School in Ohio.

Ernest Van den Haag has taught criminal justice at several universities and is author of *Punishing Criminals* (revised 1991).

Mary Stuart Van Leeuwen is professor of psychology and philosophy and resident scholar in the Center for Christian Women in Leadership at Eastern College.

Raleigh Washington is pastor of Rock of Our Salvation Evangelical Free Church, Chicago, Illinois.

David Wenham is lecturer in New Testament at Wycliffe Hall, Oxford.

Robert N. Wennberg is professor of philosophy and department chair at Westmont College.

J. Philip Wogaman is senior minister of Foundry United Methodist Church, Washington, D.C.

David F. Wright is senior lecturer in ecclesiastical history and dean of the faculty of divinity at New College, University of Edinburgh, Scotland.

John Howard Yoder is professor of theology at Notre Dame University.

Part 1

Beginning and Ending Life

1

Abortion

Last year, 45,000 people died on American highways. Every ten days or so in American abortion clinics, an equal number of human fetuses dies. In the civilized world, far more human deaths are caused by **induced abortion** than by any other cause. (Spontaneous abortions and miscarriage are not moral issues.) The sheer magnitude of the numbers—doctors perform perhaps 1.5 million abortions in the United States each year—and the powerful emotions surrounding the abortion debate accentuate the moral issues. The current campaign to permit legalized infanticide only intensifies the conflict.

Typically, partisans in the United States frame the abortion question in terms of conflicting rights, the right to life as opposed to the right to reproductive freedom. In the famous 1973 case, *Roe v. Wade*, the United States Supreme Court ruled that a woman's right to privacy based on the Fourteenth Amendment to the Constitution includes a right to abortion. Some Christians think ethics should speak only of responsibilities and not of rights. They correctly remind us that modern society encourages people to emphasize their individual rights. Our culture does not understand the biblical ideal of a community of people who willingly give up their own rights to serve others. Rights language, however, does point to abiding human values that ethical principles should preserve.

A human life begins (at least biologically) when a sperm and an ovum join to form a **zygote**. As a zygote grows, it becomes an **embryo**, and then,

21

about seven weeks later, we call it a **fetus**. Some who reject abortion find the word *fetus* objectionable; they prefer *baby* or *unborn*. *Fetus* is essentially neutral, however; general dictionaries usually say it refers to the unborn young.

The options for moral views on abortion depend on the relative value given to this developing life and to the freedom of the mother. **Pro-life** advocates stress the value of each unborn's life. Although they may feel great compassion for pregnant women caught in painful dilemmas, they ascribe greater weight to the fetus's life. **Pro-choice** supporters emphasize the value of self-determination expressed in each woman's right to reproductive choice. Although they may believe the fetus has a right to live, they claim priority for a woman's right to freedom from intrusive, often male-dominated rules that undermine her very humanity. The values at stake, therefore, are the values of life on the one hand and self-determination on the other.

Political partisans who adopt these positions often conceptualize their positions in extreme, either-or terms, using emotionally charged words to articulate their views. To one side, the developing fetus is a cuddly, unborn baby, and abortion is murder. To the other, the developing fetus is amorphous tissue, a product of conception, and abortion is a safe medical procedure. Political activists often use heavily emotive words and so obscure finer, yet important distinctions in their rush to gain rhetorical advantage.

Careful analysis reveals a spectrum of perhaps four basic positions. First, the Roman Catholic Church has denied even those abortions intended to save the mother's life. Second, some conservative Protestants justify only those abortions that save a mother's life. These are called **therapeutic abortions**. Third, other Christians identify a category of "hard cases" (extreme situations like rape, incest, or severe deformation revealed through **amniocentesis**) that may justify or even necessitate abortion. Taken together, the hard cases constitute at the very most about 7 percent of abortions in America. These three views are all broadly pro-life. Fourth, some in our society (but few conservative Christians) take the pro-choice view: society should make abortions available to any woman who needs to make that choice.

Some who take the last view want to separate questions of public policy from issues of private morality. Admittedly, the distinction between the public and private realms is often appropriate; surely a society cannot legislate against issues of private morality like lusting in one's heart. Some apply this public-private distinction to abortion. They opt for a pro-choice view in public policy in conjunction with a privately held pro-life position. For example, Christian (and formerly evangelical) feminist, Virginia Ramey Mollenkott, argues against criminalizing abortion because of what making it illegal would do to women. At the same time, she personally considers abortion morally repugnant.

Christians turn to the Bible for light on questions like abortion. Remarkably, the Scripture does not address the matter directly. Prohibiting abortion among ancient Jews, who valued descendants very highly, was no doubt unnecessary. Christians often quote Psalm 139:13–16, Jeremiah 1:5, and Luke 1:41–44 to support a pro-life position, but these texts show only obliquely that God is interested in the preborn. They do not explicitly forbid abortion. The sixth commandment, "Do not commit murder" (Exod. 20:13), is quite explicit, but its relevance depends on theological or philosophical arguments aimed at proving that the preborn are as much human persons as are adults.

Exodus 21:22–25 elicits more commentary than any other biblical text for its connection to abortion. It says that if two fighting men hit a pregnant woman and the baby comes out (Hebrew: *yatsá*) and there is no serious injury, the offenders are fined. If serious injury results, then the life-for-life principle (***lex talionis***) applies. Traditionally, most commentators, including the Jewish rabbis whose wisdom is preserved in the Talmud, have argued that this text implies a significant difference between the value of a fetus and the value of the mother. If the fetus dies, the husband imposes a fine. If the mother dies, capital punishment is in order.

Jack Cottrell questions this long tradition, however, by arguing that the Hebrew *yatsá* does not mean miscarriage (even though many English translations use *miscarriage*, implying a dead fetus). If Cottrell is right, *yatsá* does not mean stillbirth, but live birth. Thus, the text actually applies *lex talionis* to both the woman and the fetus, and this gives the fetus a significant status, not an inferior one.

The point of examining biblical texts is to find guidance on a central question: Is the fetus a human person? But this raises an even more fundamental and critical question: What is a human person? To know whether the unborn fit into the category *human*, we first need to delineate the category. In the **functionalist** definition of personhood, a human organism becomes a person as it learns to do something, that is, when it acts personally as a moral, intellectual, spiritual agent. Westmont College philosopher Robert Wennberg explains the view that a zygote grows into personhood. To be a human person is to possess certain abilities: one acts personally; therefore, one is a person. A fetus, according to this view, is a potential person, an organism that is not yet, but that will become, a person.

This view raises questions about the status of newborn babies. Can newborns act personally? Surely not. It might appear, then, that a functionalist view entails that even a healthy newborn is not yet a human person and thus does not have an inviolate right to life. Following this logic, some utilitarians like Michael Tooley, Peter Singer, and Joseph Fletcher have argued for infanticide in some cases: a newborn must pass intelligence tests. The right to live is something one must earn.

Christians and many others find these conclusions abhorrent. To avoid them, Christians who adopt functionalism distinguish the **actuality principle** from the **potentiality principle**. Functionalism combined with the actuality principle affirms that a human organism has a right to life if and only if it has already developed some capacity for self-conscious, personal thought. This implies that a newborn does not have an inviolate right to life, and on this basis, Tooley and others argue that euthanizing handicapped newborns is morally right. Functionalism combined with the potentiality principle, however, affirms that a human organism has a right to life if it either has developed or *has the natural capacity for developing* self-conscious, personal life. Every fetus, in this view, has a right to live. Evangelical functionalists, including Wennberg, choose this option.

In contrast to functionalism stands the traditional essentialist view of human personhood. In **essentialism**, a human organism is a human person and possesses a right to life simply because it is a member of the human species. Roman Catholic writer Robert Joyce defends the view that a human person is what she is by endowment, not by achievement. To be a human person is to possess the natural capacity to become what one already is: one is a person; therefore, one acts personally. According to this view, a fetus is a developing person, a person in the process of development.

Evangelicals agree in rejecting functionalism combined with the actuality principle; they find the utilitarian argument for infanticide absurd. Conservative Christians, of course, have generally adopted a pro-life view. The heart of the pro-life stance is promoting the value of human lives, and this leads us to consider what Christians should do to defend that value.

One arena of response is politics—voting for legislators who promote pro-life policies, supporting presidents who appoint pro-life judges, advocating strong policies to help disadvantaged children. Another is adoption. Yet another is more controversial: the rescue movement. The issues are so monumental and the options so stark that some pro-life activists willingly practice civil disobedience to dramatize their opposition to abortion. The rescue movement forces questions of several kinds onto the table. First, speaking broadly, is civil disobedience ever justified (see chap. 11)? If the answer is positive, then, speaking more specifically, is civil disobedience justified on this particular issue? Does rescuing fit the criteria for appropriate civil disobedience? Does it, for example, promise a likely positive resolution to the problem?

Rescuing stirs defenders of abortion to strong response as well. Pro-choice forces help women get past pro-life protestors who block abortion clinics. Defenders of abortion rights defend the right of choice everywhere they can. And they accuse pro-life activists of wanting to see children born, but caring little for them after birth. Pro-lifers, the argument goes, seem more pro-birth than pro-life.

This critique reminds us that the value worth defending is not birthing, but persons. Attitudes and policies that foster birth, but do little for disadvantaged children once they are born, may promote an abstract principle, "pro-lifeness," but they can neglect the human persons that the pro-life principle is intended to nourish. Whatever we think of civil disobedience, the body of Christ must pursue another response. Christians should articulate a compelling vision of a society in which all persons give more than they receive. Law alone cannot do the job; it changes only externals. The gospel, preached and lived, can help forge a community in which all human persons, both the born and the unborn, are loved as God loves them.

Reproductive Choice

Basic to Justice for Women

Virginia Ramey Mollenkott

During her reproductive years, a healthy woman can give birth to thirty children. Therefore, if she wishes to accomplish anything other than child birthing and childcare during her lifetime, she must learn to control her fertility. She must in fact either control her fertility or be controlled by it.

Well, then, she and her husband must use contraceptives. But these too may fail. . . . Even sterilizations and vasectomies fail.[1] How is a married woman able to plan schooling or commit herself to a career or vocation as long as her life is continually open to the disruption of unplanned pregnancies? Unless, of course, she can fall back on an abortion when all else has failed!

But in American society today, a very strong movement is afoot to outlaw abortion on the grounds that the fetus is a human person from the moment of conception. . . . Fundamentalists and even the more moderate evangelicals are fond of warning society about a "slippery slope," [on] which the legality of abortion leads the way toward increasingly degenerate behaviors. Furthermore, the argument is advanced that since God is sovereign and makes no mistakes, every pregnancy is His will and must not be interfered with. Even in cases of rape, incest, or fetal deformity, because God did not choose to prevent the pregnancy, no human being should attempt to prevent the birth.[2]

Such arguments are frightening in a society where "rape is so common that one in three women is likely to be raped during her lifetime," and where "anywhere from 9 percent to 52 percent of women were sexually victimized

1. *Point Counter Point* (Washington, D.C.: Religious Coalition for Abortion Rights, 1985), 9.
2. For an example of such an argument, see Donald Shoemaker, *Abortion, the Bible and the Christian* (Cincinnati: Hays Publishing Company, 1976).

26

as children."[3] Any act of unprotected intercourse results in pregnancy about 4 percent of the time, with rape and incest no exceptions. In fact, because incestuous relationships involve repeated abuse, pregnancy becomes even more likely. Hence, American women find themselves on a slippery slope of another type, in which they are vulnerable to sexual abuse as children, to rape throughout their lives, and should they be heterosexually active, to the disruption of unwanted pregnancies at any time. (Even marriage offers little safety. Rape occurs in at least 14 percent of marriages.)[4]

If the anti-abortion forces have their way, the victims of sexual terrorism or human error will have no access to legal abortion. Already, because of the 1977 Hyde Amendment that cut off most federal funds for abortion services, victims of incest or rape cannot obtain funding for an abortion. Neither can a woman whose fetus is severely deformed, nor a woman whose pregnancy would involve serious mental and/or physical health damage to herself. Medicaid is available only if the abortion is necessary to save the physical life of the woman involved.[5] Not surprisingly, as soon as the Hyde Amendment went into effect, the number of reported deaths due to illegal abortions increased for the first time since 1973, when the Supreme Court recognized a woman's right to choose an abortion consistent with sound medical practice. The increased deaths occurred in the poorest segment of the female population; and due to the phenomenon known as "the feminization of poverty," that segment is growing larger every year.[6]

Christian feminists, male or female, are committed to the achievement of justice for women in the social, religious, political, and economic spheres. Most of us believe that such justice entails not merely piecemeal measures but a radical restructuring of society in order to overcome the sexism that sets up and maintains oppression in psychological and biological terms. For instance, feminists believe that partnership (sexual or otherwise) should be structured according to a fluid model of reciprocity and mutuality rather than a rigid one-up, one-down model in which somebody has to be the boss.

What distinguishes *Christian* feminism from other forms of feminist commitments is adherence to personal faith in Christ as opposed to regarding the Christian religion as so inherently sexist that it must be abandoned. Among Christian feminists, *evangelical* feminists are distinguished by their insistence that when the Bible is interpreted holistically and with scholarly care, it turns out to be part of the solution rather than part of the problem.

3. "For Some Children, The Bedtime Story is Just the Beginning of a Nightmare" (Washington: Religious Coalition for Abortion Rights, n.d.).
4. See Diana E. H. Russel, *Rape in Marriage* (New York: Macmillan, 1982).
5. "The Hyde Amendment . . . An Assault on the Moral Integrity of the Poor" (Washington, D.C.: Religious Coalition for Abortion Rights, 1984).
6. See Mimi Alperin, "The Feminization of Poverty," *Women of Faith in Dialogue,* ed. Virginia R. Mollenkott (New York: Crossroad, 1987).

Although we admit that there are many reflections in the Bible of the sexist cultures in which the biblical authors were socialized, evangelical feminists argue that the overall thrust of Scripture is toward human equality and mutual empowerment.[7]

On the matter of abortion, the vast majority of Christian feminists recognize the absolute necessity of "women's right to the conditions for procreative choice," seeing women's "right to choose" as one of the most basic foundations of justice for women. Along with Beverly Wildung Harrison, who has provided important leadership, Christian feminists work to call Christian ethical discussions to accountability concerning women's well-being. Like Harrison, we work in the "hope and faith that a non-misogynist Christianity is a possibility."[8] . . .

Partly because it is difficult to avoid absorbing the unconscious misogyny of right-wing Christianity, there are people who claim to be feminist who do not favor reproductive freedom for women and therefore do not support the moral agency of women. . . . For instance, I was recently the only pro-choice plenary speaker at the fourth annual Evangelical Round Table, a national gathering of scholars discussing "The Sanctity of Life."[9] Although I was assured that a full spectrum of opinion would be represented, no fewer than nine other plenary speakers—in fact, everybody other than myself who would be touching on the abortion issue—were opposed to permitting pregnant women to decide their own destiny in relationship to God and human responsibility as they perceived it. Almost everyone was willing to use public policy to render abortion illegal, thus removing from pregnant women the opportunity of choice without which nobody can be a responsible moral agent.

I argued that according to Genesis, God gave to Adam and Eve both the power of responsible choice and the means and opportunity to choose wrongly. Although an omniscient God would certainly have known the sad results of their choice, the alternative was to create marionettes who would serve necessity rather than God. So important was human moral agency that God voluntarily limited God's own power by placing power into human hands: "Then God said, 'Let us make [humanity] in our image, in our likeness, and *let them rule* over the fish of the sea and the birds of the air, over the livestock, over all the earth'. . . . God blessed them and said to them, 'Be fruitful and increase in number; fill the earth and *subdue* it.'" (Gen. 1:26–28 NIV, emphasis mine.) Although several hundred evangelicals who heard this argument believe in the authority of Scripture and recognize the necessity of

7. The central organization of evangelical Christian feminists is the Evangelical Women's Caucus, 1357 Washington Street, West Newton, Massachusettes 02165. Phone: (617) 527-3560. Publications that are committed to evangelical feminism include *The Other Side* (Philadelphia) and *Daughters of Sarah* (Chicago).

8. *Our Right to Choose: Toward a New Ethic of Abortion* (Boston: Beacon, 1983).

9. Held at Eastern College, June 3–5, 1987.

choice in every other area of life, so committed are they to the concept of the fetus as fully human that not one single voice was raised in support of my position. One assistant district attorney did attempt to use Exodus 21:22–25 to give biblical primacy to woman's life over the life of the fetus, since loss of the fetus incurs only a fine while loss of the woman's life requires a life for a life; but he was immediately silenced by Ronald Sider's claim that a proper translation of Exodus 21 in The New International Version indicates not loss of the fetus' life, but only a premature birth.[10] Dr. Sider did not mention the fact that even the NIV translators give "miscarriage" in a footnote as an accurate alternative reading, while the King James Version, the Living Bible, The Jerusalem Bible, the New English Bible, and the Revised Standard Version all translate "miscarriage," so that *ending fetal life clearly requires only payment of a fine, while ending a woman's life requires the death penalty.* This is an important distinction because Exodus 21 is the only place where Scripture even distantly approaches the topic of abortion; and it implies the primacy of the woman's fully developed actual human life over the fetus' developing, but only potential humanity. Such a distinction is basic to conservative Christians like John R. W. Stott, who comments that the decision to abort for reasons of maternal health involves "a choice between an actual human being and a potential human being."[11]

At the Evangelical Round Table dedicated to "The Sanctity of Life," I was struck by the absence of any acknowledgment of the sanctity of woman's moral agency and the general unconcern about the well-being of women. There were a few references to "compassion," but one wonders what compassion might mean to people who are willing to support public policy that forces desperate women into back-alley life-endangering abortions. I came away wondering whether, indeed, "a non-misogynistic Christianity is a possibility," but my presence there is evidence that like other Christian feminists, I have not yet abandoned hope.[12] . . .

Like racism, misogyny rarely goes without its mask. In a campaign to control women's lives by controlling their reproductivity, the central strategy is reiteration of the simple declaration that human personhood begins at conception, so that killing a fetus is no more acceptable than any other form of murder. But such statements short-circuit ethical discussion by assuming that one particular theological viewpoint has such absolute validity that it must be imposed on others who in all honesty do not agree with it.

---

10. Although Sider did not document his claim, he was relying on Jack W. Cottrell, "Abortion and the Mosaic Law," *Christianity Today,* 16 March 1973, 8.

11. "Reverence for Human Life," *Christianity Today,* 9 June 1972, 12.

12. My speech, "'Freely They Stood Who Stood, and Fell Who Fell': Respecting the Moral Responsibility of Women," will be published in Volume III of *The Evangelical Round Table* (Princeton University Press, 1988). It will also be published in slightly different form by the Religious Coalition for Abortion Rights.

At the Evangelical Round Table, aware that the charge of civil religion might be damaging to her cause, Kay Coles James of the National Right to Life Committee claimed that fetal personhood is a biological fact rather than a theological perception. But in all truthfulness, the most that biology can claim is that the fetus is genetically human, in the same way that a severed human hand or foot or other body part is human. The issue of *personhood* is one that must be addressed through religious reasoning. . . . Except in the most materialistic of philosophies, human *personhood* has a great deal to do with feelings, awareness, and interactive experience. As the United Church of Christ puts it, "The question of when life begins . . . is primarily a theological question, on which denominations or religious groups must be permitted to establish and follow their own teachings."[13]

In a pluralistic society, wherever there is widespread diversity of opinion concerning an issue, there can never be a just law requiring uniformity of behavior vis à vis that issue. Hence, women who believe that abortion is murder may *never* justly be required to have an abortion. Anti-abortion laws would not affect such women for obvious reasons. But for women whose religious beliefs do permit them to consider abortion (and under certain circumstances require them to do so), anti-abortion legislation would forbid their following these religious convictions. Hence, anti-abortion legislation would start America [down] yet another slippery slope, in which the erosion of the first clause of the Bill of Rights, which protects freedom of religion, could lead to the erosion of subsequent clauses in the same Bill of Rights. . . .

Dr. John M. Swomley, Professor of Christian Social Ethics at St. Paul School of Theology (Missouri), asserts that "The pro-life position is really a pro-fetus position and the pro-choice position is really pro-woman." I think Dr. Swomley is right about that, as long as "pro-woman" is understood to be supportive of the woman's need to assess what is God's will for her and whether or not she can adequately undertake the lifelong covenant of caring that giving birth represents. Pro-choice feminists do not devalue the fetus or even pit the rights of the woman against the rights of the fetus. Rather, we seek to support the woman's moral agency as she weighs the complex factors that must affect her decision, including the value of the fetus as potential human life, the quality of life that she could offer the fetus after its birth, the probable impact of that birth on the already existing web of her other relationships and responsibilities, and her own mental health and general well-being.

Dr. Swomley raises the important question of whether indeed there is anything either in law or the Bible about absolute right to life. Distinguishing between a virtue and a right, Dr. Swomley points out that nobody can sue anyone else for failing to endanger their own life by diving into deep water to try to save a drowning person. (Thus, the drowning person has no *absolute*

13. Statement of the General Synod, 1981.

right to life.)[14] And there is no biblical mandate that requires us to risk our lives to save the life of someone else. To the contrary: Jesus treated it as evidence of exceptional love if anyone were willing to die for his or her friend (John 15:13). Every time a woman gives birth, she undergoes the equivalent of a major operation, whereas getting a legal abortion is seven times safer than giving birth. It is remarkable that through the centuries, so many millions of women have chosen to give birth and have gracefully entered into a lifelong covenant of caring for their children. One cannot get that quality of caring by coercive methods!

If Christians truly care about justice for women, for people of other colors than white, and for the poor as well as the rich, we will restrain ourselves from the coercions involved in civil religion and will work to assure the availability of legal, medically safe abortion services for those who need them—including the public funding without which impoverished women cannot exert their procreative responsibility. At the same time, remembering the behavior of Hitler who discredited birth control, closed contraceptive clinics, and made abortion assistance a penal offense for Germans while *forcing* Jewish and other non-Aryan women to have abortions,[15] we will also resist attempts to force sterilization onto Third World or other powerless women, and we will try to see to it that everyone is supplied with reliable, affordable means of contraception. We will try to improve the quality of life for the born as well as the unborn by finding ways to provide poor families with food, shelter, and clothing; by paying just wages for women's work; by developing adequate, affordable childcare centers and shelters for battered spouses and children; and by providing thorough sex education that teaches people to honor human dignity in their relationships.

Institutionally speaking, is a non-misogynistic Christianity really possible? And do the American people really value religious freedom enough to restrain their government from passing laws that are based on the theological perceptions of only *some* of the people? Will American women be permitted to act upon their consciences as dignified moral agents in the reproductive choices that determine their lives, their families, and their futures? Will Medicaid ever again make it possible for poor women to achieve the reproductive freedom that more affluent women currently enjoy?

Only time will tell.

From Virginia Ramey Mollenkott, "Reproductive Choice: Basic to Justice for Women," *Christian Scholar's Review* 17 (1988): 286–93.

14. *Six Ethical Questions* (Washington, D.C.: Religious Coalition for Abortion Rights, 1984).
15. Frederica F. Hodges, *Abortion and the Holocaust: Twisting the Language* (Washington, D.C.: Religious Coalition for Abortion Rights, 1987).

Abortion and the Mosaic Law

Jack W. Cottrell

Perhaps the most crucial question in the abortion debate is when (or even whether) the fetus is to be considered a human being. . . . The problem is that the biblical teaching directly relevant to the abortion debate is quite scanty. There are a few passages, such as Psalm 139:13–15, Job 3:11, Jeremiah 1:5, and Luke 1:39–44, that are often cited as evidence that God considers the unborn child fully human. . . .

Another passage of Scripture to which an appeal is being made more and more in the current debate is Exodus 21:22–25, which reads as follows in the American Standard Version:

> And if men strive together, and hurt a woman with child, so that her fruit depart, and yet no harm follow; he shall be surely fined, according as the woman's husband shall lay upon him; and he shall pay as the judges determine. But if any harm follow, then thou shalt give life for life, eye for eye, tooth for tooth, hand for hand, foot for foot, burning for burning, wound for wound, stripe for stripe.

A number of evangelicals are among those who think this passage indicates that the Bible makes a distinction between fully human life and the life of the fetus. These verses are taken to mean that a fetus is not considered to be a soul or a fully human person, and that it is therefore of less inherent value than an already born person.

Among those evangelicals who have taken this position is . . . Nancy Hardesty, who in *Eternity* quotes Exodus 21:22–25 and then says,

> It can be inferred here that the fetus was not considered a human life or "life for life" would have been demanded as it was for the mother's life or at least a

"fetus for a fetus" as was done under Assyrian law ["When Does Life Begin?," *Eternity*, Feb., 1971].

In the same issue Lloyd Kalland remarks,

> According to Ex. 21:22, it is not a capital offense to destroy a fetus. Interpreters who claim that the fetus should be treated as a person, in my opinion, have been unsuccessful in their attempt to square this assumption with the interpretation most faithful to the text. . . . "While the fetus is a precious organism, it is not yet a complete person ["Fetal Life"]. . . .

The majority of commentaries and translations are favorable to the interpretation discussed above. In numerous allusions to this text, the Talmud uniformly sees it as referring to a miscarriage, equivalent to a property loss on the part of the father. The following reference is typical: "If one hurt a woman so that her embryo departed from her, compensation for Depreciation and for Pain should be given to the woman, compensation for the value of the embryo to the husband." As John Peter Lange sees it, verse 22 refers to a case in which an abortion takes place but no other injury results *(Commentary on the Holy Scriptures)*. . . .

Most modern translations likewise present verse 22 as a reference to a miscarriage. The Revised Standard Version reads, "When men strive together, and hurt a woman with child, so that there is a miscarriage, and yet no harm follows, the one who hurt her shall be fined, according as the woman's husband shall lay upon him." . . .

In all these commentaries and translations, . . . two things are either stated or implied: (1) that verse 22 refers to a miscarriage, the death of the unborn child; and (2) that this supposed death of the fetus is the injury for which the guilty party is only fined, while any injury to the mother is considered to be *further* harm serious enough to invoke the *lex talionis* (eye for eye, tooth for tooth, and so on). . . .

Despite the widespread acceptance of this view of Exodus 21:22–25, this interpretation does not seem to me to be supported by the text itself. This is true particularly of the two points specified in the preceding paragraph. A careful examination of these verses can yield conclusions quite different from these: (1) that verse 22 refers to the premature birth of an otherwise healthy child, and (2) that an injury to the child no less than to the mother called for the application of the *lex talionis*.

There is absolutely no linguistic justification for translating verse 22 to refer to a miscarriage. The clause rendered in both the King James and the American Standard Version "so that her fruit depart" literally reads, "and her children come out" (as the marginal reading in the New American Standard Version indicates). The noun is *yeled*, which is a common word for child or offspring. (The only peculiarity is that it is plural.) The verb is *yatza'*, which has the common meaning of "to go out, to go forth, to come forth." It is often used to refer to the ordinary birth of children, either as coming forth from the loins of the father (e.g., Gen. 15:4; 46:26; 1 Kings 8:19; Isa. 39:7), or as coming forth from the womb of the mother (Gen. 25:25, 26; 38:28, 29; Job 1:21; 3:11; Eccles. 5:15; Jer. 1:5; 20:18). In the latter instances the reference is to an ordinary birth of a normal child; in no case is the word used to indicate a miscarriage. (In one passage, Num. 12:12, the word refers to the birth of a stillborn child. But this is a stillbirth, not a miscarriage; also, the concept of stillbirth is communicated not through the verb *yatza'* but through the specific description of the child itself.)

Another reason for thinking that Exodus 21:22 refers to a premature birth and not to a miscarriage is that there is a Hebrew word, *shachol*, that specifically refers to the event of miscarriage. (In some cases it means "to be bereaved.") This word is used in Exodus 23:26 and Hosea 9:14, where it refers to miscarriage among human beings. In Genesis 31:38 and Job 21:10 it refers to animals, and in 2 Kings 2:19, 21 and Malachi 3:11 it refers to land and plants that do not produce mature fruit.

Thus there seems to be no warrant for interpreting Exodus 21:22 to mean "the destruction of a fetus." . . . The expression used is indicative of nothing more than the birth of a child. The irregularity of the situation is the fact that the birth is prematurely and maliciously induced.

The second point I wish to defend is, as stated above, that any injury to the child no less than to the mother would demand the application of the *lex talionis*. This is, of course, contrary to the popular understanding in which verse 22 refers to a case in which the fetus is killed but no *other* harm ensues, the death of the fetus being considered a minor injury that deserves to be penalized only by a fine. According to this view, then, verse 23 would be talking about some *further* harm of a much more serious nature, i.e., an injury to the mother herself. Only if the mother received injury would "an eye for an eye" be required, or "a life for a life."

But it must be insisted that the text itself makes no distinction between any harm done to the child and any harm done to the mother. This is simply not the point of contrast in the passage. What is being contrasted is a situation in which harm comes to neither mother nor child, and a situation in which either one or the other is harmed. In the former situation, the premature birth of the infant is not considered to be harm at all. The text specifically says that if the woman is struck so that her children come out, "and there not be harm" then the adversary shall be fined. The fine presumably is imposed because of the danger to which mother and child are exposed and the parents' distress in connection with the unnaturally premature birth.

The illusion that the birth of the child is in itself harm or injury (even to the point of death) is created by the addition of the word *other* or *further*, either in verse 22 or in verse 23. . . . The New American Bible says that she "suffers a miscarriage, but no further injury." (Moffatt, Goodspeed, the Amplified Bible, and the New American Standard Version are similar to the NAB, although the NASV properly italicizes the word *further*.) The addition of *other* or *further* implies that some harm has already been done, namely, the alleged miscarriage; this is then judged to be relatively insignificant in that it draws only a fine. But the original text contains no such word as *other* or *further*. It clearly and simply says that this first contingency is a case in which no harm occurs. Even though the child is born prematurely, it is unharmed. The text will permit no other understanding.

Only in verse 23 is the possibility of harm introduced, and it reads literally, "and if harm occurs." The text does not say that this is *further* harm, or that it applies only to the mother. It makes absolutely no distinction between the mother and the child.

Clearly, then, the interpretation of this passage that is most faithful to the text is that which distinguishes between a premature birth that harms neither the mother nor the child and a premature birth in which one or the other is injured or even dies. In the latter case the life of the fetus is valued just as highly as the life of the mother, and the *lex talionis* principle applied to both. . . .

This conclusion about Exodus 21:22–25 will by no means settle the abortion issue. One might grant the validity of this interpretation and still in good Christian conscience be in favor of more liberal abortion practices. One might argue, for instance, that this section of the law is not intended to say anything about a non-viable fetus, and that it is therefore irrelevant to the main part of the argument. Yet at the very least, if this view of Exodus 21:22–25 is correct, then one can no longer find here a biblical justification for liberalizing abortion laws. And if it cannot be found here, then it can be found nowhere in Scripture, for there does not seem to be any other passage to which any serious appeal has been or can be made for this purpose.*

From Jack W. Cottrell, "Abortion and the Mosaic Law." Used by permission, *Christianity Today* (16 March 1973): 602–5.

*In the original, Prof. Cottrell referred to Bruce K. Waltke, "The Old Testament and Birth Control," *Christianity Today,* 8 November 1968. Waltke has modified his views, so the editors have deleted references to his essay.

The Right to Life

Three Theories

Robert N. Wennberg

. . . The abortion debate has served to provoke interest in the much larger and more fundamental question: How extensive is the class of individuals possessing full moral standing? Are human infants and human fetuses, for example, *both* included in this class? And what do we say about the severely retarded, that is, individuals destined never to function above a subpersonal level; do they possess full moral standing? And are any non-human animals to be included? So then, how are we to classify the following: fetuses, infants, children, adults, the reversibly comatose, the irreversibly comatose, the severely retarded, the less severely retarded, and non-human animals? Which of these possess full moral standing?. . .

Three principles are presently receiving considerable attention in the professional literature. Each defines the class of possessors of the right to life, and each has different implications for the moral permissibility of such activities as abortion and infanticide. Unquestionably the Christian community has a continuing obligation to give these theories (and variants of them) careful scrutiny and to be an active participant in the current discussion. Simply in terms of the pursuit of moral truth this is a significant debate. But it is also one with social ramifications that in time will impinge upon us all—Christians and non-Christians alike.

The three theories can be stated as follows:

(1) Only beings with a developed capacity for conscious self-reflective intelligence have a right to life.

(2) Beings with *either* a developed capacity or a "natural potential"[1] for conscious self-reflective intelligence have a right to life.

1. A human organism has a "natural potential" for personhood if it is possible for it to develop into a person without the necessity of outside intervention to invest it with new latent

36

(3) All members of the human species have a right to life, whether or not there is a potential for conscious self-reflective intelligence.

These theories might be labeled, respectively, the *actuality principle*, the *potentiality principle*, and the *species principle*. And if we were to stipulate that a *person* is an individual with a developed capacity for self-reflective intelligence (admittedly a narrow construal of the term), then we can state the three principles in the following way:

(1) The actuality principle: only persons have a right to life.
(2) The potentiality principle: both potential and actual persons have a right to life.
(3) The species principle: all members of the human species have a right to life, whether or not there is a potential for personhood.

The Actuality Principle

This is the most radical theory on the current scene. It maintains that an individual comes to possess a right to life only when that individual possesses self-consciousness, thoughts of the future, and hopes and aspirations for that future. This view is notable—perhaps notorious—because of the individuals which it *excludes* from possessing a right to life; among those excluded are, especially, *infants*. For to kill painlessly a newborn infant or to abort a non-viable fetus is, it is argued, to accomplish only what effective birth control measures would also accomplish, namely, preventing a personal center of consciousness from emerging. Such prevention harms no one, for there is "no one" to be harmed. To be sure, the individual who grows to adulthood will be glad not to have been killed in infancy, and glad not to have been aborted during pregnancy, but also—note—glad that his or her conception was not prevented by birth control. None of these practices—birth control, abortion, and infanticide—harm *persons* (that is, harm self-conscious beings with hopes and aspirations for the future) but only prevent persons (in that same sense of the term) from coming into existence. According to the actuality principle, however, no person has a right to *come into* existence; they only have a right to *remain* in existence.

In sum, the implications of the actuality principle look like this:

---

properties, the unfolding of which (when coupled with socialization) will yield a person. On this view, the *unfertilized* ovum does not have a natural potential for personhood because it requires the intervention of the male sperm to give it new features which only then put it on a trajectory that will yield a person. Thus if one could preserve alive an unfertilized ovum, one would always have just that—an unfertilized ovum. But if one preserves alive a fertilized ovum, there will in time emerge a person.

Possessors of a right to life	Non-possessors of a right to life:
children	fetuses
adults	infants
the *reversibly* comatose	the *irreversibly* comatose
the less severely retarded	the severely retarded
	. . .

The Potentiality Principle

But how should we meet the challenge that it makes no sense to ascribe to infants (and to fetuses) a right to life? We can, of course, argue that it does make sense—and I, in fact, happen to believe that it does. But a protracted discussion would be required to show this, with some people—indeed, people who have no sympathy whatsoever for the actuality principle—continuing to find talk of an infant's right to life conceptually problematic. And many philosophers find the whole notion of moral rights and their existence a difficult one. Further, Christians often do not warm to the notion that persons have a right to life nor to the claim that this is what makes killing wrong to begin with, for it seems to leave God out of the moral picture. After all, both the Old and New Testaments roundly condemn the killing of the innocent, but never introduce the notion of a right to life.[2] For in the biblical tradition it is not that someone's killing me violates my right to life so much as it violates God's sovereignty over life and his authority to determine under what circumstances it can be taken. In this spirit Dietrich Bonhoeffer (in remarks referring to abortion but *a fortiori* applicable to infanticide) has commented, "The simple fact is that God certainly intended to create a human being, and this nascent human being has been deliberately deprived of his life."[3] So what is wrong with infanticide? Just this: it contravenes a divine intention for that life, namely that from the infant a person is to emerge.

Therefore, what we can argue is that the life of an infant is to be respected and not taken at will because from the infant will emerge a person, a personal center of consciousness, a rational agent, a self-aware being capable of moral and spiritual agency. This is to endorse the more general principle: it is wrong to kill what will naturally and in due course develop into a person. And by arguing this way we have introduced the potentiality principle. Further, lying behind this principle, it might be pointed out, is the more general principle, in Alan Donagan's words, ". . . if respect is owed to beings because

2. Likewise Greek ethics operated without the concept of a right to life. Not until William of Ockham was the notion of possessing any kind of right explicitly introduced into moral discourse. Cf. Kurt Baier, "When Does the Right to Life Begin?" in *Human Rights*, ed., J. R. Pennock and J. W. Chapman (New York: New York University Press, 1981). For a sensitive attempt to articulate a Christian theory of rights, see Lisa Sowle Cahill, "Toward a Christian Theory of Human Rights," *The Journal of Religious Ethics* 8 (Fall 1980): 277–301.

3. *Ethics* (New York: Macmillan, 1955), 176.

they are in a certain state, it is owed to whatever, by its very nature, develops into that state."[4] Both of these principles can be accepted and understood without any reference to a right to life. So when asked why it is intrinsically objectionable to kill infants, we can say: it is wrong to kill what will naturally and in due course develop into a person. When asked why should we accept *that* principle, we can reply: "if respect is owed to beings because they are in a certain state, it is owed to whatever, by its very nature, develops into that state." Now people may choose to reject both of these principles, but they are not required to do so because the principles themselves are conceptually incoherent. Thus killing infants could be intrinsically objectionable even should infants not be the bearers of a right to life. And so also for all potential persons; they can possess an inviolate status even if it should turn out that they do not possess a right to life. The potentiality principle, then, makes a sensible and coherent claim in maintaining that the lives of those with a potential for personhood must be respected.

Now, as was stated at the outset of this paper, those who place a major emphasis upon rights usually do so with an explicit anti-utilitarian point of view, stressing basic rights which do not defer to the collective interests of society. In contrast, it is the utilitarian who characteristically eschews all talk of rights. However, to abandon talk of a right to life, as I am here suggesting, or even to abandon *all* talk of rights, does not necessarily signal pro-utilitarian sympathies, nor does it commit one to utilitarian conclusions. For the anti-utilitarian moral perspective—which I endorse and judge most compatible with a Christian perspective—can also be framed with no reference to rights at all. Indeed, principles devoid of any reference to rights can be as inviolable as rights themselves (or principles referring to rights). Thus even if "rights" are conceptually problematic, it is possible to assign moral standing to potential persons without resorting to utilitarianism. The potentiality principle remains a live option even if *a right to life* cannot be sensibly attributed to potential persons.

The implications of the potentiality principle are as follows:

Possessors of a right to life (or full moral standing):	Non-possessors of a right to life (or full moral standing):
fetuses	the irreversibly comatose
infants	the severely retarded
children	
adults	
the reversibly comatose	
the less severely retarded	

4. *The Theory of Morality* (Chicago: University of Chicago Press, 1977), 171.

And how do advocates of the potentiality principle classify non-human animals? They conceivably could grant some of them a right to life. It all depends on how they view the rational capacity of various animals. Thus chimpanzees who use American Sign Language, because of their advanced level of rationality, might be classified as holders of a right to life or possessors of full moral standing. Certainly the intelligence-level of chimpanzees is impressive, even if we agree with those who deny that chimpanzees have in fact learned to use language. However, my strong inclination is to argue that human beings have a unique value that surpasses that of any animal, including the chimpanzee. For what makes human life especially valuable is the capacity for moral and spiritual agency, and thus the capacity to relate and to be accountable to God. This capacity is absent in all non-human animals, including the most intelligent (chimpanzees, dolphins, etc.). Their life patterns are adopted instinctively and are not chosen from among alternatives, nor are they the object of moral reflection. Human beings choose the ends for which they will live, non-human animals do not. These remarks do not justify, however, the traditional Western insensitivity toward the suffering of animals and their casual use in trivial scientific experimentation. For from the fact that human beings have a unique value it does not follow that animals have no value at all. However, it *is* to say that both those with a capacity for moral and spiritual agency, and those with a potential for such agency, do have an incomparable value and claim to life.

This is a moral account that finds a congenial home in the context of the Judaeo-Christian tradition, where there is a profound sense of gratitude for life as a gift of God. Life has been given by a loving and gracious God, and that gift is itself good despite the burdens that may have to be borne to preserve and protect it. Such a gift is not to be repudiated but prized and nurtured. Additional theological support is found in the doctrine of creation, which affirms not merely that God brought the universe into existence at one time by the free exercise of his power, but also that the ongoing procreative process is to be viewed as expressive of God's creative will. Therefore the infant as viewed through the eyes of Christian faith is seen as biological human life on the way to thinking, loving, willing, and worshipping, and all this is perceived as God's intention and purpose for that life. Certainly these two theological themes, that life is a gift of God and that God the creator has intentions for biological human life, express and support a strong presumption in favor of life that characterizes the Christian tradition. This presumption means that the burden of proof rests on the shoulders of those who would destroy developing human life, and this burden is a heavy one; substantial reasons are required before human life can be sacrificed.

Nevertheless the potentiality principle is not without its problems, despite the theological compliments I have paid it. For just as the actuality principle involves the denial that infants have a right to life, so the potentiality principle involves the denial that the *severely retarded* have a right to life. To put it in more general terms, it involves the denial that killing the severely retarded is intrinsically objectionable. By "severely retarded" reference is made to all those members of the human species who by defect of birth are destined never to become personal beings. But if an individual altogether lacks the potential for personal existence, then according to the potentiality principle that individual does not have a right to life nor an inviolate status. And this denial does seem to be an awkward implication—at least at first flush, though it is not in the same category with the more offensive denial that normal infants possess an inviolate status or a right to life.

However, it may not be beyond *all* doubt that the life of a severely and permanently retarded individual is inviolate in the way that the life of a person or potential person is inviolate. To be sure, there may be *other* very good reasons for not killing such individuals, such as the considerable danger involved in drawing lines ("here rationality is adequately developed but there it is not"), or the tendency of such acts of killing to blunt our sensitivity and respect for other human life, or, finally, the danger of mistaken diagnosis and prognosis. (I want to be very clear that I am thinking of the extreme cases where individuals are unable to function above an animal level. I am not thinking, for example, of those participants in the Special Olympics for whom personal existence is present, though stunted. Such individuals are persons with an unqualified right to life. That is beyond dispute. All participants in the current debate acknowledge that fact.) Nevertheless, it is not easy to accept the claim that these are the *only* reasons for respecting the lives of the severely retarded. It may be that the grossly retarded have a unique status. For it does seem that it is more seriously wrong to kill an adult person or a normal newborn than it would be to kill a grossly retarded individual. On the other hand, it is a more serious act to kill a severely retarded human than to kill a dog or cat.

A comment by Philip Devine may prove helpful at this point, serving to reduce the moral tension that those of us who are otherwise attracted to the potentiality principle may feel. He says,

> The principle of respect for persons also extends by what might be called the overflow principle, to things closely associated with persons. Thus corpses ought not to be treated as ordinary garbage, and one might also argue that a modicum of reverence should be accorded the process by which persons come to be.[5]

The overflow principle, as Devine calls it, might also be invoked to explain the respect we feel to be appropriate to the grossly retarded. For they possess the kind of living biological organism through which personal life normally

5. *The Ethics of Homicide* (Ithaca, N.Y.: Cornell University Press, 1978), 10.

manifests itself, though in their particular case it does not and will not. The severely retarded, then, are "closely associated" with those who are persons by virtue of their sharing the same biological organism. The respect due the grossly retarded is "an overflow," meaning that it is less than that which is due a person (or potential person), but more than would be proper for a mere animal. By putting the grossly retarded in this special category, a category in which a good measure of special respect is due, we achieve several things. First, the sting is taken out of any denial that the grossly retarded have a person's right to life—for we are not thereby reducing them to mere animal status. Second, we are enabled to preserve the insight that personhood, with its attendant moral and spiritual capacities (or potential for this), on an individual by individual basis, renders human life valuable and inviolate.

The overflow principle can be articulated in terms of a Christian anthropology that views human beings as compound creatures consisting of two dimensions: (a) self-creative moral and spiritual agency, and (b) biological functioning which (normally) makes possible such agency. The respect due such compound creatures is both a product of their nature and the fact that they are a divine creation. In the case of the severely retarded, however, there is no agent-capacity since there exists a human biological organism that is critically defective. Nevertheless such organisms remain a divine creation and significantly they are of the same biological type ordained by God to be bearers of moral and spiritual agency. Because of this association a more-than-animal-respect is appropriate. We may judge them *not* to be in the image of God and not to have a person's or potential person's inviolate status, but for all that we do not relegate them to animal status (even if we have a high view of animals). So when we are confronted by any such biological organism we recognize it as a member—although a defective member—of that class of organisms divinely chosen to be vehicles for rational, moral, and spiritual life, and as a consequence we deem a considerable amount of respect for the individual to be appropriate.

The Species Principle

Once we take the potentiality principle and augment it with the overflow principle we come very close to having what amounts to the species principle, namely, the principle that declares that human life is rendered inviolate by virtue of membership in the species *Homo sapiens*. It is not, according to this view, personal characteristics nor possession of a potential for this that invests one with full moral standing. Rather it is solely by virtue of our species membership—a member of the human species being defined as any being conceived of human parents. In this there is an explicit rejection of the doctrine that an *individual Homo sapiens* has its special status by virtue of *its* being either a person or a potential person. It is sufficient simply that it be a member of the right species. Thus the life of a defective *Homo sapiens*—an anencephalic infant, for example—with no potential whatsoever for rational existence, [is] still inviolate because it is a *Homo sapiens;* that fact alone endows it with its special status.

The strength of the species principle is that it accounts very well for what many—if not most—people seem to believe, namely, that infants (who are not yet persons, in a strict sense of that term, but nevertheless are *Homo sapiens*), adult humans (who are persons in this sense and are *Homo sapiens*) and grossly retarded humans (who never will be persons but are *Homo sapiens*) all possess a shared dignity and value. The one thing they have in common is that they are *Homo sapiens.* So it is tempting to conclude that it is simply membership in the human species that endows one with a right to life. However, if the species principle is not appropriately qualified, the irreversibly comatose, who are still members of the human species but who have no prospect for conscious experience, will be possessors of full moral standing. This does seem odd. To avoid this implication the species principle can be interpreted as maintaining that only members of the human species who are *conscious or have a potential for conscious existence* have full moral standing. On this interpretation the species principle dictates the following conclusions:

Possessors of a right to life:	Non-possessors of a right to life:
fetuses	the irreversibly comatose
infants	
children	
adults	
the reversibly comatose	
the severely retarded	
the less severely retarded	

Unquestionably the most interesting and perplexing case is that posed by the grossly retarded. Such individuals are neither persons nor will they ever be persons. However, if we are of the opinion that such extremely retarded individuals have the same moral status that a normal person has and if we are not happy with the overflow principle, then we may be hard pressed to account for this opinion except by reference to considerations of species— they are *Homo sapiens* and solely because of this their lives have to be respected every bit as much as our own. For although the grossly retarded may function only at an animal level, we are understandably loathe to relegate them to mere animal status.

To be sure, some have argued *not* that the absence of personal life in the severely retarded yields the conclusion that we can justifiably treat them like animals, but rather it forces the conclusion that some animals are to be upgraded and given the same consideration we accord to persons. For if the excessively retarded lack the capacity for personal life, but still have the right to life or full moral standing, then we can't exclude animals on the grounds that *they* lack that capacity. We may not be happy with this suggestion nor content to relegate the excessively retarded to mere animal status. And for many this is precisely the appeal of the species principle—it *includes* the excessively retarded as possessors of a right to life (they are members of the proper species) but excludes animals (they are not members of the proper species).

But why does this particular species endow its members with a right to life? Providing an answer to this question is essential if one is to avoid the charge—one now frequently made—that the species principle is nothing more than an arbitrary preference for one's own species—the Planet of the Apes syndrome, if you will, or what is now standardly labeled "speciesism" (on analogy with racism and sexism). One answer that can be given is simply to contend that *Homo sapiens* is a species—and so far as we know the only species—in which rational creatures are found and that their presence in the species sanctifies the *entire* species, endowing each member with a right to life whether or not the particular member is itself a rational being.

However, on this explanation of matters we are being asked to believe that *Homo sapiens* are morally special because of the presence of personal life in the species in general, while individual *Homo sapiens* are *not* rendered "unspecial" by its total absence in them. Whereas there is no formal contradiction in such a claim, there is something contrary to common procedure in this approach. For when I assert that the life of a pet canary, say, is not inviolate, I draw that conclusion simply because I believe that *this* canary is neither a person nor a potential person, not on the basis of what I believe about *other* canaries—that none of them are persons (though I happen to believe that as well).

Nevertheless there is a theological version of the species principle which will hold attraction for those who view the image of God not as a network of special rational capacities, whether actualized or potential, but as a unique *status* conferred in a sovereign act of valuation by God. Of course such a Barthian conception of the image of God will not appeal to everyone. But for those for whom it does have appeal it will provide a theological basis for the species principle. It would be claimed that the act of divine valuation has as its object all and only *Homo sapiens,* who thereby are in the image of God and consequently protected by the biblical prohibition against killing the innocent. Thus all that is required to be in the image of God is to have the requisite status, something that can be had even if the individual never was, never could be, nor ever will be a person (i.e., a rational being capable of moral and spiritual response to God). Thus an anencephalic infant is in the image of God even though it lacks an upper brain portion and consequently has no potential for rational existence. Conceivably, then, apes and ants could have been in the image of God, for God could have conferred this status on them without having to alter their nature. But some of us may rest uncomfortable with such a view, believing instead that one's status as a special object of God's love and grace is in fact tied to one's nature as a person (or potential person) who can respond to God, enter into relationship with him, and be morally and spiritually accountable to him. It may indeed be, as Christians affirm, that this special status is something conferred on persons by God by virtue of his purposes for them, a status he could have refrained from conferring had he not had those purposes. But it doesn't follow that God confers this status on those who lack the potential for personal life and who therefore cannot participate in those purposes.

Concluding Remarks

The actuality principle has implications that will be distressing both to the Christian community and to the community at large. . . .

Nevertheless, for the Christian the choice between the potentiality principle and the species principle is a more difficult matter, though in this regard our respective views of the image of God might well prove decisive for us. If we judge that the image of God is the capacity, whether potential or actualized, for moral, spiritual, and rational agency (as I am inclined to do), then we are well on our way to accepting the potentiality principle. But if we also adopt the overflow principle (i.e., non-rational members of the human species possess a special, though *less than full,* moral status simply because they are *Homo sapiens*), then we have adopted a logic that parallels the logic of the species principle (i.e., non-rational members of the human species possess a *full* and unqualified moral status simply because they are *Homo sapiens*). In that case we must at least have a sympathy for the species principle even if we judge it not to be as finely nuanced as the alternative that we ourselves find convincing. . . .

No matter how we ultimately resolve these issues, as Christians we address them within the context of a tradition that has a profound respect for developing human life and that finds the termination of such life, even in justified circumstances, tragic and sorrowful. We affirm, therefore, the high value of fetal and neonatal life, and if such an affirmation means anything, it must mean that burdens are to be borne to preserve and protect that life. This must always be the starting point from which we begin our theorizing.

From Robert N. Wennberg, "The Right to Life: Three Theories," *Christian Scholar's Review* 13 (1984): 315–32.

When Does a Person Begin?

Robert E. Joyce

Everyone ought to be interested in his or her origins on the planet Earth. Someday little Louise Brown [born in 1978], the first "test-tube baby," will be interested. Today you and I wonder when we began as persons. . . .

What really happens in the fertilization process, and what is this being we call a *person?* These are two of the most important questions. Our responses will go a long way in helping to determine the ethical rightness or wrongness of abortion and of *in vitro* fertilization.

What is a person? When is a person? These questions are essentially philosophical. They require an integration of our knowledge of certain basic data and conclusions in embryology. But they are not specifically scientific questions. We go beyond the eyeball vision and verification involved in natural science, while taking it carefully into account, and we try to say ultimately what this tiny, microscopic creature called a human zygote really *is*. Biologically viewed, even an adult human being cannot be said to be a person. For a biologist as a biologist, you and I are simply human organisms. But for the biologist as a philosopher—and *everyone* is a philosopher to some extent—you and I can be readily recognized as persons.

However, neither biological concepts nor raw common sense offer sufficient perspective for evaluating the origins of life. Consider, for example, the common embryological term, "fertilized ovum." It can be misleading, since there really is no such thing as a fertilized ovum. Once fertilization occurs, the ovum has ceased to be, leaving in its wake cytoplasmic matter that will serve to nourish the new life. The zygote is in no proper sense a fertilized ovum. It is only figuratively so. . . .

46

What Is a Person?

A person is essentially a being that is naturally gifted (not self-gifted) with capacities or potentialities to know, love, desire, and relate to self and others in a self-reflective way. The person is—not by self but by nature—*able* to be aware of who he or she is and *able* to direct his or her own self in *accord with* this nature. A tree acts in accord with its nature, but does not direct itself that way—it is not consciously a tree. A dog or a dolphin acts in accord with its nature, but does not and cannot direct itself *as a self* in accord with its nature. A person can. The person's dignity and freedom are, at least partly, based on his or her capacity for *freely* acting in accordance with nature, rather than merely existing. Our freedom as persons resides not so much in our ability to do as we please, but in our ability to act freely and deliberately as we were gifted.

There are many alternate ways of phrasing the definition of a person, depending upon different needs of emphasis. But it would seem to be crucial that we recognize a person as a natural being and not simply as a functional being. A person is one that has the natural, but not necessarily the functional, ability to know and love in a trans-sensible or nonmaterial way. As soon as we require a person to have the functional ability for this kind of activity, we seem to slip into a subjectivistic elitism such that the comatose, senile, and retarded—even the sleeping—would not be regarded necessarily as persons. This position is out of touch with the human condition. If nature has no essential value in our knowing and judging who or what is a person, independent of accepted functional abilities, then there is little hope for recognition of an objective nature transcending the limits of our personal consciousness in anything else.

In recent years some philosophers have adopted what has been called the "developmentalist" interpretation of the beginning of a person. Daniel Callahan views it this way:

> [Abortion] is not the destruction of a human person—for at no stage of its development does the conceptus fulfill the definition of a person, which implies a developed capacity for reasoning, willing, desiring, and relating to others—but is the destruction of an important and valuable form of human life.[1]

The language of the Supreme Court in *Roe* v. *Wade* is harmonious with this perspective.

I would suggest that a person is not an individual with a *developed* capacity for reasoning, willing, desiring, and relating to others. A person is an indi-

---

1. Daniel Callahan, *Abortion, Law, Choice and Morality* (New York: Macmillan, 1970), 497–98.

vidual with a *natural* capacity for these activities and relationships, whether this natural capacity is ever developed or not—i.e., whether he or she ever attains the functional capacity or not. Individuals of a rational, volitional, self-conscious *nature* may never attain or may lose the functional capacity for fulfilling this nature to any appreciable extent. But this inability to fulfill their nature does not negate or destroy the nature itself, even though it may, for us, render that nature more difficult to appreciate and love. That difficulty would seem to be a challenge for us as persons more than it is for them.[2]

Neither a human embryo nor a rabbit embryo has the functional capacity to think, will, desire, read, and write. The radical difference, from the very beginning of development, is that the human embryo actually has the natural capacity to act in these ways, whereas the rabbit embryo does not and never will. For all its concern about potentialities, the developmentalist approach fails to see the actuality upon which these potentialities are based. Every potential is itself an actuality. A person's potential to walk across the street is an actuality that the tree beside him does not have. A woman's potential to give birth to a baby is an actuality that a man does not have. The potential of a human *conceptus* to think and talk is an actuality. Even the potential to receive actuation (called "passive potency" by traditional philosophers) is itself an actuality that is not had by something lacking it.

Underlying the common difficulty in seeing that the nature of a person is more basic than its functional characteristics lurks the perspective of utilitarianism. The sharp difference in viewpoint between the utilitarian-situationist ethic and the traditional Judeo-Christian ethic might be glimpsed by watching a swimmer. If we are on the shore of a river watching somebody swimming against the current, we might be inclined to be satisfied with a relativistic perspective. Observing how the swimmer is not making any progress against the current, relative to the dock on which we stand or to other reference points on the shore, we would rightly say, "He isn't moving." But afterward when the swimmer drags himself onto the dock, we might ask him, "Were you moving?" He would be quite rightly inclined to say yes. The difference between moving as a goal-striving behavior and moving as a natural act becomes evident.

Similarly, there is a great difference between the ideas of personhood as an achievement and personhood as an endowment. As the swimmer is essentially a swimmer by his natural acts of *being* a swimmer, and not by his success or failure at getting somewhere, so the person is essentially a person by his *being* a person, and not by his success or failure at demonstrating it. A rational definition of person is rooted in perception of a person's nature.

2. The recognition of a person involves, in part, a moral decision. This point is made effectively by John Noonan in the booklet *How to Argue About Abortion* (New York: The Ad Hoc Committee in Defense of Life, 1974), 10.

Nature does not revolve around function. Function revolves around nature. Functions can come and go, but nature is dynamically stable. . . .

A Person's Beginning

If a person is an individual entity with the natural, though not necessarily functioning, capacity to think, will, and relate self-reflectively, when does such an individual actually begin to exist in the world of space and time? There would seem to be but one reasonable point at which to acknowledge the existence of a new individual person in this world: conception. Conception is the moment when the so-called fertilization process is complete, and the point from which a genetically and physically unique individual is present and growing. . . .

Before a sperm penetrates an ovum, these two cells are clearly individual cells and are parts of the bodies of the man and woman respectively. They are not whole-body cells as is the zygote cell which they cause; they are part-body cells. The zygote is a single cell that is a whole body in itself. From within it comes the rest of the individual, including the strictly intrauterine functional organs (the placenta, amnion, and chorion), as well as the rest of the body, which is destined for extrauterine life. The sperm and ovum are not potential life; rather, they are potential *causes* of individual human life. They do not, even together, become a new human life, because they do not survive beyond conception. In the fertilization process, they become causes of the new human life.

Fertilization is a process. The process may take twenty minutes or several hours. But it has a definite conclusion. The moment at which this process terminates in the resulting zygote can be called conception. The sperm and ovum are specific, instrumental causes of the new human being. The man and woman are the main agents of this procreation: they cause the actual (not potential) existence of a person in the world.

Parental bodily matter (the sperm and ovum) is a crucial element in procreating the new being, but is not the stuff out of which this unique bodily being is adequately constituted. The bodily matter of the zygote comes into existence *by means of* the bodily matter of the parents but does *not* come *from* their bodies—it only looks that way to the unphilosophical mind. The matter of the new person is constitutively different matter. The chromosomal uniqueness of the zygote is sufficient testimony to the radical difference of both form and matter in this new being; the unique matter of the zygote has traits similar to, but in no way identical with, those of the parents. With the perspective of an evolutionist, who once said that the evolution from nonlife to life was a "leap from zero to everything," we might say that the transition from parent body to offspring is a leap from zero self to all of self. . . .

At any given moment, a whole living substance—be it a peach tree, a rabbit, or a person—either is or is not alive. Once it is alive, it is totally there as this particular actual being, even though it is only partially there as a *developed* actuality. There is no such thing as a potentially living organism. Every living thing is thoroughly actual, with more or less potential: actually itself, while potentially more or less expressive of itself. A one-celled person at conception is not a potential person, but an actual person with great potential for development and self-expression. That single-celled individual is just as actually a person as you or I, though the actual personhood and personality of the new individual are, as yet, much less functionally expressed.[3]. . .

The issue thus becomes whether we are prepared to acknowledge the *natural roots* of the individual's personality within this largely, though not entirely, undifferentiated stage. The genetic differentiation of a zygote or a blastocyst, however, must be reasonably acknowledged as the natural roots of a personality, not of a "dogality" or of a "rabbitality." The human zygote is a member of a unique *species* of creature. . . .

Conclusion

The point when an individual person begins to exist is one of the most crucial philosophical and social issues of our age. . . .

In order to put the issue of personhood and conception into its truest perspective, philosophers are being challenged to represent, clarify, and deepen our understanding of the nature of the person. Because the being of a person is, as it were, a seamless robe, our thinking must be woven from the natural, substantive, and nonfunctional level of meaning. Otherwise, "quality of life" ethics becomes the survival of the fittest and of the most functional; the ethic itself becomes a nonethic. We need an ethic sensitive to a deeper and richer vision of our dignity even as adults, who are dependently developing persons in the environment of space and time. Without appreciable insight into the inexhaustible process of personhood development, we will not be prepared to respect, reverence, and protect the prenatal person.

Natalism, the superiority of the born over the unborn, has replaced racism and sexism as the chief atrocity of our time. Fallacious thinking is polluting the atmosphere of thought regarding what a person is and when he or she begins. The philosophical forces of materialism, utilitarianism, and secular humanism press upon every pro-life thinker. Anyone who desires social justice for the prenatal child faces a tough swim against a mighty current.

Reflective advocates of social justice for the prenatal may take heart. We can learn from other swimmers, swimmers who are moving vigorously in

3. Cf., Robert and Mary Joyce, *Let Us Be Born* (Chicago: Franciscan Herald Press, 1970), 21–24.

amniotic fluid, growing stronger while they seem to be getting nowhere. They are sources of inspiration. We can learn from these prenatal children as we continue to think and communicate, gestating as we are—here in the premortal womb of time and space. When we are finally born at death, we will not be asked, "Did you succeed?" We will be asked, "Were you moving?"

From Robert E. Joyce, "When Does a Person Begin?" in *New Perspectives on Human Abortion*, Aletheia Books, ed. Thomas W. Hilgers, Dennis J. Horna, and David Mall (Frederick, Md.: University Publications of America, Aletheia Books, 1981), 345–56. Reprinted with permission of Greenwood Publishing Group, Inc., Westport, CT.

For Further Reflection

Case Studies

Anencephalic fetus. From the results of amniocentesis, a twenty-three-year old wife and mother from a solid Christian marriage learns she is carrying a baby suffering from anencephaly and spina bifida. *Anencephaly* describes a horrible genetic deformation in which the developing fetus has no upper brain and no skull; *spina bifida* is a condition in which the spinal column is not covered by skin. Since it has no upper brain, this fetus has absolutely no capacity for self-conscious intellectual life. Although its lower brain stem can sustain breathing for a short time, this child will likely die soon after birth. Medical personnel say it will not survive more than a few days. The young mother must decide whether to have an abortion or give birth to a nonviable child.

As a Christian friend, the young woman asks you for help in her painful decision. She opposes taking any human life, but wonders whether she should consider a group of cells that completely lacks potential for conscious life to be a human person. Does this fetus have a human status by endowment, or is its utter lack of potential an indication that it has no human status? What other issues become relevant in deciding what to do?

Malnourished mother. Living in squalor in a Third World country, a forty-three-year old Christian has just lost her husband. A mother of six, she now finds she is two months pregnant. If she continues with the pregnancy in her weakened condition, she faces a 30 percent chance of death during delivery since her hemoglobin level is very low. Even if she survives delivery or a Caesarian section, the trauma of the pregnancy and birth will leave her body weakened and susceptible to a variety of diseases. Of course, she does not have access to the sort of medical resources available in a Western hospital. Thus, she must decide whether to continue with the pregnancy and risk creating six orphans or to terminate the pregnancy in order to preserve her fragile health and her ability to care for her family.

You are asked to help decide what to do. You want to defend life, but whose life is most important? Can you justify abortion to save the mother's life? What role does faith in God play? Should this mother just trust God or take things into her hands or both?

Glossary

Actuality principle: A kind of functionalism affirming that a human organism has a right to life if and only if it has actually developed a minimal ability to express self-conscious, personal life (contrast with potentiality principle).

Amniocentesis: A test for a fetus's genetic health; involves examining the genetic structure of cells found in amniotic fluid drawn by needle from the amniotic sac.

Embryo: Early stage in a human's development after the zygote stage and before it takes its distinctive form; roughly the first seven weeks of gestation.

Essentialism: The view that a creature is a human person and thus has a right to life by virtue of being a member of a class, the natural kind *human,* rather than by virtue of being able to perform certain functions (contrast with functionalism).

Fetus: The individual unborn human in the later stages of development; roughly from the end of the second month of pregnancy until birth.

Functionalism: The view that an organism is a human person by virtue of its ability to function personally; a human organism is a human person if it can or will act personally, that is, if it acts as a moral, intellectual, spiritual agent (contrast with essentialism).

Induced abortion: Intentional termination of a pregnancy using any one of a variety of medical interventions; spontaneous abortion, commonly called miscarriage, happens naturally and is not morally significant.

Lex talionis: The law of retribution (eye for eye, tooth for tooth, life for life) found in Leviticus 24:17–20 and relevant to Exodus 21:22–25.

Potentiality principle: A kind of functionalism affirming that a human organism possesses a right to life if it has developed or has the natural capacity for developing self-conscious, personal life (contrast with actuality principle).

Pro-choice: An adjective describing views that regard the value of reproductive freedom more highly than the value of fetal life.

Pro-life: An adjective describing views that regard the value of fetal life more highly than the value of reproductive freedom.

Therapeutic abortion: An abortion performed to save the mother's life.

Zygote: The product of the union of a sperm and an ovum in its first days of life.

Annotated Bibliography

Batchelor, Edward, Jr., ed. *Abortion: The Moral Issues*. New York: Pilgrim, 1982. Twenty seminal essays by theologians representing a variety of perspectives.

Brody, Baruch A. *Abortion and the Sanctity of Life: A Philosophical View*. Cambridge: MIT Press, 1975. Essentialist defense of a pro-life position by a convert to that view.

Burtchaell, James T. *Rachel Weeping: The Case Against Abortion*. San Francisco: Harper & Row, 1982. Collection of five powerfully argued essays by a noted Catholic scholar.

Church and Society 71 (March-April 1981). Entire issue devoted to pro-choice arguments from liberal theological perspectives.

Congdon, Robert N. "Exodus 21:22–25 and the Abortion Debate." *Bibliotheca Sacra* 146 (1989): 132–47. Physician updates evangelical discussions on Exodus 21:22–25 since Cottrell's essay.

Cottrell, Jack W. "Abortion and the Mosaic Law." *Christianity Today* (16 March 1973): 602–5. Influential essay on the relevance of Exodus 21:22–25 to abortion.

Feinberg, Joel, ed. *The Problem of Abortion*. 2d ed. Belmont, Calif.: Wadsworth, 1984. Good collection of essays on philosophical aspects of abortion.

Gorman, Michael J. *Abortion in the Early Church: Christian, Jewish and Pagan Attitudes in the Greco-Roman World*. Downers Grove, Ill.: InterVarsity, 1982. Discussion of conflicting perspectives on abortion in the first five centuries of the church.

Harrison, Beverly Wildung. *Our Right to Choose: Toward a New Ethic of Abortion*. Boston: Beacon, 1983. Important statement of a feminist perspective on abortion by a liberal Christian.

Hilgers, Thomas W., Dennis J. Horna, and David Mall. *New Perspectives on Human Abortion*. Frederick, Md: University Press of America, Aletheia Books, 1981. Extensive anthology of pro-life essays that includes medical, legal, social, and philosophical approaches.

Hoffmeier, James K., ed. *Abortion: A Christian Understanding and Response*. Grand Rapids: Baker, 1987. Helpful collection of essays, mostly by

Wheaton College professors, on historical, biblical, ethical, and practical aspects of abortion.

Koop, C. Everett, and Timothy Johnson. *Let's Talk: An Honest Conversation on Critical Issues: Abortion, AIDS, Euthanasia, and Health Care.* Grand Rapids: Zondervan, 1992. Two Christian physicians prominent in public life discuss abortion in the context of public health.

Mollenkott, Virginia Ramey. "Reproductive Choice: Basic to Justice for Women." *Christian Scholars Review* 17 (1988): 286–93. Christian feminist, formerly an evangelical, supports a pro-choice position in public policy.

Morowitz, Harold J., and James S. Trefil. *The Facts of Life: Science and the Abortion Controversy.* New York: Oxford University Press, 1992. A discussion of abortion set in the context of human reproduction and embryology.

Pojman, Louis P., and Francis J. Beckwith, eds. *The Abortion Controversy: A Reader.* Boston: James and Bartlett, 1994. Very helpful collection of essays on abortion.

Thompson, Judith Jarvis. "A Defense of Abortion." *Philosophy and Public Affairs* 1 (1971): 47–66. Classic essay arguing that fetuses' having a right to live is consistent with a moderate pro-choice position.

Tooley, Michael. *Abortion and Infanticide.* Oxford: Clarendon, 1983. Very important work by a philosopher campaigning aggressively for both abortion and infanticide.

Wennberg, Robert N. *Life in the Balance: Exploring the Abortion Controversy.* Grand Rapids: Eerdmans, 1985. Philosophical analysis by an evangelical who argues that abortion is usually morally wrong but should not be criminalized.

2

Reproductive Technologies and Genetics

In October, 1991, Arlette Schweitzer, 42, gave birth to her daughter's twins. She bore her own grandchildren as a surrogate (substitute mother) for her daughter, Christa Uchytil, who was born without a uterus. Doctors took eggs from Christa's ovaries, fertilized them in the laboratory with her husband's, Kevin's, sperm, and implanted them in Schweitzer's womb. The twins' birth certificates list Christa and Kevin as the parents. The grandparents, Dan and Arlette Schweitzer, are delighted at the outcome.

In September, 1990, Anna Johnson gave birth to a boy for Mark and Crispina Calvert. Doctors took the Calverts' sperm and egg, united them in the laboratory, and implanted the fertilized egg in Johnson's womb. A hysterectomy prevented Crispina Calvert from carrying a baby, so the Calverts paid Anna Johnson $10,000 to bear a child for them. In this case, however, the outcome was not happy. During the pregnancy, relations between the Calverts and Johnson broke down, and both Mrs. Calvert and Johnson sought court declarations of motherhood. In May, 1993, the California Supreme Court ruled six to one that Johnson has no maternal rights to the child. This court was the first in the nation to decide who is the natural mother of a child: Is it the woman who provides the womb or the one who provides the ovum (egg)?

Until recently **surrogacy** or surrogate mothering meant that the woman chosen to bear the child (the birth mother) also provided the ovum (genetic surrogacy). Doctors artificially inseminated her with sperm from the husband of an infertile woman. The surrogate's ovum established a biological, genetic link between her and the baby. Previous court rulings, such as the Baby M. decision in New Jersey, focused on such genetic surrogacies where the birth mother is also the biological mother.

The cases of Arlette Schweitzer and Anna Johnson, however, involved a new approach—gestational surrogacy (also known as genuine surrogacy). In this situation, the surrogate carries the baby, but contributes nothing to the child genetically. In both genetic and gestational surrogacy, the child is given at birth to the couple who requested the surrogate's help. In both kinds of surrogacy, legal complications may arise. The surrogate can develop a strong maternal bond with the life inside her, prompting her to want to keep the child at birth. Justice Joyce Kennard, the dissenting court member in the Anna Johnson case, and the only woman on the court, argued that "a pregnant woman intending to bring a child into the world is more than a mere container or breeding animal; she is a conscious agent of creation no less than the genetic mother, and her humanity is implicated on a deep level." In Kennard's view, the surrogate's role should not be devalued.

The Johnson case is just one example of how law, technology, theology, and ethics intersect and overlap in the frontierland of new reproductive technologies. And it illustrates what is often the case in medical research: technology races ahead while law, theology, and ethics scramble to catch up and develop standards to govern the new procedures.

Technological assistance in the process of conception and pregnancy has accelerated rapidly in recent years, corresponding to the alarming increase in infertility among those who desire to have children. The occurrence of infertility rose almost 300 percent between 1964 and 1984. Researchers estimate that infertility affects up to 18 percent of couples in the United States, with men and women contributing equally to the problem.

A number of factors help account for the prevalence of infertility. Men are affected by low sperm count or blocked sperm ducts, possibly due in some cases to chemicals such as insecticides. Women have blocked fallopian tubes or scarred tissue in their ovaries or uterus, frequently caused by venereal diseases such as gonorrhea and chlamydia. Each year, more than three hundred thousand women lose their fertility as a result of sexually transmitted diseases. In both men and women, stress apparently contributes significantly to the rise of infertility, even if none of the physical conditions mentioned above is present. And, because of the desire to pursue career goals before having children, many couples postpone pregnancy until the middle or later thirties when it is generally more difficult to conceive.

Several methods for overcoming infertility are widely used and accepted. **Artificial insemination** (AI) involves the injection of sperm either into a woman's vagina or into her uterus. The sperm can come from either her husband (AIH) or from a donor other than her husband (AID). **In vitro fertilization** (IVF) is the process (used in the cases of Arlette Schweitzer and Anna Johnson) of removing a woman's ova or eggs, combining them with sperm in a petri dish (*in vitro* means "in glass"), and after two or three days inserting the fertilized egg or eggs into the womb that will carry the child. While semen specimens are collected through masturbation, ova are removed from the ovaries with a laparoscope. Doctors usually give drugs to the woman to increase the number of eggs produced in the month when they intend to harvest the eggs. Two other strategies are designated GIFT and ZIFT. Gamete intrafallopian transfer (GIFT) refers to the injection of ova and sperm into the fallopian tubes, with the hope that these will unite. In zygote intrafallopian transfer (ZIFT), an embryo produced in a petri dish is placed in the fallopian tube.

Embryo transfer (ET) is the process of conceiving embryos in one woman, removing them early in their development, and transferring them to another woman. Surrogate mothering, as discussed above, involves the use of another woman to carry and bear the baby.

While many people, even some Christians, welcome these technological advances, many others raise objections to them. Some object to any form of technological assistance in conception because it separates sexual union from procreation, thus going against God's intent for human relationships. God gives the gift of children to many, and those who are unable to have children naturally should recognize their situation as God's will for them. We should not interfere in the situation. Further, by artificially producing pregnancy, we diminish the importance of the sexual union since the child is not the result of an act of parental love. Others view this as a simplistic objection, asserting that the attempt to have children and to overcome infertility by technological means is no less an act of love than is the act of sexual intercourse. Rather, it demonstrates a couple's great desire for children. In this view, the objectors place too much emphasis on the sexual act.

In the first essay, religion professor Janet Dickey McDowell claims that we ought to rejoice with those who overcome infertility through the use of IVF. Rather than weakening the sexual union, IVF may relieve the stress placed on a marriage due to infertility, thereby actually strengthening the marriage and the sexual union. She resolves the problems involved with IVF by asserting that the objection is not with the technology itself, but with the wrongful use of the technology. She is cautious, however, about other procedures such as AID and surrogacy.

A different objection to the use of some reproductive technologies is the potentially profound psychological impact on children who find out they are the product of surrogacy, AID, or IVF. Initial research, though far from complete due to the relatively limited data available, supports this objection. In reply to this argument, some point out that once such technology is commonplace, there will be no stigma attached to these children. Indeed, while the first children born via IVF received a great deal of publicity, hundreds since then have been born in virtual anonymity. Researchers do not really know how these children will cope with the knowledge that they were conceived in a laboratory.

A more serious objection relates to children who were conceived with the sperm or egg of a donor, whether through IVF, ET, or surrogacy. Initial research suggests that some "products" of such technology have felt that they were abandoned and betrayed by their biological parent(s), leaving them with feelings of confusion and "lostness." The privacy of the donors, protected by infertility clinics, has made it nearly impossible to track down the biological parents. This can create problems when children need to know their genetic heritage for medical reasons.

While opinion is divided over the use of some reproductive technologies, ethicists tend to agree that surrogacy is improper except in such cases as that of Arlette Schweitzer. Many, perhaps most, evangelicals rule out AID on the basis that it breaks the important unity in marriage and family relationships (a third party—the donor—invades the sacred marriage union), and because of the potential psychological problems for the child.

There are mixed opinions on IVF, however. Perhaps the most critical concern has to do with the procedure itself. It is commonplace in IVF to produce several embryos (preferably three). Once this is done, either several embryos are placed in the woman's uterus so that there is a better chance of pregnancy, or some embryos are frozen in case the initial procedure fails. In the first case, if two or more fetuses develop, there is a chance that not all will survive birth. To increase the chances of a healthy pregnancy and birth, one or more of the developing fetuses is sometimes aborted (a process known as "selective reduction"). In the case of frozen embryos, if the first trial is successful, the couple faces the question of what to do with the remaining embryos. Will they be used later for another pregnancy, or will they be destroyed? Are they human beings? Can we justify the experimentation with and the destruction of thousands of embryos—incipient human lives—for the sake of knowledge? What price have we paid to develop our current technology? If we agree to use IVF today, are we condoning the research that has made it possible?

In his discussion, evangelical theologian and ethicist Stanley Grenz considers a wide range of issues. He not only provides a fuller evaluation of IVF and other procedures than does McDowell, but he also looks at the more foundational question of technological assistance in reproduction and two alternatives to assisted procreation: adoption and remaining child free. Not all Christians will agree with every one of his arguments and conclusions, but we can learn from his presentation and analysis of key aspects of the debate.

One other issue—**genetic engineering**—needs to be considered. In one sense, this phrase refers to any technique having to do with the manipulation of gametes (reproductive cells) or the fetus, including the various types of artificial conception already discussed, as well as methods for treating disease in the womb. Another aspect of genetic engineering concerns the manipulation of genetic material to enhance or improve human life, including attempts to manufacture human beings to exact specifications. In our comments below, we refer to this second area of genetic engineering, a field of research and experimentation that presents some of the most complex and far-reaching ethical challenges in the history of humanity.

The Food and Drug Administration approved the first genetic engineering experiment on a human on September 14, 1990. A four-year-old girl suffering from a rare immune disorder called adenosine deaminase (ADA) deficiency was the patient. ADA made her highly susceptible to infections and various forms of cancer because she is unable to form antibodies against abnormal cells. Scientists extracted her lymphocytes (white blood cells), then transplanted a functioning ADA gene into them, and infused them back into the girl. The process must be repeated monthly because the cells survive only a few weeks.

This experiment is part of the Human Genome Project, a three-billion-dollar, fifteen-year effort, begun in 1988, to identify every human gene and assign it to its chromosomal location. This is a monumental task, since each human cell contains about one hundred thousand genes. These genes, composed of deoxyribonucleic acid (DNA), direct our development from conception to adulthood and are passed on to our children. One full set of DNA (the genome) contains about three billion bits of information strung end to end. As the Human Genome Project proceeds, discoveries of disease-linked genes are being reported with increasing frequency.

While the project offers exciting possibilities for the early detection and even elimination of genetic disorders, many people are alarmed by the implications of the research. They claim that we have started down a "slippery slope," with no objective means of determining where to stop. If we can eventually identify, remove, and replace any gene in the human body, what will prevent us from trying to improve the gene pool by selecting only "superior" traits? Who decides which traits are superior?

Many other ethical questions arise. For example, may insurance companies acquire the genetic data of people before insuring them? If so, can companies rightly withhold insurances from genetically high-risk persons? Should employers have access to the genetic map of prospective or current employees? Should we choose marriage partners and decide to have children on the basis of genetic identity and predisposition? Should embryos be destroyed if they have been found to be carriers of disease-producing genes? Should a society require genetic testing of its citizens, or would mandatory testing violate human rights and individual freedoms? If there were a required national testing program, how would the fearful Big Brother scenario of the novel *1984* be avoided? Three percent of the budget for the Human Genome Project is allocated for studies on these and related ethical problems arising from the research.

In his essay, W. French Anderson, a research director at the National Institutes of Health, discusses what we are now capable of doing in the area of genetic engineering, what we will likely be able to do within a few years, and what we should do. He argues that gene therapy for the treatment of severe disease is acceptable, but we should not use genetic engineering for "enhancing" humans because we do not really understand how the complex human organism really "works."

Anderson's position seems consistent with Christian values. God has given humans the ability to find treatments for many serious ailments, and we should be able to proceed with engineering that treats human suffering. However, we certainly are complex organisms, fearfully and wonderfully designed by an omniscient God. Should we start to tinker with improving our make-up, we risk producing more harm than good. We might innocently attempt to eliminate a gene that seems undesirable, yet could prove to be important for allowing us to function normally, in the image of God. We need to remind ourselves that just because certain technological procedures are available does not necessarily mean we should use them.

Ethical Implications of In Vitro Fertilization

Janet Dickey McDowell

On December 28, 1981, Elizabeth Carr made headlines as the first child born in the United States as the result of in vitro fertilization (IVF). . . . What should be the Christian response to IVF and associated techniques?

Some Christians believe that the response ought to be uniformly negative. The earliest and strongest objections to even limited employment of IVF came from within Christian traditions committed to the indivisibility of sexual union and reproduction. Those who oppose artificial forms of birth control (notably the Roman Catholic Church in its official statements) most often do so on the grounds that these forms deliberately sever a natural—that is, biological—link between intercourse and procreation, a connection which ought not to be broken simply because to do so is unnatural. Their objection to IVF rests on the same premises. They contend that because IVF removes conception from its natural context, intercourse, it is impermissible. If sex without the potential for conception is wrong, then so, they say, is conception without sex.

These opponents to artificial birth control and IVF may be faulted at several points. Initially, one must question whether artificiality per se is reason enough to oppose a procedure like IVF. Kidney dialysis, respirators, even blood transfusions are also unnatural medical interventions, yet they are not opposed with the vigor of the Vatican's response to IVF. One may choose to distinguish between artificial birth control and a technique such as dialysis by pointing out that dialysis *supports* or *mimics* natural physiological function, whereas artificial birth control *thwarts* natural function. However, such a distinction would work against those who oppose IVF on grounds of its artifi-

63

ciality, for in fact it is far more analogous to dialysis, in that it also attempts to replace (by admittedly complex technological means) a deficient physiological function. Thus the Roman Catholic response to IVF appears inconsistent with its acceptance of other medical technologies.

A second difficulty with this most conservative rejection of IVF is that it presumes an absolute indivisibility of reproductive potential and the sexual expression of love in every single act of intercourse. The majority of Protestants (and a great many Roman Catholics who stand in tension with their tradition's stand on artificial birth control), while perceiving an important connection between reproduction and sexual love, do not assert that the reproductive purpose of sexuality needs to be served at all times. Instead, the unitive purpose of sexuality—its capacity to express love—is claimed as fundamental. Procreation will often be an outgrowth of a mature sexual relationship, but the temporary postponement of reproduction, or even a decision not to conceive children at all, is acceptable within this less naturalistic perspective.

This understanding of the values associated with intercourse would hold that love (as expressed in sexual activity) is preconditional to reproduction, and in that sense the two purposes remain linked. But because this view is less act-oriented, more concerned with the total relationship than with every instance of intercourse, there would be no reason to object to IVF. The fact that conception does not take place as the *direct* result of love made concrete through intercourse is less significant; provided that both love and the desire to procreate are elements of the couple's total relationship, IVF would not be problematic.

Other critics raise quite a different objection. They fear that IVF will encourage (by providing a means) an obsessive concern with having one's own child, a child genetically related to its parents. It is thought that those who choose to accept the discomfort, expense and inconvenience of IVF, rather than opting for adoption, may perceive parenthood too biologically. These critics are concerned that IVF candidates will fail to keep in mind that Christian parenthood is above all a moral commitment to nurture a child, not the contribution of ova or sperm.

It would seem, however, that this danger is not substantially greater for couples using IVF than for other couples. All parents are potentially prey to this sort of idolatry: a veiled worship of self and the continuation of self in future generations. Christian churches rightly ought to discourage all of its manifestations, whether in candidates for IVF or prospective parents who anticipate ordinary conception.

At the same time, it is important to remember that genetic inheritance is not incidental. A sense of lineage—connectedness to parents and grandparents and great-grandparents—while far from vital to successful family relationships, ought not to be discounted entirely. If only for very practical reasons, such as medical records, children often need to identify their genetic parents. Many contemporary adoptees testify to the psychological value of learning about those to whom one is bound by genetic ties. Additionally, a child resulting from the unique combination of the parents' reproductive cells—in a very real sense, their selves—may be a significant sign of their life together.

Kept in proper perspective, genetic parenthood is valuable. It would be unreasonable to deny couples unable to conceive without IVF the chance to experience such parenthood merely because the potential for misunderstanding exists. It is highly unlikely that Christians will ever totally disregard genetic parenthood. (Random child-swapping at birth or mandatory communal child care from very early ages would seem to be ways a community could curb a fixation on genetic parenthood. These have not, to my knowledge, been endorsed by any major Christian group.) Unless and until such a state of affairs comes about, it would be cruel to denounce as selfish or idolatrous those who desire to establish a genetically based family, even when a procedure like IVF is required.

Other objections to IVF have focused more narrowly on the technique itself. Some fear that fertilized ova created by the procedure may be destroyed or used for experimentation, rather than transferred to the uterus of the woman from whom they were obtained. Recovering and fertilizing several ova during IVF is very common; hormonal stimulation of the ovaries is a standard element of the procedure and frequently results in the production of more than one mature ovum.

Objections to possible destruction of or experimentation with fertilized ova stem from a contention that human life is worthy of moral respect (and even legal protection) from its origins in the fertilized ovum. To use fertilized ova for experimental purposes or to discard them would be, according to these critics, tantamount to abortion or human experimentation without consent.

This potentially serious reservation about IVF, however, is overcome by the particular procedure in use at the Eastern Virginia Medical School in Norfolk (the most "prolific" clinic in the U.S.). Where more than one ovum is recovered by the laparoscopy, all are exposed to sperm. Any which manifest successful cell division (and thus are "alive") are inserted into the woman's uterus and thus given an opportunity for implantation. None is used for experimental purposes or destroyed.

However, if a clinic chose to deviate from this procedure and retain some fertilized ova, the objection would be properly focused on the morality of destroying or experimenting with fertilized human ova, not on IVF itself. Setting aside the question of whether discarding a fertilized ovum *would* constitute abortion (and further, whether such abortion ought to be prohibited or discouraged), it is clear that this objection does not necessarily apply to present procedures, especially those used in U.S. clinics. Respect for human life at its very earliest stages is not inherently incompatible with in vitro fertilization and thus need not be the basis for opposing the technique.

It seems, then, that IVF is not inherently immoral. When employed to facilitate conception by loving couples, it is no more problematic than an artificial fallopian tube would be. The abuse of fertilized ova is not necessarily an element of the procedure, and those who would object on grounds of unnaturalness must be prepared to reject other medical interventions that bypass pathological conditions. Conceptions via IVF ought not simply to be tolerated; they should be celebrated, for they enable otherwise infertile couples to join in passing along the gift of life.

Nevertheless, future procedures relying in part on the IVF technique may pose moral dilemmas. Two in particular, embryo transfer (the insertion of a fertilized ovum into the uterus of a woman who did not provide the ovum) and ova and embryo banking (stockpiling frozen ova and fertilized ova), are being quietly attempted in Australia and perhaps elsewhere. Whereas IVF as currently practiced aids in the establishment of genetically connected families, these new applications run significant risks of confusing lineage, distorting traditional family structures, and/or depersonalizing human reproduction.

Defenders of ova and embryo banking argue that it need not be used in tandem with embryo transfer to a nondonor woman. They contend that frozen ova, fertilized or not, would merely be stored until such time as the donor chose to use them. Theoretically this would reduce the need for multiple surgeries to recover ova when implantation does not take place and the procedure must be repeated. This use of ova/embryo banks raises no objections not already discussed herein with regard to the basic IVF technique.

However, embryo transfer in combination with ova banking or embryo banking could be used in a variety of circumstances. For example, in the case of a woman with healthy ovaries but uterine disease (or the absence of a uterus) such that she could not carry a child, embryo transfer would make it possible for her to have her ovum removed, fertilized, then transferred to the uterus of another woman. This "genuine surrogate" would experience pregnancy and birth, and after birth the child would be surrendered to its genetic parents.

For another example, a woman with a healthy uterus who did not wish to have her own ovum fertilized (perhaps for eugenic reasons) could elect to have an ovum provided by an anonymous donor fertilized with her partner's sperm and then transferred to her uterus. Or she could choose to have an already fertilized ovum inserted. Using a donated unfertilized ovum would be strongly analogous to artificial insemination by an anonymous donor;

employing the services of an embryo bank has been likened to very early adoption.

What objections might be raised to the genuine surrogate application of IVF and embryo transfer? Primarily, one must be concerned with the attitude such a practice would engender toward the surrogate. Would she view herself merely as an incubator-for-hire, or be viewed in that light by those who employ her? Probably—perhaps even certainly. It would, in fact, be almost imperative for the surrogate to see herself in this way in order to maintain an emotional distance during pregnancy and thus be able to surrender the child at birth. She would have to guard zealously against viewing herself as a "mother," as more than a temporary "repository" for someone else's child. Do Christians wish to encourage women to perceive procreative capacities as mere services available for hire?

Further, an impersonal, businesslike attitude toward the surrogate on the part of the genetic parents seems crucial to a successful surrogate arrangement, unless the couple genuinely welcomes ongoing third-party involvement in their family life. The couple would seem to have only two choices: viewing the surrogate simply as a means to their reproductive end, or creating a new form of extended family. While the latter choice is not unthinkable (and perhaps not undesirable), the former is more likely. One must ask whether Christians wish to be the sort of people who treat one another in this way; the answer seems clearly negative. The kind of interactions among the primary parties necessary to make the genuine surrogate situation work are not those fostered by Christian values. It would be difficult (though not impossible) to structure a surrogate situation in such a way that people are fully respected as persons.

Ova banking is, as was suggested earlier, analogous to artificial insemination by donor (AID). Therefore qualms about AID—such as concern about psychological damage to the noncontributing partner, pseudoadultery, confusion of the child's genetic inheritance, and devaluation of the anonymous donor—apply also to ova banking. Large numbers of people, many of them Christian, believe that the potential pitfalls of AID can be avoided through sensitive counseling and maximum participation by the male partner during the insemination process. The fact that embryo transfer would enable a woman to experience pregnancy and the birth of the child (conceived with an ovum not her own) would ensure in this case an even greater sense of full contribution to procreation by the partner whose genes are absent. Those who permit AID should welcome ova banking; those who find AID troublesome will view ova banking in a similar light.

In contrast to ova banking, embryo banking has some genuinely novel features—features which could well rule out its use. Fundamentally, objections to embryo banking stem from its deliberate creation of nascent life not desired by either genetic parent. While unintended conceptions do occur with some frequency as a result of intercourse, such conceptions are acci-dental—perhaps even tragic—and not normative. And many couples who conceive unintentionally[,] do, upon reflection, welcome the child. But the anonymous contributors to a bank will never have such a change of heart. Presumably they will not even know whether their genetic offspring exist.

The analogy to adoption employed to defend the practice of anonymous embryo banking (and subsequent transfer) breaks down when one considers that it induces genetically broken families. The child will never have a chance to know biological kin. Adoption, in contrast, *copes with* broken bio-logical relations; it does not create them. Such deliberate scrambling of lin-eage seems to serve only the purpose of allowing a couple to experience preg-nancy and birth—a purpose that does not seem sufficiently important to warrant the possible confusion.

In summary, I have argued that IVF per se is not morally troublesome. It seems, in fact, to be a positive good in overcoming medical conditions that preclude procreation by some couples. However, other procedures relying on the IVF technique are less acceptable. Ova banking ought to be employed only with the same caution as AID. Genuine surrogate situations seem acceptable only under very rare circumstances that preserve respect for the surrogate. And the transfer of embryos provided by anonymous donors ought virtually to be prohibited altogether.

Technology and Pregnancy Enhancement

Stanley J. Grenz

Technological Assistance and the Christian

In the second half of the twentieth century medical science has responded to the problem of infertility with several technological procedures aimed at enhancing the prospects of conception for barren couples. Yet each procedure developed in recent years has been the object of heated debate not only in society as a whole but also within the church. Before looking at several of these procedures a more basic question must be addressed: the propriety of employing any technological means to enhance possibilities of pregnancy.

a. The rejection of all *technological assistance.* Opposition in principle to all technological procedures in the area of procreation has been voiced from diverse sources within the Christian community.

The most often cited of these objections focus on the relationship between sexual intercourse and procreation. Some critics argue that technological procedures ought not to be employed, because through such means human beings—e.g., doctors and the married couple—take to themselves God's prerogative in conception. Others claim that these procedures constitute an unwarranted intrusion of science into the realm of nature. But the most basic formulation of the argument reasons that such processes separate sexual intercourse and procreation, the joining of which are the intent of the Creator.

Perhaps the most lucid assertion of this argument has been offered by the Roman Catholic Church. The Catholic position on the latest technological advancements was outlined in the 1987 Vatican statement on human reproduction, *Donum vitae.*[1] Although the document's specific subject is artificial

---

1. The Congregation for the Doctrine of the Faith, "Instruction on Respect for Human Life in its Origin and on the Dignity of Procreation: Replies to Certain Questions of the Day" (Vatican City, Feb. 22, 1987), Part II, B4a.

69

insemination, the Catholic magisterium in effect spoke against any type of technological assistance in the procreative process.

Foundational to the rejection of technological means is the statement's reaffirmation of the traditional church position concerning the goal-directedness of the sex act as demanding an "inseparable connection . . . between the two meanings of the conjugal act: the unitive meaning and the procreative meaning." Technological fertilization undermines the origin of the human person as the result of "an act of giving," the fruit of the parents' love; it results in the child being "an object of scientific technology." In short, "such fertilization entrusts the life and identity of the embryo into the power of doctors and biologists and establishes the domination of technology over the origin and destiny of the human race."

b. The case for openness to technological assistance. . . . All Christians ought to applaud the Roman hierarchy for launching a commendable attempt to maintain the mystery of human procreation in the face of the unchallenged intrusion of technology into human life. Yet, the wholesale rejection of all types of technological assistance in the natural human drive to produce offspring is unfortunate. . . . [T]he rejection voiced by *Donum vitae* reflects a truncated and therefore damaging understanding of the meaning of the sex act within marriage. By insisting that the "unitive meaning" of the sex act cannot be separated from the "procreative meaning," the magisterium is maintaining virtually unaltered the Augustinian-Thomist understanding that works to limit sexual activity to procreation.

The document's understanding of the meaning of the sex act is truncated, for within the marriage bond sexual activity can carry other equally significant meanings. . . . The sex act may serve as an expression of the marriage covenant the partners share, and thereby as the "sacrament" of the marriage covenant, an outward act which repeatedly seals and signifies their inward commitment. It can be an illustration of the mutual submission that is to characterize marriage, thereby forming a spiritual metaphor, a beautiful reminder of the self-giving love of Christ. These aspects of the meaning of the sex act may exist apart from the procreative intent. In fact, rather than the procreative meaning being central for the unitive meaning, as is implied in the Vatican statement, the other aspects of the sex act are what form the context for procreation. As self-giving love is creative, so the giving of oneself in the marriage act can be procreative within the context of the marital covenant. Even the meaning most closely bound to the procreative process, namely, the couple's openness to the broadening of their love beyond the marital bond, remains when there is no possibility that pregnancy will result from the sex act.

In contrast to the position of *Donum vitae*, therefore, it would seem that a fuller understanding of the meaning of the sex act within the marital bond would welcome as God's gift, rather than discourage, technological assistance in procreation, so long as the process employed is not objectionable on other moral grounds.

Technological assistance as such, therefore, is not ethically questionable. Rather than a wholesale rejection of technological assistance *in toto,* such assistance, within certain limitations, in the process of pregnancy can be a great benefit to childless couples and therefore ought to be welcomed. The ethical issue, in other words, does not lie with the idea of assistance from medical science. Rather, each specific means must be ethically tested.

Alternatives to Technological Procreation

Of course, the availability of technological assistance does not mean that conscientious childless couples ought to sense a compulsion to employ it. The Vatican document goes too far in asserting that infertile couples are called to find in their situation "an opportunity for sharing in a particular way in the Lord's cross. . . ." Nevertheless, the suggestion that this be a valid attitude is surely correct. In addition to turning to technological assistance, two other options are worthy of consideration by couples touched by infertility: adoption and remaining "child free" for the sake of service to Christ.[2]

a. Adoption. Adoption ranks as the preferred option for couples who cannot have children through natural means. This practice carries biblical precedence. Moses, for example, was adopted. And the implication of the doctrine of the virgin birth is that Jesus was adopted as well (by Joseph). Further, the adoption of a child who for some reason is given up by his or her natural parents becomes a gracious act, for therein a couple extends a home to a homeless little one. In this way the act can serve as a reflection of the gracious compassion of God, who provides home for the homeless. Finally, adoption can also serve as a metaphor of God's adoption of human beings into the divine family.

Because of the picture of spiritual truth that it offers, adoption is a viable option. As John and Sylvia Van Regenmorter aptly declare, "For the Christian infertile couple, adoption is not 'second best.' It is simply the way that God in his wisdom can choose for us to be parents. Whether one becomes a parent biologically or through adoption, the fact is that children are not a right but a gift from God."[3]

Nevertheless, adoption is not without its difficulties.[4]

---

2. The term *child free* is offered as preferable to *childless* by Diane Payette-Bucci, "Voluntary Childlessness," *Direction* 17, 2 (1988): 39.

3. John and Sylvia Van Regenmorter and Joe S. McIlhaney, Jr., M.D. *Dear God, Why Can't We Have a Baby?* (Grand Rapids: Baker, 1986), 141.

4. For a helpful, succinct discussion of the joys and difficulties surrounding adoption, see ibid., 139–48. The difficulties involved in the adoption process are the subject of a recent *Time* cover story. Nancy Gibbs, "The Baby Chase," *Time,* 9 October 1989, 86–89.

One major problem is that of completing the adoption process. The availability of abortion and the trend toward single mothers electing to keep their babies has reduced the number of adoptable babies in the United States. As a result, waiting periods have lengthened from two to, at times, eight years. Many couples find the length of the wait, which draws out the adoption process, simply too great an obstacle to overcome. An alternative to which many have turned is the adoption of children from impoverished countries. Others have been willing to take into their homes children who are either physically or mentally disadvantaged or rejected for some other reason.[5] Such an act requires great fortitude, but also becomes an example of great love.

A second difficulty focuses on the expense surrounding the adoption process. Although some institutions may offer their services at little charge, the costs of adoption through other agencies can be high. These expenses often come after a couple have already spent a large sum of money on infertility treatment.

Finally, adoption brings a certain amount of trauma not associated with biological birthing. An adopting couple will need to cope with the implications of their pursuance of adoption, for thereby they are acknowledging that their efforts to give birth have come to an end. Family and friends might find it difficult to accept the adopted child, adding to the stress of the adjustment. And in later years the family will need to assist the adopted child in coping with the knowledge that the biological parents gave the child for adoption.[6] Despite these difficulties, adoption can be a laudable expression of the openness of the marriage partners to broaden their bond in order to welcome new life in their midst.

b. Remaining child free. Another alternative for the infertile couple is that of remaining child free. The ancient Hebrews viewed childlessness as an unfortunate, even a reproachful situation. A similar viewpoint was widespread in American culture until recently, in that children were viewed as crucial to the economic well-being of the family. But as the focus of the nature of the family shifted from production to consumption, attitudes toward childlessness began to change as well. On the heels of such changes, this option has become more acceptable and more commonplace.

Viewed from a Christian perspective, a case could be made for choosing to remain child free. A New Testament foundation for this option arises by extending Paul's argument regarding the single life (1 Cor. 7:25–40) to the already married who are contemplating having children. Just as marriage can

5. The situation of "special-needs" children is described in Richard Lacayo, "Nobody's Children," *Time,* 9 October 1989, 91–95.
6. Cases of adopted children and genetic parents finding each other are widely publicized. For a recent report, see Elizabeth Taylor, "Are You My Mother?" *Time,* 9 October 1989, 90.

distract a person from full service to the Lord (the point Paul raised), so also parenting is a time-consuming, potentially distracting occupation. Consideration of this principle could motivate a couple to remain child free for the purpose of devoting more energy to the Lord's work, just as a single person may choose to forego marriage for the same reason.[7]

It may be added, however, that just as it is not to be assumed from 1 Corinthians 7 that all Christians are to choose to remain single, so also being child free is not the norm for Christian couples. It may well be that many couples will conclude that having children in fact enhances their ministry in the Lord's work. At the same time, the choice of remaining child free for the sake of devotion to the Lord does offer an opportunity to infertile couples to see their situation as the vehicle to what for them may be greater service in the fellowship of Christ.

As in the case of adoption, the option of remaining child free is not without difficulties. First, the couple will need to cope with lingering negative attitudes from both family and society toward such a decision. It is often assumed that all couples have children and that those who do not are motivated only by selfishness. Child free couples will need to learn to pass off rude and unloving comments by others, which reflect such judgmental attitudes.

A second danger is that of falling into the temptation to live only for oneself or for one's spouse. Without the cares and financial burdens involved in raising a family, child free couples can get caught in the trap of focusing on themselves. Therefore, they might need to make a conscious effort to open their relationship beyond themselves by discovering ways of giving of themselves to others. Children who for various reasons are in need of the support and love of replacement "parents" or adult friendship and guidance offer one important means to this end. By ministering to such children, a couple with no children in the home can both extend a type of parental love to children and experience in a unique way the joys of being "parent."

Both adoption and remaining child free for the sake of devoting greater time, money, and energy to the Lord's work are worthy options for the infertile couple and therefore ought to be given careful consideration. Nevertheless, they must not be cited as the only options. For some infertile couples the desire to experience the joy of being partners with God in the mystery of procreation is a divinely given impulse that ought to be facilitated, so long as it is morally proper and technologically feasible. By developing the means to accomplish this, modern medical technology now offers hope to many infertile couples that this joy may be realized.

7. For a fuller development of the motivations for childlessness, see Diane Payette-Bucci, "Voluntary Childlessness."

Methods of Technologically Assisted Conception

The battle against infertility has produced several technological means of assisting in the process of procreation.[8] These offer to many otherwise child-less couples the hope of experiencing the joy of procreation and parenting. . . .

These various procedures [such as AID, IVF, and ET] open the door to multiple parenting situations. Perhaps the most complicated arrangement imaginable is the situation in which the sperm from a male donor fertilizes an egg from a female donor, which is then placed in a surrogate mother, all on behalf of a married couple consisting of a husband with a low sperm count and a wife who has neither functioning ovaries nor uterus.

Ethical Considerations

In a sense, technological procedures . . . are blind to ethical consider-ations. The process of assisting in the combining of sperm and egg inside a woman's womb or in a laboratory, for example, is oblivious to the source of the material being brought together and to the relationship between the donors of that material. But the purported biological neutrality of such pro-cedures does not necessarily make them ethically neutral. Nor does a theo-retical openness to the efforts of modern medicine in assisting infertile cou-ples in these ways require that Christians conclude that all such techniques are ethically acceptable.

The mere fact that medical research has made a process possible does not mean that it is morally justifiable. Whereas medical technicians may on occasion find ethical considerations irrelevant to their task, the Christian does not. The methods put forth by the medical community must be tested not only by whether they are able to assist in the process of conception, but by whether or not they maintain Christian ethical standards.

a. Technological procreation within the marriage bond. For many, artificial insemination and IVF/GIFT loom as the gateway to the strange world of technological procreation. In a sense this perception is valid, for when viewed from an ethical perspective, they stand on the border between tech-nological assistance that remains strictly within the bond of marriage and that which moves beyond this bond.

The boundary characteristic of the process arises from the ethical impor-tance of the source of the sperm and egg brought together in these proce-dures. Viewed from the technical dimension, of course, the source of the ele-

8. For a discussion of methods of technological assistance in procreation see William Walters and Peter Singer, eds., *Test Tube Babies: A Guide to Moral Questions, Present Techniques and Future Possibilities* (Melbourne: Oxford University Press, 1982), and Mary Warnack, ed., *A Question of Life: The Warnack Report on Human Fertilization and Embryology* (New York: Basil Blackwell, 1984).

ments sperm and egg is irrelevant. From the ethical perspective, however, this factor is more significant than the technological differences among the various procedures, because they employ sperm derived from different sources (for example, AIH and AID are distinct acts). AID introduces sperm from a third party, with the result that the genetic makeup of the offspring is the product of the combination of the genes of a woman and those of someone other than her husband. In AIH, only the husband's sperm is used to impregnate the wife, thereby maintaining the closed nature of the marital relationship in the procreative process. In the same way, practices such as IVF and GIFT carry differing implications depending on whose sperm is being united with whose egg.

Some ethicists have rejected all these procedures on the basis that they employ masturbation in the process. This objection, however, is not warranted. The ethical problem with masturbation does not lie in the act itself, but in the dangers that surround the practice, such as the risk of developing into a self-gratifying habit, dependent on pornography to maintain. The act of masturbation that provides sperm for procedures such as artificial insemination, however, generally does not carry these dangers. The potential problems with these procedures lie elsewhere.

Unless there are other complicating factors, procedures that use a wife's egg and a husband's sperm are gaining widespread acceptance.

Of these, AIH is the simplest, and it generally engenders no grave concerns for Christian ethicists.[9] The use of the husband's sperm maintains the integrity of both the marriage relationship and of the genetic inheritance of the offspring produced by the process. In fact, when utilized within the covenant of marriage, AIH ought to be greeted as a helpful means that assists in the formation of new life—the natural offspring of the marital union—giving expression to the creative love present in the union of that husband and wife.

Whenever it uses only the wife's egg and the husband's sperm, GIFT could also gain wide acceptance among Christians. In vitro fertilization (IVF) may likewise serve as a helpful way of bringing together the elements from an otherwise infertile married couple. But it introduces certain other complications that increase the potential for ethical problems. These will be discussed later.

b. The introduction of a third party into the marriage bond. Although many Christians find AIH relatively uncomplicated in its ethical implications, the situation with other practices, beginning with AID and including IVF and surrogacy, is somewhat more complicated.

---

9. Acceptance of AIH is not universal, however. Another argument voiced against AIH is the cleavage it produces between sexual love and procreation. See Leon Kass, "New Beginnings in Life," in *The New Genetics and the Future of Man*, ed. M. Hamilton (Grand Rapids: Eerdmans, 1972), 53–54.

Some ethicists argue that these various practices produce an adulterous situation, in that the sperm of the husband is not combined with the egg of the wife. Although there is a sense in which this suggestion poses an important ethical question, the charge of adultery as generally proposed offers an oversimplified prognosis of the ethical problem involved. The technological combining of sperm and egg, regardless of their source, does not entail adultery, simply because neither the intent to be unfaithful to one's marital vows nor the act of intercourse is present.

On another level, however, the charge of adultery does raise a difficulty inherent in all technological processes that employ sperm or egg from someone other than the marital partners. Each of these methods introduces a third party not directly into the marriage bond itself (as in adultery), but into the procreative process. Does this introduction of another person in the procreative process constitute a violation of the marital covenant? An affirmative response to this question was succinctly articulated by the 1987 Vatican statement: "The fidelity of the spouses in the unity of marriage involves reciprocal respect of their right to become a father and a mother only through each other."

The perspective offered by Judeo-Christian history on this issue is not totally unambiguous. The ancient Hebrews were characterized by a double standard. They viewed marriage as giving to the husband exclusive rights to his wife in this regard, but the exclusiveness was not reciprocated. Polygamy was practiced in the Old Testament era, but not polyandry. The church, however, has rejected this double standard. By appeal to various sources, not the least of which is the creation story in Genesis 2, it has consistently championed the practice of monogamy. In Christian history, it became simply assumed that the marriage covenant means that each of the spouses may become father or mother only through the other.

Yet, the witness of history does not confirm the Vatican statement without further consideration, for there is a sense in which the contemporary situation lacks historical precedence. Once the church came to adopt monogamy, the only way in which a married person could become a parent apart from one's spouse was through adultery. This link to adultery, perhaps more than any other consideration, led to the viewpoint reflected in *Donum vitae.* Now, however, procreation can occur within the context of marriage yet apart from the union of the sperm and egg from the marriage partners without thereby introducing either the intent or the act of adultery. The only way to find technological procreation to be adulterous is to define adultery not as the willful violation of the covenant of sexual faithfulness, but as the violation of the assumed right of each spouse to become parent only through the other.

Contrary to the language of the Vatican statement, however, the New Testament does not emphasize rights. Instead, it speaks of the willingness to give up one's rights for the sake of another. This viewpoint appeals to the example of Jesus who put aside his divine prerogatives in order to fulfill his mission and die on the cross (Phil. 2:7, 8). On the basis of this example and the New Testament emphasis, a case could be made for practices involving donor sperm or egg within the context of marriage.

Modern technological capabilities allow a married person, motivated by the desire to facilitate the wish of one's spouse to give birth to biological off-spring, to choose willingly to set aside his or her "right" to be the sole means whereby the spouse is able to become a parent. And this can be done without introducing the physical act of adultery into the marital relationship. Thus, a husband could choose to allow the technological introduction of the sperm of another male so that his wife may become the biological mother of the child they welcome into their marriage. Or a wife might consent to the introduction of the egg from another woman, for the sake of allowing her husband to be the biological father of their child. This decision need not be viewed as consent to an intrinsically unethical act, for the introduction of the sperm or egg of another occurred apart both from any intended or actual physical act of marital unfaithfulness. It is the absence of both intent and act that sets the technological process apart from situations in which actual sexual intercourse involving a third party is employed to bring about conception.

The technological introduction of a third person into the procreation process is not unethical, insofar as it does not constitute a violation of the marital bond. Nevertheless, other difficulties potentially arise from the procedure. These ought to be considered by any couple contemplating the use of such methods of technological procreation.

Several potential difficulties are psychological in nature. The knowledge that the new life was produced by neither their physical nor genetic union may make it difficult for one or the other of the spouses to extend full acceptance to the child. Similarly, the fact that one partner, but not the other, was able to be involved in the procreative process could result in feelings of guilt or incompetency[10] that potentially place undue and lasting strain on the marriage relationship.

The potential for legal complications is likewise present. For example, the question of progenitorship could become a factor should the trauma of the experience eventually lead to marital breakdown and divorce. In such a situation would each spouse continue to view the child as his or her own? And how would the attitude of each of the parties affect the divorce settlement? Likewise, the introduction of other persons into the procreative process introduces questions concerning the legal status of all such persons, which

10. See Lori B. Andrews, "Yours, Mine and Theirs," *Psychology Today* 18 (12 December 1984): 24.

could conceivably trigger litigation. Recent court cases have indicated the legal muddle that can occur when the prerogatives of each of the partners, the donor(s), or a surrogate mother must be juggled. The potential exists as well for legal entanglements in the more distant future, if the anonymity of the other person(s) involved is challenged because of the child's need to know his or her full genetic heritage for medical reasons or in order to insure against an unintentional incestuous union.

A third area of possible difficulties is the trauma which the child conceived through such means will face. This trauma arises from the fact that not only is a third party introduced into the marital relationship, but a third "parent" is added into the horizon of the child. This difficulty could be nothing more than the need to deal with the questions the child might raise concerning his or her genetic inheritance. Yet, the child's interest could develop beyond the natural inquisitiveness motivated by the desire to know about oneself and one's biological background. The couple might eventually need to deal with the issues surrounding very practical situations in which genetic history is crucial to the health or well-being of the child.

The addition of a third party into the procreative process potentially brings a third parent into the child's life. This could occur through the initiative of the child, who sets out to discover his or her genetic father or mother. But it could also arise should the genetic parent later seek to establish contact with the child.[11]

While none of these potential problems is inherently insurmountable, each ought to be considered seriously by any couple contemplating the use of these technological means.

c. Problematic dimensions of technological practices themselves. When contemplating the possible use of donors, a couple will want to give consideration to the weighty complications cited above. In addition to these, several other more technologically oriented factors add to the problems inherent in certain procedures.

(1) Problems of IVF. Apart from the potential for difficulties within the marriage and family relationships, the process of in vitro fertilization introduces several ethical problems.[12] One of the most perplexing of these is the question of "waste," which arises in several different ways. The problem of waste can arise through the inefficiency of the process. Whereas in natural reproduction as few as 25 percent of the embryos produced actually become implanted in the uterus of the mother, the failure rate of IVF is

---

11. Some donors have sought court action in order to gain the right to visit children produced by their sperm. Lori B. Andrews, "Yours, Mine and Theirs," 29.

12. For a discussion of a variety of purported ethical issues surrounding IVF, see William B. Neaves and Priscilla W. Neaves, "Moral Dimensions of In Vitro Fertilization," *Perkins Journal* 39, 1 (1986): 10–23.

even higher. As many as fifteen eggs may be required for a successful implantation.[13]

A more widely known waste problem is that of disposing of the multiple conceptions that regularly occur outside the woman through IVF. In the United States all of the embryos produced in vitro are generally placed in the uterus (which introduces the risk of a multiple pregnancy); however, the possibility is always present that some embryos may be destroyed.

Third, the problem of waste is potentially present each time human embryos are frozen for future disposal or use. Several recent court cases have involved the bizarre problems of the rights of various parties to determine what is to be done with the products of IVF which have been placed in storage.[14]

These various dimensions of the question of waste raise foundational issues, such as when life begins as well as the intrinsic worth and rights of embryos.[15] Does life begin at conception? Is a human embryo to be treated with the full respect due to a human being? And do embryos have the right to be placed in the womb so that they can possibly develop and be born? William and Priscilla Neaves offered a succinct summary of the relationship of IVF to these issues:

If the intrinsic worth of an early human embryo is no less than that of a newborn infant, IVF cannot be rationally justified. On the other hand, if the principal value of a human embryo derives from its ability to become a baby, IVF may be seen as a moral way of awakening this potential where it would not otherwise exist.[16]

The issue of waste requires that certain minimum guidelines be followed in all IVF situations. The practice of placing in the womb all the embryos so produced is surely correct. Thereby all embryos are given opportunity to implant and develop. Beyond this step, great caution must be exercised in placing embryos in storage for future use.[17]

13. Neaves and Neaves, "Moral Dimensions," 20. A recent report suggests that the success rates of infertility clinics may not be as high as they would have their patients believe. See "What Do Infertility Clinics Really Deliver?" *U.S. News and World Report*, 3 April 1989, 74–75.

14. Otto Friedrich "A Legal, Moral Social Nightmare," *Time*, 10 September 1984, 54–56.

15. David T. Ozar argues that regardless of the answers to these questions, frozen embryos ought to be kept in their frozen state until implanted in a womb or are no longer capable of surviving implantation. "The Case Against Thawing Unused Frozen Embryos," *Hasting Center Report* 15, 4 (1985): 7–12.

16. Neaves and Neaves, "Moral Dimensions," 22.

17. The guidelines for freezing embryos offered by Grobstein, Flower, and Mendeloff serve as an example: "The clinical community involved with in vitro fertilization should voluntarily limit use of embryo freezing to the initial purpose—i.e., to circumvent infertility in patients. Freezing should be carried out only with surplus embryos obtained from a clinically justifiable laparoscopy, and on thawing, embryos should be returned to the uterus of the donor, usually after an unsuccessful first attempt to transfer unfrozen embryos. Thawed embryos should be

Although certain cautions ought to be used as a general practice whenever IVF is employed, it would be ill-advised to argue against the procedure solely on the basis of the high percentage of embryos placed in the womb that do not finally attain implantation. Even in natural reproduction a great number of embryos are wasted. It seems that even God is willing to risk the loss of embryos in the process of bringing new life into the world.

(2) Problems of technological procreation in general. One crucial question must be raised concerning all procedures involving third parties: Is it ethical to use a person's reproductive capacities apart from procreating offspring within the context of marriage?

Here the issue of personal motivation arises. It is conceivable that a donor or a surrogate could be motivated purely by altruism, by the desire to assist a childless couple in having a baby. Nevertheless, it is questionable if such pure motives actually govern any such action. Technological procedures introduce the temptation of allowing less laudable motivations to surface and offer the heinous possibility that the process of procreation could be commercialized, as donors sell their wares and surrogates rent their bodies.

Steps in this direction are already visible. Donors, for example, are often students who sell sperm for economic reward. Many past donors have apparently later undergone a change of attitude, sensing both a greater responsibility for and a greater interest in their AID children.[18] Regardless of the actual motivation of the donor, the child conceived by such means may never be able to overcome his or her negative feelings toward the donor parent. As one AID child who undertook a search for her genetic father asked, "Didn't he feel any sort of responsibility for the life he was creating?"[19]

A further issue raised by technological conception in general is that of final outcome: Where will it lead? Current capabilities are already producing radical changes in societal attitudes and outlooks. Sperm banks, for example, are already a reality. Will their acceptance, together with the use of technological procedures, lead to a complete separation of procreation and childbearing from the traditional context of the inviolate bond between husband and wife that is so crucial for the psychological and spiritual development of

---

transferred to a nondonor only with the consent of the donor and an institutional review board or hospital ethics committee. Frozen embryos should be kept in storage for not more than five years or until the establishment of relevant public policy. Under such a voluntary arrangement, experience could be gained with freezing through clinical trials as an adjunct to in vitro fertilization but without public anxiety that other purposes might be served that had not been carefully considered. The purpose of the arrangement would be to avoid precipitate limitation of freezing for purposes that appear to be publicly acceptable, out of suspicion and fear of unsanctioned purposes, such as uncontrolled experimentation." Clifford Grobstein, et.al., "Special Report: Freezing Embryos: Policy Issues," *The New England Journal of Medicine* 312, 24 (1985): 1588.

18. Florence Isaacs, "High-Tech Pregnancies," *Good Housekeeping*, February 1986, 82.
19. Lori B. Andrews, "Yours, Mine and Theirs," 22.

children? Already single women and lesbian partners have sought children by AID. If such practices increase dramatically, they will call into question widely held, traditional understandings of the basis of parenthood and the nature of the marital union. Is our society prepared to deal with such changes?

Other changes are also on the horizon. Practices such as IVF and embryo transfer that provide "waste products" open the door to experimentation with embryos on the basis that they will be discarded anyway. Experimentation has already indicated the potential of fetal parts in the fight against certain diseases. Will we eventually create a society in which embryos are produced for the purpose of providing for the medical well-being of the living?[20]

Technology also holds the possibility of increased interest in eugenics. Current procedures already enable some degree of gene selection. One sperm bank was established specifically for the purpose of collecting sperm from persons of high intelligence. Future possibilities are mind boggling. For example, by combining IVF and gene-splicing procedures, technicians could attempt to eliminate genes that are undesirable.[21]

Some scientists are beginning to advise caution concerning the possibilities that loom in the not-too-distant future. Oxford University zoologist William D. Hamilton for example, after contemplating the current trend of "unnatural human reproduction," concluded at the 1987 Nobel Conference at Gustavus Adolphus College, "I would like to see sex kept not only for our recreation but also, for a long while, let it retain its old freedom and danger, still used for its old purposes."[22]

Conclusion

The consideration of these various matters leads to two conclusions. First, procedures that technologically introduce a third party into the procreative process may not constitute a violation of the marriage covenant. Therefore, they are not for that reason ethically suspect. At the same time, however, the variety of problems that potentially arise from such procedures indicates that the good they might bring simply does not outweigh the risks they involve. Janet Dickey McDowell aptly summarized the matter in terms of the genetic confusion that arises: "Such deliberate scrambling of lineage seems to serve only the purpose of allowing a couple to experience preg-

20. For a discussion of the question of fetal tissue transplants from a philosophical point of view, see Barbara Miller, "Baby Harvest: Year Two-thousand Twenty," *Contemporary Philosophy* 12, 7 (January 1989): 29–30.

21. For a discussion of this possibility, see Neaves and Neaves, "Moral Dimensions," 17–19.

22. William D. Hamilton, "Sex and Disease," in *The Evolution of Sex*, ed. George Stevens and Robert Bellig (San Francisco: Harper & Row, 1988), 90.

nancy and birth—a purpose that does not seem sufficiently important to warrant the possible confusion."[23]

Second, procedures that employ only the sperm of the husband and the egg of the wife ought to be welcomed. Although they are not free from all potential difficulties, they can serve as a means of assisting an infertile couple in producing a child that is in every respect truly their offspring. Properly limited in this manner, technological assistance need not be dangerous, but could become a God-given means of assisting happily married couples to enjoy the blessings of parenthood.

23. Janet Dickey McDowell, "Ethical Implications of In Vitro Fertilization," *The Christian Century*, 19 October 1983, 938.

Genetics and Human Malleability

W. French Anderson

Just how much can, and should we change human nature . . . by genetic engineering? Our response to that hinges on the answers to three further questions: (1) What *can* we do now? Or more precisely, what *are* we doing now in the area of human genetic engineering? (2) What *will* we be able to do? In other words, what technical advances are we likely to achieve over the next five to ten years? (3) What *should* we do? I will argue that a line can be drawn and should be drawn to use gene transfer only for the treatment of serious disease, and not for any other purpose. Gene transfer should never be undertaken in an attempt to enhance or "improve" human beings.

What Can We Do?

In 1980 John Fletcher and I published a paper in the *New England Journal of Medicine* in which we delineated what would be necessary before it would be ethical to carry out human gene therapy.[1] As with any other new therapeutic procedure, the fundamental principle is that it should be determined in advance that the probable benefits outweigh the probable risks. We analyzed the risk/benefit determination for somatic cell gene therapy and proposed three questions that need to have been answered from prior animal experimentation: Can the new gene be inserted stably into the correct target

1. W. French Anderson and John C. Fletcher, "Gene Therapy in Human Beings: When Is It Ethical to Begin?" *New England Journal of Medicine* 303, 22 (1980): 1293–97.

cells? Will the new gene be expressed (that is, function) in the cells at an appropriate level? Will the new gene harm the cell or the animal? These criteria are very similar to those required before use of any new therapeutic procedure, surgical operation, or drug. They simply require that the new treatment should get to the area of disease, correct it, and do more good than harm.

A great deal of scientific progress has occurred in the nine years since that paper was published. The technology does now exist for inserting genes into some types of target cells.[2] The procedure being used is called "retroviral-mediated gene transfer." In brief, a disabled murine retrovirus serves as a delivery vehicle for transporting a gene into a population of cells that have been removed from a patient. The gene-engineered cells are then returned to the patient.

The first clinical application of this procedure was approved by the National Institutes of Health [NIH] and the Food and Drug Administration [FDA] on January 19, 1989.[3] Our protocol received the most thorough prior review of any clinical protocol in history: It was approved only after being reviewed fifteen times by seven different regulatory bodies. In the end it received unanimous approval from every one of those committees. But the simple fact that the NIH and FDA, as well as the public, felt that the protocol needed such extensive review demonstrates that the concept of gene therapy raises serious concerns.

We can answer our initial question, "What can we do now in the area of human genetic engineering?" by examining this approved clinical protocol. Gene transfer is used to mark cancer-fighting cells in the body as a way of better understanding a new form of cancer therapy. The cancer-fighting cells are called TIL (tumor-infiltrating-lymphocytes), and are isolated from a patient's own tumor, grown up to a large number, and then given back to the patient along with one of the body's immune growth factors, a molecule called interleukin 2 (IL-2). The procedure, developed by Steven Rosenberg of the NIH, is known to help about half the patients treated.[4]

The difficulty is that there is at present no way to study the TIL once they are returned to the patient to determine why they work when they do work (that is, kill cancer cells), and why they do not work when they do not work. The goal of the gene transfer protocol was to put a label on the infused TIL,

2. See also W. French Anderson, "Prospects for Human Gene Therapy," *Science*, 26 October 1984, 401–9; T. Friedman, "Progress towards Human Gene Therapy," *Science*, 16 June 1989, 1275–81.

3. J. Wyngaarden, "Human Gene Transfer Protocol," *Federal Register* 54 no. 47 (1989): 10508–10.

4. Steven A. Rosenberg et al., "Use of Tumor-Infiltrating Lymphocytes and Interleukin-2 in the Immunotherapy of Patients with Metastatic Melanoma," *New England Journal of Medicine* 319, 25 (1988): 1676–80.

that is, to mark these cells so that they could be studied in blood and tumor specimens from the patient over time.

The TIL were marked with a vector (called N2) containing a bacterial gene that could be easily identified through recombinant DNA techniques. Our protocol was called, therefore, the N2-TIL Human Gene Transfer Clinical Protocol. The first patient received gene-marked TIL on May 22, 1989. Five patients have now received marked cells. No side effects or problems have thus far arisen from the gene transfer portion of the therapy. Useful data on the fate of the gene-marked TIL are being obtained.

But what was done that was new? Simply, a single gene was inserted into a population of cells that had been obtained from a patient's body. There are an estimated 100,000 genes in every human cell. Therefore the actual addition of material was extremely minute, nothing to correspond to the fears expressed by some that human beings would be "re-engineered." Nonetheless, a functioning piece of genetic material was successfully inserted into human cells and the gene-engineered cells did survive in human patients.

What Will We Be Able to Do?

Although only one clinical protocol is presently being conducted, it is clear that there are several applications for gene transfer that probably will be carried out over the next five to ten years. Many genetic diseases that are caused by a defect in a single gene should be treatable, such as ADA deficiency (a severe immune deficiency disease of children), sickle cell anemia, hemophilia, and Gaucher disease. Some types of cancer, viral diseases such as AIDS, and some forms of cardiovascular disease are targets for treatment by gene therapy. In addition, germline gene therapy, that is, the insertion of a gene into the reproductive cells of a patient, will probably be technically possible in the foreseeable future. My position on the ethics of germline gene therapy is published elsewhere.[5]

But successful somatic cell gene therapy also opens the door for enhancement genetic engineering, that is, for supplying a specific characteristic that individuals might want for themselves (somatic cell engineering) or their children (germline engineering) which would not involve the treatment of a disease. The most obvious example at the moment would be the insertion of a growth hormone gene into a normal child in the hope that this would make the child grow larger. Should parents be allowed to choose (if the science should ever make it possible) whatever useful characteristics they wish for their children?

5. W. French Anderson, "Human Gene Therapy: Scientific and Ethical Considerations," *Journal of Medicine and Philosophy* 10 (1985): 275–91.

What Should We Do?

A line can and should be drawn between somatic cell gene therapy and enhancement genetic engineering.[6] Our society has repeatedly demonstrated that it can draw a line in biomedical research when necessary. The Belmont Report illustrates how guidelines were formulated to delineate ethical from unethical clinical research and to distinguish clinical research from clinical practice. Our responsibility is to determine how and where to draw lines with respect to genetic engineering.

Somatic cell gene therapy for the treatment of severe disease is considered ethical because it can be supported by the fundamental moral principle of beneficence: It would relieve human suffering. Gene therapy would be, therefore, a moral good. Under what circumstances would human genetic engineering not be a moral good? In the broadest sense, when it detracts from, rather than contributes to, the dignity of man. Whether viewed from a theological perspective or a secular humanist one, the justification for drawing a line is founded on the argument that, beyond the line, human values that our society considers important for the dignity of man would be significantly threatened.

Somatic cell enhancement engineering would threaten important human values in two ways: It could be medically hazardous, in that the risks could exceed the potential benefits and the procedure therefore cause harm. And it would be morally precarious, in that it would require moral decisions our society is not now prepared to make, and it could lead to an increase in inequality and discriminatory practices.

Medicine is a very inexact science. We understand roughly how a simple gene works and that there are many thousands of housekeeping genes, that is, genes that do the job of running a cell. We predict that there are genes which make regulatory messages that are involved in the overall control and regulation of the many housekeeping genes. Yet we have only limited understanding of how a body organ develops into the size and shape it does. We know many things about how the central nervous system works—for example, we are beginning to comprehend how molecules are involved in electric circuits, in memory storage, in transmission of signals. But we are a long way from understanding thought and consciousness. And we are even further from understanding the spiritual side of our existence.

Even though we do not understand how a thinking, loving, interacting organism can be derived from its molecules, we are approaching the time when we can change some of those molecules. Might there be genes that influence the brain's organization or structure or metabolism or circuitry in

6. W. French Anderson, "Human Gene Therapy: Why Draw a Line?" *Journal of Medicine and Philosophy* 14 (1989): 681–93.

some way so as to allow abstract thinking, contemplation of good and evil, fear of death, awe of a 'God'? What if in our innocent attempts to improve our genetic make-up we alter one or more of those genes? Could we test for the alteration? Certainly not at present. If we caused a problem that would affect the individual or his or her offspring, could we repair the damage? Certainly not at present. Every parent who has several children knows that some babies accept and give more affection than others, in the same environment. Do genes control this? What if these genes were accidentally altered? How would we even know if such a gene were altered?

My concern is that, at this point in the development of our culture's scientific expertise, we might be like the young boy who loves to take things apart. He is bright enough to disassemble a watch, and maybe even bright enough to get it back together again so that it works. But what if he tries to "improve" it? Maybe put on bigger hands so that the time can be read more easily. But if the hands are too heavy for the mechanism, the watch will run slowly, erratically, or not at all. The boy can understand what is visible, but he cannot comprehend the precise engineering calculations that determined exactly how strong each spring should be, why the gears interact in the ways that they do, etc. Attempts on his part to improve the watch will probably only harm it. We are now able to provide a new gene so that a property involved in a human life would be changed, for example, a growth hormone gene. If we were to do so simply because we could, I fear we would be like that young boy who changed the watch's hands. We, too, do not really understand what makes the object we are tinkering with tick.

In summary, it could be harmful to insert a gene into humans. In somatic cell gene therapy for an already existing disease the potential benefits could outweigh the risks. In enhancement engineering, however, the risks would be greater while the benefits would be considerably less clear.

Yet even aside from the medical risks, somatic cell enhancement engineering should not be performed because it would be morally precarious. Let us assume that there were no medical risks at all from somatic cell enhancement engineering. There would still be reasons for objecting to this procedure. To illustrate, let us consider some examples. What if a human gene were cloned that could produce a brain chemical resulting in markedly increased memory capacity in monkeys after gene transfer? Should a person be allowed to receive such a gene on request? Should a pubescent adolescent whose parents are both five feet tall be provided with a growth hormone gene on request? Should a worker who is continually exposed to an industrial toxin receive a gene to give him resistance on his, or his employer's request?

These scenarios suggest three problems that would be difficult to resolve: What genes should be provided; who should receive a gene; and, how to prevent discrimination against individuals who do or do not receive a gene.

We allow that it would be ethically appropriate to use somatic cell gene therapy for treatment of serious disease. But what distinguishes a serious disease from a "minor" disease from cultural "discomfort"? What is suffering? What is significant suffering? Does the absence of growth hormone that results in a growth limitation to two feet in height represent a genetic disease? What about a limitation to a height of four to five feet? Each observer might draw the lines between serious disease, minor disease, and genetic variation differently. But all can agree that there are extreme cases that produce significant suffering and premature death. Here then is where an initial line should be drawn for determining what genes should be provided: treatment of serious disease.

If the position is established that only patients suffering from serious diseases are candidates for gene insertion, then the issues of patient selection are no different than in other medical situations: the determination is based on medical need within a supply and demand framework. But if the use of gene transfer extends to allow a normal individual to acquire, for example, a memory-enhancing gene, profound problems would result. On what basis is the decision made to allow one individual to receive the gene but not another: Should it go to those best able to benefit society (the smartest already?) To those most in need (those with low intelligence? But how low? Will enhancing memory help a mentally retarded child?)? To those chosen by a lottery? To those who can afford to pay? As long as our society lacks a significant consensus about these answers, the best way to make equitable decisions in this case should be to base them on the seriousness of the objective medical need, rather than on the personal wishes or resources of an individual.

Discrimination can occur in many forms. If individuals are carriers of a disease (for example, sickle cell anemia), would they be pressured to be treated? Would they have difficulty in obtaining health insurance unless they agreed to be treated? These are ethical issues raised also by genetic screening and by the Human Genome project. But the concerns would become even more troublesome if there were the possibility for "correction" by the use of human genetic engineering.

Finally, we must face the issue of eugenics, the attempt to make hereditary "improvements." The abuse of power that societies have historically demonstrated in the pursuit of eugenic goals is well documented.[7] Might we slide into a new age of eugenic thinking by starting with small "improvements"? It would be difficult, if not impossible, to determine where to draw a line once enhancement engineering had begun. Therefore, gene transfer

7. See, for example, Kenneth M. Ludmerer, *Genetics and American Society* (Baltimore, Md: Johns Hopkins University Press, 1972), and Daniel J. Kevles, *In the Name of Eugenics* (New York: Knopf, 1985).

should be used only for the treatment of serious disease and not for putative improvements.

Our society is comfortable with the use of genetic engineering to treat individuals with serious disease. On medical and ethical grounds we should draw a line excluding any form of enhancement engineering. We should not step over the line that delineates treatment from enhancement.

From W. French Anderson, "Genetics and Human Malleability," *Hastings Center Report* (January/February 1990): 21–24.

For Further Reflection

Case Studies

Low sperm count. Matt and Kelly love children and have a strong desire to have one or more of their own. They used birth control until their careers were in order and then tried to conceive. After two years of trying, they consulted a fertility expert and discovered that Matt has an extremely low sperm count. They tried artificial insemination (AIH), but that failed. Most of their friends have one or more children, making their own infertility more painful. They have felt their privacy invaded by fertility specialists. Worst of all, they have endured the thoughtless remarks and jokes of others concerning their childless state. They tried adoption but have been told that there simply are no babies available in the categories they prefer. The process has strained their relationship. Time after time, hope has given way to despair. They are faced with one last decision: Should they attempt conception through AID, or should they accept their infertility as God's will for them? What would you counsel them to do? What are the ethical considerations?

Sperm bank decision. Barry and Ann Friesen have been married for two years and are planning to conceive their first child in about a year, when their financial situation stabilizes. They just discovered, however, that Barry has cancer and will need extended chemotherapy. Doctors have warned that the treatment may leave Barry sterile. The Friesens are considering the possibility of storing Barry's sperm in a sperm bank so that when they wish to conceive they will be able. Some of their Christian friends are favorable to the idea, while others contend that Barry and Ann should not try to "play God" but should accept whatever happens as God's will for them. What are the issues involved in this decision, and how would you advise the Friesens if they asked for your counsel?

Glossary

Artificial insemination (AI): Injection of sperm cells either into a woman's vagina or into her uterus, with the hope that one will fertilize the woman's ovum (egg) and lead to pregnancy. The sperm may be from the woman's husband (AIH) or from someone else—a donor (AID). Quite often the donor is unknown to the prospective mother; the sperm is obtained from a sperm bank.

Embryo transfer (ET): Transfer of an embryo conceived in one womb to the womb of another woman. The embryo is transferred before it can implant it the original womb.

Genetic engineering: Term most broadly and most commonly used to refer to the use of genetics to design human descendents, and the manipulation of the entire living world for the supposed benefit of humanity. More precisely, the term denotes any technical intervention in the structure of genes, for such purposes as the removal of a harmful gene, the enhancement of a particular genetic capacity, or the changing of an organism's genetic structure. Sometimes the term is used to refer to reproductive technologies in general.

Genetics: Study of genes (the chromosome units that determine one's hereditary characteristics) and the application of that knowledge to a number of experimental and clinical uses.

In vitro fertilization (IVF): Combining of a woman's egg(s) and a man's sperm in a petri dish, followed by the insertion of the fertilized egg into the womb.

Surrogacy: Most often the process in which a couple chooses another woman (the surrogate) to be artificially inseminated with the man's sperm. In theory the surrogate will carry the baby to term, giving it up to the couple at birth (genetic surrogacy). Also refers to the process in which the parent couple's sperm and ovum are combined in vitro, and the embryo placed in the womb of the surrogate (gestational or genuine surrogacy). Again, the surrogate gives up the baby at birth.

Annotated Bibliography

Anderson, W. French. "Genetics and Human Malleability." *Hastings Center Report* 20 (January/February 1990): 21–24. Rejects any enhancement of human nature through genetic engineering, but approves of genetic technology to correct disease.

Bird, Lewis P. "Universal Principles of Biomedical Ethics and Their Application to Gene-Splicing." *Perspectives on Science and Christian Faith* 41 (June 1989): 76–86. Attempts to dispel misguided fears associated with genetic engineering, focusing instead on important issues such as universal principles, common cliches, and anxieties.

Chadwick, Ruth, ed. *Ethics, Reproduction and Genetic Control.* London and New York: Routledge, 1987. Contributors grapple with scientific, legal, and ethical problems, considering the last from the perspectives of both secular moral philosophy and theology.

Cole-Turner, Ronald. *The New Genesis: Theology and the Genetic Revolution.* Louisville: Westminster/John Knox, 1993. Theology professor helpfully considers the theological ramifications and arguments pertaining to genetic engineering.

Evans, Debra. *Without Moral Limits: Women, Reproduction and the New Medical Technology.* Westchester, Ill.: Crossway, 1989. A blistering critique of new reproductive procedures, detailing how women are victimized and exploited by technologies that disregard both medical and moral norms.

Feinberg, John S., and Paul D. Feinberg. *Ethics for a Brave New World.* Westchester, Ill.: Crossway, 1993, 207–98. Two very helpful chapters on reproductive technologies and genetic manipulation; careful presentation of and analysis of the issues from the perspective of two evangelical theology professors.

Findlay, Steven. "What Do Infertility Clinics Really Deliver?" *U.S. News and World Report,* 3 April 1989, 74–75. Reports on the findings of a nationwide survey of infertility clinics, warning against overly optimistic reports on the success rates of IVF and GIFT.

Grenz, Stanley J. "Technology and Pregnancy Enhancement." In *Sexual Ethics: A Biblical Perspective,* Dallas: Word, 1990, 142–55. Very helpful discussion of the issues from an evangelical perspective.

Hull, Richard T., ed. *Ethical Issues in the New Reproductive Technologies.* Belmont, Calif.: Wadsworth, 1990. Excellent selection of both issues and contributors, including Arthur Caplan, LeRoy Walters, Hans Tiefel, and Lori Andrews. Highly informative.

Jones, D. Gareth. *Brave New People: Ethical Issues at the Commencement of Life.* Revised. Grand Rapids: Eerdmans, 1985. Careful reflection from a scientific and Christian perspective. A valuable study.

————. "Some Implications of the New Reproductive Technologies." *Perspectives on Science and Christian Faith* 39 (March 1987): 31–38. Biblical and theological principles applied to issues of human life, infertility, and the nature of the family.

Lammers, Ann, and Ted Peters. "Genethics: Implications of the Human Genome Project." *The Christian Century* (3 October 1990): 868–72.

Views the project positively, as evidence of our "co-creatorship" with God in shaping the future of the human story.

Lauritzen, Paul. "What Price Parenthood?" *Hastings Center Report* 20 (March/April 1990): 38–46. Interacts with feminist objections to new reproductive technologies from the point of view of an infertile man.

McDowell, Janet Dickey. "Ethical Implications of In Vitro Fertilization." *The Christian Century* (19 October 1983): 936–38. Considers objections to IVF, concluding that the process per se is not morally objectionable, and that IVF conceptions should be celebrated.

Miller-McLemore, Bonnie J. "Produce or Perish: Generativity and New Reproductive Technologies." *Journal of the American Academy of Religion* 59 (Spring 1991): 39–69. Argues that the new reproductive technologies should be considered in a moral and religious context that is more sensitive to women.

3

Euthanasia

As students of logic know, Socrates was mortal. As students of history know, Socrates, the great philosopher, died when he drank poison hemlock because the senate in Athens had condemned him to die by self-inflicted capital punishment. Today medicine can delay the **death** of philosophers in ways Socrates never dreamed possible. In spite of its power, however, medicine cannot destroy death. In fact, it sometimes leaves patients in a twilight between life and death. These conflicting realities—the power of medicine to cure and the inevitability of death—give impetus to a pressing ethical question: How should we care for terminal patients?

Many values compete in discussions of terminal medical care. Some people argue that physicians should put their patients painlessly to sleep when extreme pain or incurable disease makes life not worth living. The Hemlock Society, taking its name from the drug that killed Socrates, joins other lobbying groups in campaigning for legalized **mercy killing**. Christians generally believe, however, that mercy killing is immoral because it involves intentionally destroying something of great value, namely, a human life.

Euthanasia means the deliberate act of intending or choosing a painless death for the humane purpose of ending the agony of someone who suffers from incurable disease or injury. Many people distinguish between two subtypes of euthanasia, **active euthanasia** and **passive euthanasia**. According to this distinction, *active euthanasia* denotes directly taking the life of the patient while *passive euthanasia* means acting to avoid prolonging the dying process. In other words, in active euthanasia, a physician or a friend causes

95

death (perhaps by injecting a toxin or by shooting the patient) though for merciful reasons. In passive euthanasia, however, the underlying disease or assault on the body actually causes death. The distinction emphasizes the difference between commission and omission. *Active euthanasia* signifies committing an act that kills, but *passive euthanasia* means refraining from an act that prolongs life. In both cases, however, the intention is to use death as a strategy for ending agony humanely. In euthanasia, one chooses death as a means to resolving suffering.

A growing number of ethicists, however, are dissatisfied with the active/passive distinction. The main difference between active and passive euthanasia is the physical nature of the act—whether it is an act of commission or omission. But many believe this is not the salient point. Rather, the key issue is intention. The main question to ask is, What is chosen or purposed or intended in this act? Consider, for example, two cases of cutting off a foot. In one case, a slaveowner intends to keep a slave from running away. In the second, a doctor purposes to save a patient from severe gangrene. These two physical acts are the same, but the intentions are very different. Intention, not the physical nature of the act, is the most important point.

For this reason, ethicists are increasingly distinguishing euthanasia (which means intending death as a means to ending suffering) from **letting die.** Letting die is withholding or withdrawing life-prolonging and life-sustaining technologies as an intentional act to avoid useless prolonging of the dying process. Letting die is like so-called passive euthanasia in that it never permits direct killing; the underlying disease or injury is the actual cause of death. But unlike passive euthanasia, letting die does not intend or choose death as a means to end suffering. Letting die will only choose to use other means (such as pain-suppressing drugs or emotional and spiritual support) to help people as they approach death. Further, letting die prohibits withholding or withdrawing life-prolonging and life-sustaining technologies in cases where they offer hope of continued life. So when serious disease or injury is irreversible and death is imminent, a commitment to letting die permits the medical staff to turn from an emphasis on curing the disease or injury to a focus on caring for the patient through the dying process.

It is true that in letting die, a physician *knows* that death will come. But this does not mean the doctor *intends* or *purposes* death. Those who defend letting die emphasize an important distinction between intention and foresight. If someone intends to bring about the end of a woman's life, he murders her even if the physical act is an act of omission. But in letting die, someone *foresees* the end of her life as the result of his action (say, by withholding useless surgery), but without *intending* the death.

Suppose a doctor knows that a particular surgery on a cancer patient will give that patient an extra three months of life. In choosing not to do the surgery, the physician does foresee that her patient may die in only three weeks.

But she does not intend or desire that death. Rather what she chooses—her intention or desire—is to avoid useless prolonging of life and to help the patient live as comfortably as possible in his last few weeks or months of life. So this is not a case of euthanasia (choosing the patient's death as a way to end suffering), but a case of letting die (choosing the patient's well-being in the dying process). Admittedly, differentiating euthanasia and letting die sometimes requires a fine distinction. But many ethicists argue that the contrast is morally relevant. These ethicists conclude that we are forbidden to choose death even to end suffering. Yet we are permitted, in certain cases, to choose the patient's well-being by withholding or withdrawing medical treatments that either intensify the suffering or, at best, merely postpone the moment of death for a short time.

Those who oppose the term *passive euthanasia* have another reason for rejecting its use. They contend that the phrase *passive euthanasia* serves to soften opposition to active euthanasia by eroding the distinction between mercy killing and letting die. They prefer to reserve the term *euthanasia* for any action that intends to kill (whether by omission or commission) as a strategy for ending suffering. They believe that if we speak as though one form of euthanasia (i.e., passive euthanasia) is acceptable, this makes it easier for those favoring active euthanasia to argue their case. Euthanasia proponents could say to their opponents, "You already permit one form of euthanasia (i.e., the passive form), why not be consistent and permit the other form (i.e., the active form)?" (To see how proponents of euthanasia erode the passive/active distinction in building their case, note J. P. Moreland's argument.)

In addition to the mercy killing/letting die distinction, several other contrasts are important. One of these arises from the principle of **informed consent**. Before they begin treatment, care givers must be sure that their patients understand the options and freely choose a particular treatment. This means that decisions are **voluntary** on the part of the patient. Informed consent reflects two assumptions: (1) the patient will have her own best interests at heart and will therefore likely protect them and (2) the patient has a basic right to choose the treatments she will receive. At the same time, a patient's right to determine treatment is not absolute. When physicians consider a patient's subjective desires, they do so in the context of objective medical facts. If a patient's desires alone determine treatment, her doctor becomes a technician and she a consumer.

Respecting a person's wishes is impossible, however, in cases where a patient is incoherent due either to coma or dementia. This makes treatment decisions **nonvoluntary** unless the patient has previously indicated his wishes. (**Involuntary** treatment decisions go against patient desires.) Many states permit **living wills** to cover nonvoluntary cases. In a living will, individuals specify ahead of time what treatment they would like in certain circumstances. Critics complain that living wills are vague and sometimes lead to undertreatment. Their purpose, however, is to protect the patient's right of consent and to give guidance and protection to medical personnel.

The courts also recognize several other legal ways to make decisions on behalf of incompetent patients. In **durable power of attorney**, the patient signs over to a trusted individual all responsibility for his medical decisions. (Someone with Alzheimer's, for instance, might assign durable power of attorney to a spouse.) In **substituted judgment**, a court gives one person the responsibility to make a particular decision on behalf of another.

Another distinction emerges because patients have very different potentials for recovery. This suggests that more or less aggressive treatment is appropriate for different persons. The distinction between **heroic** or **extraordinary means** and **ordinary means** is an attempt to recognize this point. Heroic means include aggressive and invasive techniques aimed at significantly improving a patient's quality of life. But in some cases, extraordinary means may offer little reasonable hope of recovery or involve undue burdens. Ordinary means are medical options that both offer reasonable hope of benefit and are not excessively burdensome. Making the ordinary/extraordinary distinction very sharp is difficult because patients are so different. The distinction, however, does press us to ask: What is the best treatment option for this patient?

The contrast between medical treatment and basic care is also important. Normally functioning humans do not need treatment to stay alive, but they do need care, including food and liquid. This raises the question of mechanically administered feeding and hydration. Assuming that it is right in certain cases to cease medical treatment, is it ever right to withdraw food and liquid? Some say mechanically administered feeding and hydration are medical treatments because they require medical equipment and expertise. But feeding by hand is basic care, not medical treatment. If this is right, then we might class withholding or withdrawing mechanically administered feeding and hydration as morally right in some circumstances. Some argue, however, that giving food and liquid—even through a tube—is not treatment, but basic care. If this is so, we might consider it morally right to stop ineffective chemotherapy, but never condone pulling a feeding tube. Christians have not reached consensus on this matter.

With these several pairs of contrasts in mind, we now look more closely at the question of mercy killing. Advocates of active euthanasia use the active/passive distinction in their bid to argue that mercy killing is sometimes morally right. Often they bolster their case in this way:

1. Passive euthanasia and active euthanasia are not different in morally relevant ways, for in both scenarios the death of the patient is intended.

2. Clearly, passive euthanasia is morally right in certain terminal cases.
3. Consequently, active euthanasia is morally right in certain terminal cases.

This argument depends crucially on collapsing the distinction between passive and active euthanasia. Philosopher J. P. Moreland addresses the argument head-on, undercutting the case for active euthanasia by attacking the first premise. He delineates several important ways in which mercy killing and letting die are very different. According to Moreland, nothing about euthanasia follows from the moral propriety of letting die.

Positively, the traditional view asserts that the basic duties of physicians to help their patients (**beneficence**) and to refrain from harming them (**nonmaleficence**) imply that intending to kill is never right. For religious people generally, and Christians particularly, these duties are grounded in respect for human spiritual or personal life that in turn is based on theological and biblical commitments. The value of human life based on the image of God is particularly important. A doctor, a person who is duty-bound to respect human life, entrusted with the patient's best interests and sworn to healing and curing, cannot fulfill her responsibility by killing her patient. For the traditional view, this makes doctor-assisted suicide unthinkable.

Yet patients do sometimes die in the course of medical care. For example, a heart patient may die on the operating table despite the medical team's best efforts. In terminal care, a doctor's administering increasing doses of painkiller with intent to relieve pain can shorten the life of his patient. The **double effect principle**, long accepted in ethical theory, shows why physicians do not act immorally in these cases. If an inherently good act has two effects, one good and one bad, a person can act morally in choosing that act provided (1) only the good effect is intended (even if the bad effect is foreseen), (2) the bad effect is not the means to the good effect, and (3) the good effect is at least equal to the bad effect. Since the physician intends the painkiller to kill the pain and not the patient, he is right to give it even though it might shorten the patient's life.

The principle of double effect hinges crucially on intention, the goal pursued in an action, that is, what one is trying to accomplish in performing an act. According to the traditional view, euthanasia does not meet the criteria of the principle of double effect. Euthanasia fails at least the first two criteria. It intends death and achieves the good effect (relief of suffering) by means of the bad effect (death). Letting die is morally right, however, in cases that meet these criteria: death is inevitable and imminent, the death is caused indirectly (that is, by disease or injury), and the intention is to care for, not to kill. In such cases, termination of medical treatment (though not of basic caring—which for some includes giving food and liquid) is an act of letting die and is morally right.

Patients who have only very minimal conscious life do pose very confusing dilemmas, however. If a painful, experimental treatment might add six
months to the life of a demented cancer patient, should doctors attempt it?
If an elderly, terminal patient refuses hand feeding, should nurses mechanically administer feeding? What about comatose patients and brain-dead
patients?

These questions depend on another issue: What is death? When does one
cease to be a human person? Theologically, the meaning of *death* is the separation of the spiritual self from the body. But how does one know death has
occurred? Death is verified by looking to medical indicators. Traditionally,
medicine has taken irreversible cessation of circulatory and respiratory functions to indicate death. But technical advances have made it possible to keep
heart and lungs functioning when the brain is entirely dead. Is a brain-dead
person alive? In response, the Uniform Determination of Death Act says that
death is also indicated by the irreversible cessation of the whole brain (**brain
death**).

This use of brain function as the indicator of death requires some clear
definitions. Brain death is the death of the entire brain, including the upper
brain (that supports consciousness) and the brain stem (that controls certain
body functions like breathing and heart rate). Upper-brain death (or neocortical death) leads to permanent loss of consciousness. But it does not always
mean the brain *stem* has died. Sometimes a patient whose upper brain is dead
will have a brain stem that still supports heart and lung activity. A person
who is upper-brain dead is called a PVS (persistent vegetative state) patient.
It is important to understand that because nerve cells do not regenerate,
brain death and upper-brain death are completely irreversible. It is also true
that in a comatose patient, the upper brain continues to function at some
level. Consequently, the comatose patient can awaken. Brain death and
upper-brain death, therefore, are very different from coma.

In cases of total brain death or upper-brain death (PVS), all agree that
heroic measures are unnecessary. Many agree that ordinary treatment is not
obligatory, and letting die is moral. Some believe it is wrong, however, to
withdraw food and hydration, allowing the body to starve. Religion professor
Gilbert Meilaender takes this view. While the stopping of medical treatment
is permissible, he argues that withdrawing food and hydration never is. Even
when no conscious life is possible, routine care is appropriate. Meilaender
defends a holistic view of the human person that implies that a functioning,
but soulless body is impossible. A functioning body, even one that lacks any
potential for conscious life, is still a member of the human race and as such
deserves routine care, including food and water.

Other Christians believe that brain-dead or PVS patients are simply bodies. Their spiritual selves have gone on to their heavenly rewards. To keep a
soulless body alive is to promote **vitalism** (the idea that physical function by

itself is sacred). Thus, withdrawing food and water from brain-dead or PVS patients is morally right. Ethicist Robert Rakestraw defends this view. He argues that without a potentially functioning brain, the body no longer sustains a soul or images God. Thus, mere biological functioning of a physical body does not constitute human life. Of course, medical personnel should always care for those with any potential for conscious life, that is, for those who are still human persons. But only misguided vitalists insist that we do everything possible to the very end of merely physical life.

For the demented cancer patient or the terminal patient who refuses hand feeding, the traditional view forbids euthanasia. What then can Christians do? Our society regards medicine as a curing profession. Given that our ability to cure sometimes reaches an end, this view of medicine implies that some patients are beyond help. In contrast to this, the Christian duty to minister to the dying never ends. We can turn from curing to caring—from "rescue the perishing" to "care for the dying." The Bible says, "give beer to those who are perishing" (Prov. 31:6 NIV). When death is inevitable, medicine can attend to easing pain and the church can focus on spiritual ministry to those who must prepare for death. This last period of life can be the context for loving ministry. No one is ever beyond help. Such service, even if it does not cure, is of great value.

James Rachels and the Active Euthanasia Debate

J. P. Moreland

The rise of advanced medical technologies, especially life-sustaining ones, has brought to center stage the importance of bioethical issues that arise in acute and long-term care contexts. The recent avalanche of bioethics committees is a witness to the importance of bioethical issues.[1] Problems about the nature and permissibility of euthanasia have been especially pressing.[2]

Roughly speaking, there are two major views about euthanasia.[3] The traditional view holds that *prima facie* it is always wrong to intentionally kill an innocent human being, but that given certain circumstances it is permissible to withhold or withdraw treatment and allow a patient to die. A more radical view, embraced by groups like the Hemlock Society and the Society for the Right to Die, denies that there is a morally significant distinction between passive and active euthanasia that allows the former and forbids the latter. Accordingly this view argues that mercy killing, assisted suicide and the like

---

1. The development of bioethics committees is well advanced in acute-care facilities but not in long-term care. For more on the nature and function of bioethics committees see *Institutional Ethics Committees and Health Care Decision Making*, ed. R. E. Cranford and A. E. Doudera (Ann Arbor: Health Care, 1984); B. Hosford, *Bioethics Committees* (Rockville, Md.: Aspen, 1986).

2. For a survey of death and dying cases see R. M. Veatch, *Case Studies in Medical Ethics* (Cambridge: Harvard University Press, 1977), 317–47.

3. For an evangelical critique of voluntary active euthanasia see M. Erickson and I. Bowers, "Euthanasia and Christian Ethics," *Journal of the Evangelical Theological Society* 19 (1970): 15–24. Erickson and Bowers consider whether voluntary active euthanasia is ever right. But they assume—correctly, in my view—that active and passive euthanasia are distinct. The major burden of the present article is to justify that distinction.

are permissible. I want to argue against the radical view by criticizing the most articulate expression of it to date—that of James Rachels.[4] . . .

The Radical View

According to Rachels, the distinctions used in the traditional view are inadequate. There is nothing sacred or morally significant about being a human being with biological life. Nor is there any moral difference between killing someone and letting him die. Thus if passive euthanasia is permitted in a given case, so is active euthanasia. Two distinctions are central for Rachels' position.

1. *Biological life versus biographical life.* The mere fact that something has biological life, says Rachels, whether human or nonhuman, is relatively unimportant. What is important is that someone has biographical life. One's biographical life is "the sum of one's aspirations, decisions, activities, projects, and human relationships."[5] The facts of a person's biographical life are those of his history and character. They are the interests that are important and worthwhile from the point of view of the person him/herself. The value of one's biographical life is the value it has for that person, and something has value if its loss would harm that person.[6]

Two implications follow from Rachels' view. (1) Certain infants without a prospect for biographical life, and certain terminal patients (e.g., comatose patients, or those in a persistent vegetative state), have nothing to be concerned with from a moral point of view. They are not alive in the biographical sense, though they may be in the biological sense. But the former is what is relevant to morality. (2) Higher forms of animals do have lives in the biographical sense because they have thoughts, emotions, goals, cares, and so forth. Thus they should be given moral respect because of this. In fact a chimpanzee with a biographical life has more value than a human who only has biological life.

2. *Killing and letting die.* Rachels believes that there is no distinction between killing someone directly or letting that person die. There is no morally important difference between these. He calls this the "equivalence" thesis. His main argument for it is called the "bare difference" argument. Rachels sets up two cases that are supposed to be exactly alike except that one involves killing and the other involves letting die:

> Smith stands to gain a large inheritance if anything should happen to his six-year-old cousin. One evening while the child is taking his bath, Smith sneaks

---

4. See J. Rachels, "Active and Passive Euthanasia," *The New England Journal of Medicine* 292 (January 9, 1975): 78–80; *The End of Life* (Oxford: Oxford University Press, 1986).
5. Rachels, *End,* 5; see also 26, 33, 35, 38, 47, 49–59, 65, 76, 85.
6. Ibid., 38.

into the bathroom and drowns the child, and then arranges things so that it will look like an accident. No one is the wiser, and Smith gets his inheritance. Jones also stands to gain if anything should happen to his six-year-old cousin. Like Smith, Jones sneaks in planning to drown the child in his bath. However, just as he enters the bathroom Jones sees the child slip, hit his head, and fall face-down in the water. Jones is delighted; he stands by, ready to push the child's head back under if necessary, but it is not necessary. With only a little thrash-ing about, the child drowns all by himself, "accidentally," as Jones watches and does nothing. No one is the wiser, and Jones gets his inheritance.[7]

According to Rachels, neither man behaved better from a moral point of view even though Smith killed the child and Jones merely let the child die. Both acted from the same motive (personal gain) and the results were iden-tical (death). Thus the only difference between the two cases is killing versus letting die, and since the cases are morally equivalent this distinction is mor-ally irrelevant.

Two implications follow from the equivalence thesis. (1) Cases where passive euthanasia is permissible are also cases where active euthanasia is permissible. (2) Situations where we let people die—for example, when we let them starve in famine situations—are morally equivalent to killing them.

Criticisms of the Radical View

1. *The biological/biographical view of life.* There are at least [two] problems with Rachels' distinction between biological and biographical life.

(1) His understanding of biographical life, far from rendering biological life morally insignificant, presupposes the importance of biological human life. He describes biographical life as a unity of capacities, interests, and so forth, that a person freely chooses for himself and that unites the various stages of one's life. It is even possible for a bigamist, says Rachels, to lead two biographical lives.

Now it is precisely these (and other) features of life that the Aristotelian/ Thomist notion of secondary substance (essence, natural kind) seeks to explain. It is because an entity has an essence and falls within a natural kind that it can possess a unity of dispositions, capacities, parts and properties at a given time and can maintain identity through change. And it is the natural kind that determines what kinds of activities are appropriate and natural for that entity.

Further, an organism *qua* essentially characterized particulars has second-order capacities to have first-order capacities that may or may not obtain (through some sort of lack). These second-order capacities are

7. Ibid., 112.

grounded in the nature of the organism. For example, a child may not have the first-order capacity to speak English due to a lack of education. But because the child has humanness it has the capacity to develop the capacity to speak English. The very idea of a defect presupposes these second-order capacities.

Now the natural kind "human being" or "human person" (I do not distinguish between these) is not to be understood as a mere biological concept. It is a metaphysical concept that grounds both biological functions and moral intuitions. In what is perhaps the most articulate modern defense of the doctrine of substance I am presenting, David Wiggins states:

> If we ask what is so good, either absolutely or to me, about my mental life's flowing on from now into the future, the answer . . . imports what makes me dear to myself—and with it my idea of myself as a continuant with certain moral or other qualities that make me fond of myself.[8]

In sum, if we ask why biographical life is both possible and morally important, the answer will be that such a life is grounded in the kind of entity, a human person in this case, that typically can have that life.

(2) Rachels' view seems to collapse into subjectivism. According to him the importance of a biographical life is that a person has the capacity to set and achieve goals, plans and interests that are important from the point of view of the individual himself. But if this is true, then there is no objective moral difference in the different goals one chooses for himself. One can only be right or wrong about the best means to accomplish these goals.[9] To see this, consider Rachels' treatment of the 1973 "Texas burn case" where a man known as Donald C. was horribly burned but was kept alive for two years in the hospital against his will and is still alive today. Rachels believes his desire to die was rational because Donald C. had lost his biographical life. Says Rachels:

> Now what could be said in defence of the judgement that this man's desire to die was rational? I believe focusing on the notion of his *life* (in the biographical sense) points us in the right direction. He was, among other things, a rodeo performer, a pilot, and what used to be called a "ladies' man". His life was not the life of a scholar or a solitary dreamer. What his injury had done, from his point of view, was to destroy his ability to lead the life that made him the distinctive individual he was. There could be no more rodeos, no more aeroplanes, no more dancing with the ladies, and a lot more. Donald's position was that if he could not lead *that* life, he didn't want to live.[10]

8. D. Wiggins, *Sameness and Substance* (Cambridge: Harvard University Press, 1980), 152.
9. Rachels, *End*, 46–47.
10. Ibid., 54.

But surely some rational life plans are more valuable than others. In fact it is possible to choose goals and interests that are immoral and dehumanizing. Suppose there is a woman named Xavier. Her life plan is to become the best prostitute she can be. She enjoys bestiality, group sex, and certain forms of masochism. Her life has value from her point of view if and only if she can achieve these goals. Now suppose that she is in an accident that confines her to a wheelchair such that she is in no pain, she can lead a relatively productive life in various ways, but she can no longer pursue her desire to be the best prostitute ever. Does it make sense to say that she would be rational to desire to die? Does it make sense to say that her biographical life is what gave her life value? Rachels' view would seem to imply an affirmative answer to both of these questions. But is it not clear that Xavier was dehumanizing herself? Some forms of life are "appropriate" for humans, and others are not. The difference seems to be grounded in the fact that a human being is a creature of value, and a choice of life plans can be devaluing to the sort of creature one is. Without objective material grounds that constitute a morally appropriate life plan, subjectivism would seem to follow. But one can be wrong about one's point of view.

Rachels denies that his view is equivalent to moral subjectivism. He argues that it is objectively true that something has value for someone if its loss would harm that person. But this is a mere formal principle, and the material content one gives it—that is, what it is to be harmed—will depend in large degree on what interests constitute one's biographical life. The case of Donald C. illustrates this. But since a choice of interests is subjective, Rachels' view is subjectivist. . . .

2. The killing/letting die distinction. The "bare difference" argument involving the Smith and Jones cases was an attempt to show that two different actions—one killing and one letting die—can have the same intentions and results and thus are both morally forbidden in spite of the difference in actions. In fact, the cases are supposed to show that the mere difference between killing and letting die is irrelevant. But the cases fail to make the point. The cases gave what some philosophers call a masking or sledge hammer effect.[11] The fact that one cannot distinguish the taste of two wines when both are mixed with green persimmon juice fails to show that there is no difference between the wines. The taste of the persimmon juice is so strong that it overshadows the difference. Similarly the intentions and motives of Smith and Jones are so atrocious, and both acts are so clearly unjustified, that it is not surprising that other features of their situation (killing versus letting die) are not perceived as the morally determinative factors in the cases.

But this observation, valid as it is, does not take us to the heart of the problem with Rachels' bare-difference argument. The main difficulty with

11. See Beauchamp and Childress, *Principles,* 117.

the bare-difference argument lies in its inadequate analysis of a human moral act. Thomas Sullivan puts his finger on the difficulty when he argues that Rachels makes the distinction between the act of killing and the act of letting die be "a distinction that puts a moral premium on overt behavior—moving or not moving one's parts—while totally ignoring the intentions of the agent."[12] But is the proper analysis of a human action—especially a human moral action—one that merely treats that action as a physical event? I think not.

There is an alternative analysis of human action in general, and human moral action in particular, that finds its classic expression in Aquinas' *Summa Theologica* 1, 2 qq. 6–20.[13] A human act, moral or otherwise, is a composite whole that contains various parts among which are these two: (1) the object, end, or intention of the act, and (2) the means-to-the-end of the act. As Richard M. Gula points out:

> The intention of the agent and the means-to-an-end form two structural elements of *one* composite action. To determine the morality of the human action, both of these elements must be taken together. The significance of this is that the physical action itself (the material event, or means-to-an-end) cannot be evaluated morally without considering the actor, especially the intention.[14]

To see this, consider the following case. Suppose a man named Jones is visited by the world's leading hypnotist. Jones is hypnotized, is told to hit the nose of the first person wearing a red shirt, and is causally determined to do so. Jones wakes up, leaves the office and strikes the first red-shirted person in the nose.

Now consider Smith. He hates his football coach because he is jealous of his good looks. His coach happens to be wearing a red shirt that day and Smith, out of hatred and jealousy and with an intent to hurt his coach, strikes him on the nose. It seems obvious that Smith's act was immoral and Jones' was not. In fact it does not seem that Jones really acted at all. What is the difference? Both acts have the same set of physical happenings or means-to-ends. The difference is that Smith intended an immoral end and Jones did not act out of intent at all.

Rachels' bare-difference cases differ in means-to-ends, but they have the same intent. Defenders of the active/passive distinction, however, do not

12. T. D. Sullivan, "Active and Passive Euthanasia: An Important Distinction?" reprinted in *Social Ethics*, ed. T. Mappes and J. Zembaty (New York: McGraw-Hill, 1982), 59.

13. For recent treatments of this view see R. M. Gula, *What Are They Saying About Moral Norms?* (New York: Paulist, 1982), 61–74; J. Finnis, *Fundamentals of Ethics* (Washington: Georgetown University Press, 1983), 37–48, 112–20; J. Fuchs, *Christian Ethics in a Secular Arena* (Washington: Georgetown University Press, 1984), 75–77. See also R. M. Chisholm, *Brentano and Intrinsic Value* (Cambridge: Cambridge University Press, 1986), 17–32.

14. Gula, *What*, 27.

ground the difference on mere physical happenings or means-to-ends. The acts of Smith's and Jones' drowning the two children differ only in physical properties. But that is just part of a human act, not the whole. Rachels leaves the intent of the two acts out of his analysis, but a defender of the traditional view would not allow such an analysis to stand. . . .

From J. P. Moreland, "James Rachels and the Active Euthanasia Debate," *Journal of the Evangelical Theological Society* 31 (1988): 81–90.

On Removing Food and Water

Against the Stream

Gilbert Meilaender

As infants we were given food and drink when we were too help-less to nourish ourselves. And for many of us a day will come before we die when we are once again too helpless to feed ourselves. If there is any way in which the living can stand by those who are not yet dead, it would seem to be through the continued provision of food and drink even when the struggle against disease has been lost. To continue to nourish the life of one who has been defeated in that battle is the last evidence we can offer that we are more than frontrunners, that we are willing to love to the very point of death.

Today this intuitive reaction is being challenged. The President's Commission for the Study of Ethical Problems in Medicine and Biomedical and Behavioral Research has suggested that for patients with permanent loss of consciousness artificial feeding interventions need not be continued.[1] A group of physicians writing in the *New England Journal of Medicine* has counseled doctors that for irreversibly ill patients whose condition warrants nothing more aggressive than general nursing care, "naturally or artificially administered hydration and nutrition may be given or withheld, depending on the patient's comfort."[2]

Court decisions in cases like those of Claire Conroy in New Jersey or Clarence Herbert in California or Mary Hier in Massachusetts are contra-

1. The President's Commission for the Study of Ethical Problems in Medicine and Biomedical and Behavioral Research, *Deciding to Forego Life-Sustaining Treatment* (Washington, D.C.: Government Printing Office, 1982), 190.

2. Sidney H. Wanzer, M.D., et al., "The Physician's Responsibility Toward Hopelessly Ill Patients," *New England Journal of Medicine* 310 (April 12, 1984): 958.

dictory,[3] but a consensus is gradually building toward the day when what we have already done in the case of some nondying infants with birth defects who were "allowed to die" by not being fed will become standard "treatment" for all patients who are permanently unconscious or suffering from severe and irreversible dementia. Those who defend this view stand ready with ethical arguments that nutrition and hydration are not "in the best interests" of such patients, but Daniel Callahan may have isolated the energizing force that is driving this consensus: "A denial of nutrition," he says, "may in the long run become the only effective way to make certain that a large number of biologically tenacious patients actually die."[4]

To the degree that this is true, however, the policy toward which we are moving is not merely one of "allowing to die": it is one of aiming to kill. *If* we are in fact heading in this direction, we should turn back before this policy corrupts our intellect and emotions and our capacity for moral reasoning. That stance I take to be a given, for which I shall not attempt to argue. Here I will consider only whether removal of artificial nutrition and hydration really does amount to no more than "allowing to die."

Why Feeding Is Not Medical Care

The argument for ceasing to feed seems strongest in cases of people suffering from a "persistent vegetative state," those (like Karen Quinlan) who have suffered an irreversible loss of consciousness. Sidney Wanzer and his physician colleagues suggest that in such circumstances, "it is morally justifiable to withhold antibiotics and artificial nutrition and hydration, as well as other forms of life-sustaining treatment, allowing the patient to die." The President's Commission advises: "Since permanently unconscious patients will never be aware of nutrition, the only benefit to the patient of providing such increasingly burdensòme interventions is sustaining the body to allow for a remote possibility of recovery. The sensitivities of the family and of care giving professionals ought to determine whether such interventions are made." Joanne Lynn, a physician at George Washington University, and James Childress, a professor of religious studies at the University of Virginia, believe that "in these cases, it is very difficult to discern how any medical intervention can benefit or harm the patient."[5] But we need to ask whether the physicians are right to suggest that they seek only to allow the patient to die; whether the President's Commission has used language carefully

---

3. See a discussion of the first two cases in Bonnie Steinbock, "The Removal of Mr. Herbert's Feeding Tube," *Hastings Center Report* 13 (October 1983): 13–16; also see George J. Annas, "The Case of Mary Hier: When Substituted Judgment Becomes Sleight of Hand," *Hastings Center Report* 14 (August 1984): 23–25.

4. Daniel Callahan, "On Feeding the Dying," *Hastings Center Report* 13 (October 1983): 22.

5. Joanne Lynn and James Childress, "Must Patients Always Be Given Food and Water?" *Hastings Center Report* 13 (October 1983): 18.

enough in saying that nutrition and hydration of such persons is merely sustaining a *body*; whether Lynn and Childress may too readily have assumed that providing food and drink is *medical* treatment.

Should the provision of food and drink be regarded as *medical* care? It seems, rather, to be the sort of care that all human beings owe each other. All living beings need food and water in order to live, but such nourishment does not itself heal or cure disease. When we stop feeding the permanently unconscious patient, we are not withdrawing from the battle against any illness or disease; we are withholding the nourishment that sustains all life.

The President's Commission does suggest that certain kinds of care remain mandatory for the permanently unconscious patient: "The awkward posture and lack of motion of unconscious patients often lead to pressure sores, and skin lesions are a major complication. Treatment and prevention of these problems is standard nursing care and should be provided." Yet it is hard to see why such services (turning the person regularly, giving alcohol rubs, and the like) are standard nursing care when feeding is not. Moreover, if feeding cannot benefit these patients, it is far from clear how they could experience bed sores as harm.

If this is true, we may have good reason to question whether the withdrawal of nutrition and hydration in such cases is properly characterized as stopping medical treatment in order to allow a patient to die. There are circumstances in which a plausible and helpful distinction can be made between killing and allowing to die, between an aim and a foreseen but unintended consequence. And sometimes it may make excellent moral sense to hold that we should cease to provide a now useless treatment, foreseeing but not intending that death will result. Such reasoning is also useful in the ethics of warfare, but there its use must be strictly controlled lest we simply unleash the bombs while "directing our intention" to a military target that could be attacked with far less firepower. Careful use of language is also necessary lest we talk about unconscious patients in ways that obscure our true aim.

Challenging those who have argued that it is no longer possible to distinguish between combatants and noncombatants in war, Michael Walzer has pointed out that "the relevant distinction is not between those who work for the war effort and those who do not, but between those who make what soldiers need to fight and those who make what they need to live, like the rest of us."[6]

Hence, farmers are not legitimate targets in war simply because they grow the food that soldiers need to live (and then to fight). The soldiers would need the food to live, even if there were no war. Thus, as Paul Ramsey has observed, though an army may march upon its belly, bellies are not the target. It is an abuse of double-effect reasoning to justify cutting off the food

6. Michael Walzer, *Just and Unjust Wars* (New York: Basic Books, 1977), 147.

supply of a nation as a way of stopping its soldiers. We could not properly say that we were aiming at the soldiers while merely foreseeing the deaths of the civilian population.

Nor can we, when withdrawing food from the permanently unconscious person, properly claim that our intention is to cease useless treatment for a dying patient. These patients are not dying, and we cease no treatment aimed at disease; rather, we withdraw the nourishment that sustains all human beings whether healthy or ill, and we do so when the only result of our action can be death. At what, other than that death, could we be aiming?

One might argue that the same could be said of turning off a respirator, but the situations are somewhat different. Remove a person from a respirator and he may die—but, then, he may also surprise us and continue to breathe spontaneously. We test to see if the patient can breathe. If he does, it is not our task—unless we are aiming at his death—now to smother him (or to stop feeding him). But deprive a person of food and water and she will die as surely as if we had administered a lethal drug, and it is hard to claim that we did not aim at her death.

I am unable—and this is a lack of insight, not of space—to say more about the analogy between eating and breathing. Clearly, air is as essential to life as food. We might wonder, therefore, whether provision of air is not also more than medical treatment. What justification could there be, then, for turning off a respirator? If the person's death, due to the progress of a disease, is irreversibly and imminently at hand, then continued assistance with respiration may now be useless. But if the person is not going to die from any disease but, instead, simply needs assistance with breathing because of some injury, it is less clear to me why such assistance should not be given. More than this I am unable to say. I repeat, however, that to remove a respirator is not necessarily to aim at death; one will not go on to kill the patient who manages to breathe spontaneously. But it is difficult for me to construe removal of nutrition for permanently unconscious patients in any other way. Perhaps we only wish them dead or think they would be better off dead. There are circumstances in which such a thought is understandable. But it would still be wrong to enact that wish by aiming at their death.

Separating Personhood and Body

Suppose that we accept the view that provision of food and water is properly termed medical treatment. Is there good reason to withhold this treatment from permanently unconscious patients? A treatment refusal needs to be justified either on the ground that the treatment is (or has now become) useless, or that the treatment (though perhaps still useful) is excessively burdensome for the patient. Still taking as our focus the permanently unconscious patient, we can consider, first, whether feeding is useless.

There could be occasions on which artificial feeding would be futile. Lynn and Childress offer instances of patients who simply cannot be fed effectively, but they are not cases of permanently unconscious patients.

Yet for many people the uselessness of feeding the permanently unconscious seems self-evident. Why? Probably because they suppose that the nourishment we provide is, in the words of the President's Commission, doing no more than "sustaining the body." But we should pause before separating personhood and body so decisively. When considering other topics (care of the environment, for example) we are eager to criticize a dualism that divorces human reason and consciousness from the larger world of nature. Why not here? We can know people—of all ranges of cognitive capacity—only as they are embodied; there is no other "person" for whom we might care. Such care is not useless if it "only" preserves bodily life but does not restore cognitive capacities. Even if it is less than we wish could be accomplished, it remains care for the embodied person.

Some will object to characterizing as persons those who lack the capacity or, even, the potential for self-awareness, for envisioning a future for themselves, for relating to other selves. I am not fully persuaded that speaking of "persons" in such contexts is mistaken, but the point can be made without using that language. Human nature has a capacity to know, to be self-aware, and to relate to others. We can share in that human nature even though we may not yet or no longer exercise all the functions of which it is capable. We share in it simply by virtue of being born into the human species. We could describe as persons all individuals sharing our common nature, all members of the species. Or we could ascribe personhood only to those human beings presently capable of exercising the characteristic human functions.

I think it better—primarily because it is far less dualistic—to understand personhood as an endowment that comes without nature, even if at some stages of life we are unable to exercise characteristic human capacities. But the point can be made, if anyone wishes, by talking of embodied human beings rather than embodied persons. To be a human being one need not presently be exercising or be capable of exercising the functions characteristic of consciousness. Those are capacities of human nature; they are not functions that all human beings exercise. It is human beings, not just persons in that more restricted sense, whose death should not be our aim. And if this view is characterized as an objectionable "speciesism," I can only reply that at least it is not one more way by which the strong and gifted in our world rid themselves of the weak, and it does not fall prey to that abstraction by which we reify consciousness and separate it from the body.

The permanently unconscious are not dying subjects who should simply be allowed to die. But they will, of course, die if we aim at their death by ceasing to feed them. If we are not going to feed them because that would be nothing more than sustaining a body, why not bury them at once? No one, I think, recommends that. But if, then, they are still living beings who ought not be buried, the nourishment that all human beings need to live ought not be denied them. When we permit ourselves to think that care is useless if it preserves the life of the embodied human being without restoring cognitive capacity, we fall victim to the old delusion that we have failed if we cannot *cure* and that there is, then, little point to continued *care*. David Smith, a professor of religious studies at the University of Indiana, has suggested that I might be mistaken in describing the comatose person as a "nondying" patient. At least in some cases, he believes lapsing into permanent coma might be a sign that a person is trying to die. Thus, though a comatose state would not itself be sufficient reason to characterize someone as dying, it might be one of several conditions which, taken together, would be sufficient. This is a reasonable suggestion, and it might enable us to distinguish different sorts of comatose patients—the dying, for whom feeding might be useless; the nondying, for whom it would not. Even then, however, I would still be troubled by the worry I raised earlier: whether food and drink are really medical treatment that should be withdrawn when it becomes useless.

Even when care is not useless it may be so burdensome that it should be dispensed with. When that is the case, we can honestly say—and it makes good moral sense to say—that our aim is to relieve the person of a burden, with the foreseen but unintended effect of a hastened death. We should note, however, that this line of argument *cannot* be applied to the cases of the permanently unconscious. Other patients—those, for example, with fairly severe dementia—may be made afraid and uncomfortable by artificial nutrition and hydration. But this can hardly be true of the permanently unconscious. It seems unlikely that they experience the care involved in feeding them as burdensome.

Even for severely demented patients who retain some consciousness, we should be certain that we are considering the burden of the treatment, not the burden of continued existence itself. In the case of Claire Conroy, for example, the trial judge suggested that her life (not simply the intervention needed to feed her) had become "impossibly and permanently burdensome." That is a judgment, I think, that no one should make for another; indeed, it is hard to know exactly how one would do so. Besides, it seems evident that if the burden involved is her continued life, the point of ceasing to feed is that we aim at relieving her of that burden—that is, we aim to kill.

Having said that, I am quite ready to grant that the burden of the feeding itself may sometimes be so excessive that it is not warranted. Lynn and Childress offer examples, some of which seem persuasive. If, however, we want to assess the burden of the treatment, we should certainly not dispense with nutrition and hydration until a reasonable trial period has demonstrated that the person truly finds such care excessively burdensome.

In short, if we focus our attention on irreversibly ill adults for whom general nursing care but no more seems appropriate, we can say the following: First, when the person is permanently unconscious, the care involved in feeding can hardly be experienced as burdensome. Neither can such care be described as useless, since it preserves the life of the embodied human being (who is not a dying patient). Second, when the person is conscious but severely and irreversibly demented, the care involved in feeding, though not useless, *may* be so burdensome that it should cease. This requires demonstration during a trial period, however, and the judgment is quite different from concluding that the person's life has become too burdensome to preserve. Third, for both sorts of patients the care involved in feeding is not, in any strict sense, medical treatment, even if provided in a hospital. It gives what all need to live; it is treatment of no particular disease; and its cessation means certain death, a death at which we can only be said to aim, whatever our motive.

That we should continue to feed the permanently unconscious still seems obvious to some people, even as it was to Karen Quinlan's father at the time he sought removal of her respirator. It has not always seemed so to me, but it does now. For the permanently unconscious person, feeding is neither useless nor excessively burdensome. It is ordinary human care and is not given as treatment for any life-threatening disease. Since this is true, a decision not to offer such care can enact only one intention: to take the life of the unconscious person.

I have offered no arguments here to prove that such a life-taking intention and aim would be morally wrong, though I believe it is and that to embrace such an aim would be corrupting. If we can face the fact that withdrawing the nourishment of such persons is, indeed, aiming to kill, I am hopeful (though not altogether confident) that the more fundamental principle will not need to be argued. Let us hope that this is the case, since that more basic principle is not one that can be argued *to*; rather, all useful moral argument must proceed *from* the conviction that it is wrong to aim to kill the innocent.

From Gilbert Meilaender, "On Removing Food and Water: Against the Stream," *Hastings Center Report* 14 (December 1984): 11–13.

The Persistent Vegetative State and the Withdrawal of Nutrition and Hydration

Robert V. Rakestraw

In recent discussions of euthanasia, coma, and the withdrawal of artificially supplied nutrition and fluids, considerable confusion exists where these topics intersect with the condition known as persistent vegetative state (PVS). For example the terms "PVS" and "coma" are sometimes erroneously used interchangeably, especially by the popular media.[1] Further, regarding the withdrawal of food and water from PVS individuals, some opponents of the practice wrongly allege the intention to kill (aiming at death) on the part of all who allow the practice.[2] Such withdrawal is sometimes incorrectly viewed as euthanasia and is grouped indiscriminately with the deliberate termination of the lives of conscious yet severely disabled persons.[3]

---

1. R. E. Cranford writes: "It makes no sense to talk about 'comfort measures' or 'pain and suffering' in patients in a persistent vegetative state. Physicians should bring to the attention of Congress the fact that the class of patients called 'chronically and irreversibly comatose' simply does not exist in any meaningful sense. The term 'irreversible coma' should be completely abandoned. Physicians should educate the public that the withdrawal of artificial feeding from patients in [PVS] does not lead to the horrible signs and symptoms attributed to this process by special interest groups; this is misleading rhetoric, not medical reality" ("The Persistent Vegetative State: The Medical Reality—Getting the Facts Straight," *Hastings Center Report* 18 [February/March 1988]: 32).

2. Failing to see the distinction between withdrawing artificial feeding and aiming at death is G. Meilaender, "On Removing Food and Water: Against the Stream," *Hastings Center Report* 14 (December 1984): 11–13.

3. The fallacy of such equation with euthanasia is exposed in R. F. Weir, *Abating Treatment with Critically Ill Patients* (New York: Oxford University Press, 1989), 413–14.

The case of Nancy Cruzan—the first "right to die" case to reach the United States Supreme Court—brought the matter of the PVS before the public and the evangelical world with a special urgency. The case of *Cruzan v. Director of Missouri Department of Health* was called a "moral watershed for our nation" and "the equivalent of *Roe v. Wade.*"[4] On June 25, 1990, the Supreme Court ruled that family members can be prohibited from ending the lives of "persistently comatose" relatives who have not made their wishes known clearly and convincingly. The parents of 32-year-old Nancy Cruzan were thus barred from ordering the removal of tubes that provided her with food and water.

After a serious car accident, Cruzan's brain had received no oxygen for nearly fourteen minutes. At the time of the high court's decision she lay in a Missouri hospital bed, receiving fluid and nutrition through a small tube into her stomach. Expected to exist in this condition for another thirty to forty years with no hope of improvement, she was said to be in a persistent vegetative state.[5] The courts subsequently permitted the withdrawal of food and water after "clear and convincing" evidence was presented that Nancy Cruzan would not have wanted to continue in such a condition. On December 26, 1990, the life of Nancy Cruzan came to an end, twelve days after her feeding tube was removed at the request of her parents. "She remained peaceful throughout [the twelve days] and showed no sign of discomfort or distress in any way," according to her parents, Joe and Joyce Cruzan, who sat by their daughter's bedside while the end approached.[6]

Concerning the morality of withdrawing mechanical feeding in cases of PVS, two main positions have emerged, even within the evangelical Christian community. Typical of the one side is Joseph Foreman, a founder of the antiabortion group Operation Rescue. Foreman called Cruzan's death a tragedy. "I think in the next few years you will see an entire industry spring up around putting people to death whom family, friends and so forth have deemed to be no longer of use to anybody," he said. "There will be wings of

---

4. J. Jankowski, "Case May Create 'Right to Kill,'" *Twin Cities Christian* (November 16, 1989): 22A.

5. Chief Justice W. H. Rehnquist used the term "persistent vegetative state" to describe Cruzan in writing the majority opinion. While the Cruzan case is the first United States Supreme Court "right to die" case, there have been over fifty cases heard in the state courts since 1976. On October 11, 1986, the Supreme Judicial Court of Massachusetts voted 4–3 to allow the removal of P. Brophy's feeding tube. Twelve days later Brophy died, becoming the first American to die after court-authorized discontinuation of artificially supplied fluid and nutrition to a "comatose" patient. J. J. Davis argues against this decision in "Brophy vs. New England Sinai Hospital," *Journal of Biblical Ethics in Medicine* 1 (July 1987): 53–56. Arguing in favor of the decision and against Davis in the same journal volume is F. E. Payne, Jr., "Counterpoint to Dr. Davis on the Brophy Case," 57–60.

6. "A Peaceful Death Ends Fight Over Nancy Cruzan," *Minneapolis Star Tribune*, December 27, 1990, 1(A), 14(A).

hospitals devoted to putting people to death like this."[7] This side considers Nancy Cruzan's death a case of euthanasia and morally wrong.

Typical of the other side is Kenneth Schemmer, a surgeon in Orange County, California, and a member of First Evangelical Free Church of Fullerton. A physician for twenty-five years, Schemmer stated his opinion before the Supreme Court heard the case. He argued that the Court "should allow Nancy Cruzan's living corpse to die." In Schemmer's view "Nancy actually died on January 11, 1983, of anoxia" as the result of her car accident, which produced cardiorespiratory arrest. Because Nancy's cerebral cortex—the seat of consciousness, reasoning, value decisions, and everything else we associate with personality—was so severely damaged that it no longer functioned, only her living "animal" body remained. Her "mammalian body" should be allowed to die.[8]

What is a proper Christian response to the issue of PVS? Specifically, should Christians ever request the withdrawal of fluid and nutrition from individuals in this condition? According to the American Medical Association there are an estimated 10,000 PVS patients in the United States. To disconnect food and water from those in PVS will almost certainly result in dehydration and starvation within seven to fourteen days. To continue to supply food and water will ensure the maintenance of bodily processes for a time, often for years (the longest PVS case on record is thirty-seven years), but will almost certainly not lead to improvement in the patient.[9]

Although much has been written on PVS,[10] there is little from a distinc-

7. Ibid. 14A. See also "Prolifers Say Cruzan Death a Signal of Things to Come," *Christianity Today*, 11 February 1991, 56.

8. K. E. Schemmer, "Nancy Cruzan Is Already Dead," [Loma Linda University Ethics Center] *Update* 5 (December 1989): 4–5.

9. The longest recorded PVS survivor was E. Esposito, who existed in this condition from 1941 to 1978 (D. Lamb, *Death, Brain Death and Ethics* [Albany: SUNY, 1985], 6).

10. Four helpful articles, from very different perspectives, discussing the Cruzan case (before the announced decision) are in *Hastings Center Report* 20 (January/February 1990): 38–50. See also the five articles on PVS in *Hastings Center Report* 18 (February/March 1988): 26–47. On March 15, 1986, the American Medical Association's Council on Ethical and Judicial Affairs issued a statement declaring that life-prolonging medical treatment and artificially supplied respiration as well as nutrition and hydration may be withheld from a patient in an "irreversible coma," "even if death is not imminent." For a helpful analysis see K. O'Rourke, "The A.M.A. Statement on Tube Feeding: An Ethical Analysis," *America* (November 22, 1986): 321–23, 331. On April 21, 1988, the Executive Board of the American Academy of Neurology issued their "Position of the American Academy of Neurology on Certain Aspects of the Care and Management of the Persistent Vegetative State Patient," *Neurology* 39 (January 1989): 125–26. Also see T. L. Munsat, W. H. Stuart and R. E. Cranford, "Guidelines on the Vegetative State: Commentary on the American Academy of Neurology Statement," *Neurology* 39 (January 1989): 123–24. The AAN statement is more detailed than that of the AMA, arrives at the same conclusion. Also in agreement on allowing withdrawal of nutrition and hydration are the report of the President's Commission for the Study of Ethical Problems in Medicine and Biomedical and Behavioral Research, *Deciding to Forego Life-Sustaining Treatment: A Report on the Ethical, Medical, and Legal Issues in Treatment Decisions* (Washington, D.C.: U.S. Government

tively Christian viewpoint.[11] The purpose of this article is to clarify some of the key issues surrounding the PVS controversy by examining the ethical question: Is it ever morally permissible to disconnect artificially supplied food and water from the PVS individual? I will first define PVS. Then I will attempt to define death, to ascertain if PVS is "death" in any sense of the term. Next I will explore the issue of neocortical destruction, the condition of the PVS individual's brain, to determine if it is irreversible as some claim. Finally I will ask whether neocortical destruction may be equated with the death of the person and what response or responses may be morally acceptable in light of the findings obtained.

Definition of Persistent Vegetative State

The persistent vegetative state may be defined[12] loosely as a condition in which there is no awareness of the self or the surroundings though the patient appears at times to be awake. The condition results primarily from severe cerebral injury and is usually associated with but not limited to functionally complete destruction of the cerebral neocortex. The electroencephalogram (EEG) reading is either very depressed or flat. Under the microscope most patients' brains show extensive cortical destruction, but a small number may have more localized damage. Individuals in PVS are seldom on

Printing Office, 1983), and the report of the Hastings Center, *Guidelines on the Termination of Life-Sustaining Treatment and the Care of the Dying* (Bloomington: Indiana University Press, 1987).

11. As of May 3, 1990, the Christian Medical and Dental Society had the issue of the treatment of PVS patients under discussion. They have already formulated a statement on the withholding or withdrawing of nutrition and hydration in general (CMDS Ethics Commission, *Opinions on Ethical/Social Issues* [Richardson: CMDS, 1991], 26). D. L. Schiedermayer, chair of the Commission, summarizes the major arguments for and against withdrawal of tube-feeding in general and concludes with an urgent call for papers and correspondence on PVS and tube-feeding ("The Death Debate," *CMDS Journal* 22 [Spring 1991]: 13–19). The theology committee of the National Association of Evangelicals is also working on the issue of PVS but as of late 1991 had not yet released a statement. In a recent volume J. P. Moreland and N. L. Geisler consider the foregoing of artificial feeding but do not specifically address the issue in relation to PVS (*The Life and Death Debate* [New York: Praeger, 1990], 78–80).

12. Because there continues to be controversy about the clinical diagnosis of PVS, some lack of precision must remain attached to the expression "persistent vegetative state" (see D. N. Walton, *Ethics of Withdrawal of Life-Support Systems* [New York: Praeger, 1987], 51–53; Wier, *Abating Treatment*, 404–5). Information for this definition and description of the PVS is taken from President's Commission, *Deciding to Forego*, 174–75; American Academy of Neurology, "Position"; Walton, *Ethics of Withdrawal*, 51–53, 79–80; Cranford, "Persistent Vegetative State," 27–32; Lamb, *Death, Brain Death*, 5–6; Schiedermayer, "Death Debate," 15–16; P. A. Emmett, "A Biblico-Ethical Response to the Question of Withdrawing Fluid and Nutrition from Individuals in the Persistent Vegetative State" (master's thesis; Bethel Theological Seminary, 1989), 4–5, 248–49.

any life-sustaining equipment other than a feeding tube.[13] The brainstem—
the center of vegetative functions (such as heart rate and rhythm, respiration, gastrointestinal activity)—is relatively intact. PVS individuals thus
breathe spontaneously, their hearts beat regularly, and they show sleep-
wake sequences. They may have a grasp reflex, may exhibit yawning or
chewing movements, and may swallow spontaneously. When food and
water are supplied the digestive system utilizes the nutrients, the intestines
produce waste products, and the kidneys yield urine. Most patients are
silent, but some groan at times. The heart, lungs, and blood vessels continue to move air and blood. "Personality, memory, purposive action,
social interaction, sentience, thought, and even emotional states are gone.
Only vegetative functions and reflexes persist."[14] The American Academy
of Neurology has concluded that PVS patients do not experience pain or
suffering. Ronald Cranford, a leading authority on PVS, states that "from
a neurologic standpoint, they simply do not experience pain, suffering, or
cognition."[15]

PVS should be distinguished from . . . brain death . . . and coma. With
brain death (sometimes called whole brain death) the entire brain—including the brainstem—is irreversibly and completely destroyed. If brain death
precedes injury to the rest of the body, all other organ systems fail within
days. It is not possible to keep the body alive indefinitely with machines in
cases of brain death.[16]. . .

Coma is an "abnormality of brain function characterized by an unconscious sleep-like state with the eyes closed." While several kinds of coma
have a high mortality rate, coma is a potentially reversible condition. . . .

Defining Death

We must next attempt to define death. This is essential because much of
the argument over the withdrawal of artificial feeding revolves around the
question of whether PVS patients are alive or dead. As noted, Schemmer
holds that Nancy Cruzan actually died in 1983. Others, such as Gloria
Miller, past president of the Right to Life League of Southern California,
argue that Cruzan was alive—not brain dead, terminally ill, or dying.
According to Miller, nurses who gave Cruzan daily care say she interacted

13. This is most commonly a small plastic "G-tube" into the stomach. Within the last few
years a new technology known as hyperalimentation has become available. By this means complete nutrition can be maintained intravenously (Payne, "Counterpoint," 56). See Emmett,
"Biblico-Ethical Response," 220–28, for a useful discussion of five methods of mechanical
hydration and nutrition.

14. President's Commission, *Deciding to Forego*, 174–75.

15. R. E. Cranford, "Patients with Permanent Loss of Consciousness," *By No Extraordinary Means*, ed. J. Lynn (Bloomington: Indiana University Press, 1986), 187.

16. Lamb, *Death, Brain Death*, 37.

with her environment and caregivers.[17] Setting aside the specific case of Nancy Cruzan (because of conflicting testimony about her condition), in what sense can it be said, as some do, that PVS individuals, correctly diagnosed as such, are dead? How do we know when death has come? If we can determine that the PVS individual is dead, then we need not hesitate to withdraw food and water. If on the other hand the patient is alive, we must not take his or her life.

Robert Veatch, director of the Kennedy Institute of Ethics at Georgetown University, has been highly influential in recent discussions of the definition and determination of death. Veatch observes that there is

> widespread agreement that two separate issues are really at stake in the debate over the determination of death. The first question is essentially philosophical, conceptual, and ethical: Under what circumstances do we consider a person dead? The question is asked in several ways. What are the necessary and sufficient conditions for a person to be alive? What is the essential characteristic of persons such that its loss can be said to constitute death? . . . Once a concept of death has been chosen, one can turn to a second, more scientific question: How, empirically, does one measure the irreversible loss of whatever functions have been determined to be essential for life?[18]

Veatch suggests four categories for defining death, based upon four different concepts of death.[19] Consideration of these categories here will be helpful in providing a basic framework for our thinking about death. The issues raised are central to the ethical question before us. . . .

1. *Failure of heart and lungs.* Veatch begins with the traditional understanding of the locus of death, focusing upon the heart and lungs. In this view the concept of death (and the presence of life) centers on the flow of vital body fluids—blood and breath. When these have irreversibly stopped flowing, death has occurred. . . .

---

17. G. A. Miller, "Nancy Cruzan Is Not a Vegetable," *Update* 5 (December 1984): 5. See also R. L. Marker, "Euthanasia, the Ultimate Abandonment," *Ethics and Medicine* 6 (Summer 1990): 24, for a summary of the court records on the Cruzan case, revealing some disturbing statements about her condition (Cruzan supposedly can hear, can see, smiles at amusing stories, cries at times when visitors leave, sometimes seems to try to form words, experiences pain from menstrual cramps, will die in pain if she is starved and dehydrated to death). Perhaps because of these statements (whether they are facts or judgments is of course highly debatable), as well as the testimony of two physicians that Cruzan is not in PVS, the Supreme Court members voted as they did. Concerning vegetative patients who exhibit organized motion as a reaction to different stimuli see Schemmer, *Between Life and Death,* 56, 58–59 n. 7.

18. R. M. Veatch, "Death, Determination of," *The Westminster Dictionary of Christian Ethics,* ed. J. F. Childress and J. Macquarrie (Philadelphia: Westminster, 1986), 144–45. See also Veatch, *Death, Dying and the Biological Revolution* (New Haven: Yale University Press, 1976), 24–25.

19. Veatch, *Death, Dying,* 25–54.

2. Separation of body and soul. Aristotle and the Greeks thought of the soul as the animating principle of life. The soul or form animates the body or matter, and when these two elements are separated, death occurs. While this concept of death approximates the language of the Bible, and while most Christians accept that when the soul or spirit departs permanently from the body death occurs, the major problem with this view is how to determine when the soul is gone. Cessation of the flow of bodily fluids may accompany the departure of the soul, but the two events are not to be equated. With this concept of death the Christian must still ask: How can I know when the soul has departed? While the permanent separation of body and soul is in the view of most Christians necessary for the ending of human life on earth, the question of sufficiency hinges on one's view of PVS. The concept of body-soul separation is a theological understanding of death but not a scientific one.[20]

3. Brain death.[21] This category, as well as the next, emerged in response to the difficulty of determining death when technical devices intervene in the natural processes of living and dying. The concept of death in this view is "the irreversible loss of the capacity for bodily integration and social interaction."[22] Because this twofold capacity is centered in the brain, it is there that the locus of death is to be found. Death is considered to have occurred when the entire brain has died. . . . Yet because of the thousands of individuals with partial brain death—with the capacity for organ-system integration but without the capacity for social interaction—some are questioning whether the concept of whole brain destruction is not too narrow a criterion for declaring life to be over in every case of severe brain damage.[23] While few today would deny that this is a sufficient condition for declaring a person to be dead, the question of necessity [is it a necessary condition?] is hotly debated and leads to our next category.

4. Neocortical death. Veatch's final category places the locus of death in the neocortex, the outer layer of the brain covering the cerebrum. This is sometimes called "cerebral death," "higher brain death," or the "apallic syndrome."[24] In this view, when neocortical functioning is irreversibly lost (as

---

20. Ibid., 11–13.

21. Veatch argues: "Terms such as *brain death* or *heart death* should be avoided because they tend to obscure the fact that we are searching for the meaning of the death of the person as a whole" (*Death, Dying,* 37 [italics his]). We will use the term "brain death" because of its widespread acceptance in the literature.

22. Ibid., 53.

23. See e.g., J. B. Brierley, J. A. H. Adams, D. I. Graham, and J. A. Simpson, "Neocortical Death after Cardiac Arrest," *Lancet* (September 11, 1971): 560–65.

24. The term "apallic syndrome" refers to the loss of the pallium, the grey cortical mantle that covers the cerebral hemispheres. There is almost total destruction of the cerebral neurons, and the cortex is replaced by a "thin gliotic and fibrous tissue" in patients who remain in this condition for several years (Walton, *Brain Death,* 77).

determined by a variety of criteria, including the EEG[25]) the person is dead, because the concept of death in this case is the "irreversible loss of consciousness or the capacity for social interaction" or both.[26] This is the condition of PVS individuals. . . .

After analyzing each of these four categories in terms of their concepts of death, Veatch concludes that "death is most appropriately thought of as the irreversible loss of the embodied capacity for social interaction,"[27] a capacity that is absent with brain death and neocortical death and, of course, with the permanent failure of heart and lungs.[28] Veatch, then, accepts not only brain death but also the irreversible loss of neocortical functioning as a satisfactory category for defining death. Schemmer agrees with this conclusion.[29]

How are we to regard the proposal of Veatch and others that neocortical destruction is an acceptable understanding of death? Those who maintain that the essential quality of life is the capacity for social interaction, so that when this is gone the individual is dead, are on shaky ground from a purely scientific standpoint. While there is at present no uniform definition of death and the diagnosis is still left to the judgment of the physician, the most widely accepted scientific definitions of death include the permanent loss of organ system integration as well as the permanent loss of consciousness and the capacity for social interaction. Charles Culver and Bernard Gert, for example, define death as the "permanent cessation of functioning of the organism as a whole."[30] And the President's Commission report states that "death is that moment at which the body's physiological system ceases to constitute an integrated whole."[31] Because the neocortical concept of death involves a major redefinition of death—something that the whole brain death concept does not do since it simply recognizes what always occurs at death—the scientific community has held back from accepting neocortical destruction as a sufficient definition of death.[32]

25. Veatch contends that the EEG alone may be sufficient empirical evidence of neocortical destruction (*Death, Dying,* 42–51).
26. Ibid., 41, 53.
27. Veatch, *Death, Dying,* 42.
28. See Emmett, "Biblico-Ethical Response," 95–96.
29. Schemmer, *Between Life and Death,* 52–58.
30. C. M. Culver and B. Gert, *Philosophy in Medicine* (New York: Oxford University Press, 1982), 181.
31. President's Commission, *Defining Death,* 33.
32. Gula, *Euthanasia,* 18–19; Emmett, "Biblico-Ethical Response," 97–99, 250–51. Lamb notes that "ultimately the concept of 'death' can only be applied to organisms not persons" (*Death, Brain Death,* 93). Conceding this point, Walton argues that "aggressive therapy [by this he includes artificially supplied fluid and nutrition] may be discontinued in some circumstances even if the patient is not certifiably dead. This approach is already widely in place. It is ultimately based on the reasoning that the patient has the right to refuse treatment" (*Ethics of Withdrawal,* 85).

What should the Christian's response be to this prevailing scientific opinion? If we accept the view that the PVS patient cannot be regarded as dead, the matter would appear to be settled. Since we must do nothing to contribute knowingly to the death of an innocent person, the artificial feeding and hydration must continue. The Christian, however, is not limited to the prevailing scientific opinion in ethical decision-making. While we must not reject or ignore valid scientific findings, and while it would appear to be unwise at present to attempt to redefine death scientifically, we may—indeed, we must—consider revelation as well in formulating ethical judgments. Before turning to Biblical and theological arguments, however, one further question needs to be asked.

Neocortical Death—Is It Irreversible?

Are PVS individuals permanently unconscious? If their condition is sometimes reversible, the decision to discontinue fluid and nutrition is a much more difficult one to make. If their condition is genuinely irreversible, the moral obligation for continuing artificial feeding is harder to establish. Do we know for sure that PVS patients cannot recover? To answer this question Schemmer presents the recent findings of Fred Plum, a professor in the department of neurology at the New York Hospital—Cornell Medical Center, and his associates. Plum has been at the leading edge in this area of neurological research. He and Bryan Jennett were the first to describe the medical condition of PVS after brain damage.[33] Plum's latest findings[34] are highly significant. . . . [They show,] according to Schemmer, . . . that for the first time since we began connecting people to machines that replace their vital organs we can now determine whether we are keeping a *person* alive or keeping a *body* functioning. He calls this a "welcome breakthrough" that "may provide us with our first truly ethical release from one aspect of the life-support dilemma." . . .[35]

At the present time, there appear to be increasingly reliable scientific criteria for establishing the totality and permanence of neocortical destruction in PVS individuals.

    33. B. Jennett and F. Plum, "The Persistent Vegetative State: A Syndrome in Search of a Name," *Lancet* (1 April 1972): 734–37.
    34. F. Plum, et al., "Differences in Cerebral Blood Flow and Glucose Utilization in Vegetative Versus Locked-in Patients," *Annals of Neurology* 22 (December 1987): 673–82.
    35. Schemmer, *Between Life and Death*, 57–58. See also Emmett, "Biblico-Ethical Response," 248–51, on procedures to determine neocortical death. On the permanence of this condition Emmett writes: "The tissue of the central nervous system does not regenerate. If it is destroyed it will not repair itself as does other tissue. . . . Other parts may take over some of the function at the cerebral level and ischemic tissue which appears destroyed (as in a stroke) may recover function to some degree. However, there is no regeneration of cells. If destruction can be shown to have occurred, it is irreversible" (p. 103 n. 24).

Personhood and Neocortical Death

What Schemmer describes as a "breakthrough" is, of course, only of major ethical significance for those who accept neocortical destruction as the death of the person. As stated above, the PVS individual is not dead in the holistic physiological sense. Yet according to Schemmer's interpretation of these recent scientific findings the cerebral neocortex, in accurately diagnosed PVS cases, is completely and permanently ruined. Might it be possible to argue from a Christian perspective that even though the PVS body is still functioning, the person himself or herself is gone from the body? In other words, can we equate neocortical destruction with the ending of personal life even though the body is still breathing? This depends of course on how we understand the term "person." Although the Bible does not provide a definition of "person," Christian ethicists are more or less compelled to offer a definition because of the frequent use of the term in bioethics, sometimes in ways hostile to Christian positions.[36]

When we seek to understand personhood and humanness, the key Scriptural concept is undoubtedly the "image of God." The fact that human beings are made in (or as) the image of God is given as the reason they have rights of personhood. For example, the right to rule over creation (Gen. 1:26–28), the right to life (9:5–6) and the right to be addressed with respect (James 3:9–10) are grounded in the concept of the image and likeness of God. What we speak of as "human rights" are rights of personhood, and these are based upon our creation in God's image. To be a human person is to be an imager of God.[37]

But this just pushes the issue back one question further: What is the image of God? The main schools of thought are well-known. The most common view is that the image is an inherent characteristic or characteristics—physical, psychological, or spiritual—within human nature, such as reason, self-consciousness, or self-determination. This position has been referred to as the substantive or structural view and is based in part upon the marked innate differences between animals and human beings (Gen. 1:24–28).

The relational view sees the image not as a quality within human nature itself but as the experiencing of relationships, either between oneself and God or between human beings. The relationship itself is the image of God. Some supporters of this view point to Genesis 1:26–27, where the male-female relationship is mentioned in close connection with creation in God's image, as if to mirror the internal communion within the Godhead.

36. A significant but unsatisfactory attempt to define "person" is by M. Tooley, "Decisions to Terminate Life and the Concept of Person," *Ethical Issues Relating to Life and Death*, ed. J. Ladd (New York: Oxford University Press , 1979), 62–93.

37. Frame, *Medical Ethics*, 33–35.

A third position, the functional view, maintains that the image of God is something that human beings do, not something they possess or something they experience. The function most commonly suggested is rulership or dominion over creation, since this activity is tied so closely to the decision of God to create humans in his image (Gen. 1:26) and is repeated just after their creation (1:27–28).

None of these views should be considered as totally without foundation, nor is it necessary to define the image in terms of only one of these views. A composite understanding of the image, incorporating each of the above positions, is not only possible but quite reasonable and harmonious with Scripture.[38]

The Scriptures give good reason to believe that the image concept has a great deal to do with our relationships, our exercise of dominion, and our mental and spiritual capacities. Rather than being a singular concept or certain specific qualities, however, the image of God might better be thought of as including all that we are and do as human beings, as embodied persons. We image God in our being and in our doing, although when we sin we disgrace the God whose image we are. We may argue, as D. J. A. Clines has done from the perspective of Semitic studies, that we are created not so much *in* the image of God but *as* the image of God, to be his representatives on earth.[39]

Whether believers or unbelievers, all human beings are created and exist throughout life as imagers of God (Gen. 9:6; James 3:9), to represent the King as his vice-regents on earth. While some never fulfill this task as God intended, others grow steadily in their character and service for God (2 Cor. 3:18; Col. 3:10), just as Jesus—the supreme imager of God (2 Cor. 4:4; Col. 1:15)—developed in his total humanity (Luke 2:40, 52).

We can propose, then, that to be "in the image of God" means that we exist as the representatives of God on earth, with certain God-given and God-like qualities and capacities, so that we may experience vital relationships with God and others and so that we may exercise dominion over the earth. As we study the Scriptures on the image-of-God concept we find that to be the representatives of God on earth presupposes some capacity, either actual or at least potential, for self-awareness and self-direction, for relationships and for the exercise of authority over creation.

---

38. Composite understanding of the image (not necessarily identical to mine) are presented by A. A. Hoekema, *Created in God's Image* (Grand Rapids: Eerdmans, 1986), 66–73; G. Carey, *I Believe in Man* (Grand Rapids: Eerdmans, 1977), 30–40.

39. D. J. A. Clines, "The Image of God in Man," *Tyndale Bulletin* 19 (1968): 53–103. On this point see also J. K. Hoffmeier, "Abortion and the Old Testament Law," *Abortion*, ed. J. Hoffmeier (Grand Rapids: Baker, 1987), 54–55; A. P. Ross, *Creation and Blessing* (Grand Rapids: Baker, 1988), 112–13. Also helpful on what it means to be imagers of God are H. Bouma III, D. Diekema, E. Langerak, T. Rottman, A. Verhey, *Christian Faith, Health, and Medical Practice* (Grand Rapids: Eerdmans, 1989), 27–34.

Given this understanding of the image concept, we may now attempt a definition of the term "person." A human person is a unique individual, made as God's image, known and cared for by God at every stage of life, with the actual ability or potential to be aware of oneself and to relate in some way to one's environment, to other human beings, and to God. The earthly life of a person thus begins at conception and ends when this ability or potential ceases.[40] According to this definition, then, the baby in the womb as well as the comatose patient is a person, whereas the PVS individual, as defined with the precision that now appears to be possible, is not. His or her potential for self-awareness, social interaction, and communication with God is irreversibly lost. This is not the case with handicapped fetuses or newborns, with Alzheimer's patients, or with the comatose. Some capacity and potential—however slight—for imaging God is present in these cases.[41] The absence of or damage to cerebral functioning is neither total nor necessarily irreversible. In true PVS cases, however, the neocortex is completely and permanently destroyed.

It appears, then, that neocortical destruction equals the end of personal life because the correctly diagnosed PVS individual is a body of organs and

40. In formulating this definition I have been helped by J. R. Nelson, *Human Life: A Biblical Perspective for Bioethics* (Philadelphia: Fortress, 1984); C. S. Evans, "Healing Old Wounds and Recovering Old Insights: Toward a Christian View of the Person for Today," *Christian Faith and Practice in the Modern World*, ed. M. A. Noll and D. F. Wells (Grand Rapids: Eerdmans, 1988), 68–86; J. Foster, "Personhood and the Ethics of Abortion," *Abortion and the Sanctity of Human Life*, ed. J. H. Channer (Exeter: Paternoster, 1985), 31–53; O. O'Donovan, "Again: Who Is a Person?" *Abortion* (ed. Channer), 125–37; C. E. Bajema, *Abortion and the Meaning of Personhood* (Grand Rapids: Baker, 1974), 15–41. See also J. J. Davis, *Evangelical Ethics* (Phillipsburg: Presbyterian and Reformed, 1985), 153–54; V. E. Anderson and B. R. Reichenbach, "Imaged Through the Lens Darkly: Human Personhood and the Sciences," *Journal of the Evangelical Theological Society* 33/2 (June 1990): 197–213.

41. I do not speak of "potential persons," an expression that is frequently used by those with a permissive attitude toward abortion. I refer, rather, to persons with potential. No living entity is a potential person. As soon as human life begins in the womb the new individual is a person—a human being with God-given potential that will become more and more actual as the life progresses. The characteristics of personhood become more evident as time passes, but the individual is not lacking personhood until these characteristics appear. Those who oppose abortion, while affirming this understanding of the fetus, sometimes fail to note the fundamental difference between the potential/actual distinction at the beginning of life and at the ending of life. It is sometimes argued that since an individual is regarded as a human being from the very beginning of life, even though there is no actual cognition or self-awareness (only potential), then a PVS patient must be regarded similarly as a human person and thus be kept alive physically as long as possible. The overlooked factor is that in the fetus the child's capacities and potentialities for cognition and self-awareness are oriented in the direction of growth and fullness of life, whereas in PVS patients these potentialities and capacities are destroyed. While there is a lack of cognition and self-awareness in both the embryo and PVS patient, this fact alone does not provide a basis for identical treatment. In the one case the potential is present, and the movement is in the direction of the actual; in the other case the potential is permanently lost because the capacity itself is lost.

systems, artificially sustained, without the personal human spirit that once enabled this body-soul unity to represent God on earth.[42] Since the Bible on occasion uses the language of the human spirit's departure—as something different from the person's life-force or final breath—to signify death (Luke 23:46; Acts 7:59–60), we may use similar language in suggesting that the spirit of the PVS individual has already returned to God.[43] While the body still has some kind of residual life, the person is dead. Speaking theologically, the individual's personal earthly existence as the image of God appears to be over. While the body is necessary for imaging God, it is not sufficient for doing so. (Similarly the neocortex is necessary but not sufficient for imaging God.) A body without neocortical functioning cannot image God according to the understanding of the image concept developed above. What is essential about humanness—namely, the capacity to image God—is irreversibly gone. Neither the ability nor the potential to live as the personal representative of Another is any longer present in the physical remains of the person. Neocortical destruction is both a necessary and sufficient condition for declaring an individual dead theologically. For this reason the discontinuance of nutrition and hydration appears to be justified.[44] The Christian, then,

---

42. I am not saying, as J. F. Fletcher does, that "neocortical function is the key to humanness, the essential trait, the human *sine qua non*" ("Four Indicators of Humanhood—The Enquiry Matures," *Hastings Center Report* 4 [December 1975], reprinted in *On Moral Medicine*, ed. S. E. Lammers and A. Verhey [Grand Rapids: Eerdmans, 1987], 276). I am saying that the essence of humanness is being the image and representative of God and that neocortical function is necessary to being that image.

43. See J. W. Cooper, *Body, Soul, and Life Everlasting* (Grand Rapids: Eerdmans, 1989), 123–27. Cooper makes a convincing case for a holistic dualism in opposition to the anthropological monism of some Biblical scholars. But whether one leans toward a dualistic or monistic view of the human constitution it may still be argued that when the conscious personal life of the PVS individual has come to an end the body need not be artificially sustained.

44. The conclusion that artificially supplied sustenance may be withdrawn in certain cases is accepted by many in the medical, ethical, and philosophical fields. See e.g., S. H. Wanzer, S. J. Adelstein, R. E. Cranford, et al., "The Physician's Responsibility Toward Hopelessly Ill Patients," *Ethical Issues in Death and Dying*, 2d ed., ed. R. F. Wier (New York: Columbia University Press, 1986), 190–91. In the same volume see J. Lynn and J. F. Childress, "Must Patients Always Be Given Food and Water?" (215–29); D. Callahan, "On Feeding the Dying" (230–33). This is also the conclusion of the President's Commission, *Deciding to Forego*, 171–96; Bouma, et al., *Christian Faith*, 295–97; R. N. Wennberg, *Terminal Choices: Euthanasia, Suicide, and the Right to Die* (Grand Rapids: Eerdmans, 1989), 169–75. Many are opposed to this conclusion. See the statement "Feeding and Hydrating the Permanently Unconscious and Other Vulnerable Persons" prepared by W. E. May, G. Meilaender, et al., in *Issues in Law and Medicine* 3 (Winter 1987). Some of the signers include H. O. J. Brown, A. T. Dyck, S. Hauerwas, J. K. Hoffmeier, D. J. Kennedy, G. W. Knight III, J. W. Montgomery, R. J. Neuhaus, and the late P. Ramsey. The statement declares, in part, that "it is not morally right, nor ought to be legally permissible, to withhold or withdraw nutrition and hydration provided by artificial means to the permanently unconscious" (211). Also opposed to the view favoring withdrawal of feeding (even in cases of brain death), from a conservative Catholic viewpoint, is R. L. Barry, *Medical Ethics: Essays on Abortion and Euthanasia* (New York: Peter Lang, 1989).

has a theological basis for distinguishing between the death of the body, with its residual movements, and the death of the person. Such an approach to the problem of the PVS patient does not ignore the findings of science but recognizes the limits of science in matters of Christian moral judgment.

Conclusion

The human body must always be respected—in death and dying as well as in life—because the person who was, while on earth, the image of God functioned as God's representative through that body. But the prolongation of biological life in the apparent absence of personal life is not mandated by the Christian principle of respect for life.[45] Because equipment is available to feed a body does not mean that it should always be used. Some who oppose withdrawal of artificial feeding tubes are unwilling to have such devices connected to themselves or their loved ones in the first place, if their prognosis should be for a prolonged and permanent vegetative state. This unwillingness to connect feeding devices reveals that such persons actually agree that whatever may be used to prolong bodily existence is not always morally obligatory. If it were obligatory, no upright person should ever hesitate to connect artificial feeding equipment to a loved one who would by this means be enabled to live possibly many more years, if only in a vegetative state.[46]

45. On the question of whether the PVS individual would experience pain after the fluid and nutrition are withdrawn, all indications are that this would not be the case. Christian physician W. S. Krabill writes that even with patients who are still alive, as in the case of dying cancer patients, death by starvation is "not a painful death if local care and moisture are provided to lips, mouth, and eyes. The rising level of waste products in the blood seems to provide a natural sedative and pain-relieving effect. When it comes to those in deep coma, there is even greater assurance that withdrawing tube feeding does not cause pain" ("Death and Dying: Prevailing Medical Perspectives," *Medical Ethics, Human Choices: A Christian Perspective,* ed. J. Rogers [Scottdale: Herald, 1988], 59). See also American Academy of Neurology, "Position," 125, for the three independent bases for their conclusion that PVS patients do not experience pain or suffering. With regard to "only caring" as opposed to continuing medical interventions on the dying, P. Ramsey notes that "we cease doing what was once called for and begin to do precisely what is called for now. We attend and company with him in this, his very own dying, rendering it as comfortable and dignified as possible" (*The Patient as Person* [New Haven: Yale University Press, 1970], 151).

46. President's Commission, *Deciding to Forego,* 73–77; Lynn and Childress, "Must Patients," 225; D. W. Brock, "Death and Dying," *Medical Ethics,* ed. R. M. Veatch (Boston: Jones and Bartlett, 1989), 342. Brock makes an important point: "A very common fear of patients, families, and physicians is that the patient will be 'stuck on machines.' To avoid this outcome, parties involved in decision making may be reluctant to try life-sustaining treatment when its benefits are highly uncertain. This has the effect of denying life-sustaining treatment to some patients for whom it would have proved to be of genuine and substantial benefit and is indeed a serious harmful consequence of the reluctance to stop life support once it is in place" (342). It may be, ironically, that those unwilling (because of a strong "pro-life" view, perhaps) to disconnect equipment already in place may be hastening the death of those who would otherwise live long if they had been sustained for a time by machines. Also see the very helpful discussion in Weir, *Abating,* 401–3.

In Christian ethics one's intention is always a key factor in determinating the morality of a given action. To disconnect the feeding tube from a PVS individual must never be done with the intention to kill—to take a person's life. Our attitude and intention should be that of turning the individual over to God's providence, allowing the condition to take its course. Yet—as with many conditions judged "hopeless" by human standards—we may hope beyond all reason for hope that God will yet quicken the loved one if that would honor him and be best for the patient. Even though we may be quite reasonably assured that the individual's personal life is over, we may hope otherwise.

F. Edward Payne, a member of the Ethics Commission of the Christian Medical and Dental Society, agrees with the decision not to pull Nancy Cruzan's feeding tube. He adds, however: "I do not agree with the decision not to feed her by mouth after the feeding tube was pulled." Payne admits that the difference between these positions may seem small, but he considers it to be morally significant. He sees the continuance of mouth feeding as necessary "warm, personal care," whereas artificial feeding is medical treatment and is not required when it no longer benefits the patient.[47] In a few PVS cases, individuals actually swallow oral feedings.[48] To disconnect the artificial feeding, while still attempting to feed the patient by mouth (even if such is unsuccessful), is to balance the desire for the patient's miraculous recovery with the desire for the body to be in as natural a condition as possible while physiological death approaches. One can "play God" by technologically prolonging death as much as by hastening death. The position presented here is not euthanasia, which is best defined as any action or omission which by intention causes the death of a supposedly hopeless person in order to end the person's suffering.[49]

47. F. E. Payne, "A Time to Be Born, a Time for Treatment, and a Time to Die," *World* (January 12, 1991): 19. See also Payne in n. 5.

48. Weir, *Abating*, 409.

49. This definition includes the three elements necessary for a clear understanding of euthanasia: (1) It involves the taking of a human life, either one's own or that of another; (2) the life taken is that of someone believed to be suffering from a serious disease or injury from which recovery cannot reasonably be expected; (3) the action must be deliberate and intentional (J. Gay-Williams, "The Wrongfulness of Euthanasia," *Euthanasia: The Moral Issues*, ed. R. M. Baird and S. E. Rosenbaum [Buffalo: Prometheus, 1989], 97–98). To discontinue or withhold artificial nutrition from PVS patients is not "passive euthanasia" as some would say. It is not euthanasia at all, since there is no intention to take a person's life. Theologically the "person" is already dead. Even if the guardian is not prepared to ascribe death to the PVS patient, the withdrawal of the feeding tube is not necessarily aiming at death. The commonly used distinction between "active" and "passive" euthanasia is more problematic than helpful and should be discontinued, leaving the term "euthanasia" to be used only with reference to intentional killing (as argued by Weir, ed., *Ethical Issues in Death and Dying*, 243–44; see also Wennberg, *Terminal Choices*, 109–12). Arguments against euthanasia (understood as intentional killing) from both special and general revelation are given by M. J. Erickson and I. E.

We cannot deny that there is some risk of error in bioethical decision making. The lines are not as sharply drawn as we would like.[50] Our admittedly difficult but not (by God's grace) impossible task is to steer a right course on the one hand between an excessive devotion to biological existence as the highest of all values and on the other hand the disrespect for human life that discards anyone—in the womb, newly born, or elderly—who does not measure up to an arbitrarily established level of intelligence or value to society. It is of course always best to be on the safe side. Wisdom calls us to err on the side of keeping someone physically alive when the spirit may be gone rather than risk killing a person. But consider the magnitude of the problem. As indicated above, there are thousands of PVS individuals in our medical institutions. Every elderly person who does not succumb to a quick death faces the prospect of having his or her life artificially prolonged. As Schemmer states: "The potential of our technological nightmare has got to end somewhere, and the only way to end it lies in courageously making some decisions concerning it."[51]

This is not to say that as Christians we are compelled to make morally wrong choices at times in order to avoid greater difficulties in the future. Sin is never necessary for the Christian. Decision-making, however, is necessary. If the PVS condition can be shown to be total and irreversible, and if the loss of personhood can be considered death in a theological sense, there appears to be strong support for disconnecting artificial feeding. Those who intend to keep their PVS loved ones sustained by mechanical means are making one choice, and it should be respected.[52] Similarly those who, after prayerful and careful reflection upon the issues in the light of Scripture, in keeping with the law, decide to withdraw nutrition and hydration are making another choice. This, too, should be respected.[53]

From Robert V. Rakestraw, "The Persistent Vegetative State and the Withdrawal of Nutrition and Hydration," *Journal of the Evangelical Theological Society* 35 (1992): 389–405.

Bowers, "Euthanasia and Christian Ethics," *Journal of the Evangelical Theological Society* 19 (Winter 1976): 21–24; Gay-Williams, "Wrongfulness," 97–102; J. V. Sullivan, "The Immorality of Euthanasia," *Beneficent Euthanasia*, ed. M. Kohl (Buffalo: Prometheus, 1975), 12–33.

50. Cranford, "Patients with Permanent Loss," 187–88.

51. Schemmer, *Between Life and Death*, 125.

52. Some are quite adamant, however, that the fluids and nutrition *ought* to be withdrawn in cases where they *may* be withdrawn. See e.g., H. Jonas, "The Right to Die," *Bioethics*, 3d ed., ed. T. A. Shannon (New York: Paulist, 1987), 205–6. See also Wennberg, *Terminal Choices*, 171.

53. A much-abbreviated version of this article appeared in *The Standard* (October 1991).

For Further Reflection

Case Studies

Elderly cancer patient. Eighteen months ago, a seventy-one-year-old Christian woman developed cancer in a kidney. Physicians removed the kidney. Now, however, the cancer has spread to other parts of her body, including her brain, so she has become permanently unconscious. Her second kidney is now failing, and she needs dialysis. Dialysis might keep her alive for six to nine months. Without dialysis, she would probably survive a couple of weeks before drifting off into a relatively painless death caused by the buildup of toxins in her body. An experimental drug that might have some effect on her cancer is just coming onto the market. If she could survive for six months, this new drug might help her fight the cancer. Despite her insurance policy, all this treatment will surely deplete the woman's considerable life savings. Only then would government programs pick up what insurance will not pay.

She never told her children how she felt about terminal care. Her son thinks death is inevitable and wants to avoid dialysis. He thinks bankrupting the family for a long shot is pointless. Her daughter, a Christian with a pro-life perspective, feels uneasy about not doing everything she can to help her mother. You are a trusted friend of the daughter; you have pro-life sympathies and a background in medicine. Your friend comes to you for guidance. What should you say?

Physically tenacious grandfather. A woman in your Sunday school class raises a question. She feels uneasy about what happened to her "Poppa." Once a gentle man, brain deterioration made the grandfather irritable and even violent. The family moved him to a nursing home. There he continued to decline, gradually becoming entirely demented. One day, he had a heart attack, and the nursing home sent him to the ER. After frantic efforts, including shocking the heart, the staff started the heart and brought the old man back. After he had been in the hospital for a week, the nurses felt relieved to return him to the nursing home. Gradually, the man's physical health improved. He refused to eat, however, so the staff started mechanically administered feeding and hydration. Since the grandfather rarely even recognized the family, they asked the doctor to enter DNR (do not resuscitate) on the man's chart in case he had another heart attack. Then, however, the man did not die. The family therefore asked the doctor to withdraw the food and liquid, and gradually the man died.

Your questioner feels guilty because she did not prevent this decision. She suspects that what the family did is illegal. Did she do the right thing? What should she do now?

Glossary

Active euthanasia: Type of euthanasia in which one directly takes the life of a patient. This could be performed by the suffering person (i.e., suicide—with or without a physician's assistance) or administered by a physician or friend who causes death though for merciful reasons; also called *positive euthanasia;* contrast with passive euthanasia.

Beneficence: Principle asserting that doctors are obligated to do good for their patients.

Brain death: Total cessation of brain activity both in the neocortical brain (upper brain) and in the brain stem.

Death: Theologically, the separation of the spiritual self from the body; traditionally indicated medically by irreversible cessation of circulatory and respiratory functions; according to the Uniform Determination of Death Act, death is indicated by the irreversible cessation of the whole brain (brain death).

Double effect principle: Principle that asserts the following: If an inherently good act has two effects, one good and one bad, a person can act morally in doing that act provided (1) only the good effect is intended, (2) the bad effect is not the means to the good effect, and (3) the good effect is at least equal to the bad effect.

Durable power of attorney: Legal means by which a patient designates another to make decisions on his behalf should the patient become physically or mentally unable to do so (see substituted judgment).

Euthanasia: The deliberate act of intending or choosing a painless death for the humane purpose of ending the agony of someone who suffers from incurable disease or injury; includes active and passive forms.

Informed consent: Principle that a patient understand treatment options and choose the course of treatment or the withholding of treatment.

Letting die: Withholding or withdrawing life-prolonging and life-sustaining technologies as an intentional act to enhance the well-being of the terminally ill by avoiding useless prolonging of the dying process. Letting die is like so-called passive euthanasia in that it prohibits direct killing (the underlying disease or injury is the actual cause of death), but unlike passive euthanasia, letting die does not intend or choose death; contrast with euthanasia of all forms.

Living will: Legal document in which a person indicates his wishes regarding treatment in order to guide medical personnel in situations where he is unable to choose treatment.

Mercy killing: A synonym for euthanasia.

Nonmaleficence: Principle asserting that doctors are minimally obligated to avoid harming their patients. This principle is more fundamental than *beneficence.*

Ordinary/extraordinary: Distinction related to the degree of pain, expense, invasiveness, or inconvenience entailed in a medical treatment in proportion to possible benefits of that treatment; ordinary means are medical options that both offer reasonable hope of benefit and require only moderate costs; extraordinary means are medical options that either offer little reasonable hope of recovery or require excessive costs in pain, expense, or inconvenience.

Passive euthanasia: Type of euthanasia in which one intends death as a means to ending the agony of a suffering person, but rather than directly taking the life, one acts to avoid prolonging the dying process, allowing the underlying disease or assault on the body to cause death; also called *negative euthanasia;* contrast with active euthanasia.

Substituted judgment: Legal declaration by the courts authorizing a person to make treatment decisions for an incapacitated patient.

Vitalism: View that physical life is in itself of highest value.

Voluntary/involuntary/nonvoluntary: Distinctions related to the way the desires of a patient are incorporated in treatment decisions; voluntary treatment options follow the patient's wishes, nonvoluntary treatment decisions are made when the patient is incapacitated and cannot decide, and involuntary treatment decisions go against patient desires.

Annotated Bibliography

Bailey, Don V. *The Challenge of Euthanasia.* Lanham, Md.: University Press of America, 1990. Extensive annotated bibliography.

Beauchamp, Tom L., and James F. Childress. *Principles of Biomedical Ethics.* 3d ed. New York: Oxford University Press, 1989. Possibly the best source on theories and principles of bioethics.

Bouma III, Hessel, et. al. *Christian Faith, Health, and Medical Practice.* Grand Rapids: Eerdmans, 1989. Stresses the sanctity of life yet recognizes the scarcity of resources; excellent list of sources.

Callahan, Daniel. *Setting Limits: Medical Goals in an Aging Society.* New York: Simon & Schuster, 1987. Argues that those who have lived a full life cannot receive full access to expensive treatments.

Carrick, Paul. *Medical Ethics in Antiquity: Philosophical Perspectives on Abortion and Euthanasia.* Dortrecht: Reidel, 1985. Scholarly work on ancient attitudes toward life, death, and medical care; discusses Hippocratic Oath.

Davis, John Jefferson. "Infanticide and Euthanasia." In *Evangelical Ethics.* Phillipsburg, N.J.: Presbyterian and Reformed, 1985, 158–92. Well-documented survey by an evangelical theologian who thinks euthanasia is a kind of murder.

Erickson, Millard, and Ines Bowers. "Euthanasia and Christian Ethics." *Journal of the Evangelical Theological Society* 19 (1976): 15–24. Biblical and theological argument against euthanasia; argues against regarding euthanasia as suicide or murder.

Gula, Richard M. *What Are They Saying about Euthanasia?* New York: Paulist, 1986. Excellent introductory overview of moral issues and positions written from a Roman Catholic perspective.

Kilner, John F. *Who Lives? Who Dies? Ethical Criteria in Patient Selection.* New Haven: Yale University Press, 1990. Biblically informed approach to deciding who gets medical care.

Koop, C. Everett, and Timothy Johnson. *Let's Talk: An Honest Conversation on Critical Issues: Abortion, AIDS, Euthanasia, and Health Care.* Grand Rapids: Zondervan, 1992. Two Christian physicians prominent in public life discuss euthanasia in the context of public health.

Lammers, Stephen E.., and Allen Verhey, eds. *On Moral Medicine: Theological Perspectives in Medical Ethics.* Grand Rapids: Eerdmans, 1987. Valuable collection of more than one hundred essays on medical ethics chosen for their theological relevance.

Maguire, Daniel C. *Death by Choice.* Garden City, N.Y.: Doubleday, 1984. Roman Catholic moral theologian argues strongly for a right to die under certain circumstances.

May, William. "What Makes a Human Being to be a Being of Moral Worth?" *Thomist* 40 (1976): 416–43. Important essay on the difference between *persons* and *human beings*; defends essentialism against the speciesism criticism.

Meilaender, Gilbert. "On Removing Food and Water: Against the Stream." *The Hastings Center Report* 14 (1984): 11–13. Argues that because giving food and water is basic care and not treatment, we should never withdraw it from a patient, even one who is permanently unconscious.

Menzel, Paul T. *Strong Medicine: The Ethical Rationing of Health Care.* New York: Oxford University Press, 1990. Discusses the serious ethical dilemmas arising from rationing terminal medical care.

Moreland, J. P. "James Rachels and the Active Euthanasia Debate." *Journal of the Evangelical Theological Society* 31 (1988): 81–90. Direct philosophical response to the pro-euthanasia view that passive and active euthanasia do not differ in morally relevant ways.

Rachels, James. "Active and Passive Euthanasia." *The New England Journal of Medicine* 292 (9 January 1975): 78–80; and *The End of Life.* Oxford: Oxford University Press, 1986. Important expressions of pro-euthanasia view that depend on collapsing the active vs. passive distinction.

Rae, Scott B. "Views of Human Nature at the Edges of Life: Personhood and Medical Ethics." In *Contemporary Perspectives on Being Human,* edited by J. P. Moreland and David M Ciocchi, Grand Rapids: Baker, 1993, 235–56. Evangelical ethicist discusses personhood in relation to seriously ill newborns, the terminally ill, and PVS patients.

Rakestraw, Robert V. "The Persistent Vegetative State and the Withdrawal of Nutrition and Hydration." *Journal of the Evangelical Theological Society* 35 (1992): 389–405. Argues that we may withdraw food and hydration from PVS patients.

Ramsey, Paul. "'Euthanasia' and Dying Well Enough." *Linacre Quarterly* 44 (1977): 37–46. Prominent ethicist's reflections on positive care to terminal patients as well as patients' right to refuse invasive treatment.

Schemmer, Kenneth E. *Between Life and Death: The Life Support Dilemma.* Wheaton: Victor, 1988. Christian physician discusses the ethical issues related to life support.

Wennberg, Robert N. *Terminal Choices: Euthanasia, Suicide, and the Right to Die.* Grand Rapids: Eerdmans, 1989. Evangelical philosopher analyzes end-of-life ethics.

Part 2

Human Sexuality

4

Sexuality, Marriage, and Singleness

"There are two kinds of people: those interested in sex and liars!" While we probably cannot trace the origin of this remark, the thought it expresses is ancient. If we are human, we are interested in sex.

Unfortunately, our curiosity and interest concerning sexuality is not always guided and nurtured in a wholesome way. Throughout childhood and adolescence, parents and guardians teach their children quite comfortably and naturally about trees, animals, electricity, cooking, and many other aspects of life in the world. They usually do not, however, teach about sexual matters with similar ease. As a result, many of us grow into adulthood with partial and distorted views of God's pattern of sexuality for the human race.

The church has not been particularly helpful in this regard. While we are frequently reminded of what we are not to do, we are seldom shown the positive biblical teaching about human sexuality. The prevalence of **pornography, rape, fornication, adultery,** and **incest,** even among Christians, attests to the urgent need for specific ethical instruction and guidance in the realm of human sexuality. For example, by age eighteen, one in three women and one in five men in the United States has experienced incest or sexual assault. These evils exist even among evangelical Christians, yet we seldom, if ever, discuss them in church. Clearly our chronic failure to address sexual issues directly and openly in our congregations has rendered the church helpless to stop the alarming rise of sexual deviations and crimes in our society and in our churches.

The word *sex,* of course, has different connotations. It may refer to **gender**—the reality of our being male or female. We thus speak of the "opposite sex." It may pertain to **erotic** awareness and arousal—the attraction toward and desire for intimacy with another. A person is said to have "sex appeal." The word *sex* is also used to indicate function—activity involving the genital organs. In this sense, people "have sex." Sexual activity within marriage should, ideally, involve all of these aspects. Even apart from marriage, however, these three dimensions of sex pervade our society, either in isolation or in combination. In this chapter the term *sex* refers not so much to gender sexuality (see chap. 8) as to erotic sexuality, genital sexuality, or both, as these issue from our being male or female.

Sex is a gift from our Creator—a part of our God-given human nature—and as such it is good. A Christian ethic of human sexuality must begin with this encouraging biblical truth. The writers of Scripture clearly endorse the celebration of human sexuality (Deut. 24:5; Prov. 5:15–20; Song of Sol.; 1 Cor. 7:3–4), even on occasion becoming quite specific about sexual delights between a man and a woman (Prov. 5:19—"may her breasts satisfy you always"; Song of Sol. 2:6; 8:3—"his right hand fondles me"). Even the strict prohibition: "You shall not commit adultery," assumes a positive understanding of physical love: "You shall find sexual enjoyment within the limits established by God." Biblical scholar David Wenham emphasizes the goodness of human sexuality while noting also that sexual union is not the most important thing in life and that our sexuality must be expressed according to the Maker's instructions.

Christian ethicists, clergy, and laypeople differ, however, on what the "Maker's instructions" are. While almost all who call themselves Christians reject adulterous and promiscuous lifestyles (in theory at least), some, such as Episcopal Bishop John Spong, contend that the traditional prohibition against all sexual activity outside marriage is out of touch with reality and not helpful today. In her essay, ethics professor Karen Lebacqz argues similarly. While not endorsing **promiscuity,** her ethic of "appropriate vulnerability" allows for genital sexual expression between unmarried people, even those who are not planning on marriage. She sees vulnerability as an important God-given purpose for human sexuality and as the precondition for both sexual union and procreation of children.

Lebacqz's position obviously clashes with the traditional teaching of the Christian church. Evangelical theologian Richard Foster challenges this new sexual ethic for singles. In his view, human sexuality, even in the unmarried, is a good and wholesome part of God's creation, whereas **sexual intercourse,** because it creates a mysterious, unique "one flesh" bond, wounds the inner spirit of those who engage in it apart from marriage.

Most conservative Christians affirm Foster's perspective. In this view, both biblical teaching (Matt. 5:27–32; 1 Cor. 5–7; Eph. 5:3–12; 1 Thess. 4:3–8; Heb. 13:4) and two millennia of church history support the traditional regard for **chastity** and approve of sexual relations only within marriage. While conservative Christian ethicists today generally reject the negative teachings about the human body and its sexual nature that have prevailed for much of Christian history, they hold that marriage is the only appropriate channel for genital-sexual expression with another person. This rules out not only intercourse, but also **petting**—fondling another's sexually excitable body parts.

But what about those who are not married? It is one thing to champion the marriage union and its value in developing a context of trust for sexual bonding. It is another matter to talk about sexual desire and sexual release for those who are not married, who see no immediate prospect for marriage, and who do not believe they have the gift of **celibacy.** Since the number of singles in our society continues to rise, this is a pressing issue. Foster speaks to those in this situation. He suggests that **masturbation,** even though it can be abused, may be an appropriate means of releasing sexual tensions in adolescents and other singles.

Many Christians applaud Foster's approach while others consider it positively wrong. Perhaps the central issue in the debate is how Christians can obey Jesus' prohibition of **lustful** thoughts (Matt. 5:27–28) while entertaining the sexual fantasies that often accompany masturbation. The fact that such a common sexual practice is never mentioned in the Bible may indicate that the act itself is not the problem. However, one's thoughts, motivations, and the degree of control or bondage regarding sexual behavior are themes of major significance in the Scriptures (Matt. 5:29–30; 1 Cor. 6:12–20; 7:9; 1 Thess. 4:3–8; Eph. 5:3–12).

An issue underlying many of the questions concerning human sexuality and appropriate sexual behavior is the purpose of sex. Why did God create us as sexual beings with such strong desires for sexual intimacy? The sex drive is, after all, from God.

Because human sexuality and the ordinance of marriage are often treated together in the Bible, we can work toward the purpose of sex by first asking, What is the purpose of marriage? Some say God's primary purpose in ordaining marriage is the procreation of children. Roman Catholic Christians, following Augustine and other church fathers, have traditionally held this view. Others, particularly Protestants, focus on the intimate union and companionship between the partners. Both are taught in the Genesis account, and it may not be necessary to choose one over the other in some rigid sense.

Those who speak of priority of purpose may be using the term *purpose* with different connotations. If *purpose* connotes the end, goal, and ultimate, long-range intention for creation as a whole, then we can place priority on the propagation of the human race. In Genesis 1, God told the first couple to "be fruitful" and "to fill the earth and subdue it" (v. 28). Nothing is said of companionship because this chapter looks at the overall creation and concentrates on function within that creation (function of the expanse, v. 6; of the land, vv. 11–12; of the heavenly lights, vv. 14–18; of human beings, vv. 26–28).

However, if *purpose* is understood more from the perspective of God's immediate plan and desire for couples, focusing not on the creation as a whole but on individuals, then the primary purpose of marriage may be viewed as companionship and union—togetherness in daily life and in the task of governing the earth. John Calvin emphasized this unitive understanding of marriage. Genesis 2 lifts out and amplifies a segment of Genesis 1 by focusing on one couple and God's purpose for them. It was "not good" for the man to be alone. God made "a helper suitable for him" (2:18). Here the focus is not on procreation, but on loneliness and the need for human sexual complementarity (2:21–25). When Jesus referred to the "one flesh" concept in Genesis, he applied it, not with regard to having children, but concerning commitment and lifelong partnership as covenant companions (Matt. 19:4–6).

A third purpose for marriage, both in general and for specific individuals, is preventative: to control sexual urges by providing an appropriate channel for their fulfillment. This purpose is not mentioned in the creation accounts since the problem of premarital or extramarital encounters did not arise until after the fall. While some, such as Martin Luther, have overemphasized this purpose for marriage, it was clearly important to the apostle Paul (1 Cor. 7:2–5, 9).

One's view of the purpose of marriage can affect one's understanding of the sexual relationship. For example, a person who understands the primary purpose of marriage to be procreative rather than unitive or preventative may have a much different view of the kinds of sexual activities permitted and of the use of birth control.

Sometimes we confuse God's purpose for marriage with God's purpose for sex since the accepted outlet for sexual activity is within marriage. But not everyone gets married. And those who do marry may live many years as sexually aware persons before and after the span of the marriage itself. All of us, married or not, are sexual beings. The above glimpse at the divine intention for marriage provides some clues regarding God's purposes for human sexuality. One purpose—the biological purpose of sex—is obviously the procreation of children. Another purpose—we may call this the relational purpose—is for mutual enjoyment and creative union between partners. God delights in the pleasures (including sexual pleasures) of couples. But these two purposes are not capable of fulfillment in single persons. Are such individuals not participating in God's design for their sexuality?

Theologian and ethicist Stanley Grenz provides a somewhat different slant on the question of the purpose of human sexuality. While not denying the more traditional emphases, Grenz sees a higher, all-encompassing design in the plan of God. Grenz focuses on what he considers to be a sexually based sense of incompleteness within everyone. Because we are sexual beings and since sexuality by its very nature reaches out to others, we are incomplete as isolated individuals. We seek completeness and community through bonding with others, either in marriage or in other interpersonal relationship. Our sexually impelled drive toward completion in human fellowship is realized most fully in this life in the bonded community of the church, and in the next life in the resurrected community of God's eternal kingdom.

Grenz thus sees human sexuality as given by God to propel every person toward vibrant beneficial relationships with others and ultimately toward God himself. This perspective, if considered carefully, may do more to help people understand, accept, and enjoy their sexuality than a dozen popular sex manuals or surveys of the issues.

Marriage and Singleness in Paul and Today

David Wenham

One of the commonest misunderstandings around—among theologians and others—is that the apostle Paul had a negative view of marriage and sex. In fact, on this, as on so many other matters, he had a positive and balanced view, which we would do well to embrace in an age when there is so much confusion and hurt in this area. We could sum up the Pauline view—and indeed the view of Scripture as a whole—under three headings:

1. Human sexuality is an important, powerful and good part of God's creation. Paul's description of the church as the radiant bride of Christ in Ephesians 5:22–23 is the most obvious evidence for his positive view of marriage. He portrays the marriage relationship as something beautiful (compare Rev. 21:2, 9), and not just as beautiful but as comparable to the intimate relationship of love between Christ and his church. And, lest anyone suppose that he has an unreal, other-worldly view of marriage (as some people do have), it should be noted that he refers specifically to marriage as something involving the bodies of husband and wife.

The Ephesians passage is not isolated in Paul's writings: in Romans 7:4, 1 Corinthians 11:3 and 2 Corinthians 11:2 (where he speaks of presenting the Corinthians to Christ "as a pure bride to her husband") he compares divine-human relationships with the relationship of husband and wife.

First Corinthians 7 is often thought to present a negative view of marriage on Paul's part quite different from that in Ephesians 5; this has been used as an argument against the Pauline authorship of Ephesians or seen as an indication that Paul underwent a major change of opinion. But this is to misunderstand the passage, and in particular to fail to recognize the problem Paul is dealing with in the chapter. The problem is that some in Corinth were putting forward the view that "it is good for a man not to touch a woman" (v. 1). What they meant, as is apparent from Paul's comments on their views, is that those who are spiritual should not have sexual relationships, and they suggested that husbands and wives should not come together (v. 3), that the unmarried should remain unmarried (v. 8, etc.), and perhaps even that the married, certainly those married to non-Christians, should divorce their partners (vv. 10ff.). So there were indeed people in the early church who were negative towards sex.

Paul, however, rejects their supposedly spiritual asceticism, and, although he does believe that there is value in singleness (a point to which we shall return), he opposes the anti-sex lobby at almost every point, arguing that husbands and wives should not deprive each other of sexual intercourse, that unmarried people, except those with the special gift of singleness, should marry, and that divorce should be discouraged not encouraged. Paul recognizes very clearly in this chapter the power of the sexual drive, and when he speaks about the dangers of immorality when people are unmarried, he is not downgrading marriage so much as attacking the dangerous foolishness of those who fail to recognize the power of sexual instincts, which should not be suppressed.

That Paul's view of marriage even in 1 Corinthians 7 is positive is hinted at in verse 4, where he speaks in a remarkable way of the equal rights of husband and wife over the partner's body. He probably has in mind here the thought that is explicit in Ephesians 5 about husband and wife becoming "one flesh;" he has referred to that creation principle (Gen. 2:23) in 1 Corinthians 6:16, when explaining that prostitution is not to be contemplated, and he probably has it in mind too in 1 Corinthians 6:18, where he says, "he who sins sexually sins against his own body." It becomes clear that for Paul sexual union expressed in marriage brings husband and wife into a profound union, such that they can be thought to have a shared body: the two have become one.[1] It is this principle which Jesus in Matthew 19 [and] Mark 10 uses as an argument against divorce and which Paul, who no doubt learned it from Jesus (cf. 1 Cor. 7:10, where he refers to Jesus' teaching), uses both to exclude immorality and to explain the mutual responsibilities of husbands and wives.

We conclude that, although Paul does not spell out his understanding of marriage in 1 Corinthians 7 (since he is not addressing the question of marriage as such in this passage, but the ascetic question), he does imply the

---

1. The biblical phrase "becoming one flesh" is not simply stating the obvious fact that the bodies of man and woman become physically linked for the moment of sexual intercourse, but it is saying that, through coming together, the partners become bound to each other in a new and intimate relationship. This new relationship represents in some sense at least a break with old family loyalties ("leaving father and mother") and the beginning of a new family unit.

same very high view of marital union as is found in Ephesians 5. The repeated comparison that he makes of marriage to divine-human relationships, and even to relationship within the Godhead (e.g. 1 Cor. 11:3f.), suggests that he saw marital union as modelled on and a reflection of divine relationships—the highest and most beautiful relationships of all.[2]

If some or most of this analysis is correct, then the idea that Paul is anti-marriage and sex is very far from the mark. In fact he has about as high a view of marital union as one can imagine, far higher than the views of many moderns who glorify sex, but who see it as little more than an animal instinct or as an evolutionary mechanism for propagating the species. The Pauline and Christian view has all sorts of implications: it means that sex is not something to be embarrassed about or ashamed of, but, as part of God's good creation, is something to be thankful for and to be enjoyed. It means that sexual feelings, thoughts and drives are natural and powerful; to experience them is normal, not something unspiritual or to be alarmed about. On the other hand, it means that the proper use of sex is vitally important. To this we will return.

2. Sex is not the most important thing in life. Paul, as we have seen, has no time for the asceticism that sees marriage and sexual union as unspiritual; he sees marriage as very good. But he does not consider it the highest good or as an essential of human life. Indeed he sees singleness as an even higher calling than marriage, not in itself, but because of the "shortness of the time" and the passing nature of this world (1 Cor. 7:7, 25–35, 38).

We are reminded of Jesus' teaching about living for eternity and laying up treasure in heaven: he announced the coming of God's wonderful and exciting kingdom and told his disciples to seek the kingdom rather than worry about the things of this present passing age (cf. Matt. 6:25–34). He also explained that marrying is a this-worldly activity, not an activity of heaven (Matt. 22:23–33). Paul reflects the same priorities in his teaching: he believes that the Christian, whether married or single, should be looking and living primarily for the world to come (cf. 1 Cor. 7:29–31), but he knows that this is simpler for the single person (if he or she has the gift of singleness)

---

2. Paul does not explicitly say that marriage is for the procreation of children; he emphasizes the relationship of husband and wife to each other in a way that is significant. However, his failure to mention the procreative purpose of marriage is probably because that was not a question he needed to address in his letters rather than because it was unimportant for him. It is probably that he presupposes the OT understanding of marriage as being "to bear fruit" (in terms of children: cf. Gen. 1:29; Rom. 7:4–5), and his teaching about marriage is regularly followed by teaching concerning family life. Although our modern context is different from Paul's (so that we need to take our responsibility in the matter of over-population very seriously), he would, we suspect, have resisted any trend towards understanding marriage as being only for the mutual benefit of the two partners. Marriage is the bringing into being a new family and household, and the model of divine relationships would suggest that it is to be an outgoing and creative relationship.

than for the married person, since married people have to work out their devotion to the Lord in the context of a very demanding this-worldly commitment. In commending singleness Paul is not being anti-marriage or anti-sex; he insists that there are different callings and that each must live the life the Lord assigns him (1 Cor. 7:17). But he is being realistic about the complications of marriage and family, and consistent in his Christian priorities. Given a belief in the kingdom of God as the supreme joy and priority in life, there is no point in single Christians getting married for the sake of it. On the contrary the single person, who has the gift of self-control, can give himself or herself undistractedly to the Lord's work in ways that others cannot. Paul was a living proof of the point, as was Jesus, as have been other great Christians since. It is a gift, given only to some, to remain single, not dissimilar to other gifts such as teaching and healing, enabling the person concerned to minister in ways that those with other gifts cannot.

The importance of this teaching is considerable. Secular society tends both to romanticize and to idolize sex, and to suggest that the person who does not get sexual fulfillment in marriage or in some other way has missed out in life. The Christian wants to affirm the goodness of sexuality and sexual relations, but to affirm also that they are not the most important thing in life. Nor is singleness the greatest disaster in life: for some who are not conscious of being gifted in this way it may be exceedingly hard to live with, and they deserve all the support and understanding that they can get; for others it is a gift that gives them opportunity for more effective service and ministry. But the ultimate fulfillment and joy for the Christian, whether married or single, lies not in this world, but in the relationships of the world to come, of which marital union is only a pale copy.

3. Use according to the maker's instructions. Paul's very high view of human sexuality leads him to insist on its proper use. We have already seen how Paul rules out immorality because it is in contradiction to the "one flesh" way God designed marriage, and how for the same reasons he urges husbands to love their wives and both husbands and wives to give each other proper marital rights. For the same reasons he tells couples intending to split up to seek reconciliation rather than remarriage, and he insists that Christians embarking on marriage must marry "in the Lord" (1 Cor. 7:10, 11, 39).

Sometimes Christian morality is seen as negative and restricting, but we can see how the Pauline view of marriage has negative implications (e.g. about immorality), but also positive implications (e.g. about the place of sex in marriage). But even the negatives of the Pauline teaching are not a reflection of a negative view of sex, but of a supremely positive view. (There is a parallel in the Christian's "negative" view of abortion, being a reflection of a very high view of human life.) It is a low view of sex which sees it as little more than a pleasurable animal function, and which accordingly says that almost anything goes sexually (except perhaps the conceiving of unwanted children). That supposedly liberated view leads to chaos, because sex is a powerful force with dangerous potential when misused; it leads to the sexual distortions, unhappiness and violence that are characteristic of the "free" societies of the West, as well as to the aborting of millions of unwanted children. The Christian and the Pauline view sees sex as a great good created by God, to be used with care in the context of a loving, ongoing relationship between one man and one woman. In that context, human sexuality can be the joyful, beautiful thing that it is designed to be, rather than the ugly thing that the human race has often made it.

Of course Christians never live up fully to the Maker's instructions. But the intended pattern is clear, and the challenge of Paul to those who are married is to live out the pattern, loving each other, giving to each other, and holding together even when tempted to pull apart. It is important in the modern world, where there is so much confusion and so many anti-Christian pressures, that we understand and teach the Christian view of sex and marriage, not just to those who are married, but to those who will marry. We need to show people that Christian "narrowness" is not negative, but liberatingly positive, and that Paul got it right!

From David Wenham, "Marriage and Singleness in Paul and Today," *Themelios* 13, 2 (January/February 1988): 39–41.

Appropriate Vulnerability

A Sexual Ethic for Singles

Karen Lebacqz

All of us spend our first years single. Most of us spend our last years single. As adults, we are single by circumstance or by deliberate choice. Given these simple facts, it is surprising how little attention and how precious little support the churches have given to singleness (except for the monastic tradition, with its very particular demands and charisms). The scriptural witness on singleness is virtually ignored, despite the fact that Jesus never married and Paul preferred singleness. Throughout history, churches have simply assumed that marriage is the norm for Christians.

Single sexuality, when it is discussed at all, falls under the category of "premarital sex." Churches clearly expect that those who are single will get married and that those who have been married and are now single through divorce or widowhood will simply disappear into the closet until they marry again. The slogan recently adopted by the United Methodist Church might stand as a summary of the traditional Christian view of sexuality: "celibacy in singleness, fidelity in marriage."

A new ethic for single sexuality is needed, for the tradition that requires celibacy in singleness is not adequate. This situation does not mean that anything goes or that the church has nothing to offer by way of a positive ethic for single people. The task is to thread our way between two views of sexuality: the "old testament" or "thou shalt not" approach exemplified by much of the church tradition, and the "new testament" or "thou shalt" approach evident in much of our current culture.

The "old testament" or legalistic approach to single sexuality is well summed up in a delightful limerick by Joseph Fletcher:[1]

---

1. Joseph Fletcher, *Moral Responsibility: Situation Ethics at Work* (Philadelphia: Westminster, 1967), 88.

> There was a young lady named Wilde
> Who kept herself quite undefiled
>   by thinking of Jesus
>   and social diseases
> And the fear of having a child.

The "thou shalt not" ethic was characterized by fear—fear of pregnancy and venereal disease—and by a series of "don'ts": don't have sex, don't take pleasure in it (at least, not if you are a woman), and don't talk about it. As the limerick suggests, sexual involvement was regarded as "defiling." "Bad girls" and "good girls" were defined according to their willingness to be sexual or not. There was no discussion of the sexuality of divorced or widowed men and women, and gay men and lesbian women simply stayed in the closet.

With the advent of the so-called sexual revolution and the birth control pill, fear of pregnancy was gone. After the "thou shalt not" of Christian tradition, we encountered the "thou shalt" of contemporary culture. Here, "love" was all that counted. Women were "liberated" and virginity was redefined as "bad." Now people talked about sex all the time, with everyone. Far from being defiling, sexual involvement was regarded as mandatory. Sex was supposed to be pleasurable, and "how-to" manuals abounded. Finally, everyone knew how—but had forgotten why. In short, fear was replaced by pressure—pressure to engage in sex, to do it right, to enjoy it, and to let the world know how much and how well you were doing it.

The result is a clash often internalized into a "Catch 22." In the wonderfully perceptive comic strip *Cathy*, Cathy Guisewite captures the confusion of many. As the almost-but-not-quite-liberated "Cathy" is getting dressed to go out on a date, she reflects: "I'm wearing the 'heirloom lace' of my grandmother's generation . . . with the conscience of my mother's generation . . . coping with the morals of my generation . . . No matter what I do tonight, I'm going to offend myself."

Neither the legalistic approach of earlier Christian morality nor the permissive approach of contemporary culture provides a satisfactory sexual ethic for singles. And without a good sexual ethic for singles, there cannot be a good sexual ethic for couples either.

Can we construct a positive, Christian sexual ethic for single people? I think so. Let us begin with Christian tradition, which affirms that sex is a gift from God. [Sex] is to be used within the boundaries of God's purposes. As part of God's creation, sex is good. Like all of creation, however, it is tainted by the fall, and therefore becomes distorted in human history. It needs redemption. Such redemption is achieved by using sexuality in accordance with God's purposes and through God's grace.

The two redeeming purposes of sexuality have always been understood as procreation and union. With these purposes in mind, Christian tradition maintained that marriage was the proper context for sex, since it was the proper context for raising children and for achieving a true union. Catholics have tended to stress procreation as the primary purpose while Protestants have stressed union, but both agree on the fundamental purposes of sexual expression.

This tradition has had enormous practical implications for singles. The tradition condemns all genital sexual expression outside marriage, on the assumption that it violates the procreative and unitive purposes of sexuality. Nongenital sexual expression is also suspect, because it is thought to lead inexorably to genital expression. Given such a view of sexuality, it is difficult for single people to claim their sexuality or to develop a positive ethic for that sexuality.

Standards within both Catholic and Protestant traditions have recently loosened, but there has been no fundamental challenge to this basic paradigm. Today, some Catholics and most Protestants accept "preceremonial" sex between responsible and committed adults.[2] Both traditions have moved toward affirming union as primary, while still upholding the importance of procreation. The meaning of the two fundamental purposes has been expanded by replacing the term "procreative" with "creative" and the term "unitive" with "integrative."[3] Thus, there is some acceptance of nonmarital sexual expression, provided it is in the context of deep interpersonal commitment.

But however important such revisions may be, they do not really accept sexuality outside marriage. Single sexuality is still difficult to claim. Neither Catholic nor Protestant tradition provides a totally satisfactory explanation of why sexuality should be fully expressed only in marriage or in a "preceremonial" relationship that will eventuate in marriage. Both traditions still uphold marriage as the ideal, but give no satisfactory reasons for that ideal.

I accept part of the *method* that has led to the traditional interpretation, but wish to offer an additional insight into the nature of sexuality that might provide a fuller appreciation of the ethical context in which sexuality is expressed. I agree with the traditional understanding that sex is a gift from God to be used within the confines of God's purposes. However, I would add to the traditional purposes of union and procreation another God-given

2. Paul Ramsey argues that this is marriage in the moral sense. See his "On Taking Sexual Responsibility Seriously Enough," in Gibson Winter, ed., *Social Ethics* (San Francisco: Harper & Row, 1968), 45ff.
3. See Catholic Theological Society of America, *Human Sexuality: New Directions in American Catholic Thought* (New York: Paulist Press, 1977), 86.

purpose of sexuality that I believe opens up a different understanding of human sexuality and of a sexual ethic for singles (as well as couples).

Sexuality has to do with vulnerability. Eros, the desire for another, the passion that accompanies the wish for sexual expression, makes one vulnerable. It creates possibilities for great joy but also for great suffering. To desire another, to feel passion, is to be vulnerable, capable of being wounded.

There is evidence in Scripture for this view of sexuality. Consider the Song of Songs (the "holy of holies") which displays in glowing detail the immense passion and vulnerability of lovers. This is not married or "preceremonial" sexuality, nor are children the justification for the sexual encounter. It is passion pure and simple. And it is graphic sex. The Stoic fear of passion is not biblical. From the Song of Songs we can recover the importance of sexual desire as part of God's creation.

It is equally important to recover the creation stories in Genesis. These are so often the grounds for our interpretation of what God intends human sexuality to be. It is from these stories that we take the phrase "be fruitful and multiply" and turn it into a mandate for procreation. It is from these stories that we hear the deep call for union between sexual partners: "This at last is bone of my bones and flesh of my flesh . . . and the two shall become one flesh."

Without denying the importance of these phrases and their traditional interpretation, I would stress another passage—one that has been ignored but is crucial for completing the picture. The very last line in the creation story in Genesis 2 reads: "And the man and his wife were both naked, and they felt no shame" (Gen. 2:25). In ancient Hebrew, "nakedness" was a metaphor for vulnerability, and "feeling no shame" was a metaphor for appropriateness. (On this topic I am indebted to the work of Stephen Breck Reid of Pacific School of Religion.) We can therefore retranslate the passage as follows: "And the man and his wife experienced appropriate vulnerability." As the summation and closure of the creation story, the verse tells us that the net result of sexual encounter—the purpose of the creation of man and woman as sexual beings who unite with one another to form "one flesh"—is that there be appropriate vulnerability.

Vulnerability may be the precondition for both union and procreation: without a willingness to be vulnerable, to be exposed, to be wounded, there can be no union. To be "known," as Scripture so often describes the sexual encounter, is to be vulnerable, exposed, open.

Sexuality is therefore a form of vulnerability and is to be valued as such. Sex, eros, passion are antidotes to the human sin of wanting to be in control or to have power over another. "Appropriate vulnerability" may describe the basic intention for human life—which may be experienced in part through the gift of sexuality.

If this is so, then a new approach to sexual ethics follows. If humans are intended to have appropriate vulnerability, then the desire to have power or control over another is a hardening of the heart against vulnerability. When Adam and Eve chose power, they lost their appropriate vulnerability and were set against each other in their sexuality. Loss of vulnerability is paradigmatic of the fall. Jesus shows us the way to redemption by choosing not power but vulnerability and relationship.

The implications for a sexual ethic are profound. Any exercise of sexuality that violates appropriate vulnerability is wrong. This includes violations of the partner's vulnerability and violations of one's own vulnerability. Rape is wrong not only because it violates the vulnerability of the one raped, but also because the rapist guards his own power and refuses to be vulnerable.

Similarly, seduction is wrong, for the seducer guards her or his own vulnerability and uses sex as a weapon to gain power over another. Any sexual encounter that hurts another, so that she or he either guards against vulnerability in the future or is unduly vulnerable in the future, violates the "appropriate vulnerability" which is part of the true meaning and purpose of our God-given sexuality. Prostitution and promiscuity are also generally wrong. In each there tends to be either a shutting down of eros or a form of masochism in which the vulnerability is not equal and therefore not appropriate. Sex is not "just for fun" or for play or for physical release, for showing off, or for any of a host of other human emotions and expressions that are often attached to sexuality. It is for the appropriate expression of vulnerability, and to the extent that that expression is missing, the sexual expression is not proper.

Nothing in what has been said so far suggests that the only appropriate expressions of vulnerability are in marriage. Premarital and postmarital sexuality might express appropriate vulnerability. Gay and lesbian unions, long condemned by the church because of their failure to be procreative, might also express appropriate vulnerability. At the same time, some sexual expression within marriage might not be an appropriate expression of vulnerability—for example, spousal rape or unloving sexual encounter. We must be aware of the deceptions through which we reduce or deny vulnerability in sexuality—both the "swinging singles" image and notions of sexual "duty" in marriage deny appropriate vulnerability.

But what about singleness specifically? Is there any need for a special sexual ethic for single people? Precisely because sexuality involves vulnerability, it needs protective structures. A few years ago, the United Church of Christ proposed a "principle of proportionality" for single sexuality. According to this principle, the level of sexual expression should be commensurate with the level of commitment in the relationship. While I have some problems with this principle, it does have the merit of suggesting that the vulnerability involved in sexual encounter requires protection. The more sexual involvement there is to be, the more there needs to be a context that protects and safeguards that vulnerability. As Stanley Hauerwas puts it, "genuine love is so capable of destruction that we need a structure to sustain us."[4]

Traditionally, monogamous marriage has been understood to provide that needed context. Whatever the actual pitfalls and failures of marriage in practice, certainly in theory the commitment of a stable and monogamous marriage provides a supportive context for vulnerable expressions of the self. Marriage at its best ensures that the vulnerability of sexuality is private and that our failures remain protected in a mutually vulnerable and committed relationship.

Singleness carries no such protections. It is an unsafe environment for the expression of vulnerability. No covenant of fidelity ensures that my vulnerability will not lead to my being hurt, foolish, exposed, wounded. In short, in singleness the vulnerability that naturally accompanies sexuality is also coupled with a vulnerability of context. Thus, singleness is a politically more explosive arena for the expression of vulnerability in sex because it lacks the protections of marriage. It heightens vulnerability.

An adequate sexual ethic for singles must therefore attend to what is needed for appropriate vulnerability in sexuality. Attention must be paid to the structural elements in the particular situation that heighten or protect vulnerability. For example, a sexual ethic for singles might take one form for those who are very young and another for those who are older. The protections of age and experience may make it sensible to permit sexual encounter for those who are older and single, while restricting it for the very young. Unequal vulnerability is not appropriate. In a culture, therefore, where men tend to have more power than women and women are more vulnerable than men, great care will be needed to provide an adequate context for the expression of sexuality.

We need a theology of vulnerability. Until such a theology is forthcoming, we can only struggle toward a proper sexual ethic. Single people will have to explore their own vulnerability to find its appropriate expressions in sexuality. Neither the "thou shalt not" of traditional prohibitions nor the "thou shalt" of contemporary culture provides an adequate sexual ethic for singles. "Celibacy in singleness" is not the answer. An appreciation of the link between sexuality and vulnerability is the precondition for an adequate sexual ethic.

From Karen Lebacqz, "Appropriate Vulnerability: A Sexual Ethic for Singles." Copyright 1987 Christian Century Foundation. Reprinted by permission from the May 6, 1987 issue of *The Christian Century*.

4. *A Community of Character: Toward a Constructive Christian Social Ethic* (Notre Dame: University of Notre Dame Press, 1981), 181.

Sexuality and Singleness

Richard J. Foster

Hell is the only place outside heaven where we can be safe from the dangers of love.

—C. S. Lewis

One of the great challenges for the Christian faith today is to integrate sexuality and spirituality within the context of the single life. We are fast approaching the day when single people will be in the majority. There are, of course, the young who are still anticipating marriage. Also, there are many who are unwillingly hurled into single life by the tragic death of a spouse. The even greater tragedy of divorce casts untold millions more into the world of the single.

The church can make an enormous contribution by helping singles grapple with their sexuality with honesty and integrity. But in order to do this we must stop thinking of single persons as somehow devoid of sexual needs. Singles—especially those with a serious Christian commitment—really struggle with their sexuality. They face many troubling questions. Is masturbation a legitimate expression of sexuality for a Christian? How do I deal with the feelings of lust that often seem to dominate my thinking? What is lust, anyway, and how is it different from appropriate sexual desire? What about physical affection? Is it an appropriate means of building a healthy relationship, or is it only a one-way street to sexual intercourse? And speaking of intercourse, why is so much significance given to the insertion of the penis into the vagina? Are there really valid biblical reasons for the ban on intercourse outside of marriage, or are these just social customs? These and many similar questions are faced by all singles who are seeking to integrate their Christianity and their sexuality.

Sexuality and Sexual Intercourse

Perhaps it is best to begin by seeking to grasp a Christian perspective on sexuality and sexual intercourse. Sometimes a person will ask, "Do you believe in premarital sex?" The answer to that question is, "yes and no." Christianity says a clear yes to that question insofar as it refers to the affirming of our sexuality as human beings. Christianity says a clear no to that question insofar as it refers to genital sex. Let us try to understand the reasoning behind both the yes and the no.

We are sexual persons. We must never try to deny or reject that in any way. We are created in the image of God, male and female. In an important sense all that we are and all that we do has sexual implications. I am trying here to overcome the really silly notion that single persons are somehow asexual.

The single person's sexuality is expressed in his or her capacity to love and to be loved. Not all experiences of intimacy should eventuate in marriage or in genital sex. Loving does not need to be genital to be intimate, and the capacity to love is vital to our sexuality. And so the single person should develop many relationships that are wholesome and caring. Deeply affectionate but nongenital relationships are completely possible and should be encouraged.

The single person's sexuality is expressed in the need to experience emotional fulfillment. The decision to reserve genital sex for marriage is not a decision to remain emotionally unfulfilled. Warm, satisfying friendships are legitimate ways single people can express their sexuality. Emotional fulfillment is completely possible for the single person, and the Church can help here by providing a context for happy and satisfying friendships to develop.

The single person's sexuality is expressed in learning to accept and control his or her sexual feelings. Individuals outside the covenant of marriage should not deny or repress their sexual feelings. Donald Goergen has noted that "feelings are meant to be felt, and sexual feelings are no exception."[1] When we try to deny these feelings we cut ourselves off from our humanity.

I hear a lot more talk about platonic love than I see in experience. Most intimate heterosexual friendships have erotic dimensions to them. And it does us no good to deny that fact of life. Rather we should accept these feelings. But to accept them does not mean to act upon them. Sexual feelings are not to control us; we are to control them. It is an illusion to think that sexual desires are uncontrollable. Just because we may feel angry enough to want to murder someone does not mean that we will do so. We control our feelings of anger so that we do not kill, and in the same way we bring our sexual feelings under our authority.

1. Donald Goergen, *The Sexual Celibate* (New York: Seabury, 1974), 181.

So far we have tried to show ways by which singles should say yes to their sexuality. What about the no side of the answer to the question of sex outside of marriage?

There is no getting around it: biblical teaching places a clear veto on sexual intercourse for single people. The question is, Why? The biblical writers were not in the least prudish about sex. God's very creation of human beings as male and female suggests a wholehearted approval of exciting sexual experience. The Song of Solomon celebrates sex as a voluptuous adventure. Paul warns spouses against withholding "conjugal rights." Why, then, would sexual intercourse be reserved for the covenant of marriage?

The Bible's ban on sexual intercourse for the unmarried is based upon a profound positive insight. According to the biblical authors, sexual intercourse creates a mysterious, unique "one flesh" bond. In the creation narrative we are told in simple, yet profound, words, "Therefore a man leaves his father and his mother and cleaves to his wife, and they become one flesh" (Gen. 2:24). When the Pharisees sought to embroil Jesus in the contemporary controversy over the grounds for divorce, he appealed to the "one flesh" concept of Genesis and added, "So they are no longer two but one flesh. What therefore God has joined together, let no man put asunder" (Matt. 19:6). In Ephesians, Paul quotes the "one flesh" account to urge husbands to love their wives, because "he who loves his wife loves himself" (Eph. 5:28). His point is a simple one: marriage creates such a bonded union that to do violence to one's spouse is to do violence to oneself.

For our purposes, however, the most graphic passage of all is found in Paul's teaching in 1 Corinthians 6. Paul is dealing with the case of a man in the Christian fellowship who had been involved with a prostitute. He writes: "Do you not know that he who joins himself to a prostitute becomes one body with her? For, as it is written, 'The two shall become one flesh'" (1 Cor. 6:16). This passage makes it unmistakably clear that Paul sees sexual intercourse as the act par excellence that produces a "one flesh" bond.

We are now in a position to see why biblical morality reserves sex for the covenant of marriage. Sexual intercourse involves something far more than just the physical, more than even the emotions and psyche. It touches deep into the spirit of each person and produces a profound union that the biblical writers call "one flesh." Remember, we do not *have* a body, we *are* a body; we do not *have* a spirit, we *are* a spirit. What touches the body deeply touches the spirit as well.

Sexual intercourse is a "life-uniting act," as Lewis Smedes calls it.[2] And Derrick Bailey has added, "Sexual intercourse is an act of the whole self which affects the whole self; it is a personal encounter between man and woman in which each does something to the other, for good or for ill, which

---

2. Lewis B. Smedes, *Sex for Christians* (Grand Rapids: Eerdmans, 1976), 128.

can never be obliterated. This remains true even when they are ignorant of the radical character of their act."[3]

Thus the reasoning behind the biblical prohibition of sexual intercourse for the unmarried goes beyond the common practical concerns of pregnancy or venereal disease or whatever. Genital sex outside of marriage is wrong "because it violates the inner reality of the act; it is wrong because unmarried people thereby engage in a life-uniting act without a life-uniting intent. . . . Intercourse signs and seals—and maybe even delivers—a life-union; and life-union means marriage."[4]

Therefore, Paul is saying no to sexual intercourse outside of marriage because it does violence to the very nature of the act itself. The act draws us into the profound mystery of a "one flesh" reality. It unites and bonds in a deep and wonderful way, wonderful, that is, when it is linked to a covenant of permanence and fidelity. When it is not, it becomes "a hollow, ephemeral, diabolical parody of marriage which works disintegration in the personality and leaves behind a deeply-seated sense of frustration and dissatisfaction—though this may never be brought to the surface of consciousness and realized."[5]

The Hebrew word for intercourse means "to know." The biblical writers understood that in sexual intercourse a special kind of knowledge was conveyed, a special kind of intimacy came into being. This reality they called "one flesh." This then is why the Bible reserves sexual intercourse for the covenant of marriage.

Where does this leave those who have engaged in intercourse outside of marriage but who now recognize that what they have done is really and truly wrong? Is the bonded reality of intercourse utterly irreversible? No, it is not irreversible, but it does demand the healing touch of God. To engage in a life-uniting act without a life-uniting intent wounds the inner spirit. Such wounds often fester and become infected so that they poison the entire spiritual life. At best, they leave ugly scar tissue.

But the wonderful news is that healing is possible. The grace of God can flow into the wounded spirit, healing and restoring. Sometimes, however, individuals are not able to do this by themselves. In such cases it is best for them to seek out a wise and compassionate physician of the soul—someone who is experienced in spiritual direction and healing prayer—who can pray for them and set them free.

In whatever way it is done, healing prayer does need to be given. We cannot just pretend that the affair never happened, no matter how casual it was. If it is not dealt with and healed, it will surface sooner or later. A friend of mine once counseled a seventy-eight-year-old woman. She had been a mis-

3. Derrick Sherwin Bailey, *The Mystery of Love and Marriage* (New York: Harper, 1952), 53.
4. Smedes, *Sex for Christians*, 130.
5. Bailey, *Mystery of Love and Marriage*, 53–54.

sionary for fifty years, but now her life, it seemed, was in shambles. She had fears day and night. She was afraid of crowds; she was afraid of stairs; she was afraid of everything. And she was depressed; a deep sadness hung over her entire life. So total was her misery that she was preparing to have shock treatments.

My friend, who is very wise in the care of souls, asked if she had been happy as a child. "Oh, yes!" she responded. The next question was a simple one, "When did you begin to feel this sadness and depression?" The reply was quick, "When I was sixteen." And so my friend asked, "Why? What happened when you were sixteen that caused the sadness?" For the first time in her life, this woman admitted that at sixteen she had had an affair with a young man. Fortunately she did not become pregnant, and the young man soon went away, but she had carried this deep wound in her spirit for over sixty years.

My friend prayed for the inner healing of this dear woman, and, wonderfully, within a matter of weeks, the fears and depression began to disappear, so that, as she put it, "I am able to remember that I used to be afraid and depressed, but I can no longer remember what it felt like!"

This ministry of forgiving and healing through the power of Christ is the common property of the people of God. We can bring so much help, so much healing, if we are willing. It is a gracious ministry that needs to abound in the fellowship of the faithful.

Sexual Fantasy

Jesus, of course, made it abundantly clear that sexual righteousness was a far deeper issue than merely avoiding sex outside of marriage. He went right to the heart of the matter by speaking of the adultery of the heart, "Every one who looks at a woman lustfully has already committed adultery with her in his heart" (Matt. 5:28). This statement was a profound advance over the external righteousness of the scribes and Pharisees. It has also caused a great deal of concern and confusion about sexual fantasies.

The single person who genuinely wants to be a disciple of Christ and who therefore reserves sexual intercourse for the covenant of marriage is often confused about how to deal with sexual fantasies. Sexual fantasies delight— they also trouble and disturb. And the confusion they cause is only heightened by the ambivalence of the Christian community. When singles turn to the Church for direction, they are usually met with either stony silence or the counsels of repression. Now, silence is no counsel, and repression is bad counsel. Desperate, however, they try to repress their sexual feelings, but their efforts always end in disappointment. The result is guilt, followed by bitterness and disillusionment. The need is great for solid practical guidance on how to deal with sexual fantasies.

At the outset we must make as clear a distinction as possible between lust and sexual fantasy. I say "as clear a distinction as possible" because we simply must admit that the lines that divide the two are sometimes shrouded in ethical mists and fogs. Although all lust involves sexual fantasy, not all sexual fantasies lead to lust. How do we know the difference?

. . . I defined lust as "runaway, uncontrolled sexual passion." Lewis Smedes has articulated the difference between the two quite well: "When the sense of excitement conceives a plan to use a person, when attraction turns into scheme, we have crossed beyond erotic excitement into spiritual adultery."[6] Lust is an untamed, inordinate sexual passion to possess, and this is a very different thing from the usual erotic awareness experienced in sexual fantasy.

Hence, the first thing that believers should do is to refuse to bear the heavy burden of self-condemnation for every erotic image that floats through their minds. Sometimes sexual fantasies signify a longing for intimacy; at other times, they express attraction toward a beautiful and winsome person. Sexual fantasies can mean many things, and we must not automatically identify them with lust.

It is also helpful to recognize the positive function of fantasy. Through fantasy we are able to hold reality at bay while we allow the imagination to roam freely. Mature people are able to utilize the imagination without ever losing touch with the real world. Some of the world's finest music and greatest inventions have come in this way.

Certainly one of the distinguishing characteristics of our human sexuality, as opposed to the rest of the creation, is our ability to reflect upon our sexuality. We can write love letters, remember the warm kiss many times over, and anticipate love's tender moments yet to come. These are sexual events, erotic experiences, and they should not be classified as lust. In fact, in marriage sexual fantasy is vitally important in awakening sexual expression. Perhaps one reason many couples are bored with sex is atrophy of their imagination.

But if sexual fantasy has its positive side, it also has its destructive side. It can be a substitute for warm friendships, which carry with them the demands and disappointments of real life. It can lead to obsession with the sexual. It can easily become a truncated preoccupation with the physical. It can be a prelude to illicit behavior.

The problem of sexual fantasies genuinely intensified in our day because of the modern media blitz. It is virtually impossible to get away from the media's constant appeal to our sexual fantasies. Advertisers know well the power of sexual fantasy and constantly exploit that power.

However, we need to realize the authority we can have over our sexual fantasies. The imagination can be disciplined. In our better moments we can choose to place our minds on true and honorable and just and pure and

6. Smedes, *Sex for Christians*, 210.

lovely and gracious things. And even in our bad moments we can confess with Paul, "It is no longer I that do it, but sin which dwells within me," and know that a deeper experience of obedience is coming (Rom. 7:17).

You see, when bad people do evil they do exactly what they want to do. But when people who are seeking to follow Jesus Christ do evil they are doing precisely what they do not want to do. As Paul put it, "I do not do what I want, but I do the very thing I hate" (Rom. 7:15). When we are faced with such a condition, we say by faith, "That is not me doing it; it is sin in me, and by the grace of God and in the timing of God I shall be rid of it."

One of the most healing ministries we can render to each other is to learn to pray for one another about our sexual fantasies. In this realm I have a friend who prays for me and I for him. The sharing is confidential, of course. The praying is spiced with laughter and joy, for it is a happy ministry to which we are called. We pray that we will be protected from sexual influences that will be destructive and harmful. We pray that Christ will enter our sexual fantasies and fill them with his light. We pray that our sexuality will be whole and full and pure. It is a gracious, wholesome, happy ministry, and I would commend it to you.

Masturbation

Masturbation is so closely related to the issue of sexual fantasy that it deserves attention at this juncture. Ethical judgments about masturbation run all the way from viewing it as a sin more serious than fornication, adultery, or rape to placing it in the same category as head scratching.[7] One thing that is certainly uncontested is the almost universal experience of masturbation. James McCary, author of *Human Sexuality,* has found that about 95 percent of men and between 50 and 90 percent of women masturbate.[8] It has been said that "no other form of sexual activity has been more frequently discussed, more roundly condemned, and more universally practiced, than masturbation."[9] Nearly all adolescents masturbate and many adults masturbate from time to time throughout their lives.

7. In the Middle Ages the Roman Catholic church stressed the evils of masturbation because of its distance from procreation, which was thought to be the only function of sex, and even the most recent Vatican statement on the subject declares that "masturbation is an intrinsically and seriously disordered act." And in the Evangelical Protestant wing of the Church, Erwin Lutzer, in *Living with your Passions,* comes very close to a direct identification of masturbation with sin. By contrast, most in the medical profession today regard it as normal and not harmful. James Dobson, in his popular "Focus on the Family" film series, accepts it as a normal part of growing up unless it becomes excessive. Charlie Shedd, in *The Stork is Dead,* speaks of it as "a gift from God," since it can help to avoid promiscuous sex. The comparison of masturbation with head scratching comes from James McCary, in *Human Sexuality,* 3d ed. (New York: Van Nostrand, 1978), 293–94.
8. McCary, *Human Sexuality,* 150.
9. "Autoeroticism," in *The Encyclopedia of Sexual Behavior,* ed. A. Ellis and Aborbanel, vol. 1 (New York: Hawthorn, 1961), 204.

The issue of masturbation is particularly acute for single people who, out of Christian conviction, have said no to sexual intercourse outside of marriage. Many important questions surface: Is masturbation a morally acceptable activity for a disciple of Christ? Even more, could it be a "gift from God," as some have suggested, to help us avoid promiscuous sex? What about the sexual fantasies that invariably crowd into the landscape of masturbation?

These questions—and many more—are of concern to all believers, but they are especially urgent to singles. Deeply concerned to do what is right, many singles find their experiences of masturbation plagued by guilt, defeat, and self-hatred. They determine never to do it again. But they do. And the pit of self-condemnation deepens.

Let us begin with a couple of indisputable facts. First, masturbation is not physically harmful in any way. On this, all medical experts agree. The old myths that masturbation will cause everything from pimples to insanity are just that—myths.

Second, the Bible nowhere deals directly with masturbation. There are no injunctions against it, as there are against homosexuality, for example. The Bible's silence on masturbation is not because it was unknown, since there are references to it in the Egyptian literature of the period. It certainly is not because the Bible is squeamish about sexually explicit topics. Now, the Bible's silence does not mean that masturbation is not a moral issue, but it does mean that any biblical help we receive will be indirect rather than direct.

Three concerns heighten the moral question of masturbation. The first is its connection with sexual fantasies. Masturbation simply does not occur in an imageless void. And many are deeply distressed by the images that do come, feeling that they qualify as the lust of the heart that Jesus spoke against (Matt. 5:28).

The second concern relates to masturbation's tendency to become obsessive. People who masturbate can become compulsive in it. They feel trapped; the practice becomes an uncontrollable habit that dominates everything. Perhaps the most distressing aspect of this obsessive process is the sense of being undisciplined and out of control.

The third concern has to do with masturbation's depersonalization. Masturbation is sexual solitaire. True sexuality leads us to a deep personal relationship with another, but masturbation is "sex on a desert island," to use the phrase of John White.

On the positive end of the spectrum, masturbation does help compensate for the uneven development that many adolescents experience in their physical, emotional, and social maturation. Many teenagers are physically ready for sex far sooner than they are for social intimacy and the responsibilities of marriage. Masturbation provides a natural "safety valve" while nature is synchronizing growth in the various aspects of life.

For married couples, masturbation can often be a mutually enriching experience when done together. Within the context of married lovemaking, it has been called "an exciting excursion into shared pleasure."[10] In fact, some couples find mutual masturbation a crucial element in the development of their full sexual potential.

What should we say to all this? Well, the first thing we should say is that masturbation is not inherently wrong or sinful. In the main, it is a common experience for most people and should be accepted as a normal part of life.

The second thing we can emphasize is its value in providing a potentially healthy genital outlet when sexual intercourse is not possible. We simply must not lay impossible moral burdens upon people, especially when we have no specific biblical teaching against masturbation. Many honest folk, told of the evils of masturbation, have prayed desperately to be set free, and in reality have been expecting God to take away their sexual desires. These expectations are completely unrealistic, and, in fact, if God were to oblige, he would be doing violence to his own creation. Sexual desire is good and needs to be affirmed, not denied.

But sexual desire also needs to be controlled, which leads us to a third affirmation: the more masturbation tends toward obsession, the more it tends toward idolatry. God is our only legitimate obsession. The body needs to be under our discipline; this is true whether we are talking about sloth, gluttony, or masturbation. The uncontrolled practice of masturbation undermines our confidence and self-esteem. Obsessive masturbation is spiritually dangerous. But we must also be aware of the opposite obsession—the obsession to quit. This obsession is especially painful because one failure can cast a person into despair. It becomes a desperate, all-or-nothing situation. And this is sad, because it is really unnecessary. We do not need to put people into impossible either/or binds. What we are after is control, balance, perspective.

Closely tied to this is a fourth affirmation: masturbation's sexual fantasies are a very real part of human life that needs to be disciplined, not eliminated. Erotic imaginings will come; the real ethical question is how to deal with them. Will they dominate every waking moment, or can they be brought into proper perspective within the far greater matters of love and human relationship? We like fantasies because they idealize life. In our fantasies we are the paradigm of sexual prowess, our partner is desirable beyond compare, and, best of all, he or she says what we want, does what we want, and never makes demands on our time and energy. This is precisely why fantasies need discipline: they can divorce us from the real world of human imperfection. And Jesus' word about adultery of the heart must never be taken lightly.

The final thing we should say about masturbation is that, although it may electrify, it can never fully satisfy. Orgasm is only a small part of a much

---

10. Smedes, *Sex for Christians*, 246.

larger whole. And that larger whole encompasses the entire range of personal human relationship. A cup of coffee together in the morning, a quiet talk in the evening, a touch, a kiss—this is the stuff of our sexuality. Masturbation will always fall short, because it seeks to perpetuate the myth of the self-contained lover. . . .

The Single Life

Some have a special call of God to a single life, as both Jesus and Paul taught. This was a genuine contribution, since before this time there was no theology of sexuality that really allowed for the single life.[11]

Jesus declared that there were those who were single "for the sake of the kingdom of heaven" (Matt. 19:12).[12] And Paul builds on this foundation by suggesting that the unmarried can focus their energies toward the work of God in a way that the married simply cannot (1 Cor. 7:32–35).

Some have railed at Paul for urging people to seriously consider the single life, but the truth is that his words are filled with practical wisdom. He was not against marriage—in fact his great contribution to Christian sexual theology is the way he compares the sexual union in marriage to the union of Christ and his Church. But Paul did insist that we count the cost. You see, no one should enter the covenant of marriage without realizing the immense time and energy required to make that relationship work. "The unmarried man is anxious about the affairs of the Lord, how to please the Lord; but the married man is anxious about worldly affairs, how to please his wife, and his interests are divided" (1 Cor. 7:32–34).

Therefore, in the Christian fellowship we need to make room for the "vocational celibate"—the person who has chosen a single life in order to focus his or her energies more narrowly on the service of the kingdom of God. Jesus himself is an example of this, as is Paul. Vocational celibacy is not an inferior or a superior way of life—it is simply a different calling.

In *Freedom of Simplicity* I have written, "We do people a disservice when we fail to proclaim the single life as a Christian option. Marriage is not for everyone, and we should say so."[13] Those who are called to the single life should be welcomed into the life and ministry of the church. They are not

11. In the main, Judaism looked upon celibacy as an abnormal state. Eunuchs, for example, were forbidden to act as priests (Lev. 21:20). The only exception I am aware of to this general rule was the Essene community of Qumran. There celibacy did exist, and Jesus was likely aware of this group since his cousin, John the Baptist, was probably involved with the Essenes.

12. The biblical term is *eunuchs,* and there is considerable debate over whether this refers to a person who has never married or to a married person whose partner has left for a pagan life who does not remarry and hence is a "eunuch for the sake of the kingdom." Whichever interpretation is correct, the practical outcome is the same—the person lives a single life for the sake of the kingdom of heaven.

13. Richard J. Foster, *Freedom of Simplicity* (San Francisco: Harper and Row, 1981), 137.

half-people or folk who somehow cannot snag a mate. They have made a positive choice of the single life for the sake of Christ and in response to the call of God. And as Heini Arnold has noted, "It is possible for everyone to find the deepest unity of heart and soul without marriage."[14]

. . . I want to speak a special word about those who are single but feel no special calling to be single. Perhaps they are widowed or divorced or have not had a chance to marry but wish they were married. The Christian community needs to have a special tenderness for these who feel shoved aside and left behind in our couple-oriented world.

In many cases their situation has arisen from circumstances completely beyond their control. For example, we tell people to marry "only in the Lord," but because of our mechanisms of evangelism and Christian nurture, we have more women than men in the Church. What are the women to do?

Or consider the plight of the divorcées in our churches. In many cases we are not sure whether to welcome them or to ostracize them. They sense our ambivalence, and in some ways it is worse than outright rejection.

To the unwilling single I would like to speak the words of trust and hope. Do not harden your heart. God is still sovereign no matter what the frustrations of your life may indicate. He can bring about that "wonder of wonders and miracle of miracles" that Motel Kamzoil sang about in *Fiddler on the Roof.* Trust in him, do all you can yourself, and live in hope. And even if marriage does not come, you can know that his grace is sufficient even for that.

In writing this chapter I have been keenly aware that it is quite easy for me to pontificate on the conditions for sexual purity for singles from the warm confines of a satisfying marriage. To put it bluntly, I do not have to face an empty bed at night or mounting sexual frustrations during the day. But whatever our station in life, we can trust the goodness of God and learn to live in his power.

14. Heini Arnold, *In the Image of God: Marriage and Celibacy in Christian Life* (Rifton, N.Y.: Plough, 1976), 161.

The Purpose of Sex

Toward a Theological Understanding of Human Sexuality

Stanley J. Grenz

The Nature of Human Sexuality

What Is Sexuality?

. . . [S]exuality is a dimension of our existence as embodied persons. There are only two ways to be human—as male or as female. At its core, this embodied existence includes a fundamental incompleteness, one which is symbolized by biological sex and is based in our fundamental sexuality. Through sexuality we give expression both to our existence as embodied creatures and to our basic incompleteness as embodied persons. In this way, our sexuality calls us to move toward completeness. It forms the dynamic that lies at the basis of the uniquely human drive toward bonding. Sexuality forms the foundation for the drive which moves male and female to come together to form a unity of persons in marriage. But this yearning for completeness also forms the basis of the interpersonal and religious dimensions of existence.

Sexuality, then, both links and separates humankind and the rest of the life order. Although sex and even sexually derived bonding are evident in the animal world, in humans sexuality offers a potential for forming personal unity that goes beyond that found among animals. Because it is less strictly oriented to procreation, it fosters the type of unity of persons spoken of as love. This potential for the sharing of love, which has its basis in sexuality, gives to humankind a special status in creation: we are called to be the image of God.

Sexuality and Our Essential Being

Sexuality denotes more than the physical distinctions that allow for the differentiation between male and female in reproductive roles, for it encompasses all the various aspects of the human person that are related to existence as male or female. This understanding suggests that sexuality is so all pervasive of the human person that it must be considered an essential dimension of what it means to be human. How we think, how we view the world, and how others view us are all affected by our sexuality. . . .

Christian theology, specifically the doctrines of creation and resurrection, support[s] the thesis of the essential nature of human sexuality. God created us embodied beings, and in the resurrection we will be recreated in like fashion. Together the two doctrines confirm a basic anthropology that includes our sexuality.

The Doctrine of Creation

In contrast to that of the Greek philosophical tradition, the Hebrew understanding of creation resulted in a basically nondualistic anthropology. Greek anthropology tended to speak of distinct substantial entities, generally termed body and soul. The Hebrews, however, viewed the human person as a unitary, embodied being. The most succinct statement of the forming of humankind is found in the opening chapters of Genesis.

In the first creation story, God is presented as simply making humankind, just as he had made the other aspects of the universe, including other living things. There is no indication that humans are to be viewed apart from the material world. They are created in the divine image, but their special creation entails no fundamental dualism in humans that gives higher status to one part of the person, the soul, which is non-material in substance, in contrast to the material body, so that the soul constitutes the "real" person. In fact, the only "dualism" in the text is the male/female distinction.

The second narrative offers more detail. God's creation of the man occurs in two steps. He forms him from the dust of the ground (material) and then breathes life into him. But even this is not to be interpreted as meaning that God constituted the man as an ontological dualism. Rather, the emphasis is placed on the fact that he is an animated being, animated by the life principle from God, just as the animals, which are likewise spoken of as "soul." In this narrative, as in the first, the important distinction that arises from creation is the dual aspect of the first human pair as male and female.

From the perspective of the Genesis stories, then, humans are the creation of God in their entire being. God created animate material creatures, each of whom comprises a unity of being. In the Genesis narrative the human person is the whole person, the embodied person.

The Doctrine of Resurrection

The basic non-dualist anthropology of the Old Testament forms a context for, and is reaffirmed in, the doctrine of resurrection. In fact, the resurrection offers the ultimate critique of all dualist anthropologies, for it declares that the body is essential to human personhood. Rather than the body being shed in order for the person to enter eternity, as taught by the Greek tradition, the human person enters eternity as an animated body, as an embodied person transformed in one's entire being through the resurrection. God's creation of humankind as animated material beings is not a temporary act. Instead, the creation of the first human as a synthesis of the material from the earth and the animating principle, evidence in Genesis, actually belongs to the human destiny as God's creation. God's intent is that humans exist as embodied persons.

This intent is confirmed by the resurrection of Jesus. The main purpose of the post-resurrection stories of the Gospels as well as the Pauline appeal to the witnesses of the appearances is to indicate that the Risen Lord was recognized as none other but Jesus of Nazareth, the one who had been crucified. He had passed through the event of transformation into eternal life; yet, Jesus remained an embodied reality. His disciples touched him, ate and conversed with him, and knew who he was. With the exception of the case of the Emmaus road disciples, he is presented as recognizable by sight to those who had known him. This would seem to suggest that the basic masculine features of Jesus of Nazareth were preserved through the transformation experience of the resurrection. The Risen Lord had remained the recognizable Jesus.

Implications for Human Sexuality

The anthropology inherent in the Hebrew-Christian doctrines of creation and resurrection indicates that sexuality is a constitutive part of the human reality as an embodied existence. With a view toward creation Genesis 1:27 declares, "God made them male and female." There is simply no other way to be a created human being except as an embodied person, and embodiment means existence as male or female. This close relationship between embodied existence and being male or female is in keeping with the discovery of modern psychology that identity formation is closely connected with our sexuality. We see ourselves as male or female, and this fundamental sexuality becomes the primary and deepest aspect of our existence in the quest to determine who we are.

The doctrine of the resurrection indicates that the foundational role played by sexuality in determining identity is not destroyed in eternity. Resurrection means that our entire person, including our body, passes through transformation. But because existence as an embodied person means existence as male or female, our sexuality must participate in the event of resur-

rection as well, and by necessity, for it is a part of the total person who undergoes transformation.

Embodiment in Christian Theology and in Secularism

The emphasis of biblical anthropology on the human person as an
embodied and therefore a sexual being offers a corrective to the secular outlook widespread in Western culture today. The biblical doctrines of creation and resurrection imply that our sexuality is basic to our sense of self
and foundational to our understanding of who we are as God's creatures.
God intends that we be embodied beings who are either male or female.
Further, because our sexuality is the product of God's intention, it constitutes an essential aspect of the way we stand before God. Humans are
responsible before God to be stewards of all they are, a stewardship that
extends to the sexual dimension as well, for our existence as male or female
is essential to our being. The Christian, therefore, takes the Pauline admonition seriously, "Do you not know that your body is a temple of the Holy
Spirit, who is in you, whom you have received from God? You are not your
own; you were bought at a price. Therefore honour God with your body"
(1 Cor. 6:19–20).

Secular anthropology, in contrast, tends to view sexuality largely as an
activity, not as a constitutive aspect of our being. Sexual expression becomes
thereby an activity in which the self engages. When viewed in this manner,
sexuality is more readily separated from the self. The secularist differentiates
between "Who I am" and "What I do," seeing "What I do" as external to
"Who I am."

This attitude toward human sexuality in general and the sex act in particular is readily linked with the modern understanding of the basic nature of the
human person. In contrast to the more socially oriented viewpoint characteristic of much of Christian tradition, there has been a growing tendency in the
modern era toward a fully individualistic understanding of human nature.
The human person, the modern view maintains, is an independent self,
whose essence is to make choices in freedom. The self is fundamentally a free
decision maker. The sex act, in turn, is viewed as one vehicle for the expression of the freely choosing self, a means whereby the individual as a free agent
of action actualizes personal freedom. In keeping with this understanding the
code words of the modern sexual revolution include "self-expression" and
"self-actualization."

The Christian viewpoint differs radically from the modern secular alternative. Because of our view of the human person as a unified being, we simply cannot follow those who maintain that the body can be indulged without
affecting the essential person. Because we are created as embodied persons,
we cannot relegate the sexual dimension of our existence to the realm of the
non-significant, as having no bearing on our relation to God. We refuse to

view our fundamental identity as human beings in terms of freedom. The human person is not primarily the freely choosing self, as if our existence as male or female were external to our essential nature. Because of its mistaken understanding of sexuality, therefore, the sexual revolution is in the final analysis an illusion.

The Social Purpose of Our Creation as Sexual Beings

Human beings are sexual creatures. The individual dimension of our fundamental sexuality is obvious. But equally important is the corporate dimension of human sexuality. We are not sexual beings in isolation from each other. Rather, our individual sexual nature is closely linked to our situation as social beings. Sexuality is significant for community. The basic purpose of our existence as sexual creatures is related to the dynamic of bonding, in that sexuality forms the fundamental drive that leads to this human phenomenon. The close relationship between bonding and sexuality is borne out by the biblical documents.

The Old Testament: The Family Bond

Human sexuality and the drive toward bonding play an important role in the Old Testament. Perhaps the most powerful statement of the relationship between the two is presented in the story of the creation of the woman in Genesis 2. According to the narrative, the creative act that brought the first woman into existence was the outworking of the divine intent, "I will make a helper suitable for him," called forth by the divine observation of the situation of the first man, "It is not good for the man to be alone" (Gen. 2:18). Although the man enjoyed a relationship with the animals, none was an appropriate bonding partner for him: "But for Adam no suitable helper was found" (v. 20). The Hebrew term *helper* also refers to one who saves or delivers and is used elsewhere with reference to God in relationship to Israel (Deut. 33:7; Ps. 33:20; 115:9). God's desire, then, was to create another who would deliver Adam from his solitude by being a suitable bonding partner for him, not merely sexually, but in all dimensions of existence. In contrast to his response to the animals, Adam immediately senses a bond with the female, bursting forth in joyous declaration: She is "bone of my bones and flesh of my flesh."

The narrator concludes the episode with the application of the story to the phenomenon of male-female bonding: "For this reason a man will leave his father and mother and be united to his wife, and they will become one flesh" (v. 24). The phrase moves beyond procreative unity to encompass the entire bond enjoyed in marriage. Hence, the narrator's comment presents the awareness of a fundamental personal incompleteness ("for this cause") as the dynamic lying behind the phenomenon of the two actions, "leaving and cleaving." This awareness, in other words, results in the drive for the bonding expressed in the relationship of husband and wife.

The Old Testament, however, finds a further outworking of the relationship between sexuality and bonding. What transpires through the union of male and female, although completed in marriage, does not end with husband and wife as an isolated union. Rather, this intimate bond becomes a first step toward the establishment of the broader human community.

The Genesis narrative carries significant implications. Because we are sexual beings, as isolated individuals we are fundamentally incomplete. Our sexuality not only participates in our incompleteness, it also allows us to sense this incompleteness, and incompleteness that in turn moves us to seek community through bonding. For many, the primary place of community becomes marriage and the family. But even in the case of unmarried persons, the drive to community, while not specifically oriented toward genital expression, is nevertheless based in the awareness of the incompleteness of the human individual apart from community.

Our sexually based sense of incompleteness also forms the dynamic lying behind the search for truth, a search which ultimately becomes the search for God. We long to have our incompleteness fulfilled, and this longing gives rise to the religious dimension of life. The message of the Bible, beginning already in the book of Genesis, claims that in the final analysis the source of this completeness is found in the community that focuses on fellowship with the Creator.

The drive for completion in fellowship is not surprising, because it is in keeping with the theological assertion that we are created in God's image. Just as God is the community of the trinitarian persons, so also God has created us for the sake of community, to find completion in fellowship with each other and together with our Maker.

The New Testament: The Bonded Community

In the New Testament era, an important change occurs. Now the primary community is no longer presented as the physical family, entrance to which occurs through natural familial heritage. Rather, the central community is the church. More important than physical ancestry (who one's parents are) is one's spiritual ancestry (who one's heavenly Father is). The highest loyalty is now directed to Jesus, and the primary bond is that which binds the disciple to him and thereby to the community of disciples.

This change in outlook was inaugurated by Jesus himself. It is embodied in his demanding challenge to discipleship, summarized in his admonition, "Anyone who loves his father or mother more than me is not worthy of me; anyone who loves his son or daughter more than me is not worthy of me" (Matt. 10:37). At the same time he promises to the loyal disciple a larger, spiritual family to compensate for the loss entailed in leaving one's natural family for the sake of discipleship: "I tell you the truth, no one who has left home or mother or father or children or fields for me and the gospel will fail to receive a hundred times as much in this present age . . . and in the age to come eternal life" (Mark 10:29–30). But what Jesus demands of his followers, he fulfils himself. He too forsook family for the sake of the cause of the kingdom of God, counting as his true family "whoever does the will of my Father in heaven" (Matt. 12:50).

Jesus' view was carried over into the early church. The Jerusalem believers, for example, looked to the community of discipleship as their primary focus of fellowship and loyalty. They were bonded to each other, and as an expression of this, they held even their material possessions in common (Acts 4:32–35).

The Genesis narrative, then, indicates that God created us as sexual beings. Our sexuality has a purpose, for it is a primary force that places in us the drive toward bonding. This drive leads to the development of social communities, beginning with marriage, family, tribe, and finally larger societies. For the Christian, however, this drive is fulfilled ultimately only through fellowship as part of the society of disciples who enjoy fellowship with God through the corporate community of believers in Christ. . . .

Conclusion

What then is the purpose of sex? God created us as sexual beings, in order to bring us to one another and to himself. God's overarching design is that we reflect the divine image by being moulded by his Spirit into the community of redeemed humanity sharing in fellowship with the Creator. To this end, our sexuality depicts our fundamental incompleteness as solitary human beings and forms the dynamic that causes us to come out from ourselves in order to become whole persons through relationship with each other and ultimately with God. As Augustine noted so profoundly, "Our heart is restless until it finds rest in thee." This restlessness, related as it is to our fundamental sexuality, points forward to the consummation of God's activity in the eschatological community of his eternal kingdom. It is in view of the biblical vision of this consummation, the vision of the day when God's dwelling will be with us, that all Christian ethics, including the Christian sex ethic, and therefore all Christian ministry must be oriented.

From Stanley J. Grenz, "The Purpose of Sex: Toward a Theological Understanding of Human Sexuality," *Crux* 26, 2 (June 1990): 29–34.

For Further Reflection

Case Studies

Pornographic videos. Hannah and Charles have been married for fourteen years and are active in their church, but they are experiencing problems in their sex life together. Charles says he is bored and has difficulty getting sexually excited without some help. He wants Hannah to watch pornographic videos with him before having sex. Hannah did this a few times, but feels that it is wrong. Charles says he selects only "mild" videos and that if Hannah does not go along with his wishes, he will be unfulfilled and in danger of yielding to temptation at work. Should Hannah cooperate? If not, what might she do to help Charles? What fundamental principle or principles regarding sex in marriage is Charles failing to grasp?

Heavy petting. Jeff and Cynthia are college juniors and are very much in love. They are planning to become engaged soon and to be married the summer after graduation. Each is a Christian and feels sure that "this is the one for me." When together, however, they are finding it increasingly difficult to control their sexual desires. Recently they started "helping" each other to orgasm by hand. After all, they say, they are still saving the best for marriage. To them, their "heavy petting" is really a way of relieving sexual pressure and thus preventing them from going "all the way." What are the moral issues involved in Jeff and Cynthia's case? Is their behavior appropriate for Christians? What principles inform your view?

Glossary

Adultery: Voluntary sexual intercourse between a married person and someone other than his or her marriage partner; also includes voluntary thoughts of such activities.

Celibacy: State of being unmarried and sexually abstinent; understood either as a gift from God or simply as a circumstance of life.

Chastity: Sexual purity and responsibility in actions and thoughts, either within or outside of marriage.

Erotic: Having to do with sexual arousal and desire.

Fornication: Voluntary sexual intercourse between an unmarried man and an unmarried woman.

Gender: Maleness or femaleness.

Incest: Sexual relations between close relatives, most commonly reported between a father or stepfather and daughter or stepdaughter.

Intercourse (sexual): Intimate sexual activity involving penile penetration; also known as coitus.

Lust (sexual): Strong desire for illegitimate sexual involvement.

Masturbation: Stimulating oneself sexually, usually to orgasm.

Petting: Fondling another person's sexually excitable body parts.

Pornography: Sexually explicit pictures, writing, or other materials designed to arouse sexual desires.

Promiscuity: Sexual behavior characterized by casual, superficial relationships and frequent changes of partners.

Rape: Sexual intercourse without the consent of one of the partners.

Sex: Either the reality of being male or female (gender), or the erotic attraction and/or genital activity between persons.

Sexuality: Quality of being male or female or (more commonly) the awareness of and responsiveness to this aspect of human existence.

Annotated Bibliography

Countryman, L. William. *Dirt, Greed, and Sex.* Philadelphia: Fortress, 1988. Scholarly yet readable study of sexual ethics in the New Testament and their implications for today; liberal conclusions.

Foster, Richard J. *Money, Sex and Power: The Challenge of the Disciplined Life.* San Francisco: Harper & Row, 1985. Contains four valuable chapters on sexuality and spirituality, sexuality and singleness, sexuality and marriage, and the vow of fidelity.

Grenz, Stanley J. "The Purpose of Sex: Toward a Theological Understanding of Human Sexuality." *Crux* 26, 2 (1990): 27–34. Views human sexuality as God's gift to bring us to one another and to himself.

———. *Sexual Ethics.* Dallas: Word, 1990. The most comprehensive evangelical theological study of sexual morality available.

Hanigan, James P. *What Are They Saying about Sexual Morality?* New York: Paulist, 1982. Helpful overview of Roman Catholic controversies in the post-Vatican II era.

Kubetin, Cynthia A., and James Mallory. *Beyond the Darkness: Recovery for Adult Victims of Sexual Abuse*. Houston and Dallas: Rapha/Word, 1992. Helpful information and guidance for those affected by sexual abuse.

Leadership 9, 1 (Winter 1988). Whole issue devoted to Christian sexual themes and problems from an evangelical pastoral perspective.

Lebacqz, Karen. "Appropriate Vulnerability: A Sexual Ethic for Singles." *The Christian Century* (6 May 1987): 435–38. Instead of celibacy for singles, argues for "vulnerability," defined as the willingness to be exposed or wounded.

Nelson, James B. *Between Two Gardens: Reflections on Sexuality and Religious Experience*. New York: Pilgrim, 1983. A liberal ethicist builds on his earlier work, *Embodiment*, arguing for a "sexual theology" rather than a theology of sexuality.

Penner, Clifford, and Joyce Penner. *The Gift of Sex: A Christian Guide to Sexual Fulfillment*. Dallas: Word, 1981. Comprehensive marriage manual; Lewis Smedes says, "The best book about sex and marriage I have ever read."

Rouner, Arthur A., Jr. *Struggling with Sex*. Minneapolis: Augsburg, 1987. An evangelical call to marriage-centered sexual life; sees "self-pleasuring" (masturbation) as acceptable for singles.

Small, Dwight Hervey. *Christian: Celebrate your Sexuality*. Old Tappan, N.J.: Revell, 1974. Well-written account of the historical development of Christian thinking about sex, and a scripturally based theology of sexuality.

Smedes, Lewis B. *Sex for Christians*. Grand Rapids: Eerdmans, 1994. Revised. Widely-read overview of sexual morality in singleness and marriage; his "responsible petting" approach is too permissive for many evangelical Christians.

Spong, John Shelby. *Living in Sin?* New York: Harper & Row, 1988. One-sided argument for abandoning traditional Christian sexual ethics; written by a highly controversial Episcopal bishop.

Stafford, Tim. *The Sexual Christian*. Wheaton: Victor, 1989. Excellent application of biblical principles to the contemporary sexual confusion.

Thielicke, Helmut. *The Ethics of Sex*. New York: Harper & Row, 1964. Very highly regarded, serious study of marriage and sexual ethics by a German Protestant theologian.

Wenham, David. "Marriage and Singleness in Paul and Today." *Themelios* 13, 2 (January/February 1988): 39–41. Sees human sexuality as very good, but not the highest good, and to be enjoyed according to the Maker's instructions.

White, John. *Eros Redeemed: Breaking the Stranglehold of Sexual Sin*. Downers Grove: InterVarsity, 1993. Biblical, personal guidance from a well-respected psychiatrist on healing from sexual sin. Includes chapters on gender confusion, forgiving family sin, Satanic ritual abuse, and masturbation (seen as both sinful and psychologically damaging).

Wilson, Earl D. *Sexual Sanity.* Downers Grove, Ill.: InterVarsity, 1984. Wise counsel for those seeking to break free from uncontrolled sexual habits.

5

Homosexuality

New York City psychotherapist Ralph Blair attended three well-known evangelical educational institutions, served on the staff of a major evangelistic parachurch organization, and is a member of the Evangelical Theological Society. Yet Blair is a **homosexual.** He founded Evangelicals Concerned, a national ministry for homosexuals and those who want to understand and assist homosexuals in their unique struggles. And he believes that a person can be both a committed Christian, acknowledging the lordship of Christ and biblical infallibility, and a **practicing homosexual** in a loving, monogamous relationship.

Is a monogamous homosexual union permissible for a Christian? No responsible Christian endorses casual promiscuous sex between homosexuals any more than between heterosexuals. But Blair and an increasingly vocal minority of Christians believe that a committed partnership between two homosexuals is another matter. The Universal Fellowship of Metropolitan Community Churches, a denomination founded in 1968, consisting mostly of homosexual members, yet affirming traditional Christian doctrines, holds a position much like Blair's. What is an acceptable evangelical response to this view?

Understanding and addressing adequately the issues involved in the subject of homosexuality requires some basic definitions. **Homosexuality** (male or female) is the persistent and predominant sexual disposition of an individual toward persons of the same sex. This definition is, of course, quite general and says nothing about the cause of homosexuality or whether the person actually engages in genital sexual activity with others.

Because the word *homosexuality* is something of an umbrella term, theorists distinguish between **homosexual orientation** (also known as **constitutional homosexuality** or **inversion**) and homosexual practice. A constitutional homosexual is a person who has such a strong attraction to those of the same sex that it is not possible to develop deep heterosexual desires. These persons frequently contend that they have been aware of their homosexual orientation from early in life, from childhood or the teen years. Many, if not most, constitutional homosexuals say they are homosexual by nature, not by nurture.

A person who practices homosexual acts is not necessarily a constitutional homosexual. A person may engage in same-sex activities for a limited time (e.g., in prison or in a same-sex boarding school), yet prefer heterosexual activity when the opportunity is present. Such a person is sometimes called bisexual although this term more precisely describes those who have an equal preference for the same or opposite sex when either is available. Homosexual persons commonly refer to themselves as **gay,** either gay men or **lesbians** (homosexual women). Homosexual practices are frequently referred to by non-gay persons as **sodomy.** In the strictest sense of the term, this is sexual union by anal penetration, whether homosexual or heterosexual, but in the broader sense it is sexual activity of any kind involving practicing homosexuals.

When used alone, the terms *homosexuality* and *homosexual* refer to the orientation, but not necessarily the practice. This enables the sensitive Christian to avoid problematic statements like "Homosexuality is sin" and "No homosexual will be in heaven." While conservative Christian ethicists agree that homosexual acts and participation in the so-called gay lifestyle are sinful, they do not generally hold that the condition itself calls down the wrath of God on a homosexual person.

Some Christians, delivered from their homosexual desires, marry someone of the opposite sex and live successfully as heterosexuals. Other homosexuals, however, seek just as earnestly to please God but still struggle with same-sex yearnings, sometimes all their lives. For them, abstinence from sexual activity with others, while difficult, is preferable to living in violation of God's moral standards, just as abstinence from sexual partnerships is preferable for committed Christian heterosexuals who are single. The term *homosexual,* then, relates primarily to what people *are* rather than to what they *do*. Thus, some homosexuals are sexually active, while others are not.

Liberal ethicist James Nelson believes that loving, same-sex relationships, including genital expression, may be just as pleasing to God as **heterosexual** unions. In addition to defending this view, Nelson outlines a fourfold typology of possible theological-ethical approaches to homosexuality. The *rejecting-punitive* position is the most negative stance toward homosexuality. This is followed, in order of increasing toleration of homosexuality, by the *rejecting-nonpunitive* view, the *qualified-acceptance* view, and the position of *full acceptance*. Because most contemporary ethicists within the Christian tradition who write seriously about homosexuality argue for either the second or the fourth view, we have focused on these positions in our selections.

Nelson's article presents the full-acceptance view succinctly and clearly. This is followed by two representatives of the rejecting-nonpunitive stance. British biblical scholar David F. Wright provides an overview of the most significant Scriptures bearing on the question of homosexuality. He challenges the popular liberal view that the biblical texts commonly used to argue against the acceptability of homosexual behavior do not apply to present-day issues. Next, psychologist Stanton Jones reasons that, while specific biblical passages clearly teach against homosexual behavior, the core of Scripture's negative assessment of homosexual actions is the positive biblical view of sexuality. He also disputes some leading gay theology arguments and urges nongays to demonstrate responsible and loving behavior toward homosexuals.

In the final selection, social activist Ronald Sider offers valuable guidance regarding the AIDS crisis. In addition, he opposes **homophobia,** the irrational fear of (and sometimes hostility toward) homosexuals, while at the same time he notes that those who oppose homosexual behavior are not necessarily homophobic. A person may, on moral grounds, disapprove of same-sex genital activity yet respect homosexuals as fellow human beings made in God's image. Biblically-oriented Christians oppose fornication and adultery, but they are not afraid of nor hostile toward fornicators and adulterers. Those who hold to the rejecting-nonpunitive view agree that homophobia and heterophobia are wrong.

How prevalent is homosexuality? For years homosexual advocates have claimed that approximately ten percent of American males are homosexual. However, the basis for this claim, a study by sex researcher Alfred Kinsey in the 1940s, is seriously flawed. A 1993 survey by the Alan Guttmacher Institute, the most thorough examination of American men's sexual practices since the Kinsey report, reveals very different statistics. According to this study, about two percent of American men have engaged in homosexual acts and one percent consider themselves exclusively homosexual. These findings are similar to recently published statistics from Britain, Canada, France, Denmark, and Norway. While the Guttmacher study did not survey female homosexuality, recent surveys by the University of Chicago's National Opinion Research Center found that while 2.8 percent of the male population say they are exclusively homosexual, 2.5 percent of women consider themselves practicing lesbians.

The cause or causes of homosexual inversion are widely debated. In the August, 1991, issue of *Science,* neuroscientist Simon LaVay of the Salk Institute in San Diego published "A Difference in Hypothalamic Structure Between Heterosexual and Homosexual Men." After studying the brain structures of gay and **straight** men, he concluded that one tiny node of the hypothalamus (a part of the brain involved in regulating sexual behavior) is nearly three times larger in heterosexual males than in homosexual males. He also reported that the anatomical form of the node (which is about the size of a grain of sand) is quite similar in women and gay men, both of whom differ substantially from straight males in this respect. While some homosexual advocates claim that LaVay's study proves that homosexuality is inborn, not acquired, further analysis of the research has cast doubt on this conclusion. LaVay, himself a homosexual, cautions that his study shows only correlation, not proof of causation. He admits that the smaller size node in gay men might just as likely result from, rather than cause, their behavior. The size of bodily organs can vary with the demands made on them. LaVay and other scientists also note that the study sample was so small as to be statistically unreliable.

Scientists are also scrutinizing and debating the 1992 and 1993 studies conducted by J. Michael Bailey and Richard Pillard on twins and homosexual tendencies, and the 1993 report by Dean Hamer and his colleagues suggesting a possible genetic basis for homosexuality. The twin study, for example, found that 52 percent of identical twin brothers of self-identified gay men were also gay, compared to 22 percent of fraternal twins and 11 percent of adoptive brothers. While these results seem to point toward a genetic factor in homosexuality, critics ask, among other questions, why are the other half of the identical twins (who are genetic carbon copies of their gay brothers) not homosexual?

Due to the nature of science, researchers will continue to investigate possible causative factors for homosexuality, just as they do for other conditions. Biblical Christians need not fear such studies. But we do need to recognize the difference between objective, well-based research, with its restrained and cautious presentation of results, and the sensational tabloid-style reporting of such findings as assured results.

David Lanier, a clinical psychologist, gives another important caution. Since at least the days of Copernicus, the relationship between science and the church has been an uneasy one. Because Christians sometimes fail to appreciate the nature of scientific inquiry, every time scientific results conflict with established religious views, and science is shown to be correct, the credibility of the gospel suffers. This is unnecessary, however. The fight between Galileo and his opponents, for example, should never have occurred since the church did not have a scriptural basis for holding the Ptolemaic geocentric view of the universe. Lanier notes that evangelicals who practically make it a doctrine that homosexuality stems from choice alone, not biology, are making the same mistake. Scientists may someday demonstrate conclusively that there is a significant genetic link to homosexuality. If this happens, and if some Christians believe they must fight the evidence to defend the faith, they may once again suffer defeat in an unnecessary war.

Even if genetic or hormonal factors are shown to influence people in the direction of homosexuality, such data do not justify homosexual activities. A number of severe mental disorders, including some that induce violent behavior, are rooted in neurological and chemical abnormalities, yet we do not legitimize violent and antisocial behaviors. We concentrate instead on prevention and cure. Since every scriptural mention of homosexual conduct is disapproving, traditional Christians believe they cannot justify such actions because some biological factors may predispose a person toward them. Predisposition toward a certain type of behavior does not necessitate or legitimize that behavior.

According to Dr. Elizabeth Moberly and other contemporary researchers, abnormalities in family life and their effect on psychological development are significant factors leading to homosexual orientation. Numerous case studies support this perspective, often showing that unsatisfactory relationships with one or both parents, or the absence of the same-sex parent, is characteristic of homosexuals in their early childhood. While direct causation is not hereby established, much evidence points to psychosocial patterns and the failure to identify successfully and early (before the age of five) with the parent of the same gender as significant factors in homosexual formation. A considerable number of scholars support the view that in at least some homosexuals, one's basic sexual tendency is fairly well established in early childhood, usually by ages five to seven. This is not something chosen nor brought about by genital arousal, although in adolescence, when erotic awareness develops, one chooses how to act sexually. The adolescent who has developed a healthy gender identification may experiment with homosexual practices for a time, but does not continue long with same-sex interests. But the one who has been homosexually preconditioned may not only experiment but participate actively in a homosexual lifestyle.

Probably no one theory can account for all cases of homosexual inversion. A combination of factors is likely. Evangelical ethicists like Stanton Jones argue, however, that whatever nonvoluntary factors have contributed to an individual's homosexual inclination, the person is morally accountable for his or her sexual behavior. Just as a person (due to environmental and possible hereditary factors) with a tendency toward alcoholism should not drink alcoholic beverages, so a homosexually oriented person needs to refrain from homosexual activities. Just as God can enable a single heterosexual to live, perhaps for a lifetime, without sexual partners, so God can enable a homosexual to live a pure life. Temptation is not sin, and God in grace has assured his children that we will not be tempted above what we are able to endure (1 Cor. 10:13).

Can a homosexual person change to a heterosexual orientation? Gay advocates vigorously deny that homosexuals ever change, arguing that those who do leave a gay lifestyle are either not genuinely homosexual or are frustrated sexually in their new life. There is abundant evidence, however, to the contrary. Bob Davies is executive director of Exodus International, a worldwide referral and resource network of eighty ministries that share the belief that homosexuals can find genuine freedom from their homosexual life-patterns. Davies and Lori Rentzel, a freelance writer and editor, have written *Coming Out of Homosexuality.* In this valuable work, Davies and Rentzel, who have worked in the field of exgay ministry since 1979, report that they know hundreds of men and women who have left behind the homosexual lifestyle, and they include testimonies of several of these in the book. Some, they say, have been free from homosexual involvement for ten or twenty years and are not just suppressing homosexual longings. There has been a true resolution of this issue in their lives. Studies of conversion from a homosexual to a heterosexual lifestyle show that from one-third to nearly two-thirds of those who desire to change are successful. However, reversal of one's sexual outlook does not happen overnight. It is usually a gradual and difficult process, and homosexual desires sometimes remain, even when they are not welcomed or acted upon.

The question of homosexuality will continue as a hot ethical issue (some say the hottest) in the church and society for years to come. While the vast majority of Christians do not approve of genital sex between homosexuals under any circumstances, they believe we should manifest the same love and compassion shown by Jesus in his contacts with those whose conduct he could not endorse. Rather than condemnation, homosexuals need genuine Christian love, understanding, and warm, trusting relationships, both male and female. (For further help on these issues, contact Exodus International at P.O. Box 2121, San Rafael, CA 94912; phone 415-454-1017.)

Homosexuality

An Issue for the Church

James B. Nelson

The Bible and Homosexuality

A brief survey of pertinent scriptural passages must begin with a word about our interpretive principles.[1] My first hermeneutical assumption—and the most fundamental one—is that Jesus Christ is the bearer of God's invitation to human wholeness and is the focal point of God's humanizing action; hence, Jesus Christ is the central norm through which and by which all else must be judged. Second, I believe that the interpreter must take seriously both the historical context of the biblical writer and the present cultural situation. Third, we should study the Bible, aware of the cultural relativity through which we perceive and experience Christian existence. And, fourth, our scriptural interpretation should exhibit openness to God's truth which may be revealed through other disciplines of human inquiry.

With these in mind, let us turn to the Bible, noting first that nowhere does it say anything about homosexuality **as a sexual orientation.** Its references are to certain kinds of homosexual **acts.** Understanding of homosexuality as a psychic orientation is relatively recent. It is crucial that we remember this,

---

1. More expanded interpretations of the scriptures on the issue of homosexuality may be found in numerous places. I am indebted to a number of authors, particularly Derrick Sherwin Bailey, *Homosexuality and the Western Christian Tradition* (1955; reprint, Hamden, Conn.: Shoe String Press, 1975); Joseph C. Weber, "Does the Bible Condemn Homosexual Acts?" *Engage/ Social Action,* 3, 5 (May 1975); Helmut Thielicke, *The Ethics of Sex,* translated by John W. Doberstein (New York: Harper & Row, 1964); and H. Kimball Jones, *Toward a Christian Understanding of the Homosexual* (New York: Association Press, 1966). Especially helpful on the hermeneutical issues in this context is James T. Clemons, "Toward a Christian Affirmation of Human Sexuality," *Religion in Life,* 43, 4 (Winter 1974).

for in all probability the biblical writers in each instance were speaking of homosexual acts undertaken by those persons whom the authors presumed to be **heterosexually** constituted.[2]. . .

What are we to make of those Old Testament passages which, in addition to rape, condemn other homosexual acts? (See, for example, the Holiness Code in Leviticus 18:22, and 20:13; also Deuteronomy 23:17 and 1 Kings 14:24, 15:12, and 22:46.) Cultic defilement is the context of these passages. Canaanite fertility worship, involving sacral prostitution and orgies, constituted a direct threat to Yahweh's exclusive claim. Yahweh was the God who worked through the freedom of human history and not, primarily, through the cycles of biological life. Thus, sexuality was not to be seen as a mysterious sacred power, but rather as part of human life to be used responsibly in gratitude to its Creator. In this context these texts are most adequately interpreted, and this central message is utterly appropriate to the norm of the new humanity which we meet in Jesus Christ.

Also, remember that a common Middle East practice during this period was to submit captured male foes to anal rape. Such was an expression of domination and scorn. As long as homosexual activity was generally understood to express such hatred and contempt, particularly in societies where the dignity of the male was held to be of great importance, any such activity was to be rejected summarily.[3]

In the New Testament we have no record of Jesus' saying anything about homosexuality, either as a sexual orientation or as a practice. The major New Testament references are found in two Pauline letters and in 1 Timothy. The context of Paul's widely-quoted statement in Romans 1:26–27 is clearly his concern about idolatry. Three things should be noted. First, concerned about the influence of paganism on the Roman Christians, Paul sees homosexual expression as a result of idolatry, but he does not claim that such practices are the *cause* of God's wrath. Second, in this passage we have a description of homosexual *lust* ("consumed with passion for one another") but not an account of interpersonal homosexual love. Third, Paul's wording makes it plain that he understands homosexual activity as that indulged in by heterosexuals, hence that which is contrary to their own sexual orientation. Thus, it is difficult to construe Paul's statements as applicable to acts of committed love engaged in by persons for which same-sex orientation is part of the giveness of their "nature." Indeed, Paul uses "nature" as a flexible concept expressing varying concerns in different contexts. An ethical position that condemns homosexuality as a violation of natural law must turn to

---

2. See John McNeill, S. J., "The Homosexual and the Church," 5. (Mimeographed address given to the first national convention of Dignity, an organization for Catholic homosexuals. No date.)

3. Ibid.

a non-biblical philosophical position—but not to Pauline material—for its content.[4]

Paul's other reference to homosexual acts (1 Cor. 6:9–10) is similar to that of the writer of 1 Timothy (1:8–11). Both passages list practices which exclude people from the Kingdom, acts that dishonor God and harm the neighbor, including thievery, drunkenness, kidnapping, lying, and the like. Thus, if it is apparent that here homosexual acts are not singled out for special condemnation, it could also be argued that there was general disapproval. What, then, are we to make of Paul's moral judgment in this case? Perhaps we should accept Paul for what he was—a peerless interpreter of the heart of the Gospel and one who was also a fallible and historically-conditioned person. If the norm of the new humanity in Jesus Christ obliges us to question the apostle's opinions about the proper status of women and the institution of human slavery, so also that norm obliges us to scrutinize each of his moral judgments regarding its Christian faithfulness for our time—including his perception of homosexuality.

Surely, the central biblical message regarding sexuality is clear enough. Idolatry, the dishonoring of God, inevitably results in the dishonoring of persons. Faithful sexual expression always honors the personhood of the companion. Sexuality is not intended by God as a mysterious and alien force of nature, but as a power to be integrated into one's personhood and used responsibly in the service of love.

Theological Stances toward Homosexuality

A typology of four possible theological stances toward homosexuality can begin with the most negative assessment.[5] A *rejecting-punitive* position unconditionally rejects homosexuality as Christianly legitimate and bears a punitive attitude toward homosexual persons. While no major contemporary theologians defend this position, and while official church bodies have moved away from it, this stance unfortunately is amply represented in Christian history.

If we have been ignorant of the persecutions of homosexuals, it is not without reason. Unlike the recognized histories of other minority groups, there has been no "gay history." Heterosexual historians usually have considered the subject unmentionable, and gay historians have been constrained by the fear of ceasing to be invisible. A conspiracy of silence has resulted. Yet, the facts are there. Stoning, sexual mutilation, and the death penalty were fairly common treatment for discovered homosexuals through centuries of the West's history. While the Church frequently gave its bless-

---

4. Weber, "Does the Bible Condemn?" 34.
5. Labels similar to mine have been used by several writers in attempts to sort out differing theological positions.

ings to civil persecutions, in its internal ecclesiastical practice its disapproval was even more frequently shown through the refusal of sacraments and ostracism from the common life.[6]

The rejecting-punitive stance today may be milder in its usual manifestations, though it continues to bear highly punitive attitudes along with its theological arguments. If the latter are based upon a selective biblical literalism, the former are rooted in familiar stereotypes. All lesbians are hard, and all male gays effeminate; homosexuals are compulsive and sex-hungry; male gays are inherently prone to child molestation; homosexuals are by nature promiscuous. Each of the preceding stereotypes has been thoroughly discounted by reliable research, but they persist in the minds of many, buttressed by untenable biblical interpretations. But the key criticism of this stance is simply the incongruity of a punitive orientation with the Gospel of Jesus Christ.

The *rejective-nonpunitive* stance must be taken more seriously, for no less eminent a theologian than Karl Barth represents this view.[7] Since humanity is "fellow-humanity," says Barth, men and women come into full humanity only in relation to persons of the opposite sex. To seek one's humanity in a person of the same sex is to seek "a substitute for the despised partner," and as such constitutes "physical, psychological and social sickness, the phenomenon of perversion, decadence and decay." This is idolatry, for one who seeks the same-sex union is simply seeking oneself: self-satisfaction and self-sufficiency. While Barth says homosexuality thus is unnatural and violates the command of the Creator, he hastens to add that the central theme of the Gospel is God's overwhelming grace in Jesus Christ. Hence, *homosexuality* must be condemned, but the homosexual *person* must not.

William Muehl argues for the rejecting-nonpunitive position from a more consequentialist stance.[8] Maintaining that "the fundamental function of sex is procreation" and that homosexuality is an illness comparable to alcoholism, Muehl then turns his major attention to social consequences. Sheer acceptance of homosexuality would have "implications for our view of marriage, the limitations appropriate to sexual activity, the raising of children, and the structure of the family." Since we are relatively ignorant concerning such potentially grave social results, Muehl argues, we should respect the historic position of the Church, which rejects homosexuality.

The rejecting-nonpunitive stance appears to rest upon two major stated arguments and two major unstated assumptions—each open to serious

6. See Louis Crompton, "Gay Genocide: From Leviticus to Hitler," address delivered to the Gay Academic Union, New York University, November 30, 1974 (mimeographed).
7. See Karl Barth, *Church Dogmatics*, vol. 3, part 4, *The Doctrine of Creation* (Edinburgh: T. & T. Clark, 1961), esp. 166.
8. William Muehl and William Johnson, "Issues Raised by Homosexuality," *Y.D.S. Reflection* 72, 4 (May 1975).

question. The first stated argument is that of natural law and idolatry. At this point Barth seems to forget our human historicity, apparently assuming that human nature is an unchangeable, once-and-for-all substance given by the Creator. Actually, our human nature is shaped in some significant part by the interaction of people in specific periods of time with specific cultural symbols and specific historic environments. Committed to this alternative interpretation, Gregory Baum fittingly writes, "In other words, human nature as it is at present is not normative for theologians . . . What is normative for normal life is the human nature to which we are divinely summoned, which is defined in terms of mutuality. This, at least, is the promise of biblical religion." After examining the evidence of mutual fulfillment in committed gay couples, Father Baum concludes, "Homosexual love, then, is not contrary to human nature, defined in terms of mutuality toward which mankind is summoned."[9]

Barth's idolatry judgments appear to rest on several additional—and equally questionable—assumptions. One is that procreative sex is divinely commanded and normative. Yet, in light of the Gospel and of our current human situation, we might better say that, while responsible love and sexual expression cannot be sundered, procreation and sex cannot be irrevocably joined. Another assumption is that there can be no "fellow humanity" apart from the opposite sex. But is it not more biblical to maintain that there is no genuine humanity apart from *community*? Still another assumption is that homosexuality means a "despising" of the other sex—an assertion without logical or factual foundation. Indeed, many homosexuals exhibit the ability to establish deeply meaningful and loving relationships with members of the opposite sex precisely because sexual "conquest," in whatever form, is excluded from the situation. And, the logic of Barth's argument at this point would seem to be that *heterosexuals* by their nature should despise members of *their* own sex. Finally, Barth maintains that homosexuality is idolatrous because it is basically self-worship. It is as if the classic syllogism were to be changed to read as follows: "I love men; Socrates is a man; therefore, I love myself." Nonsequitur. In actuality, compared with heterosexual couples, committed gay couples show no intrinsic or qualitative differences in their capacities for self-giving love.

The second major argument of the rejecting-nonpunitive position is that undesirable social consequences probably would result from homosexual acceptance. This argument appears to rest on a major unspoken assumption: that homosexuals in fact do have meaningful choice about their same-sex orientation. If one makes this assumption, then one might (as Muehl appears to do) draw a further conclusion: that societal acceptance would

---

9. Gregory Baum, "Catholic Homosexuals," *Commonweal*, 14 February 1974, 480f.

188 James B. Nelson

bring in its wake a significant increase in the numbers of those choosing homosexuality.

Such assumptions must be radically questioned. Actually, statistics show no demonstrable increase in homosexual behavior in the quarter century since Kinsey's study, in spite of *somewhat* less punitive social attitudes in recent years.[10] Further, it is probable that greater acceptance of homosexuality would have *desirable* consequences for families and childrearing: emotional intimacy among same-sex heterosexual family members would be less inhibited by unrecognized homosexual fears, and syndromes of alienation and destructive rejection of the homosexual child in the family would be lessened.

The great majority of homosexuals do not appear to have meaningful choice concerning their orientation any more than do the great majority of heterosexuals. There exists today no general agreement about the cause of homosexuality. Major theories cluster around two different approaches, the psychogenic and the genetic, but both remain in dispute. It is significant, however, that in 1973 the Trustees of the American Psychiatric Association removed homosexuality from that association's list of mental disorders, saying, "homosexuality per se implies no impairment in judgment, stability, reliability, or general social or vocational capabilities."

The minority of gay persons who have sought therapeutic treatment to reverse their sex orientation have experienced an extremely low success rate. Behavioral modification programs using aversive therapy have conditioned some homosexuals against attraction to their own sex, but most frequently they have been unable to replace that with attraction to the opposite sex, a dehumanizing result. Indeed, Dr. Gerald C. Davison, who developed and popularized the "orgasmic reorientation" technique, recently disavowed his own treatment, calling on behavior therapists to "stop engaging in voluntary therapy programs aimed at altering the choice of adult partners."[11]

The other underlying assumption appears to be this: that theological positions and ecclesiastical practices which reject homosexuality can, in fact, be nonpunitive toward those persons so oriented. This, too, must be radically questioned, and we shall do so in the context of the next major position.

The third major theological option is that of the *qualified acceptance* of homosexuality. Helmut Thielicke provides its best articulation. His argument follows several steps. First, similar to Barth's contention, Thielicke maintains, "The fundamental order of creation and the created determina-

10. Compare the Kinsey statistics with the more recent estimates of Morton Hunt. A good discussion of the comparison is in the review of Hunt's book *(Sexual Behavior in the 1970's)* by Wardell B. Pomeroy in *SIECUS Report* 2, 6 (July 1974): 5f.

11. See Kenneth Goodall, "The End of Playboy Therapy," *Psychology Today* (October 1975).

tion of the two sexes make it appear justifiable to speak of homosexuality as a 'perversion' . . . (which) is in every case *not* in accord with the order of creation."[12] But Thielicke is more open than Barth to the results of contemporary psychological and medical research. Thus, he takes a second step: "But now experience shows that constitutional homosexuality at any rate is largely unsusceptible to medical or psychotherapeutic treatment, at least so far as achieving the desired goal of a fundamental conversion to normality is concerned."[13] Further, homosexuality as a *predisposition* ought not to be depreciated any more than the varied distortions of the created order in which all fallen people share.

But what of sexual expression? *If* the homosexual can change his or her sexual orientation, such a person should seek to change. Admittedly, however, most cannot. Then such persons should seek to sublimate their homosexual desires and not act upon them. But some constitutional homosexuals "because of their vitality" are not able to practice abstinence. If that is the case, they should structure their sexual relationships "in an ethically responsible way" (in adult, faithfully committed relationships). Homosexuals should make the best of their painful situations, without idealizing them or pretending that they are normal.

More than Barth and Muehl, Thielicke is empirically informed and pastorally sensitive on this issue. But his position is still grounded in an unacceptably narrow and rigid version of natural law. As such, in spite of its greater humanness, his argument becomes self-contradictory. In effect the gay person is told, "We heterosexual Christians sympathize with your plight, and we believe than any sexual expression in which you engage must be done in an ethically responsible way—but do not forget that you are a sexual pervert!"

An ethics of the Gospel ought never forget that moral responsibility is intrinsically related to self-acceptance, and that self-acceptance is intrinsically related to acceptance by significant others and, ultimately, by God. Gay persons in our society frequently have been told by their families that they do not belong to them, by the Church that they are desperate sinners because of their sexual orientation, by the medical profession that they are sick, and by the law that they are criminals. In the face of such rejection, the amazing thing is that so many are emotionally stable and sexually responsible. If emotional problems still have a higher incidence among gay persons (as they do within any oppressed social group), we should cut through the vicious circle of self-fulfilling prophecy and recognize where the root of the problem lies—in societal oppression. Thielicke fails to do this. More humane though his position is, by continuing to label same-sex orientation

12. Thielicke, *The Ethics of Sex*, 282.
13. Ibid., 283f.

as a perversion of God's natural law, he encourages continuing punitive attitudes toward homosexuals and in consequence undercuts his own hope for more responsible sexual relationships.

The fourth major theological possibility is *full acceptance.* While it usually makes the assumption that homosexual orientation is much more a given than a free choice, even more fundamentally this position rests on the conviction that same-sex relationships are fully capable of expressing God's humanizing intentions.

Though still in a minority, the advocates of full Christian acceptance are increasing in number. In 1963 the English Friends stated in their widely-read *Towards a Quaker View of Sex:* "One should no more deplore 'homosexuality' than left-handedness . . . Homosexual affection can be as selfless as heterosexual affection, and therefore we cannot see that it is in some way morally worse."[14]

Among individual theologians, Norman Pittenger has articulated this position most fully.[15] God, he affirms, is the "Cosmic Lover," ceaselessly and unfailingly in action as love, and manifested supremely in Jesus Christ. God's abiding purpose for humankind is that in response to divine action we should realize our intended humanity as human lovers—in the richest, broadest, and most responsible sense of the term. Our embodied sexuality is the physiological and psychological base for our capacity to love.

For all of its continuity with animal sexuality, human sexuality is different. As persons our sexuality means the possibility of expressing and sharing a total personal relationship in love. And such expression contributes immeasurably toward the destiny to which we are all intended. Hence, abnormality or deviance should not be defined statistically, but rather in reference to the norm of humanity in Jesus Christ. Gay persons desire and need deep and lasting relationships, just as do heterosexual persons, and appropriate genital expression should be denied to neither.

Thus, the ethical question according to Pittenger is this: what sexual behavior will serve and enhance, rather than inhibit, damage, or destroy our fuller realization of divinely-intended humanity? The appropriate answer is a sexual ethics of love. This means commitment and trust, tenderness, respect for the other, and the desire for ongoing and responsible communion with the other. On its negative side, such an ethics of love mandates against selfish sexual expression, cruelty, impersonal sex, obsession with sex, and against actions done without willingness to take responsibility for their con-

14. Friends Home Service Committee, *Towards a Quaker View of Sex* (London: Friends House, 1963), 45.
15. See Norman Pittenger, *Time for Consent* (London: SCM Press, 1970); *Making Sexuality Human* (Philadelphia: Pilgrim Press, 1970); *Love and Control in Sexuality* (Philadelphia: United Church Press, 1974); "A Theological Approach to Understanding Homosexuality," *Religion in Life* 43, 4 (Winter 1974).

sequences. Such an ethics always asks about the meaning of any particular sexual act in the total context of the persons involved, in the context of their society, and in the context of that direction which God desires for human life. It is an ethics equally appropriate for both homosexual and heterosexual Christians—there is no double standard.

A Personal Note

It is obvious by this point that my own convictions favor the full Christian acceptance of homosexuality and its responsible genital expression. I have felt quite personally the force of each of the other stances described in this article, for at various earlier periods in my life I have identified, in turn, with each one, beginning as a teenage with the full complement of anti-homosexual stereotypes. In recent years, both through theological-ethical reflection and through personal friendships with some remarkable gay persons, I have become increasingly convinced that the positions of both Barth and Thielicke inadequately express the implications of the Gospel on this issue.

Reinhold Niebuhr has powerfully argued that Christians must learn to live with the tension of "having and not having the truth." "Tolerance" in its truest sense, he maintained, is experienced when, on the one hand, a person can have vital convictions which lead to committed action and, on the other hand, that same person can live within the reality of forgiveness. The latter means experiencing divine forgiveness for the distortion of one's own understanding and having the willingness to accept those whose convictions sincerely differ. Hopefully, it is in such spirit that this personal note is written, and in such[16] spirit the heterosexual reader is invited to wonder with me at this point about three possibilities.

One possibility is that "the homosexual problem" may be more truly a heterosexual problem. We are learning that "the Black problem" is basically the problem of white racism, and that "the woman problem" is basically the problem of male sexism. So, also, we might well wonder whether or not "the homosexual problem" could be rooted in a homophobia frequently experienced by heterosexuals.[17]

My own experience suggests this. While in the preceding paragraphs for the sake of economy, I have simply used the terms "heterosexual" and "homosexual" (or "gay"), the best available evidence indicates that we are all bisexual to some degree. True, most of us, for reasons not yet fully understood, develop a dominant orientation toward one or the other side of the

16. Reinhold Niebuhr, *The Nature and Destiny of Man,* vol. 2, *Human Destiny* (New York: Scribner's, 1943), chap. 8.
17. See George Weinberg, *Society and the Healthy Homosexual* (Garden City, N.Y.: Doubleday, 1973), esp. chap. 1. Webster defines "phobia" as "an irrational, excessive, and persistent fear of some particular thing or situation."

continuum. But Kinsey's early research repeatedly has been confirmed: on the scale of sexual orientation relatively few persons fall near the "zero" and (exclusively heterosexual) and relatively few approach the "six" mark (exclusively homosexual).

Though, for the majority of us, our adult genital expression may have been exclusively heterosexual, it is quite probable that we do experience homosexual feelings even if such are frequently relegated to the unconscious level. And males in our society generally have the greater difficulty with this, inasmuch as we have been continuously subjected to exaggerated images of masculinity. Thus, I believe it is worth pondering whether *some* of our common reactions against homosexuality might be linked to secret fears of homosexual feelings in ourselves—Freud's "reaction formation," defending against an impulse felt in oneself by attacking it in others.

Gay people may also represent threats to us in other related ways. The gay man seems to belie the importance of "super-masculinity," and his very presence calls into question so much that "straight" males have sacrificed in order to be manly. Homosexuals appear to disvalue commonly-held public values related to marriage, family, and children. Because we so frequently judge others by our own standards, those who obviously deviate from them appear to be seriously deviant. And, strangely enough, homosexuals may awaken in heterosexuals a dimly-recognized fear of death. Sometimes our hopes of vicarious immorality through our children and grandchildren are stronger than our resurrection faith. Then the presence of the gay person who (usually) does not have children may reawaken the fear of death, even though its conscious experience may be a nameless anxiety. I wonder.

Second, I wonder how much of the heterosexual reaction against homosexuality is related to male sexism. I suspect that *some* of our responses are. Surely, the more severe biblical condemnation of male homosexuality was not unrelated to the status of the male in a patriarchal society. For a man to act sexually like a woman was serious degradation (literally loss of grade). And in our own society where male sexism remains a serious problem, it is still the male who more commonly experiences homophobia. Indeed, the striking parallelism between so many arguments against homosexual acceptance with arguments against full acceptance of women-men equality ought to make us reflect on this.

Third, I wonder about the possibilities of augmented liberation for us all were a greater acceptance of homosexuality to come. Many of us have experienced some diminution of our own homophobia bringing new possibilities of tenderness, lessened competitiveness, and greater emotional intimacy with those of our own sex. Many of us males have become more conscious of the connection between the uses of violence and our needs for assurance of our virility, and we wonder whether greater understanding and acceptance of our own homosexual impulses might not well contribute to a more peaceful society. The list of liberating possibilities could be expanded, but perhaps the point is clear. In any event, I wonder about the relation between Jesus' apparent silence concerning homosexuality and Jesus as the image of authentic human liberation.

Precisely because we must live with "having and not having the truth" it is important that we share our serious wonderings. Perceptions of sincere Christians will differ on this issue, but we can all attempt to invite each other into our quests for fuller understanding of that humanity into which God invites us all. . . .

From James B. Nelson, "Homosexuality: An Issue for the Church," *Theological Markings* 5, 2 (Winter 1975): 41–52.

Homosexuality

The Relevance of the Bible

David F. Wright

It has become almost a commonplace in the contemporary discussion of homosexuality—whether ethical, theological, or ecclesiastical-disciplinary—that the Bible has little or no direct or specific light to cast on our modern problems. This verdict may be illustrated by the words of Robin Scroggs:

> Not only is the New Testament church uninterested in the topic, it has nothing new to say about it . . . *Biblical judgments against homosexuality are not relevant to today's debate.*[1]

This broad position, which is standard fare in liberal writing, may be said to rest on a single conviction—that the biblical texts are invariably found to be talking about or alluding to only something quite different from what poses the real dilemmas today. The difference may vary from text to text, but the points of reference or concern to the biblical writers do not match ours.

This paper seeks to challenge this consensus, or at least to put some sharp questions to it, by means of a re-examination of the main texts and of the processes of reasoning commonly applied to them. In the bygoing it should provoke discussion about the criteria or methods whereby we assess the relevance of biblical material to present-day issues. For convenience I will follow the biblical order—which does not imply importance or priority. Each text of course merits extended exegesis, which it is impossible to provide in this context. . . .

---

1. *The New Testament and Homosexuality* (Philadelphia: Fortress, 1983), 101, 127.

Leviticus 18:22, 20:13

The textual meaning here is not in dispute. Although the precise physical form of homosexual intercourse may not be certainly identifiable, no body of opinion claims that this is at issue—as though what is banned is only a posit in parallel to heterosexual congress, but not necessarily other forms, such as anal intercourse.

Two reasons are commonly advanced for limiting the scope of the Levitical law—the ritual context of the Holiness Code, and the cultic context of the proscription of Egyptian or Canaanite religion. They may be two sides of the same coin, and are in any case not easily separable. The claim is made that the prohibition is no more of general reference or lasting import than the ban on cutting your beard in a certain way (19:27) or making a garment out of two different materials (19:19) or intercourse during menstruation (18:19) and so on. Since we no longer entertain similar notions of ritual impurity or are faced with homosexual behaviour associated with heathen idolatry, this part of the Mosaic law has nothing to say to the permanent-loving-preference type of homosexuality.

The argument has to recognize that many other unambiguously sinful acts are also encompassed by the Levitical code, such as bestiality (18:23) and child sacrifice (18:21), the immediate neighbours of 18:22, and adultery (20:10) and incest (18:6ff). These chapters undoubtedly place a great mixture of activity and conduct under the ban, but is there no way of discriminating between the more and less grave?

Another way to pose the issue is to ask whether the Mosaic law reprobated behaviour simply because the Canaanites indulged in it. This would presumably mean that it condemned everything the Canaanites did, which is scarcely a tenable possibility.[2] Is it not eminently more reasonable to argue that the Canaanites' cultic homosexual prostitution (if that is what it was) provided a further reason for avoiding Canaanite religion—because homosexual relations were unacceptable on more fundamental grounds than their contextual association with pagan cult? After all, the Israelites did not need, one assumes, to be informed about the Canaanite practice of child sacrifice before they could know whether it was permissible for them to dispose of their children in this way. To put it another way, is it conceivable, from what else we know about Mosaic or Israelite ethics, that child sacrifice or homosexuality would have been tolerated if disinfected of their Canaanite associations?

In any case, the argument goes on, the whole of the Levitical legislation lapsed in the Christian church:

---

2. See G. Wenham, "Homosexuality in the Bible," in *Sexuality and the Church*, ed. Tony Higton (Hockley, Essex: Kingsway Publications, 1987), 31.

It would simply not have occurred to most early Christians to invoke the authority of the old law to justify the morality of the new: the Levitical regulations had no hold on Christians and are manifestly irrelevant in explaining Christian hostility to gay sexuality.[3]

This sounds like a historical statement (i.e., rather than an assertion of what they should have done, on theological or ethical grounds). In the context it considerably underestimates the early Christian citation or appeal to the two verses in question.[4] It also misses a weightier consideration which I will raise below.

Romans 1:26–27

Two or three main arguments are commonly advanced against discerning here a permanent position for Christian ethics to adopt. For many interpreters, Paul's diatribe is merely preformed tradition, typical of the strictures passed on the immoral world by Hellenistic moralists such as Philo and Plutarch. It is entirely conventional, contributes nothing distinctively Christian, and may tell us little about the behaviour of real people in Paul's day.

Others discount the passage by highlighting, as with Leviticus (and the two cases are often felt to reinforce each other), the links between idolatry and perverse sexuality. Even if it is not cultic prostitution that is in view, Paul is indicting activity that issues from corrupt religious roots (vv. 23, 25). His horizon does not extend beyond the consequences of worshipping creatures rather than the creator. He is surely not saying anything of the highly moral homosexual monogamy of faithful Christians.

And if you attempt to counter this disqualification by drawing attention to Paul's argument from nature, the reply comes back that it is a very versatile, not to say slippery or devious, device in Paul's hands: does not 'nature' teach us that long hair is degrading for a man (1 Cor. 11:14)? Nature may be nothing more than convention, fashion, common use and wont. Paul is not propounding an argument from natural law or even a conviction based on the doctrine of the creation of human nature, male and female.

John Boswell's ingenuity delivers a further coup de grâce. Paul has in view only those individuals who abandoned their own natural dispositions in order to engage in same-sex behaviour—contrary to *their* nature. They are in fact heterosexuals who defy their own heterosexuality.[5] This interpretation has not been without its followers, but need detain us least of all. Its atom-

---

3. John Boswell, *Christianity, Social Tolerance and Homosexuality* (Chicago: University of Chicago Press, 1980), 105.
4. For the evidence see my article "Homosexuals or Prostitutes? The Meaning of ἀρσενοκοῖται (1 Cor. 6:9, 1 Tim. 1:10)," *Vigiliae Christianae* 38 (1984): 125–53.
5. Boswell, *Christianity, Social Tolerance and Homosexuality*, 108–12.

istic concept of nature seems to me to require a highly contrived, not to say esoteric, reading of the passage. It also entails in Paul an awareness of the difference between homosexual and heterosexual natures that most students of the subject find nowhere in antiquity. It would enable one to distinguish between two types of homosexual practitioners—in Bailey's terms, between perverts and inverts.

What few have sufficiently weighed is Paul's linking together of male and female same-sex conduct. What is for us an instinctive association was very rare in antiquity, not least because female homosexuality is rarely mentioned.[6] Prior to Paul I know of only two writers who subject them to common condemnation—Plato and Ps-Phocylides.[7] Scroggs, who makes much of the character of the Pauline material as merely 'preformed tradition', is aware of the difficulty of pointing to any relevant 'preformed tradition' in this case, but is not thereby deterred.

The linkage has implications beyond the question of Paul's originality, to which we shall return. It bears also on his meaning, for the parallelism strongly suggests that Paul gives us something like a generic condemnation of homosexuality. This is to say, he sees beyond particular forms of same-sex relations or same-sex relations in particular contexts to what it is that enables one to lump both female and male conduct together. For if, as most scholars hold, the only pattern of male homosexuality that Paul could have known or dreamt of was pederasty, there is no counterpart on the female side. From what we know of the latter, the arguments used to limit Paul's [criticisms of] pederasty and so to disenfranchise it cannot be applied to the unnatural relations of woman with woman.

Indeed, the equivalence in Romans 1 bids us not be so dismissive toward Paul's appeal to nature. This is assuredly a widespread category in the moral writers of the Hellenistic era, particularly as a result of the influence of Stoicism. But the allusions in the chapter to divine creation (vv. 20, 25) justify us in believing that the argument from nature has to be taken with great seriousness. In my view its force is not lessened by involving the active/aggressive v. passive/receptive form of gender expectations to which it often gave rise. What has to be shown (and I firmly believe the *onus probandi* [burden of proof] lies on this interpretation) is that Paul did not believe that male and female were created for each [other] with complementary sexualities grounded in the distinctive constitutions of their sexual organs.

Before advancing certain more general considerations pertinent to Romans 1 we must turn to the last textual evidence to be considered.

---

6. See Scroggs, *The New Testament and Homosexuality*, 140–4, and B. Brooten, "Patristic Interpretations of Romans 1:26," *Studia Patristica* 18, 1 (1985): 287–91.

7. Cf. Scroggs, *The New Testament and Homosexuality*, 131, 141.

1 Corinthians 6:9, 1 Timothy 1:10

We have in fact already passed in review the major factors that lead many commentators to refuse to allow any abiding ethical significance in the occurrences in these two verses of the Greek term *arsenokoitēs*.

For Scroggs and his ilk, Paul and the Paulinist have simply taken over a conventional vice-list from the moral literature of Hellenistic Judaism or even secular Hellenistic writers. As such it tells us nothing in detail about his attitude to particular forms of behaviour; it serves merely to convey a generalized outlook on society. It bears little or no relation to the kind of people the Corinthian Christians may previously have been, or indeed to the ills of their Corinthian milieu. Its 'traditional form . . . forbids an assessment in terms of the contemporary scene, as if, for example, we had to do with a realistic description of conditions in Corinth.'[8]

The tradition determines that Paul could have in mind only the particular form of male homosexuality that was culturally dominant, namely pederasty, as analysed by Kenneth Dover and others. It is to the undesirable features of that kind of relationship that *arsenokoitēs* refers, and not in principle to same-sex intercourse. Some writers, including Scroggs, believe that we can more closely define the meaning of the term. Both of its uses condemn very specific forms of pederasty; 1 Timothy has in view 'the enslaving of boys or youths for sexual purposes, and the use of these boys by adult males', and 1 Corinthians condemns only 'the active partner who keeps the *malakos* (effeminate call-boy) as a "mistress" or who hires him on occasion to satisfy his sexual desires.'[9] Scroggs holds in particular that insufficient regard has been had by historians to homosexual prostitution, which enables us to interpret the *arsenokoitēs* as an exploitative, aggressive participant in this commerce. I think Scroggs is entangled in a deep inconsistency—between identifying the Pauline vice-lists as essentially 'preformed tradition' and discerning in the two occurrences of *arsenokoitēs* not only surprisingly precise forms of pederasty but two different expressions of it. The two elements in his case are linked together by such profound analytic insights as the following: 'it is not hard to imagine that Paul's basic attitude toward pederasty could have been seriously influenced by passing a few coiffured and perfumed call-boys in the marketplace'.[10] Chacun à sa imagination!

Professor Boswell is almost alone in questioning whether anything homosexual is involved in this Greek term at all. He concludes that it denotes 'male sexual agents, i.e., active male prostitutes, who were common throughout the Hellenistic world in the time of Paul',[11] who may have ser-

---

8. H. Conzelmann, *I Corinthians*, Hermeneia (Philadelphia: Fortress, 1975), 101.
9. Scroggs, *New Testament and Homosexuality*, 108.
10. Ibid., 43.
11. Boswell, *Christianity, Social Tolerance and Homosexuality*, 344.

viced male or female clients. He reaches this position by construing the word in a manner calculated to evoke from classical linguists only scornful derision. It does not mean 'those (males) who lie with males' but 'males who lie with' others, whether male or female. Compounds of *arren*—when spelled with *rs* instead of *rr* make it the subject or qualifier of the second element, not its object. This is patent nonsense; the difference is purely dialectal.[12]

What Boswell and many other writers (but not Scroggs) have failed to notice is the significance of Paul's choice of *arsenokoitai,* which is not attested before 1 Corinthians. Whether Paul coined it we cannot tell, but it is certainly a coinage of Hellenistic Christianity or Judaism. What should by now have occasioned more surprise is that, if Paul or his source wanted to condemn pederasty, he did not use one of the many words or phrases currently in common use to refer to it. Instead he employed a new term—and one fashioned on the basis of those Levitical prohibitions:

meta arsenos ou koimēthēsē koitēn gynaikos (18:22)
koimēthē meta arsenos koitēn gynaikos (20:13)

One clearly need look no further for the inspiration of this Jewish or Christian neologism. Scroggs recognizes this (although he inclines, in my view implausibly, to seeing the Greek term as the equivalent of the rabbis' semi-technical phrase based on Leviticus—*mishkav (b)zakur,* but the difference between us is not great at this point). But he then devises for the word a meaning that forgets its provenance. Boswell's eccentric etymology at least has this much in its favor, that it faces up to the word itself.

Confirmation of the derivation of the word from the LXX of Leviticus comes from what is probably its next occurrence, in the *Sibylline Oracles* 2:73. Here it is found in what may be one of the Christian interpolations of the Jewish base, but it is more likely to be of Jewish origin, for it appears in a section closely related to the Hellenistic-Jewish gnomic wisdom collection known as the *Sentences* of Ps-Phocylides, although *arsenokoitēs* itself does not occur in the latter. Ps-Phocylides, according to its latest editor, originated in Alexandria roughly between 30 B.C. and A.D. 40. The relevant part of the collection, which appears in very similar form in the *Sibylline Oracles,* betrays heavy Levitical influence.

Now no one claims that Leviticus had pederasty in mind! Paul has in fact adopted or fashioned a term which is little more than a substantival transcript from Leviticus (LXX) and which speaks simply of males sleeping with males. Oddly enough, despite the liberal consensus, the New Testament at

12. See my extended refutation in the article cited in note 4 above, and my paper, "Early Christian Attitudes to Homosexuality" forthcoming in *Studia Patristica,* for a broader critique of Boswell's handling of patristic material.

no point obviously refers to pederasty at all. It might be overarguing to claim that Paul in his choice of language seems to have deliberately avoided the plethora of terms current to denote pederasty, but if he had wanted to condemn only pederasty, let alone only the highly specific vices detected by Scroggs, he went a very odd way about it.

It may be thought that this argument is too etymological, recalling the shades of Kittel and the pre-Barr era. It is true of course that had Paul used an explicitly pederastic word, it would not have followed that he meant by it solely pederasty. For so dominant was the pederastic form of homosexuality that its vocabulary had come to refer to other forms, almost generically. Thus Hellenistic Jewish writers like Philo talk about the Sodomites as pederasts. This usage has persisted even to the present day; cf. our 'rent-boys', who are normally adults. The early medieval penitential literature similarly speaks of adult partners in homosexuality as 'boys'. My argument from *arsenokoitēs* does not stand alone, but forms a double cord with the distinctiveness of Romans 1:26–27.

In particular, the argument that Paul is merely retelling preformed tradition is decidedly shaky. Scroggs persists in it despite the fact that he cannot point to any source that Paul may be presumed to have known which combines a condemnation of both male and female homosexuality in the manner of Romans 1. Nor is the situation with the vice-lists quite so clear-cut with respect to the Pauline verses. Many a commentator claims that the vices itemized in these two verses derive from the common content of many such lists, but hardly anyone provides firm evidence to back this up. The exegete's and the translator's quandary over *arsenokoitēs* arises in part precisely from the lack of plain parallels in lists earlier than 1 Corinthians.[13]

It need not be a corollary of derivation from conventional moralistic wisdom that Paul/the Paulinist is not addressing a concrete context in these letters. The selection made from pre-existing vice-catalogues may reflect the writer's awareness of the local problems or the social composition of the church.[14] Is it in any case a sound or reasonable deduction from the use of traditional material that its user cannot be directing or adapting it to a live audience or real-life situation? This is a useful point at which to draw out some general considerations in conclusion.

General Conclusion

How can we determine, if Paul does not use specific language, that he has only specific abuses in view? Such an assertion is in effect the stance of

13. Cf. Conzelmann's silence in *1 Corinthians*, 102, on the occurrence of this particular term in other lists.
14. See an argument to this effect for 1 Cor. 6 by P. Zaas, '1 Corinthians 6:9ff: Was Homosexuality Condoned in the Corinthian Church?' *Society of Biblical Literature Seminar Papers* 2, 17 (1979): 205–12.

Scroggs *et multi alii*, although it has too often rested on inadequate linguistic analysis. One might ask the converse: if a writer attacks pederasty in an unmistakable manner but uses the vocabulary of 'male' rather than 'boy', would we again be required to conclude that his hostility was without prejudice to his estimate of any other form of homosexuality? I have argued that the distinctiveness of both the word *arsenokoitēs* and the content of Romans 1:26–27 at least prima facie reveals Paul's extrapolating from the particular to the general. Why should the fact that the only form of homosexuality Paul could have known about at all directly was pederasty, whether involving prostitution or not, be allowed to dictate the conclusion, in the face of linguistic evidence to the contrary, that he could not have been passing a broader judgment, and that his opinion of other patterns of homosexuality is quite indeterminable?

My rebuttal of such a position is twofold: not only has insufficient regard been taken of the precise originality of Paul's statements, but also inadequate heed has been paid to what else we know of Paul's mind, which is neither so inaccessible that we may father upon him some of the wilder speculations found in this area of discussion, nor so 'cribbed, cabined and confined' by the phenomena of contemporary society that he was incapable of formulating a moral judgment with a reach beyond the immediately observable. I find it quite inconceivable, from what else I know of Paul's mind, e.g. on the significance of the one-flesh heterosexual union, that he could have countenanced any model of same-sex genital relationship. This assessment of mine (which I merely summarize rather than substantiate at length) confirms me in my conclusions drawn from a close analysis of Paul's particular statements. Scrogg's failure is partly one of inadequate scrutiny of the trees and partly one of missing the wood for the trees.

A final issue concerns the question of originality in another sense. What if we decide that Paul has nothing to say about homosexuality that goes beyond the wisdom of the Old Testament and later Judaism? Does it devalue his strictures if they display nothing distinctively Christian? I leave aside here the question whether nothing of a distinctively Christian kind about homosexuality can be deduced from what Paul says elsewhere about sexual relations (e.g. in 1 Corinthians 6). My answer to my own question will not be hard to predict, for I have discerned special significance precisely in the fact that in *arsenokoitēs* Paul deliberately sided with the Levitical ban. But quite apart from this, Conzelmann's comment is pertinent:

> The fact that Christianity takes over the Jewish ethic must be theologically understood. Christianity regards itself not as a new system of ethics, but as a practical exercise of the will of the long-known God.[15]

15. Conzelmann, *1 Corinthians*, 101.

While I doubt if this can be viewed as wholly satisfactory as a generalization, Christianity's adoption of Jewish ethical attitudes should not of itself be treated as somehow sub-Christian or negligible. Plenty of evidence from antiquity could be advanced to show that you did not have to be Jewish, or even Stoic, let alone Christian, to condemn pederasty as contrary to nature. Why should Christianity's sharing of common ground with earlier traditions be sufficient cause not to take it seriously?

What price originality? I conclude that Paul's lay partly in being unoriginal. Although Paul said remarkably little about homosexuality (which may in itself be open to varying hypothetical explanations), what he does say reveals a remarkable originality, in part by adopting the broader perspectives of the tradition that derived from the Old Testament and from Leviticus in particular.

From David F. Wright, "Homosexuality: The Relevance of the Bible," *Evangelical Quarterly* 61, 4 (1989): 291–300.

The Loving Opposition

Stanton L. Jones

When asked why they think homosexual behavior is wrong, many Christians reply simply, "Because the Bible says it is!" The Bible does indeed condemn homosexual acts every time they are mentioned. But many Christians are unprepared for the revisionists' arguments for rejecting all the major biblical texts as either irrelevant or misunderstood.

This is a thumbnail sketch of what one will hear from critics of the traditional view:

They argue that Leviticus 18:22, 20:13, and Deuteronomy 23:18, which condemn male homosexual behavior, are irrelevant because they do not address today's homosexual lifestyles. These passages occur in the midst of a discussion of God's disapproval of the fertility cults in the pagan communities surrounding the Israelites. The only kind of homosexual behavior the Israelites knew, it is argued, was homosexual prostitution in pagan temples. That is what is being rejected here and not the loving monogamous gay relationship of persons of homosexual orientation today.

The Genesis 19 story of Sodom and Gomorrah is alleged to be irrelevant because it is a story of attempted gang rape, which was an indicator of the general wickedness of the city. The homosexual nature of the gang rape is seen as an irrelevant detail of the story.

Romans 1 is often reduced to being a condemnation solely of heterosexual people who engage in homosexual acts. They rebel against God by engaging in what is unnatural to them. This passage has no relevance today, it is argued, because modern homosexuals are doing what is natural to them and thus not rebelling against God.

In 1 Corinthians 6:9 and 1 Timothy 1:10, the Greek words that are often translated as referring to homosexual practices are said to be unclear and probably describe and forbid only pederasty, the sexual possession of an adolescent boy by an older adult man of the elite social classes.

Some of these criticisms have an element of legitimacy, but most evangelical biblical scholars concur that every one of them goes too far. The critics are right, for instance, in dismissing the view that homosexual preoccupation was the most heinous sin of Sodom and Gomorrah. Ezekiel 16:49–50 says, "Now this was the sin of your sister Sodom: She and her daughters were arrogant, overfed and unconcerned; they did not help the poor and needy. They were haughty and did detestable things before me. Therefore I did away with them" (NIV). Materialistic America in general, and not just the gay community in particular, is uncomfortably similar to this description of Sodom's sins. We are quick to condemn those we are uncomfortable with but slow to judge ourselves.

But Leviticus, Romans, 1 Corinthians, and 1 Timothy are relevant and binding. Archaeological studies confirm that the ancient world knew of homosexual desire and practice, even if the concept of a psychological orientation was not present. Thus it is striking that *every time homosexual practice is mentioned in the Scriptures, it is condemned.* There are only two ways one can neutralize the biblical witness against homosexual behavior: by gross misinterpretation or by moving away from a high view of Scripture.

Important as they are, these passages are not the cornerstone of the Christian stance that homosexual action is immoral. The core of Scripture's negative assessment of homosexual practice is the positive biblical vision of sexuality—which applies equally to homosexual persons and to heterosexual, men and women, adults and children. . . .

The heart of Christian sexual morality is this: God made sexual union for a purpose—the uniting of husband and wife into one flesh in marriage. God uses sexual intercourse, full sexual intimacy, to weld two people together (1 Cor. 6:16). God has a big purpose in mind for sex because he has a big purpose for marriage—something bigger than simply a means for us to get our sexual needs met, have fun, have kids, and not have to be lonely.

In Ephesians 5 we learn more of what this bigger purpose is. According to Paul, marriage is to model concretely here on earth what God wants in the relationship between Christ and his bride, the church. Jesus is one with the Father, and he tells us that we can be one with him. We are utterly different from God, but he wants to unite with us (1 Cor. 6:17). This reality can be uniquely modeled on earth through the union of two different kinds of human beings, male and female. Marriage is a living parable, a concrete symbol, that models for the world the mystical union of Christ and his people. According to God's original design, marriages have grand, even cosmic, meaning. And this meaning remains regardless of how pathetically short we fall of that grand design.

Interestingly, the scientific evidence supports this. If it is God's intent that sexual intercourse is to bond two people together for life in marriage, what would we expect the effect of premarital sex and cohabitation to be? Those actions should make marriage less likely to work. And that is what the facts show (especially in a recent study reported by Andrew Greeley in his book *Faithful Attraction*). The more premarital sex people have, the more likely they are to have affairs in marriage; the less likely they are to have optimal sexual relationships in marriage; and the less likely they are to be satisfied with their marriages. Numerous studies over decades have shown that people who cohabit before marriage are more likely to divorce. All of the ways we humans foul up God's design have long-term negative consequences.

If marriage occupies this place in God's plan, and if sex is so important to God's plan for marriage, we can see the vital importance of obedience to God's standards for sexuality. Sex is a gift, but it is a gift we can abuse. God's intent is that sex be used rightly inside and outside of marriage. Inside of marriage, its proper use is for pleasure, procreation, and as something to be shared lovingly and with gratitude to build up the unity of the couple. Outside of the marriage of a man and woman, the proper use of sex is to honor God by costly obedience in living a chaste life. Through this difficult commitment, we learn to value obedience over gratification and to serve God instead of serving our own lusts. Heterosexual or homosexual, the call of Christ is the same: if you find yourself unmarried, God wants you to live a chaste life.

But isn't this unfair to the homosexual person? The heterosexual single at least has the chance of marriage. The person with homosexual longings has no such chance. He did not choose to have the feelings and inclinations he does. Is it fair to Mark to argue that God is calling him to a life of chaste singleness? Is it fair to Gail to suggest that God would have her forgo motherhood because she is not married?

First, let us acknowledge that few people choose to have homosexual inclinations. The evidence suggests that genetic factors, possibly operative through brain differences, may give some a push in the direction of homosexual preference. Disordered family relationships that leave people confused at a deep level about their sexual identity seem also to play a major role. In addition, early homosexual experiences of seduction or abuse may play a role . . . And many lesbians, especially, seem to have been the targets of sexual abuse by men earlier in life, leaving them with deeply impaired abilities to trust or feel close to men later.

But the existence of inclinations, orientations, or preferences have little to do with God's moral call on our lives. Social science is finding many powerful factors that shape character and influence morally laden choices. Alcoholism, anxiety-proneness, ill-temperedness, and even the propensity to violence are made more likely by the presence of genetic and family variables.

Is it unfair, then, for God to hold up sobriety and moderation, trust and faith, self-control and patience, restraint and respect, as moral values?

No, because God is the Maker, the one who sets the design. And though God is perfectly just, he never promised to be fair by human standards. We are saved by grace, but in the race that Paul talks about—the race to press on to the high calling of Christ—some of us start farther back in the pack than others, farther back from the ideal. But that does not make the goals that God ordains illegitimate or nonbinding.

While one ideal, heterosexual marriage, is not an option for the homosexual Christian without a large dose of divine healing, the other ideal, chaste singleness, is open and accessible. And that ideal of chaste singleness holds out the possibility for true integrity and beauty, as the models of Jesus himself, Paul, and many other saints show. The fact that such chastity is difficult for homosexual persons is of little moral consequence, as it is also difficult for heterosexuals. The difficulty should be dealt with pastorally, not by changing the moral standard.

And so, the Christian vision for sexuality and marriage is our foundational reason for rejecting homosexual action as a legitimate moral option. A warning, though: many gay Christians will simply deny that this is the binding Christian view. Many advocates of a liberalization of the church's ethical stance suggest that the only element of the Bible or of the Christian tradition that is binding on all people is the general call to manifest in any relationship the kinds of loving characteristics that are described as being important in marriage—sacrificial love, honesty, and so forth. Gay relationships, it is argued, can do this as well as straight.

The first problem with this argument is that it does not truthfully reflect the Christian tradition. It is ultimately irrelevant whether or not homosexual couples can be just as loving, faithful, or monogamous as heterosexual couples. God has a distinctive purpose for sex and for marriage, a purpose that necessitates a heterosexual union.

Second, the revisionist's argument simply does not match reality. For example, male homosexuality tends to be strongly associated with promiscuity: The famous Bell and Weinberg study *(Homosexualities)* suggested that about a third of gays have had over one thousand sexual partners in their lifetimes. Very few gays are in committed, long-term relationships; Bell and Weinberg found that less than 10 percent of gays are in such relationships. Those who are in stable relationships do not tend to be sexually monogamous. McWhirter and Mattison *(The Gay Couple)* found that 0 percent of the one hundred stable male couples they studied were sexually monogamous after being together for five years. The authors of that study, themselves a gay couple, said that to be gay is to be nonmonogamous, and that monogamy is an unnatural state that some gay men attempt because of their internalized homophobia; so when you finally grow to accept your own gay-ness, you shed monogamy [as] a butterfly sheds a cocoon.

It may be that the homosexual community cannot embrace monogamy because homosexual sex can never produce what God made sex for. They turn instead to promiscuity and perversions to create sexual highs. The gay community calls these perversions "high-tech sex." Many know of oral and anal sex, but fewer know of commonly, though not universally, practiced activities such as sadomasochistic practices of inflicting pain on a partner during sex, group sex of all kinds, and more extreme distortions. When sex outside of God's will does not do what God made it to do, many people, gay and straight, search for some way to make sex deliver an ever bigger electric charge, the elusive ultimate orgasm, that can somehow make up for the absence of what sex was meant to create: unity.

In summary, persons of homosexual inclination are under the same moral call as we all are—to respond to the offer of divine mercy and forgiveness through the gift of Jesus Christ, to offer our lives as the only gift we can give in return. If we love him, we will obey his commands. And his will with regard to our sexuality is either that we live chaste lives of dependence on him, or that we strive to build a marriage that models Christ's love for the church before the watching world, aided by the uniting gift of sexual inter-course. All of us should strive anew to live by this holy standard.

Why Is the Issue Important?

Homosexual acts are like every other sin: They violate God's express will and distort God's creational design. Just as much fire from our pulpits should be aimed against greed, pride, racism, lack of compassion, and spir-itual lukewarmness as against homosexual behavior. The best estimates today suggest that 1 to 3 percent of the population engage in homosexual acts (*not* the 10 percent that badly biased research once suggested). In this light, why should homosexuality be a special concern for the church?

There are three reasons why this issue is important, and none of them has anything to do with homosexual people being especially bad or disgusting.

First, the church's historically high view of the authority of Scripture is threatened by efforts at revising the church's position on homosexuality. As was argued earlier, the only way to neutralize the biblical witness against homosexual behavior is either grossly to misrepresent the Bible or to under-mine its authority. The apologists for the "gay Christian" movement tend to do both.

While claiming to be staunchly within the Christian tradition, revisionists terribly distort biblical sexual ethics. In his book *Come Home! Reclaiming Spirituality and Community as Gay Men and Lesbians*, Presbyterian minister Chris Glasser says that *fidelity* does not mean being sexually exclusive and monogamous; *fidelity* really means only keeping your promises. So if a gay Christian companion promises to have only five other lovers per year, he is being faithful if he stays within those limits.

Episcopal biblical scholar William Countryman, in his book *Dirt, Greed, and Sex,* adopts a biblical theology that allows for homosexual practice, but he at least has the courage to admit that his method of interpretation also makes prostitution and sex with animals legitimate options for Christians (as long as such acts are done in love).

In her book *Touching Our Strength,* Carter Heyward, an Episcopal ethicist, suggests that heterosexual marriage enslaves women. She calls instead for loving sexual friendships; and there is no reason to limit these life-giving "godding" relationships to only one person or to one sex.

The majority group of the Presbyterian Special Committee on Sexuality, which authored *Presbyterians and Human Sexuality, 1991,* claimed that God's Word to us is those parts within the Bible that are just and loving, that liberate people and make them more satisfied and fulfilled; the rest is simply not God's Word. Therefore, since the prohibition against sex outside of marriage oppresses and frustrates single people and denies their sexual rights, the committee argued, then this could not be God's Word.

The second reason why homosexuality is an important issue is that what the Bible treats as an isolated *act* to be condemned (namely, people of the same gender having sex), our society treats as a fundamental element of personal *identity.* In this view, the people I described at the beginning are not people who engaged in certain acts or who have certain inclinations. Rather, they *are* homosexuals—gays and lesbians. Their sexual inclinations define most deeply who they are. If a sexual desire defines a person, then acting on that desire is essential to personhood. If we buy this logic, then to suggest that God does not want them to engage in homosexual acts is to insult their innermost beings.

The Christian response is to deny the legitimacy of defining a person by his or her sexual desires—or by any other fallen element of one's nature. In Christ, our identities are based on our status as God's adopted children. This is the foundation for understanding who we most truly are.

Paul teaches in Romans 6:16 that we do not just find or discover ourselves; rather, we build a moral and personal momentum by the choices we make. We are either becoming more a slave to sin or a greater slave to Christ. If what you mean by saying you are a homosexual is that you experience homosexual desire, that is reality. If what you mean by saying you are a homosexual is that your identity is defined by your gayness and that living out those sexual leanings is essential to your very nature, then your identity is misplaced; you are trying to build an identity on shifting sand.

It is for this reason that Christians must continue to strive to love the sinner but hate the sin, even though this saying drives the gay Christian community crazy. We can say and strive for this because we refuse to make homosexual behavior or preference the core of anyone's identity.

The third reason this issue is vital today is that there is unrelenting pressure on the church to change its historic stance. The revisionists present it as a simple issue: The church has evolved in rejecting slavery, racism, and sexism, and now it is time to stop its most deeply entrenched bigotry—homohatred, heterosexism, and homophobia.

But again we encounter a problem: We can only change our position on homosexuality by changing our fundamental stance on biblical authority, by changing our core view of sexuality, and by changing the meaning and character of Christ's call on our lives. The first two have already been addressed above; but we need to say more about the nature of Christ's call on our lives.

Christ is our perfect model of love and compassion, and we have much to learn from his love for sinners and participation in their lives. But he did not just ooze warm fuzzies; Christ also had the gall to tell others how to live their lives, to insist that his truth was the only truth, and to claim that he alone was the way to God. In short, Jesus was what many people today would call a narrow-minded bigot.

And we, the church, have been entrusted with proclaiming the message that we have received from him. When we do, we risk being called rigid and narrow-minded. We must face the reality that Christianity "discriminates." It says one path is the right way. Christians make a ridiculous set of claims: that an omnipotent God bothered to create and love us; that he let us and our forebears spit in his face in rebellion; that he chose a peculiar and unsavory primitive tribe to be his conduit for blessing; that he actually revealed what he wanted these people to believe and how they were to live; and that this God actually became a person and died for us to conquer sin and death on our behalf. That is a most unlikely story! But Christians are supposed to spread the news that this is *the* story, the only true story.

The church has, in each generation, been faced with new challenges, which are really new twists on old issues. The current movement to see gay persons as a social group that must be loved and accepted as they are is the latest form of an old challenge—the challenge to diminish the authority of God's revelation, to understand people on their own terms rather than by God's view of them, and fundamentally to amend the nature of Christ's call to take up our crosses and follow him.

What Are We to Do?

In this difficult time, there are two things that we must do. They are two things that do not naturally go together. We must exhibit the very love and compassion of Jesus Christ himself. And we must fearlessly proclaim the truth that Jesus Christ himself proclaimed and embodied.

The key to compassion is to see ourselves in another, to see our common humanity. This is what many of us cannot or will not do. A certain degree of natural revulsion to homosexual acts per se is natural for heterosexuals. All of us should be thankful that there are at least some sinful actions to which we are not naturally drawn. But a revulsion to an act is not the same as a revulsion to a person. If you cannot empathize with a homosexual person because of your fear of, or revulsion to, them, then you are failing our Lord. You are guilty of pride, fear, or arrogance. And if you are causing others to stumble, you are tying a millstone around your own neck.

The homosexual people I know are very much like me. They want love, respect, acceptance, companionship, significance, forgiveness. But like all of us sinners, they choose the wrong means to get what they want.

We, the church, have the opportunity to demonstrate, in our words and in our lives, God's love for the homosexual person. If we truly love, we will act on that love. We must start by eradicating our negative responses to homosexual people. Stop the queer jokes and insults; they hurt others. We must deal with our own emotional reactions; we must decide to love. We must repudiate violence and intolerance toward persons of homosexual orientation. We must change the church so that it is a place where those who feel homosexual desire can be welcomed. The church must become a sanctuary where repentant men and women can share with others the sexual desires they feel and still receive prayerful support and acceptance.

Are you willing to pray with, eat with, hug and comfort, share life with a woman or a man who has homosexual feelings? Frequently, we already do but do not know it. Just as we share meals with gluttons, shop with the greedy, share compliments with the vain, and vegetate with the slothful—and as others share life with us without knowing our hidden sins—so we share life, knowingly or unknowingly, with the homosexual. But we need to do so knowingly and lovingly.

Now the second part of our call—to speak the truth. If we truly love, we will not shrink from speaking God's view of homosexual behavior. Do not be deceived: increasingly today we are defined as unloving solely for viewing homosexuality as immoral, regardless of the compassion we exhibit. Nevertheless, we must strive to be loving when we voice our opposition. Compassion in no way entails an acceptance of the gay lifestyle any more than it entails affirming an adulterer's infidelity.

As people of homosexual inclination follow our Lord down the narrow road, they can pray and hope for healing. There are two prevalent distortions about healing today. The first is the conservative Christian myth that a quick, sincere repentance and prayer for healing will instantly change the person. Thankfully, few spread this damaging myth today.

The more prevalent myth is that there is no hope for healing. Anyone who says there is no hope is either ignorant or a liar. Every secular study of change has shown some success rate, and persons who testify to substantial healing by God are legion. There is hope for substantial change for some in this life.

But while our ultimate hope is secure, we do not have certainty about how much healing and change is possible for any particular homosexual person. Some will never be healed in this life. We need to balance a Christian triumphalism with a theology of suffering, a recognition that we are a hurting and beaten-down race. We must not believe the world when it tells us there is an easy answer to everything, even when the speaker is a Christian. There is dignity and purpose in suffering. The Christian homosexual's witness is not invalidated by pain and difficulty; Christians trust that there is always a deeper purpose in suffering.

Mark, my Christian brother who still longs for healing while he lives a celibate life, and many like him, need to be assured by the church of the meaningfulness of [their] pilgrimage. We need to remember that Christians witness to their faith not just in their strength and triumph, but also in their brokenness. We can be Christlike in how we bear our sufferings. We all want to be triumphant ambassadors for Christ, but few of us are. Our homosexual brothers and sisters who follow our Lord in costly discipleship have much to teach all of God's people.

While challenges are nothing new for God's body on earth, they are nonetheless real challenges. This is an important moment for the church, with many denominations and institutions debating whether to change the church's traditional teaching on homosexuality. Those of us involved in the debate must remember that we can fail in two directions.

First, we can fail by compromising (and thus undermining) God's authoritative Word, rejecting God's view of sexuality, and embracing a human-centered notion of costless acceptance. The challenge here is to resist the pressure and courageously articulate God's truth regarding sexuality.

Second, we can fail by saying the right things but in the wrong way. Too many Christians have let hate slip into their rhetoric on this issue. The challenge here is to be the loving opposition, to imitate our Lord, who chases down his sinful creatures with aggressively open arms while all the while saying no to our sins. We all need to repent of our arrogant and intolerant attitudes toward those whose struggles are different from ours. Our goal must be to become a community that embodies the welcoming grace and love of our Lord Jesus Christ.

From Stanton L. Jones, "The Loving Opposition." Used by permission, *Christianity Today* (19 July 1993): 19–25.

AIDS

An Evangelical Perspective

Ronald J. Sider

How should Christians respond to people with AIDS? Our Christian understanding of both creation and redemption tells us that people with AIDS are of inestimable worth, persons so important and precious in the sight of their creator and redeemer that God declares them indelibly stamped with the divine image. Indeed, people with AIDS are so special that the Creator of the galaxies declares that his Son's death on the cross was precisely for them. No matter how weak or frail, no matter how marginalized or despised, no matter how ravaged by wrong choices, people with AIDS enjoy the full sanctity of human life. So we offer them our love and support, no matter how inconvenient or costly. That is the first, middle, and last thing to say.

To be sure, there are other things that must be added. But only secondarily. One crucial test of our commitment to the sanctity of human life in our time will be whether as a society we will spend the money, take the time, and run the risk required to treat people with AIDS as persons, down to the last painful gasp. That basic theological affirmation does not settle many complex issues of public policy, but it does provide an essential framework for grappling with them.

How should our response to the AIDS epidemic be influenced by the fact that in many places the primary transmitters of the disease are promiscuous male homosexuals and intravenous drug users? Answering this secondary question is more complex. It is a prejudicial untruth to call AIDS a homosexual disease. AIDS is a viral disease that affects heterosexuals and homosexuals. There is no evidence whatsoever to indicate that this new virus was originally produced by homosexual practice.

212

At the same time, however, it is dishonest and unwise to minimize the fact that much of the transmission of AIDS occurs because of promiscuous (especially homosexual) sexual intercourse. Regardless of one's view of either homosexuality or promiscuity, the facts are that the only truly safe intercourse is that within a lifelong monogamous relationship, and that AIDS is closely linked with homosexual promiscuity. The December 1986 *Hastings Center Report* indicates that "many AIDS patients report 1,000 sexual partners over a single life time."[1] One third of all male homosexuals, according to an authoritative national survey cited in the report, said that they had had more than fifty to seventy partners in the previous year. Insisting, in our public-policy decisions, on the importance of the connection between homosexual promiscuity and the transmission of AIDS is not an instance of heterosexual homophobia.

What about the charge that AIDS is God's punishment for gays? For many this question might not even arise, and it is not the most important question. But it is essential to deal with it at some length, first, because some evangelicals have made this charge; second, because the media have spread the charge far and wide; and third, because some religious people discussing AIDS seem to want to ignore the biblical teaching that there is a moral order in the universe and that wrong choices have consequences.

To begin with, it is wrong to suggest that God created AIDS as a special punishment for the sin of homosexual practice. Such a suggestion ignores, for one thing, much empirical data. Apparently the virus is new. Why would God wait for millennia to design this special punishment? Furthermore, many people who have not engaged in homosexual activity have AIDS. At least five hundred babies have already been born with AIDS, and a minimum of seven hundred people have contracted the disease through blood transfusions. If AIDS is divine punishment for homosexual practice, why don't gay women get it? Are the radical feminists right that God is exclusively female? In parts of Africa, AIDS affects heterosexuals and homosexuals in approximately equal numbers.

Furthermore, there is no biblical basis for linking specific sicknesses with specific kinds of sin. Certainly sickness and death are the result, in biblical thought, of the fall, but a specific sickness is seldom related to a specific sinful act, and then only by special prophetic declaration. In the one situation where Jesus explicitly dealt with the questions, he emphatically rejected the suggestion that blindness was caused by a man's sin or that of his parents (John 9:2–3). Rather, Jesus said that the reason for the blindness was to make manifest the works of God. If Christians today offer com-

1. Dan E. Beauchamp, "Morality and the Health of the Body Politic," *Hastings Center Report* 16 (December 1986): 34.

passionate, costly care to people with AIDS, they will in a similar way bring glory to God.

Evangelicals should be able, however, to condemn homosexual practice as a sinful lifestyle without being charged with homophobia or blamed for many of the problems emerging in the AIDS epidemic. Almost all evangelicals consider homosexual practice (which must be carefully distinguished from homosexual orientation) to be sinful. And I agree, although I want to add that it is no more sinful than adultery, greed, gossip, racism, or materialism.

Ethicist James B. Nelson goes much too far when he argues that "we who call ourselves Christians bear major responsibility for the problems created by the AIDS crisis. . . . We have been the major institutional legitimizer of compulsory heterosexuality."[2] Evangelicals confess that they have been guilty of homophobia. But they reject the charge that their condemnation of homosexual practice somehow played a major role in creating the AIDS crisis. To the extent that there is a link between AIDS and homosexuality, the major point that must be made is that it is homosexual promiscuity that stands condemned, not evangelical belief that homosexual practice is wrong.

An argument similar to Nelson's is made by Dan Beauchamp in the *Hastings Center Report* (December 1986). Beauchamp contends that religious prejudice against homosexuality impedes changes in gay promiscuity, and that if it is to end, society will have to permit permanent forms of gay association, including marriage. In the name of public health he calls on health officials to work for this kind of "sexual freedom." He concludes by pleading that we keep our eyes fixed on "the central issue—the many ways in which centuries of religious and social superstitions and prejudice stand in the way of improving public health."[3]

This is largely unacceptable special pleading. Certainly there has been homophobic and misguided public restriction of private sexual acts between consenting adults, and that must end. But to demand that Christians either give up a belief that homosexual practice is wrong and endorse government sanction of gay marriage, or else accept major responsibility for the AIDS crisis, is nonsense. Gay folk can stop being promiscuous and thus end the risk of infection any time they choose. They don't need to wait for others to affirm their sexual preference.

My next comment on the issue of AIDS as punishment for homosexual practice may upset even more people than my previous point. The Bible throughout teaches that God is both loving and just, both merciful and holy, and therefore has established a moral order in the universe. Ignoring God's

2. James B. Nelson, "Responding to, Learning from AIDS," *Christianity and Crisis* 46, 8 (19 May 1986): 179.
3. Beauchamp, "Morality," 35.

law structured into nature has consequences. A major article on AIDS in a religious periodical asserted that "The God of the Christian revelation is not a God who punishes people."[4] But that is not what the Scriptures say. In fact, nowhere in the Bible is there more discussion of punishment of sin than in the words of Jesus. Furthermore, St. Paul argues the general point about there being a moral order in the universe precisely with reference to male and female homosexual practice (Rom. 1:26–28). God has created free persons who may freely choose to reject God's law, but their choices have consequences both now and in the future.

This point is just as relevant, of course, to any type of self-destructive behavior, or to acts of economic injustice, as it is to homosexual practice. (Someone has quipped that if AIDS is divine punishment, then surely the people who bring us economic oppression, environmental pollution and devastating wars should at least get herpes.) Oppressing the poor violates God's moral order and produces disruption, chaos and other evil consequences. (It is relevant to point out here that the unusually high proportion of blacks and Hispanics in the population of drug addicts, including intravenous drug users with AIDS, is surely related to the incredibly high unemployment rate for black and Hispanic teenagers, which in turn is related to racism and economic injustice. Similarly, the increasing number of female prostitutes with AIDS is related to female poverty and the tragedy of battered women.) Sexual sin is no worse than other varieties, and they all have consequences.

We cannot ignore this general truth when we come to the issue of AIDS. If the Bible teaches that homosexual practice is wrong, as I think it does, then it is right to suppose that violating God's law in this area will have negative consequences.

This is not to say that the AIDS virus is some supernatural divine creation to punish homosexual practice; I have emphasized that I reject that view. But I refuse to bow to today's widespread relativism and deny and ignore the clear biblical teaching that some actions are wrong no matter what Hollywood or Greenwich Village says. Ignoring the moral order of the universe has consequences.

As a citizen, I insist on the right to say that and to seek to shape public policy in ways consistent with that belief without being called a bigot. Evangelical Christians believe that one reason Western society today is in trouble is its widespread ethical relativism and accompanying sexual promiscuity (both heterosexual and homosexual). I do not ask that public policy enforce biblical sexual norms, but I do ask that public policy not undermine them.

It is important to add here that there are contexts in which it is appropriate, and other contexts in which it is inappropriate, to emphasize the link

4. David James Randolph, "Aid for Persons with AIDS," *Engage/Social Action* 14, 2 (February, 1986): 43.

between actions and consequences. When a person is dying of lung cancer, one does not lecture her on the dangers of smoking. When a friend is struggling to survive a heart attack, one does not denounce him for poor eating patterns or failure to exercise. Nevertheless, warnings about smoking and vigorous personal appeals to friends not to destroy their health by overwork or overeating are entirely appropriate at other times.

I have been dismayed by failures to observe this very simple distinction. In his book on AIDS, John Fortunato quotes an evangelical chaplain who began every initial conversation with gay AIDS patients with a harsh denunciation of the sin of homosexual practice.[5] Such an approach is so far from Jesus' compassionate and forgiving relationship with the adulterous woman that one wants to scream. The first thing the Christian must say to an AIDS patient is that God loves him or her so much so that if it were necessary for Jesus to experience the cross again just for that person, he would gladly do it.

But just because one does not admonish and educate at the deathbed does not mean, to quote Episcopal Bishop John Walker of Washington, D.C., that "our calling is not that of judging but of serving."[6] We must do both, albeit in different settings. Much depends, too, on what one means by "judging." Harsh, insensitive, self-righteous attitudes are never acceptable. But "not judging" in that sense is fully compatible with insisting that certain behavior is wrong. Jesus never supposed, as do some modern relativists, that his command to "judge not" means that we cannot condemn sin.

What should be the church's role in the AIDS crisis? It does not take long to say what the church should do; but actually doing it is quite another mater. One decisive test of whether the church is truly what it claims to be will be whether or not it can muster the obedience and courage to embody its teaching that all human life is sacred even in the midst of the racing panic of plague time.

The most basic role for the church is to set a good example. Thus far it has not batted a thousand. Members of one church in Florida not only led the fight to exclude three hemophiliac boys with AIDS from public school but also decided not to admit persons carrying the AIDS virus into Sunday school, worship or other church activities.[7] Many other churches, on the other hand, have exhibited a different spirit, recognizing that the AIDS virus cannot be spread by casual contact.

    5. John Fortunato, *AIDS: The Spiritual Dilemma* (San Francisco: Harper & Row, 1987), 103–4.
    6. Marjorie Hyer, "Bishop Urges Church Action on AIDS Care," *Washington Post*, 31 October 1986, 16(A).
    7. *Florida Baptist Witness*, 17 September 1987. This entire issue is devoted to the question of AIDS and the church.

Second, the church should provide direct ministry, both pastoral and other services, to people with AIDS and their families. (*Christianity Today* rightly deplores the fact that far more is happening already in this area than the media report.)[8] Third, the church can serve an indispensable role in education. Because people generally trust the church, it should be able to combat the irrational fears and rumors by presenting facts and respected counsel.

Fourth, the church should, as James Nelson suggests, engage in further theological reflection on the issues raised by the AIDS epidemic. It needs to rediscover and proclaim the full biblical understanding of the joy and boundaries of sexual expression, teach by word and example the goodness of the lifelong marriage covenant between a man and a woman, and learn better how to offer unlimited acceptance to everyone without succumbing to mushy relativism. Those four points take only three minutes to articulate. To incarnate them requires a lifetime of struggle.

Nelson is very helpful in calling for a careful balancing of individual rights and social good. The people who speak most often about the sanctity of human life should have been the very first to champion the right of people with AIDS to adequate healthcare rather than lobbying against government expenditure for AIDS research, as did the Moral Majority. And the people who speak frequently about democratic freedom and individuals' personal relationships with God ought to be among the most vigorous champions of the right to individual freedom and privacy. At the same time, Nelson rightly insists that these individual rights must be balanced by a concern for the public good so that we protect the blood supply, and the health of schoolchildren and health professionals, while wisely allocating scarce medical resources.

Finally, the topic of condom ads needs to be addressed, not because it is more important than (probably it is not even as important as) other public-policy questions such as mandatory AIDS testing or contact notification, but because it has provoked such extensive discussion among evangelicals. Some conservative Christians have vigorously, even viciously, denounced fellow evangelical Surgeon General C. Everett Koop for suggesting advertisements and education about condoms in the battle against AIDS. Koop insists that the only safe sex is that within a monogamous relationship, but he also demands that we deal with the real world where promiscuity persists and spreads the AIDS virus at a terrifying rate.

Koop is correct that we need a public education campaign that includes TV and print media encouraging people who choose to persist in high-risk behavior to use condoms. But I also find substance in the response of many people—from Sir Immanuel Jakobowits, the chief rabbi of Britain, to writers in *Christianity Today* to delegates at the 1987 Southern Baptist Conven-

8. Andres Tapia, "High-Risk Ministry," *Christianity Today* 31, 11 (7 August 1987): 15.

tion—that the promotion of condoms could easily encourage promiscuity. If we are trying to warn adolescent youngsters about the danger of promiscuity, I doubt we do it effectively by a TV ad featuring (to take one current example) a glamorous young woman who says she wants love but she is not willing to die for it.

There is a way to meet both sides' concerns. We could have TV spots featuring someone like Rock Hudson at a stage of the AIDS disease where its ravages are unmistakable. The text could read something like this:

> The only safe sex is within a lifelong monogamous relationship. I wish I had lived that way before I got AIDS. But if, in spite of today's harsh facts, you want to play Russian roulette with your life, then please use condoms. They are not fail-proof, but they do improve your chances.

Such TV spots would not glamorize promiscuity. But they would get the word out on condoms. It is highly unlikely that condom manufacturers would pay for such ads. But promoting their profits is not our agenda. (In fact, TV ads by condom manufacturers should be discouraged because their commercial interests will almost certainly override any concern for public-health education.) Rather, government agencies and private groups, including churches, should develop such spots, and stations should run them as public-service announcements.

Religious leaders today have the awesome task of helping to lead people through what may well become the most deadly epidemic in human history. I hope we will have the courage and faith to turn away from irrational fear, panic and the temptation to place personal security above compassionate care for the marginalized and ravaged. I hope that instead we will be given the grace to incarnate the belief that all persons, including our sisters and brothers dying of AIDS, are stamped with the divine image and are thus of inestimable value.

For Further Reflection

Case Studies

Gay marriage proposal. Stan grew up in a conservative Christian home and church. At age eleven, he received Christ as his Savior. In his early teen years, he became powerfully aware of his homosexual desires. For the next several years, he suppressed these inclinations although he did have a brief sexual relationship with a neighbor boy. After numerous dates with girls, Stan reluctantly acknowledged that his sexual preference was toward males. Wanting to live for God, he chose celibacy throughout his later high-school and college years. Now Norman, a man in his church whom Stan has known for some time, has asked Stan to enter a "marriage" union with him. Stan is strongly attracted to Norman, but is not persuaded by Norman's interpretation of the Bible passages on homosexuality.

What steps should Stan take to find the help he needs? How would you counsel Stan if you were his pastor or close friend?

Lesbian schoolteacher. Brenda is an elementary public school principal who recently discovered that Sarah, the third grade teacher at the school, is a practicing lesbian. An excellent teacher, Sarah is well-liked by the students and parents and does not openly flaunt her lesbianism. A committed Christian, Brenda has informed Sarah that she knows of her situation. Sarah replies that she cannot change her orientation. While she will not promote her lifestyle in the classroom, neither will she forsake her lover. In addition, she reminds Brenda that there is no way legally that the principal can remove her from her position.

Should Brenda make an issue of Sarah's presence on the faculty, informing parents of Sarah's lifestyle, or should she simply pray for Sarah and keep the matter quiet? How should Brenda's specifically Christian convictions enter into her attitude regarding Sarah's employment?

Glossary

Constitutional homosexual: A person whose sexual attraction to those of the same gender is so deeply rooted that it is part of his or her essential being. A constitutional homosexual is not necessarily a practicing homosexual. See also homosexual orientation.

Gay: Homosexual; homosexual women prefer to speak of themselves as lesbians, while homosexual men refer to themselves as gay men.

Heterosexual: Person attracted sexually to those of the opposite gender; also, pertaining to the attraction itself.

Homophobia: Irrational fear of homosexuals sometimes leading to an attitude of hostility toward them.

Homosexual: Person (male or female) with a homosexual orientation, who may or may not be a practicing homosexual; also, referring to same-sex desires and/or practices.

Homosexuality: Persistent or predominant sexual disposition (see homosexual orientation) of an individual toward persons of the same sex.

Homosexual orientation: Disposition or persistent preference of a person for same-gender sexual relationships; also known as constitutional homosexuality and inversion.

Inversion: Same as homosexual orientation.

Lesbian: A homosexual woman.

Practicing homosexual: One who prefers and regularly engages in same-sex genital activities.

Sodomy: In the strictest sense, sexual union by anal penetration, whether homosexual or heterosexual; in the broader sense, sexual activity of any kind involving homosexuals.

Straight: Heterosexual.

Annotated Bibliography

Bahnsen, Greg L. *Homosexuality: A Biblical View*. Grand Rapids: Baker, 1978. Argues that not only is homosexual practice sin, but also that one's homosexual orientation, for which one is morally responsible, is itself sinful.

Bailey, D. Sherwin. *Homosexuality and the Western Christian Tradition*. New York: Longmans, 1955. Marks the beginning of serious nontraditional thinking within the church; widely influential in the subsequent debate, especially for its prohomosexual treatment of the biblical texts.

Bartlett, David L. "A Biblical Perspective on Homosexuality." *Foundations* 20, 2 (April-June 1977): 133–47. Contends that while the specific biblical passages on the subject condemn homosexual practices, there are biblical grounds for giving full recognition to Christian homosexual relationships.

Boswell, John. *Christianity, Social Tolerance and Homosexuality.* Chicago: University of Chicago Press, 1980. Massive scholarly historical work studying the presence of homosexuals in the church and society, as well as social and religious attitudes to them; prohomosexual reinterpretation of biblical texts.

Campolo, Tony. *20 Hot Potatoes Christians Are Afraid to Touch.* Dallas: Word, 1988, 107–20. Contends that in many cases homosexual orientation is inborn; such persons can benefit by living together in celibate, lifelong homosexual "covenants."

Consiglio, William. *Homosexual No More: Practical Strategies for Christians Overcoming Homosexuality.* Wheaton: Victor, 1991. Called a "must-read book" by Elizabeth Moberly; helps homosexuals deal with the blocked emotional development that diverted them from God's heterosexual design in the first place.

Dallas, Joe. *Desires in Conflict.* Eugene, Ore.: Harvest House, 1991. Proven, practical approach to finding freedom from homosexual involvement, written directly to the homosexual person by the president of Exodus International.

Davies, Bob, and Lori Rentzel. *Coming Out of Homosexuality.* Downers Grove, Ill.: InterVarsity, 1993. A comprehensive guide to all angles of the topic: biblical, biological, psychological, social, and relational; equally weighted in addressing male homosexuality and lesbianism. A valuable handbook that is sensitive to gay concerns without approving of homosexual behavior.

Greenberg, David F. *The Construction of Homosexuality.* Chicago: University of Chicago Press, 1988. Highly significant, well-researched history of homosexuality. Argues that the ways people act sexually (or otherwise) are expressions of the customs and practices of the culture in which they live, and that there is no such thing as homosexuals as an abiding and universal category of being.

Hays, Richard B. "Relations Natural and Unnatural: A Response to John Boswell's Exegesis of Romans 1." *Journal of Religious Ethics* 14, 1 (Spring 1986): 184–215. Helpful refutation.

Jones, Stanton L. "The Loving Opposition." *Christianity Today* (19 July 1993): 19–25. Advocates traditional biblical understanding of homosexuality while affirming need for loving, graceful response.

Keysor, Charles W., ed. *What You Should Know About Homosexuality.* Grand Rapids: Zondervan, 1979. High-quality essays on key aspects of the problem: Scripture, biology, civil rights, ministry.

Lanier, David D., R. Albert Mohler, Jr., and C. Ben Mitchell. "By Choice or by Birth?" *World,* 31 July 1993, 22–25. Three evangelicals comment on studies linking homosexuality to genetic factors.

Lanning, Cynthia, ed. *Answers to Your Questions About Homosexuality.* Wilmore, Ky.: Bristol, 1988. Clear direction from evangelical experts in several fields; very useful as a practical guidebook.

Lovelace, Richard F. *Homosexuality and the Church.* Old Tappan, N.J.: Revell, 1978. Highly regarded evangelical work treating scriptural and theological issues with sensitivity and careful scholarship.

Magnuson, Roger J. *Are Gay Rights Right?* Updated edition. Portland, Ore.: Multnomah Press, 1990. Informative, helpful, and comprehensive manual by an evangelical trial lawyer in Minneapolis.

McNeill, John J. *The Church and the Homosexual.* 4th ed. Boston: Beacon, 1993. Influential study by a former Jesuit; largely accepts Bailey's exegesis.

Moberly, Elizabeth R. *Homosexuality: A New Christian Ethic.* Cambridge, England: James Clarke, 1983. A psychoanalytic interpretation focusing on root causes. Argues that the fulfillment of legitimate developmental needs has been blocked by ambivalence to members of the same sex.

Nelson, James B. "Homosexuality: An Issue for the Church." *Theological Markings* 5, 2 (Winter 1975): 41–52. Helpful for its fourfold classification of attitudes within the church toward homosexuality.

Pattison, E. M. "Homosexuality: Classification, Etiology, and Treatment." In *Baker Encyclopedia of Psychology,* edited by David G. Benner, Grand Rapids: Baker, 1985, 519–26. Valuable summary of recent literature, especially on types of homosexuality and causation.

Scanzoni, Letha D., and Virginia R. Mollenkott. *Is the Homosexual My Neighbor? A Positive Christian Response.* Rev. ed. San Francisco: HarperSan Francisco, 1994. Urges a rethinking of the biblical passages and an attitude of understanding toward homosexuals; favors practicing homosexual unions.

Schmidt, Thomas E. *Straight and Narrow? Compassion and Clarity in the Homosexual Debate.* Downers Grove: InterVarsity, 1995. Useful interdisciplinary guide to the topic. Very carefully argued, interacting with the latest research on Scripture and science.

Scroggs, Robin. *The New Testament and Homosexuality.* Philadelphia: Fortress, 1983. Maintains that the New Testament judgments against homosexual behavior are not relevant to today's debate.

Sider, Ronald J. "AIDS: An Evangelical Perspective." *The Christian Century* (6 January 1985): 11–14. Helpful presentation of a Christian response to people with AIDS.

Stott, John R. W. "Homosexual 'Marriage'." *Christianity Today* (22 November 1985): 21–28. Worthwhile overview of the biblical teachings in light of contemporary arguments; pleads against homophobia.

Thielicke, Helmut. *The Ethics of Sex,* translated by John W. Doberstein, Grand Rapids: Baker, 1964, 269–92. Maintains that while the homosexual condition is a "perversion" of God's created order, "ethically responsible" unions can be acceptable.

Ukleja, P. Michael. "Homosexuality and the Old Testament." *Bibliotheca Sacra* (July-September 1983): 259–66; and "Homosexuality and the New Testament." *Bibliotheca Sacra* (October-December 1983): 350–58. Biblical studies refuting prohomosexual interpretations.

Wood, Glenn G., and John E. Dietrich. *The AIDS Epidemic: Balancing Compassion and Justice.* Portland, Ore.: Multnomah Press, 1990. Two medical doctors produce what Joe Dallas calls "the best resource on AIDS I know of."

Wright, David F. "Homosexuality: The Relevance of the Bible." *Evangelical Quarterly* 61, 4 (1989): 291–300. High quality, conservative treatment of the key Scripture texts; addresses contemporary objectors like Scroggs and Boswell.

Yamamoto, J. Isamu, ed. *The Crisis of Homosexuality.* Wheaton: Victor, 1990. Collection of articles from evangelical contributors on the major aspects of the topic.

6

Divorce and Remarriage

Statistics abound. Social scientists, government officials, church leaders, and women's magazine editors all say the same thing: in American culture, for every two couples that marry, one couple divorces. Scripture, however, presents **marriage** as the permanent union of a man and a woman as husband and wife. Through an official ceremony of vows, the bride and groom promise faithfulness to each other, the church and society recognize these vows as having binding force, and the husband and wife consummate those vows in sexual union. But if matches are made in heaven, how should the church respond to the avalanche of marital failure on earth?

Those outside religious communities do not see **divorce** or remarriage after divorce as important moral issues even though many are beginning to recognize the profound social and psychological implications of these issues. All evangelicals agree, however, that divorce is essentially contrary to God's will even though the Bible concedes that it is sometimes necessary. Even then, however, divorce leaves a devastating aftermath. Divorce is often sinful, usually ruinous, and always tragic.

Evangelicals usually argue either that remarriage is always prohibited or that it is sometimes permitted. Bible editor and former professor Charles Ryrie articulates an argument from the Bible for his claim that any remarriage constitutes **adultery** and is sinful. New Testament professor Craig Keener argues that those who are victims of divorce due to adultery or desertion by their spouses may innocently remarry if and when reconciliation

225

becomes impossible. Many evangelicals allow remarriage under these two conditions only. But Keener claims that, in addition to the cases of adultery and desertion, a category of "other exceptions" like mental cruelty or physical abuse justifies one in seeking divorce and, if reconciliation is impossible, remarrying.

The major evangelical views are built on a common set of important biblical texts. The fundamental text is Genesis 2:24–25. Here, at the culmination of the creation story, Adam and Eve come together as husband and wife in a permanent, one-flesh relationship. Deuteronomy 24:1–4 presents the basis for exceptions to marriage permanence. As an instance of case law, it focuses on a very specific situation, it does not command divorce. It commands only that a twice-divorced woman whose first husband had found "something indecent" in her may not remarry that first husband. This text poses several sticky problems, one of which is the meaning of *something indecent*. The phrase is important because of the various interpretations offered by Jewish rabbis.

Seeking to trap Jesus, some Pharisees asked him to interpret Deuteronomy 24:1–4: "Is it lawful for a man to divorce his wife for any and every reason?" (Matt. 19:3). Jesus responded by refering to Genesis 2:24. But the Pharisees wanted Jesus to declare whether *something indecent* means adultery (the restrictive Shammai view) or if it includes just anything that displeases a husband (the liberal Hillel view). Jesus took the opportunity to teach that Moses permitted divorce, but only as a concession. Those who pursue quick and easy divorce reveal their selfish interest in finding a legalistic loophole for evading God's will. This amounts to legalized adultery.

Scholars debate the meaning and applicability of the so-called **exception clause** of Matthew 19:9—"except for marital unfaithfulness." (They also wonder why the clause appears only in Matthew.) *Marital unfaithfulness* does not translate *moicheia*, the usual word for adultery, but *porneia*. Scholars generally agree that *porneia* refers to sexual sin in general, including adultery and much more. Additionally difficult is whether the exception clause applies to the next phrase, "marries another." If it does not, then someone could divorce a spouse who is persistently unfaithful, but remarriage is never permissible. If it does, then one could divorce an unrepentantly adulterous spouse and then remarry. This interpretive issue divides the two views most commonly held by evangelicals.

Those who allow for remarriage on grounds of persistent unfaithfulness usually see in 1 Corinthians 7:15 another justification for remarriage after divorce: permanent desertion. Paul's agenda in this section is mixed marriages: What happens when a believer has an unbelieving spouse? Generally, the apostle counsels keeping the marriage intact. Peace, permanence, and reconciliation are always first options in troubled marriages. If an unbeliever insists on leaving, however, the believer is "not bound" in such cases. Does this mean (1) that a believer is no longer bound to the obligation to seek reconciliation (but should remain unmarried) or (2) that she is no longer bound to her spouse (and thus is free to remarry someone else)?

This latter view is the so-called **Pauline privilege.** Those who defend this Pauline privilege accept remarriage on the grounds of permanent desertion. (Of course, if *not bound* in this text means only that one is free of the obligation to seek reconciliation, one could still hold on other grounds that a deserted spouse may remarry.) Either way, those who see 1 Corinthians 7:15 as permitting permanently deserted spouses to divorce and remarry must still reconcile this permission with the adultery-only position of Jesus in Matthew 19.

The issue of issues for interpreting these texts on marriage and divorce is this: Can anything short of the death of one spouse dissolve a marriage? If a marriage is indissoluble, then a remarriage after divorce constitutes marriage by a married person to someone other than one's spouse and the consummation of this new marriage is by definition adultery. But if marriage is dissoluble, then a remarriage after divorce is a marriage by a single person and this is not by definition adultery (though some other factor might make it sinful). The fundamental assumption concerning the dissolubility of marriage colors exegesis and influences which of the two views one takes. The evidence for this basic assumption is critical.

Traditionally, the Roman Catholic Church has defined marriage as a sacrament, a means of God's saving grace. This entails the permanence of marriage, and it forms the foundation for an absolute prohibition of divorce. Catholic teaching permits **annulment**, an official cancellation of a marriage, but not divorce. Unlike divorce, which recognizes the legitimacy of the marriage it ends, an annulment declares that the attempted marriage never really came into being. Traditionally, the church recognized failure to consummate a marriage by sexual intercourse as the proper grounds for annulment. Today, however, interpretations of canon law have become more lax, recognizing other possible grounds for annulment.

The Reformers generally held that victims of adulterous spouses could divorce and remarry. But some evangelicals, like Ryrie in the selection to follow, argue for the indissolubility of marriage. Some point to Jesus' words, "What God has joined together, let man not separate" (Matt. 19:6), as evidence that marriages are unbreakable. But others think this argument is erroneous. Jesus did not say we *cannot* break a marriage; he said we *should not* do so. His statement is prescriptive, not descriptive. Indeed, it is precisely because marriages *are* breakable that Jesus commanded us not to break them. No moral teaching prohibits impossible actions.

Another argument for the indissolubility of marriage depends on the idea that marriage is a covenant. Some identify the word *cleave* (Gen. 2:24) as a covenantal word. Since God's covenant with humans is unbreakable, by analogy the marriage covenant is also indissoluble. In addition, the kinship legislation of Leviticus 18:6–18 shows that the "one flesh" of Genesis 2:24 is permanent. According to this view, marriage establishes kinship relationships with a new family. We can no more break covenantal-family relationships than we can sunder blood-family relationships.

Those who argue against the absolute permanence of marriage, however, do not think *covenant* implies indissolubility, and this for several reasons. First, those who see marriage as breakable believe the connection between Genesis 2:24 and Leviticus 18 is too tenuous. Second, they note that Paul uses *one flesh* to describe a relationship with a prostitute (1 Cor. 6:16), and this is clearly not a permanent relationship. Paul's usage seems to emphasize the sexual and relational aspects of one flesh, not its covenantal nature. (Those who defend permanence respond by saying that Paul is applying Genesis 2:24 analogically to a new situation, not exegeting it in its original context.) Third, the permanence of God's covenant is due to the unswerving fidelity of God, not some innate quality of covenants. Obviously, the matter of indissolubility is critical. Ryrie and Keener disagree about the breakability of marriage, and this is a major reason they disagree about remarriage.

For those who follow biblical teaching, one thing is clear: divorce is always less than ideal. The Scripture clearly commands faithful monogamy as the ideal (see chap. 4). Divorce is conceded or permitted, but never required. Divorce is one way to protect the victims of spousal neglect, irresponsibility, abuse, or betrayal. Talking about the concessions is necessary when considering difficult cases where one spouse is victimized by the other. But sometimes the less guilty spouse focuses on the technical details of the law, using the concessions as loopholes to "get out of the marriage" lawfully. Approaching the concessions of Scripture with this pharisaical attitude often reflects selfish concern for legalistic guiltlessness. While some may seek to manipulate the technicalities of the law in their own favor, God permits divorce to protect those who suffer betrayal.

The first thing to say about marriage is the good word: it is a gift from God. Good teaching about marriage properly accents the positive. Such teaching is first theological, focusing on the bright vision of God's intentions for marriage. It is next practical, emphasizing biblical principles and relational strategies designed to fulfill that vision. Only then should Christian teaching consider options for intervention in marriages where the vision is dimming or hopelessly darkened. The interpretive differences between the views we are considering relate to intervention in problem cases, but focusing on intervention can emphasize the wrong thing. The church must teach a positive and proactive theology of marriage. It must build a captivating vision of God's will for marriage. This image can be part of a preventive strategy to help stem the tidal wave of divorce in the church.

The matter of misdirected focus seems parallel to discussions of abortion where at most 7 percent of abortions involve some mitigating circumstance (what some call hard cases). We spend most of our energy discussing the 7 percent, and so we miss a simple but important point: most evangelicals believe most abortions are illegitimate. Similarly, we may wonder how many divorces are caused by unrepentant adultery or permanent desertion. Common sense suggests that the narcissism of our culture nurtures many divorces even among Christians. The complexities of the exception clause and the Pauline privilege should not blind us to an overwhelming agreement among Christians ethicists: God both hates divorce (Mal. 6:10) and loves the penitent of heart.

Several related questions deserve attention. First, does a remarried divorcee live in a permanent state of adultery? If marriages are unbreakable, the answer, it seems, is affirmative. If remarriage to another spouse means adding a second spouse to the first, then remarriage is continuous adultery or perhaps polygamy. But writers on both sides of the issue generally agree that it is the act of breaking up the marriage that constitutes sin (in cases where suing for divorce is in fact sinful). Whether those who believe marriage is indissoluble can say this consistently is a different question. The fact remains that given the circumstances, remarried divorcees cannot any longer fulfill their original commitments. So most agree they ought to remain faithful to their current spouses, and they do not repeatedly sin when they consummate those vows sexually.

Second, is one who divorces before becoming a Christian different from a Christian who divorces (since at conversion "all things are new"), and should this pre-Christian divorcee have the right *on this ground* to remarry? The view implied here denies the possibility of remarriage to those who divorce as Christians, but makes an exception for those who divorce as pre-Christians. A noble intent motivates this view: a desire to show mercy to at least some who experience marital failure. While this view offers God's grace to those whose pre-Christian marriages were tragic failures, it suggests that fuller forgiveness is possible before conversion than after. This surely is false; Christians receive God's grace, too. The timing of an illegitimate divorce and remarriage has nothing to do with whether God will forgive.

Third, a related issue is the "husband of one wife" requirement for church leaders (1 Tim. 3:2; 3:12; Titus 1:6). Whom does this phrase preclude as church leaders? Singles (at least one spouse), polygamists, or remarried divorcees (at most one spouse)? Despite the prejudices of some pulpit committees, singleness surely does not disqualify a potential church leader (see Matt. 19:12; 1 Cor. 7:32–40). Polygamy as commonly understood was apparently rather rare in the first century. Those who believe marriage is indissoluble tend to conclude that Paul has remarried divorcees in view: they are, in fact, polygamists (still technically married to a first spouse while married to a second) and thus are not the husband of one wife.

Those who see marriage as breakable, on the other hand, often interpret the phrase to mean that a church leader should exhibit an obvious faithfulness to one spouse. Robert Saucy, who takes this view, argues that the requirement does not refer to the legal marital status of an elder, but to personal qualities, an elder's character, actions, and attitudes. This phrase identifies, not those who have never sinned, but those who are now mature and faithful in their married relationships. (Incidentally, this qualification applies equally to pastors and to deacons. Whatever this phrase means, it applies to both offices.)

Most of the time, divorce does not solve problems, it evades them. It often creates more difficulties of its own. Those contemplating divorce should face these facts realistically. One quarter of first marriages fail, but two thirds of subsequent marriages end in divorce (according to the National Center for Health statistics). To lower these numbers and to help the people that these numbers represent, prevention through early detection and intervention are best. The best ways to change high divorce rates are aggressive premarital counseling, intensive postmarital resourcing, and proactive teaching and preaching about marriage, sexuality, and human relationships. Dealing with crumbling marriages only by pursuing last-ditch efforts to prevent inevitable divorces is a surefire formula for failure.

The church must offer resources to spouses, protection for victims, forgiveness to the penitent, and warning to the irresponsible. Sometimes warning is preached at the victim. Obviously, we must present the ideal sensitively so as not to add to the pain of victims. At other times grace and forgiveness are offered to the irresponsible and unrepentant. Clearly, we should solemnly proclaim the serious consequences of marital betrayal. Part of the church's difficult task is to keep these differing themes in balance as it ministers to a variety of people who are struggling to live God's ideal in this most sensitive and important area of life.

Biblical Teaching on Divorce and Remarriage

Charles C. Ryrie

Divorce and remarriage are biblical doctrines, and like other doctrines must be formulated on the basis of sound exegesis and biblical theology. Sound exegesis furnishes the raw material, the data; biblical theology correlates the results of exegesis in relation to the progress of revelation. The result provides authoritative instruction for this crucial area of life today. Undebatable authoritative truth comes from revelation. Our experience cannot create it; it should conform to it; certainly it must never compromise it.

The Teaching of the Old Testament

The Institution of Marriage (Gen. 1:26–27; 2:18–25)

The Purpose of Marriage

Marriage was instituted in the context of creation, making it an ordinance that applies to all regardless of the presence or absence of faith. God's [purposes] in giving marriage to all mankind were (1) to supply the lack a man or woman has alone; (2) to encourage a faithful, monogamous relation[ship] for the fabric of society; and (3) to establish the one flesh relationship.

The first relates to the word "helper" in Genesis 2:18. It simply means that each alone lacks what the mate can supply so that together they make a complete whole.

The second finds its basis in that God made only one wife for Adam and said that he should "cleave" to that wife (Gen. 2:24). Cleaving carries with it the idea

> . . . of clinging to someone in affection and loyalty. Man is to cleave to his wife (Gen. 2:24). Ruth clave to Naomi (Ruth 1:14). The men of Judah clave to

David their king during Sheba's rebellion (2 Sam. 20:2). Shechem loved
Dinah and clave to her (Gen. 34:3) and Solomon clave in love to his wives
(1 Kgs. 11:2).

Most importantly, the Israelites are to cleave to the Lord in affection and
loyalty (Deut. 10:20; 11:22; 13:4 . . . 30:20; Josh. 22:5; 23:8) if his blessing is
to be theirs. . . . In these verses parallel words and phrases that describe this
proper attitude to the Lord are: fear, serve, love, obey, swear by his name, walk
in his ways, and keep his commandments.[1]

The third, to provide the closest relationship, is the meaning of "one
flesh." It not only involves physical union but also a unity of spiritual, moral,
and intellectual facets of the husband and wife. Furthermore, "this union is
of a totally different nature from that of parents and children; hence marriage between parents and children is entirely opposed to the ordinance of
God."[2] Consequently, in the Mosaic legislation sexual relations, whether
within or outside the marriage relationship, with close relatives were forbidden (Lev. 18:6–18; cf. Deut. 22:30; 27:20, 22–23).[3] These prohibitions
were related not only to literal blood lines but also to "blood" relationships
created through marriage (e.g., a brother's or uncle's wife). Marriage not
only creates vertical blood relationships in the form of children, but also horizontal "blood" relationships between the couple themselves.[4] In short, "one
flesh" is analogous to kinship.[5]

If these are God's purposes in marriage, then obviously they are thwarted
by unfaithfulness, polygamy, and incestuous relationships.

The Elements of Marriage

Biblical marriage involves three elements. First, the consent of the partners and of the parents (Gen. 21:21; 34:4–6; Judg. 14:2–3; Josh. 15:16; Eph.
6:1–3; 1 Cor. 7:37–38). Second, the public avowal which could include a
marriage contract as well as legal and social customs (Gen. 29:25; 34:12).
Third, the physical consummation of the union which normally follows.
That intercourse alone did not constitute a marriage is evident from the distinction throughout the Old Testament between a person's wife or wives and
his concubines (Gen. 22:24; Judg. 8:30–31; 2 Sam. 3:7; 5:13; 1 Kings 11:3)

---

1. Earl S. Kalland, s.v. *"dābaq," Theological Wordbook of the Old Testament* (Chicago: Moody
Press, 1980), 1:178; cf. Abel Isaksson, *Marriage and Ministry in the New Testament: A Study With
Special Reference to Mt. 19:13 [sic] – 12 and 1 Cor. 11:3–16* (Lund: Gleerup, 1965), 19.
   2. Keil and Delitzsch, *The Pentateuch* (Edinburgh: T. & T. Clark, n.d.), 1:91.
   3. See also R. K. Harrison, *Leviticus*, Tyndale Old Testament Commentaries (Downers
Grove, Ill.: Inter-Varsity, 1980), 186.
   4. Cf. G. J. Wenham, *The Book of Leviticus*, NICOT (Grand Rapids: Eerdmans, 1979),
253–54.
   5. Cf. Isaksson, *Marriage and Ministry*, 20–21; Harrison, *Leviticus*, 186.

and the sequence of events involved in Deuteronomy 22:28–29 (cf. Exod. 22:16–17). The legal/contractual aspect was important and made the period of betrothal binding.

The Indissolubility of Marriage

As marriage was originally planned there was no provision for ending it except by death. This concept was behind the Lord's answer to the Pharisees in Matthew 19:4–6 where he appeals to Genesis 2:24 as the basis of his teaching that marriage is indissoluble.

Divorce and Remarriage in the Mosaic Law

Divorce

The Mosaic Law nowhere provided for divorce, though people who lived during that period practiced it. The importance of this point cannot be over-stressed, especially in light of statements by evangelicals who, after discussing Deuteronomy 24:1–3, note that "God permitted divorce within stringently defined limits."[6] In fact the passage only recognizes that divorce was being practiced, but it never prescribes it.[7]

Another passage, Deuteronomy 22:13–29, describes two circumstances where divorce is proscribed. One was the case where the husband "turned against" his wife and sought to justify a divorce by accusing her of premarital unchastity. Assuming that the charge was false, the verdict was clear: "And she shall remain his wife; he cannot divorce her all his days" (v. 19; NASB is cited, unless indicated otherwise). Does this not say something important to the reason for divorce sometimes offered today, namely, that when love dies, the marriage dies and divorce is recommended?

The other circumstance involved intercourse with an unbetrothed virgin. In this instance the man was required to marry the girl and never to divorce her (v. 29).

The betrothed couple were legally considered as husband and wife in most respects.

> At the betrothal, the bridegroom, personally or by deputy, handed to the bride a piece of money or a letter, it being expressly stated in each case that the man thereby espoused the woman. From the moment of betrothal both parties were regarded, and treated by law (as to inheritance, adultery, need of formal divorce), as if they had been actually married, except as regarded their living together."[8]

6. Jay Adams, *Marriage, Divorce and Remarriage in the Bible* (Phillipsburg, N.J.: Presbyterian and Reformed, 1980), 30.

7. Cf. Isaksson, *Marriage and Ministry*, 21, 25.

8. Alfred Edersheim, *The Life and Times of Jesus the Messiah* (Grand Rapids: Eerdmans, 1943), 1:354; cf. Roland de Vaux, *Ancient Israel*, vol. 1, *Social Institutions* (New York: McGraw-Hill, 1965), 36.

The story of Hosea and passages like Jeremiah 3:1–8 are used by some to conclude that God Himself is a divorcee (having divorced Israel as Hosea did Gomer) and therefore divorce is sometimes justified.[9]

However, it is far from clear exegetically that Hosea divorced Gomer, so at best this would be a very insecure foundation on which to build a case for legitimate divorce. Dwight Small, who praised Adams's book, has listed ten reasons why it is not possible to conclude that Hosea divorced Gomer.[10] Furthermore, it is even less tenable to conclude from the story of Hosea that God divorced Israel. The question of Isaiah 50:1 is either a rhetorical one presupposing a negative reply or it should be understood as an allegory like Jeremiah 3:8. If these illustrations are pressed to make God a divorcee, then perhaps he was also a polygamist, since he married both Israel and Judah. Nor should such poetical and metaphorical language be pressed into the service of determining the exact meaning of πορνεία in legal passages in Matthew's gospel.[11]

The point is simply that the story of Hosea and its illustration of God's relation to Israel furnishes no secure basis for concluding that there are sometimes legitimate divorces.

Remarriage

Deuteronomy 24:1–4 has been used by evangelical Protestants to demonstrate that "the divorce permitted or tolerated under the Mosaic economy had the effect of dissolving the marriage bond," therefore, with reference to our Lord's teaching in Matthew 5:32 and 19:9 "we should not expect that remarriage would be regarded as adultery."[12] In reality this is a misuse of the passage.

First, notice that

> . . . the legislation relates only to particular cases of remarriage; the protasis contains incidental information about marriage and divorce, but does not legislate on those matters. The verses do not institute divorce, but treat it as a practice already known. . . .[13]

The passage acknowledges the existence of the practice of divorce; it regards the second marriage of the divorced wife as legal; and it forbids the reinsti-

9. Adams, *Marriage, Divorce and Remarriage*, 56, 71–75.
10. "The Prophet Hosea: God's Alternative to Divorce for the Reason of Infidelity," *Journal of Psychology and Theology* 7 (1979): 133–40. See also Francis I. Anderson and David Noel Freedman, *Hosea: A New Translation with Introduction and Commentary*, AB (Garden City, N. Y.: Doubleday, 1980), 124, 220–40, who defend the same conclusion.
11. See Tim Crater, "Bill Gothard's View of the Exception Clause," *Journal of Pastoral Practice* 4, 3 (1980): 5–12.
12. John Murray, *Divorce* (Philadelphia: Orthodox Presbyterian Church, 1953), 41–42; cf. Guy Duty, *Divorce and Remarriage* (Minneapolis: Bethany, 1967), 32–44.
13. Peter C. Craigie, *The Book of Deuteronomy*, NICOT (Grand Rapids: Eerdmans, 1976), 304–5.

tution of the first marriage even after the death or divorce of the second husband. In particular, it forbids the remarriage of the first husband on the
ground that the one flesh bond with that first husband still exists, even
though divorce has been effected. Thus the passage teaches exactly the
opposite from what Murray claimed. The first marriage is not "dissolved";
otherwise, there would be no basis for prohibiting that remarriage.[14]

The indecency which caused the first husband to divorce his wife has
been variously explained. It was not premarital unchastity, since the law specifically dealt with such cases (Deut. 22:28–29). Likely it was something
short of adultery. Isaksson suggests that it meant the voluntary or involuntary exposure of the wife's pudendum [or genitalia], which would arouse his
loathing.[15] If the husband chose to divorce his wife, he had to forfeit the
dowry and may also have had to pay her a kind of alimony.

Scholars are not agreed on the basis for the prohibition of remarrying the
first wife. The suggestion that the entire law was to deter hasty divorces is
unlikely. Financial considerations would probably do that. Others suggest
that to reconstitute the first marriage would be a type of incest, on the basis
of Genesis 2:24 and Leviticus 18:6–18, because the one flesh relationship
was never dissolved.[16] One thing is certain: Deuteronomy 24:1–4 does not
teach a dissolution divorce that breaks the marriage bond as Murray and
others have taught and then applied to the teaching of the New Testament
in order to validate remarriage. In fact, the prohibition in verse 4 is based on
the enduring nature of the one flesh bond of the original marriage. Therefore, a woman cannot return to the first husband even if her second husband
dies. . . .

The Teaching of the New Testament

Most agree that the New Testament permits divorce only in two
instances: πορνεια (Matt. 5:32; 19:9) and desertion by the unbelieving partner in a spiritually mixed marriage, the mixture having occurred after the
marriage (1 Cor. 7:15). These passages contain difficult problems, chiefly
the meaning of πορνεία and the question of whether or not remarriage is
permitted in either instance.

The Teaching of Christ
The Summary of His Teaching
When the apostle Paul summarized the Lord's teaching concerning
divorce, he did not include any exception to the total prohibition of divorce

14. See G. J. Wenham, "The Restoration of Marriage Reconsidered [Deut. 24:1–4]," *Journal of Jewish Studies* 30 (1979): 36–40, and *Third Way* 1, 21 (November 3, 1977): 7–9.
15. *Marriage and Ministry*, 26.
16. Cf. Wenham, "The Restoration of Marriage."

by Christ (1 Cor. 7:11). This seems to say that Christ taught the indissolubility of marriage and that whatever he meant by πορνεια was an uncommon
meaning. Otherwise, Paul might have been expected to include a commonly
understood exception to divorce in his summary.

Furthermore, no exception appears in Mark's (10:11–12) and Luke's
(16:18) accounts of our Lord's teaching. Some have attempted to harmonize
these accounts with Matthew's inclusion of an exception by saying that
Mark and Luke state the general rule while Matthew added the exception
(usually understood as sexual immorality).

However, the disciples' reaction to the Lord's teaching when the exception was included (Matt. 19:10) was not the kind one would expect if they
understood the exception to mean immorality in general, for they were
greatly startled by his teaching. They evidently thought he was teaching the
indissolubility of marriage so clearly that they suggested it might be wiser not
to marry at all. In reply the Lord did not recommend celibacy as the better
course of action, but the very fact that the disciples rejected (v. 10) this conception of life and marriage shows that they understood his teaching to be
different from what they knew in Judaism. And the Lord did not suggest that
they had exaggerated or misunderstood his teaching.

Everything points to the exception being something uncommon, certainly
nothing as common as adultery or immorality in general.

The Background

The Hillel-Shammai debate was certainly in the minds of the Pharisees
when they asked the Lord if a Jew could divorce his wife for any cause (Matt.
19:3). The school of Hillel interpreted the words עֶרְוַת־דָּבָר in Deuteronomy
24:1 more leniently by disjoining the words and making them read
"uncleanness, or anything else." Naturally this interpretation, like the evangelical Protestant view today, enjoyed more popularity than that advanced
by the more strict school of Shammai, which allowed divorce only for some
immodesty, shamelessness, lewdness, or adultery. By asking the Lord to take
sides on this question, the Pharisees hoped to lessen his popularity with the
people, whichever side he took.

However, the Lord's response did not deal with the particulars of Deuteronomy 24 at all, but rather with God's original intention for marriage and
with an action which would result in one or the other party being involved
in committing adultery. The Pharisees were preoccupied with establishing
grounds for divorce (and doing the same today is similar to Pharisaism); our
Lord was concerned about the indissolubility of marriage.

The Interpretations of the Exception Clause

The Patristic View. This view states that when one party was guilty of
πορνεία, usually understood to mean adultery, the other party was

expected to separate but did not have the right to remarry. This was the view of all the Greek and Latin fathers, save one, in the first five centuries of the Church.[17] . . .

While this writer does not agree with making πορνεία equal to adultery or any sexual sin, he does agree that the texts do not allow remarriage without committing adultery. This is very important to the current debate, for the construction of the Matthean texts applies the exception, whatever it means, only to divorce, and not to remarriage. Had the exception clause come after "marries another" it would have sanctioned remarriage, but it does not. Therefore, it is an assumption read into the texts to conclude that if there is legitimate ground for divorce then there is automatically permission for legitimate remarriage. Actually, the texts say that such remarriage involves adultery.

The Evangelical Protestant View. This view has two variations within it. Some, like Murray, understand πορνεία to be equivalent to μοιχεία.[18] Others give it a wider sense to cover a broad range of sexual sins. James B. Hurley understands it to mean illicit sexual relations which would have called for the death sentence in the Old Testament: adultery, homosexuality, and bestiality.[19] Richard DeHaan includes premarital sex, incest, adultery, rabbinically unapproved marriage, homosexuality.[20] John MacArthur concludes that "fornication is the broad word for any kind of unlawful, shameful sexual activity."[21] All variations see the exception clause as qualifying both verbs (put away and [re]marry), thus permitting both divorce and remarriage in the case of πορνεία. Of course, divorce is not required, but it is permitted and so is remarriage. By this interpretation of πορνεία almost anyone could justify a divorce, especially if adultery is further defined as the Lord does in Matthew 5:28.

To be sure, πορνεία does sometimes include adultery. But that does not indicate its meaning in these divorce texts, in a gospel that is concerned with legal niceties in which Matthew clearly distinguishes the two terms. This is evident in 15:19 where πορνεία and μοιχεία appear side by side. Indeed, Matthew uses πορνεία only in chapters 5, 15, and 19 and μοιχεία in 15 where he distinguishes it from πορνεία. If he meant adultery in 5 and 19 why did he not use the clear word? The question is not, does πορνεία *ever* mean adultery, but does it *always* mean adultery? Lexical evidence does not

17. Henri Crouzel, *L'Eglise primitive face au divorce* (Paris: Beauchesne, 1971), and "Remarriage After Divorce in the Primitive Church: A Propos of a Recent Book," *Irish Theological Quarterly* 38 (1971): 21–41.

18. *Divorce*, 21.

19. *Man and Woman in Biblical Perspective* (Leicester, England: InterVarsity, 1981), 103–4.

20. *Marriage, Divorce, and Re-Marriage* (Grand Rapids: Radio Bible Class, 1979), 12; cf. Adams, *Marriage, Divorce and Remarriage*, 54.

21. Study notes on audiocassette 2220, 28.

require the meaning adultery in the divorce texts unless it can be proved (which it cannot) that the word always means adultery.

No reference in the New Testament equates πορνεία and μοιχεία as the proponents of this view require. The oft quoted reference of Sir. 23:23 as an example of such an equation in pre-Christian Jewish literature is far from sure. J. Jensen, who has done the most scholarly word study in print on πορνεία, translates the passage "she has wantonly committed adultery."[22] Isaksson noted already in 1965 that πορνεία in Sir. 23:23 most likely refers to the "sexual desire" that led the wife to commit adultery.[23] The same is true of πορνεία in *Herm. Man.* 4.1.3–8 and Tob. 8:7.

Acts 15:20 and 29 furnish clear examples of πορνεία used in a restricted sense and certainly not as a broad word for any kind of unlawful sexual activity.

The letter of James to the local churches of Antioch, Syria, and Cilicia forbids, in fact, four things proscribed by the Holiness Code of Lv 17–18, not only for "any man of the house of Israel" but also for "the strangers that sojourn among *them.*" . . . These were the meat offered to idols (Lv. 17:8–9), the eating of blood (Lv. 17:10–12), the eating of strangled, i.e., not properly butchered, animals (Lv. 17:15; cf. Ex. 22:31), and intercourse with close kin (Lv. 18:6–18).[24]

Here is a clear instance where πορνεία does not mean all kinds of unlawful sexual activity, but one kind only.[25]

The evangelical Protestant view is faced with another problem: the two different meanings simultaneously given to the verb ἀπολύω. Though this is not impossible, it is potentially confusing, especially when Matthew is so concerned with legal matters. First, divorce and remarriage is adultery where no instance of πορνεία is involved, implying that ἀπολύω does not terminate marriage. Second, where πορνεία is involved, Matthew must be using ἀπολύω with the meaning of divorce with the right to remarry because in the evangelical Protestant view the first marriage is terminated.

In summary, there appear to be three major problems with the evangelical Protestant view. First, it cannot substantiate equating πορνεία with μοιχεία.[26] Second, if it could, then it would not be able to account for the disciples' reaction in Matthew 19:10. Third, the position of the exception

22. "Does *Porneia* Mean Fornication? A Critique of Bruce Malina," *Novum Testamentum* 20 (1978), 172f. He places Matthew 5:32 and 19:9 in the category of forbidden marriages.
23. *Marriage and Ministry*, 133.
24. J. A. Fitzmyer, "The Matthean Divorce Texts and Some New Palestinian Evidence," *Theological Studies* 37 (1976), 209. Also H. J. Richards, "Christ on Divorce," *Scripture* 11 (1959), 29–30.
25. Cf. Bromiley, *God and Marriage*, 44–45.
26. See especially, Isaksson, *Marriage and Ministry*, 131–35.

clause in the protasis of Matthew 19:9 does not lead to the conclusion that it modifies both verbs; therefore, even if divorce is permitted, remarriage is not. These last two matters are further complicated if one presses the dictionary definition of πορνεία into the context of Matthew 19:3–12.

The Betrothal View. Few evangelicals realize that this view was the subject of a doctoral dissertation at the University of Uppsala in 1965.[27] The betrothal view builds on the fact that in Judaism a betrothed or engaged couple were considered "husband" and "wife."[28] Jewish betrothal was a legal contract which could only be broken by formal divorce or by death. If the betrothed proved unfaithful during the period of betrothal or was discovered on the first night not to be a virgin, then the contract could be broken. This is why Joseph was going to divorce Mary when he discovered that she was pregnant (Matt. 1:19). . . .

This view is quite defensible and easily harmonizes with Paul's summary of the Lord's teaching in 1 Corinthians 7:10–11. No breakup of a marriage is permitted, though dissolving an engagement is, if fornication has occurred. Its weakness lies in the technical meaning given to πορνεία. πορνεία is nowhere else used in the restricted sense of "unchastity during the betrothal period."

The Unlawful Marriage View. This view, which is the most defended among scholars over all others, has three variations. The least popular form understands πορνεία to refer to marriages to non-Christians since it would be a form of spiritual idolatry and thus unlawful.[29] Another variation sees πορνεία as a reference to intermarriage between a Jewish Christian and a gentile Christian. This could easily be the meaning in Acts 15:20 and 29 where Jewish Christians, still concerned with obeying the Mosaic law with its prohibition against marrying a gentile (Deut. 7:1–3), would be greatly offended if this were happening even between believers of mixed racial backgrounds (cf. *Jub.* 30:7, 11).

More commonly, however, πορνεία is understood by those who hold this view to indicate unlawful incestuous marriages, i.e., marriages within the prohibited degrees of kinship proscribed in Leviticus 18:6–18. The proponents of this view see the restricted meaning of πορνεία in 1 Corinthians 5:1 and especially Acts 15:20 and 29 as the key to understanding its meaning in the Matthean exception clause.

This view was published by W. K. Lowther Clarke in 1929,[30] given pref-

---

27. Cf. Isaksson, *Marriage and Ministry*.
28. Cf. Alfred Edersheim, *Life and Times*, 1:354, and G. Delling, "πάρΘενος," *Theological Dictionary of the New Testament* 5 (1967), 835 n. 59.
29. A. Mahoney, "A New Look at the Divorce Clauses in Mt. 5.32 and 19.9," *Catholic Biblical Quarterly* 30 (1968), 29–38.
30. *New Testament Problems* (New York: Macmillan), 59–60.

erence by me in 1954[31] and more recently supported by F. F. Bruce.[32] Clarke's explanation of the view is this:

> The Apostolic Decree of Acts xv. 29 promulgated a compromise. . . . Since the first three articles of the compromise are concerned with practices innocent enough to the Gentiles, the fourth must be of a similar nature. The passage in 1 Corinthians gives us the clue. *Porneia* here means *marriage within the prohibited Levitical degrees*. . . . [This] was a live issue, and *porneia* was the word by which it was known.

> Turning to St. Matthew, the problem we have to account for is the obscuring of the plain rule of St. Mark by an exception which seems inconsistent with the teaching of our Lord even in St. Matthew. If the foregoing argument holds, the reference is to the local Syrian problem. One exception is allowed to the universal rule: when a man who has married within the prohibited degrees puts away his wife the word adultery is out of place. Rather the marriage is null. . . .
> . . . There is no divorce, but causes of nullity may be recognized.

In addition to this evidence from the New Testament itself for this particular meaning of πορνεία, Joseph Fitzmyer and James R. Mueller have shown from the Qumran literature that זנות, the Hebrew counterpart to πορνεία, was used in Palestine in the first century specifically of marriage within those prohibited relationships.[33] Thus it was a meaning known to the people of the time when our Lord spoke on divorce.

This view seems completely defensible. It does not share the weakness of the betrothal view in that πορνεία does have the meaning of incest in passages other than the debated ones both within and outside the New Testament. It also accounts for the reaction of the disciples and removes any contradiction with the other Gospel accounts and with 1 Corinthians 7:10–11.

The Teaching of Paul

Concerning Marriage (Rom. 7:1–3)

In this passage Paul develops the concept that death releases the believer from his obligation to the law. He then illustrates this principle with marriage, stating that a woman is bound to her husband as long as he lives (and no exceptions). When and only when he dies is she released from the marriage relationship. If a woman is joined (that is, actual marriage, not illicit

---

31. Published in 1958 in *The Place of Women in the Church* (New York: Macmillan, 1958), 43–48.

32. *New Testament History* (Garden City, N.Y.: Doubleday, 1969), 287. Also, R. Martin, "St. Matthew's Gospel in Recent Study," *Expository Times* 80 (1969), 136; J. R. Mueller, "The Temple Scroll and the Gospel Divorce Texts," *Revue de Qumran* 38 (1980), 247–56; and many more.

33. Fitzmyer, "Matthaean Divorce Texts," 213–21; cf. A. Stock, "Matthaean Divorce Texts," *Biblical Theology Bulletin* 8 (1978), 25–28.

intercourse, since the same word is used in both parts of v. 3) to another man while her husband is alive, she will be called an adulteress. A second marriage while the first mate is living is adultery.

Concerning Divorce (1 Cor. 10–16)

The main point of Paul's counsel is clear: maintain the marriage. If separation occurs (which Paul does not approve of), then only two options remain: remain unmarried or be reconciled to the original partner. In this advice Paul said he was following the teachings of Christ, and he did not mention any exception that would sanction divorce. This reinforces the view that "except for πορνεία" means something uncommon and more peculiar to a Jewish audience.

In a spiritually mixed marriage Paul's counsel is the same: stay together. His reasons are (1) for the sake of the family (v. 14); (2) for the sake of peace (v. 15); and (3) for the sake of personal testimony (v. 16).

V[erse] 15 is understood in two entirely different ways. Some say that Paul permits remarriage if the unbelieving partner gets the divorce. Others insist he says nothing about the possibility of a second marriage for the deserted believer. The privilege to remarry is the so-called Pauline privilege of the Roman Catholic view, and the evangelical Protestant view agrees with it.[34]

Two things need to be noted. First, the departure of the unsaved spouse is not necessarily a divorce; it may only be a separation which would in no case leave the other party free to remarry.[35] Second, even if it does refer to a divorce initiated by the unsaved partner, Paul says nothing about a second marriage for the believer. Indeed, both [verses] 14 and 16 make it clear that remarriage is not the subject of verse 15 at all. Paul does not introduce that subject until v[erse] 39. What is the bondage which the believer is not under? "All that οὐ δεδούλωται clearly means is that he or she need not feel so bound by Christ's prohibition of divorce as to be afraid to depart when the heathen partner insists on separation."[36]

Like the Lord, Paul disallowed divorce. He did recognize that the unbelieving partner in a spiritually mixed marriage might leave (and subsequently divorce) in which case the believer could not prevent it. But in no case was

34. See Duty, *Divorce and Remarriage*, 100. Unfortunately Duty, earlier in his work (50) appealed to J. A. Bengel in support of his view that the exception clause qualifies both the divorce and remarriage under the circumstances given. Duty should have noted the brackets around the words that supported his view in the *Gnomen*: they signify that they are the comments not of Bengel, but the annotations of Steudel, the editor of the German edition of the *Gnomen*. If Duty would have looked at Bengel's comments at 1 Corinthians 7:15 he would have seen that Bengel apparently did not even allow the remarriage of the deserted believer.

35. D. L. Dungan, *The Sayings of Jesus in the Churches of Paul* (Philadelphia: Fortress, 1971), 96–99.

36. A. Robertson, and A. Plummer, *First Corinthians*, ICC (Edinburgh: T. & T. Clark, 1914), 143.

the believer free to remarry. The legal facet of any marriage may be dissolved, but the one flesh relationship and vows made to God do not become non-existent until the death of one of the partners.

Some attempt to justify the remarriage of divorced persons on a certain interpretation of 1 Corinthians 7:27–28.[37] It assumes that the phrase "released from a wife" (γυναικος) includes divorced from a wife.[38] However, in v[erse] 25 Paul introduces a new subject, signaling the same by using περι δε (cf. 7:1; 8:1; 12:1; 16:1); and the subject introduced is τῶν παρθένων, virgins, not divorcees.[39] Furthermore, "released" appears in the perfect tense, referring not to freedom from marriage by divorce, but to a state of freedom, i.e., the single state.[40]

Concerning Remarriage

Since v[erse] 15 does not address the question of remarriage, and since v[erse] 27 refers to a single person (most likely an engaged couple, τῶν παρθένων being the only instance of the genitive plural in the New Testament, and παρθένος in the rest of the chapter refers only to women), the only time in 1 Corinthians 7 Paul deals with the question of remarriage is in v[erse] 39. The two restrictions he places on remarriage are (1) the death of the first mate (as also implied in Rom. 7:1–3) and (2) the necessity of the new partner being a believer. Later Paul also urged younger widows to remarry (1 Tim. 5:14).

Summary

In summary, the New Testament presents a higher standard than the Old Testament. It was our Lord who announced this superior standard by going further in his teaching than the strictest Jews of his day in that he disallowed divorce altogether. Although he did not blame Moses for allowing a bill of divorce, he replaced Jewish law with God's ideal state as announced before the fall of man.

The "exception clause" apparently concerns unlawful unions and is no license to justify divorce for sexual immorality. Even if immorality occurs, forgiveness and reconciliation are the goals, not divorce. Even if a legal divorce should occur, the "one flesh" relationship cannot be severed, and that is why remarriage is disallowed. Even separation, albeit temporary, is

---

37. C. Brown, "*chōrizō*—Divorce, Separation and Remarriage," *New International Dictionary of New Testament Theology* 3 (1978), 536–37.

38. Cf. Duty, *Divorce and Remarriage*, 109.

39. For the most satisfactory of the four views of what is taking place in 1 Corinthians 7:25–38, see J. K. Elliott, "Paul's Teaching on Marriage in 1 Corinthians: Some Problems Considered," *New Testament Studies* 19 (1973), 219–25. Most writers now follow his leading.

40. Robertson and Plummer, *1 Corinthians*, 153.

not approved, and if it happens, reconciliation is still the goal. Death of a partner alone breaks all that is involved in the "one flesh" relationship.

Paul's teaching is the same. Though recognizing that separations may occur, he does not approve of them, and certainly not of divorce. He included no exception for divorce when he summarized the Lord's teaching, and he only allowed for remarriage after the death of one partner.

The practical problems of applying this teaching must have been present in the first century as they are in ours. The Scripture does not deal with all the cases that can arise, but it does give us the restrictions, the goals, and the reminder of the power of the Holy Spirit. If these were sufficient in those days, they are also sufficient for today.

Doctrine must never be compromised by cases; cases should always conform to doctrine. Let us obey God's word and never adjust it for immediate solutions. This is the only way for anyone to have fellowship and fulfillment according to God's standards. As Bromiley rightly says, people ". . . must be ready to obey God and not remarry after separation even though they might plead, as they often do, that they have a right to happiness or to the fulfillment of natural desires."[41]

Christian marriage is made an example in the New Testament of the relation between Christ and his Church. That great mystery is concretized in Christian marriage. Among other things, this surely means showing love, forgiving as often as necessary, and being faithful to the vow of commitment each made to the other until death separates.

*I am indebted to Bill Heth for making available to me the careful research he has done for a thesis and for many conversations that have sharpened my thinking.

From Charles C. Ryrie, "Biblical Teaching on Divorce and Remarriage," *Grace Theological Journal* 3, 2 (1982): 177–92.

41. *God and Marriage*, 40–41.

Final Words

Craig S. Keener

This book [. . . *And Marries Another*] has examined the New Testament teaching on divorce and has questioned how these insights might be applied today. The chapters on Matthew made it clear that if Jesus did not explicitly allow exceptions for remarriage, they were at least implicit in his words, as his disciples writing under the Spirit's inspiration understood.

Paul draws out a similar but different exception for why divorce is permissible, adding abandonment to adultery as grounds for a valid divorce. He also permits remarriage, because a valid divorce simply renders the innocent party "single" and permits remarriage in the same way that it is permitted for any single person. There are advantages to remaining single, but these apply equally to the divorced person and the never-married person.[1] . . .

But a few practical questions remain to be considered, since they could not be specifically addressed in our study above. Although the bulk of this book focuses on biblical texts and what their authors meant by them, the relevance of this book is that divorce and remarriage has become a major pastoral issue. The illustrations below are intended to provoke pastoral reflection on the principles articulated in this book.

What About "Other Exceptions"?

Matthew allows that a spouse's infidelity can dissolve the marital union. This suggests that he permits divorce in the case of unrepentant infidelity,

---

1. There may be emotional reasons unmentioned by Paul that differentiate between the two, but they seemingly level out. A divorced person must work through some deep hurts before being ready to adjust fully to a new relationship; but this person also may bring to a marriage some experience and maturity, provided he or she was the innocent party and worked hard to preserve the union. It may also be more *difficult* for a divorced person, who has tasted the blessing of intimacy, to remain single than for a Christian who has never tasted that blessing.

not that he gives an excuse to get out of a difficult marriage even though the bonds might be restored. But infidelity is clearly an exception. Paul, addressing a specific situation where nonbelieving spouses may have wanted to leave the Christian, also allows divorce and remarriage. The tenor of New Testament teaching, however, is that divorce is to be avoided at all costs.

But what happens if divorce occurs for reasons other than these two exceptions? What happens if divorce occurred before conversion? What happens if the guilty party repents, but the marriage has already been dissolved and the other partner has already begun a new relationship? Can a spouse who is physically abused get out of the situation? Can she (or he) divorce if all else fails, and must she (or he) then remain single?

These are hard questions, and they are all too relevant in our society. I have unfortunately encountered most of these situations, and a variety of others, in my limited pastoral experience; we must be ready to address such situations in our culture today. Assuming that Jesus' teaching on the subject is a general principle meant to admit exceptions (as Matthew and Paul demonstrate), and acknowledging the probability that his teaching is hyperbolic, we may allow some exceptions not addressed by Matthew or Paul because they were not specifically relevant to the situations these writers addressed.

With regard to any preconversion sin, the New Testament expressly teaches that a believer in Christ is a new creation; the old sins have passed away and are remembered no more. If Saul of Tarsus, after all he did against the Christians, could be forgiven and welcomed fully into fellowship, then a preconversion divorce should no longer be reckoned against the new believer as a sin.[2] This does not, of course, mean that no attempt should be made at reconciliation, if that possibility still lies open. Marriage is sacred, whether contracted before (as in the case of most of the believers in 1 Cor. 7 and 1 Peter 3) or after conversion. But where reconciliation is impossible, a new life qualifies the new believer to pursue a new relationship in the Lord, provided it is with the understanding that the next marriage must be fully submitted to God's teachings.

If a wife (or, in fewer cases, a husband) is being physically or sexually abused by the spouse, my own pastoral counsel would be for her to get out of the situation. In my opinion, if reconciliation and restoration of the marriage are subsequently impossible (and the innocent partner has tried), the abused person is free to remarry. The fact that the New Testament does not explicitly make an exception for this does not demonstrate that no exception could be made. I do not suppose that spousal abuse never occurred in New

---

2. Those who argue that people still have to pay for earlier crimes, for instance, if they are in jail, skew the analogy badly. *God and his church* do *not* enforce such "laws" or discipline the repentant; this is done by civil magistrates. We have not a single instance in the New Testament of the church disciplining someone already repentant.

Testament times, but I cannot honestly think of any references to it in the ancient literature; and the New Testament writers apparently thus had no immediate need to address it. Can we honestly maintain that a valid marriage exists when one spouse is treated only as an object for venting the other's repressed, violent rage? Is this not infidelity in some sense? And does not Paul's ad hoc exception, addressing a specific situation, point us to the kind of exceptions we must make in analogous situations?

Too often battered wives have been told that it is Christlike to remain in the abusive situation and have been made to bear the guilt and shame of the situation themselves, as if they accomplish some redemptive purpose for their husbands thereby. But although Peter's instructions to wives in 1 Peter 3 is prefaced by the example of our Lord's suffering, it was not addressing the situation of physical abuse. Slaves in Peter's day might have had to endure such affliction, because they could not get out of the situation. But wives today can get out of the situation, and we should not think that Peter wanted slaves to endure beatings if they could have avoided them. The early Christians in fact helped slaves to get out when they could, buying their freedom. (When early Christians used their money to have compassion on those in great need rather than on church buildings, there was for some reason more money to go around.) Paul was right to preach the gospel even in the face of persecution; he was also right to escape that persecution when the opportunity presented itself (e.g., Acts 9:24–25; 14:6; Matt. 10:23).

If it is argued that claims of abuse might be used as a phony excuse for a woman to leave a marriage, it should also be observed that the church's standard against divorce has been used by husbands as an opportunity to continue abusing their wives. Sometimes "taking sides" on whether or not a divorce is legitimate is a tough call; but when the case is genuinely too tough for us to judge, we ought to be humble enough not to judge it at all. But other times the decision is not tough; we just do not want to get involved, and so we give out pat theological formulas: No divorce under any circumstances.

I know of a woman who refused to confess her husband's abuse or be taken to the hospital after a beating; she died from her injuries. In this case she acted out of loyalty to her husband rather than from pastoral advice; but had a pastor advised her to remain in that situation, he would in my opinion share the bloodguilt of her murderer. This is, I confess, strong language. But too many churches have looked the other way while people were being broken, and my reading of the Bible says that calls for strong language: it calls us to repent of not caring enough to move beyond our pet formulas and deal with real human lives for whom Christ died.

In the past I either counseled people to stay together or left the decision entirely to the person seeking my counsel; I have never recommended divorce. But in retrospect, I think on those few occasions when I knew or suspected physical abuse, adultery, or that a parent was giving drugs to the kids, I should have recommended at least a temporary separation. Although I would still maintain that we must do everything possible to hold together a marriage until it is clear that one spouse is bent on dissolving it, there are circumstances where separation, and indeed divorce, is necessary. Some ivory-tower theologians who spend their time picking apart the grammar of New Testament texts without regard to the situations it addressed or the situations with which pastors must grapple today would do well to give attention to texts like these:

> If you had understood what Scripture says, "I want mercy and not sacrifice," you would not have condemned the innocent (Matt. 12:7).

> Whoever causes one of these little ones who believe in me to stumble, it would have been better for him to have had a millstone suspended from his neck, and to have been cast into the open sea (Matt. 18:6).

> They (the scribes and Pharisees) bind together heavy loads and lay them on other people's shoulders, but they themselves won't even push the loads with a finger (Matt. 23:4).

Pastors are shepherds, called to live among the sheep, to feed them and bind up their wounds. Indeed, all of us in the body are called to go after straying or wounded sheep (Matt. 18:10–14); and all of us are called to care for one another as for ourselves (Matt. 22:37–39), nay, to love one another even as Christ loved us, by serving one another to the death (John 13:34–35). Divorce is wrong because it violates a covenant of permanent love made before God to another person made in God's image; condemning the innocent party in a divorce is wrong because it despises the righteousness of Christ and oppresses the person who has already experienced the deepest rejection possible. Rejecting the guilty party or parties in a divorce once they have repented is wrong because it is a denial of the only forgiveness any of us can have before God (Matt. 6:14–15; 18:21–35; Col. 3:13, etc.).

Not all divorces have an innocent party, of course. Often the officially innocent party could have done much more to hold the marriage together. Often "exceptions" can becomes excuses—one spouse's urging the other spouse to commit adultery so he or she can have the excuse to file (this has happened), an unforgiveness that refuses to accept the other's repentance, an angry slap taken as physical abuse. And where do we draw the line? While day after day of subjection to menial labor and cursing is not physical abuse, it is certainly abuse of the severest sort. But then what about arguments (in which most couples engage at times)? What about insensitivity to needs, expressed or unexpressed? Disagreements over the use of money? Disagreements over who should lead in the home? "Psychological abuse" can become a catch-all phrase that permits divorce for almost any reason, as the school of Hillel did (except that either party can now file). Can a man divorce his wife "for any cause," or are there definite limitations?

Jesus' teaching on the matter was stated hyperbolically for a reason. Yes, there may be exceptions. But Jesus' point is that we dare not look for the exceptions—they are only the last resort when all else has failed. A tough marriage is not an excuse to bail out. Indeed, in Jesus' day, marriages were arranged by parents; some marriages started off with more in their favor than others, but Jesus told his followers to make their marriages work, as much as it was in their power. In the same way today, there will always be marriages more and less comfortable than our own, and we, as much as is in our power, must make our marriages healthy and enduring.

The summons of his Kingdom is to be servants, to lay down our own desires and to seek reconciliation and healing (not just repressed hostility) in our marriages. Jesus demands that we make our marriages work. Only God ultimately knows what is in our hearts, but that inward standard is the one by which we will be judged: even if all the world thinks we did our best, if we really were not doing so, he knows. Following the teaching of the Kingdom means holding neither anger nor lust, and it means not looking for ways out of our marriage vows. The exception clause may be increasingly forced on us in our culture, but we must never forget that it remains an "exception," after all else has failed.[3] The exception may come sooner or later, depending on how the breaking of the marriage is forced on the faithful partner; but to the extent that it depends on us, we must always do our best to make our marriages alive and strong.

Jesus' message to everyone is plain enough: to those contemplating divorce, don't; to those inclined to condemn without knowing the circumstances, don't; to those near a prospective Christian divorce, offer yourselves as humble agents of reconciliation and healing; to those who have repented and made restitution (insofar as possible) for a sinful choice, trust his forgiveness; to those on whom dissolution of marriage forced itself without invitation, be healed by God's grace and dare to stand for your freedom in Christ, which no one has the authority to take away from you. And whether his call after the divorce proves to be singleness or marriage, make your life a life of prayer that will minister to all believers with whom you have relationships, harboring no bitterness either against your former spouse or against a church whose fear of human pain often overshadows its willingness to heal it.

3. I greatly appreciate the vitally important material written today on building strong marriages, such as by H. Norman Wright, James Dobson, Ed and Gaye Wheat, and others. Having been part of communities besides middle-class white North Americans, I think that there is now a great need for literature to be written that will address the marriage dynamics of Christians in different cultures, but this does not diminish my appreciation for what has already been written in marriage enrichment and counseling.

Conclusion

Is God against divorce? To this we must answer a resounding Yes. But the Yes must be qualified if the other partner has already broken the marriage; Scripture certainly allows making the brokenness of the marriage official if the partner has broken it. And the divorce is made official precisely to allow the innocent party (when there is an innocent party) to remarry, after God's compassion through the body of Christ and time have wrought their healing.[4] It is not legitimate for us to think of divorced people as a category; we must differentiate between the innocent and the guilty, or discard the label altogether. The innocent should be treated as other singles (or married people, if they have remarried); the guilty should be helped first to repent and then to seek reconciliation if it is still possible.

Divorce has become common in Western society. This is a tragedy, and the church is right to take a stand against it. But it is no longer possible to "sacrifice" divorced Christians for the sake of the standard. It was never right, of course, but it has now become a stumbling block to more and more people. How long will conservative churches be able to continue evangelizing the multitudes in our society who are divorced, while forbidding them to hold offices in the church and often requiring them to remain single? Most churches, regardless of their position on divorce and remarriage, address all too little the acid agony of divorce, the problems faced by the children growing up in single-parent homes, the need of the innocent party for assurance and the need of the guilty party for correction and restoration to right relationship with God and his people. Scripture gives us some guidelines on how to make its teaching practical in our culture, just as it was when its Author first gave it. May we have the courage to obey its guidance.

Pages 104–10 of . . . *And Marries Another: Divorce and Remarriage in the Teaching of the New Testament.* © 1991 Hendrickson Publishers, Peabody, Massachusetts, used with permission.

4. It is my belief, based on inference from New Testament texts about forgiveness, that the guilty parties or party are also allowed to remarry if they have genuinely repented and done their best to make any necessary restitution. But this point is not as easily argued on the basis of explicit statements in Scripture, and I do not wish anyone to confuse it with my argument from Scripture above, which I think *explicitly* allows remarriage for the innocent party.

The Husband of One Wife

Robert L. Saucy

The question of the meaning of the qualification laid down by the apostle Paul regarding the elder's marriage relationship is impossible to answer simply from the words involved. Literally the Greek words are simply "a one woman man" or "a one wife man." Lenski translates them as "one wife's husband."[1] Whether this means one at a time or one during a lifetime depends completely on other considerations. Even the question of the meaning of "one at a time" depends on one's view of divorce as to whether a divorced man who has remarried is considered to be "one wife's husband." Since the phrase, "one woman man" is ambiguous in itself it is necessary to seek its meaning with the help of the general biblical teaching on marriage which is pertinent to this question. . . .

If divorce on the basis of adultery is legal and dissolves the marriage so that the one divorced can marry another, is the one remarried considered to be now "the husband of one wife"? It seems evident that legally such a remarried person is the husband of only one wife. He is not considered to have two wives. If this is true, then technically, he meets the requirements of the language of 1 Timothy 3:2.

The next question is whether the Bible ever indicates that even though he is the husband of one wife without any breaking of God's law, he is yet somehow disqualified as an elder. We can find no such distinction and it would seem that if there were so, it would have been indicated in far clearer terms.

The conclusion is therefore that technically the man divorced on biblical grounds meets this qualification. As will be noted later, however, this quali-

1. R. C. H. Lenski, *The Interpretation of St. Paul's Epistles to the Colossians, to the Thessalonians, to Timothy, to Titus and to Philemon* (Columbus, Ohio: Lutheran Book Concern, 1937), 579.

fication is not to be interpreted as a simple legal statement but rather as a quality of a man's life. It may be therefore that a man could legally be the husband of one wife and yet not be a faithful loving husband. This is sometimes true concerning parties that are divorced. While there may be technically an innocent party it is possible that he or she was not the faithful spouse that they should have been. Each case deserves investigation with regard to this qualification for eldership. . . .

The Evidence from the Background of the Church

The historical evidence suggests that the church of this time was made up of those that had formerly been involved in all kinds of immorality. Lenski explains this condition in relation to the qualification of the elder to be the husband of one wife.

> Paul has a reason for beginning with "*one* wife's husband." In those days mature men were chosen for the eldership, who, as a rule, were married and had families; there were no seminary graduates who were awaiting calls. The bulk of the membership from which the elders had to be chosen had come from paganism. What this means as to sexual vices is written large in the New Testament and in the moral records of the day. Even the early apostolic conference in Jerusalem warns against "fornication" and uses this wide term to cover all the prevalent pagan sexual excesses (Acts 15:29). The epistles fairly din the word into their readers' ears. There was the regular institution of the hierodouloi, pagan temple prostitutes; the common custom of having *hetaerae* ("companions," see Liddell and Scott ἑταῖρος), girls from noncitizen families who were used by unmarried and by married men; and thus, besides these standard practices, all the rest of the vileness that formed the soil from which these grew. Converts to the gospel did not at once step into perfect sexual purity. Hence this proviso regarding the "overseers": to begin with, a man who is not strictly faithful to his one wife is debarred.[2]

This picture of the background from which the church members would have come, which included divorce for all kinds of reasons, is substantiated by all sources.[3] It thus suggests that the qualification of "husband of one wife" would not mean that the person had never sinned in this area, but that as Lenski suggests they had been purified in these areas so that now they were faithful to their one wife.

---

2. Ibid., 580–81.
3. See William Barclay, *The Letters to Timothy, Titus and Philemon* (Philadelphia, 1960); Friedrich Hauck and Siegfried Schultz, "πορνη et al.," *Theological Dictionary of the New Testament*, ed. Gerhard Kittel, trans. and ed. Geoffrey W. Bromiley, vol. 6 (Grand Rapids: Eerdmans, 1968), 592; C. K. Barrett, *The New Testament Background: Selected Documents* (London, 1956), 8; Patrick Fairbairn, *Commentary on the Pastoral Epistles* (Grand Rapids: Zondervan, 1956 reprint [1874]), 428.

The Evidence from the Other Qualifications Listed

The previous conclusion is supported by a consideration of the interpretation of the other qualifications. Do these other requirements stipulated by the apostle mean that the prospective elder must never have sinned prior to the present in a way which contradicts these requirements?

In 1 Timothy 3:3, Paul states that the elder is not to be addicted to wine. Does this mean that at no time in his previous life the prospective elder was ever drunk? The elder furthermore is not to be pugnacious or contentious. Does this mean that he has never in his life been characterized by these two words? Are these characteristics to be interpreted in the sense that they were never a part of the man's life or are they to be interpreted that by God's grace they have been worked out of his life so that they are not now as he is being examined for eldership a part of his life? The answer appears obvious.

In view of these considerations it seems difficult to make this one qualification concerning the marriage state refer to the entire life as one interpreter who writes, ". . . when men were to be considered for this high office, there must be no record of divorce or other marital infidelity in the candidate, even before his conversion."[4] Why not apply this same principle to all the qualifications, if we are going to apply it to this one?

If this interpretation is correct, in view of what we have argued, (1) that adultery is probably not a continual state of sin, but can be forgiven even as a murder, and (2) that divorce does dissolve marriage so that one married again is not considered to be the husband of two wives, then it would seem reasonable to interpret this qualification of being the husband of one wife as a present quality of a man's life.

This does not mean that any person is qualified just because he is the husband of one wife any more than it means that any person is qualified just because he is no longer murdering people, or no longer getting drunk. The sinful characteristic of his life which led to sin in these areas must have been changed by God's grace. This would take time and would require in some cases long periods of observation and the living of the changed life before his fellow believers. It must be noticed that this is not simply a negative, technical quality dealing with the legality of one's marital state.

The writer in Kittel's Dictionary correctly points out, "The Old Testament prohibition of adultery is not confined to the negative avoidance of the sinful act. It finds its true fulfillment only in the love of spouses who are joined together by God (R. 13:9)."[5] Kent likewise explains the intent of the

4. Homer A. Kent, Jr., *The Pastoral Epistles: Studies in I and II Timothy and Titus* (Chicago: Moody, 1958), 129.
5. F. Hauck, "μοιχεύω et al.," *Theological Dictionary of the New Testament*, ed. by Gerhard Kittel, trans. and ed. Geoffrey W. Bromiley (Grand Rapids: Eerdmans, 1967), 734.

qualification when he says, "The phrase by Paul is stated positively. The overseer must be a one-woman man. He must be devoted to her and give her all the love and consideration that a wife deserves."[6]

The Question of Lowering the Standard

It may be questioned as to whether such a qualitative view of this requirement is not lowering the standard, as one man recently remarked, "At least my interpretation (speaking of his) maintains a high standard," implying that the view presented in this study lets down the bars. In answer to this we would suggest two thoughts.

First, this argument assumes that the bars should be up in the first place. If bars have not been erected by the Word, we have no right to erect them. Removing previously erected bars, if this is the case in this position and if they are not demanded by the Scripture, would not be wrong.

The abuse of correct laws does not allow us to change those laws. The Fifth Amendment to the Constitution has been much abused by gangsters and enemies of our country, but there is not a court or legislature in America that would abolish it.[7]

In reality we are suggesting that this argument should not bear on one's interpretation of what this qualification is. The only concern should be that our interpretation is that intended by the writer of the Word.

Secondly, I do not think that this is in reality a lowering of the standard of qualifications. In placing an emphasis on the positive characteristic of a faithful husband rather than simply upon the legal married status, this understanding actually exalts the requirement. While there are men who have been barred from eldership who on the basis of this interpretation should be permitted to occupy this position, there are others now serving as pastors or elders who under this understanding of being characteristically a one-woman man should be disqualified. Legally as far as their married state is concerned they are husbands of one wife, but their actions and attitudes demonstrate that they are not truly one-woman men.

Conclusion

The evils of sexual immorality and divorce must be taught as they are in the Word—as sin. Churches need to exercise more discipline in these areas. But it must be remembered that these sins can be forgiven and the person cleansed and changed by the saving power of God's grace in Christ. The "husband of one wife" qualification therefore, it seems to us, does not demand the absence of life-long sin in the area of marriage relationships, but

6. Kent, *Pastoral Epistles*, 130.
7. Cf. Guy Duty, *Divorce and Remarriage* (Minneapolis: Bethany, 1967), 127.

the evidence that the power of God's transforming grace is presently operative in the life of the candidate to the effect that if there has been sin in these
areas, it has been forgiven through genuine repentance, and the sinful tendencies which led to the breakdown have been overcome by the power of the
indwelling Spirit of holiness.

From Robert L. Saucy, "The Husband of One Wife," *Bibliotheca Sacra* 131 (1974):
229–40.

For Further Reflection

Case Studies

Abandoned husband. Bob married Martha eight years ago, and they quickly had three children. After six especially tumultuous months, Bob came home from work one day and found a note taped to the refrigerator: "Dear Bob, I can't keep giving anymore. I need some time for myself. Goodbye for now." The financial stress on Bob has been great since his factory wages only partly meet the needs of the family. Bob has lost his home, and the children have moved in with his parents. Two years have gone by and after repeated attempts to find her, Bob believes Martha is gone forever. He has no idea what sort of life Martha is living and has had very little contact with her. Though he is generally opposed to divorce, he comes to his pastor wondering if God will punish him if he gets divorced. "Martha isn't coming back, and my children need a mother," he says. "Would God punish me if I got a divorce and began to date again?" How should the pastor respond?

Repentant husband. William, a Christian, married for eight stormy years, decided to join the swinging-singles set. He lived the part for two years, committing adultery with many single women. Susan, his wife, pled with him to come back. Finally, she gave up, and on the advice of her family, sued for divorce. The legal move shocked William. He suddenly realized the depth of his sin and the foolishness of his actions. He was throwing away his family! He sought out his pastor, confessed his sin, and set about to reconcile with his wife. But Susan had turned a corner. She was deeply hurt. She worried about disease. She did not want William back. He had repeatedly committed adultery, and so she felt she was entitled to a divorce (Matt. 19). Despite his

255

pleadings, she finalized the divorce. Two years later, Susan remarried, claiming she was not duty-bound to reconcile. After another year, William comes to you, wondering whether he may pursue another relationship. William's brother reminds him that his predicament is his own doing. The brother argues that remarriage is always adultery. William believes he did all he could to reconcile with Susan, but to no avail. You are a Christian counselor. What would you say to William?

Glossary

Adultery: Voluntary sexual intercourse between a married person and someone other than his or her marriage partner; also includes voluntary thoughts of such activities.

Annulment: An official cancellation of a marriage; unlike a divorce, which acknowledges the legitimacy of the marriage it ends, an annulment declares that the attempted marriage never really came into being.

Divorce: A legal dissolution of a duly consummated marriage.

Divorce (sacramental view): Catholic view that considers marriage a sacred covenant before God that is unbreakable except by death; in this view, annulment is permissible under certain circumstances, but divorce never is.

Exception clause: The phrase *except for adultery* (Matt. 5:32 and 19:9); whether Jesus permits an innocent victim of divorce to remarry depends on how this phrase relates to surrounding clauses.

Marriage: A union of one man and one woman as husband and wife through an official ceremony of vows by which the man and woman promise faithfulness to each other; marriage is recognized by society as well as by the church and is consummated in a full sexual union.

Pauline privilege: The idea that an innocent Christian deserted by an unbelieving spouse is not bound to the marriage vow and is therefore free to choose remarriage; based on one interpretation of the phrase *not bound* in 1 Corinthians 7:15.

Annotated Bibliography

Achtemeier, Elizabeth Rice. *The Committed Marriage.* Philadelphia: Westminster, 1976. A theology of marriage.

Balswick, Jack O., and Judith Balswick K. *The Family: A Christian Perspective on the Contemporary Home.* Grand Rapids: Baker, 1989. Christian psychologists develop a theology of marriage.

Bromiley, Geoffrey W. *God and Marriage.* Grand Rapids: Eerdmans, 1980. Brief book outlining the theological meaning of marriage and opposing the remarriage of divorced individuals.

Duty, Guy. *Divorce and Remarriage*. Minneapolis: Bethany, 1967. Well-documented (though inelegantly written) justification of permission for innocent partners to remarry.

Ellisen, Stanley A. *Divorce and Remarriage in the Church*. Rev. ed. Grand Rapids: Zondervan, 1980. Briefly defends permission for innocents to remarry and for remarried divorcees to enter pastoral service.

Heth, William A., and Gordon J. Wenham. *Jesus and Divorce*. London: Hodder and Stoughton, 1984. Very detailed, well-documented argument against remarriage.

House, H. Wayne, ed. *Divorce and Remarriage: Four Christian Views*. Downers Grove, Ill.: InterVarsity, 1990. Four authors' views representing the spectrum of positions plus responses by each writer to the other three essays.

Keener, Craig S. *. . . And Marries Another: Divorce and Remarriage in the Teaching of the New Testament*. Peabody, Mass.: Hendrickson, 1991. Very competent analysis of New Testament cultural backgrounds; resists divorce, but permits divorce and remarriage in cases other than adultery and desertion.

Laney, J. Carl. *The Divorce Myth*. Minneapolis: Bethany, 1980. Defense of a very restrictive view that all divorce is sinful.

Mace, David, and Vera Mace. *The Sacred Fire: Christian Marriage Through the Ages*. Nashville: Abingdon, 1986. Survey of views of marriage in Christian history.

Melton, J. Gordon, ed. *The Churches Speak On—Sex and Family Life: Official Statements from Religious Bodies and Ecumenical Organizations*. Detroit: Gale Research, 1991. Compilation of official church and denominational statements about marriage.

Murray, John. *Divorce*. Reprint ed. Philadelphia: Presbyterian and Reformed, 1961 (originally 1953). Landmark evangelical statement of permission for victims of spouse's adultery or desertion to remarry.

Richmond, Gary. *The Divorce Decision*. Dallas: Word, 1988. Powerful anecdotal account of the devastating consequences of divorce.

Ryrie, Charles C. "Biblical Teaching on Divorce and Remarriage." *Grace Theological Journal* 3 (1982): 177–92. Argues against all remarriage.

Saucy, Robert L. "The Husband of One Wife." *Bibliotheca Sacra* 131 (July 1974): 229–40. Insightful discussion of "the husband of one wife" qualification for elders and deacons in light of general biblical teaching on marriage.

Steele, Paul E., and Charles C. Ryrie. *Meant to Last*. Wheaton: Victor, 1983. Statement of restrictive view of divorce and remarriage.

Stevens, R. Paul. *Married for Good: The Lost Art of Staying Happily Married*. Downers Grove, Ill.: InterVarsity, 1986. Brief marriage-enrichment

For Further Reflection

manual that defends the view of marriage as an unbreakable covenant.

Wiebe, Philip H. "Jesus' Divorce Exception." *Journal of the Evangelical Theological Society* 32 (September 1989): 327–33. Discussion of Matthew 19:9 using logical analytical techniques.

Part 3

Class Relationships

7

Race Relations

America has proclaimed Martin Luther King, Jr.'s, birthday a national holiday. Many **people of color** appear in the popular media that whites enjoy and on the athletic teams they love to cheer. Virtually every institution prints on its brochures and reports, "XYZ, Inc., does not discriminate on grounds of race, color . . ." America seems to have changed her ways. Despite all this, however, African-Americans still insist that America, "the land of the free," reeks of **racism**.

Take the devastating 1992 Los Angeles riots. An amateur videotape caught four white policemen beating an African-American man named Rodney King. When the four men were put on trial for assault, however, the jury declared them all not guilty. (A later court case did convict two of the men.) Most African-Americans saw the initial decision, acquitting all of King's assailants, as strong evidence of insidious racism. The rage some felt gradually escalated until South Los Angeles went up in flames. In line with their stereotypes, some whites took those riots as evidence that their biased views of all black people are actually true.

Because of the unique experience of slavery in America, we will focus on racism against African-Americans. But other groups victimized by racism—Native Americans, Hispanics, Jews, and Asians, not to mention peoples around the world—have their own unique concerns. At the same time, many peoples of color today experience a kinship because they have all felt the hos-

261

tility of white people and institutions. This suggests that perhaps we can transfer some of the principles of black/white interactions to relations among other people groups.

The belief of some whites constitutes racism in its classic sense. In her classic *Race: Science and Politics,* Ruth Benedict defines *racism* as

> the dogma that one ethnic group is condemned by Nature to hereditary infe-
> riority and another group is destined to hereditary superiority. It is the dogma
> that the hope of civilization depends upon eliminating some races and keeping
> others pure. It is the dogma that one race has carried progress throughout
> human history and can alone ensure future progress. (p. 98)

Nazi Germany was officially racist. The Nazis carried racism to its logical end: **genocide**. The racist claims that if one **race** retards the progress of society, then others should eliminate that race. So-called neo-Nazi groups today believe Hitler was on the right track. Many white Americans, however, find the proposal that America should now pursue a genocidal policy utterly reprehensible. But they forget that the United States did seek to destroy Native American peoples only a century ago.

Official United States government policy today does not seek genocide. The law now prohibits racial **discrimination**. Yet blacks claim that racism is still rampant. Part of the reason is that some writers in race relations now define *racism* as "racial prejudice with power." This expands Benedict's classic definition significantly. In the fuller sense, racism includes not only racial discrimination, but also white cultural ways that act as stumbling blocks to blacks. Given this, an institution like a school can be racist. A black person who enters a dominantly white environment feels like a fish out of water. An organization may proclaim itself officially nondiscriminatory, but those who control access to the institution (even those who are not white) may still follow subtle unspoken cultural ways or patterns that benefit whites. To make this point, African-Americans say, "A black man in a blue uniform is still a white cop."

The differences in these two definitions of *racism* are important. When some whites think of a racist, they imagine a skinhead. When some blacks think of a racist, they think of anyone who is white. White persons usually resent this; most have no sympathy whatever for the Ku Klux Klan (KKK). White Christians know intellectually that the gospel breaks down walls between races (Gal. 3:28). Yet black persons contnue to feel frustration. The unfamiliar and uncomfortable cultural ways of white society hold them back. They constantly swim upstream against this current, encountering subtle barriers and hostilities at every turn. Of course, whites are responsible for the flow of the river, and so nonwhites easily assume that whites are racists. Whites cannot understand this. They feel unjustly accused. Disagreement about implicit definitions brings massive misunderstanding and reinforces prejudice.

While white Americans may not be as blatant about their racism as they once were, old ideas die hard. In *The New York Times Magazine* (27 October 1985), a black mother vented her anger over a school play at a mainly white school. The teacher cast a white child as a gorilla and gave him a mask. The black children took the role of monkeys and wore no masks. Whites who take the time to listen to blacks will hear a million stories like this. Upon learning that people of color will be in the majority in America in another generation, patriotic white Americans wince, secretly fearing America's decline. These feelings betray prejudices.

Racism is a belief about a class of people. **Racial prejudice** is an attitude. Attitudes are beliefs with an evaluation attached. "The police are powerful" is a belief. The Los Angeles police chief is proud of police power; the ghetto dweller hates it. The pride and the hate are evaluations. Since attitude is belief plus evaluation, two people can have the same belief about some object and still have opposite attitudes about that object.

All humans prejudge others. When a uniformed woman in a restaurant asks me whether I would like some coffee, I prejudge that she is a waitress, even before I know her personally. Prejudgings of this sort are a normal and necessary part of life. The phrase *racial prejudice*, however, connotes a negative attitude based on racial identity. I am racially prejudiced if I see an Italian man and immediately assume that he is part of the Mafia. Prejudice in this sense allows stereotypes to control interaction between persons. Unlike prejudice (which is a broader term), a **stereotype** is a composite image of persons of a certain class. It is a stable, negative, communally recognized picture of groups of persons. According to the usual stereotype, for example, an Asian man chatters rapidly, bows all the time, and wears thick, round, wire-rimmed glasses.

Stereotypes dominate thinking in this way: meeting a real person of some class stimulates in the mind a whole constellation of preset images and attitudes. For instance, when a southerner hears a northern accent, he immediately accesses a certain file in his mental hard disk. Onto his mental screen pops his preconceived set of attributes filed under the title *northerner*: rude, fast-talking, liberal, southerner-hating. Upon meeting the northerner, the southerner looks at his own screen and sees, not the real person, but his own preset image. The real northerner merely stimulates the southerner to see his own stereotype.

When a white person sees a Hispanic, she sees a set of images and qualities that she has filed under the designation *Hispanic*. Similarly, the Hispanic person accesses his set of preconceived ideas regarding whites. Both uncover attitudes that prevent them from seeing the other person as he or she really is. When negative preconceptions dominate both individuals, the preconceptions prompt hostile interactions, at least initially. Not surprisingly, the negative experiences that the prejudices generate will reinforce the prejudices. Then, the next time these people encounter someone of another race they are even more likely to experience hostility.

Pastor Spencer Perkins of Voice of Calvary Fellowship in Jackson, Mississippi, writes about the results of these prejudices for his people. He suggests that a consistent pro-life strategy must involve more than opposing abortion. It must also include caring for those who are already born, reaching out to people who already have life but are members of another racial group. If whites win the fight against abortion, says Perkins, they can go home. The black community, however, will still have many pro-life issues to face.

The negative interactions of whites and blacks in North America have a long history. The first African slaves arrived in Portugal in 1444. The importation of African slaves ultimately led to a new justification for the institution of slavery. In the ancient world, masters and slaves among cultures around the Mediterranean Sea could be any color. As the Europeans enslaved Africans, however, they began to argue that lighter skin naturally suits some to the superior role, and darker skin to the inferior. This is classic racism.

Everyone understands today that slavery is evil. In the years before the Civil War, slave holders built theological justifications for slavery: it is "natural" and ordained by God; the Old Testament condoned slavery and the New Testament did not eliminate it; God cursed Ham and his black descendants. All Christians today see, however, that these absurd arguments require tortured exegesis, as Methodist Old Testament scholar Everett Tilson clearly argues.

Now that the slaves have been freed and civil rights guaranteed, some whites feel angered by what they perceive as black ingratitude. Perhaps they believe down deep that in 1620, the Pilgrims stepped off the Mayflower at Plymouth Rock to found America for white, English Christians (that is, for white, Anglo-Saxon Protestants—WASPs). (Many do not know that in 1619, twenty black slaves toiled for white masters in Virginia.) Whites believe non-WASPs are warmly welcomed. In reality, the non-WASPs come on WASP terms, with WASP permission, and must adapt to WASP culture. Light-skinned Europeans made this bargain and melted into the WASPs' pot. The African, identified by his skin as the German Jew was by his yellow Star of David, faced obstacles at every turn. For this reason, Malcolm X said, "We didn't land on Plymouth Rock; Plymouth Rock landed on us."

Whites who believe that Lincoln's Emancipation Proclamation solved the blacks' legal problems are naive. The Emancipation Proclamation made slavery illegal, but did not prevent racists from finding new and more subtle ways to discriminate. Soon after the demise of slavery, racist powers in the American south developed a new system of oppression: segregation. The

Supreme Court gave its blessing to the "separate but equal" principle in the famous *Plessy v. Ferguson* decision of 1896. In theory, the races were equal, but powerful whites used segregation, enforced legally by the **Jim Crow** system, to ensure that African-Americans remained very unequal.

For this reason, in the years after World War II, black leaders sought to dismantle segregation. If segregation kept blacks down, integration would allow blacks access to the American dream. In 1954, in another landmark decision, *Brown v. Board of Education*, the Supreme Court declared the Jim Crow system unconstitutional, and African-Americans began to dismantle that system piece by piece. Starting with Rosa Parks' courageous decision not to sit in the back of the bus, the nonviolent civil rights movement, led by Martin Luther King, Jr., and others, gradually made great strides in changing American public policy.

If the legal battles led to success for some blacks, however, the social prospects for others remain unchanged. Many in the African-American underclass feel hopeless. They live in a world of catch-22. The problems are only too well-known. If whites are to avoid blaming the victim, they must experience deeply and emotionally the frustration, despair, and hopelessness that pervade some urban neighborhoods. If blacks are to avoid accusing whites of causing all their troubles, they must understand that many whites feel much goodwill toward people of color. Many whites experience race fatigue, a sense of frustration at being repeatedly accused of racism and blamed for miseries they feel powerless to relieve. Each group blames the other; relations grind down into hostility and finger-pointing.

How should Christians respond? Both emancipation and integration have, in the minds of many, failed to bring just relations between the races. As emancipation destroyed the legal structure of slavery, so integration attacked the judicial framework of segregation. But the law cannot change the attitudes of racists who creatively find new ways to oppress nonwhites despite new legal requirements.

Christians must consider their response at both personal and social levels. At the personal level, white Christians can empathize with peoples of color. To *feel* what it is like to be black and despised in America will help. Christians can seek cross-cultural experience, for cultural differences repeatedly surface in interracial relations. Interracial experience must be augmented, however, with a willingness to admit failure, to learn, and to change. Otherwise, people merely dismiss culturally different groups as unnatural or bizarre. This suggests that Christians should express love, not just in theory, but in concrete and positive racial relationships. This requires a willingness to listen intentionally to fellow Christians of other races and to go the second mile.

The church faces another significant issue: the "suburban captivity" of the gospel. The values, methods, and members of evangelicalism are dominantly white and middle class. Jesus Christ has blond hair and blue eyes. Many African-Americans consider the gospel of this Jesus utterly alien. A gospel of the suburbs does not speak forcefully to the city. Some blacks choose to replace the church, believing that Islam is the religion for peoples of color. The church's response to the whiteness of the gospel (What if Jesus was dark?) and its concern for social righteousness profoundly affect its evangelistic impact. Perkins's essay speaks loudly to this problem of perception. If the church does not identify with the people, it discredits the gospel message.

At the social level, evangelicals divide on whether government should do more. Some activists think government must do much more. Many conservatives, by contrast, point out how little has changed for many peoples of color despite great legal victories and colossal social programs. This shows the limitations of government.

One area of debate between these two views is **affirmative action** policies that seek to favor formerly disadvantaged peoples in hiring and promotion. Since this works against job opportunities for whites, however, some reject affirmative action as a kind of **reverse discrimination**. Others, like conservative black scholar Shelby Steele, argue that affirmative action degrades the genuine achievements of hard-working minority persons. When racists see a minority person advancing, they give credit, not to the individual who deserves it, but to the affirmative-action plan. Others point out, however, that affirmative action is one strategy for helping to ensure that qualified persons of color are considered for positions that before had gone to whites because of *their* skin color.

In this day of huge budget deficits, America will never again have the public resources she had in the last three decades, and budget constraints will limit government initiatives in the future. As an alternative to big government, Raleigh Washington and Glen Kehrein seek to make a difference through holistic, Christian ministry. Washington, an African-American pastor, guides the Rock of Our Salvation Church in a poor neighborhood near Chicago. Kehrein, a white man from rural Wisconsin, leads Circle Urban Ministry, a Christian social agency in the same neighborhood. The two ministries support each other, and the two men intentionally model reconciliation in their relationship with each other. Together these ministries express a uniquely Christian approach to racial conflict: reconciliation in the name of Christ.

A constellation of solutions is no doubt necessary. Government can do some things in law and policy that individuals or small institutions cannot. Changed hearts and Spirit-filled lives, however, can bring reconciliation where governmental edict cannot. Some churches in declining areas actively recruit stable families to live and work in these neighborhoods. These churches can develop ministries of reconciliation that promote healing at many levels. Most basically, many people must learn to stop blaming others for the discord. The surest way to prevent reconciliation is for each person to insist that the other is solely responsible for the standoff. The church, in nurturing Christian holiness, can help its members learn the pain of confession, the relief of forgiveness, and the joy of service.

Many peoples of color are already making these sacrifices. But some have grown tired of the fight, going their own way in the belief that the majority of white Christians will never care about their plight. Whites, they argue, are benefactors of a culture that privileges them. Because of the power their skin color entails, whites should carry a larger responsibility for confronting racism and seeking reconciliation (Luke 12:48).

In a day of shrinking government resources, sacrifice by people of all colors—committed first to Christ, motivated by his love, and working in genuine partnership with other believers—is a powerful healing force. It is time for white churches to join fellow Christians of all ethnic backgrounds in the ministry of reconciliation. Overcoming racism is everyone's business.

The Prolife Credibility Gap

Spencer Perkins

Abortion—and the prolife movement—present black evangelicals with a dilemma. It is not that we question the evil of abortion; Jesus clearly would have condemned it. But for me, a black man, to join your demonstrations against abortion, I would need to know that you understand God's concern for justice everywhere.

It is hard for me, for example, not to be distracted by the faces I see leading the prolife crusade. Aren't some of these the same people who twenty years ago were calling Martin Luther King, Jr., a Communist? Are they not the same people who fifteen years ago moved out of the neighborhood in which I now live because too many blacks were moving in? Or aren't they the same Christians who opened private schools as soon as the courts ordered desegregation in the South in order to avoid any contact with us?

When it comes to abortion, these experiences have led to a credibility gap. Ever since I can remember, it has been almost axiomatic that if we blacks took a stand on an issue, conservative evangelical Christians would line up on the opposite side of the street, blocking our way. The gulf between us is so deep that it is hard to imagine us on the same side of an issue.

When Love Is Costly

When I was growing up in Mississippi, we were taught that the evidence of love for Christ was love for neighbor. I always asked if that meant that I had to love white people, too. The answer was always the same: "*especially* white people." Even after my father, John Perkins, was severely tortured and beaten almost to death by angry white men blinded by hatred and prejudice, the answer was the same: "*especially* white people." Since it was increasingly obvious in the sixties that white people did not love *us*, I wondered if there were no white Christians south of the Mason-Dixon line.

The wounds of racism and oppression still cut deep. Just how deep was made plain to me by comments made by a black single mother while she watched white antiabortion protesters on the evening news. "Do you think they would care if only black babies were being aborted?" she asked. Many of us, even now, struggle without answer. I know this sounds callous, but such sentiment demonstrates the magnitude of the gulf between us and illustrates our desperate need for reconciliation.

The issues get even more complex. For blacks who have a huge stake in the well-being of the black neighborhood, what does the reality of "zero abortions" mean? How many more female-headed households would be created? How many more young women would be strapped in the cycle of poverty and dependence on welfare? How many more gang members would these families produce? Wouldn't the ghettos be twice as large in just a few years? Wouldn't the crime rate soar? Wouldn't the prisons overflow? Who would take care of all of these children?

Am I not right in assuming that as the ghettos became larger and more dangerous, these same antiabortionists would move farther and farther into the suburbs, taking little or no responsibility for the social consequences of the lives they helped save?

Hope for Healing

These questions are real to us; before I can pick up a picket sign and join in this parade—before I can join hands with you and sing "We Shall Overcome," and certainly before I can go to jail with you—some of my fears need to be calmed. I need to feel secure that you have had a change of heart. I have heard very few Southern evangelicals admit they were on the wrong side of the race issues back in the fifties, sixties, and early seventies. I have never heard any of them say that they should have blocked the entrances to the jails where we were beaten and tortured, or taken a stand with us when we wanted equal access to "life, liberty, and the pursuit of happiness." In fact, over the past few years there have been only a few Southern, white, evangelical Christians who have asked our forgiveness and extended a hand in reconciliation. On the contrary, for every step we take in their direction, it seems that most take another step toward the suburbs.

This is the truth as we see it—the truth that needs to be heard in order for healing to take place in the Christian church, black and white. Healing will be hindered as long as Christians let their "Thus saith the Lord" on one issue be the evidence of their righteousness—at the expense of a lifestyle of justice. As Christians we are called to be "prolife," but that must have more than a narrow meaning, for life without dignity is a fate worse than death. A true prolife perspective must include a concern for justice in all its forms.

A recent incident illuminates the contradictions and frustrations surrounding the abortion issue because this broader prolife concern has not always been in evidence. One of the black women in our church was tending the nursery a few months ago while a Right to Life meeting was being held. Our church, Voice of Calvary Fellowship, is unusual for a Southern church in that the racial make-up is approximately half black and half white. Some of the white brothers and sisters of our church are passionately involved in the prolife movement, which is probably why the meeting was held at our church. One local white woman obviously did not realize our racial mix and did not prepare her children for what they would encounter. When they walked into the building, the first thing they saw was the skin color of our black children. One of the woman's boys immediately asked in disgust, "What kind of church *is* this?" His brother's response summed up what these young boys felt about their black brothers and sisters: "We'd better be careful what we touch here," he said, drawing his hands back as if fearing contamination.

I have to wonder at the answer these young white children are given in words and deeds when they ask the question, "Does loving my neighbor mean loving blacks too?"

Where Strategies Meet

Being prolife and demanding an unborn baby's "right to life" is a high calling. But I believe that God cares about a deeper principle—a "right to justice"; that is, a right to a decent *quality* of life.

It is not a simple, glib response, then, when I must counsel an unwed black teenager against an abortion, even though I believe with all my heart that abortion is morally wrong. I feel that if the love of Christ compels me to save the lives of children, that same love should compel me to take more responsibility for them once they are born. Until Christians like me are willing to offer more than counseling for prospective mothers, until the Christian church is willing to take responsibility for the quality of life of these mothers and children, whatever that may entail, then our crusade for the lives of unwanted children will continue to be perceived as lacking integrity, especially in the black community.

For me, the issue is not about abortion—whether it is wrong or right to kill unborn children. The issue for me is much deeper—whether together we will embrace a Christianity committed to justice for all, or whether we will remain apart and fight our separate battles. Perhaps the abortion controversy is the vehicle God will use to bring us together.

As for answering the question, "Where do black Christians stand on abortion?" it looks to me as if we are on the same side of a moral issue. But if, from where you stand, you insist the battle is against abortion, while we believe the battle is against injustice, our strategies must remain different. We believe your plans for an all-out-war on abortion will prove to be short-sighted. When and if you win the abortion battle, the war will be over for you and you will be able to return home. Then we will be left to undertake the reconstruction. Therefore, our strategy must continue to be the fight against injustice—a war with many battlefronts. Where abortion will rank in our battle plan will depend on the strength of the relationship we can establish in the future and on how much your burdens and concerns, because of that relationship, can become ours.

From Spencer Perkins, "The Prolife Credibility Gap." Used by permission, *Christianity Today* (21 April 1989): 21–22. Spencer Perkins is the co-author of *More Than Equals;* he is also editor-in-chief of *Urban Family: A Magazine of Hope and Progress,* and editor of "The Reconciler," a newsletter devoted to racial reconciliation, Jackson, Mississippi (1-800-354-1563).

The Racial Issue in Biblical Perspective

Everett Tilson

The Bible makes numerous references to African countries and peoples. It likewise contains reports of frequent conflicts between Israelites and Africans. But in no place does it ever suggest race as the source or focus of any of these clashes. In fact, the only race ever mentioned in the Bible is a footrace.[1] . . .

Numerous biblical teachings have moved the major branches of Christianity to call for an inclusive church in an inclusive society. Yet many Christians remain unconvinced by this summons. And some of them continue to quote the Bible in support of racial discrimination. . . .

Biblical Props for Discrimination

Numerous biblical quotations and several alleged biblical teachings have been used in defense of racial discrimination, but only a few of these have appeared with marked regularity in racist literature. Therefore we may safely limit our investigation to the interpretation of such favorite quotations and themes. This will by no means indicate the limits to which such use of the Bible has sometimes gone. It should nevertheless quite adequately demonstrate the astonishing ingenuity and dubious reliability of this whole approach to the Scriptures.

Genesis 9:18–19 and chapter 10 (see also Acts 17:24–26) often get quoted in support of the idea that God has established boundaries, by con-

1. The black-white issue, because it stands at the center of this country's race problem, will be the primary focus of this article.

272

tinents, for the Mongoloid (supposedly descended from Shem), Negroid (supposedly descended from Ham), and Caucasian (supposedly descended from Japheth) races, respectively. These passages have been favorites with those who argue for the forced return of all blacks to Africa. Proponents of this view conveniently overlook the fact that the vast majority of blacks in America did not come to this country by choice. They likewise do not mention the fact that the general application of this principle would also send most American whites back to Europe. . . .

Genesis 9:20–27 has long been employed to justify the condemnation of blacks as slaves and the objects of discrimination. The curse of God on Ham, it is argued, is irrevocable; and it applied to all members of the black race, since Ham is assumed to be their progenitor. Even a casual analysis of this passage, with the help of a good Bible dictionary, would demonstrate that this interpretation rests on a patchwork of incredible errors. The evidence shows: (1) the curse is pronounced by a man, Noah, and not God; (2) when Noah pronounces the curse, he is not sober but drunk (at any rate, he does not curse the one who has given him occasion for offense); (3) the victim of the curse is not Ham but Canaan; (4) the descendants of Canaan, despite Noah's condemnation of them to slavery, continued to be masters over Palestine for some seventeen centuries; (5) the Canaanites were not blacks but whites. . . .

[A] check of the peoples from whom such biblical figures as Abraham, Joseph, Moses, and Solomon took wives against the Genesis table of nations reveals the presence in their ancestry of numerous connections with Hamitic peoples. When Aaron and Miriam begin to murmur against Moses for his marriage to a Cushite woman, they are rebuked by the Lord (Num. 12:1–8). One might also note in the genealogy of Jesus the name of Rahab, possibly a descendant of Canaan (Matt. 1:5; see also Gen. 10:18–19; Josh. 2:1ff.), one of the four sons of Ham (Gen. 6:10)—the one, in fact, on whom the famous curse fell!

A close study of Genesis 11:1–9 reveals its use as a racist text to be equally burdened with wholly erroneous assumptions. The writer of this narrative traces the confusion of tongues to humankind's rebellion against God, not to an attempt to integrate the races. Nowhere is it suggested, as the racist interpretation of the passage would require, any coincidence between linguistic differences and racial boundaries. And history, it should be noted, offers little convincing support of any such coincidence. The people of India and China, the purity of whose racial stock is surpassed almost nowhere, speak so many different languages and dialects that they often find themselves unable to converse with others from their own country who may live only twenty miles away. In the United States, on the other hand, blacks and whites, despite racial differences, speak a common language. Appeal to this passage as proof of God's establishment of segregation by an act of special providence can only be construed as an insult to God. Who are we to say that God, if he or she had been so vitally interested in the separation of the races, could have produced no better plan of separation than one that does not separate? Besides, we must ask, does not Pentecost (Acts 2:5–13) dramatize the purpose of God in Christ to reverse the effects of the separation at Babel?

The call of Abraham to live in separation from certain peoples (Gen. 12–15) is also frequently cited as a biblical warrant for racial separation. Since this call likewise includes a demand for Abraham's separation from his own kinsmen and countrymen, it is difficult to see why, in the absence of any mention of race, one can read it as a prescription for racial separation. Moreover, when we consider the explicit repudiation throughout the New Testament of the requirements of circumcision, the mark of Abraham's separation, we can only view this reading of the passage by Christians as a shocking betrayal of the writings and faith of the New Testament.

Some champions of human separation on racial grounds view Leviticus 19:19, which puts under the ban any mixture of breeds of cattle, seed in a field, or fabrics in a garment, as sort of a golden text for their cause. Yet even children know that any suspension of such mixtures in animal or plant husbandry would obviously effect a revolution. Any merchant with so little sense as to stock 100 percent wool suits with 100 percent wool linings would soon go 100 percent bankrupt. Any application of this passage to race would obviously presuppose a ban on all mixtures of color in animals, plants, and fabrics. But who on earth would think of outlawing Dominique chickens, orchards with both Grimes Golden and Virginia Beauty apple trees, or the use of pheasant feathers in female headdress? The obvious answer is nobody. Even the people who use this text as a sanction for the racial separation of human beings, which it never mentions, do not practice the separation of animals, plants, or fabrics, which it expressly enjoins. Since Jesus derived the second half of the Great Commandment from Leviticus 19:18, it is not at all surprising to see people turning to the Book of Leviticus in search of light on the problem of race. But the use separatists make of Leviticus 19 is instructive. Whereas Jesus ignored verse 19 but quoted 18, separatists ignore 18 and quote 19. Even more surprising is their disregard of verses 33–34 of this same chapter, for these verses prescribe the proper treatment of [non-]Israelites by Israelites—and with no suggestion whatever of any distinction between Caucasian strangers and Negroid strangers. . . .

Advocates of the separatist doctrine like to appeal to Jesus' command on one occasion to go only to the lost sheep of the house of Israel. They conveniently overlook the fact that obedience to this injunction would spell the end of missionary activity to any Gentiles, white or black. They likewise ignore Jesus' replacement of this commandment with a later commission to bear witness to the gospel to all people in every place (i.e., Acts 1:8). More amazing still, they take no account of the proclamation of the gospel by the apostolic church to Jews, Samaritans, and Gentiles on a nondiscriminatory basis (Rom. 10:12; Gal. 3:28; Eph. 2:11–22). These same oversights characterize the use by racists of Jesus' reluctance in responding to an appeal from a Syrophoenician woman (Mark 7:24–30; compare John 4:7–42).

The failure of first-century Christians like Paul to attack slavery is sometimes given as a precedent for toleration of the status quo in race relations. Paul's advice to Philemon, in counseling him with respect to the proper treatment of Onesimus, a runaway slave about to be returned to him, calls into question this view of Paul's stand on slavery. In verses 15–16 he wrote Philemon thusly: "For perhaps this is why you lost him for a time, that you might have him back for good, no longer as a slave, but as more than a slave—as a dear brother, very dear indeed to me and how much dearer to you, both as man and as Christian" (NEB). This and other such passages prompted P. T. Forsyth to say of slavery: "The New Testament does not destroy it, but its gospel does."

It is sometimes argued that God's choice of Israel serves as proof of the divine subordination of certain races. This argument rests on two mistaken assumptions: (1) that the people of Israel can be identified on racial grounds; (2) that this choice carries with it privileges without price. The prophets challenge this first assumption by interpreting rebellion against God, irrespective of race, as cause for exclusion from the benefits of God's promise to Israel. By making participation in these benefits available to all on the sole conditions of faithfulness to God and loving service to neighbor, irrespective of race, Jesus and the apostles deny all possibility of identifying the people of God on racial grounds. All major contributors to both Testaments stand the second of the above assumptions squarely on its head. God's choice of Israel, along with the privilege of becoming the object of God's love, carries with it the responsibility of service as the agent of God's love and purpose. Just as God's love manifests itself to all without regard for race, we are prohibited from being choosy in determining the objects of our love. That this role entails no special privileges or immunities is amply attested by the experience alike of the people of Israel and Jesus of Nazareth. The New Testament repeatedly assures us that we can expect much the same treatment as they received as the reward for our service as the agents of God.

Biblical Warrants for Racial Inclusiveness

The practice of racial inclusiveness within Christianity has certainly not kept pace with its articulation of racially inclusive pronouncements. Yet our churches' proclamations on the issue of race, even in countries such as our own, in which for generations public statutes lent sanction to racially discriminatory practices, have for decades been remarkably free of reservation and ambiguity. . . . [E]ven if grudgingly, we had to admit that the call to action with which the Bible confronts us is a summons to work for a racially inclusive human community.

The grounds for reaching this conclusion have varied from group to group, but they have typically featured considerations to which the following five propositions (from which flow implications of great significance for combating racism) call attention.

> Proposition 1: Pride of race, like pride of any other mark of human distinction, is a denial of God's grace and a betrayal of the church's hope.

The Bible betrays an awareness of the differences that divide people into separate groups. It knows of the division of peoples by language, culture, nation, and geography. But it acknowledges only one difference of decisive significance for the conduct of human life. And that is not the difference that separates people by language, culture, nation, and geography. The only differences of ultimate importance for human existence is the difference that separates creatures from Creator, humanity from deity, the peoples of every race from the God of all races. And that difference is not one that divides people, but one that unites them. It makes them one in their absolute dependence on Another for their very existence. . . .

> Proposition 2: Denial of the gospel to any person for any reason, racial or otherwise, marks a betrayal not only of the universal love of God the Creator and Christ the Redeemer but also of the mission of the church.

The ancient Israelites' belief that they enjoyed a special relationship to God may well have taken root and flourished in henotheistic soil. However, once they had left behind this primitive theological heritage for a monotheistic theology, they lost little time in setting the stage for the transformation of biblical faith into a religion inclusive enough to match the universal sovereignty and mission of their God. They proceeded to assert our oneness in the creative and redemptive love of God. They also asserted that God has made us all targets of the gospel to which that love commits us. . . .

> Proposition 3: Any sort of exclusion from or discrimination with the Christian fellowship, save on grounds of faith and conduct, marks a betrayal of the example of Christ and the apostles and the purpose of the church.

If we would ascertain how Jesus and the apostles would have handled our race problem, we have only to look at how they handled their race problem. To say this is, of course, to deny that color is the exclusive or even primary basis for today's exclusivist and discriminatory practices against certain races. It is to agree with those who contend that "the 'race problem' with which [we] have to deal is not so much a biological as a sociological problem in which theological, cultural and psychological factors all play their part."[2] Since these were the very same factors that framed "the dividing wall of hostility" (Eph. 2:14) between mainstream Judaism and sinners, publicans, Samaritans, and Gentiles, we not only have warrant for speaking of primitive Christianity's "race problem"[3] but we are also justified, as I have already suggested, in looking to their practice and teachings for guidance in our search for the solution to our race problem. On this score the New Testament writers speak with a single voice. Just as they bear emphatic witness to the progressively inclusive character of early Christian practice, they are also clear about the conclusions to which this practice leads.

Despite laws forbidding association with sinners, publicans, Samaritans, Gentiles, our Lord and his disciples associated with all these people. Official Judaism evolved an "elaborate system of spiritual quarantine regulations"[4] for keeping law-abiding Jews from law-breaking Jews like the sinners and publicans of the Gospels. It felt that "segregation(!) alone could preserve it from extinction."[5] Yet Jesus, judging by the frequency with which his critics assail him for associating with people of this ilk, simply "became notorious"[6] for his disregard of this taboo. . . .

Proposition 4: Self-denying service to persons in need, irrespective of race or party or any such thing, is the identifying mark of Christ and his followers.

Despite the particularism of his religious heritage, the Jesus of Matthew's Gospel never mentions

race or nationality in his list of requirements for appropriation of the life in the kingdom he heralds. He offers it, not to the smug and self-satisfied, but to the poor who mourn, weep, act mercifully, seek peace, and welcome persecution ahead of compromise (5:3–10); not to those who were born aright, but to those who live aright (5:17–20); not to the legalists who never fail to bring their gift to the altar at the appointed time, but to those who love even the people who look on them as enemies (5:23–24); not to those who love only their own kind, but to those who love even the people who look on them as enemies (5:43–48). In short, salvation in Matthew hinges, not on external gifts open only to the privileged few, but on personal gifts available to all.[7]

2. W. A. Visser 't Hooft, *The Ecumenical Movement and the Racial Problem* (Paris: UNESCO, 1964), 8.
3. W. D. Schermerhorn, *Beginnings of the Christian Church* (New York: Methodist Book Concern, 1929), 93.
4. David Daube, *The New Testament and Rabbinic Judaism* (London: Athlone Press, 1956), 375.
5. W. D. Davies, *Paul and Rabbinic Judaism* (London: S.P.C.K., 1948), 61.
6. B. H. Branscomb, *Jesus and the Law of Moses* (New York: R. R. Smith, 1930), 132.
7. Adapted from my book, *Segregation and the Bible* (New York: Abingdon, 1958), 75ff.

278 *Everett Tilson*

Christian reflection on Jesus' life and practice has yielded a broad consensus concerning authentic Christian living itself. This agreement touches on many things, but it highlights, in addition to the significance of Jesus' life for us, the relative importance of words and deeds and the use of special gifts.

Christ's ministry of crossbearing service gives us the model for the conduct of life as well as the central theme of Christian worship. The life of Jesus focuses attention on the work of the God whose glory we contemplate in worship. Needless to add, such worship inevitably sets us at odds with racism's model for the conduct of life. Whereas racism bids us seek greatness in domination, we are called to follow one who found greatness in service (Matt. 20:26–28; 21:14; Luke 4:18–21; Rom. 12:16); whereas racism demands that others lay down their lives for it, we are called to follow one who bids us lay down our lives for others (1 John 3:16; 4:8–11). However, in all these things, we are called to do nothing that the caller himself did not do before us. Yet we cannot be excused for doing anything less, either, for we "are the body of Christ and individually members of it" (1 Cor. 12:27). . . .

Proposition 5: The expression of hatred for any human being for any reason, racial or otherwise, marks a failure of love for God.

The assertion that all persons are created equal, insofar as it refers to individual native endowment, is patently absurd. It likewise enjoys little support in Scriptures. The Bible does not teach that all human beings are equally able or useful. Its teaching is that all human beings are equally created and equally loved by God. Although the love of God revealed in Jesus did not originate with him, multitudes did not become aware of this love until they encountered it in Jesus. And this same Jesus, who tells us of a God who blesses the good and the evil alike, calls us not to imitate our neighbors in the bestowal of love, but to imitate God (Matt. 5:48). By implication we are asked to ponder the possibility that others may not become aware of God's love until they see it in us; that we cannot fulfill our mission from God's man for others until we become God's people for others; in short, that each of us is called to become Christ to the neighbor. . . .

When we read the Bible from the viewpoint of God's Word made flesh in Jesus Christ, the divisions of human beings by race pale into insignificance beside their bonds of union. The demands of faith push these accidents of birth into the background. The impulse to go apart on the basis of race yields place to the necessity to draw together on the basis of grace.

True enough, Christ and the apostles do not provide us with a clear example of conquest over the temptation to separate people on the basis of race. They did not face that problem. But they did encounter the temptation to separate publicans, Samaritans, and Gentiles. And they faced that problem head-on in decisive combat. What is more, by facing and solving it as they did, they gave us more than a precedent for breaking down the middle wall of partition between blacks and whites. They gave us, at the same time, an example and sanction for breaking down every wall of partition that separates one group of God's people from another group of God's people.

From Everett Tilson, "The Racial Issue in Biblical Perspective," *Quarterly Review* 3, 2 (Summer 1983): 51–68.

Where Are My Ambassadors of Reconciliation?

Raleigh Washington and Glen Kehrein

When south central Los Angeles went up in flames in April 1992, the glow lit TV sets across America. Angry blacks and worried whites were tense. Would the sparks ignite racial tensions in cities all over the United States?

The backlash in other urban areas, however, was minimal, and many Americans breathed a sign of relief. Soon the L.A. riots were as old as yesterday's news. What happened there was someone else's problem.

But the embers in urban America glow just beneath the surface. The fire has lost its heat, but the smoke can still suffocate us. The fumes are fed by hopelessness and powerlessness on one side, and indifference and insensitivity on the other. We have a crisis in our cities, a crisis that is draining the life-blood from the black community. Ominous statistics read like a medical chart in the terminal ward:

- Homicide is the leading cause of death for black males and females ages fifteen to thirty-four.
- Blacks account for 44 percent of all homicide victims, even though they make up only 12 percent of the population.
- Ninety-five percent of black homicides were committed by black perpetrators.[1]
- Infant mortality among blacks is twice as high as for white infants.[2]

1. The first three statistics are from Carl C. Bell with Esther Jekins, "Preventing Black Homicide," in *The State of Black America 1990* (New York: National Urban League, 1990), 143–55.

280

- In the ten largest urban cities, the high school dropout rate for black males is 72 percent.[3]
- The 1991 unemployment rate for black Americans was 12.9 percent—more than twice the rate for white Americans.[4]
- At the end of the 1980s, more than half of African-American children were born to single mothers.[5]
- In 1960, 78 percent of black families with children were headed by both a mother and a father—a figure that dropped to 37 percent by 1990.[6]

So why are we surprised when young black men with low self-esteem, few positive role models, and little hope for making it out of the ghetto join a gang for a sense of belonging, identity, power, and protection? Using drugs is a way to dull the pain, and the young men accept selling drugs as the only road to success in a community where too few fast-food jobs are the only alternative.

But statistics don't really tell the story. The real story of urban grief and despair is the lost lives. A sniper's bullet cut down little Dantrell Davis, age seven, as he and his mother crossed the street from their home in Chicago's Cabrini Green public housing project. Dantrell was on his way to school during an autumn day in 1992 in a location where gunfire from gangs was common. As of this writing, investigators are unsure whether Dantrell was the unintended victim of a bullet meant for someone else or actually sought by the sniper, killed to spite his great-uncle, a leader of the notorious Black Disciples. It matters little. Young Dantrell was gunned down, an innocent victim of gang-related violence.

Unfortunately, Dantrell's death is not an isolated incident. He is the third child in Jenner Elementary School (and the twenty-seventh child in Chicago) to die a violent death in a single year.[7] Can you imagine that happening in your neighborhood?

A whole generation is at risk in our inner cities. They are mainly African-American and Hispanic children, and the cancer is spreading. Gordon McLean, who ministers to many young gang members as director of the

2. LaSalle D. Leffall, Jr., "Health Status of Black Americans," in *The State of Black America 1990*, 131.

3. Mark S. Hoffman, ed., *The World Almanac* (New York: Pharos, 1992), 169. Based on the first six months of the year and projected forward.

4. Marvin McMikel, "Black Men: Endangered Species," *Club-Date* (August/September 1989): 29.

5. Andrew W. Edwards, "The Black Family: A Unique Social System in Transition," in *The State of Black Cleveland 1989* (Cleveland: Urban League of Greater Cleveland, 1989), 187.

6. Andrew Billingsley, "Understanding African-American Family Diversity," in *The State of Black America 1990*, 89–90.

7. "Special Report: Dying Young," *Chicago Tribune*, 18 October 1992, sec. 2, a.

juvenile justice ministry of Metro Chicago Youth For Christ, often intones ominously to complacent whites, "Gang violence—coming soon to a neighborhood near you."

A Fragile Peace

McLean is right. The riots in L.A. were only a foretaste of the racial tremors rumbling beneath the surface in our country. On one hand we have Louis Farrakhan, the charismatic black muslim who used to rant and rave about "white devils" while he plucked black men off the street, gave them dignity, and got them off drugs. On the other, we have David Duke, former Ku Klux Klansman and one-time Louisiana legislator who once paraded in a white sheet, preaching hate. Today, Duke and Farrakhan both dress in pinstripe suits and speak calmly, but their message is still the same: race-baiting, alienation, and separation between black and white.

Satan loves that. Ever since creation, Satan has been working overtime to alienate people from their Creator and from each other. And he's still at it.

Jack and Jenny Oliver live in Evanston, Illinois, just north of Chicago, a community that prides itself on being ethnically diverse and racially sensitive. The Olivers were shocked to discover that their next-door neighbors— the only black family on the block—had recently received several anonymous "hate letters" enumerating various complaints and telling them to get out of the neighborhood. Suspicions and accusations regarding who had sent the letters broke apart the fragile racial peace of that city block. Up to this point, except for "hi" across the fence, there had been very little relationship between the black family and the other white neighbors. Most of the whites gave as their reason certain irritations, such as late night noise, as well as the hostility of the black grandmother, who wouldn't even say hello.

What they didn't know—until the hate letters started the white neighbors talking with other members of the black family—was that, as a child, the grandmother had seen her own brother lynched by the Klan. Suddenly a glimmer of understanding broke through some of the judgmental attitudes in the neighborhood. Without knowing who had written the letters, Jack and Jenny wrote a (signed!) letter inviting all the neighbors to use the incident as an opportunity to build relationships between black and white and work out problems person to person, rather than letting them breed further distrust and alienation. It's only a step—but it's a step in the right direction.

Reconciliation: Part of Daily Living

Separation and alienation between people is nothing new. During the first century, people faced the same barriers of race, class, and sex that we have today. In fact, before Christ died, Herod's temple divided the people in all three areas. The Holy of Holies, set off by a heavy curtain into which only the high priest could go once a year, divided the people from God. The Court of Priests divided the "professional clergy" from the "lay people." The Court of Israel divided the men from the women. The Court of Women divided Jewish women from the Gentiles. Last but not least was the Court of Gentiles. Josephus, a first century [historian], informs us that a cornerstone of the fifth partition read: "Any Gentile that goes beyond this partition only has himself to blame for his ensuing death."

But when Jesus cried out from the cross, "It is finished!" the curtain that separated the Holy of Holies was torn from top to bottom The people were confused and astounded. What did it mean? They didn't yet understand what Christ's ministry was all about: the reconciliation of all people with God and with each other.

In a letter to the Corinthian church, however, Paul the apostle spelled it out clearly:

Therefore from now on we recognize no man according to the flesh; even though we have known Christ according to the flesh, yet now we know Him thus no longer. Therefore if any man is in Christ, he is a new creature; the old things passed away; behold, new things have come. Now all these things are from God, who reconciled us to Himself through Christ, and gave us the ministry of reconciliation, namely, that God was in Christ reconciling the world to Himself, not counting their trespasses against them, and He has committed to us the word of reconciliation. Therefore we are ambassadors for Christ, as though God were entreating through us; we beg you on behalf of Christ, be reconciled to God. He made Him who knew no sin to be sin on our behalf, that we might become the righteousness of God in Him. (2 Cor. 5:16–21 [NASB])

The Word of God is not just saying that reconciliation is a good idea. Rather, Paul informs us that the ministry of reconciliation is a *mandatory* part of every Christian's daily living. This passage outlines, first, the act of God in creating us anew, from the inside out; second, the purpose of God to reconcile the world unto Himself; and third, the method of God in calling all Christians to be ambassadors for Him, giving them the ministry of reconciliation.

Reconciliation has a twofold reality: it has already happened, and yet it is still in process. We have been reconciled to God through conversion; we are a new creation (v. 17). This is an accomplished fact. But this reconciliation must continue to work through us, crossing racial, social, and sexual barriers by means of the ministry of reconciliation empowered by God through Christ to work in and through us.

The result should be a newly created body of believers who no longer look at people as the world sees them (v. 16)—as potential threats or the dregs of society. We acknowledge that it is God who alone can accomplish reconciliation across the barriers of sin and separation (v. 18). We accept the responsibility not only of the message of reconciliation (v. 19), but the ministry of reconciliation (v. 18) as well, becoming Christ's ambassadors, pleading with others to be reconciled to God (v. 20).

Racial Reconciliation: Priority of the Church

With materialism, secular humanism, New Age cults, disintegrating families, perversion of sexual mores, and abortion battling for the soul of the church today, don't Christians have enough to wrestle with? Why make racial reconciliation a priority in the church? We see three reasons to urge such a reconciliation.

First, Christ made it a priority. "For [Christ] Himself is our peace, who made both groups into one . . . that in Himself He might make the two into one new man, thus establishing peace" (Eph. 2:14–15 [NASB]). The apostle Paul was referring to the historical alienation between Jews and Gentiles, which was creating conflict in the church in Ephesus. With love and compassion, Paul made the bottom line abundantly clear: Christ's purpose was to bring the two together, creating "one new [people]" in the body of Christ.

Second, the apostle Paul made it a priority. In writing to the Colossian church, he described the Christian's new being as undergoing "a renewal in which there is no distinction between Greek and Jew, circumcised and uncircumcised, barbarian, Scythian, slave and freeman, but Christ is all, and in all" (Col. 3:11 [NASB]). In one fell swoop Paul extended the priority of reconciliation in Christ beyond the Jew/Gentile issue to include all people groups regardless of race, nationality, ethnicity, class, religious tradition, or status. He assumed that all of these alienated or separated people belonged together in this melting pot called the church.

Third, the theological foundation of our faith is reconciliation. When our relationship with God was broken, God brought us back—reconciled us—to Himself through a personal relationship with His Son and our Savior, Jesus Christ. Now He has called us to be His ambassadors and has given us the ministry of reconciliation. This means, first of all, reconciling people to God through the power of the cross, and then reconciling people to people across racial, class, and gender barriers.

To be ambassadors for Christ, then, is to be reconcilers wherever relationships are broken, in whatever situation God has placed us. We believe Satan has exploited the sin of racism throughout the centuries, and certainly in this country, to alienate people from God and from each other. Small pockets of valiant believers,[8] men and women, black and white, have been "living out reconciliation" in the name of Christ against all odds, but the battle continues.

---

8. Two examples of such believers and churches are Cary Casey and Wayne Gordon and their Lawndale Community Church in Chicago's impoverished West Side community.

Our Benign Neglect

The ministry of reconciliation can never be mere passive acceptance of a theological truth, but must include active participation. Unfortunately, the Christian church at large—to state it in the most favorable way—is guilty of benign neglect. At best, we have been standing quietly on the sidelines while racism continues to wreck havoc on our society. Most Christians—white, black, Hispanic, and Asian—have not directly attacked the problems of racism. True, most of us wouldn't march with the Ku Klux Klan or hurl epithets at a minority child integrating our schools. But few of us, churches or individuals, have made it a priority to heal the divisions between black, white, brown, or yellow by deliberately and intentionally building relationships across racial lines.

Historically, through its neglect in not confronting the problem, the white segment of the church has allowed itself to unwittingly become a co-conspirator with the enemy. Scripture has been used, the church has been used, tradition has been used, social convention has been used to support every form of prejudice and oppression of ethnic minorities, including Hispanics and Asians. Consider these actions, inactions, and poor theologies used by many in the American Christian church.

- The "curse of Ham" (Gen. 9:25) was used for centuries to justify the white race subjugating the black race.
- The Southern church's tacit approval of Klan activities is well documented.
- The American church, for the most part, accepted the World War II imprisonment, denial of civil rights, and unlawful confiscation of property of Japanese-Americans because of their ancestry. Most Asian-Americans were feared as traitors while white European-Americans were honored as patriots.
- In recent times, homogeneous church-growth principles, espousing the maxim "people feel more comfortable with people like themselves," are used to justify continuing separation of believers on the basis of race and class.
- Churches have eagerly sent thousands of missionaries to dark-skinned peoples in distant lands while ignoring the plight of the inner-city immigrants at their doorstep.
- Inner-city mission programs (like foreign missions several decades ago) have too often embodied a condescending "white Bwana/ignorant blacks" attitude.
- Clapping, syncopation, or other "emotional" musical forms—qualities typical of black music—have been characterized as "of the devil."

- Where integration has "worked," it often means that blacks have assimilated white culture (a denial of black cultural strengths).
- Interracial dating and marriage—even between born-again believers— have been discouraged, forbidden (even on Christian college campuses), and feared.

Satan has used race to divide believers and make a mockery of our faith, and we as Christians have not stood against it. We sing, "They will know we are Christians by our love," but as black, white, Asian, and Hispanic Christians we harbor fear and mistrust, anger and hatred in our hearts toward each other.

Christ is holding out nail-pierced palms: "Where are My ambassadors of reconciliation? I died on the cross to heal the divisions between you; I have given you the ministry of reconciliation! Why are My children still alienated from one another? Why is the wound of racism still festering in My church? Where are My ambassadors?"

As ambassadors for Christ, we must bring the ministry of reconciliation specifically to the area of racial alienation. Our consciousness has been raised; many laws have been changed; it is even "politically correct" to be racially tolerant. But that isn't reconciliation.

After the Rodney King verdict and the riots in south central L.A., author Kurt Vonnegut was quoted in *The Chicago Tribune* as saying: "We can actually hate blacks if we want, so long as they have a fair shot at the American dream. To hell with love and everything else." That's an incredible statement, a very humanistic worldview of the problems that we're experiencing. He's saying, we've talked about love (the '60s version: "All we need is love, love, love") and it didn't work.

But Vonnegut's statement represents absolute sin, for Jesus made very clear that hate is murder. Murder and violence and destruction of the human personality and spirit begin in the heart. Vonnegut's statement is also a practical impossibility. No one is going to give African-Americans a "fair shot" at the American dream if "we can actually hate blacks if we want." In God's economy, justice and love are always inextricably linked.

Black people in this country are perishing from lack of knowledge of the saving grace of Jesus Christ. We are letting the Louis Farrakhans of the world tell them that Christianity is a "white man's religion." By our actions—and our inaction—black and white Christians are saying to each other, "I have no need of you." And Satan is having a heyday.

The Key: United in Christ

We believe the body of Christ holds the key that can unlock the stranglehold of racism in our society. That key is the ministry of reconciliation.

Christ has given us a mandate. It is high time the church as a whole, and individual believers, answered the call of Christ and became ambassadors of reconciliation in our homes and churches, neighborhoods and cities. . . .

For Further Reflection

Case Studies

Newcomer encounters racist. Ben, a white Christian, moves to a small community and eagerly joins the only evangelical church in town. One evening, Jason, a successful pharmacist and lay leader in the church, invites Ben to join some men from church to watch the Super Bowl. Jason sells medicine to minority persons. During the game, Jason complains loudly about the number of African-Americans in the National Football League (NFL). He then remarks about the many minority persons on welfare, their general laziness, and the detrimental effect they have on American society. Shocked and offended, Ben says to Jason that perhaps discrimination has something to do with this problem. The group watches in stunned silence as Jason insists that the problem lies in the inherent laziness of minority races; if they worked harder, peoples of color could easily find jobs. Though a newcomer, Ben persists. If all companies make employment decisions on merit just as they do in the NFL, minority persons would do good work at better jobs, he says. Since companies discriminate, affirmative action is necessary. Jason sweats as he loudly condemns job quotas.

The group invited you, the pastor of this church, to join the party. You see that Jason's racism puts minority persons in a catch-22: high unemployment figures prove laziness, not discrimination; because they are lazy, people of color do not deserve welfare or unemployment checks; further, society should not promote minority employment via affirmative action. Appalled by these comments, you must stand for principle, defend Ben (who finds himself in an awkward spot), and keep peace in the church. What do you do?

288

White daughter dates a Hispanic. Your white friend Paul is the parent of a sophomore at a Christian college. His daughter is dating a Hispanic classmate, a young Christian man majoring in Bible. Paul is frantic. He secretly hopes and even prays that his daughter's relationship will break off, but it continues and even blossoms. After two years of dating, Paul's daughter and her boyfriend begin talking marriage. Paul violently opposes mixed marriages. He argues to his daughter that the children of such a relationship will be of mixed descent and so will have difficulty making friends. He points out that different cultures have different ideas about marriage and family and that these differences will cause confict. The daughter angrily rejects her father's concerns, claiming they merely reflect racist attitudes. The boyfriend claims that as Christians they can overcome these issues. Paul is unconvinced. He remains bitter and angry. He thinks he is looking out for his daughter, but he feels she completely rejects him. He comes to you in despair. How would you help Paul? Is he facing only emotional questions or are there ethical issues here as well?

Glossary

Affirmative action: Policies designed to promote employment among different races by aggressively recruiting, training, and promoting qualified minority persons.

Discrimination: When based on race, treating someone differently than his merit suggests simply by virtue of his racial identity. It usually connotes treating a minority person badly just because she is a minority, but could include giving a white person an advantage because of his color.

Genocide: Attempt to kill those of a particular race; logical extension of racism in its traditional sense.

Jim Crow: A set of laws, policies, and practices that enforced segregation of African-Americans prior to the civil rights era.

People of color: Recently coined phrase incorporating all nonwhite ethnic and racial groups bound together by their common experience of oppression and discrimination due to the racism of whites.

Race: Notoriously ambiguous term for categorizing people by appearance. Sometimes people group very different cultural backgrounds in one race as when they describe both Pakistanis and Koreans as "Asians."

Racial prejudice: Attitudes, usually negative, about certain persons based on racial identity; prejudices about racial or ethnic groups are often persistent, and they powerfully affect interactions between members of different groups.

Racism: Traditionally, the belief that one racial group in the human family is inherently superior to or more virtuous or deserving than another due to inherited characteristics, that civilization has developed due to the virtues of that race, and that the future of civilized society depends on preserving the purity of that race. More recently, some describe racism as racial prejudice with power and include as an effect of racism the cultural dislocation experienced by minority peoples due to dominant cultural patterns.

Reverse discrimination: Disadvantage white males experience when those who hire workers pass them over in favor of a member of some disadvantaged group.

Stereotype: Negative, composite image of persons of a certain class; a fixed, communally recognized impression of a group of people.

Annotated Bibliography

Ansbro, John J. *Martin Luther King, Jr.: The Making of a Mind.* Maryknoll: Orbis, 1982. Philosophical analysis and critique of the sources and content of King's nonviolent philosophy.

Barndt, Joseph R. *Dismantling Racism: The Continuing Challenge to White America.* Minneapolis: Augsburg, 1990. White pastor from the Bronx describes for whites how to understand and overcome racism.

Benedict, Ruth. *Race: Science and Politics.* Rev. ed. New York: Viking, 1943. Classic study distinguishing the facts of race and the dogma of racism.

Griffin, John Howard. *Black Like Me.* New York: Houghton Mifflin, 1960. Experiences of a white man disguised as a black man in the early days of the civil rights movement.

Hacker, Andrew. *Two Nations: Black and White, Separate, Hostile, Unequal.* New York: Scribner's, 1992. Powerful, realistic, and discouraging description of the current state of race relations by a white social scientist.

Jones, Major J. *Christian Ethics for Black Theology: The Politics of Liberation.* Nashville: Abingdon, 1974. Important African-American theologian seeks a middle ground between the black power and nonviolent stances.

Kelsey, George D. *Racism and the Christian Understanding of Man.* New York: Scribner's, 1965. Classic work that disengages racism (which says human life is determined by the physical and genetic) from true Christianity (which sees human life as a function of the personal and spiritual).

King, Jr., Martin Luther. *Strength to Love.* Philadelphia: Fortress, 1963. Collection of sermons that presents King's powerful vision for justice through nonviolent social change.

Myrdal, Gunnar. *An American Dilemma: The Negro Problem and Modern Democracy.* 2 vols. New York: Harper, 1944. Monumental treatise discussing the dilemmas America faced after WWII in shaping an inclusive democracy.

Pannell, William E. *The Coming Race Wars.* Grand Rapids: Zondervan, 1993. Evangelical warns of heightened racial tension in coming years as a result of failures to deal effectively with racism.

Perkins, Spencer. "The Prolife Credibility Gap." *Christianity Today* (21 April 1989): 21–22. Essay on the need for a broader pro-life position that includes concern for the poor as well as for the unborn.

Perkins, Spencer, and Chris Rice. *More Than Equals: Racial Healing for the Sake of the Gospel.* Downers Grove, Ill.: InterVarsity, 1993. A biracial ministry team writes about reconciliation and the gospel.

Prinzing, Fred, and Anita Prinzing. *Mixed Messages.* Chicago: Moody Press, 1991. Two veterans of Christian ministry candidly discuss the interracial marriages of two of their children.

Raboteau, Albert J. *Slave Religion.* New York: Oxford University Press, 1978. Fascinating historical background on the faith of slaves.

Salley, Columbus, and Ronald Behm. *What Color Is Your God?* Rev. ed. Downers Grove, Ill.: InterVarsity, 1981. A black man and a white man join to argue that Christianity, considered purely and not in its racist forms, is a powerful force for the liberation of all persons.

Skinner, Tom. *Black and Free.* Grand Rapids: Zondervan, 1969. Early evangelical statement about the new African-American consciousness.

Steele, Shelby. *The Content of Our Character.* New York: St. Martin's, 1990. Black conservative defends integration, but emphasizes the responsibilities of blacks as well as whites in the era after civil rights.

Tilson, Everett. "The Racial Issue in Biblical Perspective." *Quarterly Review* 43 (1983): 51–68. Discussion of biblical texts on slavery and race.

Washington, Raleigh, and Glen Kehrein. *Breaking Down Walls: A Model for Reconciliation in an Age of Racial Strife.* Chicago: Moody Press, 1993. A black man and a white man working together in urban Chicago articulate their vision for a holistic, evangelical ministry.

8

Gender Issues

In 1920, American women gained the right to vote. Americans know that this happened because of laborious efforts by a group of women renowned in history as the suffragettes. Few people know two significant facts about the suffragettes. First, they represented a second wave of **feminism**. The first wave grew out of the nineteenth-century movement to abolish slavery. Second, in many cases, those who participated in the first two waves of feminism committed themselves not only to feminism, but also to Christian teachings.

After gaining the right to vote, however, women's groups disintegrated. Betty Friedan's important 1963 book, *The Feminine Mystique*, signaled a renaissance of feminism, a third wave. Unlike the original feminists, Friedan defended an inherently secular feminism. But not all feminists today are secularists. Like the suffragettes, many religious people today try to connect feminist ideas to their theological beliefs. Yet feminists of all kinds agree that **patriarchy**, a system of social life and thought that entrenches male dominance, is an evil force that mars all relationships between the genders. Patriarchy, they argue, encourages **sexism** (prejudice against women) and even **misogyny** (the hatred of women).

Contemporary feminists differ about how much the church and the Bible contribute to the oppression of women. Radical religious feminists (called revolutionary or post-Christian feminists) generally agree with secular feminists that faith in God the Father and his Son is inherently and irredeemably patriarchal. Thus, people like Mary Daly, a former Roman Catholic, and Rosemary Radford Ruether, a Roman Catholic teaching at a United Methodist seminary, argue for a distinctively feminist theology complete with new, feminine core symbols. More moderate religious feminists (called reformist or broadly Christian feminists) think this contempt for traditional metaphors is too radical. Yet, since they are theologically liberal, they do disagree with the Bible when it fails to square with their feminist agenda.

Those in a third group, **biblical feminists**, do not stand in the tradition of secular feminism, but relate instead to early Christian feminism. Thus, they do not concede that feminists must reject the Bible when it is properly interpreted. In the early 1970s, some biblical feminists organized themselves into the Evangelical Women's Caucus (EWC). As the EWC drifted left from the evangelical center, others formed Christians for Biblical Equality (CBE) in 1987.

Psychology professor Mary Stewart Van Leeuwen reflects a biblical feminism. Biblical feminists support **egalitarianism**, the view that in home, church, and society, both men and women equally may exercise leadership. Van Leeuwen discusses three forms of secular feminism: liberal feminists, Marxist feminists, and radical feminists. (Her essay shows that *feminism* refers to many very different views.) Over against secular feminism, Van Leeuwen discusses a differentiating feminism that recognizes the differences between men and women and their unique strengths and weaknesses. We have much to learn about how the genders relate, she argues, including how men and women alike see male experience as "normal" and female experience as "deviant"!

Contrasting these various kinds of feminism are traditionalists who argue for male leadership in the home and church. This point of view, sometimes called **hierarchicalism**, affirms that God's order for gender relationships places males in the role of **head** (defined as *leader* or *authority over*) and females in the role of follower. Discerning individuals who take this position are well aware that leaders can use their position for personal gain. So sensitive traditionalists emphasize that the Bible teaches husbands to lead sacrificially, to give themselves up for their wives as Christ gave himself for the church (Eph. 5:25). Church leaders are to lead by example, not by lording it over their flock (1 Peter 5:2–4). A group called Council on Biblical Manhood and Womanhood (CBMW) seeks to promote an enlightened traditional position. Advocates of this position call their view *complementarianism*, although egalitarians resist this description of hierarchalism since differentiating feminists like Van Leeuwen certainly believe that the genders complement each other.

In his essay on covenantalism, Donald Bloesch represents those who believe that God permanently ordered the creation so that men should exercise leadership over women. Because God created men and women equal in essence (who they are), a subordination of women in function (what they do) does not belittle women in any way, he argues. Quite to the contrary, following male leadership is appropriate to a woman's created nature. Just as Jesus Christ is subordinate to the Father in function yet equal in essence, traditionalists argue, women are essentially equal, even though functionally subordinate to men in home and church.

The word *patriarchy* does not express this view very well, argues Bloesch, for patriarchy connotes male leadership bent on preserving male prerogatives. In its ancient form, patriarchy saw woman as a brood mare; in its modern type, it treats woman as a sexual plaything. Both are dehumanizing. Thus, while Bloesch agrees with patriarchy in accepting a natural hierarchy of man over woman, his covenantalism is a "radically qualified" patriarchy. Remarkable New Testament commands requiring sacrificial leadership prohibit men from using male leadership for personal gain.

The first three chapters of Genesis are very important for gender issues. Genesis 1:27 speaks of God's creating both male and female in his image. Genesis 2 has God creating man first. Man then looks unsuccessfully for a "suitable helper" until God finally creates woman as man's helper. While liberals see this as contradicting Genesis 1, evangelicals believe the two chapters are consistent. Genesis 1 is a broad statement about cosmic creation; Genesis 2 is a detailed account of human creation. Important verses include 2:18: woman is man's "suitable helper"; 2:23: woman is of the same substance as man; and 2:24: man leaves his family (!) and joins woman in marriage. Evangelicals differ as to whether these chapters emphasize equality or male leadership.

Genesis 3 contains the cursing of the serpent and of the ground. It appears that man and woman are not directly cursed (see Gen. 3:14 and 3:17), but they do at least suffer the effects of the curse. Genesis 3:16 says that the wife will desire her husband and the man will rule over woman. In the past, interpreters considered this a command: in God's plan the husband ought to rule over his wife. Most today see the results of cursing as factual predictions, not moral commands. Childbirth *will* (not *ought to*) cause great pain. The fields *will* (not *ought to*) sprout thorns and thistles. Husbands *will* (not *ought to*) rule their wives. Significantly, the New Testament never quotes Genesis 3:16 as the basis for commanding wifely submission.

Van Leeuwen sees Genesis 3:16 as a tragic prediction. She also argues that women long so deeply for relationships that they sometimes sacrifice important principles and give up responsibility for their own choices. In this passive way, they sin even as men sin in their aggression. Van Leeuwen's discussion of Genesis 3:16 reflects a significant motif among biblical feminists.

The attitude of Jesus toward women is remarkable. He included women in his larger group of followers and in his ministry. He talked with them and even taught them about God. He refused to participate in the usual condemnation of women, and he held men responsible for lust. These, no respectable rabbi would do; Jewish men thanked God they were not dogs, Gentiles, or women. As remarkable as Jesus' actions were for that time and place, they do not logically require that women and men share as equal partners in home and church. Traditionalists argue that Jesus' behavior elevates women above their low status in first century Judaism without thereby implying egalitarianism. Jesus' attitudes and actions are relevant to the question of gender relationships, but not by themselves conclusive.

Critical issues arise in Pauline texts. The apostle's words ground traditionalists' objections to egalitarian marriage and women's ordination. An important facet of this debate is the meaning of *head* in texts like 1 Corinthians 11:3. Hierarchicalists take the word to imply "authority over"; many egalitarians argue that it means "source." In other places, Paul taught that women must remain silent in church (1 Cor. 14:34–35; 1 Tim. 2:12). Before women attended college in large numbers, hierarchists tended to argue that women are unsuited to teaching. Clearly, however, women were not totally silent in the early church (1 Cor. 11:5), and when women finally went to college, they proved equal to male students in intellectual ability. Traditionalists today do allow that women can speak and teach in many contexts.

Traditionalists still argue, however, that Paul's words forbidding women to teach men (1 Tim. 2:12) reflect a transcultural "divine order" and are not limited to first-century Ephesus. They reason in this way: in 1 Timothy 2:13 the ground for prohibiting women from teaching men is the order of creation. Creation precedes the fall and all sinfully tainted human culture. Since the rationale is based on the creation, the prohibition is transcultural. Although women may teach outside the church (as Priscilla did for Apollos in Acts 18:26) and they may teach children and other women (Titus 2:3–5), women may not formally teach men in the special authoritative manner reserved for pastors.

Biblical feminists believe that 1 Timothy 2:12 addressed a particular problem in Ephesus in the first century. Since Paul assumed women taught (Titus 2:3–5), prayed, and prophesied (1 Cor. 11:5), some unique factor in the first-century context presumably required special instruction. Some biblical feminists claim that Paul wrote 1 Timothy 2:12 because of threats from an early form of Gnosticism that depended on women teachers. Others argue that the general teaching of Scripture works against class discrimination. Thus, while Paul had reasons for permitting slavery in his first-century context (cf. Eph. 6:5), all Christians believe the main thrust of biblical teaching works against slavery. Egalitarians apply this same logic to gender relationships.

Drew University theologian Thomas Oden offers a theological discussion of female leadership in the church. His view is that the Holy Spirit may call qualified women, no less than qualified men, to exercise leadership in the church. Of course, he rejects any woman's claim to a *right* to ordination, but he also correctly denies any such right to a man. He concludes that no significant theological issues stand in the way of fully qualified women entering the ordained ministry. In fact, women offer the church unique gifts that are particularly suited to the calling of a shepherd. Oden concludes that the community of faith is enriched when its leadership reflects the diversity found within its ranks.

Like Oden, Stephen Clark argues theologically rather than dissecting specific biblical passages. But he rejects the ordination of women. In his view, any defense of male leadership must stand in the context of a broader view of what it means to be the people of God. If a seemingly pointless rule, an isolated item of legislation, prohibits women's ordination, the church will eventually ordain women. Clark argues that prohibiting female ordination makes sense only in the context of a comprehensive understanding of the church as the people of God with a shared rule of life and a commitment to mutual discipline. Unless the church deliberately chooses an ethos that differs from contemporary North American culture, the prohibition against ordaining women will seem bizarre.

Many Christian women live with traditionally minded men, but do not feel oppressed. The radical love that Paul demands of Christian husbands in Ephesians 5:25 significantly moderates the negative effects of patriarchalism as the world practices it. Thus, many Christian women, deeply cherished by traditional but devoted husbands, find they cannot relate to feminists' outrage over oppression. Feminist rhetoric is alien to their experience. Women like these are happy to take literally the biblical injunctions about submission to men.

These women (and many men) can gain a new perspective that grows from the lived experience of women who do find themselves oppressed or **harassed sexually**. These women deserve to hear a gospel that accords with their experience just as much as women blessed with positive relationships where love and self-denial are the norm. Women who feel crushed by men need to know that if some use traditional patriarchy (sometimes wrongly associated with Christian teaching) to keep them down, the problem is sin.

Biblical hierarchicalists recognize that the Bible prohibits male selfishness, and biblical feminists acknowledge that the Scripture forbids female independence. In the end, the Bible insists that Christians protect the most vulnerable of God's children, the poor, the fatherless, and the widows. Opposing the self-serving patriarchy of most human cultures and defending equality between the genders as we do among the races will greatly aid in that task. For this reason, biblical feminism provides a powerful critique of business-as-usual patriarchy.

Biblical traditionalists and biblical feminists alike agree that radical feminism's analysis is equally unbalanced. Bloesch points out that patriarchy and radical feminism both emphasize the independence of the sexes. Patriarchy stresses the independence of males expressed in domination; radical feminism highlights the independence of women expressed in autonomy. Biblical values sharply undercut both impulses to independence. Human persons are interdependent and ultimately dependent on God (1 Cor. 11:11–12). From the creation story on, the Bible makes clear that living comes from dying, winning from losing, and receiving from giving. These kingdom principles apply equally to women and to men.

Christian Maturity in Light of Feminist Theory

Mary Stewart Van Leeuwen

The Scope of the Present Article

. . . The topic of this article is Christian maturity in light of feminist theory. . . . [F]eminists are no more or less value-committed than other theorists of human nature; most are merely more forthright in stating their allegiances. Consequently, it seems appropriate to begin by demonstrating the extent to which value commitments, in the form of world views, inform *all* attempts to define human maturity. . . .

World Views and Traditional Conceptions of Maturity

The word "maturity," like its semantic cousins "adjustment," "normality," and "mental health," is probably the term most related to world view in all of psychology. What does this mean? Any given world view includes a fivefold set of (nonnegotiable) beliefs. The first is a set of assumptions about the origin, nature, and destiny of the universe; a second set of assumptions concerns the basic nature of human beings; a third set tries to account for the discrepancy between the actual and ideal performance of those same human beings; and a fourth set outlines the ways in which (and the degree *to* which) this discrepancy can be overcome. A fifth set of assumptions (closely dependent on the other four) is epistemological: it endorses certain methods over others for developing the theoretical implications of the first four sets of assumptions (Smart, 1983; Stevenson, 1974; Walsh & Middleton, 1984; Wolters, 1985).

Social scientists now do their work in an increasingly postpositivist atmosphere. Consequently it has become fashionable, or at least acceptable, to concede that conceptions of maturity *are* highly dependent on the world view of persons using that term. Gone, for the most part, are theorists like Abraham Maslow (1968), who was confident that a purely "scientific" definition of maturity could be developed—but then proceeded to use his own implicit definition of maturity in his choice of famous "self-actualizers," on whose personality and behavioral traits he then based his "universal," "scientifically based" value system! Nevertheless, very few psychologists have managed to step far enough back from the theoretical battle to examine at the most general level the *relatively few* competing world views that inform contemporary, Western conceptions of maturity. One notable exception is Richard Coan's (1977) *Hero, Artist, Sage, or Saint?* which he subtitled "a survey of views on what is variously called mental health, normality, maturity, self-actualization, and human fulfillment."

Coan, who is a psychologist at the University of Arizona, argued that only *three* main world view traditions inform present conceptions of maturity, and that these, in order of their historical predominance, are the Judeo-Christian world view, the Renaissance-Enlightenment world view, and the Industrial-Postindustrial world view. (His analysis is more finely grained [than] my gross periodizations suggest, but these will suffice for present purposes.) From the Judeo-Christian tradition, which generally identifies maturity with concretely visible sanctification or the fruits of the spirit, Western psychology retains the notion—now, of course, quite secularized—that *relatedness* is an essential aspect of maturity. That is, the mature person is said to be oriented toward caring, self-sacrificial interaction with others. From the same tradition, much of contemporary psychology also retains the idea of *transcendence*.

But Coan (1977) also argued, I think correctly, that these two themes form the Judeo-Christian tradition—relatedness and transcendence—get short shrift in current conceptions of maturity: they are overwhelmed by much stronger themes derived from an *individualistic* world view which emerged during the Renaissance and gained momentum during the Enlightenment. In their wake, current conceptions of maturity heavily favor the presence of individual *creativity.* (For example, both Michaelangelo and Leonardo da Vinci—key Renaissance figures—are said to have relished solitude because it gave them the change to exercise their creative and intellectual powers uncontaminated by others, and uncompelled to share their success with anyone else.) Also stressed by Coan is the possession of *inner harmony*—that is, the absence of conflict within the individual, the cooperative functioning of all parts of the person. . . .

Finally, to the individualism of the enlightenment current definitions of maturity have added a reverence for *efficiency* and *productivity* stemming from the onset of the industrial revolution. "Thus," wrote Coan (1977), "mental health (and maturity, normality, and adjustment) are attributed to the individual who displays intellectual competence, realism, independence, emotional self-control, perseverance, and productivity. These are the values of a future-oriented and achievement-minded industrial society" (p. 76). . . .

In summary, then, contemporary conceptions of maturity are lightly flavored with the Judeo-Christian values of relatedness and transcendence, more heavily laden with the Enlightenment values of individual creativity and autonomy, and ambiguously wedded to the industrial age values of efficiency and productivity. The concept of maturity is indeed thoroughly tied to the world view, in this case the hybrid product of three-going-on-four successively-dominant, Western world views.

The Concept of Maturity in Contemporary Feminism

A Liberal Feminism

If *maturity* is a controversial concept, highly related to world view, the term *feminism* is no less so. Philosopher Alison Jaggar (1983) and sociologist Elaine Storkey (1985) have both described, in separate works, three main currents of secular feminism: liberal feminism, Marxist feminism, and radical feminism. Liberal feminism, the oldest of the three, has its wellsprings in the Enlightenment commitment to individual autonomy and faith in human reason. . . .

Such liberal feminism, according to its critics, is still alive and well in groups like America's National Organization for Women (NOW), which basically accepts the political and economic *status quo* and merely works for equal access on the part of qualified women to its ranks. It is, in the minds of its critics, a thoroughly middle-class movement which, moreover, underestimates the depth and stubbornness of patriarchy in its conviction that superficial legislative tinkering will suffice to make the "American Dream" work for everyone. Let me add, parenthetically, that most Christians do not bother to make any distinctions among types of feminism, preferring instead to dismiss the entire movement with a few epigrams. But when Christians do support feminism, it is likely to be liberal feminism that they have in mind, although most would qualify this by rejecting liberal feminists' continued support of easy divorce and abortion on demand. Nevertheless, this support is a measure of the extent to which Christians of both sexes have equated a Christian world view with Enlightenment confidence in democracy and human reason.[1] . . .

On this account the mature persons are the "reasonable" persons—those who will do unto others, including women, as they would have others do unto them. But to the liberal feminist, the mature person is also, for the most part, the *androgynous* person. Since its revival in the 1960s liberal feminism

1. See for example Richey and Jones (1974) for a further treatment of this fusing of religious and national values.

has been largely androgynous in both its theory and its platform for social change: that is, it has been committed to the position that inherent sex differences are minimal, that gender-role socialization explains virtually all behavioral differences, and that human utopia can best be envisioned as the state where men and women will be psychologically and behaviorally the same—tough when appropriate, tender when appropriate, no longer the slaves of sex-role stereotyping.

Now I would be the first to concede that we have learned a great deal that needed to be learned about human maturity from the work of feminist psychologists committed to a largely androgynous view. Methodologically, they were the ones who documented the skewed nature of the psychology literature as it had accumulated up to about 1970, showing through various reviews and journal searches that, far from building up a truly general psychology, we had been constructing something much closer to a psychology of white, male college sophomores (Grady, 1980; Schwabacher, 1972). More importantly, androgynous feminist researchers of both sexes also exposed a puzzling—and indeed depressing—double standard of maturity for men and women. I am referring to the famous series of studies initiated by Inge and Donald Broverman and their colleagues in the late 1960s (Broverman, Broverman, Clarkson, Rosenkrantz, & Vogel, 1970; Broverman, Vogel, Broverman, Clarkson, & Rosenkrantz, 1972; Clarkson, Vogel, Broverman, Broverman, & Rosenkrantz, 1970), which examined the implicit assumptions held by clinical psychologists, psychiatrists, and social workers with regard to what constitutes a "healthy" person. When asked to describe "a mature, healthy, socially competent" male, *or* female, *or* adult (sex unspecified), both male and female clinicians gave, on the verge, the same descriptive profile for a healthy man as for a healthy adult of unspecified sex. But they described healthy *women* as being different from both—as being more submissive, less independent, less adventurous, more easily influenced, less aggressive and competitive, more excitable in minor crises, more emotional and easily hurt, more vain, less objective, and less fond of math and science. Later studies went on to show that these "differences" were rather clearly perceived as "deficits" by clinicians *and* lay people of both sexes—yet they were still seen as the standard for which adult women *ought* to aim![2] . . .

Liberal feminism, then, rightly stresses the common humanity and dignity of women and men. In the process of doing so, however, its adherents tend to underrate what may well be important distinctions between the sexes, and to overrate the ease with which rational discourse will bring about gender justice. . . .

2. The pattern of such responses has changed surprisingly little since the time of the Broverman et al. research, despite the influence of feminism. See for example Spence, Helmreich, & Stapp (1974) and Ruble (1983).

Marxist Feminism

. . . If liberal feminists major on a secularized reading of *creation* as the basis of their anthropology and view of maturity, Marxist feminists by contrast major on the *fall*, although again in a highly secularized fashion. Marxism is at heart a *conflict* theory of society. The Marxist looks at societal structures and functions throughout history and does *not*, like the liberal, see in them sound, functional "givens" which should be preserved with only minor modifications. The Marxist sees instead only the embodiment of capitalist (or protocapitalist) ideology and its cunning rationalization of economic privilege. . . . Thus, to the Marxist, *class* conflict is regarded as more primary than conflict between the sexes, and the oppression of women is seen largely in class terms—that is, as reducible to economic oppression and little else. . . .

According to orthodox Marxist theory, the mature, insightful person is the revolutionary—the one who has joined the movement to hasten, by violent means if necessary, the birth-pangs of the communist state. Surely this is not an ideal to which—even in a theistic form—many Christians will readily assent, liberation theology notwithstanding? . . .

Marxist feminists, in summary, have a strong sense of the fallenness of social institutions, even as they mistakenly try to reduce the cause of this corruption to the domination of capitalist economic structures. Moreover, they see tensions between the sexes purely as a spin-off from the class tensions bred by capitalism. In this they differ from radical feminists, who share with them a conflict theory of society, but portray that conflict in a very different light.

Radical Feminism

Radical feminists, in Elaine Storkey's (1985) words,

> are the ones everyone thinks they know about . . . the aggressive women, the ones always inciting other women to belligerence, the ones undermining the position of any woman who chooses to be "just a housewife." They are the ones who are against everything, the ones never content with any legal reform, the slogan-makers, the man-haters. As far as many Christians are concerned they oppose all that is good and decent in society. (p. 90)

But radical feminism is easier to stereotype than it is to define: it has a number of different emphases, and its adherents are often dispersed among many other groups, including liberal and Marxist ones. Many of its adherents are neither theorists nor activists, but simply women who have been so damaged by various forms of male abuse that only by staying vocally or surreptitiously angry can they continue to feel at all human. By this criterion, there are a great many radical feminists who would never consciously *call* themselves feminists. And not a few of these are women who have been born, raised, and continue to stay in churches whose male leaders pride themselves in following "correct" biblical practices with regard to relations between the sexes.

Perhaps the simplest way to define the *politics* of radical feminism is to note its main point of departure from Marxist feminism. Radical feminists accuse Marxist feminists of a profound naiveté in reducing women's oppression to class oppression. To them, the basic dividing line is not between capitalist and worker (whether male or female worker), but rather between men as a *sexual* class and women as a *sexual* class. Thus, patriarchy, not capitalism, is the root problem of human society—one which predates capitalism and one which, moreover, would not be erased by the coming of any socialist utopia. . . .

Radical feminists, like their Marxist sisters, lean heavily on a secularized reading of the fall. This time, however, original sin is seen not in terms of class oppression, but rather as the patriarchal oppression of women by men. Women with religious leanings who become radical feminists usually reject both the materialism and the economic reductionism of Marxism. But their perception of the nonmaterial, spiritual realm often includes some very distorted theology by the standards of orthodox Christianity. Not only does this theology tend to see sexism as the original sin; it also tends to see women as the "new creation"—at worst more sinned against than sinning, at best on their way to rediscovering within themselves the powers of the ancient, pagan female goddesses who, it is held, were worshipped for millennia before men seized social, familial, and religious control (Christ, 1979; Daly, 1973; Reuther, 1983).

All of this may sound very bizarre—indeed, almost demonic—to most Christians. But let us again ask ourselves whether we have an important lesson to relearn from the radical feminists. Christians simply cannot deny that the fall *has* distorted relationships between the sexes. To be sure, the original sin was not sexism; it was the desire of *both* sexes to be independent of God. But sexism was surely one of the more serious *consequences* of the fall. To read Genesis 3:16 ("Your desire shall be to your husband, and he shall rule over you") as either a part of the creation order, or as a desirable prescription for postfall life is simply bad exegesis. . . .

At the same time, it would be difficult for Christian counselors to deny that women often use their position of relative weakness to their advantage in ways which are immature as well as sinful. Many are capable of exhibiting passive aggression as well as calculated helplessness. Many can fight very effectively with words even when they cannot do so with their fists. Some are more than able to pass on their ill treatment at the hands of men in the form of unhealthy power relationships with their children. More subtly, women can also become so concerned about preserving existing relationships that their personal morality gets reduced to whatever will please or placate the significant others in their lives. Harvard University's Carol Gilligan (1982) has perceptively demonstrated this in her study of the decision-making process women go through when contemplating an abortion: whether they finally opted to have or to abort the child, most of her respondents made their decision according to what they thought *someone else* (the lover, the parents, etc.) wanted them to do, hoping thereby to regain the *status quo* in that particular relationship and avoid facing the perils of a more autonomous life. Significantly, it was only when those relationships dissolved *regardless* of calculated efforts to secure them that these women were able, in retrospect, to use the tragedy of the unplanned pregnancy to assume greater responsibility for their own lives.

So while it is probably true that more obvious damage has been done to women than men as a result of fallen relationships between the sexes, women are by no means more sinned against than sinning: to say otherwise is to embrace a profound heresy regarding the corporate need of *all* human beings for repentance and salvation. . . .

Thus we have both a positive and a negative lesson to learn from radical feminism about human maturity: positively, we must credit them with reminding us that the brokenness of relationships between the sexes is no trivial, passing thing, and that overcoming it involves patient, hard, never-completed work on the part of both men and women. Negatively, however, we are reminded to be wary of a feminist triumphalism that underrates the sinfulness of half the human race, and sometimes embraces idolatry to the point of resurrecting ancient, pagan goddess cults.

Postradical or "Differentiating" Feminism

. . . More recently a growing number of feminists have begun to say, in effect, "Why *should* we accept the stereotyped male profile of maturity as the normative one? What's so great about aggressiveness, or independence, or overweening personal ambition, or the repression of emotion?" If we return to the Broverman et al. studies on sex-role stereotypes, we find that there *was* a list of female-positive traits endorsed by men and women, professional and lay persons alike. Granted, it was less than half the length of the male list, but its contents were very suggestive. These socially desirable female traits included tactfulness, gentleness, empathy, quietness, greater interest in religion, art and literature, and the capacity to express tenderness easily. And while the origins and motivations of this research are largely secular, it does not take a great deal of biblical literacy to note that the female-positive list of traits has more in common than the male list with the fruits of the spirit described in the New Testament.

Thus there is a growing group of "post-radical" feminists who seem to be saying this: women are indeed different from men; those differences may well, for all we know, result from a complex blend of nature, nurture, and free choice. But whatever their origin, they are important in their own right, and must be restudied and reinterpreted by women working on their own theoretical terms, and not according to terms laid down by a male-dominated psychology which either recasts sex differences as deficits on the part of women, or assumes that maturity in either sex means acting in a stereotypically male fashion. Far from advocating androgyny, these post-radical feminists (elsewhere [Van Leeuwen, 1986] I have also called them "differentiating" feminists) plead for a more nuanced understanding of both maturity and immaturity which takes the differential life experiences of men and women seriously without ranking them in terms of moral superiority (Gilligan, 1982; Hewlett, 1986; Keller, 1985; Lloyd, 1984; Miller, 1976; Schaef, 1981; Turkle, 1984).

I pointed out earlier in this article that the majority of conservative Christians reject contemporary feminism without making the effort to understand its various expressions, while a sizable minority endorse a qualified version of liberal or "androgynous" feminism. So far, neither group has paid sufficient attention to the emerging work of postradical or "differentiating" feminists. Yet I consider this work to be important for both groups, because its basic theoretical orientation is compatible with the confession that male and female are somehow creationally distinct (something which conservative Christians are rightly anxious to retain) and also with the confession that both women and men share the image of God and the cultural mandate, with neither being more or less fallen than the other (something which many other Christians are just as rightly anxious to stress). . . .

Let me confess that, as a psychologist, I have nursed an ongoing compulsion, dating back almost 15 years, to understand as fully as possible the meaning and implications of Genesis 3:16. That is the verse in which God, announcing the consequences of the fall, says to Eve that despite the suffering that will accompany the birth of children to her marriage, "Your desire shall be for your husband, and he shall rule over you." Now, the first thing that emerges when one tries to exegete this mysterious verse is that the Hebrew word translated as "desire" occurs only three times in the Old Testament—and this, of course, make the business of understanding its intent somewhat difficult. But when biblical scholars compare the Hebrew uses and contents of this word, most conclude that the verse is referring to an unreciprocated longing for intimacy. In Gilbert Bilezikian's (1985) words,

> The woman's desire will be for her husband, so as to perpetuate the intimacy that had characterized their relationship in paradise lost. But her nostalgia for the relation of love and mutuality that existed between them before the fall, when they both desired each other, will not be reciprocated by her husband. Instead of meeting her desire. . . He will rule over her. . . . In short, the woman

wants a mate, and she gets a master; she wants a lover and she gets a lord; she wants a husband and she gets a hierarchy. (pp. 55, 229; see also Trible, 1978)

Now let us clarify what is *not* being said here. It is not the case that the positive, mutual interdependence intended between men and women at creation has totally disappeared. Creation, common grace, and redemption have mercifully assured that this will not be so. Nor is it the case that being a "master," a "lord," or a "hierarchy" is totally against the creation order. The human abuse of power is possible only because, in the first instance, human beings were created in God's image and given the freedom to exercise accountable dominion over the creation. But what I take God to be saying, in Genesis 3:16, is that as a result of the fall, *there will be a propensity in man to let dominion run wild*—to impose it in cavalier and illegitimate ways not only upon the earth and upon other men (remember Cain's murder of Abel, the first act of warfare), but also upon the person who is "bone of his bones and flesh of his flesh—the helper corresponding to his very self" (Gen. 2:18, 23—paraphrased).

Now if this were all I had to say about this text, my audience would have every right to be uneasy. For is this not saying, in effect, just what some radical feminists say—that men are constantly being heavy-handed with women, while the women always respond with self-sacrificing patience and turn the other cheek to the point of death? Is this not, in effect, saying that sexism on the part of males *is* the original sin, and that women are the new creation, exhibiting the fruits of the spirit long before Paul identified them as the marks of a redeemed Christian (Gal. 5:22–23)? Well, no—because, you see, we have not yet finished exegeting the implications of Genesis 3:16. For this is a verse that I suspect is really being quite even-handed in its prediction of sinfulness in *both sexes*. Let me explain why.

We are agreed, I think, that accountable dominion is part of the image of God in both sexes; we are agreed also, I suspect, that men and women were intended from the beginning to be mutually interdependent. Trinitarian theology tells us that right from the beginning, God was a unified plurality of persons; that is presumably why he said, "Let *us* make humankind in our own image," an image which includes, as well as accountable dominion, an inherent sociability. Thus Christians, unlike the philosopher Thomas Hobbes (1651/1962), can never say that people are inevitable individualists who grudgingly enter into a social contract with others merely in order to advance their own private interests. On the contrary, we are so unshakably created for community that we cannot even become full persons unless we grow up in nurturing contact with others. And so, just as there is something creationally legitimate about the man's desire for dominion (even though it is misused against women) there is also something creationally right about the woman's desire for complete union with a man and (as a result, and despite the attendant pain) for the creation and maintenance of a family. But because of the fall, Genesis 3:16 seems to imply, this desire on the part of women for community is also distorted by sin. For there are two *opposite* ways persons can abuse their God-given exercise of accountable dominion. The first (the man's sin) is to try to exercise dominion without regard to the creator's original intentions for human relationships. But the second—the peculiarly female sin—is *to use the preservation of those relationships as an excuse not to exercise accountable dominion in the first place.* In other words, the *woman's* congenital flaw in light of Genesis 3:16 is the temptation to avoid taking responsibility for anything outside the sphere of immediate, personal relationships. Now this is a very seductive temptation indeed, for it so easily masquerades as virtue. After all, do Christians not hold that self-sacrificing servanthood, and the desire to maintain peace and interpersonal unity, are essential fruits of the spirit? Well, yes and no, depending on the context. If women insist on peace at any price—if they settle for an abnormal quietism as a way of avoiding the risk and potential isolation that may come from opposing evil—then they are *not* exhibiting the fruit of the spirit; they are sinning just as surely as the man who rides roughshod over relationships in order to assert his individual freedom.

Of particular relevance is Koonz (1987), who shows how Nazi women used the basic misogyny of Nazism to carve out a separate (but never equal) social sphere based on so-called women's concern. A large part of this consisted of the willing glorification of domesticity, thereby creating a refuge for the many male administrators of the extermination camps. The traditional "woman's touch" and the insular joys of Nazi family life actually helped preserve the "sanity" of mass murderers and enabled these men to continue their sordid work. In Koonz' words, "As fanatical Nazis or lukewarm tagalongs, Nazi women resolutely turned their heads away from assaults against socialists, Jews, religious dissenters, the handicapped, and 'degenerates.' They gazed instead at their own cradles, children, and 'Aryan' families. Mothers and wives . . . made a vital contribution to Nazi power by preserving the illusion of love in an environment of hatred, just as men sustained the image of order in the utter disarray of conflicting bureaucratic and military priorities and commands" (p. 17). . . .

At an even deeper level, it seems that the effects of Genesis 3:16 reflect the peculiar way in which each party sinned in the garden. The man and woman were equally created for both sociability *and* dominion—or for affiliation *and* achievement (to use the more common psychological terms). But in reaching out to take the fruit, the woman overstepped the bounds of dominion; as a consequence, she obtained a distorted concern for sociability which continues to hamper the proper exercise of her talents in the world at large. By contrast the man, in accepting the fruit from his wife, overstepped the bounds of human social unity; as a consequence, he obtained a distorted sense of dominion, which has been playing havoc with his social relationships ever since. In each case, the punishment seems to fit the original crime. . . .

References

Bilezikian, G. 1985. *Beyond sex roles: A guide for the study of female roles in the Bible.* Grand Rapids: Baker.

Broverman, I. K., Broverman, D. M., Clarkson, F. E., Rosenkrantz, P. S., and Vogel, S. R. 1970. Sex-role stereotypes and clinical judgments of mental health. *Journal of Consulting Psychology* 34: 1–7.

Broverman, I. K., Vogel, S. R., Broverman, D. M., Clarkson, F. E., and Rosenkrantz, P. S. 1972. Sex-role stereotypes: A current appraisal. *Journal of Social Issues* 28, 2: 59–78.

Christ, C. 1979. *Womanspirit rising: A feminist reader in religion.* New York: Harper & Row.

Clarkson, F. E., Vogel, S. R., Broverman, I. K., Broverman, D. M., and Rosenkrantz, P. S. 1970. Family size and sex-role stereotypes. *Science* 54: 37–45.

Coan, R. W. 1977. *Hero, artist, sage, or saint?* New York: Columbia University Press.

Daly, M. 1973. *Beyond God and the father.* Boston: Beacon.

Gilligan, C. 1982. *In a different voice: Psychological theory and women's development.* Cambridge, Mass.: Harvard University Press.

Grady, K. F. 1980. Sex bias in research design. *Psychology of Women Quarterly* 4: 345–62.

Hewlett, S. 1986. *A lesser life: The myth of women's liberation in America.* New York: Morrow.

Hobbes, T. 1962. *Leviathan.* New York: Collier. (Original work published 1651.)

Jagger, A. 1983. *Feminist politics and human nature.* Totowa, N.J.: Rowman & Allenheld.

Kanter, R. M. 1977. *Men and women of the corporation.* New York: Basic.

Keller, E. F. 1985. *Reflections on gender and science.* New Haven, Conn.: Yale University Press.

Koonz, C. 1987. *Mothers in the Fatherland: Women, the family, and Nazi politics.* New York: St. Martin's.

Lloyd, G. 1984. *The man of reason: "Male" and "female" in Western philosophy.* Minneapolis: University of Minnesota Press.

Maslow, A. 1968. *Towards a psychology of being.* Princeton, N.J.: Van Nostrand.

Miller, J. B. 1976. *Towards a new psychology of women.* Boston: Beacon.

Reuther, R. R. 1983. *Sexism and God talk.* Boston: Beacon.

Richey, R., and Jones, D. 1974. *American civil religion.* New York: Harper & Row.

Schaef, A. W. 1981. *Women's reality: An emerging female system in a white male society.* New York: Harper & Row.

Schwabacher, S. 1972. Male versus female representation in psychological research: An examination of the "Journal of Personality and Social Psychology." *JSAS Catalog of Selected Documents in Psychology* 2: 20–21.

Smart, N. 1983. *Worldviews: Cross-cultural explorations of human beliefs.* New York: Scribner.

Spence, J. T., Helmreich, R. L., and Stapp, J. 1974. The personal attributes questionnaire: A measure of sex-role stereotypes and masculinity-femininity. *JSAS Catalog of Selected Documents in Psychology* 4, manuscript no. 617.

Stevenson, L. 1974. *Seven theories of human nature.* New York: Oxford.

Storkey, E. 1985. *What's right with feminism?* Grand Rapids: Eerdmans.

Trible, P. 1978. *God and the rhetoric of sexuality.* Philadelphia: Fortress.

Turkle, S. 1984. *The second self: Computers and the human spirit.* New York: Simon & Schuster.

Van Leeuwen, M. S. 1986. The recertification of women. *Reformed Journal* 36, 8: 17–24.

Walsh, B. J., and Middleton, J. R. 1984. *The transforming vision.* Downers Grove, Ill.: InterVarsity.

Wolters, A. 1985. *Creation regained: Biblical basics for a reformational worldview.* Grand Rapids: Eerdmans.

From Mary Stewart Van Leeuwen, "Christian Maturity in Light of Feminist Theory," *Journal of Psychology and Theology* 16, 2 (1988): 168–82.

Is the Bible Sexist?

Beyond Feminism and Patriarchalism

Donald G. Bloesch

In contradistinction to both feminism and patriarchalism, I propose the biblical alternative of God's covenant of grace. One can refer to this position as covenantalism, so long as it is understood not as an ideology bent on restructuring society according to the dictates of particular vested interests, but as an outlook on life that serves the gospel proclamation.

This covenantal view is based on the biblical conception of the church as the covenant community, but the Christian family as a church in miniature is to be understood in a similar way. *Covenantal* in this context refers to a relationship between male and female. Its foundation is the promise of God to man, but this is a promise that must be acknowledged in faith and obedience. To understand male-female relationships in covenantal terms is to see the two sexes as created for fellowship with God and with one another. It means that man cannot exist alone, that he can live an authentic human existence only in obedience to the commandment of God and in gratefulness for the promise of God given to all his children. It also means that man can only live a truly human life in coexistence with woman, who was created to be his covenant partner. Together they are set in the world to live a life dedicated to the glory of God and the welfare of humanity. Their life of service is based on the covenant or agreement with God at the time of their baptism or decision of faith to live wholly for his glory and not for their own happiness. This covenantal pledge is reaffirmed at the time of marriage, since marriage itself is seen as a commitment to kingdom service in a relationship of physical intimacy. Christian marriage is a sign of God's covenant with Israel and of God's love for his church. . . .

The covenantalist, as opposed to both the feminist and the patriarchalist, sees our vocation as determined not by sex or blood or race, but by faith. The goal is not to ensure the continuity of the family (as in patriarchy), nor to realize human potential (as in feminism), but to become a sign and witness of the new age of the kingdom, to be a herald and ambassador of Jesus Christ. It is not to embark on a career of our own choosing, nor to submit to a station in life that one inherits because of one's sex or place in the family hierarchy. Instead, it is to assent to an order and vocation of God's choosing which supersedes our responsibility to our immediate family and any loyalty that we might have to our own sex or peer group. Obedience to the imperatives of the kingdom takes precedence over the vocation of biological fatherhood and motherhood (cf. Luke 11:27, 28), though the latter are not negated, but are now seen in the service of the former.

Whereas feminism stresses the independence of woman from man and patriarchalism the submission of woman, Christian covenantalism stresses the interdependence of man and woman, as well as their mutual subordination. At the same time, it makes a place for a differentiation of roles, recognizing both the dependency of woman on man and the necessity of woman for man in the orders of creation and redemption. . . .

The biblical or covenantal alternative still makes a place for role differentiation, since it sees the divergency as well as the complementarity between male and female. It affirms the fundamental equality of man and woman under God, but it nonetheless acknowledges a difference in roles rooted in both biology and psychology.[1] The woman alone can be the child-bearer, and she is especially equipped to nurse the child, though the husband can certainly share in the raising of the children. Yet in the covenantal view, the woman sees her vocation not simply as the bearing of children, but as the education of children in the fear and knowledge of God. She is to be a mother in the faith even before she is a mother according to the flesh.

Similarly the husband, by virtue of the physical strength that enabled him to be a warrior and hunter as well as a tiller of the soil, became the breadwinner in the family. Because of the tremendous change in cultural patterns, both husband and wife are now equipped to work outside the home. Nevertheless, thanks to his relative freedom from child-rearing and related household duties, the husband still retains a certain responsibility in providing for and directing the family. This is a sociological observation, but theologically the husband is given the role of spiritual director and guide for his family (cf. Eph. 5:22–33; 6:1–4).

1. One can say that man and woman are created as souls infinitely and equally precious before God, but the way they are set in historical existence accounts for the fact that the feminine is subordinate to or dependent on the masculine.

Yet even here a patriarchal model is severely qualified. The headship of the husband in the family is not lording it over others, as in the pagan concept of authority (cf. Matt. 20:25, 26), but serving the members of his household not just as an earthly provider, but as a father or brother in the faith who genuinely seeks the betterment and happiness of all those in his care. . . .

Subordination in the Christian sense is not demeaning, but elevating. It signifies not servile dependence, but creative service. The subordination of woman to man is a parable of the submission of the church to its Lord. Those who reject this want the church to be equal to the living Lord. . . .

A very real danger in the patriarchal family is tyranny in which the husband uses his power to hold his wife and children in servile dependence and submission. The danger in the egalitarian or feminist family is anarchy or even matriarchy in which the resulting vacuum in leadership is then filled by the wife or the children. Patriarchy calls for male supremacy. Feminism calls for female autonomy. Covenantalism calls for male-female partnership under the Lordship of Jesus Christ.

This means that major decisions in the family are to be made wherever possible by mutual agreement between husband and wife as they prayerfully seek the guidance of the Holy Spirit. The wife will defer to her husband, however, if he definitely feels that he is being directed by God toward a particular action. Yet she must not accept even this decision uncritically, for her first authority is the command of Christ given in Holy Scripture; she is therefore obliged to weigh even the resolution of her husband in the light of God's holy Word.

The precise relationship between male and female roles in a Christian family is illuminated by recalling the order of procession in the Trinity. Just as we see the principle of superordination and subordination in the Trinity (the Son is "begotten" of the Father), so we observe this principle at work in the world—in government and in the family. Just as we perceive a distribution in the actions of the Trinity in relationship to the world, so we see a complementarity in the roles within government and within the family. Yet because the members of the Trinity are one in essence, and because each person participates in the activity of the others, these roles are not to be conceived of legalistically or rigidly. The wife participates in the headship of the husband as spiritual director or father of the family, and the husband shares in the wife's headship as mistress of the house. These are not their primary roles, but neither partner is excluded from these roles. In exceptional cases, of course, where either husband or wife abdicates or is unable to fulfill his or her responsibilities, then the woman becomes "the man of the house," and the man becomes the helper of the woman.

The movement today toward complete egalitarianism, where equality is defined in terms of sameness rather than equal opportunity, signifies a revolt against the authority of Christ over his church. Christ and the church are not equals, and this is true for husband and wife, parents and children, in the sense that their positions in the family structure do not carry the same measure of authority and accountability. They are equal heirs to salvation, they are equally precious in the sight of God, but this is not to imply that all members of a family have equivalent gifts and responsibilities. . . .

The church has rightly become sensitive to the demands of women for equal pay and equal opportunity for work, but sections of the church have unwittingly allied the faith with a social ideology (feminism), which is basically hostile to the biblical heritage.[2] . . .

In contrast to the biblical vision, feminist ideology regards subordination and obedience as anathema. Its revolt is directed against dualism and hierarchicalism, ideas that belong to the very center of the biblical interpretation of life and history. To begin with the "new awareness of a male-female world," as does Thomas D. Parker, is to impose upon the Bible an ideology. We all bring to the Bible an ideological bias, but to make this a hermeneutical principle is nonsense. In the biblical perspective the aim in life is not self-fulfillment in a career of our choosing (as in feminism), but the fulfillment of our vocation under the cross. . . .

The Bible is unashamedly monarchial, but not sexist. It stands against the exploitation of woman by man, but it nonetheless speaks of superordination and subordination, of headship and servanthood, of an above and a below. It describes Christian marriage as a sign of God's covenant with Israel, in which Christ is the bridegroom and Israel the bride. In this parable the bride is dependent on the bridegroom, but the bridegroom in turn is glorified in and through the bride. The bridegroom does not try to keep the bride down but sacrifices himself for the bride.

An ideology, in contrast to a living faith, is intolerant and fanatical; it brooks no opposition. Its rigidity masks a basic insecurity and desperation, for its votaries are painfully aware that their attempt to create meaning for themselves is their only bulwark against emptiness and chaos. Unlike an ideology, faith can afford to dialogue in a spirit of openness, since it is confident that truth is invincible and that it will finally prevail. Whereas an ideology pins its hopes on human strategy and technique, faith humbly recognizes that truth does not depend on human efforts and arguments. While an ideology claims a premature possession of the truth, faith is content to wait for the full disclosure of truth in the future beyond history.

That most feminism is ideological in the foregoing sense no competent observer would deny. Like ideologists on the left and right, the hardcore

---

2. For an incisive critique of feminism as a social ideology see Stephen Clark, *Man and Woman in Christ* (Ann Arbor, Mich.: Servant, 1980). Unfortunately Clark does not subject patriarchalism to the same kind of critical scrutiny.

feminists seek to make people conform to their own perceptions of reality for fear that these could be shown to be erroneous if exposed to the light of truth. They cannot tolerate dissent lest their own vision of life be shown to rest on a delusion. The totalitarian character of feminism as an ideology is exemplified by Simone de Beauvoir:

> No woman should be authorized to stay at home to raise her children. . . . Women should not have that choice, precisely because if there is such a choice, too many women will make that one. It is a way of forcing women in a certain direction. . . . In my opinion, as long as the family and the myth of maternity and the maternal instinct are not destroyed, women will still be oppressed.[3]

Needless to say, patriarchalism, too, is an ideology which the church must be on guard against. Indeed, in one sense patriarchalism is more dangerous than feminism, because patriarchal imagery was used for divinity in the Bible and therefore appears easily reconcilable with the witness of faith. There is no doubt that the revelation of God was given in a patriarchal culture, but what is not always clearly understood is that this revelation transformed and overcame the oppressive and purely cultural elements in patriarchy. . . .

Against patriarchalism, evangelical Christianity says that one is not born into the kingdom, but one becomes a member of the kingdom by faith. It is not by procreation but by regeneration that one is inaugurated into the family of the church.[4] Our vocation, moreover, is not to ensure posterity for the family name, but to beget spiritual sons and daughters. Biological parentage is only a preparation for spiritual parentage.

What I am presenting as the biblical alternative can be seen as a qualified patriarchalism, but it is one that is radically qualified. In tribal patriarchy, the husband is a despot and the wife a virtual slave. The man-slave relationship is transformed in the Bible; this is especially evident in Philemon. Yet there still remains the difference between employer and employee. There is still a certain hierarchy in human relationships, not because of the patriarchal world-view of that time, but because God reveals himself as encompassing and at the same time transcending hierarchy. . . .

Christian faith does not negate the abiding values of patriarchalism, but points beyond them. The Christian wife will not just care for her husband and children (as in patriarchalism), but she will give hospitality to strangers,

---

3. "A Dialogue with Simone de Beauvoir," in Betty Friedan, *It Changed My Life: Writings on the Women's Movement* (New York: Random House, 1976), 311, 312. Betty Friedan, who does not share this extreme view, makes clear her differences with the more radical feminism in her *The Second Stage* (New York: Summit Books, 1981).

4. One strand in classical Calvinism creates the impression that one is automatically in the covenant community by virtue of being born of Christian parents. Calvin himself emphasized the need for personal faith and repentance, though he, too, was sometimes led into affirming that the children of parents in the covenant community were "presumably regenerate."

she will extend a welcoming hand to the homeless. Together with other members of her family, she will minister to the bereaved. Similarly, her husband will not just provide for his wife and family, but he will give to the poor, aid destitute widows, visit the sick, and perform other acts of sacrificial service.

In the biblical, covenantal view, authentic womanhood goes beyond being a wife and mother, just as authentic manhood goes beyond being a husband and father.[5] Obedience to the divine commandment sometimes means foregoing marriage and parenthood for undivided service to the work of the church (cf. 1 Cor. 7:25ff.). It may also sometimes entail marriage without children in order to accomplish a particular task given by God.

. . . The biblical position can also be regarded as a qualified feminism. Yet in opposition to ideological or secular feminism, it takes for its criterion the divine commandment given in Holy Scripture, not the new light that is brought to bear on the current situation by the social sciences. It upholds as the ideal of womanhood not Eve, who symbolizes independence and autonomy, but Mary who epitomizes fidelity, humility, and absolute dependence on God. Its model is not the "liberated" woman, but the woman of modesty and piety, qualities associated in Hebraic literature with natural beauty. It preaches freedom—not from moral taboos that keep the social fabric intact, but from the expectations of one's peers or family or class regarding one's life-style and task in society.

The qualified, biblical feminism that I support stands in tension with the point of view of many of those who call themselves Christian feminists. While there are areas of convergence, there are also areas of divergence. Many Christian feminists will speak of submission and obedience to God or Christ, although their preference is to place the accent on cooperation with God and Christ. Their affinities are more to the God of process thought, the "fellow sufferer who understands," than to the monarchial, sovereign Lord of biblical faith. They also resist the idea of obedience to human authorities such as heads of state and church. Yet the Bible is clear that we are to give the human authorities set over us by God a relative, though not an absolute, allegiance. Christian feminists will speak of mutual submission, but not of the relative subordination of woman to man in the covenantal relationship of holy matrimony, nor of the subordination of both man and woman to the divine order which determines their place in the marital and familial relationship. . . .

5. Billy Graham's assertion that "the appointed destiny of real womanhood" is to be "wife, mother, homemaker" is at best a half-truth of Scripture. Such a view concentrates only on certain biblical passages (such as Gen. 3:16 and Titus 2:4, 5) and ignores many others (including Luke 10:42; 11:27, 28; Matt. 27:55; 1 Cor. 7:8). See Billy Graham, "Jesus and the Liberated Woman," *Ladies' Home Journal* 87, 12 (December 1970), 42.

The gulf between the various positions is dramatically revealed by comparing the fundamental ways in which they visualize woman. The model of woman in tribal patriarchalism is the brood mare; in hedonistic naturalism, she is the "bunny" or plaything; in feminist ideology, she is the self-sufficient career woman; in romanticism, she is the fairy princess or maiden in distress waiting to be rescued; in biblical faith, she is the partner in ministry. In the biblical view, she may also be a mother—and yet never just a mother, but a Christian mother.

The conflict over this question may be expressed in another way. In patriarchalism, woman is the property of man. In romanticism, woman is the object of man's dreams. In hedonistic naturalism, woman is a sex partner for man. In feminism, woman is the rival of man.[6] In biblical faith, woman is the helpmate of man. Although in this last perspective man has a certain priority over woman, he does not have supremacy (as in the patriarchal view).

How women gain their liberation or salvation is also a subject of wide dispute. In patriarchalism, women are saved by childbearing. In naturalistic hedonism, women are fulfilled in the experience of orgasm. In romanticism, women are saved by being possessed by their knight in shining armor, the man of their dreams. In feminist ideology, women are saved by asserting their independence from the male-dominated social order or from family and clan. In biblical faith, women are saved *by* divine grace and *for* a life of service to Christ and fellow-humanity. . . .

From Donald G. Bloesch, "A Biblical Alternative," in *Is the Bible Sexist?* (Westchester, Ill.: Crossway, 1982), 84–101.

6. In my reading of feminist literature, the emphasis is on husband and wife assisting each other in fulfilling separate careers rather than working together to realize a common vocation under the cross. Rivalry means trying to equal or outdo another, and it allows for cooperation as well as competition. Even though rivalry may not be intended in a marital relationship, it is virtually inevitable where the emphasis is on self-fulfillment in a career rather than on self-giving service to the forsaken and oppressed for whom Christ died.

Women in the Pastoral Office

Thomas C. Oden

From Philippians 4:2–3 we have clear evidence that women were involved in positions of leadership in the church. Paul, who was trying to settle a conflict between Euodia and Syntyche, writes affectionately of "these women, who shared my struggles in the cause of the gospel . . . whose names are in the roll of the living." Paul was gladly affirming the privilege of laboring side by side with these women for the gospel. They vitally shared his mission and struggle. There is no warrant to assume in the passage that there was any subordinate relationship, nothing except the full equality of men and women working together in the ministry of the gospel.

Similary in Romans 16:1–16, where Paul is commending a number of Christians to the church at Rome, he lists several women mentioned alongside men as "fellow workers" in Christ. . . .

It is astonishing that in Paul's deliberate account of the fellow workers whom he commends and relies upon most, so many of them are women. It is striking that women apparently had such important roles in the mission already at this exceptionally early state of the transmission of the apostolic tradition to the Roman world, especially when seen in the light of the cultural assumptions about the assumed roles and place of women.

Ephesians 5:21–23 hinges significantly on this crucial christological image: the symbol of the head (kephale). The analogy is that the husband is the head of the wife in the same way that Christ is the head of the Church. But what sort of headship does Christ have over the church? It is a headship that implies suffering for others and redemptive love. Essential to this mode of headship is self-sacrificial, radical self-giving. This passage is not talking about a coercive, authoritarian type of headship or superordination. If that were the sort of headship meant, the passage would not have proceeded so

318

consistently from its central premise: "Be subject to one another out of reverence for Christ" (v. 21). Rather, the kind of headship indicated is that of the self-giving, righteous, redemptive *kephale*, Christ the head of the church. It is precisely by that analogy and none other that man is called to be the self-sacrificial and serving "head" of the family. The analogy is not suggestive of oppression but of service. That point is further reinforced in the next phrase where the analogy takes this amazing turn: "Husbands, love your wives, as Christ also loved the church and gave himself up for it, to consecrate it, cleansing it by water and the word" (Eph. 5:25). On the basis of this pivotal analogy we conclude that the concept of subjection or *hupotassatai* does not refer specifically to an intrinsic super- and subordination of power but to self-giving service strictly seen according to the analogy of Christ's own self giving to us.

The Issue

We have been attempting to ground the office of pastor consistently in historical Christian pastoral wisdom. That makes this present turn of argument all the more challenging. For we now turn our attention squarely to deal with this exceptionally controversial subject . . . [H]ow can we affirm the scriptural canon, as we wish to do in all critical moments of a pastoral theology, and at the same time speak in good conscience of women being called and ordained to ministry?

In probing this question I want to appeal immediately to a brilliant principle of theology found in the writings of Cardinal John Henry Newman, namely, that there is a depositum of faith given in the Christ event, that is the same always, yesterday, today and forever, and yet we see historical development that bestows ever-new meaning on this complex depositum. . . .[1]

On the basis of this principle, we will argue that both women and men may be called to representative ministry, and that this view is deeply embedded in Christ's own intention for the church and in major strands of the primitive Christian tradition, even though it has had to await a dubiously meandering stream of historical development before it could to some degree become realized in living Christian community.

We do well to confess early that far too much of the Christian tradition has been unrepresentatively male dominated in priesthood and has failed to recognize adequately God's call to women in ministry. Women have always been more ready to serve than the church allowed. What they lacked was the opportunity. But historical conditions make it now more possible to fulfill the deeper intention of the historical tradition.

1. John H. Newman, *Essay on the Development of Christian Doctrine* (Philadelphia: Appleton, 1845), chapter 5; John Newman, *Apologia pro Vita Sue* (London: Everyman's Library, 1955), 15ff.

Right or Rite?

Why not view the issue of women in ministry simply as a civil right, analogous to other employment, to which equal access is rightly due? It is an important assumption of religious liberty that ordination is not a civil right, that is, it is not under government authority, but rather, is a solemn rite of the believing community. Ordination exists only by divine calling and by the outward affirmation of the believing community. So the question of whether women should be or are capable of being ordained to ministry requires a theological, not merely a legal, answer or investigation. It is not merely a question of civil law, it is a question of sound theological, exegetical, and historical reflection. Christian civil libertarians are rightly resistant to those who would superficially view the question of ordination essentially as a matter for government surveillance, judicial dispute, or legislative whim. No government can ordain. Only the church can properly call, examine, and ordain persons to ministry. This is all the more reason that it be done justly, fairly, and in good order.

Catholic and Protestant traditionalists against women's orders have rightly expressed their concern for continuity in tradition, fitting liturgical representation, and faithful exegesis. But it is now on all three of these grounds that we wish to offer plausible reasons for the ordination of women. Despite sturdy efforts at retrenchment, the theological arguments are piling high on the side of the ordination of women, from Scripture, tradition, reason, and experience.

The clearest theological beginning point is the penetrating analogy between baptism and ordination. For in baptism, all members of the body of Christ, neither one sex nor the other exclusively, are called and committed to the general ministry. By analogy, if all the baptized are to be properly represented in a representative ministry, it is fitting that neither one sex nor the other be arbitrarily excluded from the ordained ministry of word, sacrament, and care. . . .

Rather than viewing the question of ordination of women strictly as a question of revising unchangeable dogma, we do better to think of this question as a matter of evolving and debatable theological interpretation amid the changing shapes of human cultures. Properly framed, the question assumes the church's ability and responsibility to listen ever afresh to the divine address through Scripture and tradition amid changing historical circumstances. Rather than viewing this as a question of fundamental theological backtracking, we do better to see the current church as now belatedly trying to catch up with the deeper unfulfilled intention of Christ (Mark 14:3–9; Luke 8:3–11; Rom. 16:1–15; Gal. 3:28). We are now at a point of historical development in the Christian community where it is at last possible to see more deeply and insightfully into the nature of representative ministry than has been possible under previous ambiguous historical conditions. Now we can clearly grasp that which was hidden yet implicit in the earliest Christian tradition and Scripture.

If a minister is to be a representative of Christ in the midst of the church and representative of the people before God in prayer, than it seems far more reasonable that both men and women be included in that representative function. For both male and female contribute inseparably to the wholeness of the human family.

Key Biblical Passages Rethought

. . . Based on Scripture, tradition, reason, and experience, can we properly conclude that women are called into ministry as truly as men?

The first major task is to think openly about the problematic passages of Scripture that often are alleged to constitute an unanswerable argument against the ordination of women. Here are the key problematic texts that make our case challenging:

- In 1 Corinthians 11:2–12, Paul objected to women praying or prophesying bareheaded, and argued that men should exercise the same headship toward the family that Christ exercised toward the church. Yet Paul acknowledged that "in Christ's fellowship woman is as essential to man as man to woman" (1 Cor. 11:11).
- Later, in 1 Corinthians 14:33–35, Paul appealed to the Torah in enjoining women not to speak publicly to the congregation without authorization.
- Again, in Ephesians 5:21–33, everything hinges on the illuminating analogy between Christ's sacrificial self-giving love for the church and the husband's love for the wife. The notion of "headship" is decisively illuminated by Christ's own self-giving mode of headship. "Be subject to one another out of reverence for Christ. Wives, be subject to your husbands as to the Lord; for the man is the head of the woman, just as Christ also is the head of the church. Christ is, indeed, the Savior of the body; but just as the church is subject to Christ, so must women be to their husbands in everything. Husbands, love your wives, as Christ also loved the church and gave himself up for it, to consecrate it, cleansing it by water and word, so that he might present the church to himself all glorious, with no stain or wrinkle or anything of the sort, but holy and without blemish. In the same way men also are bound to love their wives, as they love their own bodies. In loving his wife a man loves himself. For no one ever hated his own body: on the contrary, he provides and cares for it; and that is how Christ treats the church, because it is his body, of which we are living parts. Thus it is that (in the words of

Scripture) 'a man shall leave his father and mother and shall be joined
to his wife, and the two shall become one flesh.' It is a great truth that
is hidden here. I for my part refer it to Christ and to the church, but it
applies also individually: each of you must love his wife as his very self;
and woman must see to it that she pays her husband all respect."

- Similarly, in Colossians 3:18–19, married men and married women are
  reciprocally enjoined to the high responsibility of building a marriage.
  Wives are called to be responsive to their husbands and husbands to
  love their wives and not be harsh with them. But this is stated in such
  a way that it could lead to an interpretation of women as subordinate.

- The last of these problematic texts combines many of the above
  themes, and adds the "saved through motherhood" theme, namely, in
  1 Timothy 2:9–15, where women are enjoined to be learners, to listen,
  and not to "domineer over man," which hinged on a traditional rabbinic interpretation of Genesis 1 and 2, that from the outset of human
  history women have led men into sin, and yet they "will be saved
  through motherhood—if only women continue in faith, love, and holiness, with a sober mind."

These are the major texts most often quoted to defend a male-only ministry. Other Pauline texts (such as Gal. 3:28) that reflect an amazingly equalitarian view of men and women in Christ are not heard through these volleys.
Although the opposite case (that ministry is inclusive) is made more challenging by the above texts, the theological discussion is far from over. The
other side of the case has not yet received a full hearing. Even though this
exclusivist evidence may appear weighty indeed, we believe the case for
women in ministry can and should be made primarily on exegetical grounds.
We are in fact currently in the middle of a wide-ranging discussion in New
Testament studies as to whether Paul at a deeper level was an advocate of
the equality of women.[2]

In 1 Corinthians 11:4–5, for example, it seems probable that Paul was
assuming that women will be in fact praying and prophesying, that they will
be speaking on important matters in the public context of the church, and
that the only question being debated was whether their heads should be
veiled or not ("a woman . . . brings shame on her head if she prays or proph-
esies bare-headed," v. 5).

It should be kept in mind that the early Christian communities were
struggling valiantly against charges of sedition, moral irresponsibility, social
corruption, and being a revolutionary danger. The social assumptions about

2. See Robin Scroggs, who argues that the apostle Paul was "the only consistent spokesman
for the liberation and equality of women in the New Testament," *Journal of the American Academy of Religion* 40 (1972): 283.

women in the first-century context took for granted that faithful women would use discreet judgment in their public appearance. That, for instance, meant that they would be covered with a veil if they went outside their home. That was not a matter of faith, but rather of a prudent choice not to upset unnecessarily the prevailing social customs about the proper public behavior of women.

Neither Paul nor the New Testament church invented that custom. Rather, it was a part of the context to which they were trying to address the gospel. It might be considered somewhat analogous to another question of cultural assumptions that was more fully treated in the New Testament, namely, whether eating certain food consecrated to heathen deities was permissible and whether that was related to faith in Christ. Paul's answer: "Certainly food will not bring us into God's presence: if we do not eat we are none the worse, and if we eat we are none the better. But be careful that this liberty of yours does not become a pitfall for the weak" (1 Cor. 8:8–9).

What is astonishing is not the familiar ancient practice of women wearing a veil. Rather, it is the fact that within such a culture there would be Christian women who would take strong initiatives in the early church, exercise significant leadership, and be long remembered for their courage in ministry.

In the light of these prevailing cultural assumptions, it is no small point that women were baptized equally with men. For that in itself sharply distinguished the Christian rite of initiation from the Jewish rite of circumcision, which was for males only. This new eschatological community of the resurrection took an enormous political risk by encouraging the primary involvement of women in the community in a way that was virtually without parallel in the ancient Near Eastern context. No serious exegete can simply extract Paul out of that context and assume that he was speaking as if in an already equalitarian society. That was not the case.

The idea that husband and wife are before God equal in distinguishable functions is developed in Ephesians 5. Husband and wife are one with each other in the same way that Christ and the church are one body and united with each other. That is hardly a customary statement of social super- or subordination, inequality, oppression, or inferiority. Rather, it is precisely and only in the differentiation of the sexes that a complementarity between equal but different persons can lead to mutual fulfillment.

Since Paul himself, in 1 Corinthians 11:7–9, appealed directly to Genesis 1 and 2, it is appropriate that we review those passages. For in Genesis 1:27 it is very clear that it is not just male, but male and female, that are created in the image of God. "So God created man in his own image; in the image of God He created him, male and female He created them" (Gen. 1:27). To view woman as the "glory of man" is hardly to demean her, or to detract from the central Yahwist affirmation that both men and women are made in the image of God.

The issue is further clarified by looking more closely at the Hebrew word that is often translated "helper," or "help." For Eve was created, it is said, as Adam's helper *(ezer)*. But *ezer* does not imply the low status or demeaning role that is often attached to the English word *helper*. For in Psalm 33:20, the same word *ezer* ("helper") is used to describe God as our helper. Elsewhere the Psalmist wrote: "Blessed is he whose help *ezer* is the God of Jacob" (Ps. 146:5). This is the same word that was used to speak of Eve. *Helper* does not in this case suggest an inferior order of dignity, or subordinate status, but a relation of mutuality and complementarity.

The quality of this complementarity is most accurately stated in 1 Corinthians, chapter 11: In communion with Christ, "woman is as essential to man as man to woman. If woman was made out of man, it is through woman that man now comes to be" (v. 12). The heart of the issue is whether men are more necessary to women than women are to men. According to Paul, they are equally necessary to each other, and God is equally necessary for both. If, in the case of one man, woman was made out of man, it should also be remembered, notes Paul, that all other men radically depend upon woman for their being, their very coming to be. Here we have a powerful image of sexual complementarity that has a great potential impact upon understanding the office of ministry, ironically found right at the heart of one of the passages most often quoted to show sexual subordination. How, we ask, can the office of ministry be a fully representative office in the church unless it represents that complementarity of humanity through both male and female ministers?

This is why the deeper stratum of Pauline thought is far better expressed in Galatians 3:28 where Paul had been talking about the law as a kind of tutor or custodian to train and instruct and guard us until Christ comes, through whom we are justified by faith. Now through faith, he says, you all are "baptized in the union with him" (Gal. 3:27). He immediately reflects on the implications of this union for the tragic aspect of human social divisions, including that between men and women. "You have all put on Christ as a garment. There is no such thing as Jew and Greek, slave and freeman, male and female; for you are all one person in Christ Jesus" (v. 28). For those who belong to Christ live in a new creation that transcends the categories of oppression, self-justification, boasting, unjust subordination, and dominance of one person over another. These are cultural-historical antipathies that were thought by Paul to be outmoded by the love of God in Jesus Christ. . . .

The Scandal of Particularity

Some argue that women cannot be ministers because Christ himself was male. That is a fact, but what it signifies is the scandal of God's coming to us personally in a particular time and place. For if God is to come into history as an individual human being, it must be either in the form of a man or a woman—for it is not possible for a single human being to be both.

Given the cultural setting in which God chose, oddly enough, to come into history as a child of a poor family, set amid the hopes and historical expectations of a particular people, the Incarnate Lord had to be either male or female. There is no third way to be a human being. It was admittedly a distinctly partriarchal history into which the saving deed of God appeared. Then, it was widely assumed that the hoped-for messiah would be male. It would have been an even more incredible surprise than Christmas already is if God had come to the Jews as a woman. That is hardly beyond the competence of God, and indeed it is a significant meditation in speculative theology to reflect on the consequences of a female incarnation. Males in ministry should not too quickly dismiss such questions.

The central scandal of Christian revelation is that the holy God chose to become known personally in a particular time and place,[3] through an individual human being who lived out of a particular history, the people of Israel in the period of Caesar Augustus. In line with the expectations of Israel, the promised one appeared through the male line of Jesse, consistent with prophetic hopes. We can not thereby conclude that there is an absolute necessity that God's self-disclosure must, therefore, have been in the male line. Rather that it occurred through the male line is a remembered event of salvation history, another scandal of particularity, which Christians the world over celebrate at Christmastide.

We have no warrant to conclude that God is male. Even though male images are frequently used in Scripture to speak of God, female images are also used (as in Isa. 49:15 and 66:11–13). Luke 15:8–10 likens the redemptive God to a woman who sweeps the house looking for a lost coin, and when she finds it she calls her neighbors together to rejoice. In one of his moments of highest pathos, Jesus used a feminine image of God as he addressed the city of Jerusalem: "The city that murders the prophets and stones the messengers sent to her! How often have I longed to gather your children, as a hen gathers her brood under her wings" (Luke 13:34–35). But that does not mean that God is female. Rather it means that personalistic, anthropomorphic language is happily employed to talk about the personal love of God, the care and anger of God, the frustration and empathy of God who transcends all human emotions. If we did not have such personalistic imagery, Scripture would be the worse for it because it would narrow its speech to objectifying, descriptive, impersonal language.[4]

---

3. Søren Kierkegaard, *Training in Christianity and the Edifying Discourse which 'Accompanied' It*, trans. Walter Lowrie (Princeton: Princeton University Press, 1944), 79ff.

4. Augustine, *The Teacher*, 3.5ff.

Indeed, Jesus was male and not female. But he was also Jewish and not gentile, born in Palestine and not Norway. He is also of Davidic descent and not of some other family descent. All of these dimensions of Jesus' identity are connected with his role in the fulfillment of the messianic promises of God to Israel.[5] Similarly, when Jesus gathered together his twelve disciples as an analogy to the tribes of Israel, if the analogy was to be consistent and credible to Jewish hearers, the symbolic twelve would most likely be Jewish free men. Given the prevailing cultural assumptions, it would have been far more difficult for twelve women to have understandably symbolized the unity of Israel.

There remains no compelling theological reason why women should be viewed as incapable of ministerial orders. Rather, there is every reason to believe that the deeper intention of the gospel is to bring men and women into a full relationship of mutuality, complementarity, covenant love, and self-sacrificial giving that is not well represented by the super- and subordination motifs. Our English translations of words like *headship* and *helper* have given us the impression that super- and subordination are normative in the earliest Christian tradition, an error long due for correction.

Article 34 among the Anglican Articles of Religion wisely reminds us that we should not confuse matters of faith with time-conditioned, culturally-determined matters of social custom: "'It is not necessary that traditions and ceremonies be in all places one, or utterly alike; for at all times they have been divers, and may be changed according to the diversity of countries, towns, and . . . manners.'"

The exclusion of women from orders is not to be found in any of the early Christian confessions. It is not an article of the Apostles' Creed, it is not mentioned in the Nicene Creed, and it was never asserted as *regula fide.*

Women may be equipped physiologically and psychically to do some tasks of ministry better than men. With a different hormonal structure that elicits differently nuanced patterns of responsiveness, women may be more natively gifted in empathy. It may be that some of the nurturing responses implied in the pastoral metaphor may come more easily for women, whose culturally conditioned chemistry promotes deep and sustained caring. This is all the more probably the case in the context of parishioners faced with miscarriage, childbirth, mastectomy, hysterectomy, and menopause, where men may have less access to the felt dynamics of feminine psychology. We say "may" in each of the above statements, hoping that further experience and research will yield more reliable conclusions in these areas.

Full participation in the sacramental life by both women and men will better symbolize to the worshipping church the full humanity that Christ intends for us all. Clergy leadership will come from a larger pool of compe-

5. Athanasius, *On the Incarnation*, 33–40.

tent people. The shepherding image is a parenting image, just as applicable to women as men, and perhaps even more so. In the human past, women have cared for flocks just as often and well as men. Women who have been socialized and acculturated to cooperate and nurture rather than to compete and dominate will profoundly affect the future of Christian ministry. Little will be taken away from ministry except its barriers.

God the Spirit is working in our time particularly to call women into significant ordained ministries, gifted ministries that will affect the life and the ethos of the church in many positive ways in the years to come.

Man and Woman in Christ

Stephen B. Clark

. . . The fact that the debate over ordaining women has arisen among Christians so recently, relatively speaking, indicates that its appearance as an issue has much more to do with the development of technological society and its influence on the Christian churches than with anything arising from within Christian tradition.

A full treatment of the contemporary issue of ordination for women is outside the scope of this book. This book concerns the social roles of men and women, and these roles are only one aspect of the discussion about the ordination of women. . . . The material presented in this book [*Man and Woman in Christ*], however, does allow some reflections on the ordination of women insofar as Christian social roles bear on the issue of ordination. This section will consider three such reflections.

First, the study done here reveals that both Scripture and tradition teach very clearly that the positions of overall government in the Christian community should be held by men. This is one of the clearest and most consistent principles concerning the structure and order of the Christian people, from the time of Christ and the apostles until a very recent period of Christian history. If any authoritative statements about order among the Christian people are undisputed in Scripture and tradition, this one is surely among them. To change it is not simply a matter of changing one rule: If this principle can be changed, the Christian people can change any feature of order, and they are not bound by Scripture and tradition in shaping their life together. The judgment to ordain women, then, involves the judgment that modern society has reached the point where Scripture and tradition cannot definitely guide the structuring of the common life of Christians.

Secondly, the study done in this book indicates that the question of who should be heads of the Christian people is actually a question of God's purposes for the human race and for how the new humanity should be formed. Government of the Christian people is not merely a secondary question of social roles that can be changed with little consequence. Rather, the question involves a broader vision of what human life should be like according to God's ideal. The ordering of governmental responsibilities is only an expression of that underlying vision. Deciding to have women acting as heads of the Christian people means deciding that the scriptural vision of the life of humans together is no longer applicable or appropriate. A decision about structure and order in this area is a decision about what a body of Christians is trying to be.

The decision to ordain women often arises from a perception that, sociologically speaking, the Christian churches have become something very different than they have been in the past. In the modern Western world, most Christian bodies function more as religious institutions providing religious services than as Christian communities.[1] They have, in short, lost much of the relationship that makes a group a "people" in the sense in which the Scriptures speak of a "people." The governing officials of a church function less as heads over the people than as administrators and policy setters in a modern social institution, and their teaching is not received (or given) as being authoritative. Church bodies are conducted according to the principles of a service institution. Eliminating the restriction on women holding governing positions simply brings the structure of the church more in line with the principles that govern other service institutions in a modern society.

Of course, the question is how the contemporary church bodies should respond to the current situation. Should they write into their constitutions, canons, and books on church order and discipline principles that ratify their current position as service institutions, or should they try to become communities? This is not an easy question to decide. There is much to be said for the value of service institutions which have accommodated structurally as much to the contemporary society as most church bodies have. As service institutions, they can preserve some Christian life among a broad number of people. To become communities like those of the early church would involve changing much more than some isolated principles of men's and women's roles. As was pointed out earlier, Christian churches today do not follow many other instructions given in the New Testament, such as instructions about Christian discipline and about relations with non-Christians and fallen-away Christians. All these instructions make sense when Christians are viewed as a people, a social body with committed relationships. In short,

1. For a fuller discussion of this difference, see Stephen B. Clark, *Building Christian Communities: Strategy for Renewing the Church* (Notre Dame, Ind.: Ave Maria, 1972), 20–46.

to reverse the balance from being a religious institution accommodated to
modern society to being more of a people would be both very difficult and
quite risky for most Christian churches. The question, then, is whether the
current situation in some way reflects an accommodation the Lord wants the
churches to make. The key issue facing the churches today as they survey
contemporary society and consider the scriptural view of the Christian people is: What kind of Christian bodies should they attempt to be?[2]

Thirdly, the study in this book also points to a problem which faces those
churches which are trying to maintain the view that women should not be
ordained. For the most part, these churches are trying to maintain this position without attempting to provide a corresponding social structure to support it.[3] For instance, they do not any longer normally teach very clearly
about a difference in the roles of men and women. Yet, unless they do, their
position on ordination will become more and more difficult for their people
to understand and accept. When rules of order do not structure social life in
a helpful way, such rules are often experienced as both restrictive and sense-
less. Of course, these churches could claim a basis other than social structure
for holding that women should not be ordained. That is, they can, for example, insist that ordination is a sacramental matter which operates by an
entirely different set of rules than the rest of life, and which should have no
consequences for social structure. The effect of such an approach, however,
would be to reinforce the already existing separation between "religion" (or
"ritual") and "real life." Ordination can then be different because it operates
in a different realm, one where only symbol is important and where sacramental actions have effects but do not order or structure the daily life of people. In short, if the churches that presently maintain the prohibition of
women's ordination do not (1) back up their position with clear instruction
on family structure, and (2) provide their people with adequate social sup-

2. Here it is instructive to read the Kenyon case of 1974 in the United Presbyterian Church
in the U.S.A. Walter W. Kenyon appeared for ordination and stated in the course of the examination that he would not ordain women to the session. He would not oppose the ordination of
women, and would even call in someone else to do it, but he would not do so himself. His position was based upon Scripture, primarily 1 Timothy 2:12. That position was not argued either
in the original examination before his presbytery (which agreed to ordain him), or in the trial
before the synod (which overruled the presbytery) or before the general assembly (which sustained the synod). The grounds given for rejecting Kenyon's ordination was his refusal to abide
by the order to the United Presbyterian Church. That decision has a great deal of wisdom
behind it. The fundamental issue in such a case is not what the Scripture says, but what kind
of a body a particular church is and what principles it follows. A summary of the case is
recorded in "Decision of the Permanent Judicial Commission of the General Assembly of the
United Presbyterian Church in the United States of America, St. Louis, Missouri, November
18, 1974. The Rev. Jack M. Maxwell, Th.D., Appellant vs. the Pittsburgh Presbytery, Appelle;
Remedial Case No. 1."
3. See Stephen B. Clark, "Social Order and Women's Ordination," *America*, 17 January
1976, 32–33.

port to live a way of life different from the technological society around them (one which includes a role difference between men and women), these churches will fail to resolve the current controversy in the area. Either the issue of women's ordination will remain a sore point, or it will contribute to an even greater separation between "sacramental" matters and the daily life of the Christian people.

Obviously these three reflections do not cover the subject of women's ordination. However, they help to place the issue in its social context—a crucial perspective if the issue is to be resolved properly. On the one hand, those favoring women's ordination are confronted with the clear, consistent, authoritative statements of Scripture and tradition. They are also faced with the prospect of choosing to become something that may be significantly different than the vision of God's people outlined in the New Testament. On the other hand, those opposing women's ordination must be ready to take more action than the mere defense of a single rule of order which seems to make little sense by itself in the present day. They, too, must face up to the full scriptural vision of the new humanity, and must be prepared to establish a whole Christian social order which will support and make sense of many of the individual prescriptions of authoritative Christian teaching. . . .

From Stephen B. Clark, "Ordination, Occupation, Legislation," in *Man and Woman in Christ: An Examination of the Roles of Men and Women in Light of Scripture and the Social Sciences* (Ann Arbor: Servant, 1980), 654–59.

For Further Reflection

Case Studies

Marriage blues. Joe's parents believe women should work only at home, so his father worked long hours at his job while his mother did all the housework. Susan's parents shared housekeeping tasks because they both worked outside the home much of her growing-up years. Susan thought it normal that husbands do a fair share of work at home. After their wedding, Susan sought a job to help with college loans and a down payment on their house. Recognizing their need for the money, Joe did not complain. But when he came home from work, he assumed his wife would do all the house work just as his mother had. Susan, however, believed that a husband who really loved his wife would not just "bring home the bacon" but would also "help fry it." Having seen these patterns all their lives, Joe and Susan each felt their way was right. Joe felt indignant that Susan expected him to do "woman's work"; Susan felt frustrated at being asked to carry a disproportionate load at home.

As their friend, you must help mediate the quarrel. What moral principles should Joe and Susan consider in resolving this dilemma and to what extent is this a cultural problem? What should they expect from each other? Is either one using a biblical model of gender relationships?

Missionary strategy. Two women missionaries serve in a remote tribal context. The fledgling church in their care needs leadership, so one of the women seeks ordination in order to preach and give the sacraments. Another missionary in the next valley, however, opposes women's ordination. So he decides to take hazardous plane rides to the women's area, taking time away from his duties, so he can preach for the women. He believes God will bless the mission if it honors the divine order for male and female roles. The field leader for the mission believes that the church should not normally ordain women, but he also thinks that in unusual circumstances, women should preach and give the sacraments. The women believe the man is intruding and trivializing their ministry. The man is acting out of strong convictions.

What should the field leader do? Are concessions possible or would they compromise important principles? How can the field leader best affirm his missionaries and preserve the ministry?

GLOSSARY

Biblical feminism: Feminism of those who combine evangelical commitments with their defense of egalitarianism.

Egalitarianism: View that in home, church, and society, qualified men and women equally may exercise leadership; does not imply that women and men are *identical* in personal qualities, interests, skills, or gifts.

Feminism: Movement of any, male or female, who advocate laws and social policies that promote social, political, and economic equality between the genders.

Head: Key Greek word (*kephalē*) for understanding 1 Corinthians 11:13–16 and Ephesians 5:21–33; often interpreted by biblical traditionalists to mean *authority over*; some biblical feminists say it means *source*.

Hierarchicalism: View that males must fill certain leadership roles in social relationships; it is God's design, in certain contexts, that women must follow the leadership and/or authority of men.

Misogyny: Latent or explicit hatred of women.

Patriarchy: Systems of social life and language that preserve male privilege; feminists argue that patriarchy oppresses women.

Sexism: Gender-based prejudice.

Sexual harassment: Unwelcome sexual advances, whether verbal, nonverbal, or physical, that create a hostile work or learning environment, make submission to the abuse a condition of employment or the basis of performance evaluation, or cause stress, anxiety, or embarrassment for the person harassed.

Annotated Bibliography

Bilezikian, Gilbert. *Beyond Sex Roles: A Guide for the Study of Female Roles in the Bible*. Grand Rapids: Baker, 1985. Helpful, detailed study of biblical texts representing a biblical feminist perspective.

Bloesch, Donald G. *Is the Bible Sexist? Beyond Feminism and Patriarchalism*. Westchester, Ill.: Crossway, 1982. Prominent theologian crafts a qualified hierarchicalism as an alternative both to traditional patriarchy and to contemporary feminism.

Bruland, Esther Byle. "Evangelical and Feminist Ethics: Complex Solidarities." *The Journal of Religious Ethics* 17 (Fall 1989): 139–60. Essay on the difficulty of combining the theological methods of feminism with the biblical commitments of evangelicalism.

Clark, Stephen B. *Man and Woman in Christ.* Ann Arbor: Servant, 1980. Lengthy, detailed, and competent book defending traditional views on gender roles.

Clouse, Bonnidell, and Robert Clouse, eds. *Women in Ministry: Four Views.* Downers Grove, Ill.: InterVarsity, 1989. Essays and responses representing a spectrum of Christian views.

Daly, Mary. *The Church and the Second Sex.* New York: Harper & Row, 1968. Ground-breaking critique of sexism in Roman Catholicism by former Catholic, now radical feminist.

Dayton, Donald W. *Discovering an Evangelical Heritage.* New York: Harper & Row, 1976. Documents evangelical influences in early feminism.

Evans, Mary J. *Woman in the Bible.* Downers Grove, Ill.: InterVarsity, 1983. Notable study by a British scholar committed to careful study of the Bible.

Foh, Susan T. *Women and the Word of God: A Response to Biblical Feminism.* Philadelphia: Presbyterian and Reformed, 1979. Traditionalist responds directly to biblical feminists.

Friedan, Betty. *The Feminine Mystique.* New York: Dell, 1963. Magna Carta for third-wave feminism, the contemporary, secularized feminism.

Grenz, Stanley J., with Denise M. Kjesbo. *Women in the Church: A Biblical Theology of Women in Ministry.* Downers Grove, Ill.: InterVarsity, 1995. Careful, evangelical presentation of the case for full participation of women in the life of the church, including church leadership.

Groothius, Rebecca Merrill. *Women Caught in the Conflict: The Culture War between Traditionalism and Feminism.* Grand Rapids: Baker, 1994. Argues that both traditionalism and secular feminism reflect cultural patterns that contradict biblical norms.

Hardesty, Nancy A., and Letha Dawson Scanzoni. *All We're Meant to Be: A Biblical Approach to Women's Liberation.* 3d rev. ed. Grand Rapids: Eerdmans, 1992. Defense of evangelical feminism from an EWC point of view.

Hurley, James B. *Man and Woman in Biblical Perspective.* London: InterVarsity, 1981. Comprehensive traditionalist discussion of problems in biblical interpretation regarding gender roles.

Keener, Craig S. *Paul, Women and Wives.* Peabody, Mass.: Hendrickson, 1992. Very detailed analysis of key Pauline texts in light of early Christian literature.

Knight, George W., III. *Role Relationship of Men and Women.* Rev. ed. Chicago: Moody Press, 1985. Brief traditionalist essay on women's roles in marriage and the church.

Köstenberger, Andreas J., Thomas R. Schreiner, and H. Scott Baldwin, eds. *Women in the Church: A Fresh Analysis of 1 Timothy 2:9–15.* Grand Rapids: Baker, 1995. A detailed exegetical study of 1 Timothy 2:9–15 from a hierarchical perspective.

Moo, Douglas J. "1 Timothy 2:11-15: Meaning and Significance." *Trinity Journal* 1 (1980): 62–83. Detailed exposition of a central passage on women's ordination by a strong traditionalist.

Oden, Thomas C. "Women in the Pastoral Office." In *Pastoral Theology: Essentials of Ministry.* San Francisco: Harper and Row, 1983, 35–46. A theological defense of the ordination of qualified women.

Piper, John, and Wayne Grudem, eds. *Recovering Biblical Manhood and Womanhood.* Westchester, Ill.: Crossway, 1991. Concerted response to biblical feminism by twenty-two essayists representing the CBMW position.

Ryrie, Charles C. *The Place of Women in the Church.* Chicago: Moody Press, 1958. Well-known exposition of traditionalist thinking.

Schmidt, Ruth. "Second-Class Citizens in the Kingdom of God." *Christianity Today* (1 January 1971): 13–14. Significant essay bringing feminist consciousness into a major evangelical magazine; first suggestion in evangelical circles that women are oppressed.

Sommers, Christina Hoff. *Who Stole Feminism? How Women Have Betrayed Women.* New York: Simon and Schuster, 1994. Secular feminist criticizes a small but powerful and vocal group of radical feminists who have coopted the feminist movement.

Spencer, Aída Besancon. *Beyond the Curse: Women Called to Ministry.* Nashville: Thomas Nelson, 1985. Evangelical seminary professor presents a biblically-argued case for women's call to ministry and ordination.

————, et al. *The Goddess Revival.* Grand Rapids: Baker, 1995. An in-depth critique of the radical feminist goddess-spirituality movement and the question of the gender of God, from an evangelical egalitarian perspective.

Van Leeuwen, Mary Stewart. "Christian Maturity in Light of Feminist Theory." *Journal of Psychology and Theology* 16 (1988): 168–182. Psychological insights applied to understandings of Christian maturity.

————. *Gender and Grace.* Downers Grove, Ill.: InterVarsity, 1990. Emphasizes the distinctions of male and female as they approach work, church, and family life.

Part

Stewardship
of Creation

9

Wealth and Economics

Today thirty-five thousand people died in a major calamity. Several facts make this tragedy especially gut-wrenching. For one, all its victims were children. Further, it is indirectly related to the affluent lifestyle I live. Worst of all, this disaster will happen again and again: thirty-five thousand poverty-stricken children die of malnutrition and starvation 365 days a year.

A wheat farmer in Nebraska can, using his machines, cultivate thousands of acres. In George Washington's day, that much farmland required hundreds of farmers. Machines make the difference, dramatically increasing productivity, the amount of goods and services a worker can produce in a given amount of time. Due to productivity gains in the last two centuries, both **income**—economic power one anticipates receiving—and **wealth**—economic power one has already accumulated—have increased at historically unprecedented rates. Should we use that wealth to feed the hungry children?

Many have invested wealth in other good things: education, medicine, science, the arts, and technology. Thus, a fundamental question for economics is, How should a society decide where to allocate its wealth? One answer is the **free market** or laissez-faire approach. In Adam Smith's famous metaphor, an invisible hand guides a society's use of wealth as each person in the economy simply makes decisions in his own self-interest (not selfishness). If I manufacture mouse traps, it is in my best interest to make the best mouse trap for the best price. If you are looking for a good deal in mouse traps, my self-interest motivates me to work in your best interest. In a free-market system, this law of the marketplace, not a dictatorial person or group, guides the most efficient use of wealth.

Although government enforces laws requiring fairness and honesty, the free-market approach is fundamentally individualistic. Individuals make their own economic decisions without any overarching social plan or vision. This leads to the best results for the group. Free-market advocates like philosopher Ronald Nash find this system not only more efficient but morally and biblically superior as well. Significantly, though Nash does not make this point, the free-market system is culturally suited to America. Americans strongly value individualism. They do not see economics from a macroscopic or systems point of view. For this cultural reason, among others, this individual-oriented, free-market view is commonly held by evangelicals in the United States.

One group that has gained some influence among conservative Christians specifically defends free-market economics as part of its larger agenda. **Theonomists** (also called reconstructionists) hold that Christians should make the governing structures of the United States distinctively Christian. This includes both reshaping the law of the land in light of biblical law (including Old Testament civil law) and promoting a free-market economy. Although theonomists are among the most vigorous advocates of the free-market system, they are not its only defenders.

In contrast to defenders of the free-market view, advocates of the **guided-market** views criticize the laissez-faire approach on both economic and moral grounds. Ethicist Philip Wogaman argues that private interests cannot achieve certain social goals (like building a highway system). Further, the individualistic free-market philosophy promotes principles like freedom, but neglects group-oriented values.

For instance, the free-market system permits self-interested acts that assault the common good. This is the **problem of the commons**. Sending pollutants into the atmosphere is the cheapest way for polluters to make mouse traps at the lowest price. (The second cheapest way is for polluters to fund political candidates who will veto clean air legislation.) But this is not in the best interest of society as a whole. Industrialists sacrifice clean air—owned by no one in particular since we hold it in common—for their personal gain.

Guided-market theories therefore agree on the need for some central governmental power to control the economy. In Western economies, the state exercises some control while permitting some market forces freer reign. Planned economies associated with **communism** give the government significant power to control the economy. In cases where these governments are not accountable to voters, however, history shows they become both inefficient and self-serving. They do not contain incentives to encourage people to do the work and take the risks that create wealth. The recent collapse of Marxist regimes graphically illustrates the weaknesses of communist economics in a totalitarian nation. Some radical Christians in the West defend and practice a kind of voluntary communism in which a commune shares housing, transportation, and work. Involuntary communism on a national scale, however, often resorts to coercion.

Wogaman argues that without a middle road, the problems of a free-market system will lead to totalitarian **socialism**. His alternative is the mixed economy, a system in which the public and private sectors exist side by side, each contributing to the total economic life of a nation. One by one, the capitalist economies of Europe and North America have abandoned pure **capitalism** and adopted mixed capitalism. Free-marketers decry this. They believe that in mixed economies, the state steals wealth through taxes and then redistributes it inefficiently. (Thus some theonomists derisively call mixed economies **redistributionist** and **interventionist**.)

In third-world nations, **liberation theology**, which first emerged in Latin America, has genuine appeal. This form of Christian theology adapts a Marxist analysis of economic and political structures and links it to biblical themes. Liberationists begin their theology with the lived experience of oppressed peoples. They interpret great disparities in wealth as the primary manifestation of sin. They typically interpret salvation as the personal, economic, and political liberation of oppressed persons in this life. Evangelical people are generally hesitant about liberation theology's analysis. Both its use of Marxism and its tendency to interpret Scripture in line with its own agenda seem troublesome. Nevertheless, conservative Christians should take seriously the criticisms that liberationists make of unjust economic structures.

Liberationists point to the huge new problems that the industrial revolution created. For the earth, industrialization and the large population growth it supports have wreaked havoc on the environment (see chap. 10). For nations, new wealth has only enlarged the gap between rich and poor. The disparity between the economies of the northern and southern hemispheres is huge. In many cities, some of God's children live in inhumane squalor only blocks away from others who live the lifestyle of the rich and famous.

For individuals who have accumulated wealth, their economic status raises the age-old spiritual and moral question, How does **money** affect relationships to God and other persons? The Bible does not speak directly to modern economics at national and international levels. What the Bible says about economics at the social level is general: merchants should use honest weights; government must use its power for the public good; societies should aid the poor.

When the Bible speaks about finances, it is often at a personal level. Jesus, for example, warned of the addictive power of **mammon**: "You cannot

serve both God and Money" (Matt. 6:24; Luke 16:13). *Mammon* is a trans-
literation of the Aramaic word for money or wealth. It appears only four
times in the New Testament, three of these in the context of Luke 16:13. As
Jesus used it, *mammon* is money as an egocentric force, a power that capti-
vates the heart and mind, alienating a person from God. Mammon is money
deified.

According to those who defend a **simplicity gospel**, Jesus is remarkably
and consistently negative in his view of wealth. They point out that Jesus told
the rich young man to give away his wealth (Matt. 27:57). Jesus said rich
people will have a hard time getting into heaven (Luke 18:24–25). Most
Western Christians, fabulously wealthy by world standards, are accused of
deploying ingenious strategies to blunt their Master's words: "Wealth is not
sinful if your attitude is right." Advocates of the simple lifestyle stress obedience. Rationalization, they say, is not an appropriate Christian response to
wealth.

Richard Foster in *Freedom of Simplicity* and Ronald Sider in *Rich Christians in an Age of Hunger* and *Living More Simply* adopt this point of view.
The gospel of simplicity teaches wealthy Christians to live with less rather
than more. It encourages them to buy a second-hand car instead of a new
one or a bike instead of a car. Simplicity has its advantages: less environmental abuse, more financial help for the needy, less waste of resources, and
more devotion to the kingdom of God. Sider argues specifically that a simpler lifestyle will free up huge resources for relief and evangelism.

A classic on wealth, *Money and Power*, written by Jacques Ellul in 1954,
takes an extreme view of money. In Ellul's view, the Christian gospel fundamentally opposes all power, including especially political power. Money is
mammon, and mammon is an evil power. Just by using money, therefore, a
Christian becomes guilty of participating in an evil system. Instead, he
should take radical and individual responsibility for this problem. He can,
for example, profane the god Mammon by giving liberally to the poor.

Other evangelicals, reflecting a more middle-class view, find the simplicity gospel unbalanced. It is selective in its use of the Bible, they argue. God
financially blessed Old Testament saints. Proverbs extols the wisdom of
those who work diligently, save for the future, and conduct business skillfully. The simplicity gospel ignores the fabulous wealth of Abraham and the
straightforward claim, "Prosperity rewards the righteous" (Prov. 13:21).

Evangelicals who adopt middle-class values regularly criticize Ellul for
failing to distinguish *money* and *mammon*. Money is simply a medium of
exchange; it makes human society function economically. Without it, we
would return to barter, a cumbersome and ultimately unworkable financial
system. Money as such is neutral. Mammon, money turned into a god, is evil
as Ellul rightly points out. Thus, many evangelicals emphasize Paul's point
that the *love* (*agape*) of money, not money itself, is evil (1 Tim. 6:10).

The element of truth in the usual evangelical view is this: what God creates is good, not evil. Everything, including physical, fleshy stuff, is good. Indeed, if money were inherently evil, why would Ellul give it to the poor? Would he give them poison? If money is inherently evil, better to destroy it as we do disease-infested bandages. Contra Ellul's overstatements, evil is the distortion, corruption, or destruction of what is good.

From this premise, those who succeed economically sometimes infer that an affluent lifestyle is morally acceptable if someone earns it: "I worked for it; I deserve it; it's mine!" As long as a wealthy Christian gains his money legally and tithes regularly, wealth is acceptable. The **prosperity gospel** (also called the health-and-wealth gospel) takes "I earned it; it's mine" to an extreme. This view sees wealth as a blessing promised by God to all faithful Christians. Prosperity and physical well-being are the believer's birthright; they are available to all who exercise appropriate faith. But this teaching is heretical, inhumane, and economically impossible. It sees the poor, who supposedly fail to exercise the right sort of faith, as second-class citizens in the kingdom of God. It teaches the rich to love God for what he gives, rather than for himself.

Others reject "I earned it; it's mine." Simple-lifestyle advocates often assume that the affluent amass their wealth at others' expense. They tend to see wealth as evidence of oppression, the exercise of economic power in burdensome and cruel ways. Defenders of the free market contend, however, that this analysis is flawed because it sees economic exchanges as zero-sum exchanges. In a zero-sum game, only one side wins and the other loses. In the race for the America's Cup, only one boat gets the trophy.

As Nash points out, however, economic exchanges are positive-sum games: both sides win. Suppose I buy some lumber, build a garage, and sell you the building at a profit. You use the garage to make a profit fixing trucks. Our friend buys an old truck, gets it fixed in your garage, and makes a profit hauling lumber. In turn, I buy his lumber to make someone else a garage. We all win. Hard-working persons can gain while helping others get ahead.

In the selection from *Rich Christians in an Age of Hunger*, Sider argues that although some economic transactions benefit both parties, not all do so equally. Suppose ABC Coffee Corp. holds a monopoly. ABC forces José, its coffee bean supplier, to accept its outrageously low offering price for coffee beans. Since no one else will buy his crop, José's only alternative is sitting on a rotting pile of coffee beans, and so he caves in and sells. As a coffee lover, I benefit from ABC's lower coffee prices. ABC sells more coffee and raises its dividends. José supports his family on $1.79 per day. This deal is said to be a positive-sum game since it benefits José. José, of course, is better off getting something than getting nothing, but he would no doubt find the arrangement unjust.

What is a Christian's responsibility for the poor? Some believe that a Christian ought to help others only in cases where the individual is the direct cause of another's suffering. If our friend crashes his truck into your new garage, he ought to fix it. But should I help you in your need, even if I am not to blame for it? Sider answers in the affirmative. Consider this analogy. If a person's sin is not my fault, am I still responsible to witness to him about the gospel of forgiveness? Of course! Similarly, Sider argues, even if the poverty of another is not my fault, I may still have a Christian duty toward that person. If Sider is right, the debate about what causes the poverty of the southern hemisphere is relevant, but not central. Loving one's neighbor as oneself is central.

If Sider is right, Christians should help individuals in need. If a relief agency helping starving children in Minneapolis or Mozambique needs funds, many will give. But should Christians take the next step and help change the economic structures that contribute to starvation? Some Christians believe this is too socialistic. Individually oriented evangelicals tend to see personal laziness as the root of poverty. But the causes and the solutions of poverty—both personal and systemic—are much more complex. Large international economic structures, in concert with other problems, make relief necessary.

Wealth and possessions no doubt comprise an area where many North American evangelicals not only live *in* the world, but follow the values *of* the world. Some think the idolatry of possessions is evangelicalism's greatest sin. On the other hand, God does bless his children and meet their needs. Proverbs 30:8–9 and 1 Timothy 6:6 remind us of the spiritual value of contentment rooted in God's presence, not in earthly possessions. God's people can make a difference by following kingdom values. If fifty million evangelicals in the United States sought these spiritual values, this could be a new world after all.

Does Capitalism Pass the Moral Test?

Ronald H. Nash

Even a casual reading of recent Christian writings on the subject of capitalism makes one thing clear: most of the Christian scholars writing about economics these days show little regard for capitalism. Such writings often exhibit adulation for socialism and contempt for capitalism. Consider, for example, the following claims by a Latin American Protestant, Jose Miguez-Bonino:

> [T]he basic ethos of capitalism is definitely anti-Christian: it is the maximizing of economic gain, the raising of man's grasping impulse, the idolizing of the strong, the subordination of man to the economic production. . . . In terms of their basic ethos, Christians must criticize capitalism radically, in its fundamental intention. . . .[1]

It is regrettable that Bonino's confused zealotry is typical of the approach toward capitalism taken by a growing number of Christians.

For Christians like this, capitalism is supposed to be un-Christian or anti-Christian because it allegedly gives a predominant place to greed and other un-Christian values. It is alleged to increase poverty and the misery of the poor while, at the same time, it makes a few rich at the expense of the many. Socialism, on the other hand, is portrayed as the economic system of people who really care for the less fortunate members of society. Socialism is represented as the economics of compassion. Some writers even go so far as to claim that socialism is an essential part of the Christian gospel.[2]

---

1. Jose Miguez-Bonino, *Christians and Marxists* (Grand Rapids: Eerdmans, 1976), 115.
2. This outrageous claim is certainly one implication of the argument contained in Andrew Kirk's book, *The Good News of the Kingdom Coming* (Downers Grove, Ill.: InterVarsity, 1985).

This article has two jobs. First of all, it will examine the most widely used arguments that attack capitalism on moral grounds.[3] It is arguments like these that appear most frequently in the writings of religious critics of capitalism. Second, I will defend the claim that capitalism is superior to socialism on moral grounds. Few people question the economic superiority of capitalism. But, many of its critics maintain, a market system must be restricted or even abolished because it allegedly fails important moral tests.

Before the moral arguments for and against capitalism are presented, it is necessary to eliminate a source of much confusion on this issue. Many times, critics of capitalism demonstrate that they have no idea what capitalism is. The capitalism they attack is a caricature, a straw man. The stereotype of capitalism that is the target of most such attacks often results from an incorrect association of the word *capitalism* with existing national economies that are in fact better described as interventionist. More attention needs to be given to the inappropriateness of regarding interventionist policies of the United States as a paradigm of capitalism.[4]

Capitalism should be viewed as a system of voluntary human relationships in which people exchange within a framework of laws that prohibits force, fraud, and theft. Capitalism is not economic anarchy. It recognizes several necessary conditions for the kinds of voluntary relationships it recommends. One of these is the existence of inherent human rights, such as the right to make decisions, the right to be free, the right to hold property, and the right to exchange what one owns for something else. Capitalism also presupposes a system of morality. Capitalism does not encourage people to do anything they want. There are definite limits, moral and otherwise, to the ways in which people should exchange. "Thou shalt not steal" and "Thou shalt not lie" are part of the underlying moral constraints of the system. Economic exchanges can hardly be voluntary if one participant is coerced, deceived, defrauded, or robbed.

Moral Objections to Capitalism

Exploitation

Capitalism is often attacked on the ground that it exploits people and poor nations. A crucial but often unstated assumption of this view is the

---

3. In two earlier books I considered a more extensive list of objections to capitalism. See Ronald Nash, *Social Justice and the Christian Church* (Grand Rapids: Baker, 1986), chaps. 10–11; and *Freedom, Justice and the State* (Lanham, Md.: University Press of America, 1980), chap. 6.

4. The need to condense my views obliges me to omit many important things that I might otherwise wish to say. Fortunately, more complete statements of my position are available in my *Social Justice and the Christian Church* and in my *Poverty and Wealthy: The Christian Debate over Capitalism* (Westchester, Ill.: Crossway, 1986). It would be nice to think that friends and foes of my views will consult the longer expositions of my positions in these books.

belief that the only way some can become rich is by exploiting others. Poverty is, such critics believe, always the result of exploitation and oppression by someone who profits from the poverty of others. To carry the argument even further, the reason some nations are poor is because they have supposedly been exploited by richer and more powerful nations. To be specific, the West is supposed to be responsible for the persistent poverty of lesser developed nations.[5]

The exploitation model of poverty is simplistic. It is also an excellent example of the ease with which some contemporary Christians insist on reading Marxist ideology into the Bible. It is certainly true that Scripture recognizes that poverty *sometimes* results from oppression and exploitation. But Scripture also teaches that there are times when poverty results from misfortunes that have nothing to do with exploitation. These misfortunes include such things as accidents, injuries, and illness. And of course the Bible also makes it plain that poverty can result from indigence and sloth (Prov. 6:6–11; 13:4; 24:30–34; 28:19). When the problem of poverty is approached with a mind unbiased by ideology, it is easy to see that while some poverty does result from exploitation, some does not. Sometimes people are poor because of bad luck or as a consequence of their own actions and decisions.

Free Exchange Is a Zero-Sum Game

The myth about exploitation lends support to a related claim that often functions as a ground for rejections of capitalism. Capitalism is denounced because of the mistaken belief that market exchanges are examples of what is called a "zero-sum game." A zero-sum game is one where only one participant can win. If one person (or group) wins, then the other must lose. Baseball and checkers are two examples of zero-sum games. If A wins, then B must lose.

The error here consists in thinking that market exchanges are a zero-sum game. On the contrary, market exchanges illustrate what is called a "positive-sum game." A positive-sum game is one in which both players win. We must reject the myth that economic exchanges necessarily benefit only one party at the expense of the other. In voluntary exchanges, both parties may leave the exchanges in better economic shape than would otherwise have been the case.[6] Both parties to a voluntary exchange believe that they gain

5. I explore this particular charge in detail in chapter 17 of *Poverty and Wealth*.
6. Of course, it is still true that economic exchange *may* be marred by exploitation. But it is difficult to imagine an example where exploitation characterizes an exchange that does not compromise the essential conditions of a *free* exchange. A free exchange is one in which force, fraud, and theft are absent. But even if such examples exist, the important question here is whether exploitation is a necessary and unavoidable feature of market exchanges. Obviously it is not.

through the trade. If they did not perceive the exchange as beneficial, they would not continue to take part in it.[7]

Selfishness

Capitalism is also despised because it is thought to encourage a number of character traits that are incompatible with Christian values. The two sub-Christian traits most often thought to be encouraged by capitalism are selfishness and greed.

Scripture clearly does condemn *selfishness*. But the catch is that selfishness should never be confused with the quite different characteristic of *self-interest*. When Jesus commanded us to love our neighbor as our self (Matt. 22:39), He gave implicit approval of self-interest. When a person is motivated by selfishness, he seeks his own welfare with no regard for the welfare of others. But when a person is motivated by self-interest, he can pursue his welfare in ways that do not harm others.

There is nothing sinful in caring about what happens to one's family or oneself. In fact, the New Testament condemns those who lack such concern (1 Tim. 5:8). Since the kinds of voluntary exchanges that characterize the market are mutually beneficial (in other words, are a positive-sum game), selfishness is not an *inherent* feature of capitalism. People who exchange on the basis of market principles engage in activities that benefit themselves and others. The conditions of a free market oblige people to find ways of helping themselves at the same time they help others, whether they do this consciously or not. Self-interest can serve as a powerful engine that pulls society along the road to economic progress.

Greed

Capitalism is also criticized for encouraging greed. However, the mechanism of the market actually neutralizes greed as individuals are forced to find ways of serving the needs of those with whom they wish to exchange. There is no question but that market exchanges often bring us into contact with people motivated by greed. But so long as our rights are protected (a basic condition of market exchange), the possible greed of others cannot harm us. As long as greedy individuals are prohibited from introducing force, fraud, and theft into the exchange process, their greed must be channeled into the discovery of products or services for which people are willing to trade. Every person in a market economy has to be other-directed. The market is one area of life where concern for the other person is required. The market therefore does not pander to greed. It is rather a mechanism that allows natural human desires to be satisfied in a nonviolent way.

---

7. An exchange can also be regarded as beneficial if it is the lesser of two evils. A businessman may sell some product at a loss because, in the circumstances that prevail, not selling would entail even greater costs.

Money and Wealth

Capitalism is rejected by many Christians because of a faulty understanding of what Scripture teaches about money and wealth. A good example of such confusion is Jacque Ellul's book, *Money and Wealth.*[8] Ellul's selective and often tortuous reading of Scripture leads him to three bizarre conclusions: (1) The New Testament condemns wealth; (2) The Bible hates the rich; and (3) Christians sin if they save money for their future. Such extreme claims are clearly incompatible with the teachings of Jesus who saw nothing inherently evil in money, wealth, or private ownership. While Jesus clearly condemned materialism and the compulsive quest for wealth, he never condemned wealth per se. Jesus did not teach that being rich means necessarily being evil.[9] Jesus did not see anything sinful in the ownership of houses, clothes, and other economic goods. Jesus had wealthy friends and followers (Luke 14:1), stayed in the homes of wealthy people, and ate at their tables (Luke 11:37).

A number of Jesus' parables provide insights into his view on wealth. In Luke 16:9 and the accompanying parable, Jesus taught that his followers should use their resources with the same dedication and keen judgment as the unjust steward. In the parable of the rich farmer (Luke 12:16–21), Jesus did not condemn the farmer for making money but rather for this single-minded concern with his own wealth and happiness. The man was a fool because he was a self-centered materialist who had forgotten God, not because he was a successful businessman. The parable of Lazarus and the rich man (Luke 16:19–31) does not teach that a person's eternal destiny is determined by his possessions in this life. It is clear that the rich man went to hell because of a godless and self-centered life, a fact made evident by the way he used his wealth and by his indifference to the poor. The parable also implies that Lazarus was a believer. Any interpretation of the parable that suggests the poor man entered heaven because of his poverty would contradict everything the New Testament teaches about regeneration.

Even Gospel passages that stress our obligation to use our resources for God's purposes presuppose the legitimacy of private ownership.[10] Other obligations made clear in Jesus' teaching require that one first have certain

---

8. Jacques Ellul, *Money and Power* (Downers Grove, Ill.: InterVarsity, 1984 [originally published 1954]). Upon learning that Ellul's book teaches that money is evil, many readers inquired if InterVarsity gives the book away free. It does not! Much of Ellul's confusion results from his failure to draw a clear distinction between money (anything that may be used as a means of exchange) and Mammon (which is money personified and deified). Ellul is right in saying that money often assumes a sinister power over human lives. But whenever this happens, money (something ethically neutral) has become Mammon.

9. For the Old Testament view on this subject, see Ecclesiastes 5:19.

10. See Luke 16:1–3; 19:11–27; Matthew 25:24–30. These parables also commend those who demonstrate their ability to increase their wealth.

350   Ronald H. Nash

financial resources.[11] Jesus often spoke about wealth without condemning it.[12] When Jesus did call on people to renounce their possessions, his demands reflected special conditions, for example, situations where people had made their possessions their god (Luke 18:22–24). Instead of condemning wealth, then, Jesus' teaching offered an important perspective on how people living in materialistic surroundings should view the material world.

What should concern the believer is not money (something necessary for many economic exchanges) but wrong attitudes toward money. Similarly, it is not wealth per se but the improper use of wealth along with wrong attitudes toward wealth that deserve condemnation. Every Christian, rich or poor, needs to recognize that whatever he or she possesses is hers temporarily as a steward under God. Wealth that is accumulated in a dishonest way or that becomes a controlling principle in one's life is subject to condemnation. Wealth resulting from honest labor and wise investment, handled by people who recognize they are God's stewards, is not.

Morality and the Market System

Many of capitalism's religious critics fail to appreciate that capitalism can be defended not only on grounds of its economic superiority, but also on moral grounds.

Help for the Masses

Critics of capitalism fail to see the extent to which the market process is a force for improving the lot of the masses. History shows that the poor have benefited greatly from market systems. It is impossible to ease, reduce, or eliminate poverty through a continued division of the economic pie into increasingly smaller pieces. There is simply not enough wealth to go around. What the poor of any nation need is not continually larger pieces of a pie that keeps getting smaller. They need a larger pie. Instead of arguing over how the economic pie should be divided, attention should be directed toward the production of a bigger pie. As economist Henry Hazlitt notes:

Capitalism has enormously raised the level of the masses. It has wiped out whole areas of poverty. It has greatly reduced infant mortality, and made it possible to cure disease and prolong life. It has reduced human suffering. Because of capitalism, millions live today that would otherwise have not even been born. If these facts have no ethical relevance, then it is impossible to say in what ethical relevance consists.[13]

11. For example, Jesus taught that children have an obligation to care for their parents (Matt. 15:3–9) and that his followers ought to be generous in their support of worthy causes (Matt. 6:2–4). It is rather difficult to support parents or charities unless one has certain financial resources.
12. Matthew 13:44–46; 21:33–46.
13. Henry Hazlitt, *The Foundations of Morality* (New York: Van Nostrand, 1964), 325.

Social Cooperation

Capitalism does more than make it possible for people to make money. It provides the basis for a social structure that encourages the development of important personal and social virtues such as community and cooperation.

One of the major advantages of the market system is that it encourages cooperation rather than competition. This is in rather direct contrast to the usual labeling of a free market, private property system in that such an economy is said to be a competitive one. It is true that competition will exist in a market-based private property system, but competition is prevalent in any society in which scarcity exists. An advantage of the market process is that those who are the best "competitors" are those who best cooperate with, or satisfy others in the society. In order to get ahead in a private property system individuals must engage in voluntary transactions, that is, they must offer a "better deal" than competitors. This encourages cooperative behavior by focusing creative impulses and energy on adding to the satisfaction of others. The person who does this best is the one who succeeds in the market.[14]

Michael Novak finds it ironic that while capitalism is attacked for allegedly encouraging competitive individualism and possessiveness, it actually "seems to favor in its citizens forms of generosity, trust, extroversion, outgoingness, and reliance upon the good faith of others." But while voluntary economic exchanges in a market system are building community and trust, "existing socialist societies seem to narrow the circles of trust, as groups competing for the same allocations run afoul of each other's interests. Collectivism pits man against man. A system which encourages each to seek first his own interests yields liberty and receives in return loyalty and love."[15] Voluntary exchange, therefore, not only benefits all participants in the exchange, it also encourages social cooperation.

Human Dignity

Several economists have drawn attention to the way in which capitalism provides society with an important support for human dignity. Unlike socialism, Brian Griffiths explains, capitalism allows individuals "the freedom to buy and sell, save and invest, choose their preferred form of employment, and develop the skills which they feel appropriate. It allows minorities exactly these same rights too. Socialism does not."[16] Peter Hill carries this same idea even further by noting how capitalism "allows the strong and the

14. Peter J. Hill, "Private Rights and Public Attitudes: A Christian Defense of Capitalism" (Master's thesis, Dept. of Economics, Montana State University, n.d.), 8.
15. Michael Novak, The Spirit of Democratic Capitalism (New York: Simon and Schuster, 1982), 226.
16. Brian Griffiths, The Creation of Wealth (Downers Grove, Ill.: InterVarsity, 1985), 89.

weak, the skilled and the unskilled, the powerful and the powerless, to interact for their *mutual* benefit. The strong don't dominate or exploit the weak;
rather they find it to their own advantage to seek out those individuals and
offer them an exchange that will advantage both."[17] Of course, none of this
entails that everyone in a market system will end up with equal power or
equal possessions. For that matter, neither does socialism.

Political Freedom

I trust that even Christian critics of economic freedom will concede that
political freedom is an important human value. But economic freedom is a
necessary condition for personal and political liberty. No one can be free in
the political sense if he lacks economic freedom. Economic freedom aids the
existence and development of political liberty by helping to check the concentration of too much power in the hands of too few people. As long as a
large percentage of the people in a society exercise ownership control, power
within that society will be more widely diffused. No one can be free when he
is dependent upon others for the basic economic needs of life. If someone
commands what a person can or cannot buy or sell, then a significant part of
that individual's freedom has been abridged. Human beings who are dependent upon any one power for the basic essentials of life are not free. When
that master becomes the state, obedience becomes a prerequisite to employment and to life itself.

Economics is not simply a matter of finding the most expedient way of
organizing economic life. There is a necessary connection between economic freedom and political-spiritual freedom. Because collectivism in the
economic sphere means the end of political and spiritual freedom, economics is the front line in the battle for freedom. While capitalism is not a sufficient condition for political freedom in the sense that its presence guaran-
tees political freedom, it is difficult to find examples of nations with a
significant degree of political freedom that have not made provision for economic freedom.

Private Ownership and Moral Behavior

More attention needs to be given to the important ways in which private
ownership can serve as a stimulus to the development of moral behavior.
British economist Arthur Shenfield explains:

> Every time we treat property with diligence and care, we learn a lesson in moral-
> ity. . . . The reason for the moral training of private property is that it induces
> at least some of its owners to treat it as a trust, even if only for their children or
> children's children; and those who so treat it tend to be best at accumulating it,

17. Hill, "Private Rights," 19.

contrary to popular notions about the conspicuous consumption of the rich, the incidence of luck or of gambling. Contrast our attitudes to private property with our treatment of public property. Every army quartermaster, every state school administrator, every bureaucratic office controller, knows with what carelessness and lack of diligence most of us deal with it. This applies everywhere, but especially in socialist countries where most property is public.[18]

Shenfield is right. People do treat their own personal property differently than they treat public property or the property of others. This fact can be used to teach people some important moral lessons.

Everything Has a Cost

Once people realize that few things in life are free, that most things carry a price tag, and that therefore we will have to work for most of the things we want, we are in a position to learn a vital truth about life. Capitalism helps teach this truth. But, Shenfield warns, under socialism, "Everything still has a cost, but everyone is tempted, even urged to behave as if there is no cost or as if the cost will be borne by somebody else. This is one of the most corrosive effects of collectivism upon the moral character of people."[19]

Conclusion

Many religious critics of capitalism focus their attacks on what they take to be its moral shortcomings. In truth, the moral objections to capitalism turn out to be a sorry collection of arguments that reflect, more than anything else, serious confusions about the true nature of a market system. When capitalism is put to the moral test, it more than holds its own against its competition. After all, it makes little sense to reject one system on moral grounds when all of the alternatives turn out, in the real world, to have far more serious problems. To quote Arthur Shenfield again, among all of our economic options, only capitalism

> operates on the basis of respect for free, independent, responsible persons. All other systems in varying degrees treat men as less than this. Socialist systems above all treat men as pawns to be moved about by the authorities, or as children to be given what the rulers decide is good for them, or as serfs or slaves. The rulers begin by boasting about their compassion, which in any case is fraudulent, but after a time they drop their pretense which they find unnecessary for the maintenance of power. In all these things they act on the presumption that they know best. Therefore they and their systems are morally stunted.[20]

18. Arthur Shenfield, "Capitalism Under the Tests of Ethics," *Imprimis* 10 (December 1981): 5.
19. Ibid.
20. Ibid.

The alternative to free exchange is coercion and violence. Capitalism is a mechanism that allows natural human desires to be satisfied in a non-violent way. Little can be done to prevent human beings from wanting to be rich. But what capitalism does is channel that desire into peaceful means that benefit many besides those who wish to improve their own situation.

> The alternative to serving other men's wants is seizing power over them, as it always has been. Hence it is not surprising that wherever the enemies of capitalism have prevailed, the result has been not only the debasement of consumption standards for the masses but also their reduction to serfdom by the new privileged class of Socialist rulers.[21]

Capitalism is quite simply the most moral system, the most effective system, and the most equitable system of economic exchange. When capitalism, the system of free economic exchange, is described fairly, there can be no question that it, rather than socialism, comes closer to matching the demands of the biblical ethics.

From Ronald H. Nash, "Does Capitalism Pass the Moral Test?" *Evangelical Journal* 5 (1987): 35–45.

21. Ibid.

Who Should Set Social Priorities?

J. Philip Wogaman

Prior even to the question of what our priorities should be is the question of who should set them. . . . [And] even that is a hotly debated subject. Power questions always are vigorously debated, and the power to determine the goals and direction of economic life is unimaginably important. This question is center stage in the economic debates of the 1980s, and it will continue to be fought over for years to come. There are three broadly divergent kinds of answers to the question of who should decide on the priorities. Opting for one or another of these answers will not in itself tell us what the priorities ought to be, but it is a very important first step.

Letting the Free Market Decide

One option is suggested by Milton Friedman: "economic order can emerge as the unintended consequence of the actions of many people, each seeking his own interest."[1] That statement echoes the famous view of Adam Smith:

> Every individual is continually exerting himself to find the most advantageous employment for whatever capital he can command. It is his own advantage, indeed, and not that of society, which he has in view. But the study of his own advantage naturally, or rather necessarily, leads him to prefer that employment which is most advantageous to the society. . . . he is led by an invisible hand to promote an end which was no part of his intention.[2]

1. Milton and Rose Friedman, *Free to Choose: A Personal Statement* (New York: Harcourt Brace Jovanovich, 1980), 5.

355

This is a striking idea: *Nobody* should attempt to set priorities for the whole society. If each of us will just look after her or himself, that will also yield the best results for society as a whole. Smith argued that the free-market mechanism does what no individual or group of individuals could hope to do. It motivates everybody to contribute their best efforts, because otherwise they will not have anything to exchange. But it also leaves everybody free to exchange what they have for whatever they want, thereby assuring that the greatest good will result—by an "invisible hand." So priorities of production and distribution are both taken care of even though all participants in the economy are acting on the basis of their own interests as they understand them. In effect, nobody really has to care about what the economy is doing as a whole; that takes care of itself. And in a free-enterprise economy that is functioning properly it takes care of itself very well indeed. . . .

Limitations to the Free-Market Mechanism

The case for allowing the free market to establish priorities is obviously persuasive to many people and, as we have said, it has enjoyed a resurgence in the past few years. Many more people, including even some socialists, believe that some use should be made of free-market institutions in the allocation of goods and services. But that would be as a part of a wider overall plan. Those who believe in real free-market allocation do not see this as part of a broader scheme; they see it as the place where the decisive priority-setting occurs. If they are right, then there is little point in further examination of values and social priorities—except, perhaps, in advising one another about the best stewardship of our own personal resources. There would be no vantage point from which one could see the whole picture and no leverage point at which policy decisions could be reached to implement economic priorities for the entire community. So we are facing a watershed issue when we decide for or against reliance on the market mechanism to establish our priorities for us.

During the first half of the twentieth century, most of the Western capitalist countries decided they simply could not rely on this mechanism, at least not without combining it with a good deal of social planning. Practically speaking, too many people were being hurt economically in the process and too many public concerns were being neglected. In retrospect, one wonders how on earth President Reagan could ever have concluded that it hasn't "worked" to use the taxing power of government for purposes of social change. If anything hasn't *worked*, it would appear to be overreliance on the free market to do everything.

2. Adam Smith, *An Inquiry Into the Nature and Causes of the Wealth of Nations* (London: Printed for W. Strahan and T. Cadill, 1776), book 5, chap. 2.

Economic historian Karl Polanyi makes this point in considerable depth in his *The Great Transformation.*[3] The free-market mechanism did prove to be an enormous stimulus to production. It was indispensable to the breakup of medieval feudalism and to the emergence of the whole Industrial Revolution which, in turn, has been the source of vast increases in wealth and well-being. But the human consequences were often appalling. Polanyi finds it striking that despite broad intellectual agreement in the early nineteenth century on the virtues of laissez-faire capitalism, one after another of the societies committed to free-market principles found it absolutely necessary to intervene for the sake of people and social objectives that were not being served by those principles. . . .

The outpouring of legislation in the Progressive and New Deal eras of twentieth-century America came in direct response to human need and social pressure. The exploitation of child labor (and of the labor of men and women), hazardous working conditions, dehumanizingly long hours of work, low wages, periodic times of depression with high unemployment, shoddy and dangerous products, ruin of the natural environment, racial, religious, and gender discrimination all evoked social exposé, popular outcry, and governmental intervention. Left alone, the free-market mechanism was increasing production all right, but it was devastating human society. It was widely perceived that some outside force had to intervene in the market to establish and protect social goals transcending sheer economic efficiency. It was as though society instinctively rebelled against the triumph of instrumental economic values over intrinsic social ones.

But the inadequacies of laissez-faire capitalism also extend to its ethical justification. The personalistic values of freedom and individual creativity are important ones, to be sure. But in their one-sided presentation is concealed a faulty understanding of human nature. Each of us is a unique individual, a center of freedom and creativity. But we are also social by nature. The most serious philosophical failing of laissez-faire capitalism is its neglect of the social nature of human beings. Neoconservatives are more aware than their predecessors were of the social reality, but their conception of society is one of exchange: you do this for me, and I will do that for you. Even George Gilder's claim that capitalism had its origins in primitive acts of giving suggests a kind of self-interested individualism: A few venturesome people give gifts to others in the hope (though not with the assurance) that they will return the favor.

Through the gifts or investments of primitive capitalism, man created and extended obligations. These obligations led to reciprocal gifts and further obli-

---

3. Karl Polanyi, *The Great Transformation: The Political and Economic Origins of Our Time* (1944; reprint, Boston: Beacon Press, 1957).

gations in a growing fabric of economic creation and exchange, with each giver hoping for greater returns but not assured of them, and with each recipient pushed to produce a further favor. This spreading out of debts could be termed expanding the money supply.[4]

Similarly, the various writings of Ayn Rand portray society as the sum of the (largely economic) transactions of free and independent persons—although Rand is explicitly contemptuous of any display of altruism, whether or not it conceals an expectation of return.[5]

But human beings are not just individuals, and society is not just the sum of the individual transactions of people who have something to gain from one another. Human life is *shared* life. It is a sharing of perceptions and values and language and purposes and identity. We are born and nurtured in a social environment or we do not survive. Our very consciousness is mediated through language and the perception of others, to which we in turn contribute.

The neoconservatives have hold of half the truth, for no conception of human nature is adequate that neglects individual personhood, and no ethical vision is whole that neglects freedom. But the neglect of our social nature is a fatal error. Turned into an economic or political philosophy, it invites a kind of principled selfishness wherein people are led to believe that social good is only a byproduct of individual good and that it is a sufficient goal for each person to look out for him or herself.

Locke's view of property is also riddled with illusion, especially when attempts are made to apply it in the modern world. For one thing, we know in ways that Locke could scarcely have imagined that the natural world is limited. In his time the whole new continent of North America had opened up, with vast reaches of uncharted wilderness occupied and defended by a very small number of aboriginal inhabitants. It was easy enough for Locke to model a conception of property on the opportunity for settlers to stake out their claims in North America, to clear the land, and to till the soil. They only had to have the will to work. But that frontier is gone now, almost everywhere on earth. Now it is a question of access to the raw materials of nature, and not a question of imaginative labor alone.

But for another thing, Locke's individualism obscures the extent to which property is created socially. It is truly a difficult thing to sort out the relative importance of the contributions many people have made even to the solitary flash of an individual's genius, not to mention the obviously social character of mass production. It is asserted that the market will set wages and salaries

4. George Gilder, *Wealth and Poverty* (New York: Basic, 1981), 22.
5. See especially Ayn Rand, *The Virtue of Selfishness: A New Concept of Egoism* (New York: New American Library, 1964).

in accordance with the actual contributions of each person to the process, but that is largely an illusion too. There is more evidence that wages are based upon a complex and largely inherited set of relationships and expectations derived only *somewhat* from the identifiable talents and contributions of individual workers or managers.[6]

Free-Market Efficiency as Social Inefficiency

There are other problems with relying on the free market alone to establish social priorities. These have to do with the market when it is most successful—when it is doing exactly what the theory says it is supposed to do.

First, there is the problem of how one is to achieve a much-desired social result from one's purely private transactions. Being geared to private exchange, the market creates a strong bias toward individual forms of consumption. But nobody wants to limit consumption to individual goods and services. The market performs best in providing food, clothing, shelter, entertainment, and other things we want and need. It is an awkward mechanism for providing communitywide facilities in education and recreation and communication. It is a virtually impossible mechanism for providing highways and national defense. It is possible to stretch the free-market model theoretically to cover all these things, with associations of private persons banded together to purchase land for highways, with all parks and recreation facilities handled like Disneyland, with all schools handled on a private basis along with fire and police protection, with due care being taken to ensure that everybody paid for exactly the goods and services received, and so on. . . . But why go at things in such an awkward way? It reminds one of the quip that some people know the cost of everything and the value of nothing. If the community is to realize itself as a community it has a stake in directing the economic process toward some kinds of ends, including those things the existence of which ought to be *guaranteed.* We all benefit from the overall quality of community life. It is quite impossible to calculate exactly the proportions by which each of us benefits over the course of time. And it seems ridiculous even to try to calculate such things. Relative priorities must be established and, doubtless also, some means of calculating the cost of social facilities and services relative to each other and to private forms of consumption. But the effort to calculate exactly what each social service is worth to each recipient or user seems fatuous on the face of it. More than that, it reveals a one-sidely individualistic view of our humanity.

But there is another problem, present precisely when the market is functioning exactly as it is supposed to do—that is, when it is that form of disci-

6. See Lester C. Thurow, *Dangerous Currents: The State of Economics* (New York: Random House, 1983), 173–215, for a perceptive account of why a purely economic "price auction" model cannot account for actual wages.

plined efficiency the theory has always proclaimed it to be. Efficiency, in the pure model, is a result of the discipline of competition. Less efficient enterprises lose ground in their competition with more efficient ones. There is the strongest possible incentive to provide the market exactly what it wants (or can be induced to want) at the lowest possible price. Firms with high costs either destroy their own profit margins or no longer remain competitive. This often works out beneficially, in practice as well as in theory. Consumers find prices going down in competitive markets and quality going up. Entrepreneurs are motivated to develop new products to enrich the lives of people further.

But free-market competition also creates incentives to cut costs in ways that are damaging to people and to the community. The cheapest way to dispose of waste products is generally to dump them into the nearest stream or landfill or to let them belch forth into the skies without using expensive filtering devices or transporting them to safer places or refraining altogether from using productive techniques that threaten the environment. It also costs more to install safety devices on machinery and to pay more wages than the market strictly requires and to provide socially desirable fringe benefits. Irresponsible firms that evade such necessary costs may, thereby, secure favorable competitive markets. The market thus provides an incentive to irresponsible behavior when it saves money to be irresponsible. Somehow the rules of the game have to be structured in such a way that all participants are rewarded for good, not irresponsible, behavior. But that requires priority-setting from some vantage point outside the market mechanism itself. Somebody (or some group) has to decide whether the productive efficiencies gained by harmful practices are worth the cost to the community and to the people who face the impact of those practices most directly. . . .

Priority-Setting by Elites

If the free market is not an adequate way to go about setting social priorities, what is? One obvious way to deal with that problem is to turn it over to the people who really seem *qualified* to do it. . . .

There are, of course, public or governmental elites. . . . Social planning conjures up images of a Robert Moses literally transforming the face of New York City with his vast public works projects. It is popular sport to ridicule planners and bureaucrats and social engineers, and sometimes with good reason. One generation of elite planners may create the next generation's disaster. In the United States, urban high-rise public housing projects often seem to qualify for such criticism, as do some ventures in educational planning. In Britain, debate centers on economic planning. One senses that the resentment is as often directed at the paternalism or even arrogance with which some elites go about planning the lives and circumstances of all their fellow citizens as it is disapproval of the choice of priorities. But it is also the case that elitism in social planning always looks better if one is in the elite or if one can designate the elite than if one is on the outside looking in. There are usually several competing versions of utopia at any one time, each claiming the authority of genuine rationality. It would all be easier if there were a generally acknowledged class of experts upon whom all could agree and (most important of all) experts who could be counted on to agree among themselves.

Marxism maintains that there is a scientific analysis of society which provides humanity with the truly authentic picture of the direction of history. The historic role of the Communist Party is to give leadership in facilitating that all-important revolutionary transformation of society. The party does not include all members of society; it is in fact always a rather small percentage of the population in Marxist societies. But the party—actually the leadership of the party—considers itself to be the representative of the true interest of all the masses. This version of scientific socialism is familiar to all students of European Communist parties. Third World Marxist liberation movements generally have a more populist character, with some effort to consult the peasantry in the decision-making and priority-setting process. But even here there is often more than a touch of elitism. Note . . . the statement by Canaan Sodido Banana, the president of Zimbabwe: . . . "The party directing and maintaining the favour of the masses does not need to be formed by all the people of the country."[7] To qualify for party membership, one must have qualities of leadership and "other attributes not readily available to all." In his personal life President Banana has provided striking support for egalitarianism (even turning part of the beautiful grounds of his presidential palace into an agricultural and poultry cooperative, with himself working alongside others as an ordinary member). But he also clearly believes that true knowledge of the appropriate direction for society is only available for some people, and they should provide the leadership for all the rest.

If everybody agreed with the Marxist vision (if even all the Marxists agreed among themselves), it would make it easier for us to say that the party elite should set the priorities for all of us. But there is no such consensus, and the countries under Marxist domination have been all too ready to run roughshod over dissenters. Equality of opportunity to participate in the political process and freedom of expression are values that do not have high priority in most of these settings. Some people are believed to know best, and they are willing enough to insist that everybody else conform.

7. Canaan Sodido Banana, *The Theology of Promise: The Dynamics of Self-Reliance* (Harare, Zimbabwe: College Press, 1982), 49.

Laissez-faire critics of all forms of social planning have a strong point when they criticize elitism as showing disrespect for human beings. To a lesser degree they also have something of a point in noting the inefficiencies that often accompany both left- and right-wing paternalism. They are usually blind to the same elitist paternalism when it develops in a free-market setting, and they are complacent about the negative results of reliance upon that setting to establish social priorities automatically. Is there no other way?

Social Priorities in the Responsible State

The socialist Michael Harrington once observed that if the state owns the economy it is a very important question "who owns the state."[8] If, somehow, social priorities have to be established by and for the whole society, it is critically important how the people who are affected by this are to be involved in the process. Will they ultimately "own" it? Will decisions be made in their name without their being consulted?

Any conceivable approach to the setting of social priorities, from the free market of laissez-faire capitalism to the highly planned and centralized socialist state, is bound to have outcomes that are offensive to many people. Society is closely enough integrated that we are all affected by the decisions of others.

But it does make a difference whether everybody has the opportunity to participate in the process of decision-making. The laissez-faire school asserts that everybody does have that right in the free-market system, voting, as it were, with their decisions as workers and consumers. But the number of such "votes" available to different people is grossly inequitable. We vote with our dollars (or pounds, or yen, or lire), but some people have many more dollars than others and some have scarcely any at all. Decisions reached by the marketplace do not reflect the democratic outcome implied by those who speak of the democracy of the marketplace.

Moreover, as we have seen, it is awkward to the point of impossibility for people to use their consumer and labor "votes" to set priorities for public consumption, even if that is what they most want to do. People cannot take their individual resources and go out and buy a rapid transit system for their city—nor can most afford to buy parks or streets or police and fire protection. Theoretically they can respond, with their money, to the imaginative entrepreneur who establishes widely desired institutions or services. But the result is awkward, piecemeal, and sometimes profoundly destructive when taken as the sole approach to the provision of social institutions and services. There needs to be an arena of decision-making in which all can participate

8. Michael Harrington, *Socialism* (1972; reprint, New York: Bantam, 1973), 185.

in making those crucial decisions of social priority which affect the quality of life available for each and all.

This is exactly what the First Assembly of the World Council of Churches meant when, through its call for a "Responsible Society," it defined such a society in part as one where "those who hold political authority or economic power are responsible for its exercise to God and the people whose welfare is affected by it."[9] Most of the neoconservatives doubt that this can be done. They are inclined to regard government as being inescapably irresponsible, at least when it deals with economic questions. A governmental bureaucracy, like the Marxist party, may claim to speak for all the people, but conservative critics believe that in actual fact the bureaucracy is beyond social control. It can do what it wishes with the people's tax money—even using that money to perpetuate itself in power against their wishes. It, the bureaucracy, represents a large and powerful interest group, a "new class" with identifiable interests and with all the necessary means at hand to preserve and enhance them. Unlike business corporations it does not have to confront the disciplines of the market, and unlike the politicians it does not even have to run for reelection.

There is some truth in every caricature, including this one. But that is still a largely inaccurate caricature of what actually happens in the governments of democracies like the U.S. and Canada and Britain. All such countries have large numbers of dedicated public servants who are ultimately accountable to elected officials and, through them, to the people at large. In nearly twenty years of living and working at the seat of the U.S. government in Washington, D.C., I have observed several things about how the federal bureaucracy relates to the elected government and to the people:

1. The harshest criticisms of the civil service sometimes occur not because the "bureaucracy" is unconcerned about the public interest, but because it *is* concerned. Regulatory agencies may be fully responsive to the real political will of the vast majority of the people—for instance, in enforcing regulations to protect the environment or to preserve occupational safety—but that will not spare them criticism from those whose freedom to pollute or to endanger has been constricted.

2. When government agencies appear to be defending selfish interests (which, often enough, they do), they may in fact be reflecting, not resisting, the wider political process. It is interesting to observe how this or that governmental agency can be related to particular political leaders, and, through

9. This idea is reiterated and enlarged by the recent call from the 1975 Nairobi Assembly of the WCC for a "just, participatory, and sustainable society." The ecumenical concept of social responsibility is elaborated in Walter G. Muelder, *Foundations of the Responsible Society* (New York and Nashville: Abingdon, 1959) and *Religion and Economic Responsibility* (New York: Scribner's, 1953). The emphasis on "sustainability" is elaborated by Robert L. Stivers, *The Sustainable Society: Ethics and Economic Growth* (Philadelphia: Westminster, 1976).

them, to particular popular constituencies. Often the most powerful leaders of legislative committees have determinative influence in the particular agencies related to the work of those committees. The chairperson of the Senate Agriculture, Nutrition, and Forestry Committee is likely to have substantial influence in the Department of Agriculture, the chairperson of the Armed Services Committee similarly in the Pentagon, and so on. Is this irresponsible? It may well be. But the power wielded by the legislator is part of an intricate balance of power as interest confronts interest on Capitol Hill. Agricultural policies favorable to the people of Iowa or North Dakota (as represented by lawmakers from those states) may be supported indirectly if not directly by legislators from New York and Pennsylvania in return for similar support for grants for major cities, and so on.

3. Civil servants lacking strong political support are usually forced to give way when their policies or procedures are challenged by Congress. They can sometimes be resourceful in protecting their budgets and even in squirreling away reserves for unclear purposes, provided nobody cares enough to scrutinize or challenge what is going on. But they can be and not infrequently are stopped cold by law and by the withholding of budgetary support—if there really is a political will to do so.

4. The civil service is a much-needed source of competence and continuity in informing and giving force to the public will. Without this instrument the public truly would be frustrated.

I suspect similar observations could be made in London, Ottawa, Bonn, or any other capital city of a Western democracy—along with some non-Western ones as well.

Bureaucracy, whether private or governmental, is an inescapable fact of life in the modern world. Much of the setting and implementing of social priorities will inevitably be done by bureaucracies. The real question is whether they are truly accountable to the public will. The shortcomings of the market as final arbiter of social priorities mean that we shall be driven, in the final analysis, to turn the direction of society over to some irresponsible, perhaps even faceless, elite unless we can find ways to adopt our most fundamental goals democratically. Even at best, the democratic process is undoubtedly more complicated than is suggested by idealized accounts of it. But when it is reasonably open and healthy, that process can do two things: It can establish and review the most important social priorities, and it can choose leaders who will reflect the values of those who elected them and be accountable to the people. . . .

We may note in passing that economic life in a number of democratic Western countries is more accountable to the people than it is in most of the officially Marxist societies. In the latter, the Communist Party claims to embody the true will and interest of "the masses," but there are no effective channels of political review and accountability whereby these "masses" are empowered to affect economic priorities fundamentally. These democratic Western countries are largely capitalist, but in principle these countries could at any time be transformed into socialist states by the adoption of appropriate laws. Short of that, these countries have political systems through which any economic question can be reviewed. The fact that these countries are in fact more accurately described as "mixed economies" (rather than pure capitalist ones) already helps make the point. For mixed economies are ones in which there exists a substantial public sector alongside the private market, with government acting as regulator, producer, and distributor of goods and services to a substantial extent. In all of these countries, the governmental involvements in economic life reflect the outcome of many political battles fought over a long period of history and with substantial public involvement.

What about those who disagree with the outcomes of the democratic process? Questions of social priority are rarely decided by unanimous consensus. There truly is a sense in which the social priorities of the majority are usually "forced" on those who oppose them. It should be news to no one that social life in general imposes the discipline of having to accept things that one would prefer not to accept, and that is preeminently true of the political order. The issue is not whether one is or is not "forced" to accept the priorities of others with which one is not in agreement. That will inevitably happen from time to time to everybody, regardless of the political and economic system. The important question is whether or not the outcomes are a fair representation of majority views and whether those who are in opposition are free to express their opposition through speech and press and organized political action. The question is whether today's defeated minority viewpoint can hope to persuade enough people to become tomorrow's majority opinion.

Good democratic theory is thus not limited to the proposition of majority rule; it also includes those minority rights without which an opposition could never express itself. We may be coerced into accepting certain priorities in the national budget that we find repugnant, but we may not be coerced out of the political process itself.

Are Democratic Decisions Necessarily Wise Ones?

The results of the democratic process can, of course, be deplorable. George Bernard Shaw once remarked, however, that while democracy may not be the best form of government, it is that form under which we best can guarantee that people will get what they deserve. Overall, the wisdom of democratic decision-making can be compared without embarrassment to that of any alternative form, but that does not mean that grievous errors and injustices will not ever occur. Even Shaw's remark misses the point that

J. Philip Wogaman

those who lose in the democratic process may not at all deserve the folly visited on the whole society by an unwise majority. But still, it is the process that best reflects the mind of the community, whereby the community's true priorities can best be given effect. And it is the process that is most open to the correction of its previous errors.

From J. Philip Wogaman, "Who Should Set Social Priorities?" in *Economies and Ethics: A Christian Inquiry* (Philadelphia: Fortress, 1986), 14–31.

Structural Evil and World Hunger

Ronald J. Sider

In the early 1950s Northeast High School in Philadelphia was famous for its superb academic standards and its brilliant, long-standing athletic triumphs. The second oldest school in the city, Northeast had excellent teachers and a great tradition. And it was almost entirely white. Then in the mid-fifties, the neighborhood began to change. Black people moved in. Whites began to flee in droves to the Greater Northeast, a new, all-white section of Philadelphia. Quite naturally, a new high school became necessary in this developing, overwhelmingly white area.

When the excellent new school was completed in 1957, it took along the name Northeast High School, with its fond memories and traditions and many connotations of academic excellence and athletic triumph. The inner-city school was renamed Edison High. The new school took all the academic and athletic trophies and awards, school colors, songs, powerful alumni, and all the money in the treasury. Worst of all, the teachers were given the option of transferring to the new Northeast High. Two-thirds of them did.[1]

The black students who now attended Edison High had an old, rapidly deteriorating building, frequent substitute teachers, and no traditions. Nor did the intervening years bring many better teachers or adequate teaching materials. The academic record since 1957 has been terrible. But, Edison High has one national record. More students from Edison High died in the U.S. Army in Vietnam than from any other high school in the United States.

---

1. "Edison High School—A History of Benign and Malevolent Neglect," *Oakes Newsletter* 5, no. 4 (14 December 1973), 1–4; and "Northeast High Took the Glory Away," *Sunday Bulletin*, 27 January 1974, sect. 1, p. 3.

Who was guilty of this terrible sin? Local, state, and federal politicians who had promoted de facto housing segregation for decades? The school board? Parents who had, at best, only a partial picture of what was going on? Christian community leaders? White students at the new Northeast High whose excellent education and job prospects have been possible, in part, precisely because of the poor facilities and bad teachers left behind for the black students at Edison? Who was guilty?

Many would deny any personal responsibility. "That's just the way things are!" And they would be quite right. Long-standing patterns in jobs and housing had created a system which automatically produced Edison High. But that hardly silences the query about responsibility. Do we sin when we participate in evil social systems and societal structures that unfairly benefit some and harm others?

The Bible and Structural Evil

Neglect of the biblical teaching on structural injustice or institutionalized evil is one of the most deadly omissions in many parts of the church today. What does the Bible say about structural evil, and how does that deepen our understanding of the scriptural perspective on poverty and hunger?

Christians frequently restrict the scope of ethics to a narrow class of "personal" sins. In a study of over fifteen hundred ministers, researchers discovered that the theologically conservative pastors spoke out on sins such as drug abuse and sexual misconduct.[2] But they failed to preach about the sins of institutionalized racism, unjust economic structures and militaristic institutions which destroy people just as much as do alcohol and drugs.

There is an important difference between consciously willed, individual acts (like lying to a friend or committing an act of adultery) and participation in evil social structures. Slavery is an example of the latter. So is the Victorian factory system where ten-year-old children worked twelve to sixteen hours a day. Both slavery and child labor were legal. But they destroyed people by the millions. They were institutionalized, or structural, evils. In the twentieth century, as opposed to the nineteenth, evangelicals have been more concerned with individual sinful acts than with our participation in evil social structures.

But the Bible condemns both. Speaking through his prophet Amos, the Lord declared, "For three transgressions of Israel, and for four, I will not revoke the punishment; because they sell the righteous for silver, and the needy for a pair of shoes—they that trample the head of the poor into the dust of the earth, and turn aside the way of the afflicted; a man and his father go in to the same maiden, so that my holy name is profaned" (Amos 2:6–7). Biblical scholars have shown that some kind of legal fiction underlies the

2. Rodney Stark et al., "Sounds of Silence," *Psychology Today,* April 1970, 38–41, 60–67.

phrase "selling the needy for a pair of shoes."[3] This mistreatment of the poor was *legal*! In one breath God condemns both sexual misconduct and legalized oppression of the poor. Sexual sins and economic injustice are equally displeasing to God. God revealed the same thing through his prophet Isaiah.

> Woe to those who join house to house,
> who add field to field,
> until there is no more room,
> and you are made to dwell alone in the midst of the land.
> The LORD of hosts has sworn in my hearing:
> "Surely many houses shall be desolate,
> large and beautiful houses, without inhabitant . . .
> Woe to those who rise early in the morning,
> that they may run after strong drink,
> who tarry late into the evening
> till wine inflames them! (Isa. 5:8–9, 11)

Equally powerful is the succinct, satirical summary in verses 22 and 23 of the same chapter: "Woe to those who are heroes at drinking wine, and valiant men in mixing strong drink, who acquit the guilty for a bribe, and deprive the innocent of his right!" Here God condemns in one breath both those who amass large landholdings at the expense of the poor and those who have fallen into drunkenness. Economic injustice is just as abominable to our God as drunkenness. . . .

Another side to institutionalized evil makes it especially pernicious. Structural evil is so subtle that one can be ensnared and hardly realize it. God inspired his prophet Amos to utter some of the harshest words in Scripture against the cultured upper-class women of his day: "Hear this word, you cows of Bashan . . . who oppress the poor, who crush the needy, who say to [your] husbands, 'Bring, that we may drink!' The LORD God has sworn by his holiness that, behold, the days are coming upon you, when they shall take you away with hooks, even the last of you with fishhooks" (Amos 4:1–2).

The women involved may have had little direct contact with the impoverished peasants. They may never have realized clearly that their gorgeous clothes and spirited parties were possible partly because of the sweat and tears of toiling peasants. In fact, they may even have been kind on occasion to individual peasants. (Perhaps they gave them "Christmas baskets" once a year.) But God called these privileged women "cows" because they profited from social evil. Before God they were personally and individually guilty.[4]

If one is a member of a privileged class that profits from structural evil, and if one does nothing to try to change things, he or she stands guilty before

---

3. John Bright, *A History of Israel* (Philadelphia: Westminster, 1959), 241, n. 84.
4. Compare Isaiah 3:13–17.

God.[5] Social evil is just as displeasing to God as personal evil. And it is more subtle.

In the first edition of this book [*Rich Christians in an Age of Hunger*], I said that social evil hurts more people than personal evil. That may be true in the Third World, but I no longer believe that it is true in North America and Western Europe. Within the industrialized nations, the agony caused by broken homes, sexual promiscuity, marital breakdown, and divorce probably equals the pain caused by structural injustices. That is not to deny or deemphasize the latter. It is merely to underline the fact that both kinds of sin devastate industrialized societies today.

The prophets told how the God of justice responds to oppressive social structures. God cares so much about the poor that he will destroy social structures that tolerate and foster great poverty. Repeatedly God declared that he would destroy the nation of Israel because of both its idolatry *and* its mistreatment of the poor (for example, Jer. 7:1–15).

The *both/and* is crucial. We dare not become so preoccupied with horizontal issues of social justice that we neglect vertical evils such as idolatry. Modern Christians seem to have an irrepressible urge to fall into one extreme or the other. But the Bible corrects our one-sidedness. God destroyed Israel and Judah because of both their idolatry and their social injustice.

Here, however, our focus is on the fact that God destroys oppressive social structures. Amos's words, which could be duplicated from many other places in Scripture, make this divine response clear:

Because you trample upon the poor and take from him exactions of wheat, you have built houses of hewn stone, but you shall not dwell in them. (5:11)

Woe to those who lie upon beds of ivory, and stretch themselves upon their couches, and eat lambs from the flock, . . . but [who] are not grieved over the ruin of Joseph! Therefore they shall now be the first of those to go into exile. . . (6:4, 6–7)

Hear this, you who trample upon the needy, and bring the poor of the land to an end, saying, "When will the new moon be over, that we may sell grain? And the sabbath, that we may offer wheat for sale . . . and deal deceitfully with

5. This is not to deny that the degree of responsibility and guilt has some relationship to the degree of one's awareness, understanding, and conscious choice. See my more extended comments in "Racism," *United Evangelical Action* 36 (Spring 1977): 11–12. At the same time, it is important to remember that we regularly *choose* not to learn more about topics that we know would challenge and demand a change in our current thinking and living. For an excellent, extended treatment of systemic evil (including a discussion of the Pauline concept of the "principalities and powers"), see Stephen C. Mott, *Biblical Ethics and Social Change* (New York: Oxford University Press, 1982), chap. 1.

false balances, that we may buy the poor for silver and the needy for a pair of sandals. . . . (8:4–6)

Behold, the eyes of the Lord God are upon the sinful kingdom, and I will destroy it from the surface of the ground. . . . (9:8)

Within a generation after the time of the prophet Amos, the northern kingdom of Israel was completely wiped out. . . .

Institutionalized Evil Today

What does this biblical teaching mean for affluent people today? If Amos were alive, would he deliver the same judgments on us as he did against the unrighteous Israelites of his own day?

The answer, I think, is yes. A former president of World Vision has written of "the stranglehold which the developed West has kept on the economic throats of the Third Word." He believes that "the heart of the problems of poverty and hunger . . . are human systems which ignore, mistreat and exploit man. . . . If the hungry are to be fed, . . . some of the systems will require drastic adjustments while others will have to be scrapped altogether."[6] Together we must examine the evidence for this evaluation.

In citing the disturbing data which follows, I do so neither with sadistic enjoyment of an opportunity to flagellate the affluent, nor with a desire to create feelings of irresolvable guilt. God has no interest in groundless "guilt trips." But I do believe the God of the poor wants us all to feel deep pain over the agony and anguish that torment the poor. And I also believe we must call sin by its biblical name.

All developed countries are directly involved. So too are the wealthy elites in poor countries. Ancient social patterns, inherited cultural values, and cherished religious and philosophical perspectives in developing countries also contribute in an important way to create and preserve poverty.[7] In some cases, laziness and sinful choices about alcohol, sex, and drugs have created poverty. And some poverty results from natural disasters, or lack of the right tools to create wealth. The causes of poverty are complex. It would be naive to simplify complex realities and isolate one scapegoat.

6. W. Stanley Mooneyham, *What Do You Say to a Hungry World?* (Waco: Word, 1975), 117, 128.
7. See especially Piero Gheddo, *Why Is the Third World Poor?* (Maryknoll: Orbis, 1973). But see also Laurence Harrison, *Underdevelopment Is a State of Mind* (Lanham, Md.: The Center of International Affairs, Harvard University and University Press of America, 1985). Michael Novak is surely correct in insisting that religio-cultural values in Latin America itself are one major cause of its poverty. Unfortunately he grossly understates the extent to which the U.S. political and economic power is also at fault. See his *The Spirit of Democratic Capitalism* (New York: Simon and Schuster, 1982).

The affluent North is simply *not* responsible for all the poverty in the world. There are many causes. In fact, even if the rich were not responsible for causing *any* part of global poverty, we would still be responsible to help those in need. The story of Lazarus and Dives (Luke 16:19–31) does not suggest that Lazarus's poverty resulted from oppression on the part of Dives. Dives merely neglected to help. His sin was the sin of omission. And it sent him to hell.

I do believe, however, that affluent nations have played a part in establishing economic structures that contribute to some of today's hunger and starvation. Surely our first responsibility is to understand and change what we are doing wrong.

How then are we a part of unjust structures that contribute to world hunger? . . .

Consider export agriculture in Central America. Today, the bulk of the staple foods (beans, corn, rice) eaten by the poor in Central America are grown by small farmers on marginal lands. At the same time, as a recent study shows, "virtually all the fertile, flat agricultural lands in the region [are] used for export oriented crops."[8]

The story of beef since the 1950s helps one understand.[9] In the 1950s, almost all beef slaughtered in Central America was eaten locally. Then the first beef packing plant approved by the U.S. Department of Agriculture (USDA) was built in 1957. By the late 1970s, three-fourths of Central America's beef was exported.[10] By 1978, Central America provided the U.S. with 250 million pounds of beef a year. U.S.-backed development programs built roads, and provided credit to facilitate the expansion of beef exports. From 1960–1980, over one-half of all the loans made by the World Bank and the Inter-American Development Bank for agriculture and rural development in Central America went to promote the production of beef for export.[11]

Wealthy elites made great profits. But large numbers of poor farmers growing basic foodstuffs were pushed off the land as the ranchers demanded more and more grazing land to grow beef for export. In El Salvador, before the first USDA-approved beef packing plant was opened, 29 percent of rural households were landless. By 1980, one-half of all El Salvador's beef was going to the U.S. And 65 percent of the rural households were landless.[12]

8. J. Jeffrey Leonard, *Natural Resources and Economic Development in Central America: A Regional Environment Profile* (Washington: International Institute for Environment and Development, 1987), 179–80.

9. See the careful study by Robert G. Williams, *Export Agriculture and the Crisis in Central America* (Chapel Hill: University of North Carolina Press, 1986).

10. Ibid., 109.

11. Beverly Keene, "Export Cropping in Central America," *BFW Background Paper*, no. 43 (Jan. 1980).

12. Williams, *Export Agriculture*, 170.

The poor protested, but the ranchers succeeded in painting the peasant activist as communists. The national security forces trained by the U.S. often used repressive tactics including torture and murder to repress peasant protesters. "Local ranchers in this way got free eviction forces, armed and trained at U.S. taxpayers' expense."[13]

I do not mean to suggest that Central America should not export any beef. It does have a competitive advantage over many areas in producing grass-fed beef. With different policies it might have been possible to expand beef exports in a way that did not oppress the poor or destroy the environment (vast tropical forests were burned to provide the new pasture lands). But it was not done that way.

Instead, the poor suffered to produce cheap hamburgers for American consumers. Since the 1960s, beef consumption within Central America has declined 20 percent. The poor cannot compete with us. A study by the Pan American Health Organization showed that between 1969 and 1975 malnutrition rose by 67 percent among children five years and under. In fact, 50 percent of the children in Central America were dying before the age of six—largely because of malnutrition and related diseases.[14] You don't need communists to tell you that is a bad deal.

Not all the examples come from Latin America. In 1988, in the Philippines, seventy-three of one thousand infants died before the age of five, and forty-four before the age of one. Between 1977 and 1987, 50 percent of the urban population and 64 percent of the rural population was below the absolute poverty level.[15]

Again the tragic story goes back to colonial days. Before the Spanish conquerors in the Philippines arrived in the early 1600s, local villages owned land cooperatively. But the Spanish demand for surplus crops for taxes allowed the better-off Filipinos who collected the taxes for the Spanish colonialists to amass larger and larger holdings. After the United States replaced Spain in 1898, export cropping (and land concentration) increased still further. After 1960 export cropping grew even faster, as American pineapple producers moved from Hawaii to the Philippines to take advantage of cheaper wages. (They saved 47 percent in production costs.) From 1960 to 1980 the amount of land devoted to export crops increased from 15 percent to 30 percent.

The government of President Ferdinand Marcos promoted a national development policy based on export crops by ruthlessly suppressing movements of workers who pressed for higher wages or land reform. (The aver-

13. Ibid., 160.
14. Keene, "Export Cropping."
15. James P. Grant, *The State of the World's Children 1990* (Oxford: Oxford University Press for UNICEF, 1990), 76–77, 86–87.

age wage for a sugar-cane laborer working thirteen to fourteen hours a day was $7.00 a week.) Both Amnesty International and the International Commission of Jurists documented the existence of thousands of political prisoners. Electric shock torture, water torture, extended solitary confinement, and beating were widespread. Meanwhile, American military aid to Marcos continued.[16]

In February 1986, a nonviolent revolution overthrew Marcos.[17] Hope surged through the Philippines. President Cory Aquino promised both democracy and justice for the poor. Unfortunately, there has been very little land reform and the majority of the people continue to live in poverty.

Who is responsible for the children dying in Central America or the Philippines? The wealthy national elites who want to increase their affluence? The American companies that work closely with the local elite? The Americans who eat the beef needed by hungry children in Central America?

Once again we dare not make the simplistic assumption that if we stop eating food imported from the poor nations, hungry children there will promptly enjoy it. Ending all food imports is not the answer. What *is* needed is the economic empowerment of the poor masses so that they can be productive and earn a decent living. . . . My purpose here is simply to show that our eating patterns are interlocked with destructive social and economic structures that leave millions hungry and starving. . . .

The Story of Bananas

On April 10, 1975, North Americans learned that United Brands, one of three huge U.S. companies that grow and import bananas, had arranged to pay $2.5 million (only $1.25 million was actually paid) in bribes to top government officials in Honduras. Why? To persuade them to impose an export tax on bananas that was less than half of what Honduras had requested.[18] In order to increase profits for a U.S. company and to lower banana prices, the Honduran government agreed, for a bribe, to cut drastically the export tax, even though the money was desperately needed in Honduras.

The story actually began in March 1974. Several banana-producing countries in Central America agreed to join together to demand a one-dollar tax on every case of bananas exported. Why? Banana prices for producers had not increased in the previous twenty inflation-ridden years. But the costs for manufactured goods had constantly escalated. As a result the real pur-

16. Ricki Ross, "Land and Hunger: Philippines," *BFW Background Paper*, no. 55 (July 1981).

17. See chap. 3 in Ronald J. Sider, *Non-violence: The Invincible Weapon?* (Waco: Word, 1989). Published in Great Britain under the title, *Exploring the Limits of Non-violence* (London: Hodder and Stoughton, 1988).

18. *Philadelphia Inquirer*, 10 April 1975, 1–2.

chasing power of exported bananas had declined by 60 percent. At least half of the export income for Honduras and Panama came from bananas. No wonder they were poor.

What did the banana companies do when the exporting countries demanded a one-dollar tax on bananas? They adamantly refused to pay. Since three large companies (United Brands, Caste and Cooke, and Del Monte) controlled 90 percent of the marketing and distribution of bananas, they had powerful leverage. In Panama the fruit company abruptly stopped cutting bananas. In Honduras the banana company allowed 145,000 crates to rot at the docks. One after another the poor countries gave in. Costa Rica finally settled for twenty-five cents a crate; Panama, for thirty-five cents; Honduras, thanks to the large bribe, eventually agreed to a thirty-cent tax.[19]

One can easily understand why a UN fact-finding commission in 1975 concluded, "The banana-producing countries with very much less income are subsidizing the consumption of the fruit, and consequently the development of the more industrialized countries."[20]

Why don't the masses of poor people demand change? They do. But too often they have little power. For much of the last thirty years, dictators representing tiny, wealthy elites working closely with American business interests ruled many Latin American countries.

The history of Guatemala, also a producer of bananas for United Brands, shows why change is difficult. In 1954 the CIA helped overthrow a democratically elected government in Guatemala. Why? Because it had initiated a modest program of agricultural reform that seemed to threaten unused land owned by the United Fruit Company (the former name of United Brands). The U.S. secretary of state in 1954 was John Foster Dulles. His law firm had written the company's agreements with Guatemala in 1930 and 1936. The CIA director was Allen Dulles, brother of the secretary of state and previous president of United Fruit Company. The assistant secretary of state was a major shareholder in United Fruit Company.[21] In Guatemala and elsewhere change is difficult because U.S. companies work closely with wealthy, local elites to protect their mutual economic interests. . . .

John Newton was captain of a slave ship in the eighteenth century. A brutal, callous man, he played a central role in a system which fed thousands to the sharks and delivered millions to a living death. But eventually, after he gave up his career as captain, he saw his sin and repented. His familiar hymn overflows with joy and gratitude for God's acceptance and forgiveness.

---

19. See "Bananas," *New Internationalist*, August 1975, 2.
20. "Action," *New Internationalist*, August 1975, 32.
21. Carl Oglesby and Richard Schaull, *Containment and Change* (New York: Macmillan, 1967), 104; and Stephen Schlesinger and Stephen Kinzer, *Bitter Fruit: The Untold Story of the American Coup in Guatemala* (Garden City, N.Y.: Doubleday, 1982).

Amazing grace! How sweet the sound,
that saved a wretch like me;
I once was lost, but now am found,
was blind but now I see.
'Twas grace that taught my heart to fear,
and grace my fears relieved;
How precious did that grace appear
the hour I first believed.

John Newton became a founding member of a society for the abolition of slavery. The church which he pastored, St. Mary Woolnoth in the city of London, was a meeting place for abolitionists. William Wilberforce frequently came to him for spiritual counsel. Newton delivered impassioned sermons against the slave trade, convincing many people of its evil. He campaigned against the slave trade until he died in the year of its abolition, 1807.

We are participants in a system that dooms even more people to agony and death. If we have eyes to see, God's grace will also teach our hearts to fear and tremble, and then also to rest and trust.

But only if we repent. Repentance is not coming forward at the close of a service. It is not repeating a spiritual law. It is not mumbling a liturgical confession. All of these things may help. But they are no substitute for the kind of deep inner anguish that leads to a new way of living.

Biblical repentance entails conversion; literally the word means "turning around." The Greek word *metanoia,* as Luther insisted so vigorously, means a total change of mind. The New Testament links repentance to a transformed style of living. Sensing the hypocrisy of the Pharisees who came seeking baptism, John the Baptist denounced them as a brood of vipers. "Bear fruit that befits repentance," he demanded (Matt. 3:8). Paul told King Agrippa that wherever he preached, he called on people to "repent and turn to God and perform deeds worthy of . . . repentance" (Acts 26:20).

Zacchaeus should be our model. As a greedy Roman tax collector, Zacchaeus was enmeshed in sinful economic structures. But he never supposed that he could come to Jesus and still continue enjoying all the economic benefits of that systematic evil. Coming to Jesus meant repenting of his complicity in social injustice. It meant publicly giving reparations. And it meant a whole new lifestyle. . . .

For Further Reflection

Case Studies

Expensive lake home. Five years ago, a Christian carpenter built himself a lake home. He went all out, building in all the extras. He thought the home would increase in value while his family enjoyed using it. He spent $10,000 of his own money and borrowed $105,000 from the bank. Last year, the carpenter began volunteering for Habitat for Humanity. Building simple homes for poor people changed his perspective, and he began to think that a second home is not really justified. In addition, mortgage payments on the cabin were straining the family budget. Tithing stopped. He considered selling, but promptly hit a snag. He had overbuilt for the area. Other cabins on this lake are very modest. The market is down due to a local environmental problem. After the real estate fee, he can expect to net no more than $86,000 although he still owes the bank $101,000, to say nothing of the $10,000 he originally invested. Real-estate agents say that in a few years, once officials resolve the environmental problem, the value could go up.

The carpenter comes to you for advice. He wants to focus more on the needs of others, and he needs to reduce the budget strain at home. Yet, he thinks it is bad stewardship to take a $25,000 loss, especially since he would have to borrow $15,000 to pay off his mortgage. What should he do?

Price of gadgets. The XYZ Gadget Company has the best product in the field. Patents protect its design, so others cannot copy it. Since its gadget is superior, XYZ has 65 percent of the market. XYZ can control pricing because smaller competitors generally follow XYZ's lead. Because municipal water systems must have this gadget, price hikes lead to some complaining, but not to canceled orders. So XYZ has gradually boosted the price to ten times the cost of production and is reaping huge profits. Further, XYZ sells 79¢ replacement parts for $29.

The pastor of ABC Church believes these prices are excessive. By overcharging municipalities, XYZ takes money from taxpayers. The owner of XYZ, one of his deacons, argues that the prices are justified. By working for years to engineer the gadget and risking everything to build the company, he produced something that benefits society. The market sets the price, and he reaps the reward. Furthermore, he does give 10 percent of his very high income to the church. He feels guilty charging these prices, but obviously needs the salary he earns so he can care for his family. A salesman for XYZ, also a member of ABC, sees both points of view. What should he do?

Glossary

Capitalism: Economic system that connects with political democracy to form a social system that emphasizes individual freedom, limited government, and free enterprise.

Communism: Economic system that emphasizes collective or state ownership of property and in which central planners (not market forces) make economic decisions so that all citizens share wealth equally.

Free market: Economic environment in which individuals make economic decisions about production and consumption independently, with a minimum of state interference.

Guided market: Economic environment in which central planners seek to guide an economy toward certain desirable goals using a variety of strategies (e.g., taxes, tariffs, subsidies, monetary policies, and others).

Income: Economic power or money that one receives periodically in exchange for labor or the use of capital (see wealth); a person with a high income may not be wealthy.

Interventionism: Derisive word some advocates of the free-market view use to describe the guided-market approach.

Liberation theology: Third-World (especially Latin American) movement that defines sin as economic oppression and salvation as personal, economic, and political liberation of the poor.

Mammon: Wealth and money seen as a power or deity.

Money: Any medium of economic exchange; a common unit of material value in terms of which someone assigns values to all other objects.

Problem of the commons: The problem of how to protect resources that belong to no one in particular but are necessary to the well-being of everyone.

Prosperity gospel: View that a Christian has a spiritual birthright that includes material wealth (also called the health-and-wealth gospel).

Redistribution: Derisive term used by some free marketers for any strategy by which government takes money from the wealthy and gives it to the poor.

Simplicity gospel: View that Christians ought to live plain, simple lives in order to challenge the materialistic philosophy of secular society and to free up resources for Christian work.

Socialism: A social system in which the public owns the means of production and the government actively redistributes income with the aim that all citizens receive an equitable share of goods and services.

Theonomy: Movement that supports God's law, including the Old Testament civil law, as the basis of human society and defends free-market economics as a biblical means to that end.

Wealth: Stored economic power; money that is already accumulated and can be used as capital for investment (see income).

Annotated Bibliography

Barron, Bruce. *The Health and Wealth Gospel*. Downers Grove, Ill.: InterVarsity, 1987. Critical yet balanced assessment of the prosperity gospel.

Blue, Ron. *Master Your Money*. Nashville: Thomas Nelson, 1986. Christian financial planning guide.

Campolo, Tony, and Gordon Aeschliman. *Fifty Ways You Can Feed a Hungry World*. Downers Grove, Ill.: InterVarsity, 1991. Brief book of practical suggestions for helping the poor; good lists of resources.

Chilton, David. *Productive Christians in an Age of Guilt Manipulators*. Rev. ed. Tyler, Tex.: Institute for Christian Economics, 1985. Caustic theonomist response to Ronald J. Sider.

Clouse, Robert G., ed. *Wealth and Poverty: Four Christian Views of Economics*. Downers Grove, Ill.: InterVarsity, 1984. Each of four authors defends his economic theory as the best Christian option.

Copeland, Gloria. *God's Will Is Prosperity*. Tulsa, Okla.: Harrison House, 1978. An example of prosperity-gospel theology.

Davis, John Jefferson. *Your Wealth in God's World*. Phillipsburg, N.J.: Presbyterian and Reformed, 1984. Firm defense of free-market economics.

Ellul, Jacques. *Money and Power*. Translated by LaVonne Neff. Downers Grove, Ill.: InterVarsity, 1984. Extreme but influential statement of the power of money. Published originally in 1954.

Gish, Arthur G. *Living in Christian Community*. Scottdale, Penn.: Herald Press, 1979. Radical call to a simple lifestyle through Christian communal living by the author of *Beyond the Rat Race*.

Halteman, Jim. *Market Capitalism and Christianity.* Grand Rapids: Baker, 1988. Primer on economic theory that defends a guided-market form of capitalism.

Mooneyham, W. Stanley. *What Do You Say to a Hungry World?* Waco, Tex.: Word, 1975. Past president of World Vision states his case for Christian relief.

Nash, Ronald H. "Does Capitalism Pass the Moral Test?" *Evangelical Journal* 5 (Spring 1987): 35–45. Clearly written response to moral objections to capitalism.

———. *Poverty and Wealth.* Westchester, Ill.: Crossway, 1986. Staunch defense of free-market capitalism.

Neuhaus, Richard John, ed. *The Preferential Option for the Poor.* Encounter Series. Grand Rapids: Eerdmans, 1988. Set of discussions on a theme often associated only with liberation theology.

Oostdyk, Harv. *Step One: The Gospel and the Ghetto.* Basking Ridge, N.J.: SonLife International, 1983. Concrete plan for developing a total ministry to the urban poor in America.

Owensby, Walter L. *Economics for Prophets.* Grand Rapids: Eerdmans, 1988. Introduction to economic theory plus a theological evaluation of current American economic practice.

Perkins, John. *With Justice for All.* Ventura, Calif.: Regal, 1982. African-American Christian leader discusses the plight of the urban poor.

Schmidt, Thomas E. *Hostility to Wealth in the Synoptic Gospels.* Journal for the Study of the New Testament Supplement Series, vol. 15. Sheffield: JSOT Press, 1987. Stark documentation of Jesus' harsh words about wealth.

Sider, Ronald J., *Rich Christians in an Age of Hunger.* 3d ed. Waco, Tex.: Word, 1990. Updated presentation of a classic work defending the simple lifestyle; later editions are much more balanced than the first.

Simon, Arthur. *State of the Hungry World.* Washington, D.C.: Bread for the World, 1984. Founder of Bread for the World (a Christian lobbying and educational movement) assesses the world situation; updated each year.

Sobrino, Jon. *The True Church and the Poor.* Maryknoll: Orbis, 1984. Good example of Latin American liberation theology.

Tiemstra, John P. "Christianity and Economics: A Review of Recent Literature." *Christian Scholar's Review* 22 (1993): 227–47. Very helpful overview of literature and issues with extensive bibliography.

Wogaman, J. Philip. *Economics and Ethics.* Philadelphia: Fortress, 1986. Defense of guided-market economics as the most ethically responsible system.

10

Care for the Environment

The last time my mechanic changed the oil in my car, I paid him a dollar to dispose of the oil properly. Selfishly, I would rather put the money toward a cup of coffee and a muffin at my favorite Dutch restaurant. Some North Americans, after changing their own oil, dump it into the environment and avoid the fee. Why should I pay that dollar?

Taken together, those who dump their used motor oil cause as much pollution as major oil-tanker accidents. This pollution is considerable since the used motor oil from just one engine can contaminate as much as one million gallons of water. This raises again the problem of the commons (see chap. 9): dumping the oil brings short-term benefit to someone (polluters save a dollar—or a billion dollars), but sometime, somewhere, somehow, someone pays.

Today, more and more of us are paying. The problems span the world: population growth, water scarcity, deforestation, desertification, resource depletion, species destruction, urbanization, ozone depletion, and global warming. Cataracts and skin cancer cases caused by holes in the ozone layer ignore national boundaries. Such problems seem to require international response and cooperation on a scale never achieved in human history.

These dilemmas interpenetrate intractable economic issues as well: poverty, joblessness, and starvation among millions of our southern neighbors. Families in desert areas compete for cooking fuel and cut down trees. This increases the size of the desert, making it more difficult to grow crops. So

381

they move to a new area, cut down more trees, and hope to scratch out a living in the poor soil. Soon the soil is depleted of nutrients, and so they move off to what little forested land remains, competing with poor families from other areas who experience the same problems. This is a vicious cycle. It occurs because human populations can grow beyond the **carrying capacity** of an ecosystem.

The carrying capacity of an ecosystem is the number of inhabitants that system can support without suffering permanent damage. When population exceeds carrying capacity, the environment degrades. The degredation decreases carrying capacity further. Now, as population continues to increase while carrying capacity decreases, we are running out of earth. For this reason, some ecologists say that the human race must recognize the limits to economic growth. In a famous pronouncement by the Club of Rome in 1970 as well as in the classic book, *The Small World*, by Ernst Schumacher, commentators prescribed a steady-state world economy and population. Unless the human race can stop growing, it will suffocate itself and the world too.

But not everyone accepts this analysis. What we call a *frontier model* shaped North American attitudes about the environment. For three centuries, this continent offered vast territories for the white man to conquer and control. This experience encouraged North Americans to think that if one place was poisoned, they could always move on to new, unspoiled vistas, full of potential and free of pollution. Eventually, however, the explorers hit the Pacific Ocean, and their descendants settled down to pave the Golden State. Now the frontier model, with its assumption of unlimited resources, seems less appropriate than the *spaceship model*: earth is a spaceship with no new, uncharted resources, and the provisions are running low.

The frontier model emphasizes conquering the wilderness. Well before the concrete for those California freeways dried, some began crafting more romantic visions of the wilderness. John Muir, a disciple of Thoreau, rejected his family's Protestant faith and founded the Sierra Club to preserve California's forests as a sort of temple of God. Following the dust-bowl era, forester and professor Aldo Leopold drove home the need for an ethic of the land in a 1948 work, *A Sand County Almanac*. Land and human communities are fellow citizens, interrelated and interdependent. In 1962, Rachel Carson's *Silent Spring* ignited the contemporary ecology movement. She graphically showed how DDT kills the birds that announce the spring with their singing. On 22 April 1970, the first Earth Day, ecology hit the front page. These efforts emphasized preserving the wilderness.

This rise in ecological consciousness coincided with a significant criticism of Christian ethics: ecological orthodoxy blames Christian teaching for environmental degradation. Lynn White published the most influential statement of this thesis in his infamous 1967 essay, "The Historical Roots of Our

Ecologic Crisis." In White's view, the biblical concept of *dominion* (Gen. 1:28—"let them have dominion over . . .") encouraged Westerners to plunder nature for personal profit. In *Design with Nature*, Ian McHarg even more forcefully blames the biblical story for its role in the environmental crisis. According to White and McHarg, ecological salvation requires rejecting the Christian teaching that nature exists to serve humanity.

White's argument paints Christian teaching as opposed to ecology just when Western attitudes are increasingly favorable to ecology. This is troublesome to Christians because ardent environmentalists accept White's thesis as gospel. Thus, those who have acquired an environmental consciousness and who seek spiritual foundations for ecology feel compelled to look somewhere other than to the Christian faith.

The so-called Gaia hypothesis fits the bill. Scientist James Lovelock chose the word *Gaia* to describe the interaction of life and nature. In the usual evolutionary view, the conditions for life emerged by chance, and life adapted to them. According to Lovelock's Gaia hypothesis, however, organisms actually help shape the conditions needed for life to remain. In other words, life and nonlife interact as though they were a single organism. A life force helps create the climate in which biological life can evolve.

Environment mystics, especially those of a New Age orientation, have recently co-opted Lovelock's word: Gaia is Earth, our Mother! They have made it more a religious theme than a scientific hypothesis, however. They assume that native peoples experience oneness with and live in harmony with nature. They scour a variety of sources—paganism, native American religions, Taoism, and certain forms of Christian mysticism—looking for environmentally sensitive spirituality. They use these sources to create a **deep ecology**, a spiritual (but not Christian) sense of wholeness and of connection to Gaia. Matthew Fox and Thomas Berry reconstruct Christianity to fit the new paradigm. Their Christianity is creation spirituality that rejects the biblical balance between the themes of sin and redemption, emphasizing instead the original blessing of creation.

All this paints into a corner any environmental ethicists who wish to be orthodox Christians. On the one hand, they feel compelled to certify ecological concern to other Christians. Because of deep ecology, some conservative Christians wrongly associate any environmental concern with New Age thought. Some cult detectives, probing every viewpoint for New Age influence, reject any ecological viewpoint. In other camps, those with interest in end-time biblical prophecy question any activity except "soul-saving." If Christ is coming back soon, why waste energy slowing down pollution of an earth that is destined for destruction anyway?

On the other hand, orthodox Christian environmentalists also want to defend Christian teaching from the caricature propounded by White and his followers for whom Genesis 1:28 is a central cause of ecological disaster.

Dispassionate commentators agree that White overstated his case. First, blaming Christian teaching for environmental abuse ignores many cases of serious pollution perpetrated by civilizations and societies that have no biblical heritage. Second, no mere idea could possess by itself all the destructive power White ascribes to it. Third, as an alternative to White, Christians can argue that the intellectual warrant for abusing creation comes from the modern mentality with its roots in the Renaissance and Enlightenment. An ethic that justifies raping the land is a secularized distortion of Christian teaching.

What then is an appropriate biblical environmental ethic? One sophisticated Christian view on all these issues is a complex of ideas we can call the **dominion view** or the growth philosophy. This view has an *anthropocentric* emphasis: although the earth belongs to God, it exists to serve human needs. Since the earth does not exist in exactly the form that best serves human needs, humans should reshape the earth to fit human purposes. This requires an economic philosophy that stresses individual property rights and the profit motive as the incentive to produce the goods that humans need. Government's role is to free entrepreneurs of excessive regulation: government should prevent theft, fraud, and violence—and then stay out of the way and allow economic growth. Professor Calvin Beisner's essay expresses the dominion view.

The dominion view raises questions as to why we should value creation. Should we do so for itself or for some other purpose? And if for some other end, does the earth exist for humans or for God? Since God owns the creation, Christians cannot justify the wanton destruction of nature. Sensitive to this point, Beisner clearly agrees that pollution is evil. Pollution is immoral, however, primarily because it hurts other humans. If you destroy my property, my little piece of creation, I have the right to seek damages from you. The threat of a lawsuit restrains environmental degradation.

Beisner believes that the ecology movement is self-serving. Environmentalists have a vested interest in painting a gloomy picture of the future. He points out that scientific research on issues like global warming makes questionable assumptions. Thus, some ecological messages are propagandistic. Human ingenuity and the free market will yet produce new technologies to forestall the ecological Armageddon environmentalists predict. According to Beisner, society must continue to strive for economic growth.

Parenthetically, Beisner's point is well-taken. For example, early computer models predicting global warming needed refinement. When scientists plugged 1880 data into one model, the computer predicted a five degree rise in global temperatures a century later. In fact, they rose one degree. Responsible scientists admit that normal fluctuations in weather can explain the hot temperatures of recent years; the current temperatures are within the range of temperatures the earth has experienced over the last 160,000 years. Yet improved computer models have led those responsible scientists to agree that the huge amounts of greenhouse gases produced by our many cars and cows (yes, cows!) will, if unchecked, lead to global warming, thus changing world weather patterns.

Some find a dominion view untenable because it is too centered on human needs. They choose instead a **citizenship view**. This position, much more closely aligned to the mainstream environmental movement, stresses that humans, like all other species, are members of the biosphere; they are citizens of nature. This model is *biocentric*, focusing systematically on all life. It requires a more radical response to the environmental crisis. Society should promote, not just more catalytic converters on nonnegotiable cars, but a new, sustainable lifestyle that treats the environment as the nonnegotiable and questions the necessity of cars.

Staking a middle ground is the **stewardship view** defended by British geneticist R. J. Berry. This view partially agrees with the others, but it is distinguished by some differences of emphasis. Like the dominion view, it recognizes that humans should use the earth to meet human needs. In fact, significant economic growth must happen or else people already alive are doomed to marginal existence at the very best. Unlike the growth philosophy, however, a stewardship view gives more weight to a basic tenet of the environmental movement: humans are biologically related to and dependent on earth. Thus, while economic growth is necessary, it must be **sustainable growth** (defined as economic development that meets the needs of various groups while preserving the resources and carrying capacity of the environment). We must not live in God's creation as though we could treat it just any way we please.

Like the citizenship view, of course, the stewardship view accepts basic ecological premises. It sees citizenship, however, as too biocentric, as compromising the human place in nature. While humans are rooted in the earth biologically, they also transcend creation due to the image of God. Citizenship views make humans just another animal race. The dominion views are too anthropocentric. Berry sees the stewardship approach as *theocentric*.

In truth, these views are not sharply delineated; they are distinguished by their emphases. The word *stewardship*, for example, is notoriously slippery. All three views recognize both that pollution is evil and that some economic growth is necessary, especially in the Third World. Ironically, while economic growth creates pollution in the First World, the *lack* of economic growth now causes the world's poor to follow highly destructive practices like deforestation. Thus, the environmental debate is very complex both theoretically and practically.

Some of the activities recommended for "saving the earth" are shortsighted. For example, since much newspaper is made from trees planted specifically to create paper, recycling newspapers may not mean that existing trees are saved so much as it means that fewer trees are planted. The gasoline used and pollution created in picking up and transporting glass bottles for recycling may be greater than what is saved by using the recycled glass. When old-fashioned glasses replace styrofoam cups to help with landfill problems, more water is used washing the glasses after each use. These practices may create more of an illusion of ecological sensitivity than anything. Really helping the environment may turn out to cost us more than recycling does.

The real problem is that these activities (as helpful as they are when done properly) do little to alleviate intractable global problems like population growth, deforestation, desertification, resource depletion, species destruction, and global warming. The current situation seems to call for theoretical understanding and international cooperation on a new scale. Of course, policies of the industrialized nations will reflect the concerns of their voters. Thankfully, citizens and leaders of nations are coming to see the connection between environmental degradation and the quality of human life.

One thing seems obvious: the human race cannot go on as it has. Even if the growth philosophy were right for the near term, it cannot go on being right forever. Is there any hope at all? Paul Brand, a former medical missionary, reminds us that a sense of wonder at what God has created can lead to decisions that are not just grounded in short-term utility. Preserving mud may not make short-term economic sense, but it is critical to the well-being of future generations. The earth is capital. Capital can produce interest and support life. It is impossible to spend capital, instead of interest, forever. Only if present generations live responsibly do future generations—to say nothing of the poor of today's Third World—have a chance at decent life. Preserving God's beautiful creation brings glory to God and a future for the children of all the world's peoples.

Managing the Resources of the Earth

E. Calvin Beisner

Toward the end of the parable of the laborers in the vineyard, Jesus portrays the landowner—who represents God—as saying to a grumbling laborer, "Friend, I am doing you no wrong; did you not agree with me for a denarius? . . . Is it not lawful for me to do what I wish with what is my own?" (Matt. 20:13, 15). The phrase "doing . . . no wrong" translates the Greek *akiko,* a form of the verb *adikeo,* "to wrong [by] any violation of human or divine law," to "treat someone unjustly," to "injure."[1] *Adikeo* signifies action opposite to *dikaioo,* to "show justice, do justice."[2] The stem of both verbs is *dike,* "justice,"[3] meaning whatever is in accord with the law, whatever is right according to the authoritative standard of right and wrong. Hence we should find it no surprise that *adikeo* may be translated "injure," a word derived from the Latin privative prefix *in-* and the stem *jus* or *juris,* "right, law," the same stem that we find in our words *just, justice, judge, judgment, jurisprudence,* and *jurisdiction.*

What the landowner said amounts to, "Friend, I am not violating the law in my action toward you. . . . Is it not [therefore] lawful for me to do what I wish with what is my own?" The comment rests on the fundamental principle that one may lawfully do whatever he wishes with what belongs to him so long as he does not in so doing violate God's Law in relation to someone

1. Walter Bauer, *A Greek-English Lexicon of the New Testament and Other Early Christian Literature,* 2d ed., trans. William F. Arndt and F. Wilbur Gingrich, rev. F. Wilbur Gingrich and Frederick W. Danker (Chicago: University of Chicago Press, 1979), 17.
2. Ibid., 197.
3. Ibid., 198.

else. So long as we use our property consistently with the Fifth through Tenth Commandments, civil law should protect our liberty rather than limiting or infringing it. . . .

Defining the Subject

The title of this chapter is "Managing the Resources of the Earth." The surface simplicity of such a title quickly gives way to deep complexities upon analysis. It will be instructive to look at those complexities. Let's take each element of the title in reverse order.

In What Sense Does the Earth Have Resources?

What does it mean to speak of resources *of the earth*? Should we take *of* as a possessive preposition: resources that belong to the earth, that are its property? No doubt some idolaters of the environment think of resources that way, seeing even man as belonging to the earth. But Scripture doesn't see things that way. It sees the earth and everything in it as belonging to God, and God as having entrusted all of this to man as His vice-regent, giving to man some strange thing called "rule" or "dominion" over everything in the earth, instructing man to "fill the earth, and subdue it" (Pss. 24:1; 8:3–8; Gen. 1:26–30). The earth owns nothing. So what we mean when we speak of resources *of the earth* is not resources belonging to the earth, but resources that we find here.

But that in its turn is misleading. To put it rather crudely, we don't *find* resources anywhere on, in, or over the earth—at least not in their natural state. For in their natural state things are not resources at all. Indeed, they often are obstacles, sometimes dangerous ones. No, the earth—poor as it is, owning nothing—is not generous. It gives us no ready-made resources. Instead, we find *raw materials*. And these are to be distinguished most carefully from *resources*.

Raw Materials vs. Resources

Raw materials *become* resources only by the application of human ingenuity to them. Until then they contribute little or nothing to our needs—with the important exceptions of things like air and gravity,[4] from which we benefit without conscious action. Pretty much everything else in our environment becomes a resource to us only when we have developed it in some way. In other words, we don't *find* resources, we *make* them.

---

4. Even air and gravity, of course, now have many uses that were unknown generations ago. Compressed air can inflate tires or keep someone breathing under water or blast loose paint off the side of a house. Gravity can be used to produce electricity, as when water, pulled downward by gravity, turns a turbine. Who knows what other uses we'll find for these and thousands of other things in the future?

Take petroleum, for instance. No less an authority than the *Encyclopedia Britannica* (1969 edition) declares this invaluable resource, for the control of which major military strategy in this century's two world wars was largely devised, "practically useless." "Practically useless," that is, "in its crude state." But when refined—when turned from a raw material into a resource—"it supplies fuels, lubricants, illuminants, solvents, surfacing materials and many other products," including plastics, inks, fabrics, and dyes. I dare say most of this book's readers are wearing a fair amount of that sticky black stuff that our ancestors less than two centuries ago considered, at best, an ugly, smelly nuisance and, at worst, a dangerous, bubbling pit into which to fall.

Now, this distinction between raw materials and resources is not a mere academic nicety. It is of essential importance to our whole approach to the question of managing resources. It has at least three major implications in this regard:

(1) Nothing is a resource until someone has thought of a way to use it, and usually the use requires some modification of it. . . .

(2) Lots of things may be resources tomorrow that are not today. . . .

(3) Discoveries of new supplies of raw materials for which we already have found valuable uses may at any time turn sober and respected projections of future supplies into bad jokes. . . .

Resource Management Policy Must Be Elastic

These three points, when brought together, have two important implications of their own. First, any resource management policy that restricts the elasticity of the resource marketplace or slows the adaptation of society to new knowledge and states of affairs regarding resources is necessarily harmful to society. While this point in itself deserves extensive discussion, let me simply say for the moment that this means, in general, that making resource management primarily, or even significantly, the responsibility and authority of civil government is inherently harmful, for the civil government, by its very nature, lacks the ability to respond quickly and innovatively to changing circumstances.[5]

Second, resource development—the extraction and manipulation of raw materials so as to make them useful to man—will happen most rapidly and on the largest scale in a society in which people are rewarded for contributing to it and are not restricted from using their inventiveness. In other words, free societies, where legal restrictions are placed only on such things as fraud, theft, and violence, are likely to progress more rapidly in the development of

---

5. The perennial inability of most government agencies to keep their recordkeeping computer capabilities at or near state-of-the-art, while most large private businesses do this routinely, is one simple demonstration of this weakness in civil government.

resources than centrally controlled societies, where restrictions apply to far more activities than fraud, theft, and violence. Societies, of course, tend to fall somewhere on a continuum between free and centrally controlled, but in general we can infer—and empirical investigation confirms—that the freer a society is, the more rapidly and comprehensively it will develop resources. Anyone who doubts this might try comparing the number of international patents originating in free societies with the number originating in centrally controlled societies. . . .

Principles of Resource Management

Managing the resources of the earth, then, means planning and controlling how the raw materials we find about us are developed and used for the benefit of mankind. How best to do that is a question that can be analyzed in several ways: (1) What theological and moral standards should guide and limit the use of resources? (2) Who should do the planning and controlling? (3) What ends, or goals, should be pursued in managing resources? Let's look briefly at each of these questions.

Theological and Moral Standards

Five chief standards appear in Scripture for the management of resources:

The Dominion Mandate

In what theologians have long called the "dominion mandate" in the opening chapter of Genesis, God says, "Let Us make man in Our image, according to Our likeness; and let them *rule* [or "have dominion"] over the fish of the sea and over the birds of the sky and over the cattle and over all the earth, and over every creeping thing that creeps on the earth." And, having made man male and female, He says to them, "Be fruitful and multiply, and fill the earth, and subdue it; and rule over the fish of the sea and over the birds of the sky, and over every living thing that moves on the earth" (Gen. 1:26, 28, emphasis added). Let me suggest three observations about this mandate.

First, the dominion mandate, or cultural mandate, as it is also called, is, as Old Testament scholar R. Laird Harris put it, "far from specific. To have 'rule over' the earth might as easily refer to the free use and development of resources as to our responsibility for their conservation. To 'rule over' the animals does not specifically say high dams for power should be rejected so as to avoid bringing an exotic type of little fish to extinction."[6] In other words, the dominion mandate cannot be packed as a pistol in the holster of either the devotees of untouched nature or the rapists of mother earth.

---

6. R. Laird Harris, "The Incompatibility of Biblical Incentives with the Driving Forces of World Economic Systems" (unpublished address to the Chavanne Scholars' Colloquium on the Application of Biblical Propositions to Business and Economics, Baylor University, June 7–10, 1988), 3.

Second, while it may be ambiguous about other things, the dominion mandate clearly means that the earth, with everything in it—though it all belongs to God (Ps. 24:1)—was intended by God to serve man's needs. Man was not made for the earth; the earth was made for man. It is man, not the earth or anything in it, who was created in the image of God. To make man subservient to the earth is to turn the purpose of God in creation on its head.

Third, the dominion mandate does not tell us what particular uses of the earth are best suited to man's service. From this we can legitimately infer two things: (a) that God intended there to be considerable liberty regarding the ways in which we rule the earth, particularly since we differ about how we want the earth to serve us; (b) that difficult scientific and practical issues are involved in determining how best to make the earth serve us. From these two inferences we can derive a third: that we owe it to each other to be moderate and humble in our judgments of each other's views about resource management lest we mistakenly impose our own standards rather than God's.

Private Property

Scripture clearly approves of the ownership of private property, forbidding, as it does, all forms of theft (Exod. 20:15). In the context of resource management, granted the prevalence of statist attempts to control people's uses of property, it is particularly important to note that the Bible assigns to the owner of property absolute control over it within the limits of God's moral law (Acts 5:4; Matt. 20:13, 15). This principle tells us that owners of resources may use them as they wish so long as they do not violate the rights of others—rights delineated in the Ten Commandments and the case laws derived from them.[7]

Justice

The third theological and moral standard governing our use of resources is the broad biblical principle of justice. It is important, however, that this principle be rightly understood. Biblically considered, *justice* means rendering impartially to everyone his due in accord with the right standard of God's moral Law revealed in Scripture.[8] What the Law prohibits, we

---

7. The principle here stated should not be understood to conflict with the biblical requirement that owners of agricultural fields permit needy persons to glean in them (Lev. 19:9, 10; 23:22; Deut. 24:19, 20). The gleaning laws are case laws built on the Sixth and Eighth Commandments (against murder and theft, respectively), showing that our respect for others' lives must extend to permitting them access to food necessary for survival and that our property rights are limited by that respect for life.

8. For extensive development of this concept from Scripture, see E. Calvin Beisner, *Prosperity and Poverty: The Compassionate Use of Resources in a World of Scarcity* (Westchester, Ill.: Crossway, 1988), chapters 4, 5.

392 E. Calvin Beisner

should neither do nor permit others to do; what the Law permits, we may not prohibit.

Furthermore, the principle of justice prohibits force for any purpose other than to prevent or punish violations of God's moral Law. Force may not be used to induce compliance with anyone's wishes outside those countenanced by that Law. Reward, not punishment, is the proper incentive to lawful economic action; punishment should be restricted solely to violations of biblical moral Law.[9]

Liberty

From these first three theological and moral principles follows a fourth: liberty. If God's instruction that we "rule over" the earth and everything in it is far from specific, and if a biblical understanding of justice prohibits the use of force except to prohibit, prevent, prosecute, and punish violations of God's moral Law—the doing of *injustice*—then it follows that in all activities not proscribed by God's Law we have, and are to grant to others, liberty.

This brings us back to the observations with which we began, based on the landowner's comments in the parable of the laborers in the vineyard. So long as we do no injury (literally, *in-justice*) to another, we may use what belongs to us as we please—at least, we may do so without fear of human judgment. (God's judgment is another thing. He looks on the heart, not only on the outward action. He knows whether we have done something just from an unjust motive, and He judges us for that motive as well as for the act. But such judgment is impossible for human minds.)

But liberty does not mean license to do whatever we please. Others' rights define our liberty, put outside boundaries on it. Liberty means the freedom to do what is lawful, not what is unlawful, as the apostle Paul makes clear in Romans 6. The person who has been set at liberty from sin has been made a slave of righteousness. Thus sin—which Scripture defines as lawlessness (Rom. 6:19)—is not an option within real liberty.[10]

Love

But the dominion mandate, private property, justice, and liberty do not exhaust the biblical principles governing resource management. A final principle is love, the selfless act of caring for the needs of others in conformity with the requirements of God's Law (Rom. 13:8–10). While justice gives us

---

9. See E. Calvin Beisner, "Biblical Incentives and the Assessment of Economic Systems," in *Biblical Principles and Economics: Foundations,* ed. Richard C. Chewning (Colorado Springs, Co.: NavPress, 1989).

10. See this theme developed in E. Calvin Beisner, *Taking Every Thought Captive to the Obedience of Christ* (unpublished address to the annual meeting of Immanuel's Men, Immanuel Baptist Church, Rogers, Arkansas, March 4, 1989, available from the author).

the minimum standard of action, love is the high goal toward which every child of God is called to aim.[11] It is not enough that we should refrain from injuring our neighbors; we must do them positive good.[12]

This said, however, it is essential to note that love cannot be forced. It must be voluntary. Hence no appeal may properly be made to civil government to force actions above and beyond the minimum standard of justice. Because civil government is by nature an entity of force, the principle of love falls largely outside its capacities. It exists to enforce justice, not love.

Applying Principles to Resource Management

How might these general principles be applied to problems related to resource management? Let's look briefly at two basic points. These do not comprise an exhaustive list, but they do suggest some directions in which we might go.

First, the dominion mandate means at least that man, not the environment, is primary. Certainly the environment should be protected, but it must be protected for the sake of man, not for its own sake. Anything else is idolatry of nature.[13]

Second, the biblical principles of private property, justice, and liberty mean at least that no entity, private or public, has proper authority to restrict others' use of property—including any resources they own—in any way other than that required by God's moral law. Civil law should prohibit and punish actual injuries (injustices, violations of God's moral Law); it has no authority to use its legal monopoly of force for any other purpose.[14]

This does not mean, however, that just anything goes. Pollution—whether toxic chemicals, noxious odors, bothersome noises, or solid waste—that causes injury to others or their property should be subject to redress through the courts. The redress, however, should be in the form of restitution to those injured, not of fines to the state, which exists to protect and vindicate citizens' God-given rights, not to usurp those rights and the reparation for their violation to itself. Scripture provides for restitution of losses due to misuse of property (see, for example, Exod. 21:28–36; 22:6). However, real damage to or trespass upon property or person—not just

11. On the relationship between justice and love and on the role of civil government in enforcing justice but its inability to coerce love, see Beisner, *Prosperity and Poverty*, 149–53.
12. See Beisner, "Biblical Incentives and the Evaluation of the Individual's Economic Choices."
13. See Herbert Schlossberg, *Idols for Destruction: Christian Faith and Its Confrontation with American Society* (Nashville: Thomas Nelson, 1983), 171.
14. See Beisner, "Biblical Incentives and the Assessment of Economic Systems," and Beisner, *Prosperity and Poverty*, chapter 11, especially 152–59, and chapters 12, 13.

394 E. Calvin Beisner

diminution of exchange value of property (or labor)—must occur in order for restitution to be justified.[15] The mere fact that someone's offering a competing product reduces the market value of a product I offer is no cause for restitution.[16] Similarly, someone's locating a new housing development close to one in which I live, and so increasing the local supply of housing relative to demand and therefore reducing the market value of my house, is no injury to me, and I should have no coercive means of preventing it.

Some major difficulties arise at this point. Since the Industrial Revolution, civil courts have adopted conflicting notions of property rights and pollution-related torts. Furthermore, ever-growing state ownership of property—public lands, in particular—sometimes obscures the identities of both perpetrators and victims of pollution-related torts. In addition, technology has enabled us to observe and measure levels of physical invasion—by sound, light, and liquids, solids, and gases—heretofore unnoticed and thought inconsequential. Finally, determining actual causation in some cases of injury to property and person simply can be beyond our technical capacity, particularly when several different agents can have the same effects and it is impossible to determine which was the agent responsible for the effect in a given instance. In such cases, mere demonstration of correlation should not be accepted as an adequate substitution for proof of causation, and where causation cannot be proved, liability should not be adjudged. These four facts greatly complicate problems related to pollution tort policy.

Extensive discussion of these problems is, of course, impossible in this context. However, both biblical principle and prudence indicate that they are better solved by tightening up the understanding of private property and its attendant rights and responsibilities than by transferring such rights and responsibilities increasingly to the state—the latter being the tactic of choice for many theorists and courts.[17] Further, *the current crisis in tort actions in our nation's courts cannot be overcome until Americans learn to trust anew in the loving providence of God* and so to accept most of life's inevitable suffering as from His gracious hand rather than thinking all of it must be blamed on someone else who must make restitution.

15. For greater development of biblical principles of liability and restitution, see the discussion of legal restraints on pollution in E. Clavin Beisner, *Prospects for Growth* (Westchester, Ill.: Crossway, 1990), chapter 8 and the references in notes to that section.

16. For an insightful discussion of problems of definition of pollution, see Gary North, *The Sinai Strategy: Economics and the Ten Commandments* (Tyler, Tex.: Institute for Christian Economics, 1986), 170–72.

17. An outstanding collection of essays on this subject was published by the Cato Institute. See *The Cato Journal* 2, no. 1 (Spring 1982), Cato Symposium on Pollution. Available from the Cato Institute, 224 Second Street SE, Washington, D.C. 20003.

Let us turn briefly, now, to two final questions: (1) Who should plan and control resource use? (2) What should be the goals of resource management?

Who Should Plan and Control Resource Use?

Planning and control of resource use should, except perhaps under the extremities of war,[18] be left to the owners of the resources, within the limits of biblical moral Law. There simply is no biblical justification for civil government's attempting to control the use of private property, including natural resources, beyond those limits.

Making this work is not always simple. Problems arise in which property rights are difficult to define and determine. Ownership of water in aquifers or running streams or rivers, for instance, is difficult to define, as is ownership in lakes, oceans, and the atmosphere. In some instances, it seems that the state, acting on behalf of its citizens, must take on the role of owner of some such resources. In those instances, however, the state must function as nearly as possible the way private persons function as owners of property. If it fails to enforce its own property rights vigorously enough, its citizens will suffer losses due to abuse. If it exercises too vigorous control over the resources of which it asserts stewardship, its citizens may be deprived of considerable economic advantage and production.

Devising appropriate policies in this regard is not easy, but keeping three fundamental principles in focus should at least provide a sound basis for formulating policy: (1) Resources exist to serve man; man does not exist to serve them. Therefore they should be used, to the greatest extent possible, in manners best suited to the desires of the greatest numbers of people. Those desires should be measured largely by market forces: willingness and ability to pay. (2) The state is a monopoly of force. Therefore it always faces the temptation to exert its will beyond proper boundaries. Safeguards against this must be built into every policy. (3) State officials and employees are subject to the same moral frailties as private persons. Their access to the coercive capacities of the state, however, makes them potentially more dangerous to others' rights than most private persons. Strict systems of accountability, therefore, must always be part of policy.

An implication of these three principles is that policy ought to aim toward the least possible state possession and control of resources, not toward the most possible, and toward the constant reduction of state ownership of resources as technical and legal means of defining and protecting property rights advance.

18. Even in wartime the state's control of the economy should be kept to a minimum and will be most efficient if the state simply acts as a major consumer, directing the forces of the market by pressure on the demand side rather than by attempting to control the supply side by coercive regulation.

What Should Be the Goals of Resource Management?

Consistent with the dominion mandate's insistence that the earth, with everything in it, was made for man, not man for the earth, the goal of resource management should be to increase the degree to which the world serves man. Since, however, different people have different needs and desires, no generalization is possible regarding what particular uses serve that goal and what ones don't. Within the limits of God's moral Law, any use of resources that serves people is permissible; the more efficiently it serves them, the better it is. But any policymaker who thinks he can determine in advance what uses are best is a sad victim of *hubris*. Freedom, not constraint, must be the rule here.

What sort of public policy will best serve this principle of resource management? In general, expansion—not contraction—of private property rights, and even the transfer of more and more property into private rather than state hands, should be the goal of resource management policy. Such a policy will tend to keep the power of the state within its proper bounds, and so will diminish opportunities for oppression. It will also increase people's liberty within the bounds of God's Law and, simultaneously, increase their enjoyment of the goods and services that can be provided by the creative imagination as it seeks ever more ways to use resources.[19]

From *Prospects for Growth: A Biblical View of Population, Resources, and the Future* by E. Calvin Beisner, copyright ©1990, 155–68. Used by permission of Good News Publishers, Crossway Books, Wheaton, Illinois 60187.

19. This chapter is adapted from an address delivered to the New Agenda for Justice conference in Arlington, Virginia, in January 1989, sponsored by the Christian Public Policy Council.

Christianity and the Environment

Escapist Mysticism or Responsible Stewardship

R. J. Berry

Jim Lovelock, High Priest of Gaia[1] (he calls himself shop steward for non-human organisms) identifies the chief villains in damaging the atmosphere as cars, chain-saws and cows.[2] Can Christians—speaking as Christians—say anything about cars, chain-saws or cows?

1. Lovelock's Gaia hypothesis, named after the Greek Earth Goddess (James Lovelock, *Gaia* [New York: Oxford University Press,1979]), 10 proposes that the temperature and composition of the Earth's surface are actively regulated by living organisms and held by homeostatic regulation close to values that are necessary or comfortable for their continued existence (Margulis & Lovelock, 1989), in contrast to the traditional assumption that life is surrounded by and adopts to/is created for an essentially stable environment. As such, it is an entirely proper scientific hypothesis, subject to experimental test in the normal way (Craik, 1989). However, many people have made theological or metaphysical extrapolations from the original theory, encouraged in part by Lovelock's own expositions (e.g., Lovelock, 1988). Montefiore (1985) has interpreted the fact that the Earth's atmosphere is maintained well away from thermodynamic equilibrium (which is the observation that led Lovelock to his hypothesis) as evidence for the anthropic principle (Clifton, 1990; Osborn, 1990), and believes that Gaia is an indication of "the probability of God." Others have speculated even more widely (Myers, 1984; Allaby, 1989).

2. Global warming (the "greenhouse effect") is now generally accepted (IPCC, 1990) although existing data are still possible to interpret as normal climatic fluctuations. There are a number of "greenhouse gases" blanketing the earth, but quantitatively the most important one is carbon dioxide, which is produced in human-influenced increased amounts by motor exhausts, burning of fuel (often cut by chain-saws), and large numbers of cows, whose metabolism leads to much more carbon dioxide release than by other organisms'.

St. Francis of Assisi, appointed by the Pope as 'Patron Saint of Ecology', preached to the birds and talked to the flowers.[3] Can science say anything about this—other than recoiling in bewilderment?

Ian McHarg, a Glaswegian who became Professor of Landscape Architecture and Town Planning at the University of Pennsylvania, has described Genesis 1:26, 28 ('God said, "Let us make human beings in our image, after our likeness, to have dominion over the fish in the sea, the birds of the air, the cattle, all wild animals on land, and everything that creeps on the earth. . . . and said to them, "Be fruitful and increase, fill the earth and subdue it. . . ."') as 'one text of compounded horror which will guarantee that the relationship of man to nature can only be destruction, which will atrophy any creative skill. . . . which will explain all of the despoliation accomplished by western man for at least these 2000 years; you do not have to look any further than this ghastly, calamitous text'.[4] The Genesis story 'in its insistence upon dominion and subjugation of nature, encourages the most exploitative and destructive instincts in man rather that those that are deferential and creative. . . . God's affirmation about man's dominion was a declaration of war on nature'.

An American historian, Lynn White, has written similarly, albeit more temperately: 'By destroying pagan animism, Christianity made it possible to exploit nature in a mood of indifference to the feelings of natural objects'.[5]

What can the Christian reply to all this? Is it possible to do anything except repent and apologize? Does the 'environmental crisis' expose the stu-

---

3. Francis of Assisi's (1182–1240) language and thought (best known through his "Canticle of the Creation," on which the hymn "All creatures of our God and King" is based) is more like that of Eastern mystics or the North American Chief Seattle's approach than that of the Judaeo-Christian tradition. He extended the commandments to love God and one's neighbour to include all creation, in a way that seems to blur the divisions and distinctions between humans and nature. However, his attitude was primarily one of accepting God's goodness in everything, rather than the pantheism of which he is often accused. His worship was centered on Christ's work, and this led him to a deep personal humility (Santmire, 1985: 105–19). In 1980 Pope John Paul II declared him to be the patron saint of ecology.

4. McHarg (1969: 28). Stott (1984: 109–21) takes McHarg as his main example of secular attack on a Christian understanding of the environment.

5. White's (1976) essay on "the historical roots of our ecologic crisis" has been reprinted many times (see, for example, Schaeffer, 1970), and quoted as a proof of Judaeo-Christianity applying God-given human dominion. Although his paper had had considerable influence (see, for example Passmore, 1974: 5), it has been challenged on historical grounds (Welbourn, 1975; Attfield, 1983). Many of the ideas castigated by White are derived from the Greeks rather than the Bible. Notwithstanding, White correctly identifies the anthropocentrism of traditional Christian approaches to nature. However, this was combined throughout most Christian history with a clear understanding and acceptance of humans as God's vice-regents (i.e., stewards accountable to God) (Glacken, 1967; Black, 1970; Attfield, 1983). This interpretation of history has been challenged by Passmore (1974), but his arguments have been strongly countered by Attfield (1983). On the reification of nature, see note 24 (an argument dealt with particularly by Faricy, 1982).

pidity (or worse, the danger) of Christian faith? There are certainly many people who see our environmental problems as a clear indication of the failure of traditional belief, and seek hope from a mystical identification with the earth and the life, which they claim to find in hypothetical unifying forces, and on which they build a 'creation spirituality' instead of a Christ-filled life.[6] Jonathan Porritt, environmental guru *par excellence*, for example, sees the 'new' Christianity as one which substitutes an immanent for a transcendent God, not recognizing that the Bible God is both immanent and transcendent. (These proposals are a re-run of the gnostic heresy which occupied the first centuries of the Christian era).[7]

There are some interesting parallels to be drawn in these doctrinal writings with the various evolutionary debates over the past century or so— (There is nothing new under the sun): Paley's God was essentially transcendent; Darwin's demolition of the assumed fixed world of the deists brought God back into the world from remoteness above 'the bright blue sky';[8] there were a host of 'inner essence' theories produced by paleontologists during the 1920s to explain the apparent differences between the fossil record and genetical evolution (these were all shown to be unnecessary and misleading when the neo-Darwinism synthesis emerged during the 1930s[9]); and the repeated attempts to find an evolutionary ethic (associated particularly with

6. "Creation-centered spirituality" is associated particularly with two North American Roman Catholics, Matthew Fox (1983, 1990), and Thomas Berry (1988). It concentrates on the "original blessing" of God in creation, rather than on sin (and redemption). In many ways, it is a version of the fallacy that we are morally evolving beings, an idea linked particularly in recent years with Teihard de Chardin (q.v. Jones, 1969). Suffering is interpreted as the birth pangs of a new creation, a necessary part of the journey to new life. Support for such thinking is claimed from so-called Celtic spirituality (e.g., Van De Weyer, 1990; see also Martin & Inglis, 1984), Francis of Assisi and mediaeval mysticism.

7. Q.v. Porritt & Winner (1988), especially pp. 252–53. The links between contemporary "green" thinking and the Gnostics and Manichaeans of the early centuries of the Christian church have been explored by Derrick (1972). The classical refutation of gnosticism is, of course, Paul's Colossian letter, and this repays study in the face of demands by some for a new environmental theology, much of which would seek to add to Christ's work (q.v. Lucas, 1980).

8. Up to the end of the eighteenth century, there was every reason to assume that the world was only a few thousand years old, and in much the state that it was at the Creation (complicated by the Fall). The recognition that change has taken place in the natural world (much of it independent of human action, such as the extinction of the dinosaurs and other taxa at the end of the Tertiary) effectively destroyed the possibility of belief in perfect adaptation of organisms to their environment and the operation of deterministic natural laws (Ospovat, 1981). There is considerable irony in realizing that the biblical God who is both immanent and transcendent was brought back to common acceptance through the Darwinian revolution, which led to the demise of deist assumptions, popularly represented by Paley's parable of God as a Divine watchmaker.

9. The debate between paleontologists and geneticists was resolved scientifically, without recourse to or incorporation of mystical elements (Fisher, 1954; Mayr & Provine, 1980; Berry, 1982).

Julian Huxley, C. H. Waddington, G. G. Simpson, Peter Singer) have never found wide acceptance, perhaps because they do not fully explain human aspirations and needs.[10]

I wish that some history would underlie environmental proselytizing! But this is not the place to develop these warnings.

Error and Orthodoxy

Has basic Christian orthodoxy anything positive to contribute to the environmental debate? Can the church do any better than affirm it has something more to say than putting the Benedictine tradition of management alongside the more contemplative Franciscan one,[11] or pointing out that the Japanese, the Russians and (say) the Nepalese have been no more effective in looking after their environment than the reviled Judaeo-Christians of the West?[12] Indeed it has, and there has been significant work by a host of theologians (Santmire, Moule, Austin Baker, Montefiore, Gregorios, etc.)[13] and churches. . . .

Christian Stewardship and Sustainable Development

Darwin came to his recognition of natural selection by combining the concept of a struggle for existence with the observation of biological variation. If we follow a similar procedure, and bring together the notion of divine activity with the nature of mankind, we are faced with a clear call to a Christian stewardship over the whole creation—not as commonly applied in

10. Huxley, 1947 (see also Paradis & Williams, 1989); Simpson, 1950; Waddington, 1960; Singer, 1981. Rachels (1990) has reviewed the search for an evolutionary ethic: he argues the case for "moral individualism" which, translated into theological language, is not far distant in its outworking from the personal accountability rediscovered by the Reformers.

11. René Dubos has suggested that Benedict (480–550) ought to be the patron saint of ecology. Benedict reacted against the mostly solitary and frequently severe asceticism which infiltrated the church of his time from the Christian East; his order was based on combining physical work with contemplation (*ora et labora*). Dubos (1970: 126) argues that humanity needs an "ecologically sensitive but activist spirit" involving "creative intervention in the earth," rather than the more passive Franciscan approach.

12. Introducing a Conference on Environmental Ethics, Jacques Delors, President of the European Community, commented: "I have to say that the Oriental religions have failed to prevent to any marked degree the appropriation of the natural environment by technical means. . . . In other words, despite different traditions, the right to use or exploit nature seems to have found in industrialized countries the same favour, the same freedom to develop, the same economic justification" (Bourdeau, Fasella & Teller, 1990: 22).

13. Moule, 1964: Montefiore, 1975; Taylor, 1975; Gregorios, 1978; Elsdon, 1981; Moss, 1982; Santmire, 1985; Granberg-Michaelson, 1987; Bradley, 1990; Cooper, 1990.

church circles, but over all plants and animals, over living and non-living resources alike, over landscape and community. And stewardship involves management, not preservation;[14] it entails looking after the world primarily for God to whom it belongs by creation and redemption, and only secondarily for ourselves and our fellow humans. Conservation is about God in the first place, not human survival or comfort. For, as Paul wrote to the Colossians, Christ Jesus has 'the primacy over all creation. In him everything in heaven and on earth was created. . . . He exists before all things, and all things are held together in him. . . . God chose through him to reconcile all things to himself making peace through the blood of the cross—all things, whether on earth or in heaven' (Col. 1:15–20). The Bible does not, like the Greeks, look back to a recoverable paradise; it begins in a garden (which itself needs management) and ends in a city.

The truth, of course, is that we have failed in our stewardship. It does not matter whether or not we acknowledge our commitment to be stewards, there can be no dissent we have misused and abused our world to the extent that permanent damage may have been caused. We have followed too uncritically the lead of Bacon and Descartes who set the social values that enjoin us to 'effect all things possible' and to 'render ourselves the masters and possessors of nature'.[15] In words used originally, I think, by Ruskin but repeated by many including Mrs. Thatcher, 'we are stealing the inheritance of our children'.[16] The Brundtland Commission restated time after time the crucial need for sustainable development if we are going to have (in the title

14. There is a tendency in both secular and religious writings to look back to a supposedly ideal time, and to seek ways of reversing current trends (Glacken, 1987). For example, Milton's *Paradise Lost* has exercised an enormous influence. From the Christian point of view, part of the problem lies in different exegeses of Romans 8:19–22, which has been understood by some to mean that "nature" will be restored, but in context refers specifically to the Spirit's work in humans; the passage speaks of creation's suffering as a consequence of human sin. Kidner (1967: 73) describes the situation as "leaderless, the choir of creation can only grind in discord." In other words, Paul is writing of the failure of human stewardship rather than the causal decay of environment; his argument is that as long as we refuse (or are unable through sin) to play the role created for us by God, the natural world will be dislocated and frustrated. The Romans passage is therefore about relationships, and complements the understanding and implication of human nature shaped by God's image.

15. See Russell (1985), especially chapter 4.

16. Ruskin wrote: 'God has lent us the earth for our life; it is a great entail. It belongs as much to those who are to come after us and whose names are already written in the book of creation, as to us; and we have no right, by anything we do or neglect, to involve them in unnecessary penalties, or deprive them of benefits which it was in our power to bequeath. . . . Men cannot benefit those that are with them as they can benefit those who come after them; and of all the pulpits from which human voice is ever sent forth, there is none from which it reaches so far as from the grave.' Jacques Delors (1990: 23) expressed this as: 'We have not inherited the earth from our ancestors, we have borrowed it from our children'; Mrs. Thatcher (q.v. *This Common Inheritance*, 1990: 10) has reminded us that 'we do not have a freehold on our world, but only a full repairing lease.'

of their Report), any Common Future at all.[17] Chris Patten laid it on the line at a speech in the City a few months ago.[18] He said, 'Only through development which is sustainable can countries such as ours continue to grow. And more importantly, only in this way can less well developed countries break the vicious downward spiral of poverty leading to environmental degradation, leading to greater poverty, and so on.'

Environmental Ethics

Where does all this get us? Do Christians have anything to say to the world about the environment? I believe we do. In 1986 the World Wildlife Fund (as it then was) held its 25th anniversary celebrations at Assisi, and called upon the world's religions to assert their commitment to conservation. Declarations on 'man and nature' were produced in the name of Buddhism, Christianity, Hinduism, Islam, and Judaism.[19] The Christian statement was not strong, and the Duke of Edinburgh (who is President of WWF International) subsequently convened a series of meetings at Windsor on 'the Christian Attitude to Nature'.[20] He challenged those attending with a question, 'There must be a moral as well as a practical argument for environment conservation. What is it?'

The answer, of course, is responsible stewardship and this is the key to the values which determine our actions toward the environment.

Exactly the same answer was given at a conference convened by the Economic Summit Nations last year,[21] which defined an environmental ethic as involving:

17. The Brundtland Commission is the name by which the World Commission on Environment and Development (WCED) is usually known, after its chairman, Dr. Gro Harlem Brundtland, one-time Prime Minister of Norway. The WCED was set up by the United Nations Organization in 1983 on the pattern of the Brandt Report (on economics) and the Palme Report (on disarmament) to:

1. Re-examine the critical issues of environment and development and to formulate innovative, concrete, and realistic action proposals to deal with them.
2. Strengthen international co-operation on environment and development and to assess and propose new forms of co-operation that can break out of existing patterns and influence policies and events in the direction of needed change.

The Brundtland Commission Report was published in 1987; an assessment of its achievements so far has been compiled by Starke (1990).

18. At Coopers & Lybrands, 27 March 1990. Sustainable development can be defined as 'a process of social and economic betterment that satisfies the needs and values of all interest groups, while maintaining future options and conserving natural resources and diversity'.

19. The intention of the Assisi meeting was 'to link the secular movement for the conservation of nature with the religious perception of nature as the creation of a supreme being' (Edinburgh & Mann, 1989: 11).

20. Edinburgh & Mann (1989).

21. The sixth annual bioethics conference of the Economic Summit Nations was held in Brussels in May 1989 on 'Environmental ethics: man's relationship with nature, interactions

Stewardship of the living and non-living systems of the earth in order to maintain their sustainability for present and future, allowing development with equity. Health and quality of life for humankind are ultimately dependent on this.

A surprising number of consequences follow the acceptance of such an ethic. It involves characteristics which can be regarded as belonging to all good citizens or organizations, such as truthfulness, freedom of choice, justice and so on. But more importantly, it implies obligations such as that all environmental impacts should be fully assessed in advance for their effect on the community, posterity, and nature itself, as well as on the individual interest; that regular monitoring should be undertaken; that support should be provided for basic environment research; facilities for technological transfer; regular review of environmental standards and practices; rigorous implementation of the 'polluter pays' principle; etc. There is a clear convergence between the implications of both sacred and secular arguments.

Does the Christian point of view help or hinder environmental conservation? Certainly there are no grounds for agreeing with McHarg that Christianity is an inevitable environmental disaster. Indeed without the constraints of non-utilitarianism, it would be easier to justify self-interest, short-term solutions, parochial or 'not-in-my-backyard' considerations, and justification of extreme anthropocentric or naturalistic/preservationist situations. Christian doctrine provides a regulator for our environmental attitudes which can come from the application of strict common sense, but which are likely to be more consistent if based on underlying principle rather than mere pragmatism.

Environment and Gospel

But there are other considerations affecting our environmental attitudes. In the middle of the Acts of the Apostles are three verses which record Paul's only address to those outside mainstream religious thought.[22] There are plenty of examples in the New Testament of sermons directed to educated Jews, to academics who suspect that there is a supernatural, or to believers

---

with science' (Bourdeau, Fasella & Teller, 1990). In his opening address, Delors called for an environmental code of practice, on the grounds that 'the values which have been accepted up to now by all industrial societies, whereby our natural habitat has become no more than a commodity, must be replaced by different values and a different approach to the environment'. The Brussels Conference set up a Working party to devise such a code, which was presented in May 1990 to a follow-up conference on science to the Brundtland Commission (Berry & Bourdeau, 1990; Berry, 1990).

22. Stott (1990: 231) writes on this passage: 'Although what Luke includes is only a very brief extract of Paul's sermon, it is of great importance as his only recorded address to illiterate pagans. It invites comparison with his sermon to religious and educated Jews in the synagogue at Pisidian Antioch, which is the only other one that Luke chronicles during the first missionary journey'.

In the same context of wondering and learning from the natural world, it is worth remembering also, that the Genesis creation narratives are in part at least, a theodicy.

with incomplete understanding. How does Paul challenge the sort of audience which will probably predominate during this coming week? You might think that he would take the opportunity to preach 'Christ and him crucified', the incarnation, or resurrection, or reconciliation, or the warmth of church fellowship. He does none of these things. His message is simple, it is one of hope and of the good news of God at work; it is a straightforward plea to take the facts of human folly and the works of God in nature at their face value. Paul says,

> The good news we bring tells you to turn from your follies to the living God, who made heaven and earth and sea and everything in them. In the past ages he has allowed all nations to go their own way; and yet he has not left you without some clue to his nature in the benefits he bestows; he sends you rain from heaven and the crops in their seasons, and gives you food in plenty and keeps you in good heart (Acts 14:15–17).

In a world when we are increasingly having to question the regularity of the seasons or the trustworthiness of the rains, let us seize on the clue to God's nature that he has given us in the benefits we receive. Our world is not a chance collection of atoms, nor are we simply generalized higher apes. We live in a world created by God, and we are responsible to him for our treatment of it. Let us not apologize for the faith of our fathers. The God of Abraham, Elijah, and David is the God of history, who is active today. Our ways are in his hands; he is the God of 1990 A.D. just as much as he was of 1990 B.C. and 990 A.D.

On the gates of the old Cavendish Laboratory (Physics Department) in Cambridge is carved the text (Ps. 111:2),

> Great are the words of the Lord,
> pondered over by all who delight in them.[23]

23. Kidner (1975: 397) comments on this verse, 'Because the Lord's works are made 'in wisdom' (Ps. 104:24) they repay research, as recent centuries of rigorous study have shown us abundantly. . . . But while this verse is well taken as God's charter for the scientist and the artist, verse 10 must be its partner, lest "professing to be wise" we become fools, like the men of Romans 1:18–23'. Verse 10 is

The face of the Lord is the beginning of wisdom,
and they who live by it grow in understanding.

It is worth recalling (although some will find this ironic) that the anthem composed by F. W. Bridge for Charles Darwin's funeral in Westminster Abbey was based on a similar proposition in Proverbs 3:13, 14:

Happy is he who has found wisdom,
he who has acquired understanding,
for wisdom is more profitable than silver,
and the gain she brings is better than gold.

Let us ponder the words of the Lord, and let us use them as his own clues to his continuing work in the world. May they direct us to the Christ who has brought all things together, male and female, white and black, sacred and secular, and above all things sinner with salvation.

References

Allaby, M. *Guide to Gaia*. London: Macdonald (1989).

Attfield, R. *The Ethics of Environmental Concern*. Oxford: Blackwell (1983).

Berry, R. J. *Neo-Darwinism*. London: Edward Arnold (1982).

Berry, R. J. Environmental knowledge, attitudes and action: a code of practice. Sci. publ. Affairs 5, 13–23 (1990).

Berry, R. J., and Bourdeau, P. L. In *Sustainable Development, Science and Policy*: 345–357. Oslo: Norwegian Research Council for Science and the Humanities.

Berry, T. *The Dream of the Earth*. San Francisco: Sierra Club (1988).

Black, J. *The Dominion of Man*. Edinburgh: Edinburgh University Press.

Bourdeau, P., Fasella, P. M., and Teller, A. (eds.). *Environmental Ethics. Man's Relationship with Nature Interactions with Science*. Luxembourg: Commission of the European Communities.

Bradley, I. *God is Green*. London: Darton, Longman & Todd (1990).

Clifton, R. K. Review of John D. Barrow and Frank J. Tipler: *The Anthropic Cosmological Principle*. Sc. Christian Belief 2, 41–46 (1990).

Cooper, T. *Green Christianity*. London: Spire (1990).

Craik, J. C. A. The Gaia hypothesis—fact or fancy? J. mar. biol. Assoc. **69**, 759–768 (1989).

Delors, J. Opeining address. In *Environmental Ethics*: 19–28. Bourdeau, P., Fasella, P. M., and Teller, A. (eds.). Luxembourg: Commission of the European Communities (1990).

Derrick, C. *The Delicate Creation*. London: Stacey (1972).

Dubos, R. *Reason Awake: Science for Man*. New York: Columbia University Press (1970).

Edinburgh, HRH Duke of, and Mann, M. *Survival or Extinction*. Windsor: St. George's House (1989).

Elsdon, R. *Bent World*. Leicester: IVP (1981).

Faricy, R. *Wind and Sea Obey Him*. London: SCM (1982).

Fisher, R. A. Retrospect of the criticisms of the theory of natural selection. In *Evolution as a Process*: 84–98. Huxley, J., Hardy, A. C., and Ford, E. B. (eds.). London: Allen & Unwin (1954).

Fox, M. *Original Blessing*. Santa Fe, New Mexico: Bear (1983).

Fox, M. *The Coming of the Cosmic Christ*. San Francisco: Harper & Row (1990).

Glacken, C. *Traces on the Rhodian Shore*. Berkeley, Cal.: University of California Press (1967).

Granberg-Michaelson, W. (ed.). *Tending the Garden. Essays on the Gospel and the Earth*. Grand Rapids, Michigan: Eerdmans (1987).

Gregorios, P. M. *The Human Presence*. Geneva: World Council of Churches (1978).

406   R. J. Berry

Huxley, J. S. *Evolution and Ethics*. London: Pilot (1947).

IPCC [Inter-Governmental Panel on Climatic Change]. *Climate Change*. Cambridge: Cambridge University Press (1990).

Jones, D. G. *Teilhard de Chardin. An analysis and assessment*. London: Tyndale (1969).

Kidner, D. *Genesis*. London: Tyndale (1967).

Kidner, D. *Psalms 73–150*. Leicester: IVP (1975).

Lovelock, J. E. *Gaia*. New York: Oxford University Press (1979).

Lovelock, J. E. *The Ages of Gaia*. Oxford: Oxford University Press (1988).

McHarg, I. L. *Design with Nature*. New York: Natural History (1969).

Margulis, L. and Lovelock, J. E. Gaia and geognosy. In *Global Ecology*: 1–30. Rambler, M. B., Margulis, L., and Fester, R. (eds.). London: Academic (1989).

Martin, V., and Inglis, M. *Wilderness. The Way Ahead*. Forres: Findhorn (1984).

Mayr, E., and Provine, W. B. (eds.). *The Evolutionary Synthesis*. Cambridge, Mass.: Harvard University Press (1980).

Montefiore, H. (ed.) *Man and Nature*. London: Collins (1975).

Montefiore, H. *The Probability of God*. London: SCM (1985).

Moss, R. *The Earth in Our Hands*. Leicester: IVP (1982).

Moule, C. F. D. *Man and Nature in the New Testament*. London: Athlone Press (1964).

Myers, N. *Gaia: an Atlas of Planet Management*. Garden City, N.Y.: Doubleday (1984).

Osborn, L. H. A. A theological perspective on Barrow and Tipler's *The Anthropic Cosmological Principle*. Sc. Christian Belief **2**, 47–52 (1990).

Ospovat, D. *The Development of Darwin's Theory. Natural History, Natural Theology and Natural Selection 1838–1859*. Cambridge: Cambridge University Press (1981).

Paradis, J., and Williams, G. C. *Evolution and Ethics*. Princeton, N.J.: Princeton University Press (1989).

Passmore, J. *Man's Responsibility for Nature*. London: Duckworth (1974).

Porritt, J., and Winner, D. *The Coming of the Greens*. London: Fontana (1988).

Rachels, J. *Created from Animals*. Oxford and New York: Oxford University Press (1990).

Russell, C. A. *Cross-currents. Interaction Between Science and Faith*. Leicester: IVP (1985).

Santmire, H. P. *The Travail of Nature*. Philadelphia: Fortress (1985).

Schaeffer, F. *Pollution and the Death of Man*. London: Hodder & Stoughton (1970).

Simpson, G. G. *The Meaning of Evolution*. New Haven: Yale University Press (1950).

Singer, P. *The Expanding Circle. Ethics and Sociobiology*. Oxford: Clarendon (1981).

Starke, L. *Signs of Hope*. Oxford: Oxford University Press (1990).

Stott, J. R. *Issues Facing Christians Today*. Basingstoke: Marshall (1984).

Taylor, J. V. *Enough is Enough*. London: SCM (1975).

This Common Inheritance. Britain's Environmental Strategy. Cm 1200. London: HMSO (1990).

Van De Weyer, R. *Celtic Fire.* London: Darton, Longman, Todd (1978).
Waddington, C. H. *The Ethical Animal.* London: George Allen & Unwin (1960).
Welbourn, F. B. Man's dominion. Theology **78**, 561–568 (1975).
White, L. The historical roots of our ecologic crisis. Science, N.Y., **155**, 1204–1207 (1976).

From R. J. Berry, "Christianity and the Environment: Escapist Mysticism or Responsible Stewardship," *Science and Christian Belief* 3 (1991): 3–18.

"A Handful of Mud"

A Personal History of My Love for the Soil

Paul W. Brand

I grew up in the mountains of South India. My parents were missionaries to the tribal people of the hills. Our own life was about as simple as it could be, and as happy. There were no roads. We never saw a wheeled vehicle except on our annual visit to the plains. There were no stores, and we had no electricity and no plumbing. My sister and I ran barefoot, and we made up our own games with the trees and sticks and stones around us. Our playmates were the Indian boys and girls, and our life was much the same as theirs. We absorbed a great deal of their outlook and philosophy, even while our parents were teaching them to read and write and to use some of the tools from the West.

The villagers grew everything they ate, and rice was an important food for all of us. The problem was that rice needs flooded fields in the early stages of growth, and there was no level ground for wet cultivation. So rice was grown all along the course of streams that ran down gentle slopes. These slopes had been patiently terraced hundreds of years before, and now every terrace was perfectly level and bordered at its lower margin by an earthen dam covered by grass. Each narrow dam served as a footpath across the line of terraces, with a level field of mud and water six inches below its upper edge and another level terrace two feet below. There were no steep or high drop-offs, so there was little danger of collapse. If the land sloped steeply in one area, then the terraces would be very narrow, perhaps only three or four feet wide. In other areas where the land sloped very little, the terraces would be very broad. Every one of the narrow earth dams followed exactly the line of the contours of the slope.

Every few feet along every grassy path were little channels cut across the top of the dam for water to trickle over to the field below. These channels were lined with grass and were blocked by a grassy sod that the farmer could easily adjust with his foot to regulate the flow of water. Since each terrace was usually owned by a different family, it was important to have some senior village elder who would decide whether one farmer was getting too much or too little of the precious water supply.

Those rice paddies were a rich soup of life. When there was plenty of water, there would be a lot of frogs and little fish. Herons and egrets would stalk through the paddy fields on their long legs and enjoy the feast of little wrigglers that they caught with unerring plunges of their long beaks. Kingfishers would swoop down with a flash of color and carry off a fish from under the beak of a heron. And not only the birds enjoyed the life of the rice paddies—we boys did too. It was there that I learned my first lesson on conservation.

One day I was playing in the mud of a rice field with a half-dozen other little boys. We were catching frogs, racing to see who would be the first to get three. It was a wonderful way to get dirty from head to foot in the shortest possible time. But suddenly we were all scrambling to get out of the paddy. One of the boys had spotted an old man walking across the path toward us. We all knew him and called him "Tata," meaning "Grandpa." He was the keeper of the dams. He walked slowly, stooped over a bit, as though he were always looking at the ground. Old age is very much respected in India, and we boys shuffled our feet and waited in silence for what we knew was going to be a rebuke.

He came over to us and asked us what we were doing. "Catching frogs," we answered.

He stared down at the churned-up mud and flattened young rice plants in the corner where we had been playing, and I was expecting him to talk about the rice seedlings that we had spoiled. Instead he stooped and scooped up a handful of mud. "What is this?" he asked.

The biggest boy among us took the responsibility of answering for us all. "It's mud, Tata."

"Whose mud is it?" the old man asked.

"It's your mud, Tata. This is your field."

Then the old man turned and looked at the nearest of the little channels across the dam. "What do you see there, in that channel?" he asked.

"That is water, running over into the lower field," the biggest boy answered.

For the first time Tata looked angry. "Come with me and I will show you water."

We followed him a few steps along the dam, and he pointed to the next channel, where clear water was running. "That is what water looks like," he said. Then he led us back to our nearest channel, and said, "Is that water?"

We hung our heads. "No, Tata, that is mud, muddy water," the oldest boy answered. He had heard all this before and did not want to prolong the question-and-answer session, so he hurried on, "And the mud from your field is being carried away to the field below, and it will never come back, because mud always runs downhill, never up again. We are sorry, Tata, and we will never do this again."

But Tata was not ready to stop his lesson as quickly as that, so he went on to tell us that just one handful of mud would grow enough rice for one meal for one person, and it would do it twice every year for years and years into the future. "That mud flowing over the dam has given my family food every year from long before I was born, and before my grandfather was born. It would have given my grandchildren food, and then given their grandchildren food forever. Now it will never feed us again. When you see mud in the channels of water, you know that life is flowing away from the mountains."

The old man walked slowly back across the path, pausing a moment to adjust with his foot the grass clod in our muddy channel so that no more water flowed through it. We were silent and uncomfortable as we went off to find some other place to play. I had gotten a dose of traditional Indian folk education that would remain with me as long as I lived. Soil was life, and every generation was responsible for preserving it for future generations.

Over the years I have gone back to my childhood home several times. There have been changes. A road now links the hill people with the plains folk, for example. But traditional ways still continue. The terraced paddy fields still hold back the mud. Rice still grows in the same mud, and there is still an overseer called Tata—although he is one of the boys I used to play with sixty-five years ago. I am sure he lays down the law when he catches the boys churning up the mud, and I hope the system lasts for years to come. I have seen what happens when the old order breaks down, as it did in the Nilgiri Hills. I remember going there for a summer holiday with my family in 1921, when I was a boy.

The Nilgiri Hills, or Blue Mountains, were a favorite resort of the missionaries from the plains during the hot season. We hill folk did not need any change of climate, but we went because of the fellowship. The Nilgiris were steep and thickly forested, with few areas level enough for cultivation, even with terraces. The forestry service was strict and allowed no clearing of the trees except where tea plants or fruit or coffee trees were to be planted. These bushes and trees were good at holding soil, and all was well. I can remember, as a child, the clear streams and rivers that ran down the valleys, and the joy of taking a picnic to the waterfalls and wading in the pools.

Thirty years later—in the 1950s—I was back in India, now a doctor and a missionary myself, with a wife and a growing family. Now I was living on the hot plains at Vellore Christian Medical College. Everything about India brought back memories, but what I longed for most were the mountains, to remind me of my childhood. My wife and I started a tradition of taking our children to the Nilgiris every summer holiday, and they reveled in the cool air and enjoyed the forests and mountain peaks. But something was different, or soon became so.

A new breed of landowners began to take possession of the mountain forests. During the great struggle for independence in India, a number of people had suffered imprisonment, and they now claimed rewards from a grateful country. Free India had much goodwill but little money, so it gave land to these political sufferers, and some of that land was the forests of the Nilgiri Hills. These new landowners had not been farmers before. They had never known any Tata to teach them the value of mud. They wanted to make money, and make it fast. They knew that the climate was ideal for growing potatoes, and that there was a market for them. So they cleared forests from sloping land and planted potatoes. Two, even three crops could be harvested every year, and they made good money. But the land suffered. Harvesting potatoes involves turning over the soil, and monsoon rains often came before the new crop could hold the soil. . . .

One summer holiday our bus struggled up the winding road, and the heat of the plains gave way to cool breezes. We looked for the streams and waterfalls that I had loved. But now the water looked like chocolate syrup; it oozed rather than flowed. What we were seeing was rivers of mud. I felt sick.

There was a dear old Swiss couple, Mr. and Mrs. Fritschi, who lived in Coonoor, on the Nilgiri Hills. They had been missionaries of the Basel Mission in Switzerland but were long retired and now owned a nursery of young plants and trees. They loved to help and advise farmers and gardeners about ways to improve their crops. It seemed to me that these devoted people would know if there was some way to advise the landowners about ways to save their soil. I went to ask Mr. Fritschi about the havoc that was being wreaked by potato farming and to find out if there was anything that we could do. Mr. Fritschi despaired about the new landowners. His eyes were moist as he told me, "I have tried, but it is no use. They have no love of the land, only of money. They are making a lot of money, and they do not worry about the loss of soil because they think it is away in the future, and they will have money to buy more. Besides, they can deduct the loss of land from their income tax as a business depreciation." In the United States today this would be called agribusiness rather than farming, and indeed, the attitudes of agribusiness are much the same.

Thirty more years have passed, and my children have grown up and scattered, and we have left India. But we love it still, and every year I go back to visit my old medical college in Vellore and take part in the leprosy work there. I don't really enjoy going back to the Nilgiri Hills anymore, although many parts of them are still beautiful. I look up to the slopes that used to be covered with forests and then were planted with potatoes year after year.

There are large areas of bare rock now, of no use to anybody. The deforested areas that still have some soil look like stretches of gravel. The streams and springs that ran off from these areas ran clear sixty years ago, flowed mud thirty years ago, and today are dry. When the rains come, they rush over this land in torrents; the land floods, then goes dry. . . . Oh, Tata! Where have you gone? You have been replaced by businessmen and accountants who have degrees in commerce and who know how to manipulate tax laws, by farmers who know about pesticides and chemical fertilizers but who care nothing about leaving soil for their great-grandchildren. . . .

Outside of India I have seen another drama of trees and soil and water and human starvation working its tragic sequence that so often seems inevitable. This drama is unfolding in Ethiopia.

I first saw Ethiopia at the beginning of the nineteen-sixties when I went to Addis Ababa on behalf of the International Society for the Rehabilitation of the Disabled. My task was to negotiate the establishment of an all-Africa training center for leprosy workers, with an emphasis on rehabilitation. I had to meet the emperor Haile Selassie and his minister of health as well as ministers of agriculture and commerce, and the dean of the university medical college, which was just beginning. I also met representatives of American AID and the Rockefeller Foundation. Later, when the new training center was established, I went to work there. My job was surgery; I was teaching reconstruction of the hand and foot. But, as has happened so often in my life, it was the trees and the soil and agriculture that caught my attention. This was partly because most of our patients were farmers, and their future had to be in farming if they were not to be dislocated from their families and villages.

The emperor was very gracious as we talked about the problem, and he allowed our patients to farm tracts of the Royal Lands. The Swedish churches had sent farmers into Ethiopia to teach the patients how to farm more efficiently, and it was a joy to see acres of *tef*, the local food grain, growing to harvest. Patients with leprosy were learning how to work without damaging their insensitive hands. We were grateful to the benevolent old emperor; all seemed to be going well. Gradually, however, we began to see the real problems of that tragic country. When we visited distant treatment centers, we camped along the way, and we were impressed by the way the countryside was fissured with deep canyons where streams had eroded the soil on their way to join the blue Nile. That mighty river flowed from Lake Tana through the deepest canyon of all on its way to Egypt and the Mediterranean Sea. Farmers on the edges of these canyons were having to retreat year by year as their soil slipped away into the rivers. Once there had been trees and forests on this land, but the trees had been felled for timber and firewood, and to make way for grazing and cultivation.

What impressed me most, however, were the poor crops and stony fields that were cultivated by the peasant farmers. Every field seemed to be cov-

ered with great stones and boulders. Many of these stones could rather easily have been levered up and rolled away to the edges of the fields, where
they would have made walls to hold the soil in and keep marauders out. It
did not take much inquiry to find out why such simple improvements had
never been made, and why the peasants put up with the constant irritation
of having to till and harvest between these rocks. They knew, and were frank
to tell us, that if ever they made their fields look good, they would lose them.
The ruling race of Amharas, based in the capital city, included all the lawyers and leaders of the country. An Amhara could claim any good piece of
land simply by stating that it had belonged to his ancestors. Supporting documents were easy to obtain. In court the peasant had no chance. Thus his
only hope of being allowed to continue farming his land was to make it
appear worthless.

Both the Ford Foundation and the Rockefeller Foundation had considered sending help to teach good farming methods and to halt erosion, but
both insisted to the emperor that land reform had to come first. Only if the
land were owned by the people who farmed it would it be taken care of in a
way that would preserve it for generations to come. The peasants had to have
confidence that their handful of mud would still be there for their children.
If not, why not let it be washed down into the river?

The emperor tried to introduce land reform, but he failed. The Amharas
were too strong for him. The established church, the old Ethiopian Orthodox church of which the emperor was head, had a vested interest in the status quo, and so was on the wrong side of real justice. This has happened
often in the past when churches have gotten comfortable and wealthy.

On a state visit to Egypt the emperor walked down to the banks of the
River Nile. He kneeled to scoop up two handfuls of the rich, fertile mud and
raised his hands. "My country," he said. The Blue Nile had carried Ethiopia
to Egypt, and the old emperor knew it. He could not send the mud upstream
again, and he did not have the courage to make the changes that would have
arrested further loss.

Today Emperor Selassie is dead. Every cabinet minister with whom I
negotiated for our training center is dead. They were killed by the firing
squads of the Revolution. I loved some of those men. Ato Abebe Retta, the
Minister of Health, was a courteous gentleman of culture, and he had good
plans for medical education. I enjoyed meals with him in his home, and we
talked about leprosy control. He and the minister of agriculture were blind-
folded and shot by a firing squad. The emperor, who gave us all that land—
that regal figure who was the first president of the Organization of African
Unity and who presided at the opening of our training center—died in
prison. I could weep for them, but if I do, can I at the same time weep for
the hundreds of thousands of peasants who are dying at this very moment
because of famine? There might not have been a famine today if the trees had

414 Paul W. Brand

not all been cut down, if the land had not eroded away, if the absentee land-lords of Ethiopia had not been so greedy, and if the church had insisted that justice should prevail. I did not like the Revolution or the foreign invaders who brought it about, but they would never have succeeded if the people had not been laboring under a sense of injustice. Ethiopia was ready for revolution. The new Marxist government has not succeeded in bringing back the trees or the land, and it has spent its energy in war. But the roots of Ethiopia's problems stem from generations ago, before the time of the leaders who recently died for their collective sins. . . .

I would gladly give up medicine and surgery tomorrow if by so doing I could have some influence on policy with regard to mud and soil. The world will die from lack of soil and pure water long before it will die from lack of antibiotics or surgical skill and knowledge. But what can be done if the destroyers of our earth know what they are doing, and do it still? What can be done if people really believe that free enterprise has to mean an absolute lack of restraint on those who have no care for the future?

All is not lost if there are still people who have faith and people who care. God still has a church that produces people who care. In the final analysis it is not knowledge or lack of it that makes a difference, but concerned people. A sense of concern for the earth is still transmitted by person-to-person communication and by personal example better than by any other method. Old Tata still lives on. He lives in the boys who played in the mud, and they will pass on his concern for the soil and his sense of the importance of it for future generations. Old Mr. Fritschi still lives on. The love of trees that he tried to promote in the Nilgiri Hills is now being promoted by his son, Ernest, on the plains of Karagiri. This is the place that I love to visit because I get a sense that the earth is being revived. If it can happen in one place, then why not everywhere? A single dedicated person giving a good example is better than much wringing of hands and a prophecy of doom.

Ernest grew to love India, and he became a citizen and married a lovely Indian woman. He studied at Madras University and became a doctor, then an orthopedic surgeon. Working with leprosy patients, he joined the leprosy mission and worked in many countries, including Ethiopia. Eventually he became director of the Schieffelin Research and Training Center at Karagiri, near Vellore.

The land for the center was once barren gravel, with not a tree anywhere, and water was hard to locate. I remember walking over the large acreage before we started to build on it and thinking that it was no surprise that the government had donated it so freely, since it was good for nothing else. But Ernest had faith in the land and was determined to prove that it could be productive of more than buildings and a hospital. Other directors had made a good start, but Ernest made a rule for himself that every year he would plant trees and more trees. To follow his rule, he collected seeds and seedlings from everywhere and nourished them in his own garden until they were strong. Then he planted them just before the rains, and had them watered by staff and patients until they had root systems deep enough to survive. The hill that formed one border of the Karagiri land was bare and rocky, and the rains would send a rushing flood of water over the gravel of the hospital grounds. So Ernest built contour ridges of gravel and soil that held the water long enough for it to soak in.

I remember the hospital and the staff houses and chapel that grew up around it. They were gray and white and stood out against the skyline. They were the only structures to break the monotony of the gravel slopes for miles. When I approach that hospital today, it is invisible, hidden in a forest that is higher than the tallest buildings. The place has been declared a sanctuary by the Environmental Department of the government. The whole area is full of birds; we counted and identified about forty species in one afternoon. The water table, which is falling in most places, was rising last year under the gravel at Karagiri. Soil is being built up, not lost.

What are a few lush acres among the million barren ones? It is important to me because it sounds a message: one man can make a difference. Dedication is what is needed, and faith. It is important, too, because the man who brought about this little revolution is not a professional farmer or a government official. He is simply a doctor who loves trees and soil and water. He was sometimes criticized by his board of directors, who said that his goal and objectives should be to treat leprosy patients and help rehabilitate them. Money should not be diverted to other goals like farming and reforestation. But Ernest has proved that concern for soil and trees benefits patients too. Buildings do not need to be air-conditioned when they are shaded by trees. Patients who see and participate in good practices on the land learn to reproduce these practices when they go home.

Not far away is the Vellore Christian Medical College, founded by the beloved American doctor Ida S. Scudder. She loved trees, and she insisted on building the college on an extensive piece of land where there would be room for growth and breath and gardens and trees. She was followed by others who had the same view. The first Indian director was also a woman, Dr. Hilda Lazerus. She doubtless had claims to fame in her own medical specialty, but I remember her for her love of trees. From time to time she would go on inspection tours around all the buildings, including the staff houses. All waste water from basins and baths was discharged over the ground outside the houses by separate waste pipes from each sink or basin. Hilda Lazerus always spotted the waste pipe that was without a tree or a vegetable plot to nourish. She would call up any householder, even a senior professor in the college, and would insist that a papaya tree be planted to use the waste water from the pipe. The next day a seedling or even just a seed would be delivered to his door.

Hilda Lazerus is long gone, but her trees remain, and her philosophy remains too. The doctors who received their training at Vellore are teaching their undernourished patients that they can stay well by using every drop of water to grow plants and fruit trees. The same philosophy has guided new outreach developments in public health and community medicine that are an important part of the work of the college. In my day we used to get excited and concerned about new drugs and new diagnostic equipment, but today when I visit, I find that the director of RHUSA, a center for community health, is more likely to be excited about preserving the water table, growing the right kinds of crops, and preserving the soil. This is health, and this is hope for the future, because the students who graduate from this college go all over India, and they go with concern for trees and water because they know that that is how life is sustained. I love to return to Vellore every year. It tells me that all is not lost, and that each of us can make a difference. There is still life in the land, and God still blesses those who recognize that "the earth is the Lord's."

I am a grandfather now. My grandchildren do not call me Tata, but I rather wish they would. It would not mean much to them, but it would remind me that in addition to the immortality of the spirit, we all have a kind of immortality of the flesh. If the children called me Tata, it would remind me that, down through the centuries, there may be many generations of people who will bear my humanity and who will enjoy life or who will suffer in proportion to the care that I now take to preserve the good gifts that God has given to us. Part of that care is exercised in teaching and in example. My grandson is called Daniel, and the next time he comes to visit me, I shall take him out into my garden and I shall scoop up a handful of mud and I shall ask him, "Daniel, what is this?"

From Paul W. Brand, "'A Handful of Mud': A Personal History of My Love for the Soil," in *Tending the Garden,* ed. Wesley Granberg-Michaelson (Grand Rapids: Eerdmans, 1987), 136–50. Used by permission.

For Further Reflection

Case Studies

Taxol. Scientists discovered in 1979 that 30 percent of ovarian cancer patients respond to a drug named taxol. Taxol comes from the bark of the Pacific yew, a scrubby conifer that loggers once discarded. It takes sixty pounds of bark from three one hundred-year-old trees to produce enough medicine for one patient. Because Bristol-Myers holds an exclusive patent on taxol, costs for a single patient could reach $250,000. Since twelve thousand women die of ovarian cancer each year, producing taxol for all of them would quickly wipe out the Pacific yew; one lobbyist maintains that taxol production could wipe out the trees in five years. Environmentalists contend that making taxol is living on capital; it is destroying an irreplaceable resource to gain a short-term benefit. But cancer patient Sally Christensen argues that she wants to live. She states quite simply that people are more important than trees. Indeed, these trees have no other economic value. Some claim that scientists will synthesize taxol within two years, cutting its cost by one thousand times. Christensen cannot wait.

In your church are state officials who must decide about harvesting the Pacific yew. What choice is best? Should society sacrifice the Pacific yew to save lives until scientists synthesize taxol? Since production of natural taxol cannot meet the demand, who decides who would receive treatment? (Reported in *Newsweek*, 5 August 1991. Christensen died early in 1992. In November 1992, scientists synthesized taxol.)

Pollution and anencephaly. Six poor mothers, in and around Brownsville, Texas, gave birth to anencephalic babies during six weeks in March to April 1991. For all of 1991, six more mothers had babies with the same birth

417

defect, a fatal condition in which an infant's brain is incomplete or missing. With five thousand births a year, Cameron County should have an anencephalic birth every other year. What caused all the birth defects? Speculation centers on the hundred or so factories just across the Rio Grande in Matamoros, Mexico. Matamoros is a boom town where U.S. companies have built manufacturing facilities to take advantage of cheap labor and lax environmental enforcement. Open ditches in the area are evidence that officials look the other way. The ditches are full of gunk—oil, chemicals, substances of every kind. The parents of the anencephalic babies quickly blame these pollutants.

The Chamber of Commerce in Brownsville resists this causal connection, however. The Chamber notes that unwarranted negative publicity will cause U.S. firms not to locate in Cameron County, condemning residents to continued poverty. A study by the Center for Disease Control is inconclusive; it notes that the mothers of the deformed babies were poor, had little prenatal care, and ate inadequate diets. Lawyers for the mothers do not trust the study, believing that government studies must please many powerful interests. Which side should the church support? Should Christians press to clean up the environmental mess? Suppose someone proves it did not cause the birth defects? Does the need of church members for jobs require accepting some pollution?

Glossary

Carrying capacity: The number of organisms an ecosystem can support without degrading.

Citizenship view of ecology: Theory of environmentalism stressing that humans are part of the biosphere just like all other species.

Deep ecology: A deeply spiritual approach to ecology based on nature mysticism or pantheism.

Dominion view of ecology: Christian theory of environmentalism emphasizing the right of humans to use creation for their own needs; destruction of nature is prevented by individuals who own property rights over nature.

Stewardship view of ecology: Christian theory of environmentalism focusing on the responsibility toward God for protecting the environment.

Sustainable growth: Economic development that meets the needs of various groups while conserving the resources and carrying capacity of the environment.

Annotated Bibliography

Beisner, E. Calvin. *Prospects for Growth*. Westchester, Ill.: Crossway, 1990. Evangelical defense of a dominion view of ecology.

Berry, R. J. "Christianity and the Environment: Escapist Mysticism or Responsible Stewardship." *Science and Christian Belief* 3 (1991): 3–18.

Claims the Christian worldview can support a positive environmental ethic; includes a good bibliography.

Berry, R. J., ed. *Environmental Dilemmas: Ethics and Decisions.* London: Chapman & Hall, 1992. Influential British scientist and Christian edits a selection of essays addressing dilemmas faced by scientists working on real-life environmental issues.

Berry, Thomas. *The Dream of the Earth.* San Francisco: Sierra Club Books, 1988. Good example of a deep ecology approach to the environment.

Brand, Paul W. "'A Handful of Mud': A Personal History of My Love for the Soil." In *Tending the Garden,* edited by Wesley Granberg-Michaelson, Grand Rapids: Eerdmans, 1987, 136–50. A very personal narrative about valuing the earth.

Carson, Rachel Louise. *Silent Spring.* Boston: Houghton Mifflin, 1962. Influential book on the consequences of pesticide use on bird populations; a turning point in the ecological movement.

Derrick, Christopher. *The Delicate Creation.* Old Greenwich, Conn.: Devin-Adair, 1972. Witty, pessimistic discussion of a theology of nature from a traditional Catholic perspective.

DeWitt, Calvin B. *The Environment and the Christian.* Grand Rapids: Baker, 1991. Collection of essays focused on New Testament teachings about the environment.

Gore, Al. *Earth in the Balance.* New York: Houghton Mifflin, 1992. A U.S. vice president describes various environmental problems.

Granberg-Michaelson, Wesley. *Ecology and Life.* Waco, Tex.: Word, 1988. Readable defense of Christian responsibility to protect the environment; appendix reprints Lynn White's essay.

Granberg-Michaelson, Wesley, ed. *Tending the Garden.* Grand Rapids: Eerdmans, 1987. Fine collection of biblically and practically oriented essays; includes a response to New Age views on ecology.

Hardin, Garrett James. *Filters Against Folly: How to Survive Despite Economists, Ecologists and the Merely Eloquent.* New York: Penguin, 1985. Unique evaluation of simplistic and short-sighted economic and environmental analyses.

Kjos, Berit. *Under the Spell of Mother Earth.* Wheaton: Victor, 1992. Critique of pagan and New Age understandings of environmentalism.

Leopold, Aldo. *A Sand County Almanac.* New York: Oxford University Press, 1966 (originally published 1948). Influential naturalist writes about land use and the need for an ethic of the land.

Lovelock, J. E. *Gaia.* New York: Oxford University Press, 1979. Original source of Gaia hypothesis co-opted by environmentally minded New Agers.

McHarg, Ian L. *Design with Nature.* Garden City, N.Y.: Doubleday, 1969. Professor of landscape architecture and town planning strongly implicates Genesis in the ecological crisis.

Miller, Alan S. *Gaia Connections.* Savage, Md.: Rowman & Littlefield, 1991. Expression of holistic deep ecology.

Nash, James A. *Loving Nature.* Nashville: Abingdon Press, 1991. Discusses theological, ethical, and political dimensions of the ecological crisis from a mainline Protestant viewpoint.

Passmore, John Arthur. *Man's Responsibility for Nature.* London: Duckworth, 1980. Philosopher rebuts nature mysticism and Christian stewardship and then argues that secularized Western civilization provides the best resources for dealing with the environment.

Santmire, H. Paul. *The Travail of Nature.* Philadelphia: Fortress, 1985. Ambitious attempt, based on a history of theology, to rebut Lynn White.

Schaeffer, Francis A. *Pollution and the Death of Man.* Wheaton: Tyndale House, 1970. Early evangelical essay on the theological foundations for ecology.

White, Lynn, Jr. "The Historical Roots of Our Ecologic Crisis." *Science* 155 (1967): 1203–7. Classic essay famous for laying blame for the ecological crisis on biblical teaching about dominion (Gen. 1:28).

Wilkinson, Loren. *Earthkeeping in the Nineties.* Rev. ed. Grand Rapids: Eerdmans, 1991. Influential explorations of the many dimensions of the ecological crisis by evangelical scholars representing a stewardship view.

Part 5

Law and Government

11

Civil Disobedience

In April 1989, some fifty protesters broke the law when they spread out across two sides of an intersection adjacent to the National Institutes of Health in Bethesda, Maryland. In an action sponsored jointly by People for the Ethical Treatment of Animals (PeTA) and In Defense of Animals, the protesters blocked traffic for several minutes with a banner saying, "Animal Rights: An Idea Whose Time Has Come." Animal-rights activists have also broken into laboratories, videotaped conditions in the animals' cages, and rescued the animals.

Because of their opposition to military expenditures by the government, war-tax protesters break the law by withholding or otherwise seeking to avoid paying a sizable percentage of their income tax due. Some opponents of abortion stage "rescue" demonstrations at abortion clinics, breaking trespass laws as they sit at the entrances and block expectant mothers' access to the buildings.

Animal-rights activists, war-tax protesters, and antiabortion rescuers all break the law to achieve their goals. All are practicing **civil disobedience** (CD), the nonviolent, public violation of some law or policy, as an act of conscience, to protest the injustice of the law or policy and (in most cases) to effect or prevent change in the law or policy. While no definition of CD is without controversy, this one, or something like it, is commonly accepted.

Civil disobedience is nonviolent, not necessarily because its advocates believe that violence is wrong in principle (although many do), but because violence does not appear to be the best strategy for accomplishing the desired ends. CD is also public. Protesters desire to draw as much attention as possible to their cause. By contrast, when Christians under a repressive government, meet secretly to bury their dead, worship their God, and baptize new believers, they disobey their government, but their actions are not generally what ethicists refer to as CD. The same is true of those who hid Jews from the Nazis. By definition CD is public, although in popular usage, nonpublic acts of disobedience against government are sometimes designated CD.

Civil disobedience by Christians has been practiced since the days of the early church. In 298, Marcellus the centurion was killed for refusing to serve any longer in the Roman army because of his abhorrence of both the idolatry and the bloodshed required of those in military life. In the seventeenth century, John Bunyan was arrested three times and spent thirteen years in prison for failing to attend the Church of England and for preaching without a license. During the Nazi Holocaust, Martin Niemöller, Dietrich Bonhoeffer, and others in the Young Reformation Movement publicly opposed the Nazis through their sermons, writings, and other activities. For their actions, Niemöller received seven years in Dachau, and Bonhoeffer was hanged. In the early 1980s, Everett Sileven, pastor of the Faith Baptist Church in Louisville, Nebraska, spent months in jail because of his refusal to obtain a state license for his church-sponsored elementary school.

Theorists distinguish civil disobedience from illegal **conscientious objection** or conscientious refusal, based both on the grounds of the actions and the intention of the protesters. According to some ethicists, CD involves illegal actions that are political in nature, that is, the grounds for protesting are *commonly held* principles of justice and the good of society. Conscientious objection, however, applies to actions that are compelled more by *personal* moral and religious beliefs. Further, many hold that in CD, properly speaking, a person intends to effect or prevent change in a law or policy, whereas in conscientious objection, the protester is primarily bearing witness to a law or policy she considers evil. She is drawing attention to certain moral principles, but is not necessarily attempting to coerce others. As in the case of military-draft resistance during the Vietnam War, however, actual practice often blurs these distinctions. This explains why definitions of CD are controversial.

Theorists also recognize that CD is not revolution. In some cases, CD may pave the way for revolution, as when the American colonists refused to pay the stamp tax to the British government. But in CD as traditionally defined, protesters are not seeking to overthrow the established government. Revolution, by contrast, is the forcible overthrow of an established government by the people governed.

Another distinction is between direct CD (the violation of a law considered immoral) and indirect CD (disobedience to an admittedly just law as a means of protesting some other law or policy). Activists who violate the laws against trespassing in order to protest the use of nuclear power are clearly using indirect CD.

Scholars also distinguish between permissible CD and obligatory CD. In the first, the illegal protest action is considered permissible but not obligatory for everyone. With obligatory CD, the protest action is viewed as mandatory for all; the law is so evidently wrong that morally sensitive people must disobey. Christians differ, of course, on just which actions are permissible and which are obligatory. Some, for example, consider rescuing babies at abortion clinics permissible while others consider it obligatory.

Christians face two broad categories of obligatory CD: when the government commands them to do what is contrary to God's Word (as in Daniel 3 when the king ordered the Hebrews to worship the golden image) and when the government prohibits them from doing what God's Word commands (as in Acts 4 and 5 when the Sanhedrin forbade the apostles to preach the gospel). The first category necessitates passive CD—refusing to support the law by not doing what it requires. The second category calls for active CD—doing something illegal to protest the law. (Or it might call for conscientious objection at least.) If the government requires Christian schoolteachers to teach the equal value of all religions, they should practice passive CD. If Christian students are forbidden to pray quietly together in school lounges, they might practice active CD. Active CD requires greater courage than passive CD, and moral justification for active CD is more difficult to establish. Many Christians who readily support passive CD are hesitant about endorsing active CD.

Evangelical ethicist Stephen Mott explains the nature of CD (in its classical form) as subordination to government rather than defiance of government. An advocate of CD may consider a particular law unjust, but respects the system generally. Mott presents five criteria that must apply in order to justify a given protest action as an acceptable instance of CD: the law opposed is immoral, every possible nondisobedient recourse has been exhausted, the protest is not clandestine, there is a likelihood of success, and there is a willingness to accept the penalty for breaking the law.

In Mott's view, Christians may protest a law that violates the civil rights of a minority. Thus, in 1960, when four black students sat down at a segregated Greensboro, North Carolina, lunch counter and refused to leave after being denied service, their action met the necessary qualifications for CD. Their public disobedience, which prompted some seventy thousand others in the next year and a half to act similarly, and which led to the desegregation of eating places in over one hundred southern communities, is justifiable in Mott's view.

Mott points out that the method of CD is strategic noncooperation—a way of seeking justice through selective, socially potent forms of nonconformity. This does not imply, however, that all strategic noncooperation is CD. The

California grape controversy, for instance, involved strategic noncooperation, but it was not CD. The conflict between grape pickers and growers involved not only employee noncooperation in the form of strikes but customer non-cooperation in the form of grape boycotts in several cities across the nation. In no case, however, did the strikers or boycotters break laws. Civil disobedience is the best known, but not the only, form of strategic noncooperation.

Conservative theologian Charles Ryrie is much more restrictive than Mott in his understanding of CD. According to Ryrie, whenever a Christian feels compelled to disobey the government, "he must be sure it is not because the government has denied him his rights but because it has denied him God's rights." This view prohibits illegal protests intended to eliminate discrimination against people of a certain color or sex. Near the end of his article, Ryrie states that he believes CD is justified only when the government forbids one to worship God. Earlier in the essay, however, he presents the broader principle that CD "seems justified when the authority requires a believer to disobey the laws of God." Overall, Ryrie's article is a strong denunciation of present-day CD in almost every instance.

Norman Geisler, evangelical apologist and philosopher of religion, presents a helpful distinction for thinking about CD. He speaks of antipromulgation CD and anticompulsion CD. According to the first position, Christians should disobey their government when it promulgates (puts into effect and upholds) unbiblical laws or policies, even though these laws or policies do not compel Christians to do something wrong. In this view, Christians should rescue at abortion clinics, even though the government never requires them to obtain or perform abortions. According to the second position, CD is justified only when the law *requires* them to do evil. Geisler supports anticompulsion CD, but is against the antipromulgation position.

Baptist pastor and scholar John Piper, who has been arrested for rescuing at abortion clinics, favors antipromulgation CD. Because the 1973 Supreme Court decision, *Roe v. Wade,* upholds the purported right of women and doctors to abort life in the womb, Christians are justified in using CD to oppose the government. Piper contends, however, that rescuers are not really offending against the no-trespassing law, but against *Roe v. Wade.* He argues, contrary to Geisler, that the Bible supports activities that parallel abortion-clinic rescues.

Civil disobedience—not only to oppose abortion but for numerous other causes—is controversial among Christians because of the tension between submission to government and resistance to injustice. Both norms are biblically grounded, but the application of relevant Scriptures to specific cases is often difficult. The challenge to the church is in knowing how to contend for justice in an often unjust society, while respecting the God-given authority of government and while loving our neighbors—even abortionists, racists, and militant atheists—as ourselves.

Civil Disobedience as Subordination

Stephen Charles Mott

Civil disobedience accords with the major characteristics of the biblical teaching on the relationship of the believer to society. It is nonconformity with the world as in conflict with the new life under God. It is undertaken in order to establish justice. But in its classical form it also expresses subordination to government.

Civil disobedience, as it has been defined in modern times, is a limited tactic. It is based on the principles which regulate civil life.[1] In principle it recognizes the prima facie claim of governmental authority, and in method it appeals to moral sympathy in the general populace. Civil disobedience seeks to bring law and morality into greater congruence, and this congruence underlies respect for law.[2] Those who employ civil disobedience act within the framework of acceptance of the legitimacy of a particular system of law. The action taken implies that the system is generally worthy of support. Such an act respects rather than defies the authority of the government, and thus legitimate civil disobedience entails certain qualifications. (This does not mean that other forms of disobedience or resistance are never ethically valid. The nature of the action contemplated may be incompatible with the restrictions of civil disobedience. For example transportation of slaves through the Underground Railroad obviously could not be a public act.[3] Or in a highly repressive political regime, such as in Nazi Germany, the chances

1. John Rawls, "The Justification of Civil Disobedience," in *Civil Disobedience*, ed. H. A. Bedau (New York: Pegasus, 1969), 247.
2. Elliot M. Zashin, *Civil Disobedience and Democracy* (New York: Free Press, 1972), 127.
3. James F. Childress, *Civil Disobedience and Political Obligation: A Study in Christian Social Ethics* (New Haven: Yale University Press, 1971), 8.

of success may be negligible and the cost too high for it to be worthwhile to engage in public disobedience and accept the penalty.)[4]

Qualifications of Civil Disobedience

1. The law opposed is immoral. Because of the prima facie duty of subordination to government, the first characteristic of genuine civil disobedience[5] is that the law to be protested must be in conflict with a higher prima facie claim. The law stands in contrast to what is basic to life, dignity, and social harmony—indeed to the very purpose of law. The law violates values fundamental to personal morality and allegiance to God.

It must be recognized that subordination to government makes it impossible to avoid totally involvement in every instance of injustice. No social institution is entirely free from evil, and participation in any existing society involves compromise with the ideal of the Reign of God.[6]

The thought of Thomas Aquinas on obedience to civil law is relevant to contemporary considerations of civil disobedience. He wrote that laws can be unjust in two ways. A law is unjust if it is unfair or unconstitutional. It may be beyond the scope of the power which has been granted to the authority. For example, a law may not interfere with matters which depend on "interior movements of the will" (conscience), are essential for life, or are voluntary and private, such as contracting marriage or a vow of chastity. We would say that such a law interferes with basic liberty. A law is unfair if the ruler acts for personal interests, rather than for the common good, which is the legitimate basis for law and the possession of power. Laws are also unfair when they lay burdens unevenly on the governed. A law which violates the civil rights of a minority, we might say today, could be disobeyed because it fails to provide equal protection and thus distributes justice unevenly. Because these laws are not legitimate, says Aquinas, they are acts of violence rather than true laws. He quotes Augustine, "A law that is not just, goes for no law at all." Such a law is therefore not binding on the conscience; it has no power of obligation although one might go the second mile and obey it to avoid scandal or turmoil.

The second way in which Aquinas says that a law may be unjust is that it may be in conflict with the good itself, with God. This would include any-

---

4. Sanford Jay Rosen, "Civil Disobedience and Other Such Techniques: Law Making through Law Breaking," *George Washington Law Review* 37 (1968/69): 454.

5. James Luther Adams was the first to note the similarity between the criteria for civil disobedience and for just war ("Civil Disobedience, Its Occasions and Limits," in *Political and Legal Obligation*, ed. J. R. Pennock and J. Chapman [New York: Atherton, Nomos 12, 1970], 302). In both cases concern for basic prima facie duties imposes strict qualifications upon the actions taken.

6. Cf. Kent Greenawalt, "A Contextual Approach to Disobedience," in *Political and Legal Obligation*, ed. J. R. Pennock and J. Chapman, 347.

thing which is against the divine law. An oppressive law may contradict God's commands of justice for the oppressed or love for the neighbor. Aquinas states that such a law is not lawful at all. It *must* be resisted. One is obliged to disobey.[7] Accordingly, laws directly contrary to one's basic moral integrity and conscience should not be obeyed.[8] They are not legitimate; they do not exemplify the authority spoken of in Romans 13.

If it is a sin not to respect legitimate law and order, it also is a sin to fail to oppose unjust law and order. Disobeying unjust law has always been part of the struggle for justice. . . . [William] Booth wrote:

> Some men go to a goal because they are better than their neighbors, most men because they are worse. Martyrs, patriots, reformers of all kinds belong to the first category. No great cause has ever achieved a triumph before it has furnished a certain quota to the prison population. The repeal of an unjust law is seldom carried until a certain number of those who are labouring for the reform have experienced in their own persons the hardships of fine and imprisonment.[9]

To protest an unjust law, one may have to disobey a different one. How does one oppose a voter qualification law when one does not have a vote? How does one protest the absence of a law by disobeying it? The law actually disobeyed should not be a law that protects or provides for a value with a higher moral claim than the one opposed. One would not destroy property to protest discrimination in the mail service, a service which is a subsidiary good. One chooses the least important law which will allow an effective protest.[10] The effectiveness of the protest will usually depend on the relevance of the substituted law to the one protested.

It is important to reiterate that civil disobedience is a matter of *moral* dissent. Unacceptable motivations include self-interest, prejudice, unexamined emotional reaction, and unconfirmed factual claims.[11] One supports one's judgment with reference to moral principles—to a higher law. This criterion of civil disobedience, as well as those which follow, refutes the argument that civil disobedience is not different from any other type of law breaking.

2. Every possible nondisobedient recourse has been exhausted. Because civil disobedience affirms obligations to the legal system, one must first vigorously attempt to change the law through the means of change that the system pro-

7. Thomas Aquinas, *Summa Theologica*, 1.2, qu. 96, art. 4.
8. Michael Bayles, "The Justifiability of Civil Disobedience," *Review of Metaphysics* 24 (1970): 13; cf. Helmut Thielicke, *Theological Ethics*, vol. 1, *Foundations* (Philadelphia: Fortress, 1966), 1.533.
9. Booth, *In Darkest England and the Way Out* (London: International Headquarters of the Salvation Army, n.d.), 174.
10. Bayles, "Justifiability of Civil Disobedience," 17–18.
11. Ibid., 11.

vides. Some would apply this qualification legalistically to stifle any civil disobedience. However, there are situations in which the political processes are
flagrantly inefficient, and there are times when immediate action is necessary.
The meanings of "exhaust" and "possible" will be tempered by the context.[12]

3. *The protest is not clandestine.* The clearest sign of the affirmation of legal
authority in civil disobedience is the fact that it is carried out in full view of
the agents of law enforcement and of the public. This indicates that one is
not trying to benefit from disobedience or subvert the system. Openness is
required not only for the sake of principle but also for the strategy of appeal
to public opinion. There should be a clear statement of the purpose of the
act, and one should relate one's actions to one's goals in such a way that this
relationship will be clear to the outside observer.[13] For the same reasons the
act should be nonviolent. . . .

4. *There is a likelihood of success.* Michael Bayles distinguishes between two
types of civil disobedience. In the first, *personal civil disobedience,* obedience
is incompatible with one's moral integrity. One acts solely for the sake of
conscience, not for social change. Here the criterion of likelihood of success
is inapplicable. The second type is *social civil disobedience,* in which the purpose is to change or protest a law.[14] Since we are considering strategies for
social change, we are primarily concerned with this type. Because the violation of the duty to submit to governmental authority is a grave act, one does
not seek change through civil disobedience without some assurances that
one's purpose is attainable. Consideration should also be given to the proportion between the good that may probably be accomplished and the probable evil effects accompanying the good. The latter might include disrespect
for the law, violence, social conflict, as well as the disadvantages of the punishment that could follow.[15]

5. *There is a willingness to accept the penalty.* Because civil disobedience is
carried out in the context of support for the legal system as a whole, the participant in civil disobedience does not try to evade arrest, trial, or the penalty
which the legal system may assign to him or her. The rule of law means
indictment of all persons whom it is reasonable to believe have violated the
law, and acceptance of the rule of law includes a commitment to the equal
enforcement of the law. Therefore, respect for the system means accepting
the application of legal punishment to oneself.[16]

This criterion is closely connected with the openness of the act. One does
not flee prosecution or sentence. One does not try to hide one's act. By

12. Cf. Adams, "Civil Disobedience," 304–5.
13. Rosen, "Civil Disobedience," 455.
14. Bayles, "Justifiability of Civil Disobedience," 13–14.
15. Adams, "Civil Disobedience," 306–10.
16. Bayles, "Justification of Civil Disobedience," 20.

accepting the penalty, one reaffirms one's membership in the community. By accepting the penalty, one also admits that one's judgment is fallible. One might be wrong and society right after all.[17]

This criterion does not mean that one does not use all the means of defense available through the law. Using the legal system is one aspect of affirming it. In addition, the court process often provides the public and legal attention which the act of disobedience sought.

Civil disobedience contributes to the legal order. No constitutional process is so perfect that it avoids injustice entirely. Civil disobedience, stepping into the breaches of constitutional order, gives justice a second chance.[18] If it were not for the possibility of civil disobedience, departures from justice would have less chance of being corrected. Pressure for justice and resentment against injustice could be ignored and continue to build up until there was a threat of violence and revolt. Without the disturbance of civil disobedience,

> the legal system and the social order can become a stagnant haven of injustice, a harbinger of violence or of revolutionary action. When other checks and balances in the society and the government do not function adequately, civil disobedience can step into the breach and promote the fundamental values of a just democratic society.[19]

Thus civil disobedience can truly be a way of paying our obligations of respect and honor to the political system (Romans 13:7).

The method of civil disobedience is strategic noncooperation. . . . Civil disobedience aims at changing law. Real change of laws and customs is a long process, but the first step is to alter public opinion and to stir people to action. Civil disobedience may be considered effective when it contributes to either or both of these ends.

Civil disobedience shares the limitations of other forms of strategic noncooperation. It is a criticism of the social system but inadequate by itself for the positive achievement of justice.[20] It is not an alternative to political action within the system but a component of such action.[21] Strategic noncooperation is most effective when it can feed back into the constitutional system. For example, in the successful black civil rights struggle, the protests and boycotts were accompanied by the intervention of federal power. Civil disobedience contributed to the racial integration of public schools, but it

17. Greenawalt, "Contextual Approach to Disobedience," 347.
18. Richard A. Wasserstrom, "Obligation to Obey the Law," in *Contemporary Political Theory*, ed. A. de Crespigny and A. Wertheimer (New York: Atherton, 1970), 287.
19. Adams, "Civil Disobedience," 328.
20. Ibid., 330.
21. Childress, *Civil Disobedience*, 239.

had little effect until there was a federal decision, which in turn required the cooperation of a whole network of individuals and public agencies.[22] Because civil disobedience exists in the framework of a government the authority and legitimacy of which it supports, it accepts its place beside other aspects of the political activity of that system.

Civil disobedience is not the normal path to justice, but the situations which demand it in a world hostile to God are not uncommon, and they often involve the most crucial issues of justice.

22. Zashin, *Civil Disobedience*, 315. On this point, cf. 313–16.

The Christian and Civil Disobedience

Charles C. Ryrie

The Justification of Civil Disobedience on Philosophical Grounds

Various philosophical criteria have been offered to justify instances of civil disobedience. The first that is often heard is that no laws are to be broken other than clearly unconstitutional ones. The obvious fallacy in this is the question of what is clearly unconstitutional? The tendency of the Supreme Court in recent years to interpret the Constitution liberally makes it difficult to establish with certainty the constitutionality of any law. No one can meet the criterion of certainty of the unconstitutionality of a law in order to justify civil disobedience simply because certainty cannot be established. When there is doubt a citizen may become deliberately disobedient in order to test the law in relation to the Constitution. This was done, for instance, in testing the validity of the "Monkey Law" in Arkansas. However, it must be remembered that the one who breaks the law must submit to the penalty of the law if the case is lost. It may be observed, too, that under our legal system testing a law in court does not require mass violations of it in order to bring it to that test.

A second proposed criterion for justifying civil disobedience is that it must be used only as a last resort after all available grievance procedures have been exhausted.[1] But, again, who is to decide when we have arrived at that last resort which will justify an act of civil disobedience? Furthermore, someone might well decide that normal legal procedures for expressing

1. Cf. Abe Fortas, *Concerning Dissent and Civil Disobedience* (New York: New American Library, 1968), 75ff.

grievances would consume too much time and therefore he cannot wait until the matter comes to a last resort. The physician may need to make an immediate decision concerning an abortion without waiting for legal procedures to justify his act. He may do the right thing medically by not waiting, but not legally nor justifiably according to this criterion.

A third possibility, and one that is heard loudly today, is that civil disobedience is justifiable if done conscientiously. "Justification is by appeal to the incompatibility between political circumstances and moral convictions."[2] In other words, self-interest or personal gain is supposedly absent as a motive for the disobedience while appeals to morality and conscience are the bases. The obvious problem with this criterion is the difficulty of judging the conscientiousness of an action. Such judgment is in all instances subjective. Furthermore, as ex-Justice Abe Fortas put it: "But good motives do not excuse action which will injure others. The individual's conscience does not give him license to indulge individual conviction without regard to the rights of others."[3]

A fourth suggested criterion is that civil disobedience in order to be justified must be accompanied by complete submission to arrest and punishment. "Law presents a clear alternative: to obey this law or suffer this penalty. It is a precious right to be able to say to government: 'I will not obey this law, but I will accept the punishment connected with that disobedience. I will endure your penalty rather than commit an injustice.' . . . The law cannot say simply 'do this or do not do this.' It must say, 'do this or do not do this—or else.' And the 'or else' provides an essential alternative *within* the structure of law. . . . The man who acts in defiance of law with the intent to escape both the command and the punishment is acting outside the law. The man who says 'NO' to the law's command and stands still for the law's 'or else' is operating within the law."[4]

The problem with this viewpoint, though seemingly incontrovertible, is simply that it can be made to justify any act of civil disobedience whether or not constitutionality seems to be involved, whether or not it is as a last resort, and whether or not it stems from a moral judgment about the matter. Punishment for breaking the law is commonly regarded as a moral retribution, not as a perfectly respectable choice freely open to everyone.

It is significant that all of these philosophical criteria involve a large measure of subjective judgment in using them. Who decides what is clearly unconstitutional? When have we come to the last resort? Whose conscience is to be trusted as right in a matter? Who can decree that willingness to accept punishment justifies breaking the law? In other words, philosophy

2. Hugo A. Bedau, "On Civil Disobedience," *The Journal of Philosophy* 58 (1961): 656.
3. Fortas, *Concerning Dissent*, 28.
4. Darnell Rucker, "The Moral Grounds of Civil Disobedience," *Ethics* 76 (1966): 143–44.

offers no authoritative working basis that is not subject to whatever amount of flexibility the person trying to relate to that basis wants to use.

The Biblical Teaching on Civil Disobedience

Some may insist that the biblical teaching is open to subjective interpretation too. To the philosopher we point out that at the most it could be no more subjective than these philosophical bases. But there is a very major difference between philosophic bases and the biblical basis. However one interprets or interacts with the biblical teaching, it has the authority of God behind it, whereas all other criteria are man-made and thus authoritative only to the extent that any one or any group chooses to make them so. Christian doctrine has an existential dimension to it, but it is in the *use* of that doctrine, and not in its *content* which is God-given.

1. *Didactic data.* Our Lord clearly taught that His followers are citizens of two worlds and that they must discharge responsibilities in both realms. His classic statement on the subject was: "Render to Caesar the things that are Caesar's, and to God the things that are God's" (Mark 12:17). In relation to the spiritual kingdom, God's servants do not fight (John 18:36); but soldiers, even repentant ones, are a legitimate part of the order of this world's kingdoms (Luke 3:14).

It is the apostles, however, who gave more detail concerning the believer's responsibility to the government under which he lives. Paul commanded submission to the government (Rom. 13:1–7) because authority is ordained of God (v. 1) (notice that nothing is said about only certain forms of government being ordained of God), because resistance to government is ultimately resistance to God (v. 2), because government opposes evil (v. 4) and because conscience tells us to be subject (v. 5). Interestingly, no exceptions are given to these four reasons for obeying government that would justify civil disobedience. In the contrary, ways are spelled out to show obedience; and they are dues (personal taxes), tribute (probably export and import taxes), fear and honor.

Eight or nine years later, after having had much personal involvement with the Roman government under which he lived (including several imprisonments), Paul had not changed his mind about the teaching he had written before in Romans. He said again essentially the same thing: "Put them in mind to be subject [this is the same verb as in Rom. 13:1] to principalities and powers [this is also the same word as in the previous passage], to obey magistrates, to be ready to [do] every good work" (Titus 3:1). Maltreatment at the hands of the Roman government had evidently not provided Paul with sufficient existential grounds for changing his teaching (cf. 1 Thess. 2:2).

About the same time as Paul was writing to Titus, Peter wrote a similar word on submitting to government (1 Peter 2:13–17). The reasons he lists for obeying are: in order to show by obeying God-ordained government our obedience to God Himself (v. 13), because it is the will of God (v. 15), and it is a part of a good testimony to the unsaved (v. 15). This obedience, according to Peter, should extend to every ordinance and to all rulers. Again no exceptions are indicated either because of the type of government or the conscience of the believer. Actually the principle underlying this concept of civil obedience is the believer's position as a servant of God (v. 16). In summary, the didactic data of Scripture [teach] complete civil obedience on the part of Christians and [do] not indicate any exceptions to this principle.

2. *Historical data.* Both the Pauline and Petrine teaching were written under the reign of the Emperor Nero (54–68). Romans was written during the first period of his reign, the celebrated quinquennium, which was characterized by good government and popularity. It is reported that Seneca said of Nero that he was incapable of learning cruelty. Royal intrigue, however, led by his mother, resulted in her death in A.D. 60 and in a definite change of pattern of life and government on the part of Nero. He plunged deeper and deeper into personal dissipation and brought the empire into bankruptcy. On July 18, 64, Rome began to burn, and whatever Nero's part may or may not have been in this, the populace wanted a scapegoat and suspicion surrounded Nero. To divert this from himself he attempted to lay the blame on the Christians. Tacitus described the process in this way:

"Wherefore in order to allay the rumor he [Nero] put forward as guilty, and afflicted with the most exquisite punishments those who were hated for their abominations and called 'Christians' by the populace. . . . Therefore first of all those who confessed [to being Christians] were arrested, and then as a result of their information to a large number were implicated, not so much on the charge of incendiarism as for hatred of the human race. They died by methods of mockery; some were covered with the skins of wild beasts and then torn by dogs, some were crucified, some were burned as torches to give light at night. . . . Men felt that their destruction was not on account of the public welfare but to gratify the cruelty of one [Nero]" (*Annals*, xv. 44).

Though not unquestioned, many place the writing of 1 Peter shortly after the beginning of this Neronian persecution. If Peter was in Rome at this time (which may be likely from 1 Peter 5:13), this makes his teaching about civil obedience even more significant.

3. *Illustrative evidence.* Thus far we have discovered no grounds for civil disobedience in the didactic or historical data. Are there illustrations which would give guidelines for possible exceptions to the principle of submission? Peter's responses to the Sanhedrin (Acts 4:19; 5:29) are usually cited as examples of proper civil disobedience on the part of the believers. They are not the best because the disobedience was not directed against the civil power, Rome, but against the religious authority of the Jewish Sanhedrin. And yet, in a certain sense these are good examples, for the jurisdiction of

the Sanhedrin was rather wide at the time of Christ. It had authority to order arrests by its own officers and to judge cases which did not involve capital punishment. Nevertheless, the area of jurisdiction and the cases judged were, as far as New Testament examples are concerned, in the realm of religious and not strictly civil matters. But from these instances in Acts a principle does emerge: disobedience of higher authority seems justified when the authority requires a believer to disobey the laws of God.

Failure to distinguish between civil and religious authority in the time of Christ has led some to picture our Lord as an example of civil disobedience. One underground newspaper caricature recently described Him as "a threat to established law and order" while another pictured Him as "conspiring to overthrow the established government." It is true that our Lord was a threat to the religious establishment, but He Himself stated that He was not concerned about the kingdom of Rome, and Pilate understood Him clearly (John 18:33–38). This is a most interesting dialog, for when Pilate asked the Lord if He were King of the Jews, the Lord immediately countered by asking Pilate from whose viewpoint he asked the question. From a Jewish viewpoint He admitted to the claim, but from the Roman viewpoint He had no designs to be king. And the Roman context was all that concerned Pilate; thus he declared Him innocent. This shows that our Lord was not an anarchist trying to overthrow the Roman government.

When Shadrach, Meshach, and Abednego were brought into direct conflict with Nebuchadnezzar's decree to worship the golden image because of their God-given religion, they disobeyed. In this case, God vindicated their actions by delivering them from the fiery furnace punishment. The same was true for Daniel who disobeyed the unalterable law of the Medes and Persians and who also was delivered from the den-of-lion punishment. In neither of these cases was there any possibility of changing the law of the land. But the principle illustrated is the same as in Acts: subjection to the law of God takes priority in a believer's life over obedience to the laws of man.

It should not be assumed, however, that the path of civil disobedience in the name of obedience to God will always result in divine intervention for deliverance. "Others were tortured . . . others had trial of cruel mockings and scourgings . . . of bonds and imprisonments; they were stoned, they were sawn asunder, were tempted, were slain with the sword; they wandered about in sheepskins and goatskins, being destitute, afflicted, tormented" (Heb. 11:35–37). When civil law and God's law are in opposition, the biblical illustrations seem to sanction, if not oblige, the believer to disobey.

Indeed, our Lord's words concerning rendering to Caesar the things that are his and to God the things that are God's in effect deny to the state control over man's relations with God. Whenever a believer feels obliged to disobey his government, he must be sure it is not because the government has denied him his rights but because it has denied him God's rights.

438 *Charles C. Ryrie*

The Contemporary Ramification
of the Doctrine of Obedience

The doctrine of civil obedience is but a part of the larger teaching of Scripture on subjection to constituted authority. Angelic beings are subject to Christ (1 Peter 3:22); believers are to be subject to one another (1 Peter 5:5); the church is subject to Christ (Eph. 5:24); the Son shall be subject to the Father (1 Cor. 15:28); servants are subject to their masters (1 Peter 2:18); children are under their parents (1 Tim. 3:4); wives are subject to their husbands (Col. 3:18); young people are to be subject to their elders (1 Peter 5:5); church members are to be governed by their leaders (Heb. 13:7, 17); and believers are to be subject to their government. It is part of a total doctrine of obedience.

At least one educator has recognized the integral relationship between all these facets of life. Dr. Max Rafferty lays the blame for the present disorder on misdirected ministers, soft judges, permissive psychologists, but mostly on parents who have abdicated their parental authority.[5] Whether or not one agrees with his analysis, it is difficult to deny the fact that many areas of obedience to authority are interrelated in the Scriptures. Therefore, breakdown in one will likely involve breakdowns in the others, and that is exactly what is happening in our contemporary society. Civil disobedience is only a public display of ecclesiastical disobedience which in turn is the fruit of disobedience in the home, and so on. If this is true, then the Christian should demonstrate orderliness within the various spheres to which he is related. When he is under authority he should submit obediently; when he is in authority he should lead decisively. It is nothing short of hypocrisy for a Christian to decry public acts of disobedience while he perpetrates private ones.

The Eschatological Ramification of Disobedience

But the world seems to be plunging rapidly down the path of increasing lawlessness in many areas of life. Where will it all end? The Bible answers that question quite plainly and vividly in 2 Timothy 3:1–5. There are listed eighteen characteristics of the hard times of the last days, and many of them reflect lawlessness. Blasphemy is lawlessness against God; disobedience to parents is lawlessness in the family; [acting] without natural affection is lawlessness against one's own body; truce-breaking is lawlessness with others; fierce means untamed which speaks for itself; despisers of those that are good is lawlessness in respect to the established order; heady means reckless, and so it goes. No city, country, no class, no institution is exempt from this rampant lawlessness.

5. Max Rafferty, "Mom and Pop Deserve Blame for Syndrome," *Dallas* (Texas) *Morning News*, 31 March 1969, 14C.

I can think of no better situation into which a dictator could more easily move than into this state of lawlessness. Perhaps you read or saw *The Rise and Fall of the Third Reich.* The pieces of that picture should never have fit together. There was the unknown fanatic who was disliked and distrusted by almost everyone except his small band of followers; there were intelligent, civilized, and cultured people who should have seen what was happening, and there was a democratic government that should have prevented such a takeover. The pieces would not have fit together except for one ingredient which was present in the situation and that was lawlessness. In the wake of lawlessness Hitler was swept to power. The impossible happened, and the lawless situation was replaced by the law of a lawless dictator. And this is exactly what will happen on a worldwide scale before long. The lawlessness of our day is ripening the world for a takeover by some who will promise to bring order, even by the use of force, out of this chaos. Such a one will arise—to be sure after the church has gone to meet the Lord in the air—and, paradoxically, he is called the lawless one (2 Thess. 2:8). History will repeat itself, only this time on a much larger scale. Christians today must be certain they are not contributing to this climate of lawlessness in any sphere of life.

Is not the Christian to take leadership in trying to correct the ills of society and will not this responsibility sometimes involve and justify acts of civil disobedience? Certainly the believer has a social responsibility and in a word it is to do good to all men and especially to other believers. But he also has a civic responsibility and that is to be an obedient citizen. If the government under which he lives allows for means of legitimate protest and change, he surely may use them. But to take the law into his own hands finds no support in the Scriptures. The only exception seems to be if the government forbids his worshipping God. To serve Caesar and even fight for him, the Christian must do; to worship Caesar, he must not do. It is well to remember that the New Testament writers did not crusade against one of the worst social ills of their day—slavery. Paul advised Christian slaves not to let it matter to them (1 Cor. 7:22). He did not advise them to become martyrs in the cause of liberation. Indeed even when writing to a Christian master about a runaway slave who had become a believer, he only suggested that he be taken back and not punished. He never even hinted that the master should free his slaves because this was the Christian thing to do (Philem. 17).

The Christian's primary responsibilities are evangelism and godly living. Through witnessing he changes men; through righteous living he affects society; through private and public obedience he honors God.

From Charles C. Ryrie, "The Christian and Civil Disobedience," *Bibliotheca Sacra* 127 (April 1970): 153–62.

Biblical Submissionism

Disobedience to Government Is Sometimes Right

Norman L. Geisler

There is general agreement among Christians that there are times when a Christian should engage in civil disobedience. The real problem is where to draw the line, and there are two positions on this. One view holds that government should be disobeyed when it promulgates a law that is contrary to the Word of God. The other view contends that government should be disobeyed only when it commands the Christian to do evil. . . .

The difference between the two views can be brought out by a couple of illustrations. According to the antipromulgation position, a citizen should disobey the government when it forbids the teaching of creation in the public schools, because this pronouncement is contrary to the Word of God. This, they claim, limits the freedom of creationists to express their views, which are based on the Word of God. However, according to the anticompulsion position, the Christian should not disobey this law because it does not compel him to believe or teach that creation is false, nor does it negate his freedom to teach creation outside the public school classrooms. If a government commanded that creation could not be taught anywhere, that would be oppressive and could be disobeyed.

Abortion is another issue that focuses the difference between the two viewpoints. Agreeing that abortion is contrary to the Word of God . . . , the antipromulgation view insists that a citizen has the right to engage in civil disobedience in order to oppose abortion. Here the antipromulgationists are split between two camps: those favoring such violent actions . . . as bombing clinics, and others favoring only such nonviolent disobedience as illegal clinic sit-ins.

Anticompulsionists, on the other hand, believe that it is wrong to disobey the law in order to protest abortion. This is because there is a difference between a law that permits abortions and one which commands abortions. We should legally protest unjust laws, but we should not disobey them. It is one thing for a government to allow others to do evil, but it is another thing for it to force an individual to do evil. Only in the latter case is civil disobedience justified.

The Biblical Basis for the Anticompulsion Position

There are several biblical instances of divinely approved civil disobedience. In each case there are three essential elements: first, a command by divinely appointed authorities that is contrary to the Word of God. Second, an act of disobedience to that command. And finally, some kind of explicit or implicit divine approval of the refusal to obey the authorities.

Refusal to kill innocent babies—In Exodus 1:15–21, Pharaoh commanded that every male Hebrew baby be killed by the midwives. But the Hebrew midwives Shiphrah and Puah "feared God and did not do what the king of Egypt had told them to do; they let the boys live" (v. 17). As a result "God was kind to the midwives and the people increased and became even more numerous. And because the midwives feared God, he gave them families of their own" (vv. 20–21).

Refusal of Pharaoh's command not to worship God—Moses requested of Pharaoh, "Let my people go, so that they may hold a festival to [the LORD] in the desert" (Exod. 5:1). But Pharaoh said, "Who is the LORD, that I should obey him and let Israel go? I do not know the LORD, and I will not let Israel go" (v. 2). But the children of Israel left Egypt with a spectacular display of miraculous interventions on their behalf (Exod. 7–12).

Refusal of prophets to be killed by Queen Jezebel—In 1 Kings 18:4, wicked Queen Jezebel "was killing off the Lord's prophets." In defiance of her orders, the prophet Obadiah "had taken a hundred prophets and hidden them in two caves, . . . and had supplied them with food and water." Although explicit approval of his act is not stated, the whole context and manner of presentation implies that his action was divinely approved (see vv. 13–15), since the government has no right to compel the killing of innocent servants of God.

Refusal to worship an idol—In Daniel 3, the government commanded that everyone in the kingdom "must fall down and worship the image of gold that King Nebuchadnezzar has set up" (Dan. 3:5). But three Hebrew children defiantly replied, "we want you to know, O king, that we will not serve your gods or worship the image of gold you have set up" (v. 18). As a result, God blessed them and miraculously preserved them from the fiery furnace into which they were thrown (3:25–30).

Refusal to pray to the king and not to God—Few biblical stories are more famous than Daniel in the lions' den. It is a classic example of divinely approved civil disobedience. The king had ruled that anyone who prayed "to any god or man [except him] during the next thirty days shall be thrown into the lions' den" (Dan. 6:7). Daniel defied the order when "three times a day he got down on his knees and prayed, giving thanks to his God, just as he had done before" (Dan. 6:10). Here again God richly blessed the civil disobedience of Daniel who emerged from the lions' den confidently proclaiming, "My God sent his angel, and he shut the mouths of the lions. They have not hurt me because I was found innocent in his sight" (6:22).

Refusal to stop proclaiming the gospel—Although the authorities were religious, not civil, the principles are the same here as in the other cases of divinely approved disobedience. The authorities "commanded [the apostles] not to speak or teach at all in the name of Jesus" (Acts 4:18). But Peter and John replied, "Judge for yourselves whether it is right in God's sight to obey you rather than God" (v. 19). The text goes on to say that "the people were praising God for what had happened" (v. 21), thus indicating God's approval of their refusal to obey this mandate not to preach Christ.

Refusal to worship the Antichrist—During the tribulation period, the faithful remnant of believers will refuse to worship the Antichrist or his image. John said the false prophet "ordered them to set up an image in honor of the beast who was wounded by the sword and yet lived" (Rev. 13:14). But they refused and "overcame him by the blood of the Lamb and by the word of their testimony; they did not love their lives so much as to shrink from death" (Rev. 12:11). God rewarded them with "the crown of life" (Rev. 2:10).

All of these divinely approved cases of civil disobedience follow the same pattern. In each case the believers are compelled to act contrary to their beliefs. God has commanded in his Word that we worship him and not idols, that we not kill innocent people, that we pray only to him, and that we proclaim the gospel. But each civil command given in these illustrations compels believers to act contrary to God's commands. The civil commands do not simply allow others to act contrary to God's law; they force believers to disobey God's law. This is oppressive and should be disobeyed. . . .

It is legitimate civil disobedience to flee, if possible, from an oppressive government, and not to fight it. Israel fled from Egypt, and Obadiah and Elijah fled from wicked Jezebel. But none of them engaged in a war against the government. So whenever a government is tyrannical, a Christian should refuse to obey its compulsive commands to do evil, but should not revolt against it because of its unbiblical commands that permit evil.

This does not mean, of course, that we should not peacefully, legally, and actively work to overcome oppression. It simply means that we should not take the law into our own hands, since "the authorities that exist have been established by God" (Rom. 13:1). And when we cannot accept their command to do evil, then we must either flee or submit to punishment.

An Objection to the Anticompulsion View

Some have argued that the Bible commands us to rescue the innocent. Proverbs 24:11 says, "Rescue those who are being taken away to death." On this basis they insist that it is right to disobey government when innocent lives are at stake, such as the Jews in Nazis Germany or the unborn in societies in which abortion is legal. But there are several serious problems with this position.

First, Proverbs 24:11 does not support civil disobedience to prevent legal abortion. In fact, in this very chapter God enjoins civil obedience on the believers and warns against even associating with lawbreakers (v. 21). Furthermore, those being led away to death (v. 11) are probably victims of lawbreakers, not those being put to death in accordance with the law. There is no indication at all in the text or its context that the command is to interrupt the God-ordained adjudication of the law, even in capital cases.

Second, the comparison between German Jews and the unborn is invalid, since there are significant differences. The Holocaust was mandated by the state, whereas legalized abortion in America is only permitted by the state. The former would allow for civil disobedience but the latter would not. Furthermore, the Jews were unwilling to go to the gas chambers but the mothers (who are responsible for the life in their womb) are willing to have the abortion. Forced abortion is another matter; it would justify civil disobedience. In addition, failure to disobey the law to kill unwilling Jews is tantamount to assisting in the crime. However, failure to disobey the law that permits abortion is not assisting in the crime. Finally, the humanity of an adult Jew is obvious to all, but the full humanity of the unborn is hotly debated. In legalized abortion both the state and many doctors or aides have told the mother that the baby is only a "tissue" and not fully or legally human. These factors make it invalid to argue that because civil disobedience is justified to save Jews from a Nazi holocaust it is also right to engage in civil disobedience to prevent willing mothers from having legal abortions.

Third, the same logic could lead Christians to hinder people going into Hindu, Buddhist, or Mormon temples so as to prevent them from committing idolatry. It could also lead us to snatch alcohol and cigarettes out of unbelievers' hands so as to prevent their (and others') deaths. Likewise, it would justify civil disobedience to hinder a state-executed capital punishment simply because we believe the person to be innocent. But this is to presume one's personal belief can override the God-ordained governmental process of civil justice (Rom. 13:1).

From Norman L. Geisler, "Ethical Issues: Civil Disobedience," in *Christian Ethics* (Grand Rapids: Baker, 1989), 239–55.

"Rescue Those Being Led Away to Death"

John Piper

. . . Proverbs 24:11 says, "Rescue those being led away to death; hold back those staggering toward slaughter."

This is a general statement. No specifics are given. No illustrations. And the reason for this is so that we will not limit it to one group of humans and try to leave out another group. We must not limit it to Jews or white people or healthy people or rich people or intelligent people. It is general, not specific.

What does it teach us to do? It teaches us this: "If a group of humans is being taken away to death who ought not be taken away to death, the people who fear God in the vicinity ought to try to rescue them." What is being commanded here is some kind of intervention from us when we become aware of neighbors being killed who ought not to be killed.

I strongly believe Proverbs 24:11–12 is God's Word today to [his people] concerning the slaughter of abortion. I believe this text is a clear call to action (see also Ps. 82:3–4; Isa. 58:6–7; James 1:27; 2:14–17; 1 John 3:16–17). . . .

[T]he kind of rescue efforts that involve trespassing are biblically legitimate. This is not the only way to obey Proverbs 24:11. But I want to show that it is one right way and that conscience may well require it of some of us.

When I was arraigned in Ramsey County Court the first time January 6, [1989], I was given an opportunity to address the court. This is what I said to Judge James Campbell:

Suppose I lived next door to a very mean-spirited man who was so hostile that he put up "Do Not Trespass" signs all over the fence around his house mainly to keep me out.

One day I hear children screaming from his backyard. I run to the fence and notice a little child choking on something. Instinctively I jump the fence and try to save the child. I'm too late.

After a few days this mean-spirited man seeks a warrant for my arrest. I go into court and the judge, for reasons beyond his control, finds me guilty of trespassing and fines me $50. Would I be disrespectful of the law if I refused to pay?

Judge Campbell answered, "In that case you should appeal the decision, because of a special legal reality called the law of necessity. But there are distinguishing facts between that case and this one."

So I asked if he would be willing to tell me what facts. He paused and said, "The Supreme Court has ruled in *Roe v. Wade* that abortion is not a crime."

Here is my defense for those who oppose trespassing at abortion clinics. Judge Campbell said very plainly that I should appeal the sentence if I were found guilty of trespassing to save the life of a child.

I would *not* be guilty because of "the law of necessity." You are *not guilty* of crime or wrongdoing when you trespass to save life. That is what the judge said. That is what your conscience says.

Then why are all these people being arrested and found guilty? It is not really because of the trespass law. Every judge in this country would ignore the trespass law when saving life is at stake. This is not the law that is sending hundreds to jail. The reason I got arrested is not the trespass law; it is *Roe v. Wade.*

If *Roe v. Wade* had not stripped the unborn of their humanity, it would be no crime to trespass to save them. Therefore when we trespass to try to save them, we are not offending against the trespass law at all. We are offending against *Roe v. Wade.*

Some have argued that trespassing does not qualify as a biblical instance of legitimate civil disobedience. They say the Bible only condones breaking a law that "requires an act which is contrary to God's Word," or "prohibits an act which is consistent with God's Word."

The trespass law, they say, is a good law and does neither. So it is not right to break it. Moreover, there are no biblical examples of civil disobedience that parallel the contemporary rescues.

My response is twofold. First, *Roe v. Wade* does, in effect, "prohibit an act which is consistent with God's Word," namely, the (legal) protection of children. Legal because as Judge Campbell said, the "law of necessity" overrules the law of trespass when saving life is at stake. You are not guilty when you trespass to save innocent life.

But *Roe v. Wade* is a law that tries to stop you from doing this by stripping the unborn of their humanity. Therefore it is a wicked and indefensible law. It should not be obeyed when it, in effect, prohibits trespassing to save innocent life—a perfectly legal act (except for the intervention of *Roe v. Wade*).

My second response is it is not true that the Bible gives no examples of civil disobedience parallel to contemporary rescues.

Esther is a remarkably parallel example. King Ahasuerus sanctions the unjust killing of Jews throughout his kingdom. Esther is urged by Mordecai to intervene. She protests that it is against the law to approach the king unbidden.

It is remarkable that this is a kind of trespass law Mordecai wants her to break. "For any man or woman who approaches the king in the inner court without being summoned the king has but one law: that he be put to death" (Esther 4:11a).

Nevertheless Esther decided to risk it. She was not sure what the outcome would be, but said, "I will go to the king, even though it is against the law. And if I perish, I perish" (4:16). So she broke a royal trespass law to save those whose murder had been unjustly sanctioned by the king.

It is the climax and celebrated center of the book. It is not an incidental event. This parallel is close enough to make me feel in very good company when I am trying to rescue children by trespassing.

There are two other close parallels. The king of Jericho sanctioned the capture of Jewish spies. It wasn't even a bad law that spies should be turned over to the authorities (just like the trespass law is ordinarily a good law).

But Rahab contravened this (ordinarily good) law in order to rescue the spies. She was commanded to stop interfering with the arrest of the spies (Josh. 2:3). But she refused.

The other biblical parallel is Obadiah. Queen Jezebel sanctioned the slaying of the prophets of the Lord. But Obadiah intervened, at the risk of his life, to rescue a hundred of them (1 Kings 18:4, 13).

Rahab and Obadiah had not been commanded to harm prophets or spies, just as we are not commanded to have abortions. Rather they were prohibited to physically rescue those who were endangered by legal sanction as we are prohibited to physically intervene in abortion.

I find it very strange how eager some evangelicals are to discover a legal technicality that makes these biblical examples of "illegal" rescues right, but the rescue of innocent, unborn children wrong, even though *it is not illegal to trespass to save innocent life!*

A law which prohibits the justified effort to "rescue those being led away to death" is the kind of law Esther broke to save Jews, Obadiah broke to save prophets, Rahab broke to save spies, Corrie ten Boom broke to save Jewish refugees, and which some of us have broken—and will break again—to bear witness to the truth that even in a pluralistic land there is a limit beyond which government may not violate the law of God without physical resistance.

From John Piper, "Rescue Those Being Led Away to Death," *The Standard* (May 1989): 27–32.

For Further Reflection

Case Studies

Forbidden worship. You are a "tentmaker" missionary, working as an engineer in a country hostile to Christianity. The government tolerates foreign Christians if they do not evangelize citizens of the country, but the authorities severely persecute citizens who convert from the national religion. At times, depending on the whim of local judges, the state takes children away from their Christian parents. Some Christians have even given their lives for their faith. While many Christian citizens live in the country, they meet covertly in small groups and communicate with other believers secretly. Recently some became convinced, through a study of Acts 4 and 5, that they should no longer hide their faith. They have spread the word that in two weeks they will conduct a public baptism ceremony by the river outside the city as the beginning of a regular Sunday service schedule on the site. They are fully prepared to accept persecution. Because of your theological education and maturity, the national Christians in your city look to you for counsel. Should you advise your friends, some of whom are married with children, to engage in active CD by attending this baptismal service, or should you advise against it? What are the arguments for and against participation in the service?

Rescue the children. Your section of the city is well-known as the center of a large "adult movie" industry. Several major film makers of pornographic videos and movies operate in the area, allegedly within the law. The local authorities say they would like to remove the businesses, but claim their hands are tied. Although the film studios insist that only adults participate

447

as actors, some preschool children accompany the actors into one of the studios every morning. When questioned by the child-protection agency, the studio owner claims (truthfully, the authorities learned) that the preschoolers are children or stepchildren of the actors. The studio operators say they are merely providing child care for the employees. The film maker's high-powered lawyers have successfully blocked further investigation even though seemingly well-grounded rumors persist that these same children appear regularly in illegal "kiddie porn" movies.

More and more concerned Christians are seriously considering civil disobedience. They intend to violate the trespassing law by blockading with their bodies the entrances to the studio before the employees and children arrive. Their purpose is to draw such media attention to the situation that the studio will either be forced to close or at least be kept from having children on its premises. Some Christians in your church intend to "rescue" the children by blockading the studio, but others say they cannot condone breaking the law. What are the criteria for determining whether civil disobedience is justified, and how do they apply in this case? Should you participate in the blockade?

Glossary

Civil disobedience: Nonviolent, public violation of some law or policy, as an act of conscience, to protest the injustice of the law or policy and (in most cases) to effect or prevent change in the law or policy.

Conscientious objection: Refusal to submit to some governmental requirement, such as mandated military service, out of personal, moral, or religious beliefs, as a means of bearing witness to the perceived wrong in the law or policy.

Annotated Bibliography

Alcorn, Randy C. *Is Rescuing Right?* Downers Grove, Ill.: InterVarsity, 1990. Thorough argument for and defense of the anti-abortion rescue movement.

Childress, James F. *Civil Disobedience and Political Obligation.* Yale Publications in Religion, vol. 16. New Haven: Yale University Press, 1971. Superior examination of the major aspects of CD, including theological dimensions; a widely recognized work.

Davis, John Jefferson. *Evangelical Ethics.* 2d ed. Phillipsburg, N.J.: Presbyterian and Reformed, 1993, 189–206. Argues from Scripture that both CD and revolution are right in some cases.

Geisler, Norman L. *Christian Ethics.* Grand Rapids: Baker, 1989, 239–55. While CD in some instances can be justified scripturally, revolution cannot.

Hastings Center Report 19 (November-December 1989): 23–45. Helpful articles evaluating CD related to abortion, AIDS, and animal rights.

Laffin, Arthur J., and Anne Montgomery, eds. *Swords into Plowshares: Nonviolent Direct Action for Disarmament.* San Francisco: Harper & Row, 1987. Articles and first-person accounts defending the CD methods and experiences of nuclear-arms protesters.

Mawdsley, Ralph D. "Civil Disobedience and Christian Schools: A Biblical Perspective." *Christian Education Journal* 4, 1 (1983): 59–66. Valuable discussion of CD in general, using Christian schools as an example.

Mott, Stephen Charles. *Biblical Ethics and Social Change.* New York: Oxford University Press, 1982, 142–66. Defends CD under the broader category of strategic noncooperation.

Piper, John. "Rescue Those Being Led Away to Death." *The Standard,* May 1989, 27–32. A defense of abortion-clinic blockades.

Rawls, John. "The Justification of Civil Disobedience." In *Moral Problems: A Collection of Philosophical Essays,* edited by James Rachels, San Francisco: Harper & Row, 1975, 181–94. Careful philosophical analysis of the grounds for CD.

Robertson, O. Palmer. "Reflections on New Testament Testimony Concerning Civil Disobedience." *Journal of the Evangelical Theological Society* 33 (September 1990): 331–51. Valuable overview of fifty-seven New Testament passages that relate to the question of CD.

Ryrie, Charles C. "The Christian and Civil Disobedience." *Bibliotheca Sacra* 127 (April 1970): 153–62. Strongly opposes almost all CD.

Schaeffer, Francis A. *A Christian Manifesto.* Revised. Westchester, Il.: Crossway, 1982. Calls for force (even violence in extreme cases) to overthrow unjust laws.

Stevick, Daniel B. *Civil Disobedience and the Christian.* New York: Seabury, 1969. At times dated, yet still valuable overview of the subject.

Wallis, Jim, ed. *The Rise of Christian Conscience.* San Francisco: Harper & Row, 1987. Key articles, both descriptive and prescriptive, most published originally in *Sojourners* magazine, advocating CD.

12

Capital Punishment

Capital punishment is barbaric, discriminatory, and counter-productive; it should be abolished. Capital punishment is just, pro-life, and a deterrent against violence; it is a tragic but necessary duty of government. Both views are not only present in our society but are held by sincere Christians. As with so many ethical issues, no one position is endorsed by Christians universally. Advocates of both sides (and of positions in between) skillfully and passionately use scriptural, philosophical, and pragmatic arguments to defend their views.

Capital punishment derives its name from the Latin *caput,* meaning, among other things, *head, top,* or *leader.* Capital offenses are thus the most serious, those at the top of any list of offenses, those that call for the most extreme punishment—death. In the past, governments have used decapitation and hanging, but modern societies more customarily use the firing squad, electrocution, or lethal injection.

Christian proponents and opponents of capital punishment both use the Bible to support their positions. Opponents point out that the Lord did not kill some of the best-known murderers in the Bible. The stories of Cain (Gen. 4), Moses (Exod. 2), and David (2 Sam. 11–12), for example, show God's attitude toward even first-degree murderers to be in favor of life, not death. They also point to the story of the woman caught in adultery (John 8:1–11). Even though the story is probably not part of the original text of Scripture, it quite likely conveys accurately an event in Jesus' life. Opponents

451

of capital punishment say that the story shows that, however the death penalty for adultery was enforced in the Old Testament era, Jesus clearly taught pardon and repentance rather than capital punishment.

Advocates of capital punishment usually admit that the death penalty under the Mosaic law is not necessarily reproducible in exact fashion today. But they believe that capital punishment is God's way for human governments to punish serious offenders. The two major texts these advocates use today, Genesis 9:1–7 and Romans 13:1–5, carry weight independently of the argument from Mosaic legislation. In the Genesis passage, we find God commanding Noah and his sons to be fruitful and multiply throughout the earth. The Lord was concerned to repopulate the earth after the flood. To guarantee this, God put a fear of human beings within the animals so that they would not easily kill the few people then on earth. God also allowed humans to use the animals for food, as long as they did not eat meat with the lifeblood still in it. It is from this mention of animal blood, in the context of God's concern for the expansion of humankind, that the matter of human bloodshed is raised. Both animals and people who shed human blood will be required to give an accounting to God.

Genesis 9:6 is pivotal: "Whoever sheds the blood of man, by man shall his blood be shed; for in the image of God has God made man." Some scholars debate whether the first statement is prescriptive or descriptive. Is God demanding death for murderers (prescriptive) or stating what will inevitably happen if people resort to killing other people (descriptive)? Some ethicists, assuming that the text does authorize capital punishment, question whether the death penalty is mandatory or merely permissible. Further controversy revolves around the second statement of the verse. How does the image of God connect with the previous assertion? Is the divine image mentioned because, in effect, the killer is assaulting God's presence in the person? Or does the image, being from God, give human beings the authority to take the life of a murderer?

John Murray, the late Reformed theologian, discusses some of the questions in the Genesis 9 debate, arguing that this chapter, as well as the Bible as a whole, prescribes the death penalty for murder, for the duration of human history. To him, rather than showing disregard for human life, capital punishment for murder emphasizes the sanctity of human life.

Eric Hobbs and Walter Hobbs, an attorney and a retired university professor respectively, present a different perspective on the Scriptures. They agree that capital punishment is not intrinsically wrong, since God authorized it as part of the Mosaic law. But they hold that there is no clear biblical mandate for capital punishment today. Further, even if we could interpret some Scriptures as allowing the death penalty, the overarching thrust of biblical revelation argues against capital punishment as practiced in contemporary society.

Another issue that emerges from Genesis 9 is how and why the shedding
of blood enters into the argument. Does the author of Genesis understand
blood to be the essence of physical life, so that bloodshed calls for legal retribution? Or does blood symbolize the sacredness of life, so that the shedding of a killer's blood (whether animal or human) is viewed in a ceremonial,
atoning sense, needed to cleanse the earth from the defilement of sin? On
this issue, most writers hold to the former view and claim that Genesis 9
enunciates the life-for-life principle. Some, however, like Mennonite theologian John Howard Yoder and the Hobbses, adopt the latter interpretation.
Yoder argues in his article that in Noah's day, the killing of a murderer was
not a civil, nonreligious matter as in societies that practice the death penalty
today. It was, rather, a sacrificial act, developed in the course of humanity
and permitted by God, as a ceremonial compensation for a previous wrongful taking of life.

Those favoring capital punishment often point to Romans 13. Verse four
speaks of government's power to "bear the sword" and refers to the one who
rules as "God's servant, an agent of wrath to bring punishment on the
wrongdoer." The Hobbses again differ from Murray in that they see the
sword as the state's guarantor, not necessarily its means, of punishment.
They understand the sword as a symbol of authority, the ultimate coercive
power of the state, rather than as an executioner's weapon.

In his article for this chapter, Yoder raises an important hermeneutical
question: How do the Old and New Testaments interrelate and speak
authoritatively to ethical issues in society today? Those opposed to capital
punishment tend to favor the priority of the New Testament over the Old in
determining God's will regarding the punishment of criminals. In their view,
the law of love, demonstrated most fully in the life and death of Jesus, means
that we should seek the preservation of the offender both in body and in soul.
Further, since we all share in the guilt of the criminal by not doing all we can
to improve the society that produced him, we ought to search for remedies
other than killing.

In addition to discussing biblical arguments, we can bring other issues to
the fore by asking, Why does society punish criminals? More specifically,
what are the purposes of capital punishment? This question is relevant to the
debate because certain key arguments for and against the death penalty
depend on whether the claimed purposes for the execution are actually
accomplished by it. Some of the most commonly discussed purposes for
capital punishment include **retribution, deterrence,** and the protection of
society.

Retribution is that which is given or exacted in return for a wrong done.
Central to the concept is the idea of recompense or equivalent compensation. Many regard the law of retaliation, or *lex talionis,* as the key biblical
basis for retribution (Lev. 24:17–21). They argue that the *lex talionis* man-

dates government execution of those who take human life. But biblical scholars now understand this requirement of "eye for eye" and "life for life" as a general principle, not an exact legal requirement. In other words, the law of retaliation tells us that a penalty should fit the crime and must not exceed it. It does not appear that, even in Old Testament times, governing authorities exacted actual eyes or teeth from those who injured others.

Apart from the biblical material, however, retribution, or retributive justice, is given as the chief purpose of capital punishment. The murderer deserves to die. Since he ended the life of another, justice demands that his life also end. If retribution in this sense of exact retaliation is a valid purpose for capital punishment, it obviously accomplishes its purpose.

Most or all who advocate the death penalty, and even many of those who oppose it, agree that the murderer deserves to die. But according to opponents of capital punishment, retribution that involves the killing of a human being decreases the value of human life in a society. Rather than an act of vengeance, a lengthy prison term, even life imprisonment when called for, is adequate retribution for serious crimes. Christian opponents of the death penalty add that a spirit of exact retaliation smacks more of revenge than of justice and is thus ruled out by the New Testament teaching on forgiveness, mercy, and concern for the rehabilitation of the offender. Christian proponents reply that while we should forgive and extend mercy at a personal level, the state must demand capital punishment for capital crimes. The requirements of justice must be satisfied.

Both sides see retribution as a legitimate purpose for punishment, but the definition of retribution varies with the position taken on capital punishment. Defenders of the death penalty often (but not always nor necessarily) stress the principle of exact recompense, and some even insist on the validity of revenge. Opponents agree that punishment should generally fit the crime, but do not believe this requires either exact proportionality or a spirit of vengeance.

Another possible purpose of capital punishment is deterrence. This raises the question: Does the death penalty have a deterrent effect on potential killers? Writers have used more ink debating this question than they have in discussing perhaps any other aspect of the capital-punishment controversy. Proponents highlight statistical materials that show how the death penalty deters would-be murderers. Abolitionists emphasize data, however, that rebut the deterrence theory. Further, they claim, as the number of legal executions increases in a society, so does the number of murders. In their interpretation, government-approved killing actually brutalizes society and lowers the perceived value of human life.

Opponents of the death penalty also claim that the theory of deterrence assumes that most murders are premeditated so that would-be murderers weigh the pros and cons of their intended action. But since the majority of murders are committed in the anger and turmoil of the moment, thoughts of the death penalty do not affect the killer. Defenders reply, however, that if a society consistently applied capital punishment for those who deliberately kill, others would hesitate to murder—even in the midst of a heated argument. They point out, furthermore, that the Bible says clearly that the death penalty is a deterrent (Deut. 13:10–11; 17:12–13; 21:20–21). (These Scriptures, however, speak of crimes other than murder.) Given all this, many scholars on both sides concur that the arguments and statistical data for and against deterrence are inconclusive and that the debate must be decided by the consideration of more fundamental themes and values.

Although the deterrence factor is highly debatable, the death penalty, if carried out, obviously prevents that person from killing again. Defenders of capital punishment cite the protection of society from identified murderers as another purpose. Some argue that it is justifiable, and in some cases even necessary, to kill a murderer to prevent that person from taking more lives. Since many murders in our society, including many in prison, are committed by previously convicted murderers, hard-core killers should be put to death. If the killer is spared and he kills again, the government may bear some responsibility, at least indirectly, for the death of the victims. Opponents of this line of reasoning reply that while an executed killer will not kill again, his death only devalues life further, and this indirectly encourages more murders.

Among numerous objections to capital punishment, in addition to those discussed above, are the charge of discrimination and the argument from economic cost. Regarding the first, statistics consistently indicate that a higher proportion of criminals who are less-educated, poor, or people of color are sentenced to death than are those who are white, well-educated, or economically sufficient. Ernest Van den Haag, a criminal-justice scholar, addresses this objection, arguing that even though some inequalities do exist in the judicial process, justice nevertheless demands that society punish the guilty even if others who are guilty manage to escape similar punishment. Reform of the justice system, not abolition of capital punishment, is the answer to the problem of inequalities. Additionally, like Murray, Van den Haag contends that the sacredness of every human life and the good of society demand that when life is taken, the destroyer of life must himself be destroyed.

Another objection pertains to the economic cost of capital punishment. When the expense of all appeals is added to the cost of the initial trial, executing a prisoner is actually more expensive than imprisoning him for life. Florida, for example, the state second only to Texas in the number of executions since 1976, averages $3.2 million per execution. This is six times Florida's average cost of life imprisonment. Defenders of capital punishment reply that if justice were meted out more swiftly and carefully, fewer appeals and delays could lower costs.

The number of executions in the nation will no doubt continue to rise and fall periodically. The fate of convicted murderers will depend on what new studies are released, how the media cover the issue, which view seems politically advantageous, and which moral arguments gain or lose persuasiveness in the hands of ethicists and political commentators. As always, the responsible Christian, while taking contemporary data and analysis seriously, will above all seek to discern scripturally grounded moral norms and to apply them in a context of neighbor-love, guided by justice and mercy.

The Sanctity of Life

John Murray

As respects man in his relation to man the main question in this passage is whether the clause, 'by man shall his blood be shed' is a statement of fact or a command. As far as construction is concerned it could be either.[1] If the clause is simply a statement of fact, the thought is that divine retribution will take its course and will sooner or later catch up with the murderer; he that takes the sword will perish with the sword. God's providence will insure this outcome even though the human agent of execution will not necessarily be prompted by the motive or intent of bringing to effect the divine law of retribution.[2] There are considerations which favour the other interpretation, namely, that here a charge is given to man to execute the death penalty.

(1) If the text of verse 5b were simply, 'the blood of him who sheds the blood of man I will require', then the thought could well be that God will require it and will order it so in the movements of his providence. But the terms of the text, 'at the hand of man, at the hand of man's brother will I require the life of man', point definitely to a requirement laid upon the man's brother, that is to say, that God will require the retribution to be executed by another who is called the man's brother. (2) The final clause in verse 6, 'for in the image of God made he man', when taken in conjunction with the *requirements* expressed in verse 5, is most naturally interpreted as providing the reason why man is to inflict the death penalty upon the murderer. It would not be impossible to regard it as stating the reason why God orders it to fall out this way in the arrangements of his retributive providence. But since verse 6 follows upon the stipulation of verse 5b, we should expect verse

---

1. יִשָּׁפֵךְ could be Jussive as well as Imperfect Niphal of יִשָּׁפֵךְ:.
2. Cf. Calvin: *Comm. ad* Genesis 9:6.

6b to enunciate the reason for this requirement rather than the reason for what, as a matter of fact, is not overtly mentioned in the passage as a whole. (3) The later provisions of the Pentateuch respecting manslaughter distinctly require that the murderer be *put to death* and that he be put to death at the hand of the avenger of blood (cf. Num. 35:16–21). We may conclude therefore that it would be quite contrary to the analogy of Scripture, as well as to the natural force of the whole passage, to regard Genesis 9:6 as anything else than a charge given to man to execute the death penalty, and that verse 6b enunciates the reason why this extreme penalty is to be exacted.

Another question that arises in connection with verse 6 is whether the concluding clause states the reason why man should be given the authority to execute the death penalty or why the death penalty should be exacted. On the first alternative the thought would be that the image in which man is created and the consequent authority with which he is invested warrant[s] the exercise of this prerogative. On the other alternative the stress falls upon the heinousness of the offense; an assault upon man's life is a virtual assault upon the life of God. So aggravated is this offense that the penalty is nothing less than the extremity.

It must be said that both of these interpretations are in accord with the context. In favour of the first it may be said that the emphasis placed upon the requirement that each man's brother should exact the penalty may be regarded as carried over to verse 6 for the purpose of reinforcing man in the discharge of this obligation by reminding him of the prerogative that belongs to him in terms of the image of God in which he was created. In favour of the second alternative is the consideration that the clause in question does provide the answer to the insistent question: Why is such an extreme penalty exacted for the shedding of blood? Furthermore, it is more feasible to take the concluding clause of verse 6 as more directly related to what immediately precedes, namely, that the blood of the murderer is to be shed. The first view appears to load the thought that it is by *man* that the blood of the murderer is to be shed with more weight than the sequence and emphasis of the clauses warrant.

In either case, however, the accent falls upon the divine image in man as the rationale of the execution of the death penalty. Whether the fact of God's image in man is the reason why man is charged to take the life of another, or whether it is the reason why life is taken, we must perceive that the institution of capital punishment is grounded in the fact that the divine image constitutes man's uniqueness. And we cannot deny that, in this ordinance, capital punishment is established as the retribution to be meted out to the person who wantonly and willfully takes the life of his fellow. When we ask about the perpetuity of this institution, no consideration is more pertinent than this: the reason given for the exacting of such a penalty (or, if we will, the reason for the propriety of execution on the part of man) is one that has permanent relevance and validity. There is no suspension of the fact that man was made in the image of God; it is as true today as it was in the days of Noah. To this must be added the observation that, in respect of our relations to men, no crime is as extreme and, as concerns the person who is the victim, none is as irremediable, as the crime of taking life itself. Furthermore, in no other instance of biblical jurisprudence is the reason for the infliction of a penalty stated to be that man is made in the image of God. That consideration is reserved for this particular crime and for the sanction by which it is penalized. The institution of capital punishment for murder is, therefore, in a different category from those other provisions of the Pentateuch in which putting to death was required for many other offenses. Not only do the time and circumstances of the institution differ; the reasons which underlie the sanction in this case are radically different. We have good reason, therefore, for maintaining that the institution is of permanent obligation.

Of the ten words of the decalogue it is the sixth, 'Thou shalt not kill', that is based upon and enunciates the principle of the sanctity of life. The commandment is the brief and concrete way of formulating this principle which had been recognized and applied long before Sinai. In our modern context the translation 'Thou shalt not kill' needs to be guarded against misinterpretation. The commandment is not in the general terms of prohibiting the putting to death of another, as our word 'kill' might suggest. The term used in the commandment is the specific one to denote what we call murder. What is in view in the prohibition is violent, willful, malicious assault upon the life of another. The Mosaic revelation, which had the decalogue at its center, prescribed the death penalty for a great many offenses, and the sixth commandment could never have been understood as prohibiting the infliction of death as retribution for certain sins. Any argument against capital punishment based upon the sixth commandment does not have even the semblance of plausibility; it could be used only by those who abstract the sixth commandment from the total context in which it appears. . . .

Is there evidence to show that the ordinance of capital punishment is applicable in the order which the New Testament has introduced? In the Old Testament we found that it is correlative with the sixth commandment and is based upon the same principle which the sixth commandment embodies, namely, the sanctity of life. We have also found that the reason given for the execution of capital punishment is a reason that has permanent validity; man is made in the image of God and assault upon man's life is assault upon the life of God. The sin of murder does not become any less heinous under the New Testament; it gathers greater proportions with the increase of revelation respecting the sanctity of life.

It is conceivable that the progress of revelation would remove the necessity for the penal sanction. This is the case with the death penalty for adultery. And the same holds true for many other penal sanctions of the Mosaic economy. Does the same principle apply to the death penalty for murder?

In answer to this question it is necessary to keep in mind two considerations: (1) the specific character of the sin of murder and its peculiar gravity, (2) the time and circumstance in which capital punishment for murder was instituted. In reference to the first we must take into account the fact that, of all the sins which are concerned with our relations to our fellowmen, murder is the capital sin. As a violation of the summary commandment, 'Thou shalt love thy neighbour as thyself', it is in a unique category because, as far as this world is concerned, there is no way of being reconciled to the victim of our wrong-doing, no way of remedying the breach, no way of securing his forgiveness. As far as our relations to the victim are concerned, murder is an irremediable sin. Furthermore, the gravity of this offense is emphasized by the fact that only in this case is the divine image in man pleaded as the reason for the penalty inflicted; assault upon man's life is assault upon the life of God 'for in the image of God made he man'. In reference to the second consideration the ordinance of capital punishment was instituted at the epochal stage in human history when there was, as it were, a new beginning. There is a note of universality analogous to the institution of animal food and the covenant of perpetual preservation (Gen. 9:3, 8–17). For these reasons it should cause no surprise if this ordinance should stand apart from the other ordinances of the Mosaic economy which involved the death penalty for other kinds of sin. There is an unquestionable uniqueness attaching to the sin and to the reason for the infliction of the penalty, and, to say the least, this uniqueness would demand hesitation before we apply to this ordinance the abrogation which we find in the case of the death penalty for other sins under the Mosaic economy. With these considerations in view we are in a better position to examine the New Testament evidence.

First of all, we do not have in the New Testament anything pertaining to this institution that is parallel to what must be interpreted as our Lord's abrogation of the death penalty for adultery. Our Lord instituted divorce for adultery (Matthew 5:31, 32; 19:9); by implication he abrogated the Mosaic death penalty.

Secondly, the teaching of the New Testament regarding the power and use of the sword as the prerogative of the civil magistrate carries with it express warrant for the infliction of death. To suppose that the sword (Rom. 13:4; cf. 1 Pet. 2:14) can be restricted to lesser forms of punitive infliction and does not imply the extreme penalty is to go in the face of that which 'the sword' properly and obviously symbolizes.[3] This passage (Romans 13:4)

---

3. It is well expressed by F. A. Philippi: 'But this passage certainly contains a *dictum probans* for the position that even the N.T., instead of abolishing, expressly ratifies the right of governors to inflict the penalty of death; for while the sword stands here as a symbol of government,

therefore distinctly implies that to the civil magistrate is given not only the power but, as the minister of God, the right, the authority, to use the sword for the infliction of death as the penalty for crimes which merit this retribution. If we were to attempt to draw up a catalogue of such crimes we would encounter difficulty. But one thing is plain; in terms of biblical teaching the one crime that is placed beyond all question as falling into this category is that of murder. The right of the sword implies at least one crime for which death may be inflicted. That one crime, if there should be only one, is the crime of murder. This, above all others for the reasons given, warrants and demands the *jus gladii*.

In the third place, the apostle Paul, who penned Romans 13, in his defense before Festus said, 'If therefore I do wrong and have committed anything worthy of death, I refuse not to die' (Acts 25:11). Here we have a few eloquent facts. (1) Paul recognized that there were crimes which were worthy of death. How many or how few he considered worthy of such a penalty we do not know. But the biblico-theological background of Paul's thought would have settled for one beyond all question, the crime of murder. (2) Paul protests that he would not offer resistance to the infliction of the death penalty if he had been worthy of it. Paul's conscience was so attuned to the demands of justice that he would plead no deviation from rectitude even though he himself were to be the victim of its demand. And he would not plead deviation in the case of another, because Paul's ethic was governed by the command, 'Thou shalt love thy neighbour as thyself'. (3) Implicit in Paul's protestation is his recognition that some authority had the right to put to death. What authority he considered as invested with that right, whether the Roman government only or the Jewish people through the Sanhedrin,[4]

---

punitive authority in general, it describes that authority precisely in its uttermost expression as *jus gladii* in the proper sense of the word. It is therefore perfectly absurd, when the apostlE applies to the culminating form of the punitive authority of rulers an expression whose historically and juridically fixed signification cannot for a moment be called in question, to wish to assert that he denied to authority the right of exercising that which the sword *properly* symbolizes; comp. Matthew 26:52; Revelation 13:10; and respecting the actual exercise of the *jus gladii*, Acts 12:2' (*Commentary on St. Paul's Epistle to the Romans*, vol. 2, translated by J. S. Banks, (Edinburgh, 1879), 299.

4. On the moot question whether the Sanhedrin had authority in Paul's time to pronounce and execute the death penalty cf. Emil Schürer, *A History of the Jewish People in the Time of Jesus Christ*, trans. T. A. Burkill, et al. Edinburgh, 1890; reprint, Clark 1973, 1890),1; 187f.; Sidney B. Hoenig, *The Great Sanhedrin* (Philadelphia: Dropsie College for Hebrew and Cognate Learning, 1953), 88f.; Alfred Edersheim, *The Life and Times of Jesus the Messiah* (New York: Longman, Green, & Co., 1910), vol. 2, 556f., 569f. Undoubtedly the chief priests and the whole Sanhedrin sought to put Jesus to death and condemned him to be worthy of death (Matthew 26:59, 66; Mark 14:55, 64; Luke 22:71; John 19:6, 7) and Pilate said to the chief priests and officers 'Take him yourselves and crucify him: for I do not find any crime in him' (John 19:6). Yet, in answer to a similar reply on Pilate's part, the Jews said, 'It is not lawful for us to put any man to death' (John 18:31). The question is then simply that of the right of putting the

it does not concern us now to try to determine. It is sufficient to know that Paul assumed the right to exist and that he would not appeal from a judgment to execute the death penalty if he had been guilty of a crime warranting it.

We can scarcely overlook this same kind of conscientious regard for, and sensitivity to, the demands of justice in the penitent thief upon the cross when he replied to the other malefactor's railing: 'And we indeed justly; for we receive the due reward of our deeds: but this man hath done nothing amiss' (Luke 23:41). His recognition of just retribution for crime is consonant with the transformed state of mind which his prayer addressed to the Lord himself evinced. It is an eloquent index to the nobility of thought which sainthood carries with it; not only is it wholly diverse from the ranting and railing of the impenitent thief, but it has no affinity with the sentimentality that knows little of the sanctity of life or of justice.

We have sufficient evidence, therefore, for the conclusion that the institution of capital punishment is not abrogated in the New Testament but that it is one of the prerogatives of that civil magistracy which is an ordinance of God and therefore one of the respects in which we must needs be subject not only for wrath but also for conscience sake. The perpetuity of this sanction accentuates the gravity of the offense involved in murder. Nothing shows the moral bankruptcy of a people or of a generation more than disregard for the sanctity of human life. And it is this same atrophy of moral fibre that appears in the plea for the abolition of the death penalty. It is the sanctity of life that validates the death penalty for the crime of murder. It is the sense of this sanctity that constrains the demand for the infliction of this penalty. The deeper our regard for life the firmer will be our hold upon the penal sanction which the violation of that sanctity merits.

From John Murray, *Principles of Conduct* (Grand Rapids: Eerdmans, 1957), 107–22. Used by permission.

---

death penalty into effect. On the question of responsibility, as distinct from the authority to put into execution, cf. N. B. Stonehouse, 'Who Crucified Jesus?' in *The Westminster Theological Journal* 5, 2, 137–65.

Contemporary Capital Punishment

Biblical Difficulties with the Biblically Permissible

Eric E. Hobbs and Walter C. Hobbs

[I]n the United States today the death penalty neither is nor can be administered consistently with biblical standards.

This is not to say that we hold Scripture to forbid capital punishment. To the contrary, the death penalty was established by God in ancient Israel as the required response to a variety of wrongs, and civil authority as well as the "blood avenger" (the victim's next of kin) was empowered and expected to adjudicate accusations of capital offenses and to execute the guilty.

God's holiness does not change through time. It is preposterous to us to imagine that what in one era he viewed as sin he might later decide is righteous, or that what once he called holy he could later call evil. If at one time his moral purity accommodated capital punishment, it is not possible that at another time such punishment could be morally repugnant *per se.* Unlike blasphemy (for example) which is never biblically permissible regardless of circumstances, the death penalty is not intrinsically contrary to the character of God. He has himself at times directed that it be used. Any biblical indictment of capital punishment must rest instead on considerations extrinsic to the punishment itself.

On the other hand, God does often change the manner of his dealings with humankind. The history of his involvement with people from Adam to Noah to Abraham to Moses to David to the dispersion to Christ to Paul to us today is a history of changing circumstances within which we detect different ways by which God communicates his changeless character. He has always detested sin, and he judges it. But the satisfaction of that judgment

463

(by Jesus Christ) is illustrated sometimes by the sacrifice of animals, sometimes by liturgy, and sometimes by a variety of expressions of penitence he generously invites from the believer. It is similarly the case with capital punishment. In one era the capital offense might be persistent disobedience to parents (Deut. 21:18–21), in another it might be disobedience in warfare by the keeping of prohibited spoils (Joshua 7) and in another it might be a crime against the state (2 Sam. 1:1–16).

For us the question is not whether capital punishment *per se* is biblically invalid. In our view the answer is clear: it certainly is not. The question we face instead is whether capital punishment is biblically invalid in contemporary society. For reasons to be elaborated below, we submit that it is.

Many people, however, understand Scripture to require—not merely to permit under given conditions—civil authority today to continue to use capital punishment as an instrument of justice and social control. We shall examine their arguments first.

Is Capital Punishment Required in Scripture?

The thesis that God intends government to execute persons guilty of various offenses rests primarily on three texts other than Mosaic law (which arguably is directed solely to ancient Israel); these are Genesis 9:1–7, Acts 25:1–12, and Romans 13:1–5.

Genesis 9:1–7. The Genesis passage was addressed to Noah immediately following the flood, and it is therefore deemed by some to be applicable to all of human society: "I will require satisfaction of your life-blood from every animal, and from a man also I will require satisfaction for the death of his fellow-man. He that sheds the blood of a man, for that man his blood shall be shed: for in the image of God has God made man" (vv. 5–6). Even should one assume, however, the universal applicability of the principle expressed in the passage, there is yet cause to question the traditional interpretation that the death penalty is here mandated for murder (the text is silent about other conceivable capital offenses):

(a) To find such a mandate in the passage requires that one take the text prescriptively, when it is more reasonable to take it predictively. Yahweh is not shy about speaking in the imperative, as is evident from verses 1–4 and 7. But in verses 5–6, on which rests the thesis that capital punishment by civil authority is required in response to murder, Yahweh is instead stating what he shall do and what therefore will occur.[1] Whether he accomplishes that result by human agency or another means (including his own intervention)

---

1. It had not always been thus. When Abel's "blood cried to God out of the ground," God punished his murderer, Cain, not by death but by hardship and banishment. Cain, however, feared that others would seek to kill him. (Presumably he did not think that they would *need* a command!) But God specifically protected Cain from such capital retribution (Gen. 4:3–15).

is not indicated, but nothing demands the view that civil authority is or must be his instrument.

(b) Few if any persons today suggest that they find in this passage basis for the "execution" of animals that "murder" people. Society may for its own protection destroy animals that have killed or injured its members, but the moral and legal vocabulary of murder and execution, so pertinent when used with reference to human beings who kill others, is simply useless when the killers in question are beasts. Yet in verse 5 of this passage, which is alleged to require capital *punishment for murder,* God expressly includes animals among the killers to be killed in turn, drawing no distinction between their amorality and humankind's capacity to do evil: "I will require satisfaction of your life-blood from every animal, and from a man also will I require. . . ." We submit that the moral distinction is ignored here because the morality of murder is not at issue. We are aware that others disagree, holding the theme of this passage to be the image of God in humankind. Our view, in contrast (see [c] below), is that at this time in history God is attaching exceedingly high symbolic importance to the shedding of blood, and he is here making the point vividly. Whatever one's own position may be, however, the unavoidable reality persists that a text which is said to demand capital punishment for murder includes within its reach animals incapable of such immorality, thereby casting serious doubt on the interpretation.

(c) We have suggested that the substantive focus of the passage is on the significance of blood. The traditional interpretation treats "blood" as a euphemism for "life" *(per v. 4),* and the shedding of blood as equivalent to death. But blood in Scripture is not solely a metaphor. It is also invested by God with a covenantal importance, playing a distinctive role in his remedy for sin by signifying the satisfaction of his judgment (Heb. 9:10–22). "Without the shedding of blood there is no forgiveness." We submit that in this Genesis passage, the central significance of blood in the divine plan of redemption is being heralded to the new social order. To dilute the covenantal significance of that announcement, therefore, by treating the passage as if it were a call to the use of capital punishment, is in our view to miss the profound message of the text.

Acts 25:1–12. Here many people find New Testament warrant for the continued validity of the use of capital punishment as a civil measure. Given our view expressed above that capital punishment is not of itself biblically invalid, we need not be further persuaded that it is permissible under other than Old Testament circumstances. But we do resist any suggestion that the passage in Acts 25 reflects a requirement that capital punishment be generally employed.[2] In the incident reported there, Paul is undertaking his own

---

2. See, for example, Gordon H. Clark, "Capital Punishment," in *Baker's Dictionary of Christian Ethics,* ed. Carl F. H. Henry (Grand Rapids: Baker, 1973), 84.

legal defense before a lawfully constituted (though biased) Roman tribunal against accusations brought by Jewish leaders whom he insists are lying. Festus, the governor before whom Paul is being tried, wishing to ingratiate himself with those leaders, asks Paul if he is willing to be tried in Jerusalem, a change of venue advantageous to Paul's adversaries. Paul says no; this forum is the appropriate one. I haven't done anything unlawful against the Jews, and you know it. If I'm guilty of a capital offense—the only plausible legal charge, but one which can well be tried in Rome—then I'm ready to accept the death penalty. (Paul did not fear death, he welcomed it! See Phil. 1:23.) Otherwise, I ought to be set free. Rather than go to trial in Jerusalem, I appeal to Caesar.

Paul was willing to stand before a Roman court on a Roman offense which carried Rome's death penalty. But he was quite unwilling to stand trial in a kangaroo court made especially accessible to people who sought to destroy him with lies (if not first by ambush; see v. 3). It was a sensible position to take, and it prevailed. His appeal was indeed taken to Caesar (v. 12). But it is hardly evidence that God expects civil authority everywhere to employ capital punishment against the unruly.

Romans 13:1–5 includes the assertion that government "does not carry the sword without reason; it is God's agent to bring deserved punishment upon the evildoer" (v. 4). The passage is perhaps the most commonly cited ground for the view that God intends civil government to punish various offenders by death. But again, it is not without its difficulties, and two in particular compel us to a contrary position.

(a) The reason God's agent carries the sword, says the text, is to bring deserved punishment on the evildoer. In Paul's day as now, most offenses visited penalties on the offender far short of death, because death was simply too extreme a response to lesser violations of law and morals. It was not "deserved," even under the relatively harsh codes then in force. We do not read the term "sword," therefore, to be a synonym for execution. Rather we hold it to be the state's ultimate power of coercion available to insure that all punishment, no matter how slight or severe, is meted out. Stated differently, we understand the passage to say the sword is the state's guarantor, not necessarily its means, of punishment.[3]

(b) Verse 4 warns that inasmuch as government does have power to punish evildoers, the one who does wrong should be alarmed. In the traditional interpretation, verse 4 means that because "the sword," i.e., capital punishment, is designed to deter the evildoer, one does well to keep it in mind when contemplating action. We have no concrete data concerning the actual deterrent effect of the death penalty on first century people comparable to

3. For a more thorough elaboration of the point, see John H. Yoder, *The Politics of Jesus* (Grand Rapids: Eerdmans, 1972), 205–6.

the data reported above from the twentieth century. But we know that not even the terrifying prospect of crucifixion dissuaded the faithful in the time of Antiochus Epiphanes, 167–166 B.C., nor the insurrectionists in the time of Alexander Jannaeus, *circa* 88 B.C., nor the insurgents in the time of Varus, 4 B.C., nor the rebels in the time of Florus, A.D. 66, nor those who withstood for a time the siege of Titus, A.D. 70.[4] It is possible, we grant, that the noble motives of such victims places them in a class separate from that of the common criminal whom the sword is allegedly intended to deter. But we are skeptical. Presumably, those who put these thousands to death saw them also as common criminals. And we note that in eighteenth and nineteenth century England the likelihood of execution for petty criminality exercised apparently little deterrent effect. Consequently, we are inclined to doubt that the general public of Paul's day would be any more responsive than others who came before or after them to injunctions that they fear the sword. To insist, therefore, that the passage endorses capital punishment as a deterrent means of social control, is, in our view, probably to insist that Paul (Scripture) was oblivious to social reality. We prefer to forsake the popular position that the word represents execution and adopt the view stated above that the sword is the ultimate coercive power of the state.

The ultimate coercive power of the state to punish offenders, however, may seem at times to be no more a deterrent generally than is capital punishment specifically. Have we simply refined terms without impairing the basic thrust of the traditional interpretation of the passage? Again, we think not. We believe that the traditional interpretation misunderstands what and how legal penalties deter as they do. To the limited extent that they serve as deterrent, they deter only the "rational" offense (including, we recognize, *bona fide* first degree murder *et al.*, all other things being equal—which, of course, they seldom are). But as our anecdotes earlier suggested, punishment is virtually powerless against crimes of passion and, though only intimated above, against "crimes of survival" as well. In response to such behavior, punishment serves principally the illegitimate cause of revenge.[5] Romans 13:1–5, we submit, fits only a social system whose members can control their passions and whose needs are met. And that is precisely the community to whom the passage is addressed. Paul is there telling *Christians* that the penalties which may be visited on them by government for wrong behavior are of God—so watch out! "It behooves us to be law abiding both because of punishment and for conscience' sake" (v. 5). The passage is not,

4. D. H. Wheaton, "Crucifixion," in *The New Bible Dictionary*, ed. J. D. Douglas (Grand Rapids: Eerdmans, 1978), 281.
5. Revenge is to be distinguished from retribution. The latter is the painful consequence of unacceptable behavior, inflicted by God or his authorized representative. Revenge, on the other hand, is the vindictive, hate-driven, egocentric "getting even" which is forbidden to the Christian.

we are suggesting, a discourse on penology for the guidance of society at large. Paul is speaking only to Christians who profess to love the Lord their God with all their minds. His comments are offered not as justification for legal punishment based on a deterrence theory impugned by data, but as instruction to believers concerning their responsibilities and vulnerabilities to God-ordained civil government, "God's agent . . . who does not carry the sword [the ultimate power underlying law-enforcement] without purpose."

On the grounds of the three foregoing textual reviews, we find no basis for the principle that civil authority is obligated by God to bring capital punishment to bear on persons who are guilty of various grave wrongs. At most, capital punishment is a biblically valid option available to government when no other considerations rob it of legitimacy. In the United States today, however, capital punishment does not, in our view, pass biblical muster, primarily because the criminal prosecutorial system does not do justice. That system instead metes out punishment demonstrably disproportionately, laying a much heavier hand on the poor and the weak than on others. It claims in part to serve as deterrent, but appears to us chiefly to satisfy revenge.

Three Further Biblical Objections

Yet even if the criminal justice system were refashioned to make it just indeed, and even if revenge were to play no part in executions in the United States, the Christian would still be faced with three additional problems drawn from Scripture: (1) the finality of capital punishment; (2) the nature of capital offenses; and (3) the means of execution.

1) *Finality.* There are two branches to the difficulty posed by the finality of execution, and each considerably worsens the impact of the other. One is that death ends all hope of profound evangelism. The alternative to execution, namely, imprisonment, is understandably considered by many persons to be a fate worse than death. But the Christian knows that no matter how hellish our prisons may be—and terribly hellish they are—hell itself holds far more horror for the unredeemed. We recognize that Scripture does not permit the finality of death to preclude the death penalty absolutely, but we are also reminded that where Yahweh expressly authorized civil government to inflict the punishment, that government was in theory his own, operating under his direction.

In our culture, moreover, we wrestle with a complicating aspect of finality that heightens the difficulty of the first, namely the uncertainty (not to be confused with "unfairness") of our criminal justice procedures. On occasion "the real murderer stands up" just in the nick of time or, more tragically, too late. Unlike Yahweh, we mere humans have no assurance that we are not ushering into hell someone who did not deserve to be put to death. In our view, the possibility is itself sufficient to counsel caution.

2) *Offenses.* The nature of the capital offense—*which* deeds ought to be punishable by death?—is a question that should vex every student of Scripture who endorses capital punishment in our day. Except for the Mosaic law, God's Word is almost completely silent on the matter. In that law, murder of course is included, and manslaughter is not (Exod. 21:12–14). Also included are kidnapping (Exod. 21:16) and particular forms of incest (Lev. 20:12). But included too are the striking and the cursing of one's parent (Exod. 21:15 and 17), adultery (Lev. 20:10), homosexual intercourse between males (Lev. 20:13) and bestiality (Lev. 20:15–16). On what grounds then shall the Christian today affirm capital punishment for murder but not for adultery; for kidnapping but not for homosexual encounters among males; for treason or rape which are not found in Scripture's catalog of capital offenses,[6] but not for cursing one's parent, which is? How much, if anything, of ancient Israel's law is operative here, and what is set aside? On what authority?

If one holds that the determination of offenses considered capital is properly the function not of Mosaic law but of whatever government is in power (Rom. 13:1), then on what grounds should we, the sovereign people, hold forcible heterosexual rape to be punishable by death, but not homosexual rape or statutory rape or spousal rape? If murder should be punished by death, should that include the mercy-killing by an elderly wife of an octogenarian suffering excruciating pain in a terminal illness? If not, why not? This is not a mistake that would gain one sanctuary in a city of refuge; it is a deliberate killing (Num. 25:6–25). Where shall the Christian citizen, legislator, or judge turn for such answers if not to Scripture? And what will he or she find, whether driven elsewhere or to the Word? Such unanswerable questions lead us to doubt the practicability of a doctrine of capital punishment allegedly grounded in the Sacred Text.

3) *Means of execution.* By stark contrast, Scripture does address clearly the means of execution, but in terms most unpalatable to many in the contemporary Western world, Christians included. Are we biblically compelled to stone the murderer or to have the victim's kin (the "blood avenger") kill him? Would those who contend that Acts 25 or Romans 13 mandate capital punishment also insist that we must crucify the offender or behead him or run him through with a sword? Are we biblically prohibited from using less violent means, e.g., overdoses of a sleep-inducing drug? Again, if not, why not? Considerations of humaneness can not save us here, for if they suffice to overwhelm the biblical methods of capital punishment they suffice also to overwhelm the punishment *per se* in favor of gentler alternatives. The mandate of Scripture for given means of execution is as clear as the mandate for execution itself.

6. Rape is a capital offense only when the victim is "betrothed"; see Deut. 22:25–29.

One might argue that death, not torture, is the biblically prescribed penalty, so the least traumatic death is the one that ought to be inflicted. But (a) that principle is nowhere found in Scripture, and (b) it clearly was not practiced by Yahweh: even in ancient Israel, less traumatic means than stoning could have been devised by which to execute an offender. Moreover, would not softening the means of execution be a detriment to the alleged deterrent function of capital punishment? Ought we not, as DiSalle suggested, return to public executions televised for all to see? And if we do, would not stoning, or crucifixion, or beheading, or running through with a sword all be considerably more effective than lethal anesthesia?

In short, even if unlike us one works his or her way through the two earlier problems of finality and the nature of capital offenses, one may be impaled at last on the horns of a twentieth-century Christian's dilemma: Does one return to the methods by which offenders in Scripture were publicly executed, or does one repudiate at this juncture the very document on which is grounded the assertion that capital punishment is morally and socially required?

Conclusions

(a) We find no biblical evidence that God mandates the use of capital punishment by civil government today. At most, it is permissible when other scriptural concerns are met.

(b) We entertain serious reservations, however, about the just application of the death penalty by the criminal justice system in the United States today, and so we believe that capital punishment fails of biblical validity on those grounds.

(c) Moreover, even were the system revised to cure the flaws which now preclude the just use of capital punishment, we would still caution against cutting off an offender from additional opportunity of conversion.

(d) Similarly, we believe that the capacity of the criminal justice system for error poses too grave a risk to the innocent, given especially the eternal consequences of the penalty.

(e) In addition, we find no clear guidance in Scripture or elsewhere as to which offenses ought to be punished by death.

(f) Finally, what comment there is in Scripture concerning the means of execution of an offender is wholly incompatible with contemporary practice and sensibilities.

From Eric E. Hobbs and Walter C. Hobbs, "Contemporary Capital Punishment: Biblical Difficulties with the Biblically Permissible," *Christian Scholar's Review* 11 (1982): 250–62.

Noah's Covenant and the Purpose of Punishment

John Howard Yoder

The case for the death penalty as an institution in modern societies has several quite different roots. Different advocates appeal to quite different reasons in its favor. . . .

The first religiously based argument, . . . for most Christians, comes from the story of Noah. As we range around the argument, seeking the most solid ground, this is one obviously right place to begin. It appears literally to be a direct divine command:

> Whosoever sheds the blood of Man
> In Man shall his blood be shed
> For in the image of God
> he made Man.[1] (Gen. 9:6)

Does This Text Prove What It Has Been Assumed To?

The first task of the biblical interpreter . . . is not to read a text as if "from scratch," or as if its meaning were self-evident to every well-intentioned reader, but rather to protect the text from misuse, even to "liberate" its original meaning from the deposit of interpretations which have already been laid over it by centuries of readers. To say this is not to suggest that earlier readers were dishonest or insincere. It is merely to take seriously the fact that

---

1. The noun translated "man" (Hebrew *adam*) here is generic; it means humankind. The Hebrew reader's mind is thrown back to the beginning of chapter 2, where *adam* meant the human race, without gender division or individuation. That Creation narrative was the only place where God's "image" had previously been referred to.

they were prisoners of their cultures, as we are of ours, even as the text we are seeking to read was the product of its own culture.

We need to make a self-conscious effort to understand the focus of the worldview implicit in the culture from which any ancient text comes to us. Some tend to read a text like this as if it were legislation, providing, prehistorically, at no particular time but with validity for all times, that there should be a particular institution, equivalent to what we call the state, the basis for civil law, to protect threatened social values.

God's covenant with Noah was not that. We need to step back from such modernizing assumptions if we are to have any hope of understanding how the sanctity of life was really understood in the ancient Israelite setting where these words were first recited.

"Recited" is the right description of how this ancient text was originally used. This rhythmic quatrain (further rhythmic in that in Hebrew the words "blood" and "man" rhyme) is not part of a code of laws, though such codes did exist at that time in the ancient Near East. It was formulated as oral lore, recited by sages and priests, repeated by the old, and remembered by the young. It is part of the deep symmetry of things, fitting in with the seasonal, rhythmic reliability of nature:

> As long as earth lasts
> sowing and reaping
> cold and heat,
> summer and winter
> day and night
> shall cease no more. (Gen. 8:22 JB)

This is not legislation for a government to apply. It is wisdom, a prediction, a description, of how things are in fact, in primitive and ancient societies. The nature of things did not come to be this way only because God said these words, as if without the words, or before God spoke them, matters would have been different. That is true of some kinds of human laws, nonexistent before, which come into being only when voted by a legislature or promulgated by a king or other authority.

We also err when we tend to read this text as if the defense of life through the threat to life were a new arrangement, established only after the Flood. It hardly can be taken that way, as the text of Genesis now stands.[2] Things were already that way before the covenant with Noah; in

2. Expert Scripture scholarship has projected diverse hypotheses as to the original dates and original authorship of the several strands of the Mosaic literature. That speculation would call into question some simple arguments based on the assumption that a text like that of Genesis was originally a literary unity. There is, however, no serious scholarly claim according to which Genesis 9 would be older than Genesis 4.

fact, that was the way it was as soon as the first murder was reported. That arrangement is already presupposed in the account of Cain, in Genesis 4. There the first murderer, called to account for the life of the brother he had killed, said:

> My punishment is greater than I can bear;
> behold: you drive me from this ground.[3]
> I must hide from you and be a fugitive and wanderer over the earth.
> Whoever comes across me will kill me. (Gen. 4:13f JB)

What Cain feared was, as it were, a defensive reflex of society as a whole, of "everyone who sees me." There is no account of there having been a previous divine command demanding blood for blood. The response of Yahweh to the jeopardy under which Cain saw himself was to intervene, to protect his life by a "mark"[4] and to announce the threat of retaliation. Thus, the first intervention of God in Genesis, counter to the ordinary reading, is not to demand that murder be sanctioned by sacrificial killing, but to protect the life of the first murderer. Far from demanding the death penalty for murder, Yahweh saved Cain from it. That is the first and the most characteristic action of the God of the Bible with regard to our subject.[5]

Yet, the pattern of violence continued and escalated out of all proportion. Cain's descendant, Lamech, boasted:

> I have slain a man for wounding me,
> a young man for striking me.

---

3. The ground is personified. "The voice of your brother's blood cries to me from the ground" (4:10); the metaphor of "blood" for life is the same as in chap. 9. Yet the "cry" of the blood is not to be satisfied. God intervenes to save the murderer.

4. Patristic symbolic theology speculated that the "sign" given to Cain to protect him was *tau* or the cross. Biblical scholars hypothesize that it may have been the trace of a tattoo worn by metalworkers; in the ancient world smelting was thought of as a secret stolen from the gods of the underworld (Lloyd R. Bailey, *Capital Punishment: What the Bible Says*. Nashville: Abingdon, 1987).

5. JHWH (usually pronounced "Yahweh") is the proper name of God. "Lord" in the AV and in Jewish piety is a reverent substitution. Jehovah and Yahweh are hypothetical reconstructions of the name. Bailey (39 and 107) suggests that Yahweh made a mistake; that if vengeance against Cain had been permitted, then "violence in the earth" would not have escalated so as to necessitate the Deluge. This would take more argument than either Bailey or Genesis provides. Genesis 6:6 says that what God regretted was having created mankind, not having protected Cain. Bailey also makes much of the claim (40, 70) that narrative texts should not be taken as bearing moral instruction. This is an assertion without an argument. Of curse each genre of literature should be read in its own terms. Bailey would have done well to distinguish more than he does between Genesis 9 and the Mosaic civil code, or between "moral" and "civil" texts. But narrative can be the vehicle of moral instruction, especially in settings called *etiological*, i.e., texts which deal with why and how things came to be, or in texts exhibiting God's or Jesus' character.

> If Cain is avenged sevenfold,[6]
> truly Lamech seventy-seven-fold! (Gen. 4:23f.)

This is the normal pattern; fallen humanity responds to evil with *escalating* vengeance. Primitive peoples show the same pattern as Lamech, from the intertribal wars of Borneo through the bloody gang justice of the Sicilian hills and the American underworld, to the proverbial "feudin' hillbillies" of the Appalachians. Each *particular* act of vengeance is thought of as "setting things right" or as "defending the peace," but in fact the spiral escalation of vengeance and counter-vengeance raises the toll of suffering brought about by any one offense, far beyond any proportion to the original damage done.

Having opened our minds to the awareness that the reason for primitive revenge was not the same as our modern arguments, we can and should move on to note what is different about the agents of the action.

The ancient quatrain does not say who the "man" is who shall shed the killer's blood. Certainly, it was not a constitutional government by means of a trial by judge or jury. Historians tell us that it was the next of kin, called "the avenger" (*goel*, the same Hebrew word as "redeemer") who executed family-based vengeance. The mechanism of retaliation, once unleashed, had to run its course. Later laws spell this out. If a corpse was found with no way to know whom to punish, very special ceremonies were needed on the part of the elders of the nearest town to "cover" them against the blood-vengeance which was due (Deut. 21:1–8). A person who killed accidentally could be protected only by taking refuge in one of six designated "cities of refuge" and staying there for the entire life of the high priest (Num. 35:11–28, cf. Deut. 4:42f; 19:1–10). No ransom was possible for blood guilt, even when the death was accidental (Num. 35:32f). Nor was bloodshed the only occasion for such sanctions. Death was the penalty as well for dozens of other offenses. . . .

There are others who read the Noah story as if it belonged in Exodus or Leviticus, as part of a body of rules set out to govern the particular nation of Israel, to be established much later in the land of Canaan, in the light of the sovereignty of Yahweh, in whose name Moses was to make of his mixed multitude (Exod. 12:38) a nation. It was not that. When that civil legislation did arise later, it too was to have provision for the death penalty, as we shall see, but not for the same reasons, and for many other kinds of offenses.

The context of Genesis 9 is that of ritual sacrifice. The anthropologist will call it "cultic" or "sacred." These four rhyming lines about human killing do not

---

6. Lamech's reference to Cain should not mislead us to think that he was escalating what had been said before by Yahweh. (a) The vengeance threatened in Genesis 4:15 was to be inflicted by Yahweh, but Lamech avenged himself; (b) the threat of 4:15 was successful in deterring harm to Cain, and was not carried out.

stand alone. In the same breath, the text had just been describing animal sacrifice. As contrasted with the vegetarian arrangement implied before the Deluge, animal flesh may now be eaten, but only subject to a ceremonial sense of the holiness of animate life as such, which is represented by the blood:

> Every living and crawling thing shall provide food for you
> no less than the foliage of plants
> I give you everything, with the exception
> that you must not eat flesh with the life
> —that is, the blood—in it
> I will demand an account of your life blood
> I will demand an account from every beast and from man
> I will demand an account of every man's life
> from his fellow man
> he who sheds man's blood. . . . (Gen. 9:6 JB)

The setting of our text is thus the account, after the Flood, of God's authorizing the killing of animals for human consumption. In the context, it is evident that the subject of the passage is sacrifice. The sacredness of human life is described in the same breath with God's exclusive claim on the blood of the sacrificially slaughtered beasts, and as an extension of the same. To kill animals for food is not like picking fruit from a tree, pulling turnips from a garden, or cutting wheat in a field. It is an interference with the dynamics of animal life, represented by the flow of blood through the body, which humans share with the animal world. Every killing is a sacrifice, for the life of the animal, represented by its blood, belongs to God. To kill an animal is a ritual act; the blood belongs not to the killer but to God. There is no "secular" slaughtering of animals in ancient Israel. The blood of the animal is given to God by being sprinkled on the altar or poured out on the ground. The act of eating that meat is an act of communion with God. The provision for shedding the blood of a human killer is part of the same sacrificial worldview.

The closest approximation in the later Mosaic laws to the sense of the sacred which sanctions killing in Genesis 9 is the prohibition of serving another god (Deut. 13:1–16). This text emphasizes the responsibility of any individual to be the agent of retaliation, even against one's closest kin. A whole town could need to be slaughtered and even the property destroyed.

Other ancient societies, primitive or highly developed, used human sacrifice for many other purposes. The God who renews with Noah his life-saving covenant with humanity permits human sacrifice—for that is what is prescribed here—*only* on one specific grounds, namely, to correct for a previous wrongful taking of human life.

Thus, it is not at all the case that in addressing Noah God intervenes to make blood vengeance a duty, when it had not been so before. The pattern was already old. It is then a mistake to read the word to Noah as if it were a command, ordering its hearers to do something which they would otherwise not have done. It is not that: it is a simple description of the way things already are, an accurate prediction of what does happen, what will happen, as surely as summer is followed by winter, seedtime by harvest. That killers are killed is the way fallen society works; it is not a new measure which God introduced after the Deluge to solve a problem that had not been there before, or for which God had not yet found a solution. It rather restates, as a fact and as a prediction, in the framework of the authorization now being granted to sacrifice and eat animals, that the sacredness of human life, already stated when God had saved the life of the murderer Cain, still stands. Spoken just at the place in the story where the killing of animals is for the first time authorized, the point of God's word in Genesis 9 is to reiterate the prohibition of the killing of humans.[7]

Motives and Meanings for Primitive Revenge

The careful cultural historian will have to ask at this point which of several descriptions or explanations best fits the primitive fact of blood revenge. We cannot yet review fully the several answers to this question as they are operative in modern debate,[8] but we must at least recognize the wrongness of leaping past it to too simple an answer. What were the possible meanings for Cain's contemporaries or Noah's descendants of shedding a killer's blood?

1. It might be more precisely described as eradication, getting rid of the source of trouble. The Old Testament speaks of "purging" evil from the Israelite people.[9] This would be the social equivalent of what white blood cells do to microbes or what exterminators do to vermin. The organism defends itself against a threat by removing whatever threatens. The threatening organism has no rights of its own. It is removed because it is bad, not because of a particular bad behavior.

2. It might be described as imitation, *mimesis*. I do to you what you did to my friend, not out of some general theory of social hygiene but rather, primitively, reflexively, because it does not occur to me to do anything else.[10] You "have it coming."

3. It might be understood as intimidation. If as a general pattern it is known that those who harm others are harmed in return, this may keep them

---

7. Some have argued that "by man shall his blood be shed" is a simple future rather than an imperative; a prediction but not an authorization. That is too little. God avows that the retributive process is under his rule: "I will require a reckoning." Yet, what God thus owns is an extant practice; he does not create a new institution nor decree a new duty.

8. I shall describe the variety of views more fully on pp. 156ff. [of *The Death Penalty Debate*].

9. Bailey, 32.

10. [T]he ethnologist René Girard uses "mimesis" as a far-reaching interpretation of the origins of violence and of government.

from doing it. This interpretation has several levels of meaning. One is the more narrow, mental, and therefore more modern sense. The thought is that an individual, premeditating an evil deed, will "think twice" about the cost, and will therefore renounce the evil deed on cost/benefit grounds. "Deterrence" is another modern term for this. Intimidation also has a less mental, more primitive, more "educational" sense. The generalized practice of avenging certain offenses, it is held, tends to be one way a society has of trying to teach people what deeds are offensive, not to be considered, therefore hoping to make it less likely that they will occur.

4. Both of the above concepts, "imitation" and "intimidation," can be understood to be founded in "retaliation." The root *-tal-* means "such" or "like." One may believe that God or the gods or "the moral order" should be understood in terms of a kind of balancing exercise, whereby each harmful act needs to be "paid back" or "set right" by another harmful act of the same kind and dimensions. When the "moral order" is thought of in analogy to a courtroom, we may also speak of the *talion* as "vindication,"[11] but in the old Semitic setting the courtroom is not the best symbol for that.

5. None of the above is quite what we mean when we use the word *revenge*. Usually the term *revenge* connotes an element of passion.[12] To do something "with a vengeance" suggests disregard for proportion, or for limits or barriers. It reaches beyond "eye for eye." A vengeful society, or the individual avenger, demands retaliation, claims moral legitimacy for the vindictive act, and may draw emotional satisfaction from carrying it out. Some would avow "anger" as a valid description of the motivation that is at work in so punishing the offender, and some would disavow it. Others would say that there is no anger in justice.

6. None of the above is quite what we mean by "expiation." This term points past the harm done to the social order, to the offense against the will of God or the gods. The divine anger must be placated, or the cosmic moral order must be set back in balance, the offender must "pay." In some religious and cultural settings the divine wrath is understood very anthropomorphically: God gets "mad." In others, the claim is that the "balance" needing to be restored by punishment is quite dispassionate, objective like a court's judgment, and holy.

Certainly, these several possible characterizations of why killers are killed are not all the same. The differences are significant. . . . But now we want merely to understand the Noah story. Which of them most adequately describes the facts? Which of them is morally most or least acceptable?

On the above scale, most of those who today hold the death penalty to be

---

11. The analysis of the texts sometimes is thought to teach most firmly the divine demand for symmetrical retaliation.

12. Under "retribution" we shall return later to the question of emotion.

morally justified would hold to a somewhat sanitized, modernized version of "legislation" combined with "intimidation." This is what we previously referred to under the broader heading of "deterrence." It has the least basis in the ancient text.

One the other hand, most historians studying where the legal killing of humans actually came from in ancient society, including ancient Israel, would point to one of the more angry versions of "vengeance" combined with "imitation." Journalists watching in our own times the public outcry after some particularly brutal killing would agree with the historians.

Our debate to this day is skewed by the difference between these two interpretations. Is killing a killer a vengeful action against the evildoer himself? Or is it the restoration of divine moral balance through sacrifice?

For now, this first overview of the spectrum of reasons is intended only to provoke the reader's vigilance. We need to be warned against the assumption that we know easily just which of those meanings the Genesis text originally had for its first hearers and against the assumption that the ancient meaning has any direct connection with the reasons for the modern death penalty.

The provision of Genesis 9:6 is thus not a moral demand, saying that for every pain inflicted there must be another pain inflicted to balance the scales of justice. It is not an educational demand, teaching the offender (or destroying the offender in order to teach others) a lesson to the effect that crime does not pay. It is not a political order describing how to administer a healthy city.

The order underlying the words in question is ritual; human life, human blood is sacred—whoever sheds it forfeits his own. The demand for that "forfeiting" is not vengeance on the part of the victim's family, although it easily degenerates into that; it is the organic society living in immediate awareness of the divine quality of human life. The death which sanctions death is ceremonial, celebrative, ritual.

The killing of a killer is not a civil, nonreligious matter. It is a sacrificial act. The blood—i.e., the life—of every man and beast belongs to God. To respect this divine ownership means, in the case of animals, that the blood of a sacrificed victim is not to be consumed. For humans, it means that there shall be no killing. If there is killing, the offense is a cosmic, ritual, religious evil, demanding ceremonial compensation. It is not a moral matter; in morality a second wrong does not make a right. It is not a civil, legislative matter: it is originally stated in a setting where there is no government.

Ritual Worldview and Cultic Change

One way that the ritual worldview differs from our own is that there is no concern for personal accountability. The death penalty applied to an ox which gored a man. It applied to unintended or accidental killing. If the ritual worldview of Genesis 9:6 were to be applied to our culture literally, there would be no provision for exculpating minors or the mentally ill, no separating of degrees of homicide according to intention. We would execute the contractor whose bridge collapses, the engineer whose train is wrecked, the auto driver whose brakes malfunction, if death results. For every death, blood must flow.

Christians in recent centuries, in order to attempt to understand and describe how the laws of the Old Testament ought to be respected since Christ, have proposed to divide them into civil, ceremonial, and moral laws. They then explain that the "moral" laws continue to apply in all times, but that the ceremonial ones are abrogated when the sacrificial order is fulfilled in Christ as the final sacrifice and the final high priest. Some of the civil laws, it is held, should apply to modern states, and others were intended only for the government of ancient Israel. This threefold (really fourfold) distinction may help to organize our thought, but careful study of the death penalty provisions of the books of Moses makes it clear that the distinction is alien to that world.

The covenant given to Noah involved no such distinction either, but the elements we call "moral" and "civil" were not stated, not separated. We saw that Genesis 9 speaks of the blood of animals and of fellow humans as belonging to God—certainly a sacrificial concept. The covenant given through Moses was no less holistic. Just as the Christ who was to come would be prophet, priest, and king all at once, so the covenant established through Moses was moral, ceremonial, and civil all at once, not one of them in distinction from the others. For centuries after Moses there was in Israel no king, nothing specific to call "civil."

The distinction between different types of law has served, although in an indirect, illogical way, to make room for a valid point. The valid point, which these distinctions alluded to, is that there was going to have to be change over time in how the laws would apply, and that in those changes the sacrifice of Christ was to make the biggest difference.

It is the clear testimony of the New Testament, especially of the Epistle to the Hebrews, that the ceremonial requirements of the Old Covenant find their end—both in the sense of fulfillment and in the sense of termination—in the high-priestly sacrifice of Christ. "Once for all" is the good news. Not only is the sacrifice of bulls and goats, turtledoves and wheatcakes at an end; the fact that Christ died for our sins, once for all, the righteous one for the godless (Heb. 9:26–28; 1 Peter 3:18), puts an end to the entire expiatory system, whether it be enforced by priests in Jerusalem or by executioners anywhere else.[13]

---

13. Cf. Karl Barth, "The Command of God the Creator," in *Church Dogmatics,* vol. 3/4 (Edinburgh: Clark, 1961), 442f.: "Which category of particularly great sinners is exempted from the pardon effected on the basis of the death penalty carried out at Calvary? Now that Jesus Christ has been nailed to the cross for the sins of the world, how can we still use the thought of expiation to establish the death penalty?"

Thus, by asking where killing began, and finding in the stories of both Cain and Noah what is said and what is not said there, we have been led to the most precise statement of the specifically Christian reason for the death penalty's being set aside. There are other reasons as well, more widely effective in our world, in which Anglo-Saxon democracy has spelled out the implications of the Hebrew and Christian heritage, but this is the reason closest to the heart of the gospel.

That shedding blood exposes the killer to killing is expiation in the name of the cosmic order. The death of Christ is the end of expiation.

The Ritual Nature of Social Behavior

To kill a killer is a ritual act, we have begun to see, not primordially or only in a political sense. When people gather for the funeral of a public figure, when they build a wall around their house or buy an assault gun, when they fly a flag or take off their hats, the event is not adequately interpreted by asking about a specified moral imperative, or about a pragmatic social goal. We have just attempted briefly to explain something of this sense of the sacred as it shows in the Noah story; now let us note that it is still the case today.

When society takes a life, the action is, obviously, not being undertaken for the well-being of that person. Counter to the general moral rule, most simply stated in modern times by Immanual Kant, that a person is always to be treated as an end and not as a means, when a person is killed, that cannot be an action in that person's interest. It is a public ritual, celebrated in the interest of others, in the interest of the society's controlling elite and those who support them, and their vision of the society's well-being.

When a parent or a teacher spanks a child, when an offender is put in prison or fined, it can be *claimed* that it is done in order to "teach" that guilty person something. Even then, the careful psychologist or social scientist will warn us that the real "learning" resulting from that event is probably something else. A child trained by spanking may grow up to become a teenage gangster or an abusive parent. What beating a child teaches most effectively may well be less "don't get into the cookie jar" than "might makes right," or "if you cannot reason, use force." The same may be true of other punishments as well. The petty pilferer sent to prison may learn there the skills of the professional burglar.

So the claim to "teach him a lesson" is often factually wrong. Nevertheless, it may be sincerely so intended. The sincere intention may be that the offender himself should learn that "crime does not pay," so that he does not repeat the offense. The time behind bars may lead him to think differently.

Rationales for Rehabilitation

This notion of changing the offender, ordinarily called "rehabilitation," *can* be given as a serious reason for depriving the offender of his liberty. He is shown how wrong his actions were. He may become convinced that he is under society's control. He may be led to promise (sincerely or not) that he will not repeat the offense. He may be given time to show by his actions that his promise to behave is credible, and he may even be taught a trade or helped to finish school. This is why prisons were once called "penitentiaries," places to repent. Some persons, after a prison term, do not return to crime. As long as the prospect of a future life in freedom is real, there is *some* chance that this may succeed. Yet even in these cases it is not clear that the time in prison or other kind of punishment is what made the most difference in a person's readiness to become a good member of society.

But when the line of life is crossed, the entire "teach-a-lesson" rationale becomes a lie. The only persons who can "learn" from a lethal public ritual are the others.

- the victims of the past crime (if they are alive) or their relatives can take comfort from the fact that the person who hurt them has been hurt in return: "vengeance" is the ordinary word for this. Vengefulness, taking comfort in the pain of others, is not a good moral quality in an individual, but some feel that it becomes right when the killing is done by the authorities.
- those who stand to lose by a crime are reassured that it may be less likely to happen to them—although this confidence in the "deterrent" effect is as we have seen [earlier in this book] often mistaken.
- persons who have not committed a crime should be warned that they should not think of doing so, out of the fear that they may be caught and punished. Yet, in fact, the limitations of our enforcement system do not make that threat very real in the minds of most potential offenders.
- the civil authorities celebrate and reinforce their posture of social control. In the Aryan feudal roots of our common law, the authority to dispose of the life of one's subjects was what defined a lord's sovereignty. The killer claims to be the instrument of God; he celebrates that his authority to rule is legitimate, by having the right to destroy some of his subjects.

The purpose thus far of our itemizing a few of the diverse modes of motivation has not been to be complete, but only to be broad enough to open for the reader a sense of the complexity of things, and of the inadequacy of simple explanations.

From the book *The Death Penalty Debate,* H. Wayne House and John Howard Yoder (Dallas: Word, 1991). Permission granted by the authors. This section is a selection from a larger exposition of related matters. In the book, House has replied to some of Yoder's arguments reprinted here.

The Collapse of the Case against Capital Punishment

Ernest Van den Haag

Justice and equality. Regardless of constitutional interpretation, the morality and legitimacy of the abolitionist argument from capriciousness, or discretion, or discrimination, would be more persuasive if it were alleged that those selectively executed are not guilty. But the argument merely maintains that some other guilty-but-more-favored persons, or groups, escape the death penalty. This is hardly sufficient for letting anyone else found guilty escape the penalty. On the contrary, that some guilty persons or groups elude it argues for extending the death penalty to them. Surely "due process of law" is meant to do justice; and "the equal protection of the law" is meant to extend justice equally to all. Nor do I read the Constitution to command us to prefer equality to justice. When we clamor for "equal justice for all" it is justice which is to be equalized and extended, and which therefore is the prior desideratum, not to be forsaken and replaced by equality but rather to be extended.

Justice requires punishing the guilty—as many of the guilty as possible, even if only some can be punished—and sparing the innocent—as many of the innocent as possible, even if not all are spared. Morally, justice must always be preferred to equality. It would surely be wrong to treat everybody with equal injustice in preference to meting out justice at least to some. Justice then cannot ever permit sparing some guilty persons, or punishing some innocent ones, for the sake of equality—because others have been unjustly spared or punished. In practice, penalties never could be applied if we insisted that they cannot be inflicted on any guilty person unless we can make sure that they are equally applied to all other guilty persons. Anyone familiar with law enforcement knows that punishments can be inflicted only on an unavoidable capricious, at best a random, selection of the guilty. I see no more merit in the attempt to pursue the courts to let all capital-crime defendants go free of capital punishment because some have wrongly escaped it than I see in an attempt to persuade the courts to let all burglars go because some have wrongly escaped imprisonment.

Although it hardly warrants serious discussion, the argument from capriciousness looms large in briefs and decisions because for the last seventy years courts have tried—unproductively—to prevent errors of procedure, or of evidence collection, or of decision making, by the paradoxical method of letting defendants go free as a punishment, or warning, or deterrent, to errant law enforcers. The strategy admittedly never has prevented the errors it was designed to prevent—although it has released countless guilty persons. But however ineffective it be, the strategy had a rational purpose. The rationality, on the other hand, of arguing that a penalty must be abolished because of allegations that some guilty persons escape it, is hard to fathom—even though the argument was accepted by some Justices of the Supreme Court.

The essential moral question. Is the death penalty morally just and/or useful? This is the essential moral, as distinguished from constitutional, question. Discrimination is irrelevant to this moral question. If the death penalty were distributed quite equally and uncapriciously and with superhuman perfection to all the guilty, but was morally unjust, it would remain unjust in each case. Contrariwise, if the death penalty is morally just, however discriminatorily applied to only some of the guilty, it does remain just in each case in which it is applied. Thus, if it were applied exclusively to guilty males, and never to guilty females, the death penalty, though unequally applied, would remain just. For justice consists in punishing the guilty and sparing the innocent, and its equal extension, though desirable, is not part of it. It is part of equality, not of justice (or injustice), which is what equality equalizes. The same consideration would apply if some benefit were distributed only to males but not equally to deserving females. The inequality would not argue against the benefit, or against distribution to deserving males, but rather for distribution to equally deserving females. Analogously, the nondistribution of the death penalty to guilty females would argue for applying it to them as well, and not against applying it to guilty males.

The utilitarian (political) effects of unequal justice may well be detrimental to the social fabric because they outrage our passion for equality, particularly for equality before the law. Unequal justice is also morally repellent. Nonetheless unequal justice is justice still. What is repellent is the incompleteness, the inequality, not the justice. The guilty do not become innocent or less deserving of punishment because others escaped it. Nor does any innocent deserve punishment because others suffer it. Justice remains just, however unequal, while injustice remains unjust, however equal. However much each is desired, justice and equality are not identical. Equality before the law should be extended and enforced, then—but not at the expense of justice.

Maldistribution among the guilty: a sham argument. Capriciousness, at any rate, is used as a sham argument against capital punishment by all abolitionists I have ever known. They would oppose the death penalty if it could be meted out without any discretion whatsoever. They would oppose the death penalty in a homogeneous country without racial discrimination. And they would oppose the death penalty if the incomes of those executed and of those spared were the same. Abolitionists oppose the death penalty, not its possible maldistribution. They should have the courage of their convictions.

Maldistribution between the guilty and the innocent: another sham argument. What about persons executed in error? The objection here is not that some of the guilty get away, but that some of the innocent do not—a matter far more serious than discrimination among the guilty. Yet, when urged by abolitionists, this too is a sham argument, as are all distributional arguments. For abolitionists are opposed to the death penalty for the guilty as much as for the innocent. Hence, the question of guilt, if at all relevant to their position, cannot be decisive for them. Guilt is decisive only to those who urge the death penalty for the guilty. They must worry about distribution—part of the justice they seek.

Miscarriages of justice. The execution of innocents believed guilty is a miscarriage of justice which must be opposed whenever detected. But such miscarriages of justice do not warrant abolition of the death penalty. Unless the moral drawbacks of an activity or practice, which include the possible death of innocent bystanders, outweigh the moral advantages, which include the innocent lives that might be saved by it, the activity is warranted. Most human activities—construction, manufacturing, automobile and air traffic, sports, not to speak of wars and revolutions—cause the death of some innocent bystanders. Nevertheless, if the advantages sufficiently outweigh the disadvantages, human activities, including those of the penal system with all its punishments, are morally justified. . . .

The value of life. If there is nothing for the sake of which one may be put to death, can there ever be anything worth risking one's life for? If there is nothing worth dying for, is there any moral value worth living for? Is a life that cannot be transcended by—and given up, or taken for—anything beyond itself more valuable than one that can be transcended? Can it be that existence, life itself, is the highest moral value, never to be given up, or taken, for the sake of anything? And, psychologically, does a social value system in which life itself, however it is lived, becomes the highest of goods enhance the value of human life or cheapen it? I shall content myself here with raising these questions.[1]

Homo homini res sacra. "The life of each man should be sacred to each

---

1. Insofar as these questions are psychological, empirical evidence would not be irrelevant. But it is likely to be evaluated in terms depending on moral views.

other man," the ancients tell us. They unflinchingly executed murderers.[2] They realized it is not enough to proclaim the sacredness and inviolability of human life. It must be secured as well, by threatening with the loss of their own life those who violate what has been proclaimed as inviolable—the right of innocents to live. Else the inviolability of human life is neither credibly proclaimed nor actually protected. No society can profess that the lives of its members are secure if those who did not allow innocent others to continue living are themselves allowed to continue living—at the expense of the community. To punish a murderer by incarcerating him as one does a pickpocket cannot but cheapen human life. Murder differs in quality from other crimes and deserves, therefore, a punishment that differs in quality from other punishments. There is a discontinuity. It should be underlined, not blurred.

If it were shown that no punishment is more deterrent than a trivial fine, capital punishment for murder would remain just, even if not useful. For murder is not a trifling offense. Punishment must be proportioned to the gravity of the crime, if only to denounce it and to vindicate the importance of the norm violated. Wherefore all penal systems proportion punishments to crimes. The worse the crime the higher the penalty deserved. Why not then the highest penalty—death—for the worst crime—wanton murder? Those rejecting the death penalty have the burden of showing that no crime ever deserves capital punishment[3]—a burden which they have not so far been willing to bear.

Abolitionists insist that we all have an imprescriptible right to live to our natural term: if the innocent victim had a right to live, so does the murderer. That takes egalitarianism too far for my taste. The crime sets victim and murderer apart; if the victim died, the murderer does not deserve to live. If innocents are to be secure in their lives, murderers cannot be. The thought that murderers are to be given as much right to live as their victims oppresses me. So does the thought that a Stalin, a Hitler, an Idi Amin should have as much right to live as their victims did. . . .

From Ernest Van den Haag, "The Collapse of the Case against Capital Punishment," *National Review* (31 March 1978), 397, 402–7.

2. Not always. On the disastrous consequences of periodic failure to do so, Sir Henry Maine waxes eloquent with sorrow in his *Ancient Law* (408–9). [Reprinted as Sir Henry Maine, *Ancient Law*, Everyman's Library (History), ed. Ernest Rhys (London: J. M. Dent and Sons, 1917), 228–29.]

3. One may argue that some crimes deserve more than execution and that the above reasoning would justify punitive torture as well. Perhaps. But torture, unlike death, is generally rejected. Therefore penalties have been reduced to a few kinds—fines, confinement, and execution. The issue is academic because, unlike the death penalty, torture has become repulsive to us. (Some reasons for this public revulsion are listed in chapter 17 of my *Punishing Criminals*, Basic Books, 1975) . . . [T]he range of punishments is bound to be more limited than the range of crimes. We do not accept some punishments, however much deserved they may be.

For Further Reflection

Case Studies

Murderer turns evangelist. Robert Kelly was sentenced to death for the kidnapping, rape, and murder of two eight-year-old girls. He was twenty at the time, and this was his first violent crime. After his conviction, he became a Christian through the ministry of a prison Bible-study group. Admitting that he deserved to die for his crime, he allowed his attorneys to seek life imprisonment for him instead of execution. During his years in prison he found great joy in testifying for Christ. Christian magazines published two of his articles. He committed himself to an evangelistic ministry in prison for as long as he lived. After six years on death row and several stays of execution, however, he went to the electric chair. Should cases of genuinely repentant murderers be treated differently from those who show no remorse? Why? Do the Scriptures teach that the death penalty for murderers today is mandatory in all cases, permissible but optional, or totally unacceptable? Discuss retribution, deterrence, and the protection of society as they pertain to Robert Kelly's case.

Wrongful Conviction. Charles Bernstein sat in a Washington, D.C., jail, minutes from execution, when a messenger arrived with the news that his sentence had been commuted to life imprisonment. Two years later authorities found positive evidence of his innocence. He was released from prison and soon after received a full pardon. The question arises, What if the messenger had been detained in traffic? (Jerry and Laura Gladson, "Should We Restore the Death Penalty?" *Presbyterian Journal,* 5 April 1979, 8). How substantial is the argument that because irreversible mistakes are sometimes made and innocent persons are sometimes executed, capital punishment should be abolished?

Glossary

Capital punishment: Legal execution by the government of a person convicted of a serious crime.

Deterrence: As a theory related to capital punishment, the idea that enforcement of the death penalty in a society will prevent would-be criminals from committing crimes they might otherwise have committed. As a political stance, one that relies on the possession and threatened use of weapons—especially nuclear—to discourage or prevent attack.

Retribution: Something given or demanded in return for and in proportion to a wrong done; may or may not include the notion of exact retaliation.

Annotated Bibliography

Baker, William H. *On Capital Punishment.* Chicago: Moody Press, 1985. Overview of the key biblical texts and arguments; defends the validity of the death penalty.

Barth, Karl. *Church Dogmatics.* Vol. 3, pt. 4: *The Doctrine of Creation.* Edinburgh: T. & T. Clark, 1961, 437–50. Because Christ took on himself the death penalty imposed on all human beings, capital punishment has no place in the ordinary life of the state; only in extreme cases is it justified.

Bedau, Hugo Adam, ed. *The Death Penalty in America.* 3d ed. New York: Oxford University Press, 1982. Widely used anthology with selections for and against the death penalty.

Colson, Chuck. "Society Wants Blood." *Sojourners* 8 (July 1979): 12–15. An interview with the founder of Prison Fellowship who strongly opposes capital punishment with several practical arguments.

Henry, Carl F. H. "Does Genesis 9 Justify Capital Punishment? Yes." In *The Genesis Debate,* edited by Ronald F. Youngblood, Grand Rapids: Baker, 1990, 230–50. Supports the argument for capital punishment from Genesis 9 with other Old Testament texts.

Hobbs, Eric E., and Walter C. Hobbs. "Contemporary Capital Punishment: Biblical Difficulties with the Biblically Permissible." *Christian Scholar's Review* 11, 3 (1982): 250–62. Authors agree that capital punishment cannot be intrinsically wrong, but contend that, as practiced today, it lacks biblical validity.

House, H. Wayne, and John Howard Yoder. *The Death Penalty Debate.* Dallas: Word, 1991. House argues in favor of capital punishment and

488   For Further Reflection

Yoder argues against it, and then each offers a response to the other's argument. Helpful annotated bibliography.

Llewellyn, Dave. "Restoring the Death Penalty: Proceed With Caution." *Christianity Today* (23 May 1975): 10–17. Urges death-penalty advocates to examine whether or not their view is based on a careful and consistent biblical hermeneutic.

Moreland, J. P., and Norman L Geisler. *The Life and Death Debate.* New York: Praeger, 1990, 103–21. Discusses rehabilitationism, reconstructionism, and retributionism; opts for the third and provides helpful critiques of the first and second.

Murray, John. *Principles of Conduct.* Grand Rapids: Eerdmans, 1957, 107–22. Thoughtful defense of capital punishment from Scripture.

Reid, Malcolm A. "Does Genesis 9 Justify Capital Punishment? No." In *The Genesis Debate,* edited by Ronald F. Youngblood, Grand Rapids: Baker, 1990, 230–50. High-quality argument against the more common view.

Van den Haag, Ernest. "The Collapse of the Case against Capital Punishment." *National Review* (31 March 1978): 395–407. Argues that the death penalty is constitutional, useful, and morally justifiable.

Van Ness, Daniel W. *Crime and Its Victims.* Downers Grove, Ill.: InterVarsity, 1986. Superb, scripturally oriented study by the director of Justice Fellowship.

———. "Punishable by Death." *Christianity Today* (10 July 1987): 24–27. Chuck Colson's associate examines seven cautionary principles from Mosaic law for the administration of capital punishment; suggests that today's executions do not always conform to these guidelines.

13

Peace and War

In World War I, thirty-nine million people (thirty million of them civilians) died. World War II killed fifty-one million (including thirty-four million civilians). Since the end of World War II, approximately 150 wars have killed an estimated sixteen million people. In 1987, the nations of the world spent $930 billion (U.S. dollars) just on military equipment and supplies.

Preparation for **war** and the fighting of wars have been part of human experience since the beginning of civilization. Christians agree that war is evil, at least in the sense that it is always caused by moral failure and that it results in terrible pain and devastation of human life and dignity. But is every declaration of war morally wrong? Can a Christian fight (and kill), without sinning, in at least some wars? No biblically sensitive Christian treats these questions lightly. Faithful believers do, however, disagree on the answers. Contemporary Christians adopt one of three basic positions regarding the believer's involvement in war and military service: activism, the just war view, and pacifism.

Activism holds that Christians are to support a military effort whenever their country declares war. Governments are ordained by God. We are told in Scripture to submit to our political rulers (Rom. 13:1–7; 1 Peter 2:13–14). Typically, we do not have access to the classified information available to our military leaders. For these reasons, we must trust their judgment that a war is necessary. While few Christians will admit to holding the activist view in theory, a great many tend to follow it in practice. Since they have a

489

deep sense of patriotism and since their government always presents some justification for every war, they actually support all of their country's wars.

One major objection to activism is that two nations about to go to war with one another can (and usually do) each claim moral justification for the war. Yet, logically, at most one side is justified in fighting. In every war, some soldiers fight an unjust war. Activists reply that even if this is the case, blame for an unjust fight rests with their government, not with individual soldiers. Their duty is to obey. Furthermore, disobedience to government leads to anarchy—a condition possibly worse than organized war. Because few Christians hold to activism in theory, however, we will move to the just war view—the position of most Christians.

The **just war** position, or **selectivism,** holds that Christians may support and fight in some wars—those waged for a morally defensible cause. Just war theorists distinguish between the conditions necessary for declaring war in the first place (*jus ad bellum*) and the guidelines to be followed once a war is underway (*jus in bello*). The first *ad bellum* condition for declaring war is that there must be a just cause, usually said to be unwarranted aggression. Self-defense is clearly justified. However, some just war advocates also approve of preventive wars and crusades, defending not only defensive conflicts but offensive campaigns as well. When an enemy nation is clearly preparing to attack our own, we may launch a **preventive war.** When conditions within another nation are intolerably evil, even though that nation is not aggressive toward us, we may launch a **crusade** against it. Thus, when surrounding African nations overthrew Idi Amin's bloody reign of terror in Uganda, their action was just.

Another *ad bellum* criterion is just intention. Those going to war must pursue only a just peace, not revenge, territorial conquest, or ideological supremacy. Then, too, a just war is one that is declared by a lawful authority, and that only as a last resort, after all peaceful means of resolving the conflict have failed. Further, a government should carefully consider the likelihood of victory. Unwinnable wars are not just. Finally, the principle of general proportionality (proportionality of intention) requires that the total good achieved by a victory will by all indications outweigh the total evil and suffering the war will cause. No one should prescribe a cure that is worse than the disease.

Just war advocates suggest two major *jus in bello* criteria, the principles of noncombatant immunity and of proportionate means. The principle of discrimination, or noncombatant immunity, forbids direct, intentional attacks on nonmilitary persons. The principle of proportionate means limits the use of force and violence to genuine necessity. A just government ensures that the means of war are proportionate to the tasks of war.

Christians who support the just war perspective follow several lines of argument. One involves biblical evidence. Throughout the Old Testament,

God's people fought in just wars. God not only permitted war, but at times commanded it (Josh. 8:1–29; 11:1–23; 1 Sam. 23:1–5). Even before the Mosaic law, Scripture records (with God's apparent blessing of the action) Abraham's just war to rescue his nephew Lot from the forces that had taken him and his family captive (Gen. 14). These texts imply that participation by God's people in at least some wars is morally right. Since God's moral nature does not change, what he sanctions in one phase of human history cannot be inherently evil. Further, the Bible apparently endorses capital punishment (Gen. 9:5–6; Rom. 13:4). Christians can rightly act as agents of duly constituted government when they apply the death penalty to murderous armies as well as to murderous individuals.

A second line of argument for the just war view is based on the intuitive sense of justice within most people. When we hear of a terrorist's killing innocent children, we instinctively feel that society should stop him—by shooting to kill if necessary. Likewise, if an army invades a peaceful country and engages in raping, looting, and killing, most people want a more powerful military force to stop the invaders. A standard of conscience that is held this widely must emerge from a sense of natural law that is instilled in humans by their creator.

A third argument is that the just war theory provides a moral basis for foreign policy. Even though Christians are not "of the world," they live "in the world." Christians, therefore, should act as salt and light in the national life of their society. Selectivists argue that the pacifist view is so idealistic and unworkable that national leaders will not take it seriously. The activist view, on the other hand, does not take seriously enough the possibility of self-deception among governmental and military leaders. The just war position, however, gives an ethical framework for a genuinely workable military policy. It shows that Christians can contribute significantly to the society in which they live.

New Testament scholar George Knight presents a case for Christian involvement in just wars, distinguishing between the responsibilities of the individual Christian and those of the state. While the individual must not avenge himself or herself, God has authorized the state to avenge evil and punish evildoers. Christians who serve their country in warfare are not violating Jesus' command to love their enemies, because they are not acting in personal retaliation. Following Knight, Bible teacher Jerram Barrs answers three objections levied against the just war view from the pacifist perspective.

Pacifism and **nonviolent resistance** form the third general position on the morality of war. Defenders argue that while the just war theory sounds fine in principle, any war violates many of the criteria. For example, the widespread killing of civilians (as indicated by the statistics cited above), even if not intended, violates the principle of proportionate means. And the principle of last resort is often ignored.

The perceived failure of just war criteria, however, is not the major reason most pacifists adopt this view. Christian pacifists ground their view on several deeply held convictions. One of the most fundamental is the argument from the nature of Christian discipleship. Jesus Christ lived nonviolently even when he had just cause for violence. He loved and died for his enemies and taught his followers to love their enemies without retaliation (Matt. 5:38–48; Luke 6:27–36). Since Christians are exhorted to obey Christ's teachings and to imitate Christ in his nonviolent life (1 Peter 2:18–23), war is untenable for them. Christian pacifists look on their position more as a way of life than as a theory about war. The way of the world is viewed as radically opposed to the way of the cross, and the Christian is to glory in the foolishness of the cross and the nonviolent advancement of God's kingdom (Rom. 12:19–21). As John Howard Yoder observed, Christians do not have a duty to make history come out right, since that is God's business. They do have a duty, however, to obey the teachings of their Lord.

A second conviction, held by most pacifists, is that since human life is sacred and a gift of God, no one has the right to end another's life. With this is the corollary that since Christ died for all people, offering them abundant life both now and for eternity, we cannot kill others and rob them of an opportunity to receive that gift of life in Christ. If Christians kill non-Christians, they deny them the privilege of ever knowing the redemption Christ died to give. If Christians kill Christians, as often occurs in war, they kill their own brothers and sisters. A minority of pacifists do not oppose all killing, but allow capital punishment in extreme cases. This minority group opposes war, however, because of its massive and usually indiscriminate destruction of human life (civilian as well as military), but it believes justice can be meted out fairly and individually to hard-core murderers.

A third conviction supporting pacifism is the concept of redemptive witness. Because of the courageous testimony of nonviolent Christians over the centuries, many unbelievers have been won to Christ. Others have at least received a powerful witness to the gospel of peace. The phenomenal growth of the church in the early Christian centuries, for example, is attributed in part to the other-worldliness—including nonviolence—of the followers of Christ. Patristic scholars agree that we have no evidence whatever of Christians in the army from the end of the New Testament period until A.D. 170. The early Christians did not enlist in the Roman army, but lived and died in the way of nonretaliation. And many joined the ranks of Christians due to this powerful witness of self-sacrificing love for one's enemies. However, even if none came to Christ through nonviolent witness, the message of God's love for all people—including his enemies—is still proclaimed through Christian pacifism.

Other arguments for the pacifist position are given by Ronald Sider, a seminary professor, and Richard Taylor, a parish services coordinator. They work especially with Jesus' Sermon on the Mount and the nature of war in the Old Testament. David Hoekema, a college academic dean, then answers five objections to pacifism as it is commonly perceived.

Pacifism comes in different degrees. Just as we cannot simplistically lump together all who support Christian participation in war, so we cannot view all pacifists as one. It is best to consider pacifism not as one unified position but as a continuum of perspectives ranging from the most *deontological* view on the one end to the most *consequentialist* view on the other. Deontological positions emphasize the wrongness of war in principle because it violates the fundamental law of God against killing, the obligation to love one's neighbor (and enemy), and the duty of Christians to imitate Christ in his total way of life, including nonresistance unto death if necessary. Consequentialist or *teleological* positions focus on the results of war more than on principles and norms. Some pacifists object to war primarily because the consequences are so horrendous. Death, disablement, poverty, and hatred between subsequent generations lead some pacifists to reject in fact what they might allow in principle.

Nuclear pacifism is a consequentialist form of pacifism. It justifies some forms of conventional warfare, but holds that the just war criteria rule out at least strategic nuclear weapons. Strategic nuclear war involves the most powerful warheads, delivered by missiles or bombers, targeted on the enemy's homeland, and, in many cases, directed not only against military personnel and equipment, but also against the general population. To nuclear pacifists, the large-scale death of noncombatants violates the principle of discrimination, and the destruction of the natural environment and danger to generations yet unborn violate the principle of general proportionality. Many nuclear pacifists oppose even the possession of nuclear weapons for **deterrence.** A few nuclear pacifists, such as John Stott, allow the use of tactical nuclear weapons when no other recourse is possible. Military experts define tactical nuclear weapons as those with very limited yield, directed against specific concentrations of combatants and military equipment.

A couple of other distinctions are necessary to understand pacifist thinking. *Force* is best defined as the imposition of physical strength. Most pacifists do not oppose all use of force, since force need not be used with the intent to injure or kill. Violence, however, is any physical act intended to injure, damage, or destroy a person or thing. Force need not be violence, but all violence involves force. Many (but not all) pacifists oppose all use of violence, but some pacifists oppose all use of force. Both pacifists and just war defenders frequently use these terms interchangeably, leading to considerable confusion.

This distinction between force and violence leads some to distinguish pacifism from nonviolent resistance. These two views agree that war is immoral. But nonviolent resisters will take an active role against war. They

often see pacifism as too passive. The Christian duty is not merely to withhold support from war, but to work actively against it. The distinction
between pacifism and nonviolent resistance is important, but both positions
use the same sorts of arguments in their opposition to war. While we include
Sider, Taylor, and Hoekema within the broad pacifist camp, because they
hold its basic principles, we may more accurately refer to them as nonviolent
resisters. They believe in actively crusading against war.

Many major issues—such as the relationship between Old and New Testaments, the diversity and unity of Scripture, and the application of Jesus'
ethic for Christians today—affect the debate between just war and pacifism.
In this life, it is not likely that Christians will ever fully agree on the question
of war. We can agree, however, on the terribly tragic nature of war and the
indispensability of actively waging peace. Beginning with the peace of God
ruling in our hearts individually, we can teach and live the message of peace
in our homes, churches, neighborhoods, places of work and influence, and
through our conscientious participation in government. "Blessed are the
peacemakers, for they will be called children of God" (Matt. 5:9).

Can a Christian Go to War?

George W. Knight III

War in [Southeast Asia], war between Arabs and Jews, strife and warfare in Northern Ireland: these shake the world, as well as the countries directly involved. Before these recent conflicts we had the world wars, and one could keep tracing war back in history to the epochs represented by the New and the Old Testaments.

Where were Christians in these wars and conflicts? More important, where should they have been? Should they have refused to participate in any and all wars as pacifists? Or should they have been willing to participate in some, though perhaps not all, as a duty owed to God? In view of the abiding relevance of this question and especially in view of the ambiguity of some recent conflicts, Christians should reflect again on the principles concerning war found in the Word of God.

A central point of departure is an appeal to the sixth commandment, "You shall not kill." There are those who say that this settles the issue once and for all: since God here prohibits killing human beings, this command prohibits war. It means, according to this view, that no one, individual or nation, has a right at any time to take another's life.

But the Old Testament also gives the express command of God to men to put a murderer to death: "Whoever sheds man's blood, by man his blood shall be shed, for in the image of God he made man" (Gen. 9:6). This in itself goes to show that every death inflicted is not a violation of the sixth commandment, which prohibits *murder*. Genesis 9:6 gives to men acting collectively, designated today as the state, the right—indeed, the responsibility—to inflict death on those who unjustly kill others.

This awesome responsibility of men extends not only to capital punishment for the murderer but also to the waging of war and the slaying of enemies. The Old Testament on a number of occasions speaks of God's instructing his people about war, both war waged to capture the land and war in defense (cf. Exod. 17:8ff.). Deuteronomy 20 is an entire chapter devoted to instructions from God for conducting the battle:

> When you go forth to battle against your enemies . . . you shall not be afraid of them; for the LORD your God is with you. . . . The LORD your God is he that goes with you. . . . When you draw near unto a city to fight against it, then proclaim peace unto it. . . . And if it will make no peace with you, but will make war against you, then you shall besiege it [vv. 1, 4, 10, 12].

The God and Father of Abraham, Isaac, and Jacob, and of our Lord Jesus Christ, instructed his people of old to wage war when necessary and to slay the enemy. Such a forthright statement as that of Deuteronomy 20 makes it impossible to assert that the command "You shall not kill" was intended to prohibit war. Further, these explicit instructions by God make it impossible to maintain that God prohibits the believer from engaging in war under any circumstances.

Before leaving this passage we should note that the nation addressed is a theocracy, the people of God as the nation Israel. This point is important as we consider the bearing of this passage upon the situation of today, in which the people of God are a trans-national and supra-national entity, the Church, and no nation may be considered the people of God. Although this passage, and others like it in the Old Testament, gives evidence that war is not prohibited, it does not thereby give warrant to a Christian group or to a nation to apply this passage directly to itself to warrant its initiating war, for neither is the special theocratic people of God.

Perhaps this distinction is highlighted by God's insistence that the Israelites utterly destroy their enemies in the land. This is explained as the just recompense of God upon those enemies because their iniquity is full (cf. e.g., Gen. 15:16; Lev. 18:24ff.). This is an intrusion or breaking into human history of God's justice upon men's sins. And this intrusion is done by God's special command through special revelation. Although God may and does accomplish such justice by other nations throughout human history (cf. Habakkuk and Cyrus in Isaiah), no nation or group of people may apply what was a special command in a particular situation to themselves to warrant [their] initiating warfare.

Does not this consideration make an appeal to the Old Testament invalid and useless? No, because it still recognizes the basic principle under consideration, that war itself is not always ruled out as contrary to God's will. Even though nations today, or groups of Christians, may not claim the right to act for God in initiating a war of conquest and punishment, a nation or an individual may, like Israel, defend itself or others, as Israel did and as the Old

Can a Christian Go to War?

Testament shows others' doing on many occasions (cf. e.g., Israel, David, Samson).

But what of Jesus Christ, the authority for the Christian? Anti-war appeal is more often made to him, who urges us to turn the other cheek. Soldiers don't seem to turn the other cheek and don't seem to love their neighbors, and so therefore, by implication, we have Jesus' authority against war and being a soldier.

But the appeal to Jesus as the authority against serving as a soldier seems to ignore the fact that his highest words of praise are found for a soldier, the centurion who asked that Jesus should heal his servant by speaking a word at a distance. Jesus marveled at this faith and said, "I say unto you, I have not found so great faith, no, not in Israel" (Matt. 8:10). It is noteworthy that Jesus does not demand that the centurion cease being a soldier and in Matthew 8:11 speaks of him as being a member of the kingdom of heaven. John the Baptist, when asked by soldiers in service what they must do, does not demand that they leave the army, but only that they not misuse their power for their own sinful goals in exacting by force from civilians what was not theirs by right (Luke 3:14). Peter is sent to Cornelius, the centurion soldier. The narrative speaks of that soldier as Godfearing, as one that works righteousness, and as acceptable to God (Acts 10).

In none of these encounters are these soldiers told that they must give up what they are doing because being a soldier is incompatible with their Christian faith.

But how can Jesus speak about turning the other cheek and yet recognize Christians as soldiers? Are these not mutually exclusive? Perhaps we begin to find the solution when we realize that the soldier, or any Christian, must on the one hand accept abuse and even death rather than deny Christ, [and] on the other hand defend himself, others, and a nation against attack as a responsibility laid on him by faith in Christ. Perhaps the distinction Paul makes between the individual Christian and the state in Romans 12 and 13 will point us in the direction that will help clarify this solution.

The individual Christian is not to avenge himself, he is to live peaceably, he is to feed his enemy (Rom. 12:17–21), and he is to love his neighbor and therefore not kill (Rom. 13:8–10). But significantly, right in the middle of those words, the power or authority of the state is delineated in other terms (Rom. 13:1–7). The state is to avenge. It is a terror to evil. It is a minister of God and is given no less than the sword (v. 4), and it bears the sword not in vain but as an avenger who brings wrath upon the one that does evil. We pay taxes to support this very activity upon which the state is to attend continually (v. 6). Paul says pointedly that "it [the state] does not bear the sword for nothing" (v. 4). We could say in our day that he is not armed needlessly. In using the sword, or gun, the state is expressly called a minister of God, not an opponent of God, or one that disobeys or fails to recognize His commands.

Yes, the state must serve as a police force, and therefore it must also fight, do battle, make war when needed against evil. When a mob is destroying a city with Molotov cocktails, burning, and shooting, we recognize the right of policemen to shoot to kill, if necessary, in order to save lives. And when the state or policemen or soldiers are doing so, we as Christians are called on to support them in every way, with money and with service as a policeman or soldier ourselves, if called to do so, just as the aforementioned Christian soldiers did (Rom. 13:6, 7).

Paul says to us Christians that since the state is a minister (servant) of God, "it is necessary to be in subjection, not only because of wrath, but also for conscience' sake" (v. 5). Further, we are not to resist the God-ordained powers because to do so is to withstand the ordinance of God (vv. 1 and 2). These verses, which call for subjection, are much needed in our day. The forces of rebellion and revolution are opposing not only men but God. Finally, we need to remember that Paul writes these words not about a nice so-called Christian nation but about heathen and militant Rome.

So we see that God gives to the state the power of the sword, the right to wage war against evil, and calls on Christians to honor and support this authority and activity. This much is clear. Christians should not miss this clear teaching nor be misled by the misuse of other passages.

Within these two chapters we see an important distinction made. It is highlighted by the fact that the individual Christian is not to avenge himself (Rom. 12:19) and the state as a minister of God is called on to be an avenger for wrath to him that does evil (Rom 13:4). Here we see that the Lord's teaching on turning the other cheek is not to be applied to the state in its relation with evildoers. And any attempt to do so is to fly in the face of Christ's apostle and the teaching Christ has given him.

But where does this leave the individual Christian? Here also the account of Romans 12 and 13 is helpful in the realistic qualification it gives to individual Christian conduct. The command is indeed "be at peace with all men" (Rom. 12:18). But the qualification is also there: "If it be possible, as much as in you lies . . ." or, as the NIV translates it, "If it is possible as far as it depends on you, live at peace with everyone." Peace is the keynote, even as it was in the capturing of the promised land (cf. Deut. 20:10, 11). But it is the keynote with a recognition that it is not always possible.

This qualification of Paul puts Jesus' hyperbolic and principal statement in its larger context: "Resist not him that is evil: but whosoever smites you on your right cheek, turn to him the other also. And if any man would go to law with you, and take away your coat, let him have your cloak also" (Matt. 5:39, 40). May a Christian be stripped of his clothing just because someone has learned that by a literal application of this verse he can get anything he wants from a Christian? Certainly all would agree that this is not a correct application of that part of the passage. Likewise, we should recognize by analogy that ruling out any self-defense is not an appropriate application of the other part of the passage. And Jesus did not intend it to be. He wants to drive home a principle, realizing that it is best communicated in starkness and absoluteness. Both he and the Apostle Paul do not seem to have felt constrained always to apply this teaching literally. Jesus did not offer the other cheek when struck but rather challenged his being struck—"Why do you smite me?" (John 18:23). Paul responded similarly in Acts 23:3: "God shall smite you, you whited wall: and you sit to judge me according to the law, and command me to be smitten contrary to the law?" His challenge is based on the law itself. The apology that seems to follow later is to deny not the challenge but the sharpness with which he addressed the one in authority.

Our Lord's teaching does indicate that Christians should bear verbal abuse and even physical abuse at times as Christians. But its correlation with the foregoing passages, especially Romans 12:18, indicates that they need not refuse to defend themselves or others. To be very practical: the Christian boy or girl should take a hit or two on the school playground in Christian grace, meekness, gentleness, love, and forgiveness, without feeling the necessity of avenging himself. But when that does not bring peace and cessation of the blows, then it becomes no longer possible to live at peace with that attacker, and the Christian may defend himself or herself if aid from an authority figure to stop the fight is not available. The same applies to the adult Christian when his physical life or that of others is endangered. And no less than David, a man after God's own heart, the Christian may even kill to defend himself or others.

What the Christian may do as an individual, he may do also as part of a nation, which God describes as bearing a sword and using it (Rom. 13).

This is not the end of the matter. Would that it were so simple! There is another aspect of the question. Paul presents the "normal" situation. But sometimes the state misuses its power and authority. Sometimes it uses the sword against good. The book of Revelation pictures civil government corrupt and against the true Church. Peter and the apostles had to face the authorities in Jerusalem who imprisoned them, beat them, and demanded that they stop preaching Jesus. They refused, claiming that they must obey God rather than men (Acts 4:19ff.; 5:29, 40–42). They did not protest about this or that personal right, but they did disobey when the choice was to obey God or the state. This did not become a misused fetish for the disciples, but something that they stood for when this supreme issue was at stake. The example reminds us that our obedience to the state is relative, our obedience to God, absolute. We must not absolutize patriotism or the motto "My country—right or wrong." To do so is to demand that Christians . . . must fight . . . no matter what the situation may be.

In the light of all the foregoing considerations, the Christian Church has recognized that the Christian must fight for his country in a just war and must refuse to fight in an unjust war, with the burden of proof being on the Christian more than on the state. If he dissents, as he may, he must be willing to take the consequence of his dissent.

We may not limit the just war to that of self-defense, as some have said. True, the European countries and Great Britain had a right to defend themselves against the Nazis as did the United States against Japan in World War II. But the United States did not need to be attacked by Japan to justify its warring against the Nazis to help Great Britain and Europe.

What of the war in Viet Nam? Were the aggressors Communist North Vietnamese who sought to spread godless Communism to the sea in the Orient? Was it wrong for America or other countries to help South Viet Nam defend itself and also to hold back at that point the conquest by Communism? Can it be conclusively proved to have been unjust? There may be reasons to say that continued involvement by America was unwise or unnecessary, but this is something other than saying that this war, or the American position in it, was contrary to biblical teaching. Finally, for the Christian, the defense of one's own country or the aid given to another depends not upon the form of government or upon the morality of those in authority but simply on the justice of that defense or self-defense.

These considerations do not mean that the Christian delights in war or is a militarist. The Christian has a deep antipathy to war, even though he recognizes its inevitability in a world of sin. Like James, he recognizes that, as a general principle, all conflict is rooted in man's sin and lust (James 4). But he also remembers the words of Jesus that there will be wars and rumors of wars until He returns, so that he will not fall into the idealistic folly of speaking of the war to end all wars. Even though the Christian may be caricatured by the non-Christian as the hopeless idealist, he is truly realistic in that he takes sin, which James speaks of, seriously and therefore realizes that he may be involved in a war of defense.

From George W. Knight, III, "Can A Christian Go to War?" Used by permission, *Christianity Today* (21 November 1975): 4–7.

The Just War Revisited

Jerram Barrs

Should We Not Trust in God Rather Than in Weapons?

In support of this view various passages from the Old Testament are quoted.

No king is saved by the size of his army;
    no warrior escapes by his great strength.
A horse is a vain hope for deliverance;
    despite all its great strength it cannot save.
But the eyes of the LORD are on those who fear him,
    on those whose hope is in his unfailing love,
to deliver them from death
    and keep them alive in famine (Psalm 33:16–19 NIV).

It is better to take refuge in the LORD
    than to trust in man.
It is better to take refuge in the LORD
    than to trust in princes (Psalm 118:8–9 NIV).

The pacifist will argue on the basis of such passages that our calling is to pray for peace, to trust in God, and to put no emphasis on developing, stockpiling and being prepared to use sophisticated weapons of deterrence. Israel's defense was God's concern: their actions in war were basically irrelevant or unnecessary. God gave victory to Israel by miraculous intervention so that the victory was the Lord's alone. This should be our model for today.

There are two problems with this position. God did sometimes deliver the Israelites by miraculous means without their having to fight; for example, the drowning of Pharaoh's army in the Red Sea. However, it is untrue to say that Israel's actions in war were always superfluous if they were faithfully trusting God. When Jericho was captured, God brought down the walls by his power

501

at the sound of the shout and trumpet blast. Yet it was the Israelite army which had to kill with the sword every person in the city (Joshua 6:20–21). The same is true on many other occasions. In the battle against the Amalekites, Moses prayed all day, and the army fought under Joshua's leadership, so that the text declares both that the 'Lord is at war against the Amalekites' and 'Joshua overcame the Amalekite army with the sword' (Exodus 17:8–16). Even Psalm 118, quoted above, continues: 'All the nations surrounded me, but in the name of the Lord *I* cut them off' (v. 10).

The pacifist's argument here makes a false antithesis between God's action and human action. It is parallel to those who teach that in the Christian life we do nothing, the Holy Spirit does everything; our calling is simply to trust and watch the Spirit at work. Neither on the personal level, nor on the national level, can such an antithesis be supported biblically, no matter how spiritual such an approach appears to be. Rather, in every area we are called both to pray and to act.

Secondly, we cannot draw an exact parallel between Israel and any modern nation. . . . God's miraculous dealings with Israel were unique in history, for Israel had a unique calling. We do not have the right to expect God's direct intervention into the courts of civil justice, though Israel was promised this (Exodus 28:30; Numbers 27:21; Deuteronomy 1:17). Nor do we expect that God will call us to 'holy' wars, as he did the Israelites when they entered Canaan, and many times in their later history through the period of the judges and the prophets. The pacifist cannot have it both ways. He cannot insist *both* that the Old Testament does not apply at all, that the forceful resistance of evil is for the Old Testament only, *and* that miracle will be the normal means of God's delivering nations today, as he argues it was for Israel in the Old Testament. My contention instead is that God's concern for justice is basic in both testaments, and that the principles for the practice of justice seen in both testaments must apply both nationally and internationally.

We are to work for a sound defense, and we are to pray for the Lord's help. We know at the same time that the nations are in God's hands, and that if he desires to judge our nation there is nothing we can do about it except work and pray for repentance that such judgment be averted.

Are Today's Weapons So Appalling That the Just War Theory No Longer Applies?

This is the position put forward by the nuclear pacifist: nuclear weapons are so destructive, they would involve the killing of so many civilians, that the rules of the just war are irrelevant. Therefore, it is said, the only right Christian response is to work for unilateral disarmament and totally reject the making of, dependence on, or use of nuclear weapons. It would be better for us to be overrun by an enemy than to continue maintaining a nuclear deterrent. The principle of the sacredness of civilian populations must take precedence over the prudence of being armed with a nuclear arsenal.

This argument rests on the assumption that nuclear weapons are qualitatively different from other weapons used in history. But are they? Surely they are quantitatively different, capable of greater destruction than conventional weapons, but not of a quite different order. Man has shown, again and again, that he can kill millions of people with quite simple weapons (Julius Caesar's wars in Gaul are one example). The ability to kill many with one bomb is not qualitatively different from killing many with swords or guns.

The just war theory required that war be directed against combatants, not against civilians. However, while the desire to keep civilians out of battle is obviously praiseworthy, we have to recognize that this is sometimes difficult. Have there in fact been any wars in history in which civilians have not suffered? Even within a country, as soon as the police are faced by an armed gang instead of by one individual, it is almost impossible to avoid the involvement of non-combatants. As the level of attack increases so the problems increase. A situation where a government is faced by guerrilla attacks from within ordinary communities is an obvious example of this. A government should not abandon the pursuit of justice in such situations and stand idly by while the killing continues. Rather it has to recognize that the guerrillas are representatives of the people among whom they hide, and by whom they are supported, and so reprisals have to be taken which cannot be precisely discriminate.

In war the same holds true. Weapons ought to be aimed at military targets, munitions factories and the like, but the inevitability of civilian involvement increases with the level of force necessary to resist an enemy.

Of course everyone wishes that nuclear weapons had not been invented. Everyone longs for multilateral disarmament. The question that must be faced by all is how to deal with the threat of an enemy armed with nuclear weapons, and with the danger of nuclear destruction. The nuclear pacifist must recognize that he is for practical purposes a total pacifist, given our moment of history. Unilateral disarmament by the United Kingdom might have the effect of destabilizing the situation in the world, rather than furthering peace. Further, those who suggest unilateral disarmament ought to consider the consequences of their advice, as George Will said in a *Newsweek* article: 'When the subject is nuclear weapons, everyone, and especially persons propounding radical and dubious new religious duties inimical to deterrence, should remember the duty to be clear in their own minds about where their logic leads, and to be candid with others about the probable real-world consequences of the behaviour they favour.'[1]

This issue of the awfulness of modern warfare raises a further question which must be considered in relationship to it.

1. George F. Will, "Religion and Nuclear Arms," *Newsweek*, 21 December 1981.

Is War Always the Worst Alternative?

In many discussions of war today it appears to be taken for granted that we should strive for peace at any price, that war is always the worst option. Is this necessarily true? Vladimir Bukovsky, an exiled Russian dissident, comments on the First World War and the Revolution in Russia. 'The Russian people were in any case so fed up with the war by then that they did not care. Anything seemed better or at least not worse. After three years . . . in which some 20 million people were slaughtered or died of starvation, cold, and typhoid (i.e., *ten* times as many as were killed at the front during the whole of World War I) the war came to seem a trifle by comparison, a sort of frontier skirmish somewhere in the Byelorussian swamps.'[2]

Vietnam is a more recent example. Twice as many people have been killed in Vietnam in the [10] years since the war ended than were killed in the whole 30 years previously, and yet one still finds statements such as: 'At last America withdrew its troops and peace could finally be established.'

Such a statement should make us ask: 'What is peace?' As Christians, we have to answer that peace is not simply the absence of war. Peace cannot be had in the world simply by protesting against war, or by disarming unilaterally. Of course we should pray for peace, and work for peace, but peace cannot come unless, and until, there is justice. This is why there are far more prayers for justice in the Bible than there are prayers for peace (Psalm 94; 96; 97; 100). As in our relationship with God peace came through Christ's receiving our justice, so in human society it is impossible to have peace where there is injustice. This is true within a nation: there can be no peace while criminals are at large. It is true internationally: there can be no peace in the world while the world is full of injustice. Peace is not the absence of war, it is the restoration of justice in relationships.

If, therefore, we long for peace in the world, our prayers and our efforts ought to be devoted to the establishment of justice. That will mean both the preparedness to be armed with whatever weapons are necessary to deter an enemy, and also the readiness to fight wars to resist evil when no other way forward can be found.

From Jerram Barrs, "The Just War Revisited," in *Pacifism and War*, ed. Oliver R. Barclay (Leicester, England: InterVarsity, 1984), 155–60.

2. Vladimir Bukovsky, "The Peace Movement and the Soviet Union," *Commentary* (May 1982): 25. The following paragraph in the text is a view of Vietnamese refugees who have fled to the West. We shall of course never have accurate data of this type given us by the present government. However, the United Nations estimates that at least 350,000 Vietnamese have been lost at sea while attempting to escape. Numerous newspaper and periodical articles have also referred to killing within Vietnam on a huge scale.

Jesus and Violence

Some Critical Objections

Ronald J. Sider and Richard K. Taylor

Jesus' Nonviolent Life

In both actions and words Jesus rejected lethal violence. At the triumphal entry Jesus clearly disclosed his nonviolent messianic conception. Both Matthew 21:5 and John 12:15 quote Zechariah 9:9 to underline their belief that Jesus' action fulfilled this Old Testament prophecy. Modern commentators agree that Jesus consciously chose to fulfill the eschatological prophecy of Zechariah precisely because it depicted a humble, peaceful Messiah.[1] Zechariah's peaceful vision contrasts sharply with most messianic expectations:

> Lo, your king comes to you;
> triumphant and victorious is he,
> humble and riding on an ass,
> on a colt the foal of an ass.
> I will cut off the chariot from Ephraim
> and the war horse from Jerusalem;
> and the battle bow shall be cut off,
> and he shall command peace to the nations. (Zech. 9:9–10)

Here is a picture of the Messiah riding not a warhorse but a humble donkey. Echoing many prophets who had denounced Israel's reliance on chariots and cavalry, the text foresees the abolition of instruments of war. Messianic peace prevails. . . .

1. For example, see C. E. B. Cranfield, *The Gospel According to Mark*, The Cambridge Greek New Testament Commentary (Cambridge: Cambridge University Press, 1963), 353–54.

In the final crisis, Jesus persisted in his rejection of the sword. He rebuked Peter for attacking those who came to arrest him: "All who take the sword will perish by the sword" (Matt. 26:52). Not even the defensive sword should be used. We find it significant that Jesus' rebuke to Peter gives a general reason for not using the sword, not just an objection to use in this special case. "He is obviously not thinking of just this special situation since he takes pains to lay down the general truth that they who take the sword shall perish with it."[2]

Similarly, Jesus informed Pilate that his kingdom was not of this world *in one specific way*—namely, that his followers do not use violence: "My kingship is not of this world; if my kingship were of this world, my servants would fight, that I might not be handed over to the Jews; but my kingship is not from the world" (John 18:36).[3] Jesus obviously did not mean that the messianic kingdom he had begun had nothing to do with this world. That would have contradicted the kingdom values he announced, and it would have made nonsense of the very prayer he taught his disciples: "Thy kingdom come *on earth* as it is in heaven."

Jesus' high priestly prayer is perhaps the best commentary: "The world has hated them because they are not of the world, even as I am not of the world. I do not pray that thou shouldst take them out of the world, but that thou shouldst keep them from the evil one" (John 17:14–15).

In this statement, as in John 18:36, the preposition *of* points to the source, not the location, of authority, methods and norms.[4] This Gospel-of-the-Word-become-flesh would never have said that Jesus was not very much *in* this world. But his authority and methods did not derive from the fallen order. Fighting—even defensive violence to prevent the most unjust arrest in human history—belongs to the old sinful order. Jesus' followers, however, must live according to the norms of the new messianic age. Therefore, Jesus says, they will not fight.

Jesus' Nonviolent Teaching

Jesus not only lived the way of nonviolence, he also taught it. Matthew 5:38–48 is the central passage.[5]

You have heard that it was said, "An eye for an eye and a tooth for a tooth." But I say to you, Do not resist one who is evil. But if any one strikes you on the right cheek, turn to him the other also; and if any one would sue you and take

2. Culbert G. Rutenber, *The Dagger and the Cross* (New York: Fellowship Publications, 1950), 39. Matthew 26:53–54 does go on to say that he will not call on legions of angels to protect him because he must die. But that in no way denies that the saying, "All who take the sword will perish by the sword" is a saying with general implications beyond the particular setting.

3. It is important to note one significant implication of this statement for Christians in the just war tradition. At the very least, Jesus means to forbid the use of violence to defend or extend his kingdom. Christians who defend war to protect Christians from "godless Communism" need to ponder Jesus' clear prohibition of fighting to protect his kingdom and its members.

4. So Rutenber, *Dagger and the Cross*, 39.

your coat, let him have your cloak as well; and if any one forces you to go one mile, go with him two miles. Give to him who begs from you, and do not refuse him who would borrow from you. You have heard that it was said, "You shall love your neighbor and hate your enemy." But I say to you, Love your enemies and pray for those who persecute you, so that you may be sons of your Father who is in heaven; for he makes his sun rise on the evil and on the good, and sends rain on the just and on the unjust. For if you love those who love you, what reward have you? Do not even the tax collectors do the same? And if you salute only your brethren, what more are you doing than others? Do not even the Gentiles do the same? You, therefore, must be perfect, as your heavenly Father is perfect.

To a people so oppressed by foreign conquerors that over the previous two centuries they had repeatedly resorted to violent rebellion, Jesus gave the unprecedented command: "Love your enemies." Martin Hengel believes that Jesus formulated this command to love one's enemies in conscious contrast to the teaching and practice of the Zealots.[6] Thus Jesus rejected one currently popular political method in favor of a radically different approach.

Jesus' command to love one's enemies contrasts sharply with widespread views that Jesus summarizes in verse 43: "You have heard that it was said, 'You shall love your neighbor and hate your enemy.'" The first part of this verse is a direct quotation from Leviticus 19:18: "You shall love your neighbor as yourself." But who is one's neighbor? The first part of Leviticus 19:18 indicates that the neighbor is a "son of our own people." This was the normal Jewish viewpoint. New Testament scholar John Piper, in his extensive study of pre-Christian thinking about love for neighbor, shows that in Jewish thought the neighbor that one was obligated to love was normally understood to be a fellow Israelite.[7] Thus love for neighbor had clear ethnic, religious limitations. A different attitude toward Gentiles was expected. Seldom, however, did the Old Testament command or sanction hatred of foreigners or enemies.[8] But Jewish contemporaries of Jesus did. The Zealots believed that "slaying of the godless enemy out of zeal for God's cause was

5. For a careful analysis of this whole text and its relationship to Luke 6:27–36, see John Piper, *"Love Your Enemies,"*: *Jesus' Love Command in the Synoptic Gospels in the Early Christian Paraenesis* (Cambridge: Cambridge University Press, 1979), 50–60, especially his words against speculation. He rejects the view that only antitheses 1, 2 and 4 of Matthew 5:38–48 go back to Jesus. Piper finds no reason for thinking that Jesus is not the source of it all (52–53). Generally, Piper considers Matthew original and Luke an adaptation (58–59).

6. Martin Hengel, *Victory over Violence* (Philadelphia: Fortress, 1973), 76.

7. Piper, *Love Your Enemies*, 21–48. See also W. F. Albright and C. S. Mann, *Matthew*, Anchor Bible (New York: Doubleday, 1971), 71, and Eduard Schweizer, *The Good News According to Matthew* (Atlanta: John Knox, 1975), 132: "The principle, 'love your neighbor' (Lev. 19:18), to be sure, was always interpreted so as to apply to fellow Israelites, not to others."

8. Piper, *Love Your Enemies*, 33. Some psalms, however, do speak of hating those who hate God.

a fundamental commandment, true to the rabbinic maxim: 'Whoever spills the blood of one of the godless is like one who offers a sacrifice.'" And the Qumran community's Manual of Discipline urged people to "love all the sons of light . . . and . . . hate all the sons of darkness."[9] Jesus' way was radically different. Loving those who love you (v. 46), Jesus says, is relatively easy—even great sinners like tax collectors can do that. In fact even the pagan Gentiles act kindly toward the people in their own ethnic group. Jesus totally rejects that kind of ethnic or religious limitation on love.

For the members of Jesus' messianic kingdom, neighbor love must extend beyond the limited circle of the people of Israel, beyond the limited circle of the new people of God. This text says explicitly what the parable of the Good Samaritan (Luke 10:29–37) suggests: All people everywhere are neighbors to Jesus' followers and therefore are to be actively loved. And that includes enemies—even violent, oppressive, foreign conquerors!

The difficulty of actually implementing this command has led to many attempts to weaken its radical demand. Martin Luther did that with his two-kingdom analysis. He restricted the application of these verses on love of enemies to the personal sphere and denied their application to the Christian in public life. Luther went so far as to tell Christians that in their roles as public officials, "you do not have to ask Christ about your duty."[10] The emperor supplies the ethic for public life. Exegetically, however, that seems highly questionable. As Eduard Schweizer says in his commentary on Matthew, "There is not the slightest hint of any realm where the disciple is not bound by the words of Jesus."[11] The context demonstrates clearly that Jesus intends the command to apply to the public sphere. In verses 39–41, Jesus discusses issues that clearly pertain to the public sphere of the legal system and the authorized demands of the Roman rulers.

When Jesus rejects the principle of "an eye for an eye," he is not merely offering some admonitions for private, interpersonal relationships, but rather he is transcending a basic legal principle of the Mosaic and other near-Eastern legal systems (see, for example, Exod. 21:24).[12] (Obviously Jesus understood his action as the fulfillment of the law. . . .) Instead of demanding what the law permitted, namely, full retaliation, Jesus commanded a loving response governed by the needs of the other person. One should even submit

9. Schweizer, *Matthew*, 132; also Piper, *Love Your Enemies*, 40–41.
10. Quoted in John Stott, *Christian Counter-Culture* (Downers Grove, Ill.: InterVarsity, 1978), 113.
11. Schweizer, *Matthew*, 194.
12. Also, Leviticus 24:20; Deuteronomy 19:21; so Piper, *Love Your Enemies*, 89. Arthur Holmes's suggestion that Matthew 5:39 means only that individuals are to be nonresistant and not take the law into their hands in private schemes of retributive justice is quite wrong. The *Lex talionis* ("eye for an eye") refers not to private retaliation, but to a basic principle of the Mosaic legal system. See Arthur Holmes's contribution to *War: Four Christian Views,* ed. Robert G. Clouse (Downers Grove, Ill.: InterVarsity, 1981), 71.

to further damage and suffering rather than exact equal pain or loss from the unfair, guilty aggressor. In no way should we allow the other person's response to govern our action. Verse 20 ("If anyone would sue you and take your coat, let him have your cloak as well") also clearly speaks of how one should respond in the public arena of the judicial system.

Verse 41 ("If anyone forces you to go one mile, go with him two miles") deals with how to respond to Roman rulers who demand forced labor. The verb translated as "force" is a technical term used to refer to the requisition of services by civil and military authorities.[13] Josephus used the word to speak of compulsory carrying of military supplies.[14] The Roman rulers could and did demand that civilians in conquered lands perform such services. Thus they had the right to demand that Simon of Cyrene carry Jesus' cross (Matt. 27:32). The Latin origin of the word *mile* confirms the fact that Jesus refers to the requisitioning of forced labor by the Romans. It is hardly surprising that the Zealots urged Jews to refuse this kind of forced labor.[15] Jesus, on the other hand, condemns the Zealots' violent, angry response, even to the Romans' unjust demands.

Nonresistance or Nonviolence?

But this raises a pressing problem. Is Jesus forbidding all forms of resistance to evil? It seems some forms of coercion are fully compatible with love and respect for the other person as a free moral agent while others are not. In the home with children, in the church in disciplining brothers and sisters, and in the marketplace with economic boycotts, coercion can be applied which still respects the other persons' freedom to say no and accepts the consequences. Lethal violence is different. When one engages in lethal violence, one cannot lovingly appeal to the other person as a free moral agent responsible to God to choose to repent and change.[16]

13. Schweizer, *Matthew*, 130.
14. Albright and Mann, *Matthew*, 69.
15. Schweizer, *Matthew*, 130.
16. See further Ronald J. Sider, *Christ and Violence* (Scottdale, Pa.: Herald, 1979), chap. 2. Reinhold Niebuhr, of course, denounces this kind of attempt to distinguish between nonviolence and nonresistance and then justify nonviolent resistance on the authority of Jesus. See, for instance, his "Why the Christian Church Is Not Pacifist," *Christianity and Power Politics* (New York: Scribner's, 1946), 10. As the following discussion shows, we believe that Jesus calls not for total nonresistance in the face of evil, but rather costly love so governed by the needs of the neighbor that it does not retaliate, does not reciprocate evil for evil and persists with love regardless of the other's response. That kind of love is fully compatible with economic boycott, prophetic condemnation, and political pressure, but it is not compatible with lethal violence. In the former cases, one can genuinely love the other person and call on him as a free person to repent and change, but it makes no sense to call a person to repentance as you put a bullet through his head.

Police activity, as currently performed, sometimes involves lethal violence. The long tradition of unarmed British "bobbies," however, demonstrates that unarmed police can be very

510		Ronald J. Sider and Richard K. Taylor

When Jesus said, "Do not resist one who is evil," did he mean to forbid all forms of resistance? To interpret Matthew 5:39 in that way is surely to prove too much. If we are to interpret it literally, then we must consistently apply it in a literal fashion in every area. If the text calls for literal nonresistance, then that means absolute nonresistance toward evil persons in the home and in the congregation just as much as in the search for justice in the marketplace or in the political arena. It is plainly inconsistent to apply the text literally to conclude that Jesus' nonresistance forbids boycotts and strikes and then to apply the text in a less rigid fashion with regard to the home and the congregation.

Jesus' own actions demonstrate that he did not intend to forbid all forms of resistance. Jesus constantly opposed evil persons in a forthright, vigorous fashion. He unleashed a blistering attack on the Pharisees. Denouncing them as blind guides, fools, hypocrites and a brood of vipers, he uttered a harsh public condemnation of their many errors, including their preoccupation with tithing in small matters while neglecting more important things like justice and mercy (Matt. 23:13–33).

Nor was Jesus nonresistant when he cleansed the temple, driving the animals out with a whip, dumping the money tables upside down and denouncing the moneychangers as robbers. If Matthew 5:39 means that all forms of resistance to evil are forbidden, then Jesus contradicted his own teaching. Jesus certainly did not kill the moneychangers. Indeed, we doubt that he even used his whip on them. But he certainly resisted their evil in a dramatic act of nonviolent resistance.

Nor did Jesus silently submit to aggression at his trial when a soldier unjustly struck him on the cheek (John 18:19–24). Instead of turning the other cheek, he protested! "If I have spoken wrongly, bear witness to the wrong; but if I have spoken rightly, why do you strike me?" Apparently Jesus thought that protesting police brutality or engaging in civil disobedience in a nonviolent fashion was entirely consistent with his command not to resist one who is evil. We assume Jesus did not disobey his own teaching. Therefore we must make some kind of distinction between lethal violence and nonviolent coercion even though the text of Matthew 5:38–48 does not explicitly contain this distinction. . . .

Jesus' command not to resist evil must be understood in light of the preceding verse. To exact an eye for an eye was the accepted norm. Its fundamental principle was retaliation—limited to be sure by the nature of the offense. But Jesus rejected all retaliation. Instead of hating or retaliating, Jesus' followers are to respond lovingly in light of the need of the other per-

---

effective. We would favor creative efforts to expand the many ways that police can use nonlethal coercion. In any case, police work is radically different from warfare; see especially John Howard Yoder, *Politics of Jesus* (Grand Rapids: Eerdmans, 1972), 206.

son. And that love is to be so clear and costly and so single-mindedly focused on the needs of the other that it will even accept additional insult and injury from the aggressor—even a blow with the back of the hand, the most insulting of all physical blows in Jesus' day. But that does not mean that we cannot offer any form of resistance to the evil person. That would contradict Jesus' own actions. Rather it means costly, aggressive love, controlled by the genuine needs of the other person. The members of Jesus' new messianic kingdom are to love opponents, even oppressive persecuting enemies, so deeply that they can wholeheartedly pray for their well-being and actively demonstrate their love in actions that exceed unjust demands. . . .

Some Critical Objections

Does the Old Testament support the just war traditions? [Some Christians] . . . argue that the Old Testament's call to arms is still normative. Christians through the ages have done that. The Crusaders' favorite text was Jeremiah 48:10: "Cursed is he who keeps back his sword from bloodshed." The Crusaders conquered Jerusalem on 15 July 1099 after enormous bloodshed. Christian chroniclers joyfully reported that the Christian troops then beheaded ten thousand Muslims in the great Mosque, choking the area with blood and corpses.[17]

In his defense of warfare, Loraine Boettner insists that the Old Testament's endorsement of warfare is still normative for Christians. The Scriptures, our only rule of faith and practice, teach one consistent doctrine. In dozens of places in the Old Testament, God commands war for righteous ends. The Canaanites' horrible sexual practices and human sacrifice justified their slaughter by Israel. In light of Canaanite crimes, "their forthright execution by the Hebrews seems manly and dignified, if not even merciful." They were "too degraded and sinful to live."[18] The New Testament, Boettner argues, is silent on warfare because the Old Testament had already revealed God's final word about war.

This view . . . assumes, contrary to the overwhelming evidence we have just examined, that Jesus and the apostles said nothing about the basic problem of violence. The church of the first three centuries certainly thought otherwise. But it also mistakenly supposes that the Old Testament teaching on war supports the traditional just war tradition of the church. Taken at face value, the Old Testament proves both vastly too much and vastly too little to serve as a support for Christians in the just war tradition.

Certainly it proves too much. As we have seen, the immunity of noncombatants is a central element of the just war tradition. The same is true of

17. See John Gray, *A History of Jerusalem* (London: Robert Hale, 1969), 236–37.
18. Loraine Boettner, *The Christian Attitude toward War* (Grand Rapids: Eerdmans, 1940), 22; see all of chap. 3.

proper treatment of prisoners of war. To kill civilians and prisoners of war is murder according to the just war tradition. But the Old Testament's holy war teaching commands almost exactly the opposite. Joshua 10:40 says God told the invading Israelites to wipe out "all that breathes." Samuel told Saul to defeat Amalek and to annihilate all survivors: "And Samuel said to Saul, 'The LORD sent me to anoint you king over his people Israel; now therefore hearken to the words of the LORD. Thus says the LORD of hosts, ". . . Now go and smite Amalek, and utterly destroy all that they have; do not spare them, but kill both man and woman, infant and suckling, ox and sheep, camel and ass""" (1 Samuel 15:1–3).[19] No contemporary Christian ethicist believes Christians should treat noncombatants and prisoners of war that way.

The Old Testament also records God's command to destroy Israelites for idolatry and sexual misconduct. When Moses discovered that the people were worshiping idols, he ordered the Levites to slay thousands of Israelites: "Thus says the LORD God of Israel, 'Put every man his sword on his side, and go to and fro from gate to gate throughout the camp, and slay every man his brother, and every man his companion, and every man his neighbor'" (Exodus 32:27). Judges 19–20 says Yahweh ordered the tribal armies to punish a gross sexual offense in the tribe of Benjamin. "And the LORD defeated Benjamin before Israel; and the men of Israel destroyed twenty-five thousand one hundred men of Benjamin that day" (20:35).[20] Christians today do not believe that we should kill heretics, adherents of other religions or sexual offenders.

The Old Testament proves entirely too much for those who seek its endorsement for killing. But it also proves much too little. Old Testament scholar Millard C. Lind has recently explored the theology of warfare in ancient Israel.[21] He shows that at the heart of Israel's holy war tradition is the belief that Yahweh himself miraculously intervenes to fight for Israel. Often Israel did not lift an armed finger. When God wanted the people themselves to fight, he summoned them to battle by a prophetic word. Even then it was very clear that victory was by divine act, "not by your sword or by your bow" (Joshua 24:12). "Faith meant that Israel should rely upon Yahweh's miracle for her defense, rather than upon soldiers and weapons. The human agent in the work of Yahweh was not so much the warrior as the prophet."[22]

The miraculous deliverance at the exodus was the basic paradigm. The very early poem in Exodus 15:1–18 says the escaping Israelites did not fight at all when the Egyptian army drowned in the sea. There are numerous

19. So too many other texts; for example, Numbers 31:17; Deuteronomy 20:10–18; Joshua 8:18, 24–25.
20. See Millard Lind's discussion in *Yahweh Is a Warrior* (Scottdale, Pa.: Herald, 1980), 104–5.
21. Ibid. Lind has an excellent overview of the literature on pp. 24–31 and in his notes.
22. Ibid., 23.

accounts where divine intervention alone brought victory.[23] When Yahweh's prophet ordered Israel to fight, it was still abundantly clear that the victory came from God, as Israel's defeat of Jericho, Gideon's defeat of the Midianites, and David's defeat of Goliath show. The text of Judges explicitly explains that God pared down Gideon's army so that the Israelites could take no credit for the victory (7:2–3).

Lind summarizes this early Israelite theology of warfare as follows: "Obedience to Yahweh's word and trust in his miracle are alone decisive. Israel's faith in Yahweh as warrior led her to reject the military expediency of developing sophisticated weaponry such as horses and chariots even to the time of David, weapons that would have made Israel competitive with her Philistine and Canaanite enemies."[24]

Later, Israel rejected Yahweh's kingship and asked for a human king to lead them into battle. The kings militarized Israelite society with standing armies, cavalry and chariots. But the prophets denounced this trust in advanced military technology.[25] Psalm 20:7 reflects this view: "Some boast of chariots, and some of horses; but we boast of the name of the LORD our God." Hosea, like other prophets, harshly condemned Israel's trust in military might:

> You have plowed iniquity,
>   you have reaped injustice,
>   you have eaten the fruit of lies.
> Because you have trusted in your chariots
>   and in the multitude of your warriors. (Hos. 10:13)

Since God himself fights for Israel, she need not rely on chariots, horses and a large army. Even three hundred soldiers armed with torches and pitchers will do if Yahweh leads the host.

That is the heart of the Old Testament's theology of warfare. Such a theology, if it is normative for Christians today, hardly authorizes them to support our current national reliance on ever more sophisticated, ever more powerful and destructive weapons. "Imagine what an uproar there would be if a United States President announced that God had promised victory for the United States provided we did away with our nuclear weapons and fought only with horns, pitchers and torches."[26]

---

23. E.g., 1 Samuel 5–6 (Lind, *Yahweh*, 97); 2 Kings 18:13–19:36 (Lind, *Yahweh*, 140–41). See Lind, *Yahweh*, 46ff., for a discussion of the escape at the sea.

24. Ibid., 171.

25. For example, Isa. 2:6–8; 31:1; Hos. 10:13–15. In Zech. 9:9–15, in the vision of the peaceful Messiah, chariots and cavalry disappear.

26. Richard McSorley, *New Testament Basis of Peacemaking* (Washington, D.C.: Center for Peace Studies, Georgetown University, 1979), 61.

The holy war tradition is almost as problematic for Christians in the just war tradition as it is for Christians who reject all war. It demands what the just war tradition forbids in its summons to annihilate civilians and prisoners of war. And it forbids what the just war tradition supports in its call to trust in Yahweh rather than sophisticated military technology. If the biblical holy war tradition is still normative today, then we have done many things that we ought not to have done and we have not done many things that we ought to have done.

The mystery of God's justice and love. The fundamental problem, however, still remains. The Old Testament Scriptures tell us that in Israel's history, God did many things that seem incompatible with the nature of the God revealed at the cross. How can we reconcile this picture of God with the New Testament teaching that God is love?

First, we must recognize that the God portrayed in the New Testament is not a God whose only characteristics are love and mercy. The New Testament, just as much as the Old, insists that God both restrains and punishes sin. God restrains evil lest it destroy his good creation. Further, both within history and at its culmination, God executes divine wrath and retributive punishment against sin. The world's supreme messenger of God's love, our Lord Jesus, consistently taught that at the last judgment, sinners will face God's just wrath and punishment for sin. Paul is equally clear: Those who stubbornly disobey God store up wrath for the final day of judgment where there will be "wrath and fury" against sin (Rom. 2:5, 8).

This aspect of God seems understandable and just. If there were not a natural order of regularity in nature, human freedom and responsibility would have no meaning. Moral order in the universe is essential. If defiance of the moral order had no consequences, human freedom and responsibility would have little meaning. Both testaments insist that there is a moral order. The wages of sin is death—both now and later.[27] God punishes sin both within history, as the consequences of evil choices unfold, and at the final judgment. This divine maintenance of a moral order makes sense. As philosopher A. E. Taylor says, "The retributive character of punishment . . . [is] a doctrine really indispensable to a sound ethics."[28] But God's ways remain mysterious and unfathomable. Why he suddenly punishes the lies of Ananias and Sapphira (Acts 5:1–11) and withholds punishment from worse sinners we cannot explain.

We can only acknowledge that the sovereign Creator is different from us. As the Creator of all life, he can give or take life as he chooses. He has chosen

27. Paul's concept of God's wrath has a double time frame. God's wrath operates within history as God allows the evil consequences of sinful choices to work themselves out. (That is the clear teaching of Rom. 8:18–32.) But there will also be a final day of wrath (Rom. 2:4–8).

28. *The Faith of a Moralist,* Series I (London: n.p., 1951), 183, quoted in Leon Morris, *The Cross in the New Testament* (Grand Rapids: Eerdmans, 1965), 386. . . .

to create a world where he withdraws the gift of life through earthquakes and floods, disease and old age. He also withdraws life, the Scriptures say, as punishment for sin.

Some say that they cannot believe in a God who takes life. Do they, then, believe that God gives life, that God alone is Creator? That all life is in God's hands? Do they believe that all life belongs to God: that life continues with God after this time of testing is over? These truths about conditions of life assert God's sovereignty over life. If we do not believe them, we do not believe there is a God.[29]

Even so, our questions and doubts refuse to depart. Why God would repeatedly order the annihilation of men, women and children we do not understand. Certainly it helps to remember that the Old Testament gives reasons. The abominable sexual practices and hideous human sacrifices of the Canaanites merited punishment (Numbers 33:50–56; Deuteronomy 18:9–14). And God did not want their idolatrous practices to seduce Israel into idolatry (Deuteronomy 20:17–18).

Yet we still struggle. Were these sinful practices sufficient reason to destroy entire cities? Only God has the right to make such decisions. We can only confess in faith that he is the sovereign Creator and Lord of life. He promises us that he is both just and merciful. And we know that his justice and love met at the cross.

We also know that in the final revelation given by his incarnate Son, God summons us to love our enemies. And he explicitly commands us to leave vengeance to him (Romans 12:19). We dare not confuse these two issues. To insist that the Sovereign of the universe has the right to execute vengeance and retribution on sinners is one thing. To claim that we should imitate that aspect of God is quite another.

From Ronald J. Sider and Richard R. Taylor, "Jesus and Violence: Some Critical Objections," in *Nuclear Holocaust and Christian Hope* (Downers Grove, Ill.: Inter-Varsity, 1982), 106–13, 138–43.

29. McSorley, *New Testament Basis of Peacemaking*, 69.

A Practical Christian Pacifism

David A. Hoekema

I have grown increasingly dissatisfied with the gulf separating pacifists from defenders of just war. The church in which I was raised, the Christian Reformed Church, is what one draft board, in refusing a friend's request to be recognized as a conscientious objector during the Vietnam war, aptly termed a "war church." Calvinist theology has long been hostile to pacifism, and most Reformed churches' reflections on war begin by distinguishing justified from unjustified wars. Yet the Reformed perspectives on the nature of the person and of society can actually support a realistic form of pacifism—a version that has received too little attention in either the "peace churches" or the "war churches."

Pacifism need not be politically naïve, nor need it place undue faith in human goodness. These may be telling objections to some pacifists, but a careful articulation of the pacifist vision can meet them. By the same token, pacifists ought not deride just war theory as merely *Realpolitik* in vestments, for the just war tradition, when taken seriously, is just as stringent in its demands as is pacifism. . . .

Why is the pacifist vision of a healing and reconciling ministry of nonviolence not universally embraced in the churches? I would single out five prominent arguments to which pacifists, if they are to make their own position cogent and realistic, must respond.

Pacifism is surrender. "The pacifist viewpoint is appealing in principle, but in practice it means surrendering to the aggressor," is a charge heard often. "Capitulation to the forces of evil cannot be moral."

The problem with this objection is that it equates pacifism with passive nonresistance. Pacifism is not synonymous with "passivism": the pacifist rejection of war is compatible with a great many measures for defense against

516

aggression. In fact, pacifist theorists have urged the development of a civilian-based nonmilitary defense, which would encompass organized but nonviolent resistance, refusal to cooperate with occupying forces, and efforts to undermine enemy morale.

The tendency to equate pacifism with "passivism" and capitulation reflects how little we know of the remarkable historical successes nonviolent tactics have achieved, even in the face of brutal repression. From the courageous Swedish and Danish resistance to Nazism to the transformation of Polish society by the Solidarity labor movement, and from the struggle for Indian self-rule led by Gandhi to the struggle for racial equality in the United States led by Martin Luther King, Jr., and others, nonviolence has been a creative and effective force. Whether nonviolent resistance can always overcome aggression and whether its cost in suffering and death will in every case be less than that of war is difficult to say, but at least it cannot be said that pacifism is merely a policy of capitulation.

Pacifism extolls purity. "The main problem with pacifism," runs a second objection, "is that the pacifist places a higher value on his or her own purity of conscience than on saving others' lives. If we are going to fulfill our obligations, we have to be willing to get our hands dirty and not hold ourselves on some higher moral plateau than everyone else. Pacifists enjoy the freedom that others ensure by their willingness to resort to arms."

This objection rests on two confusions. In the first place, pacifism is an objection to war per se, not merely an objection to personal participation in war. Pacifists do not ask for a special exemption because of their high moral views or delicate sensibilities; they refuse to participate in war because it is immoral. Their exemption from military service is simply the compromise position that has developed in a society in which moral objection to war is not unanimously shared.

A second confusion in this argument is the notion that taking part in war shall be regarded as a lesser evil, rendered necessary by extreme circumstances. Such a claim has no part in traditional just war theory—or, indeed, in any coherent moral theory. The just war proponent believes that war is sometimes required by justice, in which case it is not the lesser of two evils but is itself a good. The issue is whether intentional killing in war is ever a good thing, not whether one ought to grit one's teeth and bravely commit one wrong rather than another.

Pacifism is based on optimistic humanism. "Pacifism links a noble ideal—the avoidance of violence—to naïve and implausible assumptions about the inherent goodness of human nature. If I thought that I could trust people and nations to resolve their differences peaceably and fairly, I would be a pacifist too. But history teaches us differently."

This objection brings us near the heart of the theological argument against pacifism. Indeed, it is a telling argument against some forms of pacifism. Gandhi, for example, was sustained by a deep faith in the goodness of human nature, a goodness he thought nonviolent action could call forth. "If love or non-violence be not the law of our being," he wrote, "the whole of my argument falls to pieces."[1] Similar optimism about human nature seems to have motivated some Quaker writers and much of the pacifism of American church leaders following the First World War. Such optimism requires a selective and unrealistic assessment of human behavior and human capacities. If pacifism rests on a trust that people have a natural capacity and an irrepressible tendency to resolve their differences justly and harmoniously, then pacifism is a delusion, and a dangerous one.

Such trust is not, however, essential to pacifism. There can be a realistic pacifism, a pacifism that gives due weight to the sinfulness and perversity of human nature.

Pacifists and defenders of just war can agree that every life is tainted with sin, and that evil will inevitably arise, but still disagree about how we ought to respond when it does arise. An essential companion to the doctrine of sin is the doctrine of grace. Though human nature is corrupted by sin, it is also illuminated by God's presence and guidance; God's grace shows itself in countless ways in the lives of Christians and non-Christians alike. In light of this fact, evil demands a response that overcomes rather than compounds evil. Such a pacifist stance differs significantly from a Gandhian or humanistic faith in the capacity of the human heart for goodness, while retaining the conviction that there are other remedies for sin besides war.

It should be noted, further, that realism about human nature cuts two ways: if it undermines a pacifism based on optimism, it also undermines the assumption that weapons of destruction and violence intended to restrain evil will be used only for that purpose. The reality of human sinfulness means that the instruments we intend to use for good are certain to be turned to evil purposes as well. There is therefore a strong presumption for using those means of justice that are least likely to be abused and least likely to cause irrevocable harm when they are abused. An army trained and equipped for national defense can quickly become an army of conquest or a tool of repression in the hands of an unprincipled leader. But a nonviolent national defense force, or a peacekeeping force bringing together citizens of a dozen nations, is of little use except for its intended purpose.

Pacifism confuses moral categories. "The basic confusion of pacifists is their assumption that the principles of Christian morality which we ought to follow in our individual lives can be applied to governments. Only individuals

1. Mahatma Gandhi, *Gandhi on Non-Violence*, ed. Thomas Merton (New York: New Directions, 1964), 25.

can truly be moral; governments are by their very nature 'immoral,' if we judge them as we would judge individuals. Killing is wrong for individuals, but for states an entirely different standard must be applied."

The notion that morality applies to individuals and not to governments is completely contrary to a central doctrine of Reformed theology which is endorsed, in varying forms, by other Christian traditions as well: that Jesus Christ is the Lord not just of the church, nor of a special sphere of religious activity, but of all of the natural and human world. We are called to live as followers of Jesus Christ in every human activity. Thus, we must obey God's demands for justice and reconciliation not only as families and churches but as societies. There is no room in Christian social thought for excluding governments from the realm of morality. If Christian ethics permits killing in certain circumstances, then violence is legitimate as a last resort, both for individuals and for governments. But if, on the other hand, Jesus did in fact demand that the members of the new Kingdom he inaugurated renounce all killing then we must restructure both our personal and our institutional lives to fulfill that demand.

Pacifism is too patient. "To suffer wrong rather than harm another, to return nonviolent resistance for violent oppression, might have been appropriate at an earlier stage in our struggle. But the violence inflicted on us for so long leaves us no choice but to use force in return. We can endure no more; only arms can bring justice now."

This argument, the cry raised in Soweto and San Salvador, is painfully familiar, and it is impossible to hear it without feeling the deep pain of those who make it. I am not sure whether this argument can be answered. Those of us who regard it at a comfortable distance may not know the possibilities that remain to those whose lives have been stunted by violence.

Are there wrongs so grave that only violent means can set them right? I do not believe there are, but I do believe that the historical point at which one faces this question is significant. Nazism would surely have been destroyed by sustained nonviolent resistance had Christians and others not averted their gaze from its evil for so long. But whether Nazism could have been destroyed by nonviolent means in 1939 is a far more difficult question. Similarly, the Christian churches of South Africa, both black and white, could once have ended the policy of apartheid through nonviolent reforms, but today, as the black death toll mounts into the thousands, it is difficult to imagine that the system will fall unless commensurate force is brought to bear against it.

Situations of extreme oppression do not invalidate the pacifist vision of nonviolent change. Active but nonlethal resistance is both theologically and practically defensible even in seemingly hopeless circumstances—as the courageous work of André Trocmé in Vichy France and of several church leaders in South Africa today makes evident. Yet many in such situations turn to violence as their last hope in the struggle for justice. We may dispute their conclusion, but our response should be more one of solidarity than of condemnation.

From David A. Hoekema, "A Practical Christian Pacifism." Copyright 1986 Christian Century Foundation. Reprinted by permission from the October 22, 1986 issue of *The Christian Century*.

For Further Reflection

Case Studies

A just war in the Gulf? Merrill was an American officer in the 1991 Persian Gulf War against Iraq. While most of his friends agree with him that the conflict was a just war, Don disagrees. From the *jus ad bellum* standpoint, Don contends that the war did not meet the criterion of last resort, because the international blockade against Iraq was cutting deeply into Iraq's economy and would have eventually undermined its military capabilities.

In addition, the targeting of water and sanitation systems used by civilians, the relentless air attacks against retreating Iraqi troops (resulting in the needless slaughter of tens of thousands), and the use of fuel-air explosives, which suck up all the oxygen in an area of hundreds of square yards (effectively suffocating all human and animal life), violate the *jus in bello* criteria of noncombatant immunity and proportionate means.

Merrill presents the other side of the picture. He argues that the war was necessary because of the need to stop Iraqi leader Saddam Hussein's aggression against Kuwait (not to mention his ruthlessness against his own people) and to keep the control of U.S. oil supplies out of unfriendly hands. Furthermore, even if some of the just war criteria were not met in the Gulf War, a Christian is to be subject to his country's leaders (Rom. 13:1–7; 1 Peter 2:13–17). Since the president and the heads of the military have the inside information on international conflicts, the duty of Christians is to support whatever war the country enters, as long as the leaders are seeking to uphold standards that Christians generally consider right.

Do you agree with Merrill's interpretation of Romans 13 and 1 Peter 2? Do you agree that the military's failure at times to follow some just war criteria (giving Don the benefit of the doubt for the sake of argument) under-

521

522 For Further Reflection

mines the validity and usefulness of the criteria? Do you agree with Don when he says that Christians who support a just war view, in order to follow the logic of their position, should demand legal exemption from military service for *selective* conscientious objectors who claim that a *particular* war is unjust? (Ideas from Ronald J. Sider and L. Lamar Nisly, "A Just War or Just Another War?" *ESA Advocate*, March 1991, 1–3).

Noncombatant military service. With his country at war, Bernard was drafted into military service. Since he was a member of a "peace church"—one that opposes Christians' involvement in war—he could have received an exemption to the draft. However, because of the reported atrocities of the enemy, he chose to answer the call to service, while praying that he would never have to fight. He felt that he could never kill another human being. To his great relief he was assigned to the maintenance and repair of military equipment.

After the war, his church friends criticized him for his participation in violence. They said he was inconsistent, and that he should have been willing either to kill or to refuse to assist the war effort in any way. Neither his military buddies nor his church friends supported his way of thinking.

You are a member of a nondenominational church where Bernard has recently started attending. He admits to you his ambivalence on the issue of noncombatant military support, and says that he experiences guilt about his part in the war. What are the most important questions Bernard needs to ask and to answer? How can you help him focus on specific issues and a workable solution to his quandary?

Glossary

Activism: View that a citizen must support all wars his or her country fights.

Crusade: A war waged to remedy past or ongoing atrocities, especially one recognized as such for religious reasons.

Deterrence: Political stance that relies on the possession and threatened use of weapons—especially nuclear—to discourage or prevent attack.

Jus ad bellum: The conditions—such as just cause, just intention, declaration by lawful authority, and last resort—that must be met in order for a just war to be declared.

Jus in bello: The conditions—such as noncombatant immunity and proportionate means—that must be met in the conduct of an ongoing war for it to be considered just.

Just war: A war that satisfies both *jus ad bellum* and *jus in bello* criteria.

Nonviolent resistance: View that Christians should not merely avoid participation in war, but also actively resist war using nonviolent means.

Nuclear pacifism: View that while warfare with conventional weapons may at times be justified, nuclear warfare can never be, due to the uniquely destructive nature of nuclear weapons.

Pacifism: View that it is wrong to participate in war, whatever its cause.

Preventive war: A war begun not in response to an act of aggression, but in anticipation of such, to prevent the other side from striking first.

Selectivism: View that it is morally right to participate in some wars—those that are just—but not in all wars.

War: Armed conflict between or among nations or other groups of people.

Annotated Bibliography

Adeney, Bernard T. *Just War, Political Realism, and Faith.* Metuchen, N.J.: Scarecrow, 1988. Superb analysis of just war reasoning in the nuclear age.

Bainton, Roland H. *Christian Attitudes Toward War and Peace: A Historical Survey and Critical Re-evaluation.* Nashville: Abingdon, 1960. Valuable historical overview and framework; standard work.

Barrs, Jerram. "The Just War Revisited." In *Pacifism and War,* edited by Oliver R. Barclay, Leicester, England: InterVarsity, 1984, 138–61. Defends the just war, particularly from the standpoint of justice, in an excellent volume of "When Christians Disagree" series.

Clouse, Robert G., ed. *War: Four Christian Views.* Revised. Downers Grove, Ill.: InterVarsity, 1991. Herman Hoyt for "Nonresistance"; Myron Augsburger for "Christian Pacifism"; Arthur Holms for "Just War"; and Harold O. J. Brown for "Crusade or Preventive War." Each replies to the others. Good annotated bibliography.

The Evangelical Quarterly 57, 2 (April 1985). Whole issue on war, with contributions from the Old and New Testaments, church history, and biblical/theological perspectives.

Faith and Philosophy 2, 2 (April 1985). Three views on pacifism from two proponents (Stanley Hauerwas and John Howard Yoder) and one just war defender (Richard Mouw).

Geyer, Alan, and Barbara G. Green. *Lines in the Sand: Justice and the Gulf War.* Louisville: Westminster/John Knox, 1992. Raises questions about the justice of the Persian Gulf war by examining just war criteria in light of actual realities before, during, and after the war.

Hoekema, David A. "A Practical Christian Pacifism." *The Christian Century* (22 October 1986): 917–19. Answers five common arguments against pacifism.

Holmes, Arthur F., ed. *War and Christian Ethics.* Grand Rapids: Baker, 1975. Valuable anthology of writers on war from Plato to Paul Ramsey.

Johnson, James Turner. *Can Modern War Be Just?* New Haven: Yale University Press, 1984. Argues that the just war tradition is still relevant in this nuclear age and that it can help to form strategy.

————. *The Quest for Peace: Three Moral Traditions in Western Cultural History*. Princeton, N.J.: Princeton University Press, 1987. Excellent analysis of sectarian pacifism, utopian "superstate" thinking, and (to a lesser extent) the just war view, by a highly regarded just war defender.

Knight, George W., III. "Can a Christian Go to War?" *Christianity Today* (21 November 1975): 4–7. Scriptural support for just war thinking.

Macgregor, G. H. C. *The New Testament Basis of Pacifism*. Revised. London: Fellowship of Reconciliation, 1953. One of the fullest and most thoughtful studies of the NT evidence.

Miller, Richard B., ed. *War in the Twentieth Century: Sources in Theological Ethics*. Louisville: Westminster/John Knox, 1992. Valuable anthology of nonpacifist materials from Protestant and Roman Catholic writers, reasoning practically, rather than abstractly, about wars from the Manchurian crisis in the early 1930s to the Allied war against Iraq in 1991.

"Nuclear Deterrence—A Debate." *Transformation* 5, 1 (January-March 1988): 1–19. Bernard Adeney argues against nuclear deterrence; Dean Curry contends for its necessity and morality. Each replies to the other.

Ramsey, Paul. *The Just War: Force and Political Responsibility*. Reprint. Lanham, Md: University Press of America, 1983 (originally 1968). Perhaps the most widely used serious introduction to the meaning of just war teachings, by one who, until his death, was the leading defender of the view.

Sider, Ronald J., and Richard K. Taylor. *Nuclear Holocaust and Christian Hope*. Downers Grove, Ill.: InterVarsity, 1982. Influential defense of pacifism, with specific presentation of how nonmilitary defense works.

Stassen, Glen H. *Just Peacemaking: Transforming Initiatives for Justice and Peace*. Louisville: Westminster/John Knox, 1992. Valuable third alternative to just war and pacifist approaches; offers "just peacemaking" theory, grounded in the Sermon on the Mount and Paul's epistle to the Romans, with concrete, practical steps of action that both pacifists and just war theorists can support.

Stott, John. *Decisive Issues Facing Christians Today*. 2d ed. Grand Rapids: Baker, 1990, 82–112. Evangelical pastor and scholar argues for nuclear pacifism, yet allows, in situations of "utmost urgency," that very limited nuclear weapons may be morally permissible.

Wells, Ronald, ed. *The Wars of America: A Christian View*. Grand Rapids: Eerdmans, 1981. Superb analysis of U.S. wars, examining the moral issues.

Yoder, John Howard. *When War Is Unjust: Being Honest in Just-War Thinking*. Minneapolis: Augsburg, 1984. A noted pacifist challenges just war theorists to examine closely whether just war criteria are actually followed in so-called just wars.

Glossary

Active euthanasia: Type of euthanasia in which one directly takes the life of a patient. This could be performed by the suffering person (i.e., suicide—with or without a physician's assistance) or administered by a physician or friend who causes death though for merciful reasons; also called *positive euthanasia*; contrast with *passive euthanasia*.

Activism: View that a citizen must support all wars his or her country fights.

Actuality principle: A kind of functionalism affirming that a human organism has a right to life if and only if it has actually developed a minimal ability to express self-conscious, personal life (contrast with *potentiality principle*).

Adultery: Voluntary sexual intercourse between a married person and someone other than his or her marriage partner; also includes voluntary thoughts of such activities.

Affirmative action: Policies designed to promote employment among different races by aggressively recruiting, training, and promoting qualified minority persons.

Amniocentesis: A test for a fetus's genetic health; involves examining the genetic structure of cells found in amniotic fluid drawn by needle from the amniotic sac.

Annulment: An official cancellation of a marriage; unlike a divorce, which acknowledges the legitimacy of the marriage it ends, an annulment declares that the attempted marriage never really came into being.

Artificial insemination (AI): Injection of sperm cells either into a woman's vagina or into her uterus, with the hope that one will fertilize the woman's ovum (egg) and lead to pregnancy. The sperm may be from the woman's husband (AIH) or from someone else—a donor (AID). Quite often the donor is unknown to the prospective mother; the sperm is obtained from a sperm bank.

Beneficence: Principle asserting that doctors are obligated to do good for their patients.

Biblical feminism: Feminism of those who combine evangelical commitments with their defense of egalitarianism.

Brain death: Total cessation of brain activity both in the neocortical brain (upper brain) and in the brain stem.

Capitalism: Economic system that connects with political democracy to form a social system that emphasizes individual freedom, limited government, and free enterprise.

Capital punishment: Legal execution by the government of a person convicted of a serious crime.

Carrying capacity: The number of organisms an ecosystem can support without degrading.

Celibacy: State of being unmarried and sexually abstinent: understood either as a gift from God or simply as a circumstance of life.

Chastity: Sexual purity and responsibility in actions and thoughts, either within or outside of marriage.

Citizenship view of ecology: Theory of environmentalism stressing that humans are part of the biosphere just like all other species.

Civil disobedience: Nonviolent, public violation of some law or policy, as an act of conscience, to protest the injustice of the law or policy and (in most cases) to effect or prevent change in the law or policy.

Communism: Economic system that emphasizes collective or state ownership of property in which central planners (not market forces) make economic decisions so that all citizens share wealth equally.

Conscientious objection: Refusal to submit to some governmental requirement, such as mandated military service, out of personal, moral, or religious beliefs, as a means of bearing witness to the perceived wrong in the law or policy.

Constitutional homosexual: A person whose sexual attraction to those of the same gender is so deeply rooted that it is part of his or her essential being. A constitutional homosexual is not necessarily a practicing homosexual. See also *homosexual orientation.*

Crusade: A war waged to remedy past or ongoing atrocities, especially one recognized as such for religious reasons.

Death: Theologically, the separation of the spiritual self from the body; traditionally indicated medically by irreversible cessation of circulatory and respiratory functions; according to the Uniform Determination of Death Act, death is indicated by the irreversible cessation of the whole brain (brain death).

Deep ecology: A deeply spiritual approach to ecology based on nature mysticism or pantheism.

Deterrence: As a theory related to capital punishment, the idea that enforcement of the death penalty in a society will prevent would-be criminals from committing crimes they might otherwise have committed. As a political stance, one that relies on the possession and threatened use of weapons—especially nuclear—to discourage or prevent attack.

Discrimination: When based on race, treating someone differently than his merit suggests simply by virtue of his racial identity. It usually connotes treating a minority person badly just because she is a minority, but could include giving a white person an advantage because of his color.

Divorce: A legal dissolution of a duly consummated marriage.

Divorce (sacramental view): Catholic view that considers marriage a sacred covenant before God that is unbreakable except by death; in this view, annulment is possible under certain circumstances, but divorce never is.

Dominion view of ecology: Christian theory of environmentalism emphasizing the right of humans to use creation for their own needs; destruction of nature is prevented by individuals who own property rights over nature.

Double effect principle: Principle that asserts the following: if an inherently good act has two effects, one good and one bad, a person can act morally in doing that act provided (1) only the good effect is intended, (2) the bad effect is not the means to the good effect, and (3) the good effect is at least equal to the bad effect.

Durable power of attorney: Legal means by which a patient designates another to make decisions on his behalf should the patient become physically or mentally unable to do so (see *substituted judgment*).

Egalitarianism: View that in home, church, and society, qualified men and women equally may exercise leadership; does not imply that women and men are *identical* in personal qualities, interests, skills, or gifts.

Embryo: Early stage in a human's development after the zygote stage and before it takes its distinctive form; roughly the first seven weeks of gestation.

Embryo transfer (ET): Transfer of an embryo conceived in one womb to the womb of another woman. The embryo is transferred before it can implant in the original womb.

Erotic: Having to do with sexual arousal and desire.

Essentialism: The view that a creature is a human person and thus has a right to life by virtue of being a member of a class, the natural kind *human*, rather than by virtue of being able to perform certain functions (contrast with *functionalism*).

Euthanasia: The deliberate act of intending or choosing a painless death for the humane purpose of ending the agony of someone who suffers from incurable disease or injury: includes active and passive forms.

Exception clause: The phrase *except for adultery* (Matt. 5:32; 19:9); whether Jesus permits an innocent victim of divorce to remarry depends on how this phrase relates to surrounding clauses.

Feminism: Movement of any, male or female, who advocate laws and social policies that promote social, political, and economic equality between the genders.

Fetus: The individual unborn human in the later stages of development; roughly from the end of the second month of pregnancy until birth.

Fornication: Voluntary sexual intercourse between an unmarried man and an unmarried woman.

Free market: Economic environment in which individuals make economic decisions about production and consumption independently, with a minimum of state interference.

Functionalism: The view that an organism is a human person by virtue of its ability to function personally; a human organism is a human person if it can or will act personally, that is, if it acts as a moral, intellectual, spiritual agent (contrast with *essentialism*).

Gay: Homosexual; homosexual women prefer to speak of themselves as lesbians, while homosexual men refer to themselves as gay men.

Gender: Maleness or femaleness.

Genetic engineering: Term most broadly and most commonly used to refer to the use of genetics to design human descendants, and the manipulation of the entire living world for the supposed benefit of humanity. More precisely, the term denotes any technical intervention in the structure of genes, for such purposes as the removal of a harmful gene, the enhancement of a specific genetic capacity, or the changing of an organism's genetic structure. Sometimes the term is used to refer to reproductive technologies in general.

Genetics: Study of genes (the chromosome units that determine one's hereditary characteristics) and the application of that knowledge to a number of experimental and clinical uses.

Genocide: Attempt to kill those of a particular race; logical extension of racism in its traditional sense.

Guided market: Economic environment in which central planners seek to guide an economy toward certain desirable goals using a variety of strategies (e.g., taxes, tariffs, subsidies, monetary policies, and others).

Head: Key Greek work (*kephalē*) for understanding 1 Corinthians 11:13–16 and Ephesians 5:21–33; often interpreted by biblical traditionalists to mean *authority over*; some biblical feminists say it means *source*.

Heterosexual: Person attracted sexually to those of the opposite gender; also, pertaining to the attraction itself.

Hierarchicalism: View that males must fill certain leadership roles in social relationships; it is God's design, in certain contexts, that women must follow the leadership and/or authority of men.

Homophobia: Irrational fear of homosexuals sometimes leading to an attitude of hostility toward them.

Homosexual: Person (male or female) with a homosexual orientation, who may or may not be a practicing homosexual; also, referring to same-sex desires and/or practices.

Homosexuality: Persistent or predominant sexual disposition (see *homosexual orientation*) of an individual toward persons of the same sex.

Homosexual orientation: Disposition or persistent preference of a person for same-gender sexual relationships; also known as constitutional homosexuality and inversion.

Incest: Sexual relations between close relatives, most commonly reported between a father or stepfather and daughter or stepdaughter.

Income: Economic power or money that one receives periodically in exchange for labor or the use of capital (see *wealth*); a person with a high income may not be wealthy.

Induced abortion: Intentional termination of a pregnancy using any one of a variety of medical interventions; spontaneous abortion, commonly called miscarriage, happens naturally and is not morally significant.

Informed consent: Principle that a patient understand treatment options and choose the course of treatment or the withholding of treatment.

Intercourse (sexual): Intimate sexual activity involving penile penetration; also known as coitus.

Interventionism: Derisive word that some advocates of the free-market view use to describe the guided-market approach.

Inversion: Same as *homosexual orientation*.

In vitro fertilization (IVF): Combining of a woman's egg(s) and a man's sperm in a petri dish, followed by the insertion of the fertilized egg into the womb.

Jim Crow: A set of laws, policies, and practices that enforced segregation of African-Americans prior to the civil rights era.

Jus ad bellum: The conditions—such as just cause, just intention, declaration by lawful authority, and last resort—that must be met in order for a just war to be declared.

Jus in bello: The conditions—such as noncombatant immunity and proportionate means—that must be met in the conduct of an ongoing war for it to be considered just.

Just war: A war that satisfies both *jus ad bellum* and *jus in bello* criteria.

Lesbian: A homosexual woman.

Letting die: Withholding or withdrawing life-prolonging and life-sustaining technologies as an intentional act to enhance the well-being of the terminally ill by avoiding useless prolonging of the dying process. Letting die is like so-called passive euthanasia in that it prohibits direct killing (the underlying disease or injury is the actual cause of death), but unlike passive euthanasia, letting die does not intend or choose death; contrast with euthanasia of all forms.

Lex talionis: The law of retribution (eye for eye, tooth for tooth, life for life) found in Leviticus 24:17–20 and relevant to Exodus 21:22–25.

Liberation theology: Third-World (especially Latin American) movement that defines sin as economic oppression and salvation as personal, economic, and political liberation of the poor.

Living will: Legal document in which a person indicates his wishes regarding treatment in order to guide medical personnel in situations where he is unable to choose treatment.

Lust (sexual): Strong desire for illegitimate sexual involvement.

Mammon: Wealth and money seen as a power or deity.

Marriage: A union of one man and one woman as husband and wife through an official ceremony of vows by which the man and woman promise faithfulness to each other; marriage is recognized by society as well as by the church and is consummated in a full sexual union.

Masturbation: Stimulating oneself sexually, usually to orgasm.

Mercy killing: A synonym for euthanasia.

Misogyny: Latent or explicit hatred of women.

Money: Any medium of economic exchange; a common unit of material value in terms of which someone assigns values to all other objects.

Nonmaleficence: Principle asserting that doctors are minimally obligated to avoid harming their patients. This principle is more fundamental than *beneficence.*

Nonviolent resistance: View that Christians should not only avoid participation in war, but also actively resist war using nonviolent means.

Nuclear pacifism: View that while warfare with conventional weapons may at times be justified, nuclear warfare can never be, due to the uniquely destructive nature of nuclear weapons.

Ordinary/extraordinary: Distinction related to the degree of pain, expense, invasiveness, or inconvenience entailed in a medical treatment in proportion to possible benefits of that treatment; ordinary means are medical options that both offer reasonable hope of benefit and require only moderate costs; extraordinary means are medical options that either offer little reasonable hope of recovery or require excessive costs in pain, expense, or inconvenience.

Pacifism: View that it is wrong to participate in war, whatever its cause.

Passive euthanasia: Type of euthanasia in which one intends death as a means to ending the agony of a suffering person, but rather than directly taking the life, one acts to avoid prolonging the dying process, allowing the underlying disease or assault on the body to cause death; also called *negative euthanasia*; contrast with *active euthanasia*.

Patriarchy: Systems of social life and language that preserve male privilege; feminists argue that patriarchy oppresses women.

Pauline privilege: The idea that an innocent Christian deserted by an unbelieving spouse is not bound to the marriage vow and is therefore free to choose remarriage; based on one interpretation of the phrase *not bound* in 1 Corinthians 7:15.

People of color: Recently coined phrase incorporating all nonwhite ethnic and racial groups bound together by their common experience of oppression and discrimination due to the racism of whites.

Petting: Fondling another person's sexually excitable body parts.

Pornography: Sexually explicit pictures, writing, or other materials designed to arouse sexual desires.

Potentiality principle: A kind of functionalism affirming that a human organism possesses a right to life if it has developed or has the natural capacity for developing self-conscious, personal life (contrast with *actuality principle*).

Practicing homosexual: One who prefers and regularly engages in same-sex genital activities.

Preventive war: A war begun not in response to an act of aggression, but in anticipation of such, to prevent the other side from striking first.

Problem of the commons: The problem of how to protect resources that belong to no one in particular but are necessary to the well-being of everyone.

Pro-choice: An adjective describing views that regard the value of reproductive freedom more highly than the value of fetal life.

Pro-life: An adjective describing views that regard the value of fetal life more highly than the value of reproductive freedom.

Promiscuity: Sexual behavior characterized by casual, superficial relationships and frequent changes of partners.

Prosperity gospel: View that a Christian has a spiritual birthright that includes material wealth (also called the health and wealth gospel).

Race: Notoriously ambiguous term for categorizing people by appearance. Sometimes people group very different cultural backgrounds into one race as when they describe both Pakistanis and Koreans as "Asians."

Racial prejudice: Attitudes, usually negative, about certain persons based on racial identity; prejudices about racial or ethnic groups are often persistent and powerfully affect interactions between members of diffferent groups.

Racism: Traditionally, the belief that one racial group in the human family is inherently superior to or more virtuous or deserving than another due to inherited characteristics, that civilization has developed due to the virtues of that race, and that the future of civilized society depends on preserving the purity of that race. More recently, some describe racism as racial prejudice with power and include as an effect of racism the cultural dislocation experienced by minority peoples due to dominant cultural patterns.

Rape: Sexual intercourse without the consent of one of the partners.

Redistribution: Derisive term used by some free marketers for any strategy by which government takes money from the wealthy and gives it to the poor.

Retribution: Something given or demanded in return for and in proportion to a wrong done; may or may not include the notion of exact retaliation.

Reverse discrimination: Disadvantage white males experience when those who hire workers pass them over in favor of a member of some disadvantaged group.

Selectivism: View that it is morally right to participate in some wars—those that are just—but not in all wars.

Sex: Either the reality of being male or female (gender), or the erotic attraction and/or genital activity between persons.

Sexism: Gender-based prejudice.

Sexual harassment: Unwelcome sexual advances, whether verbal, nonverbal, or physical, that create a hostile work or learning environment or make submission to the abuse a condition of employment or the basis of performance evaluation, or cause stress, anxiety, or embarrassment for the person harassed.

Sexuality: Quality of being male or female or (more commonly) the awareness of and responsiveness to this aspect of human existence.

Simplicity gospel: View that Christians ought to live plain, simple lives in order to challenge the materialistic philosophy of secular society and to free up resources for Christian work.

Socialism: A social system in which the public owns the means of production and the government actively redistributes income with the aim that all citizens receive an equitable share of goods and services.

Sodomy: In the strictest sense, sexual union by anal penetration, whether homosexual or heterosexual; in the broader sense, sexual activity of any kind involving homosexuals.

Stereotype: Negative, composite image of persons in a certain class; a fixed, communally recognized impression of a group of people.

Stewardship view of ecology: Christian theory of environmentalism focusing on the responsibility toward God for protecting the environment.

Straight: Heterosexual.

Substituted judgment: Legal declaration by the courts authorizing a person to make treatment decisions for an incapacitated patient.

Surrogacy: Most often the process in which a couple chooses another woman (the surrogate) to be artificially inseminated with the man's sperm. In theory, the surrogate will carry the baby to term, giving it up to the couple at birth (genetic surrogacy). Also refers to the process in which the parent couple's sperm and ovum are combined in vitro, and the embryo placed in the womb of the surrogate (gestational or genuine surrogacy). Again, the surrogate gives up the baby at birth.

Sustainable growth: Economic development that meets the needs of various groups while conserving the resources and carrying capacity of the environment.

Theonomy: Movement that supports God's law, including the Old Testament civil law, as the basis of human society and defends free market economics as a biblical means to that end.

Therapeutic abortion: An abortion performed to save the mother's life.

Vitalism: View that physical life is in itself of highest value.

Voluntary/involuntary/nonvoluntary: Distinctions related to the way the desires of a patient are incorporated in treatment decisions; voluntary treatment options follow the patient's wishes, nonvoluntary treatment decisions are made when the patient is incapacitated and cannot decide, and involuntary treatment decisions go against patient desires.

War: Armed conflict between or among nations or other groups of people.

Wealth: Stored economic power; money that is already accumulated and can be used as capital for investment (see *income*).

Zygote: The product of the union of a sperm and an ovum in its first days of life.

Index

Informed consent, 97–98, 133
Inglis, M., 399n
Integration, racial, 265
Intention, 107–8, 130
International Commission of Jurists, 374
Interventionism, 341, 346, 378
Intimacy, 158
Intimidation, 476–78
Inversion. *See* Homosexual orientation
Isaacs, Florence, 80n
Isaksson, Abel, 232n, 233n, 235, 238, 239n

Jaggar, Alison, 301
Jakobowits, Immanuel, 217
James, Kay Coles, 30
Jankowski, J., 117n
Jekins, Esther, 280n
Jennett, Bryan, 124
Jensen, J., 238
Jesus Christ
    attitude toward women, 295–96
    authority over the church, 313–14, 328
    compassion, 209, 216
    on divorce, 235–36, 248
    incarnation, 325–26
    lordship, 313, 519
    nonviolence, 505–6
    norm for humanity, 183–85, 190
    on race relations, 276–79
    on war, 497–99
    on wealth, 349
Jim Crow laws, 265, 289
Joblessness, 381
John Paul II, 398n
Johnson, Anna, 57–59
Johnson, James Turner, 523
Jonas, H., 131n
Jones, D., 301n
Jones, D. Gareth, 92
Jones, H. Kimball, 183n
Jones, Major, 290
Jones, Stanton L., 181, 221
Josephus, 283, 509
Judaism, 164n
    on divorce, 239
Judeo-Christian tradition, 300–301

Jus ad bellum, 490, 522
Jus in bello, 490, 522
Just war tradition, 490–92, 500, 502–3, 511–12, 514, 517, 522
Justice, 268–71, 391–92, 393, 455–56, 468, 470, 477, 482–85, 491, 504
    and civil disobedience, 431–32

Kalland, Earl S., 232n
Kalland, Lloyd, 33
Kant, Immanual, 480
Kass, Leon, 75n
Keene, Beverly, 372n, 373n
Keener, Craig S., 257, 335
Kehrein, Glen, 291
Keil, C. F., 232n
Keller, E. F., 306
Kelsey, George, 290
Kennard, Joyce, 58
Kennedy, D. J., 128n
Kent, Homer A., Jr., 252n, 253n
Kenyon, Walter W., 330n
Kevles, Daniel J., 88n
Keysor, Charles W., 222
Kidner, D., 401n, 404n
Kierkegaard, S., 325n
Killing. *See* Just war; Mercy killing; Murder
Kilner, John F., 135
King, Martin Luther, Jr., 265, 268, 290, 517
King, Rodney, 261, 286
Kingdom of God, 146–47, 172, 248, 506, 519
Kinsey, Alfred, 179, 188, 192
Kinship, 232
Kinzer, Stephen, 375n
Kirk, Andrew, 345n
Kittel, G., 200
Kjesbo, Denise M., 334
Kjos, Berit, 419
Knight, George W. 128n, 335, 524
Knowledge, and intimacy, 158
Koonz, C., 308
Koop, C. Everett, 217
Köstenberger, Andreas J., 335
Krabill, W. S., 129n
Ku Klux Klan, 262
Kubetin, Cynthia A., 175

Sodom and Gomorrah, 204
Sodomy, 178, 220
Solidarity labor movement, 517
Somatic cell gene therapy, 85, 86–88
Sommers, Christina Hoff, 335
Soul, 122, 167
South Africa, 519–20
Southern Baptist Convention, 217–18
Spaceship model, 382
Species destruction, 381, 386
Species principle, 37, 42–45
Speciesism, 44, 113
Spence, J. T., 302n
Spencer, Aída Besancon, 335
Sperm banks, 80
Spong, John Shelby, 140, 175
Spousal abuse, 245–47
Stafford, Tim, 175
Stapp, J., 302n
Stark, Rodney, 368n
Starke, L., 402n
Starvation, 381
Stassen, Glen H., 524
State. *See* Civil magistrate
Steele, Paul, 257
Steele, Shelby, 266, 291
Steinbock, Bonnie, 110n
Stereotype, 263, 290
  sex role, 302, 305
Sterilization, forced, 31
Stevens, Raymond, 257
Stevenson, L., 299
Stevick, Daniel B., 449
Stewardship, 169, 400–402
Stewardship view (ecology), 385, 418
Stivers, Robert L., 363n
Stock, A., 240n
Stoicism, 197, 202
Stonehouse, N. B., 462n
Storkey, Elaine, 301, 303
Stott, John R. W., 29, 223, 403n, 493, 508n, 524
Strategic noncooperation, 425–26, 431
Structural evil, 344, 368–76
Stuart, W. H., 118n
Subjectivism, 105–6, 434
Substituted judgment, 98, 134
Suffering, 88, 211, 344
Suffragettes, 293

Sullivan, J. V., 131n
Sullivan, Thomas, 107
Surrogate motherhood, 57–58, 66–67, 75, 91
Sustainable growth, 385, 400–402, 418
Swomley, John M., 30

Talmud, 23, 33
Tapia, Andres, 217n
Taylor, A. E., 514
Taylor, Elizabeth, 72n
Taylor, J. V., 400n
Taylor, Richard K., 524
Technology, 394
  and reproduction, 58–60, 69–82
Teller, A., 400n, 403n
Temptation, 182
Ten Commandments, 391, 459
Thatcher, M., 401
Theonomy, 340, 379
Thielicke, Helmut, 175, 183n, 188–89, 191, 223, 429n
Third World, 385, 386
Thompson, Judith Jarvis, 55
Thoreau, Henry, 382
Thurow, Lester C., 359n
Tiemstra, John P., 380
Tilson, Everett, 291
Titus, 467
Tolerance, 191
Tooley, Michael, 23, 55, 125n
Torture, 470, 485n
Transcendence, 300–301
Trespass law, 445–46
Trible, P., 307
Trocmé, André, 519
Truth, 210–11
Turkle, S., 306

Ukleja, P. Michael, 223
Underground Railroad, 427
Uniform Determination of Death Act, 100
United Brands, 374–75
United Church of Christ, 30, 153
United Methodist Church, 149
Universal Fellowship of Metropolitan Community Churches, 177
Urbanization, 381